CW00674726

A History of German Theatre

Covering German-language theatre from the Middle Ages to the present day, this study demonstrates how and why theatre became so important in German-speaking countries. Written by leading international scholars of German theatre, chapters cover all aspects of theatrical performance, including acting, directing, playwriting, scenic design and theatre architecture. The book argues that theatre is more central to the artistic life of German-speaking countries than almost anywhere else in the world. Relating German-language theatre to its social and intellectual context, the History demonstrates how theatre has often been used as a political tool. It challenges the idea that German-speaking countries were a theatrical wasteland in the seventeenth and early eighteenth centuries, provides a thematic survey of the crucial period of growth in the late eighteenth and nineteenth centuries, and discusses modern and contemporary German theatre by focusing in turn on directors, playwrights, designers and theatre architecture.

SIMON WILLIAMS is Professor and Chair of the Department of Theater and Dance at the University of California, Santa Barbara. He has published widely in the fields of European continental theatre, the history of acting, Shakespearean performance, and operatic history. His major publications include *German Actors of the Eighteenth and Nineteenth Centuries* (1985), *Shakespeare on the German Stage, 1586–1914* (Cambridge, 1990), *Richard Wagner and Festival Theatre* (1994), and *Wagner and the Romantic Hero* (Cambridge, 2004). He has contributed numerous articles in his fields of speciality to edited volumes and leading periodicals. He was co-editor of the 'Lives of the Theatre' series. He is also an active director and reviewer of opera.

MAIK HAMBURGER was a dramaturge and director at the Deutsches Theater, Berlin, where he was involved in many productions of German, English, American and Spanish classical and contemporary drama. He has taught in Berlin at Humboldt Universität, the Schauspielschule 'Ernst Busch' and the Universität der Künste, and also in Leipzig and Graz. He contributed the chapter on the DDR to Wilhelm Hortmann's *Shakespeare on the German Stage: The Twentieth Century*. Hamburger has translated into German plays by Shakespeare, Sean O'Casey, Arthur Miller, Tennessee Williams, Alonso Alegria and others. He has also translated and edited a volume of John Donne's poetry, *Zwar ist auch Dichtung Sünde*.

A HISTORY OF
German theatre

Edited by Simon Williams and Maik Hamburger

CAMBRIDGE
UNIVERSITY PRESS

CAMBRIDGE UNIVERSITY PRESS

Cambridge, New York, Melbourne, Madrid, Cape Town, Singapore, São Paulo,
Delhi, Dubai, Tokyo

Cambridge University Press
The Edinburgh Building, Cambridge CB2 8RU, UK

Published in the United States of America by Cambridge University Press, New York

www.cambridge.org
Information on this title: www.cambridge.org/9780521833691

© Cambridge University Press 2008

This publication is in copyright. Subject to statutory exception
and to the provisions of relevant collective licensing agreements,
no reproduction of any part may take place without
the written permission of Cambridge University Press.

First published 2008
Reprinted 2010
Printed in the United Kingdom at the University Press, Cambridge

A catalogue record for this publication is available from the British Library

Library of Congress Cataloguing in Publication data
A history of German theatre / edited by Simon Williams and Maik Hamburger.
    p.   cm.
Includes bibliographical references.
ISBN 978-0-521-83369-1
1. Theater – Germany – History.   I. Williams, Simon, 1943–   II. Hamburger, Michael.
PN2641.H57   2008
792.0943–dc22

                                                            2008030238

ISBN 978-0-521-83369-1 hardback

Cambridge University Press has no responsibility for
the persistence or accuracy of URLs for external or
third-party internet websites referred to in this book,
and does not guarantee that any content on such
websites is, or will remain, accurate or appropriate.

To the memory of Adolf Dresen (1935–2001)

Contents

Illustrations

Contributors

DAVID BARNETT is Senior Lecturer in Drama at the University of Sussex. He has published a monograph on Heiner Müller (*Literature versus Theatre*, 1998) and articles on contemporary German and English-language drama, post-dramatic theatre, and metadrama. He researched and wrote *Rainer Werner Fassbinder and the German Theatre* (2005) as a Fellow of the Humboldt Foundation.

GEORGE W. BRANDT received his Ph.D. from Bristol University's Drama Department, and he joined the faculty there in 1951. He stayed in Bristol for thirty-five years, serving as Head of Department for several years. He created the first media course at any British university, directed numerous stage productions and films and was appointed Chair of Film and Television Studies. He retired in 1986 and was Professor Emeritus and Senior Research Fellow until his death in 2007. Publications include editing of *British Television Drama* (1981), *British Television Drama in the 1980s* (1993), *German and Dutch Theatre, 1600–1848* (1993) and *Modern Theories of Drama* (1998); as well as contributions to *The Cambridge Guide to Theatre* (1995), *The Continuum Companion to Twentieth Century Theatre* (2002) and the *International Dictionary of the Theatre 1 and 3* (1992 and 1996).

HILDA MELDRUM BROWN is Senior Research Fellow at St. Hilda's College, Oxford and Emeritus Professor of German in the University of Oxford. In 2006 she was awarded an Emeritus Fellowship by the Leverhulme Trust to carry out research into the theory and practice of the 'Gesamtkunstwerk' in the nineteenth century. She has a long-standing association with the works of Heinrich von Kleist and has published extensively on many aspects of his work. In addition to her interest in literary forms and, in particular, German drama, her work reflects a bias towards interdisciplinary studies and hybrid forms, ranging from the 18th century landscape garden and nineteenth-century book illustration, to German Romantic opera and the music dramas of Richard Wagner. Her books include *Kleist's Lost Year and the Quest for 'Robert Guiskard'* (1981), *Leitmotiv and Drama: Wagner, Brecht and the limits of 'epic' theatre* (1991; reprint 1993), *Heinrich von Kleist: The Ambiguity of Art and the Necessity of Form* (1998) and *Critique and Creativity: E. T. A. Hoffmann and the Development of the Serapiontic Principle* (2006).

MARVIN CARLSON is the Sidney E. Cohn Professor of Theatre and Comparative Literature at the Graduate Center of the City University of New York. He has received an honorary doctorate from the University of Athens, the ATHE Career Achievement Award, the ASTR Distinguished Scholarship Award, the George Jean Nathan Award for Dramatic Criticism, and the Calloway Prize. He is the founding editor of the journal *Western European Stages*. He is the author of over one hundred scholarly articles in the areas of theatre history, theatre theory and dramatic literature, and his work has been translated into fourteen languages. Among his books are *The Theatre of the French Revolution* (1966), *The German Stage in the Nineteenth Century* (1972), *Goethe and the Weimar Theatre* (1978), *Theories of the Theatre* (1984), *Places of Performance* (1989), *Performance: A Critical Introduction* (1996), *The Haunted Stage* (2001) and *Speaking in Tongues* (2006).

WILLIAM F. CONDEE is the J. Richard Hamilton/Baker and Hostetler Professor of Humanities at Ohio University, as well as Professor of Theater and Director of the School of Interdisciplinary Arts. Professor Condee is the author of two books, *Coal and Culture: The Opera House in Appalachia* (2005) and *Theatrical Space: A Guide for Directors and Designers* (1995), as well as 'Architecture for the Twentieth Century: Imagining the Theatre in the 1920s', in *Experimenters, Rebels, and Disparate Voices* (2003). His articles on theatre space have appeared in many leading architectural and theatre journals. He has taught at the University of Leipzig, the University of Wales and Vassar College, and has served as Director of the Ohio–Leipzig European Center. He was also dramaturge for the London Young Vic–West End production of *A Touch of the Poet*. He appears regularly on Broadway as a clown in the Macy's Thanksgiving Day parade.

ERIKA FISCHER-LICHTE is Professor of Theatre Studies at the Freie Universität Berlin and Director of the Interdisciplinary Centre for the

Arts and Aesthetics. Between 1995 and 1999, she was President of the International Federation of Theatre Studies. Her publications include more than twenty books and two hundred articles, among them *The Semiotics of Theatre* (1983, Engl. 1992), *The Dramatic Touch of Difference: Theatre, Own and Foreign* (1990), *History of European Drama and Theatre* (1990, Engl. 2002), and *The Show and the Gaze of Theatre* (1997, Engl. 1998). Her most recent publications are *Aesthetik des Performativen* (2004) and *Theatre, Sacrifice, Ritual: Exploring Forms of Political Theatre* (2005).

MAIK HAMBURGER studied at Aberdeen and Leipzig. For 30 years, until 1996, he was a dramaturge and director at the Deutsches Theater, Berlin, where he was involved in dozens of productions of German, English, American and Spanish drama. He has taught in Berlin at Humboldt Universität, the Schauspielschule Ernst Busch and the Universität der Künste, also in Leipzig and Graz. He has written and lectured in England and the USA on Shakespeare, O'Casey, Brecht, theatre in the GDR and problems of translation. He contributed the chapter on the GDR to Wilhelm Hortmann's *Shakespeare on the German Stage: The Twentieth Century*. Hamburger has translated into German plays by Shakespeare, Sean O'Casey, Arthur Miller, Tennessee Williams, Alonso Alegria and others. He also translated and edited a volume of John Donne's poetry, *Zwar ist auch Dichtung Sünde* (Leipzig, 1982/1985). For many years he was Vice-President of the Deutsche Shakespeare-Gesellschaft and is a member of the German P.E.N. Centre.

WILHELM HORTMANN is Professor Emeritus of the University of Duisburg. He taught English Literature at the universities of Frankfurt (1959–1973) and Duisburg (1973–1994), and European Drama at the University of California Santa Barbara in 1998. His areas of interest and research are English literature of the nineteenth and twentieth centuries, literary history and aesthetic theory, Shakespeare and theatre, the relation of politics and culture, and urbanism. His major publications include *Englische Literatur im 20. Jahrhundert* (1965), a popular history of twentieth-century English literature in German, *Wenn die Kunst stirbt* (1976), a study in German on the aesthetic and social theories of Herbert Read and the question of committed art in general, and *Shakespeare on the German Stage: The Twentieth Century* (1998, Ger. 2001). At present he finds ghost-writing an interesting (and lucrative) sideline.

CHRISTOPHER INNES holds the Canada Research Chair in Performance and Culture, together with the title of Distinguished Research Professor at York University, Toronto, and is a Fellow of the Royal Society of Canada. He is the author of thirteen books ranging from *Erwin Piscator's Political Theatre* (1972) and *Modern German Drama* (1979) to *Edward Gordon Craig: A Vision of Theatre* (1998), *Avant Garde Theatre* (1993), and *Modern British Drama: The Twentieth Century* (1992), as well as (most recently) *Designing Modern America: Broadway to Main Street* (2005). He is also the author of over 100 articles on various aspects of modern drama. He is editor of the Cambridge 'Directors in Perspective' series, and co-editor of the 'Lives of the Theatre' series. He is also a contributing editor to *The Cambridge Guide to World Theatre*, and has been co-editor of the quarterly journal *Modern Drama*.

THOMAS IRMER has taught American literature and drama at Leipzig University (1992–96), and at the Freie Universität Berlin, John F. Kennedy Institute, since 2003. From 1998 to 2003, he was editor-in-chief of the monthly *Theater der Zeit*, and, from 2004 to 2006, dramaturgical advisor for the international theatre program 'Spielzeiteuropa' at Berliner Festspiele. Books include *Frank Castorfs Volksbühne* (2003), *Die Bühnenrepublik – Theater in der DDR* (2003), and *Theater und Ritual – Luk Perceval* (2005). He is author and co-director of two documentary films on theatre, *Die Bühnenrepublik* (2003) and *Europa in Stücken* (2004).

ANTHONY MEECH is head of the Department of Drama and Music at Hull University. He has published on Brecht and the theatre of the former GDR. A founder member of the University's Centre for Performance Translation and Dramaturgy, his translations of German texts from Lenz, Lessing and Büchner to Brecht, Christoph Hein and Botho Strauss, have been staged by the Royal National Theatre and the Edinburgh Festival in the UK, as well as in Australia, South Africa, Canada and the USA.

MICHAEL RAAB is a translator, journalist and lecturer and lives in Frankfurt am Main. He received his Ph.D. at the University of Hamburg and worked as dramaturge at the Staatstheater Stuttgart, the Staatstheater Mainz, the Munich Kammerspiele and the Schauspiel Leipzig. He has written books on Shakespearean productions in Germany and England, the portrayal of the entertainment industry in contemporary British drama, the director Wolfgang Engel, and on English plays in the 1990s. His main field of work is new British and Irish drama on which he has published numerous articles and essays. He has taught at various universities and acting schools and translated plays by Catherine Hayes, David Hare, Kevin Elyot, Mark O'Rowe, Catherine Johnson, Lee Hall, Paul Tucker, J. B. Priestley, Kenneth Lonergan, Eugene O'Brien, Gregory Burke, Robert W. Sherwood, Melissa James Gibson, Michael Frayn, Simon Gray, Jonathan Lichtenstein, Laura Wade and Paul Jenkins.

ECKEHARD SIMON teaches medieval studies at Harvard University as Victor S. Thomas Professor of German. Among his undergraduate core courses is The Medieval Stage which reconstructs performances of early European plays in their original settings. To put their learning into practice, undergraduates do research on and perform a medieval play. Eckehard Simon has written books and articles on the court poet Neidhart and his school, on a Gutenberg imprint, and on early theatre. He edited research reports on *The Theatre of Medieval Europe* for Cambridge University Press (1991) and wrote a history of German non-religious theatre based on newly collected performance records (2003). He has worked with manuscripts, especially with those in Harvard's Houghton Library, and published texts from them, including the previously unknown *Swabian (Constance) Christmas Play* (1417). Fellowships from the Guggenheim and Fulbright Foundations and the National Endowment for the Humanities have supported his research.

SIMON WILLIAMS is Professor and Chair of the Department of Theater and Dance at the University of California, Santa Barbara. He has taught at universities on four continents, including the Universities of Regina and Alberta, Cornell University and, since 1984, UCSB. He has published widely in the fields of European continental theatre, the history of acting, Shakespearean performance, and operatic history. His major publications include *German Actors of the Eighteenth and Nineteenth Centuries* (1985), *Shakespeare on the German Stage, 1586–1914* (1990), *Richard Wagner and Festival Theatre* (1994), and *Wagner and the Romantic Hero* (2004). He has contributed numerous articles in his fields of specialty in edited volumes and leading periodicals. He was co-editor of the 'Lives of the Theatre' series. He is also an active director and reviewer of opera.

STEPHEN WILMER is Associate Professor in Drama at Trinity College Dublin and former Director of the Samuel Beckett Centre for Drama and

Theatre Studies. He has been a Visiting Professor at Stanford University and the University of California at Berkeley. He is a playwright and has published numerous articles in scholarly journals and chapters in books. He is the author of *Theatre, Society and the Nation: Staging American Identities* (2002), and (with Pirkko Koski) *The Dynamic World of Finnish Theatre* (2006). Other publications include: *Beckett in Dublin* (1992), *Portraits of Courage: Plays by Finnish Women* (1997), *Writing and Rewriting National Theatre Histories* (2004), (with Hans van Maanen) *Theatre Worlds in Motion: Structures, Politics and Developments in the Countries of Western Europe* (1998), and (with Helka Mäkinen and W. B. Worthen) *Theatre, History and National Identities* (2001).

Introduction

MAIK HAMBURGER AND SIMON WILLIAMS

Theatre occupies a unique position in German-speaking Europe. Not only does each major city have its own heavily subsidised repertory theatre, usually with two or three stages of differing sizes, but it has its own opera house as well. Smaller cities that, in most countries, would probably never see professional theatre also support both a drama and an opera company, often performing on the same stage. A well-run theatre is, it seems, as necessary to the health of the community as a good public school system, a research university, a well-stocked library, a symphony orchestra, or even an efficient hospital and clinics. In brief, theatre in Germany matters.

For the last hundred years, German theatre has also made its impact upon the international community. The spectacular historicist productions of the Duke of Saxe-Meiningen in the 1880s and the brilliantly theatrical ensembles of Max Reinhardt a generation later were the first exports that drew world attention to German theatre. Since then, German theatre artists have been at the forefront in most of the major movements that have transformed international theatre. Since the 1920s, German scenic designers have revolutionised our concept of stage space, German directors have made the highly influential, though much contested claim that they are the key artists in a theatre performance, and German playwrights, most notably Bertolt Brecht, have provided models for a theatre that aims to change the very fundamentals of the society in which we live.

But German theatre was not always flourishing. In the late sixteenth century, when countries such as England, France and Spain were countering the decline of the great European tradition of religious drama with the rise of a secular, professional theatre, in Germany there were no cities large enough to host a vigorous and continuous theatre life. Furthermore, the extreme political fragmentation of Central Europe, not to mention the devastating economic and social damage wrought by the Thirty Years' War (1618–48), the consequences of which were felt well into the eighteenth century, meant that there was no opportunity for Germany to develop a coherent and unified theatre culture. Theatre was not absent from Germany during this extended period. For all of the seventeenth and most of the eighteenth centuries, it was practised by troupes of strolling actors, who were initially of foreign, later of German extraction, and they may well have provided theatre of considerable vitality. Likewise, the French and Italian companies, housed in the many theatres attached to the ruling courts in the capitals of the myriad states that composed Germany at that time, were highly skilled in their various modes of performance. But however lively theatre might have been, until late in the eighteenth century it lacked a tangible presence in Germany; it was not organised as an institution that could interpret the public, and the private, world to its audiences and therefore make an imprint upon that world and contribute towards change, be it personal, social or political. But then, over the fifty or so years that spanned the turn of the eighteenth into the nineteenth century, the German theatre was transformed. Over this period, it achieved precisely the public profile that it had previously lacked. This book is in part the tale of how that transformation was prepared for, what it actually was, and how it has influenced and even guided the development of the German theatre to the present day.

The history of German theatre has, of course, its unique characteristics, and these have determined the organisation of this volume. First, theatrical and political growth did not go hand in hand in Germany. In fact, the theatre became a salient institution in German-speaking lands several decades before those lands achieved political unity. The great transformation that was initiated at the end of the eighteenth century came about primarily because the French and Italian companies that had occupied the court theatres for much of the century were dismissed and the travelling troupes of German-speaking actors took their place. Other troupes eschewed aristocratic patronage and settled into civic or municipal theatres. Yet others were hired by 'national theatres', which were founded in certain cities, often under royal or governmental patronage and protection. This process of settlement and the consequent elevation of the public profile of German actors occurred when Germany was still in a state of political fragmentation, a condition that only continued after the Congress of Vienna in 1814. This meant that, in contrast to other European countries where the nation state was already strong and unified under a central Government residing in its capital, in German-speaking Europe no one city became politically or culturally dominant. At the start of the nineteenth century, Vienna as the capital of Austria had the most diverse theatre culture, but throughout the century, Berlin became increasingly important as a centre of theatrical life, and soon after it became capital of a unified Germany in 1871, it began to supersede Vienna. But neither of these two cities absorbed the entire resources of the German theatre. On the contrary, German-language theatre maintained its provincial character and theatrical talent was spread evenly over the entire network of theatres. This means that, in the eighteenth and nineteenth centuries, not only did large cities such as Hamburg, Mannheim, Dusseldorf, Dresden, Leipzig, Frankfurt, Cologne, and Munich, make lasting contributions to the development of German theatre, but smaller towns, such as Weimar, Bayreuth, and Meiningen, did so as well. They could attract notable theatre artists and through the unusual quality and character of the work done on their stages exercise considerable influence over the theatres of larger cities.

The provincial nature of German theatre means that a history that focuses primarily on the growth of the stage in the capitals is incomplete. In the twentieth century Berlin and Vienna consolidated their positions as cultural capitals, so in the later chapters especially there is much discussion of their theatre, but not exclusively so. It would even be possible to organise a history of German theatre mainly around each of the cities,[1] but this geographical approach might not speak to the interests of English-speaking readers. We have assumed that they may be more concerned to discover the characteristics and functions of German-language theatre as a whole.

The question of function has provided one of the main organising principles of this volume. Germans, more perhaps than other Europeans, have been very much involved with the pragmatic influence that theatre exercises over society. Even before the establishment of 'standing' theatres at the end of the eighteenth century, vigorous debate had been conducted by such theoreticians and critics as J. E. Schlegel, Lessing, Schiller, and others as to what the purpose of theatre is. Much of the first half of this volume is therefore organised to highlight some of these purposes. After two chapters on the medieval German theatre, the Baroque theatre, and the strolling players, which give ample evidence that Germany was not a theatrical wasteland prior to the changes at the end of the eighteenth century, several of the following chapters centre upon one of the different functions that characterise the German stage through to the beginning of the twentieth century. These chapters are to be read as parallel stories, each one of which describes a stratum of German theatre history. Together it is to be hoped that they will display a rich and complex performance culture that has attempted to serve its society in multiple ways.

Perhaps the most distinctive stratum of German theatre as it organised itself in the late eighteenth century was its declared mission to nurture within its audiences that uniquely German quality of *Bildung*, a concept that, as we learn in chapter 3, was most completely developed by Weimar Classicism. It aimed to make audiences not only into better citizens but into complete human beings with a capacity to live with confidence, even serenity in a conflicted world; theatre has rarely been granted a more elevated function. However, theatre cannot only elevate its audiences, it should also reflect and articulate their values and beliefs, so in chapter 4, the tradition of realism in playwriting, acting and production is mapped out, in order to display how the German theatre came to act as a cohesive force within society as a whole. As one of the few public institutions that bridged the fractured landscape of German-speaking Europe, the theatre also provided a means of generating a sense of national unity among a politically divided people; chapter 9, therefore, explores how the theatre and performance events tried to instil in the populace a sense of national identity and then, after a unified nation was achieved in actuality, how the theatre was used in the twentieth century to foster a heightened sense of national pride that led to the catastrophic consequences of Nazism and the Holocaust.

One of the most surprising moments in German theatre history is the seemingly sudden explosion of dissident, experimental performance in the decades immediately prior to and following the First World War. To a considerable degree, these were precipitated by the premonition and then by the actuality of social collapse. But the theatre was not entirely unprepared to represent this crisis in German history, as it had a reservoir of drama formally capable of addressing these themes. Hence, in a book that is devoted first and foremost to the performed theatre and drama, two chapters centre, one partly, another in whole, on the important matter of drama that was unperformed in its time. Chapter 5 traces the way in which the intense subjectivism of romanticism, a key movement in German cultural history, did not initially find a theatre that was artistically suited to its expression, but by the late nineteenth century it was beginning to do so and in so doing prepared the ground for the experiments of the twentieth century. But even more significantly, there had been a subterranean tradition of social protest in drama from *Sturm und Drang* on, which provided the basis for both expressionism and the epic theatre of Bertolt Brecht. Most of the plays in this tradition, which are discussed in chapter 6, had to wait for up to a century to be performed, both because censorship kept them from performance and because the rough and seemingly disjointed nature of their language and action was unsuited to the production modes and acting styles of the time. The eruption of these plays onto German stages in the early twentieth century makes discussion of them in the context of the time in which they were written a crucial element in a history of German theatre.

As this volume proceeds and, in the second half, comes to focus primarily on theatre in the twentieth and twenty-first centuries, there is a shift in the organising principle away from the multiple functions of the theatre and more towards categories of artistic work within the theatre. In large part this shift is caused by the singular phenomenon of the director who, as many contributors to this volume point out, occupies a position of unusual power. Today in many countries the director is, for good or ill, the dominant artist in most theatrical productions, but it was in German-speaking Europe that the director, as one whose vision unifies the diverse disciplines of performance, first emerged. Chapter 7 explores the institutional and artistic reasons for the rise of the director and traces, into the middle of the twentieth century, the advancement of this figure whose imagination becomes the prime shaping force within performance. Given the continued gravitation of the modern and contemporary German repertoire towards the classics, the director has maintained this pre-eminent position, as variety in the interpretation of a familiar canon of dramatic work is one of the major attractions drawing audiences into the theatre today. But as chapters 11 and 13 both demonstrate, the director and the stage designer are capable of arousing great antipathy as well as enthusiasm; they are at one and the same time the *bêtes noires* and the golden boys and girls of the contemporary German theatre.

Even though performance of the classics is central to the German theatre, Germany has also been the source of many plays that have both passed into the international repertoire and had a strong influence upon playwrights elsewhere. For example, while Germany was the home of expressionist theatre, expressionism was as effectively practised, both as a theatrical medium and as a dramatic form, in the United States. Similarly the great revival of British theatre that began in the late 1950s and has never really died out since would be unthinkable without the example of Brecht's epic theatre, which provided a model both for productions in Britain of Shakespeare and other classic dramatists and for a whole generation of playwrights who used the stage to address the injustices and inequities of social and political life. Germany is still a leader in the field of playwriting, though, as we discover in chapter 12, the newest work is leading the theatre away from the aesthetic of dramatic representation upon which most performance has been based into a 'post-dramatic phase' in which the very concept of representation is called into question. Where the German theatre will go from here is uncertain.

One thing is certain – theatrical performance will continue to be a spatial medium. Indeed, the precise and imaginative use of space has always been a precondition for the success of almost any theatrical performance. From the building of the Bayreuth Festival Theatre in 1876, Germany has been to the fore in experimentation with different configurations of the auditorium and stage in order to maximise the potential for communication between audience and actors. Chapter 10 chronicles these experiments.

The stratified approach to history tends to highlight the work of those theatre artists who achieved significance because their work was seminal to more than one of the different functions exercised by the German theatre. Hence, in the eighteenth century Lessing, Goethe and Schiller appear as key figures not only in the development of theatre as an agency of *Bildung*, but also in the growth of a realistic theatre, so they are central to both chapters on those themes. Similarly the nineteenth-century figures of Wagner and the Duke of Saxe-Meiningen loom large in several chapters, not only because their work was crucial in the development of a realistic scenography, but because it had other ramifications as well; the Protean Wagner, for example, can be found in the chapters on realism, romanticism, nationalism, and theatre architecture. In the twentieth century Reinhardt and Brecht feature most frequently. In each instance when a multifaceted artist's name appears, different aspects of his or her work are stressed; it is hoped that, by the end of the book, the reader will have a clear idea of the manifold significance of such artists' work.

A particular challenge that faces any historian of German theatre is to determine what exactly 'Germany' is. After all, Germany did not become a nation until the Treaty of Versailles in 1871 and even then very significant areas of German-speaking Europe were not included in the new nation, most notably Austria and German Switzerland. By the term 'German', therefore, this volume assumes all of German-speaking Europe and the German-language theatre that was performed in this large area. This should not be interpreted as a claim that the theatre history of all German-speaking countries can only be understood as a part of the larger whole. On the contrary, Austrian theatre in particular has its own distinctive styles and traditions that distinguish it from all other European countries and to do these justice a separate volume would be necessary. Swiss theatre also has its own distinctive quality which cannot be adequately discussed in a volume like the present one.

A further question arises as to what materials a theatre history should consider. As the performance on stage is the central matter of this volume, all the separate arts that compose the work of performance are treated, in the first half of the book in association with each other, but in the latter half separately. Opera occupies a particularly privileged position in German theatre because the theatrical aspects of the genre have, arguably, been more readily acknowledged in Germany than elsewhere. Much scenic innovation has occurred in the name of opera and experiments in the staging of canonical operas have been more frequent and, in the view of many critics, more extreme, than in other countries. This history refers then to the performance of both spoken drama and opera, though in its discussion of the texts of theatre greater emphasis has been placed upon playwriting than upon operatic scores. These are touched upon briefly, mainly in chapter 5, but are not discussed from a musical point of view.

Finally, although many chapters are concerned with the impact theatre has upon society, it is the theatrical work as experienced by audiences that is the core of this history. It does not, therefore, contain discussion of theatre management, actor training, professional regulation, and other important institutional matters. These, we hope, will be the subject of future histories of the German theatre.

1 German medieval theatre: Tenth century to 1600

ECKEHARD SIMON

The beginnings

Medieval theatre began in the Christian church during the tenth century. On Easter morning, three monks dressed as the Marys walked up to the church altar, representing Christ's tomb, where a fourth brother, playing a white-robed angel, chanted *Quem queritis* ('Whom are you seeking?'). 'Jesus of Nazareth', the Marys responded. 'He is not here', the angel informed them, 'the Lord has risen'. Liturgical dramas were also performed at Christmas, around the visitation of the three Kings and shepherds worshipping at the manger, and later, in the twelfth century, clerics composed and performed Latin Christmas pageants on subjects such as the Beauvais *Play of Daniel* and the Tegernsee *Play of the Antichrist*. Church people abominated theatre as a pagan vanity, so they considered their 'offices' or 'orders of worship' purely as embellishments to hourly or canonical services and the Mass, the only purpose of which was to represent the story commemorated by the feast.

German gradually found its way into these Latin plays. During Easter around 1160, as clerics in Salzburg cathedral finished chanting the liturgical play of the three Marys' visit to Christ's tomb, the cantor instructed the lay audience to sing the Easter hymn *Christ ist erstanden* ('Christ has risen'), which is probably the first time that the German language was used in drama. Some decades later, around 1230, scribes in an Austrian abbey entered a Passion play into the song collection, *Carmina Burana*. In this Mary Magdalene sang courtly love songs and the Virgin Mary lamented the death of her crucified son in German. In these verses, expressing joy and sorrow, the 'mother language' of German began to replace the 'father language' of Latin. By 1250, Franciscan friars were reaching larger audiences by preaching in German, while mystics used German to express their visions. German religious theatre began as part of that new spirituality. Around 1260, a cleric, probably in Zurich, inserted German verses into a Latin Easter play. This *Osterspiel von Muri (Easter Play of Muri)* – named for the monastery where fragments of the vellum scroll on which it was inscribed were found – was a pageant of some 1,200 verses of which 612 survive, featuring Mary Magdalene, the ointment merchant, and soldiers at the tomb. In the north, a cleric near Nordhausen, Thuringia, used north or Low German for a Passion play dramatising the life and death of Jesus. Only tiny snippets of the vellum manuscript, which were discovered in the Himmelgarten monastery, survived; on them are recorded the Flight to Egypt, the Three Magi, Satan tempting Jesus, Jesus calling his disciples, and the Wedding at Cana. This constitutes the first Passion play written in a European vernacular language.

Secular German theatre dates from over a century later, with one High and one Low German text. Around 1370 a scribe, probably from Schwäbisch Gmünd, entered the *St Paul (Swabian) Neidhart Play* of 58 verses into a formulary collection, which is now in the Austrian Abbey of St. Paul, Carinthia. Anticipating Carnival theatre, this play features the legendary court poet Neidhart (d. *c.*1240), a 'knight' who tricks peasants because they disgrace him by replacing the first violet of spring, a love token he meant to give to his patroness, an Austrian duchess, with a pile of faeces. At the same time, in the Osnabrück region, a medical man wrote down a sketch of 60 verses in which seven women woo the same man. Probably performed by young men during Carnival, the farce is a pastiche of an Old Testament passage in which the prophet Isaiah castigates the wanton women of Jerusalem, who, having lost their men in war, are desperate for husbands.

The repertory

Thousands of religious and secular plays, written by anonymous clerics, school teachers, town clerks, merchants and craftsmen, were performed between 1250 and 1550, but only about 300 of these texts have survived. Because many of these performances, even in churches, were sponsored by municipal authorities, records of their production are plentiful. Treasurers recorded subsidies for stage construction and payments to actors, town councillors licensed and prohibited public theatricals, and chroniclers reported major performances. Town archives of the period[1] show that from 1400 on theatre was performed in virtually every German town. Indeed, throughout Europe, theatre was the most important medium of public entertainment and communication.

The various dialects of German were spoken over a wider area than the boundaries of present-day Germany. We have records of German performances from Riga (Latvia), Danzig/Gdansk, and Breslau/Wroclaw (Poland) in the north to Pressburg/Bratislava (Slovakia), Sterzing/Vipiteno and Bozen/Bolzano (Italy) in the south, from Eger/Cheb (Bohemia) in the east, to Arnhem and Deventer (the Netherlands) and Strasbourg and Colmar (France) in the west. Theatre was most prolific between 1450 and 1550. Some regions and towns became performance centres, in particular Thuringia, the Rhineland and Hesse (Mainz, Frankfurt am Main, Alsfeld), Nuremberg and Lübeck (for Carnival plays), Switzerland (Lucerne, Basel, Bern, Zurich), and the South Tirol (Sterzing, Bozen).

Religious plays

The ritual function of drama dictates that each play conform to a type. An Easter play has a distinct form, no matter when or for which church a cleric wrote it. About two thirds of all religious plays were staged during the Easter season. Easter plays dramatise the Resurrection, with soldiers guarding the tomb in vain, the Marys buying ointments from a merchant, and the risen Christ harrowing Hell. Passion plays extend these events backwards in time to dramatise the life of Christ, especially his crucifixion. They usually include Mary's semi-operatic lament (*Marienklage*) beneath the cross, which was peculiar to German theatre and often staged separately on Good Friday. On Ascension Day, churches enacted Christ's ascension to heaven; on Corpus Christi, townspeople, venerating the Eucharist, performed the entire history of salvation.

Plays about the end of time – on the Five Wise and Five Foolish Virgins, the Coming of Antichrist, and the Last Judgement – were sometimes put on at Christmas. Most plays staged during the twelve days of Christmas, however, depicted Old Testament prophets foretelling the Saviour's birth in a stable, the nativity, the shepherds and the Three Kings bringing gifts, and the flight of Mary and Joseph into Egypt to escape Herod's murderous rage. Townspeople staged plays to commemorate saints, from the feast day of Saint Paul (25 January) to Saint Margaret's (13 July). Morality plays, featuring allegorical figures, virtues and vices battling for the human soul, were less popular in Germany than in England, France, and the Low Countries, but a three-day morality play dramatising gospel parables was performed in Erfurt prior to 1448. Morality plays were staged during Carnival in Lübeck after 1439 and Strasbourg put on Sebastian Brant's *Tugent Spyl*, featuring a contest between Lady Virtue and Lady Lust in 1518. Swiss towns performed political moralities, especially after the Reformation.

Playwrights not only dramatised the four gospels, but stories from the apocryphal gospels (Nicodemus, Pseudo-Matthew, Thomas, Mary Magdalene), which were eliminated by the church after the Reformation. They also drew on Old Testament stories prefiguring events of Christ's life and a rich body of fairytale-like saints' legends. As performance was tied to the liturgical calendar, virtually all religious plays were performed during the first half of the year.

Secular plays

Most secular plays were staged at Carnival, the days preceding Ash Wednesday being a prime festival time. Swiss schools and towns often staged plays at New Year. Among these was a political morality by Balthasar Spross of Zurich, first performed in 1514, which deplores the split between farmers who founded the Swiss confederacy and their sons, who hire themselves out as mercenaries. The New Year's festival also provided a dignified setting for patriotic pageants such as Jakob Ruf's *Spyl von dem ersten Eydgnossen Wilhelm Thellen* (*New William Tell Play* – Zurich, 1545). There are fewer instances of performances of secular than religious plays; 150 texts have survived and there are records of roughly 300 performances in fifty-nine towns. The majority of Carnival plays (*Fastnachtspiele*) – 109 texts – came from Nuremberg, most being short comic sketches, dwelling on the bodily functions. In 'court plays', plaintiffs and defendants engage in bawdy argument before a court with judge and jury, whose verdict, if they reach one, is usually a joke, while other plays dramatise comic tales. But not all Nuremberg plays are farces. Hans Rosenplüt (c.1400–65) wrote political plays attacking the gentry and the church, and Hans Folz (c.1435–1513), on behalf of the city council, wrote anti-Judaic plays as Nuremberg was attempting to drive out its Jews. Between 1510 and 1535 the play director Vigil Raber, notably during his years in Bozen (1510–22), wrote script booklets of some thirty Carnival plays. Brief descriptions from the company's books indicate that between 1430 and 1523 the Circle Confraternity of Lübeck performed some 76 plays on their wagon stage during Carnival. The Lübeck plays had a greater literary quality and were more morally focused than the Nuremberg variety, dramatising stories from classical history and heroic legend (Charlemagne, King Arthur), as well as romances, fables, and proverbs. Moralities exemplifying honesty, loyalty and trust as personal and civic virtues were a unique feature of Lübeck Carnival theatre. Lübeck merchants had imported these play types, as they did the wagon stage, from Flemish cities like Bruges. In a morality play from 1484, the wise fool Littlejohn (Henselin) leads three brothers in a search for justice among the estates, only to find it in their own hearts. During the Reformation, Swiss playwrights like Pamphilus Gengenbach (c.1480–1525) of Basel and Niklaus Manuel (c.1484–1530) of Bern turned Carnival plays into political and confessional theatre.

Early playwrights drew no sharp line between the religious and the secular. They also mixed the comic and the tragic into what would come to be called 'tragi-comedy'. In Easter and Passion plays the marketplace quack with his surly wife and sassy servant sells ointment to the Marys walking to Christ's sepulchre, braggart knights guarding Christ's tomb fall asleep, then flee in terror at the flash of the Resurrection, and Lucifer and filthy devils engage in bawdy horseplay. In Nativity plays, Joseph hires slovenly maid-servants to mind the Christ child, boils porridge, sips from the bottle, and joins shepherds and angels in singing and dancing around the cradle. Carnival also provided opportunities for townspeople to perform Old Testament, Antichrist, and Saints plays, such as Daniel saving Susanna, Saint George slaying the dragon, and the priest Theophilus pacting with the devil.

Writing plays

The profession of playwright did not exist in the early theatre. Even the prolific Nuremberg playwright Hans Sachs made his living as a shoemaker; his notable precursors were also craftsmen: Hans Rosenplüt, an armourer and gunsmith, and Hans Folz, a surgeon and part-time printer. Pamphilus Gengenbach was a printer, and Niklaus Manuel a distinguished painter who became a town councillor. Jörg Wickram (c.1500–1562) of Colmar was a town clerk, Hans Salat (1498–1561) was court scribe in Lucerne, then became a German teacher in Fribourg. Zacharias Bletz (1511–70) succeeded Salat as court scribe. Balthasar Spross (c.1490–1521) taught school, as did Jacob Wimpfeling (1450–1528) and Johannes Reuchlin (1455–1522), both of whom produced Latin or Humanist drama.

It was during the Renaissance and Reformation that artistic identity began to matter and bureaucratic bookkeeping preserved it. Most of the earlier plays were written by men who did not record their names, but even when we have their names, nothing is known about their lives. Dietrich Schernberg of Mühlhausen, Thuringia (fl. 1482–1502), who wrote the remarkable *Spiel von Frau Jutten* (*Miracle Play of Pope Joan*, c.1485) about an ambitious Englishwoman who, with the devil's help, rises to become pope, was a vicar and notary, while Arnold Immessen (*fl.* 1480–90), who dramatised the Fall of Man and his Redemption, served as priest in Einbeck, Lower Saxony. Starting in 1430, the Circle Company stewards in Lübeck recorded the names of the four playmakers they appointed each Christmas, two of whom were to write the Carnival play of the year. Although they were allowed to farm out the writing, probably to Lübeck teachers and other literati, the young merchants presumably composed most plays themselves. We do not know the names of earlier playwrights, most of whom were probably clerics or schoolteachers with a clerical education.

But poor record-keeping alone cannot be blamed for the anonymity of early German playwrights. Playwrights wrote for performance, so they did not disseminate their handiwork by asking patrons to commission multiple manuscripts. Play-scripts were open game; directors did not hesitate to adapt older plays to fit their needs, the playing space available, or the skills of their actors. A good example is the priest and notary Henrich Hültscher (*c.*1475–1547) of Alsfeld, near Frankfurt am Main, who, in 1510–11, with four associates, revised and enlarged the Alsfeld Passion play based on Frankfurt. They added speeches from other plays, inserted new liturgical chants, and scripted a prompt-book and part-sheets for the actors. Similarly between 1400 and 1440, a West Carinthian scribe compiled six religious plays to which four later hands added corrections, variants, and stage directions.[2] The playbook, now at Eger/Erlau, Hungary, is like a kind of bank from which playwrights could draw their own performance scripts as needed. Plays did not belong to a single author, but to the community. The author therefore saw no need to inscribe his name.

The same was true for secular plays. Carnival plays were part of a performance tradition and early writers did not leave their names. Hans Rosenplüt, who settled in Nuremberg in 1426, is the first named author of a Carnival play, which is probably no accident because Rosenplüt raised the Carnival play to the level of literature. Hans Folz was to continue this tradition. Both Rosenplüt's and Folz's plays found their way into manuscripts of short verse poems targeted at readers, which Nuremberg scribes started to compile around 1450. This practice meant that Nuremberg Carnival plays survived in large numbers (109 plays in twelve manuscripts written before 1500). In other towns, scripts were lost. Because plays were revised and changed in the process of being copied, we can never be sure what a particular playwright contributed. For example, when Vigil Raber went to Bozen in 1510, he encountered an active local tradition of Carnival plays. In 1510–11 Raber copied fifteen of these plays into small booklets, adding six more by 1520. In so doing, he introduced new characters, added dialogue, and inserted new personal and place names. We know this because twelve of the pieces he expanded came down from Nuremberg where they had been written prior to 1490. By rewriting and expanding them, Vigil Raber made them his own.

There is no reliable evidence as to how the Nuremberg plays made their way across the Brenner Pass to Bozen. Perhaps Nuremberg merchants travelling to Venice brought them as printed booklets. Although principally written for local production, some plays did reach other towns. The vicars of the Abbey of St Bartholomew, where the Frankfurt Passion play was first performed in about 1330, must have taken copies of the play north to Friedberg and Alsfeld. Vigil Raber would copy plays he was asked to direct in other towns: a Passion play in Trent (1517), for example, and an Ascension play in Cavalese (1518). In 1391, the scribe Johannes, probably working in Schmalkalden, Thuringia, wrote down three remarkable plays, among them the famed *Innsbrucker Osterspiel* (*Innsbruck Easter Play*) and Europe's first Corpus Christi play. By 1445, the play-book had reached Neustift Abbey in Brixen/Bressanone, South Tirol.[3]

In large-scale marketplace performances, spectacle mattered more than words, so scripts are not of high literary quality. They are more like librettos, providing opportunities for music, movement, gestures, props, and colourful costumes. Spectators standing between mansions, leaning from windows, and crouching on rooftops could not hear all the verses, especially when the wind was blowing. Everyone knew the plot, so it was the production that mattered. Most play-scripts comprised plain, work-a-day verses, devoid of poetry. Like sermons, the medium they resemble in their social function, plays were not meant to be read but heard and seen.

Hans Sachs of Nuremberg (1494–1576) was the most prolific early German playwright, writing some 85 Carnival plays, 70 'comedies' and 58 'tragedies'. After sending their son Hans to one of Nuremberg's Latin schools, the tailor Jörg Sachs and his wife Christina apprenticed him at fifteen to a shoemaker, while the weaver and mastersinger Lienhard Nunnenbeck taught him how to write poetry and compose music. Between 1511 and 1516, Sachs travelled as a journeyman shoemaker to cities like Munich, Würzburg, and Frankfurt, the only years he would spend outside of Nuremberg. He married Kunigunde Creutzer in 1519 and advanced to master-shoemaker a year later. In 1542, he bought a house near the Holy Spirit Hospice where he lived the rest of his life. While making and repairing shoes Sachs found time to write some 6000 literary works, 4300 of which were *Meisterlieder*. The impact Martin Luther had on him can be measured by the fact that he stopped writing between 1520 and 1522. In an influential broadside of 1523, Sachs declared his public allegiance to 'the nightingale of Wittenberg'. Luther's teachings gave his writings a moralistic tone: he never entertained without teaching a lesson. Sachs did not belong to the patrician oligarchy that controlled Nuremberg. The city council censored some of his works and Sachs had to obtain their permission whenever he wanted to put on a play.

A voracious reader, Sachs turned everything he read into verse. His works constitute a library of his age, from Roman histories to Boccaccio. With his Carnival plays, starting in 1517 with *Das hoffgsind Veneris* (*The Courtiers of Venus*), Sachs was able to connect with the Nuremberg play-making tradition, but he eschewed obscenity and concluded each piece with a moral. His 'tragedies' and 'comedies' replaced religious drama and set the foundation for German playwriting to come. Unfamiliar with Aristotle, Sachs adhered to the simplistic medieval definition that when the hero or heroine dies, it is a tragedy; when they live, a comedy. As he does in the *Tragedia von der Lucretia* (1527), his first tragedy, Sachs takes his plots from histories (Livy for *Lucretia*), European literature and the Bible. Unlike the Humanists, Sachs does not imitate Greek and Latin plays. Given to spurts of astonishing productivity, Sachs wrote about one hundred plays between 1550 and 1560. In 1551, he started directing his own ensemble and acting himself. Sachs's group staged his plays in Nuremberg's Martha church and, after 1556, in the church of the dissolved Dominican monastery, using a proscenium stage without scenery, backed by curtains.[4]

Producing scripts

Play directors needed a master script to produce a play and actors part-sheets to memorise their lines. The playmaking rules of the Lübeck Merchant Confraternity[5] instruct their 'Carnival poets' to hand out part-sheets to the brothers who had been drafted to act about three weeks before the first performance on Carnival Sunday. Records of the seven-day Passion play directed by Vigil Raber in Bozen in 1514 suggest that the task of producing scripts fell to those willing to write for little pay, like school-masters and their students. The German schoolteacher Michl took fourteen days to compile two master copies of the entire play for Raber's use. His fellow teacher Anndre Tanner bound them. Their colleague Alexius, who played Jesus, wrote some part sheets or booklets himself, but made his pupils copy most of them.[6] Most of these performance scripts and part-sheets were used up in the process of producing plays. Some surviving play-books are in half-folio format so that the director could hold them easily. They contain stage directions written in red ink (rubrics) and the entire spoken text. A few feature more detailed stage directions, sometimes in larger script, but give only the first two verses of each 'speech' the players had to deliver. The director's scroll for the earliest version (c.1330) of the Frankfurt Passion play consists of seven vellum sheets glued into a strip some four metres long and rolled up on wooden end-sticks. Presumably the director stood on the centre of the platform in the Frankfurt marketplace and unrolled the scroll as he 'conducted' the Passion. Erasures and additions indicate that Frankfurt clerics used the scroll for several performances.[7]

Most plays have come down, like the Nuremberg Carnival plays, in copies produced for readers who stored them in their libraries or archived them for future performances. The court clerk Johannes Kremer, after directing the 1492 Frankfurt Passion play, made a clean copy of the script that was to serve as a master for future performances in 1498 and 1506. Kremer's copy is the only complete text of the Frankfurt Passion to survive. In a lifetime of copying and directing plays, the diligent Vigil Raber – the most important entrepreneur of early German theatre – amassed more than 58 plays, the largest collection of master copies extant.

The son of a Sterzing baker, Vigil Raber (c.1480–1552) appears to have had little formal schooling. He made his living as a craftsman, gilding, wood carving, illuminating, and, occasionally, painting altar panels. Much of this work connected him to the theatre, which was his true vocation. Until 1522, he lived mainly in Bozen where, in 1510, he began his collecting career by copying Carnival plays circulating in the town. As became his habit, he changed and expanded the scripts to fit production needs, often adding passages, such as a prologue, a part he often played. In 1514, he worked for three months, at good pay, to design and build the stage, rehearse the actors and direct the seven-day performance of the Bozen Passion play. After directing plays in other towns as far south as Trent, Raber, from 1533 on, became the driving force behind theatre productions, both religious and secular, in his native Sterzing. After he died in December 1552, the Sterzing mayor moved quickly to purchase, for a modest sum, play-books, costumes, and properties from his widow. The community of Sterzing still owns the play-books.

Although Hans Folz printed two of his Carnival plays on his own press between 1483 and 1488, this was only for Nuremberg readers. The systematic publication of plays for distribution beyond the immediate community began late in 1513 or early 1514, when the Basel printer Nikolaus Lamparter published an anonymous Zurich Morality that satirises European politicians by assembling them to play cards. After 1514, playwrights like Pamphilus Gengenbach and Niklaus Manuel started marketing their plays in printed editions so that people could buy them and possibly stage them. On Carnival Sunday 1515, the 'honourable and skilled burghers of the praiseworthy city of Basel' staged Gengenbach's Morality *Die .X. alter dyser welt* (*The Ten Ages of Man*) in the Basel Kornmarkt. It features an old hermit who exhorts men from each of the ten decades of life to repent. Only the old men aged 90 and 100 are properly contrite, which is appropriate as no one expected to live so long at that time. Taking advantage of the market this public performance created, Gengenbach printed the play, illustrating it with woodcuts, which proved an instant success. Printers in Memmingen, Augsburg, and Munich issued reprints, and Jörg Wickram, who staged the play in Colmar in 1531 and 1542, produced a revised text. With a total of twenty-seven editions and nineteen performances – including one in the Sterzing parish church[8] – *Die .X. alter dyser welt* became the first hit play of the German stage.

Playing in churches

As they were part of the liturgy, Easter and Christmas plays in Latin were chanted and staged in churches. Common wisdom has it that European playmaking had to escape the confines of the church to become fully fledged theatre, but this is untrue. Latin church drama flourished between 1200 and 1500 when most of the approximately 1000 Easter plays preserved in service books were composed, three quarters of which were for German churches.[9] Church drama and vernacular theatre therefore flourished side-by-side. By the fourteenth century, Latin church pageants could be very theatrical. For an Ascension play in the church of Moosburg, Bavaria, clerics placed a statue of Christ atop Mount Sinai, a cloth-draped wooden scaffold in the middle of the church. Beneath it, a chorister chanted Jesus's verses. The Ascension was staged by the statue being pulled by a rope until it disappeared through a hole in the vaulting.[10] Because such stagecraft was needed, all German Ascension plays were performed in churches. In the Bozen parish church, Jesus and his angels stood in wicker baskets as strong hands winched them through this 'heaven hole'. Some towns like Zwickau performed Easter plays in churches. The churches in Tirolean towns had aisles equal in height to the nave, out of which they created a large 'theatre' with excellent sight lines. Bozen and Sterzing therefore staged all religious plays with the exception of Corpus Christi pageants in their parish churches. The weather sometimes determined if plays were staged in church or outside. The opening rubric of the *Marienklage* of Bordesholm near Kiel (*c.*1475) states that clerics could stage the Lament on Good Friday either inside the parish church on a raised platform before the choir or outside 'if the weather is fair'.[11]

Playing in marketplaces

In the thirteenth century,[12] German towns began to stage plays in their marketplaces. Although layouts varied with the proportions of the square, town carpenters built platform stages in two major configurations. The simpler was a large platform in the centre of the marketplace or against one of the buildings. The platform constructed after Easter 1460 on the Weinmarkt in Memmingen for a two-day Passion play measured 45 by 100 metres.[13] When the Passion Play Confraternity of Strasbourg presented its play in the Rossmarkt, the city ordered its carpenters to build a platform out of trestles and boards from the arsenal.[14] The second configuration was more elaborate, involving separate scaffolds placed around the square. These scaffolds served as 'houses' identified with groups of players, such as the Marys, Jesus and the disciples, Herod, Pilate and their courts, or the Jews. In the performance of their Passion plays, Villingen and Lucerne distinguished between roofed scaffolds, known as 'houses', and unroofed, known as 'courts'. According to the stage plans drawn up for the 1583 two-day Passion Play in Lucerne (see fig. 1), scaffolds were arranged along the two sides of the Fischmarkt (later called the Weinmarkt). Those housing righteous figures stood on the right hand of God, those peopled with wicked characters on the left. God and his angels sat in the sacred east, on a balcony-like scaffold built between two oriels jutting out from a tavern façade. Opposite, in the west, glowered Hellmouth, a dragon's head with jaws propped open by a door. This layout mirrored the Christian world view. From opposite sides, God and Satan had their eyes on the worldlings enacting the story of their salvation.

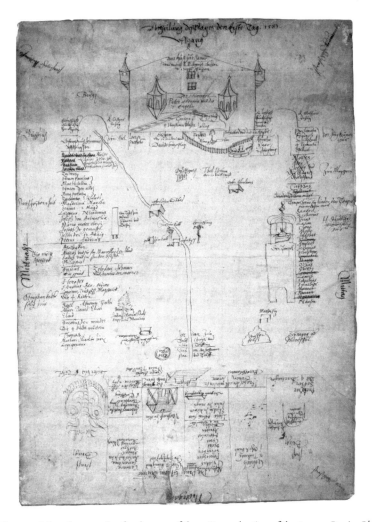

1 Renward Cysat's stage plan for day one of the 1583 production of the *Lucerne Passion Play.*

The spectators saw the actors at all times. Nothing was hidden, there was no backstage. Before Christ rose from the sepulchre, the audience must have seen him walking to the tomb, escorted by angels. The dramaturgical advantage of simultaneous staging was that it enabled the director to present two or three scenes at the same time. This was effective in showing how certain Old Testament events were believed to prefigure Christ's life. Those watching the *Heidelberger (rheinhessisches) Passionsspiel* (1514), probably in a Mainz square, saw four episodes enacted at the same time and were encouraged to contemplate how they were related. While Jacob was speaking with Joseph, a prefiguration of Christ, his brothers, who would sell Joseph, were minding flocks in the field. At the same moment, Judas agreed to betray Jesus for thirty pieces of silver while his master was eating at the house of Simon the Leper.[15] This mindset pervaded early Christian art. In old masters' crucifixion panels, Jesus appears in background scenes that precede and follow the crucifixion: Pilate condemns him, soldiers flog him and crown him with thorns, he carries the cross and is nailed to it; Nicodemus and Joseph of Arimathia take Jesus from the cross and entomb him, then the risen saviour breaks down Hellmouth to free the patriarchs. Medieval Christians commemorated the history of salvation as an eternal present, which is why artists and play directors represented Christian history as though it were taking place in the here-and-now. Church liturgy – Latin responses, antiphons, and hymns – remained part of outdoor productions. When some fifty-five actors staged the *Innsbrucker (thüringisches) Spiel von Mariae Himmelfahrt* (*The Innsbruck Play of Mary's Ascension* – manuscript dated 1391) in a three-day marketplace performance, well-trained choristers chanted thirty-two responses and antiphons. When priests and choristers intoned the liturgy, as in the Frankfurt and Alsfeld Passion, they added a theological commentary to the performance, which underlined church authority.

Marketplaces were also used to stage Carnival plays. The oldest known record of the performance of a secular play is that of a Neidhart play in the marketplace of Arnhem on Shrove Tuesday 1395.[16] Other towns along the Lower Rhine (Deventer, Geldern, Wesel, Dortmund), in Switzerland (Basel, Bern, Lucerne) and South Tirol produced Carnival plays in public squares, at times with multiple scaffolds. Although Lübeck confraternities pulled their wagon stages through the streets – a practice resembling the English one of announcing or 'banning' a play – they stopped them in order to perform, most likely in the marketplace before the town hall. Playing on a wagon in front of the town hall, attested in Flemish towns since about 1410, constitutes a variant of the marketplace stage. It offered frugal merchants the advantage of re-using the same stage every year. Although Lübeck performed its public Carnival plays on the afternoons of the three days before Ash Wednesday, most towns limited outdoor performances to Carnival Sunday. After Mass, townspeople would be at leisure to watch a play. But the main reason for the restriction was economic; Sunday was the only day merchants and traders did not need the marketplace to set up shop.

The marketplace was the town's economic centre. As the town hall and the parish church flanked it, it became the forum of political and religious authority. Players had to ask the mayor and town council for permission to use the marketplace, which incurred considerable expense. The town paid carpenters to build and tear down the stages and placed constables to guard the platform with its hangings and valuable properties and to control the spectators. They also paid musicians to play flourishes and interludes. During the performance they closed the town gates, set watchmen in the towers and posted firewardens in church steeples. The costs could be high, especially if the performance lasted several days and cut short the working week. Frankfurt staged its Passion play on the four days following Pentecost (1498), starting each day at noon and stopping when church bells rang in the night. The two-day performances of the Alsfeld and Lucerne Passion plays took all day, from 6 a.m. to 6 p.m. During these days no one could work, all marketplace trading stopped, and shops closed. But the town fathers willingly expended large amounts of public money because they regarded this as an investment. Public performances, like festivals today, fashioned the town's image and impressed countryside nobles and visitors from other towns. With marketplace performances, at Easter and Carnival, a town could place itself on the cultural map.

Playing in procession

The papal bull of 1311, instituting the Feast of Corpus Christi (*Fronleichnam*) on the Thursday after Trinity Sunday, specified that churches must display the Eucharist in a procession. Priests placed it in a monstrance and processed from the church through the streets allowing the faithful to venerate the host they believed to be the body of Christ. This explains why Corpus Christi plays, enacting the history of salvation from Creation to Doomsday, were staged in procession. Although they were popular in Europe, only about a dozen German towns sponsored them. Freiburg im Breisgau and Dresden enacted *tableaux vivants* on 'pageant' wagons used in northern English and Spanish towns. In Schwäbisch Hall, where the *Künzelsauer Fronleichnamspiel* was probably performed, actors and spectators walked through the streets, stopping at three platforms to perform brief biblical episodes, whose significance the 'rector of the procession' explained in a versified sermon. In Bozen, clerics and guildsmen enacted episodes in pantomime or a few spoken verses, while walking through the streets. The procession ended at the Musterplatz where plays featuring the Three

Kings and St George killing the dragon, employing a painted cloth over a wooden frame, were staged.[17] The Corpus Christi fraternity of Vienna enacted a Passion play in procession. Starting from St Stephen's cathedral, the brothers walked through the streets, stopping at four scaffolds to play (Neumann 2834, 2844).[18] Performing in the streets required the same regulations and expense as marketplace theatre. When Dresden staged its processional play on the feast of John the Baptist, the town asked citizens to remove wood and rubbish piles, merchant stands and carriages. To guard against fires, houseowners had to place water buckets in attics and in front of houses, while the town posted wagons with ladders and firehooks at street crossings.[19] Because spectators walked with the actors, the procession being part of the liturgy, they presumably had a more intense religious experience than just watching a marketplace show. Houses along the route were decorated, children spread flowers, leaves, and grass, and priest and players joined spectators in singing antiphons and hymns.

Playing indoors: House-to-house, town halls and schools

On 28 December 1417, the Day of the Innocents, the choirboys of the Constance Minster, led by their boy bishop, visited several houses, performing a short Nativity play and asking for gingerbread and pennies as they were leaving 'for Egypt'.[20] This is the earliest attestation of playing house-to-house. On their annual day of licence and revelry choirboys had been visiting houses and soliciting gifts since the twelfth century. By 1417, they used this occasion to put on Christmas sketches, performing house-to-house being the principal way in which Carnival plays were staged. This was probably common by 1417, but record keepers took no notice of such small-scale and private theatricals so there is virtually no documentation of them. This also goes for Nuremberg, the metropolis of Carnival plays. It is only because the method of performing Nuremberg Carnival plays is inscribed in the 109 texts we have that we are able to reconstruct it. On Carnival evenings, young men of all classes, including the Patriciate, would invade houses and taverns where revellers were feasting by oil lamp and candle light. Pushing aside tables and benches, they acted their sketches in a large room devoid of scenery, more in a presentational than a representational manner (see fig. 2). Players traded barbs with revellers, who no doubt responded in kind. As they finished, the minstrels struck up, the players danced with the women, then solicited wine, Carnival crêpes and small change as they left. In a dimly-lit room, where faces were hard to recognise,

2 *The Carnival Play of Ourson and Valentine.* Woodcut (1859) after Pieter Bruegel the Elder (*c.*1530–9).

this intimate chamber theatre was the ideal venue for bawdy Carnival playlets. Because revellers tolerated only brief interruptions, the typical Carnival play was short, about 200 verses.

The only set of records comes from a private source, an expense book, listing tips for players, kept by the stewards of a Lübeck merchant confraternity, the Greveraden Company. Between 1495 and 1539, pupils of town and church schools and choirboys, teachers and tradesmen put on 182 skits in the company clubhouse. Casts were small, on average three or four players. Up to sixteen small ensembles visited in one Carnival season, up to three would perform during a single evening. It was only when Carnival ensembles performed their plays in town halls or marketplaces that records can be found of them. Mayors, councillors, and judges with their wives celebrated Carnival in the meeting chamber of the town hall, usually located on an upper floor, which also served as a theatre. In Bozen and Sterzing, Raber and others staged Carnival plays in the town hall, a practice also recorded for the towns along the Lower Rhine (Deventer) and in Eger. These formally arranged productions, supported by public funds, called for longer Carnival plays of between 600 and 1000 verses. The performances took up a good part of the evening and would not be repeated elsewhere.

In contrast to the dignified ambience of religious plays, 'street theatre' of all kinds surrounded Carnival plays. Sons of the town elite and visiting noblemen staged jousts in the marketplace, other young men hunted down the 'Wildman', or hitched unmarried young women to ploughs and tree logs. Masked and costumed mummers paraded through the streets pulling ships or magnificent floats, which they set afire in front of the town hall on Ash Wednesday. In Nuremberg, *Schembart* maskers escorted dancing butchers holding sausage-like leather rings. Young men danced through the streets and squares of many German towns, linked together by hoops, arrows, or even axes and ropes. In Lübeck, after the afternoon Carnival plays, players directed by the 'Carnival poets', danced through the dark streets to the light of torches. Morris dancers leapt and twisted their bodies to win the favour of a 'Lady' holding an apple in the centre of their round. Sword dances were the most popular group dances for craftsmen. In Nuremberg, every seven years these were performed by the cutlers, who displayed their prized swords of Nuremberg steel. These revellers probably performed some Carnival plays as skits without formal scripts.

When Humanist scholars and teachers began to write plays – in Latin, but also in German, sometimes in Greek – their students performed them in schools, universities or palaces. Starting in 1495, Jakob Locher's students staged his plays at Freiburg University. In 1497, Johannes Reuchlin's Heidelberg students put on his Terentian comedy *Scenica Progymnasmata* (*Schooling through Theatre*) or *Henno*, based on the famed Parisian farce *Maître Pierre Pathelin* spiced up with the Italian *commedia dell' arte*, in the residence of chancellor Dalberg. In this performance, Reuchlin introduced the convention of signalling a change of location by having the actors leave the stage.[21] Konrad Celtis (1459–1508), the 'Arch Humanist' and first German to be crowned 'poet laureate' (1487), was instrumental in reviving the comedies of Terence and Plautus and Seneca's tragedies which his students would perform at Vienna University. Celtis introduced processions, music, and dancing into Latin festival plays he wrote to honour his patron, Emperor Maximilian I. At Carnival 1501, he joined learned friends in staging his *Ludus Dianae* (*Play of Diana*) in Linz castle, where the goddess Diana and her train presented the emperor, a passionate huntsman, with hunting weapons. Celtis's three festival pageants can be seen as precursors to Baroque court opera (see chapter 2). Some Humanist playwrights in the 1520s adapted the 'Terence stage' as depicted in the newly-discovered writings of Vitruvius. They closed the back of the platform stage with a wall depicting the street front of houses, each featuring a door through which characters would enter and exit. Humanist drama was mainly performed in the auditoriums of schools and universities, sometimes outside in gardens or courtyards.

Directors and actors

Records tell us little about the directors of early theatre. Clerics of various kinds constituted the most active group in the early centuries, as most drama originated in and was centred on the church. The first instance of town clerks directing comes in 1489 when Hans Pölsterl and Conrad Gärtringer produced the Sterzing Passion play.[22] In 1549 the Lucerne court clerk Zacharias Bletz directed the Antichrist and Last Judgement, standing in the centre of the Fischmarkt wearing a red cloak 'in the Roman manner', script in one hand, a gilded staff in the other, as he cued the actors and conducted the musicians.[23] The best known town clerk director is the obsessively thorough Renward Cysat of Lucerne (1545–1614) who directed the Passion play and Carnival pageants for several decades. Vigil Raber of Sterzing was the most prolific director of his age while Wilhelm Rollinger (c.1470–1521), a noted woodcarver, directed several performances of the Vienna Passion play.

In Carnival plays, the leader of the ensemble routinely recited prologues and epilogues. The Lübeck Circle Confraternity required the senior of the four Carnival poets to introduce the play to the crowd and conclude the performance with an epilogue.[24] In religious theatre, directors like Raber often served as *precursor* or *proclamator* as the prologue was called. Garbed like a herald, the precursor led the players to the stage, clearing a path through the crowd with his staff. He began the performance by calling for silence. Because spectators had no programme, he introduced the play and summarised what was to happen. Some plays used the herald to guide the audience through the complexities of the performance. In Gotha, a two-day pageant dramatised the destruction of Jerusalem, in which the herald Ottober explained changes in setting, introduced new characters, and repeated important messages. His part-sheets, the only piece of the script to have survived, allow us to reconstruct the performance.[25]

The first actor whom we know by name is Antonius, who played Mary Magdalene in the *Osterspiel von Muri*, probably in Zurich in 1260. As interlocutor of Jesus, Antonius ran the gamut of emotions from lament and despair to love and joy. Because he could speak in public and chant in

Latin, Antonius was probably a cleric.[26] The most demanding role was that of Jesus in the Passion plays. In the four-day Frankfurt Passion play of 1498, five priests took turns to play Christ.[27] Directors of Passion plays usually asked priests or vicars to play Christ; because, as they knew the liturgy and were trained to chant, they would portray the saviour with dignity. Directors found Judas the hardest role to cast because no one wished to play it. In Lucerne, an actor from another canton was hired for a fee and the town had to pay for his yellow robe and red wig.[28] Raber had to play Judas in the Bozen Passion play of 1514, but with characteristic energy he added lines to the part. The devils, however, attracted many prospects. In contrast to divine figures, who were serene and silent, devils were noisy and comic, with much leaping and shouting. They engaged in pyrotechnics as in the Winterthur Easter play of 1566 when, wielding tubes blazing with gun powder, they set the Hellsmouth scaffold afire.[29] The satanic body was believed to be anal, stinking, and erotic, so actors sometimes stepped out of bounds. The leatherer Daniel Frey, playing a devil in the 1507 Nördlingen Corpus Christi play, got carried away, grabbed women watching the procession and 'mated them like a dog', conduct for which the town council understandably jailed him.[30]

Townsmen volunteered to act in large numbers. By the fifteenth century, religious plays included minor characters barely mentioned in the Bible stories and saints' lives. Local youth clamoured to act, prompting dramatists and directors to create as many parts as possible.[31] Henrich Hültscher and his associates recruited about 200 actors for the Alsfeld Passion plays of 1511 and 1517. Since Alsfeld had a population of 2000, of whom at least half were women, about 20 per cent of the town's male population would have participated. Many actors were students and teachers, others came from confraternities. Lübeck merchant confraternities had a religious foundation, but over time became more like social clubs, one of whose functions was to produce the public Carnival plays. Religious confraternities staged plays in Vienna, Alsfeld, and Friedberg and many other towns. With the exception of the Corpus Christi play in Freiburg, German towns depended less heavily on guilds than English towns did. Actors paid for their costumes and props and received no fees. When a town staged a Passion play during the working week, the actors gave up their wages.

In casting religious plays, it was common for directors to engage the town's most prominent citizens to play authority figures. In the 1496 Sterzing Passion play, the master of the Teutonic Knights' hospice played

Nicodemus while a judge bestrode the parish church scaffold as Herod.[32] A church provost played Herod in the 1495 Bozen Passion play, while Raber, for the 1514 Bozen Passion, persuaded the mayor Sinseder to play the High Priest Caiaphas.[33] Men from Alsfeld's governing élite comprised about one-fifth of the Passion play cast; the mayor Johannes Coppersmedt played Pilate and Enders Gans, a military officer in the Landgrave's service, played the Roman centurion. Officials probably felt obliged to participate in community theatre because they regarded it as a significant cultural event. The church, moreover, proclaimed acting in religious plays to be a species of good work. In Lucerne, Mainz, Strasbourg and Vienna, church authorities promised actors remission of their sins, thus shortening their time in purgatory. In 1502, the papal legate Raimund Peraudi granted the burghers of Calw in Württemberg an astonishing 240 years remission for performing their Corpus Christi play.[34] Men of means were able to afford the magnificent costumes these authority roles required, while their busy lives benefited from having few lines to memorise. Seeing their dignified provost or sober judge rant as the evil tyrant Herod or their mayor represent the arrogant Jewish High Priest Caiaphas in the garb of a medieval bishop must have evoked in audiences feelings ranging from laughter and glee to quiet dread.

Producing and rehearsing a large religious play took several months. To perform a Passion play at Easter, Lucerne directors cast roles in November and began rehearsals in January. An ensemble in Solothurn needed only ten weeks to memorise and rehearse the two-day Saint Maurice and Saint Ursus play in 1581, a feat described as 'truly fast'.[35] The only device that helped actors remember their lines was the cue rhyme: the first verse a character speaks rhymes with the last verse of the preceding speaker. Raber inserted cue rhymes systematically into the Carnival plays he copied. Because they were shorter, Carnival plays were easier and less expensive to produce. Records call the performers 'gesellen', young fellows of all social classes, not just journeymen of the crafts and trades as scholars once believed. In Nuremberg sons of the Patriciate performed Carnival plays as did students and court scribes. Young merchants put on Lübeck's public Carnival plays, while journeymen and apprentices specialised in presenting Neidhart plays, such as the weavers of Burghausen in 1519 and the bakers of Salzburg from 1497 to 1558.[36] Because pieces were short and productions informal, ensembles could take Carnival plays to neighbouring towns. In Colmar (Alsace), Biel

(Switzerland), Sterzing and Bozen, groups from surrounding towns and villages performed in their region's major urban centre.

Throughout Europe, women did not perform on stage. The only exceptions were nuns, notably Hildegard of Bingen (1098–1179). The learned abbess, an exception in everything she did, probably directed her nuns, dressed colourfully as the Virtues, to sing and act her Morality play *Ordo Virtutum*. When Hildegard, born south of Mainz, was eight years old, her noble parents 'tithed' her as their tenth child to the Benedictine monastery of Saint Disibod where she rose to succeed her mentor, the anchoress Jutta as abbess in 1136. After Pope Eugene III recognised her as prophetess in 1147–48 at the synod of Trier, Hildegard went on to found her own convent on the Rupertsberg in Bingerbrück in 1150. By the time she died in 1179, Hildegard – mystic seer, poet, composer, preacher, and scientist – had achieved fame as the most powerful religious woman of her age, using prophecy as a charismatic gift to establish female authority. At the end of her first visionary book, *Scivias Domini (Know the Ways of God)*, Hildegard depicts the human soul on its pilgrimage through life, yearning for God's love, falling victim to selfish greed, and then returning to the true life with the help of the Virtues, positive powers of the monastic spirit (Chastity, Humility, World-Rejection, Heavenly Love, Patience, Obedience, Discipline *et al.*). In the *Ordo Virtutum* she dramatised this vision, composing solo and choir music of astonishing power and originality. While singing, Hildegard believed, the Christian soul remembers the lost music of paradise and responds to the harmonic nature of God from whom it came. Thus the devil, embodying the vices, the *Ordo*'s only male character, shouts his lines instead of singing them. Directing her twenty aristocratic nuns, Hildegard may have performed the music drama in 1152 to consecrate the Rupertsberg church. Since the manuscript contains no staging directions, however, the nuns could have simply sung it to embellish the liturgy.

According to texts and records, nuns staged Latin Easter plays, playing the Three Marys, in convents in Essen, Nottuln near Münster, and notably Gernrode abbey church around a stone Easter sepulchre still standing today. The only continuous performance tradition was among the aristocratic nuns (canonesses) of St George's convent on Prague's castle hill, who, from the twelfth to the fifteenth century, chanted and performed Easter plays in their church.[37] In all these performances, however, priests and deacons continued to play Christ resurrected, the angel at the tomb and the disciples Peter and John. The first woman to act in a German play was Martine Keldrer who played one of the three Marys in the 1496 Sterzing Passion play; Mathias Keldrer – presumably her brother – played the Virgin Mary.[38] In the Bozen Passion of 1514, Raber cast local women as the daughter of Cananea, Martha, and Mary Magdalene.[39] Records show that women assisted in many productions, sewing costumes, building small props, and preparing food.

As plays were performed by amateurs, the calibre of acting, while no doubt enthusiastic, was uneven. Precursors routinely ask the audience not to laugh when actors forget their lines. Only those playing authority figures like God, Pilate, Herod and the High Priests spoke while seated on thrones and chairs; others stood up to speak and sat down when done. To speak to characters played by other actors, actors walked to the centre of the stage known as the 'common place', which they transformed through 'spoken stage directions' into different localities. A choir of angels often intoned the song of 'Silence' to quiet the crowd after rambunctious devil episodes or to signal the end of an episode. The director also cued musicians to play appropriate background music or cover unexpected pauses in the production.

Sets, properties, stage machinery and costumes

Scenery came to be used only late in the period. A stage direction in the Zurich *Hiob* (*Job*, 1535) once attributed to Jakob Ruf notes that Job's house could be painted on linen so that it might be pulled up on ropes, presumably into a stage loft. Before that directors employed mainly stools, chairs and tables. In the first Frankfurt Passion play (*c*.1330), two barrels in the middle of the platform represented the temple pinnacle and the mountain where Satan tempts Jesus. A barrel served as Lucifer's post in many Easter plays. In some potentially dangerous scenes, directors substituted carved statues or life-size dolls for the actor. Some Marian Laments employed a wooden statue of the crucified Christ with moveable arms. In Vienna's processional Passion play, the crucified Christ was a statue, which Joseph of Arimathia and Nicodemus took down and – presumably after folding the arms – placed in the Virgin Mary's lap. Then they carried the statue into a chapel where priests intoned the 'Burial of the Cross' chant and lowered it into a tomb.[40] To represent Judas's suicide, the devils in the early Frankfurt Passion hung his effigy from the gallows. But by the time the people of Villingen (or Lucerne) staged the *Donaueschinge Passion-spiel* (*c*.1475), reserve had given way to graphic realism; Judas first hung himself from a tree, then, after hooking his body to a pulley, a devil rode him along a rope to the top of Hellmouth while tearing open his belly out of which tumbled fake intestines.

The best source for early stagecraft can be found in the notebooks Renward Cysat made for the Lucerne Passion play. He drew the well-known stage plans for the 1583 production (fig. 1). These included a trench with flowing water diagonally crossing the Fischmarkt to represent rivers like the Jordan; when Moses struck the rock, water flowed; Peter caught live fish in the Fischmarkt fountain before Jesus called him as disciple; a stage hand operated a pulley strung from the top window of the 'Heaven' tavern to the fountain column at the centre of the major scaffold; as the angel Gabriel announced to Mary that she is to give birth, the stage hand lowered a caged dove, representing the Holy Spirit hovering over her; when the Three Kings rode into the Fischmarkt, a star was pulled ahead of them until it stood over the stable. Not all of these tricks worked. In 1583 when Jesus expired on the cross, he pulled a string to raise a lid covering the hollowed top of the cross; from here a dove representing the Holy Spirit leaving Christ's body should have flown forth, but it opted to stay put; in 1597 Cysat scratched this trick. Cysat, whose father came from Milan, was familiar with advanced Italian stage craft and some of his effects may have anticipated Baroque theatricals to come. Yet even by the 1540s, directors in Protestant towns like Basel were employing complicated stage effects. To simulate the lightning that struck Saul on the road to Damascus – in Valentin Boltz's *Tragicocomoedia Sant Pauls Bekerung* (*The Conversion of St Paul*) – one stage hand fired a rocket from the balcony of a house representing Heaven while others produced thunder by rolling barrels filled with rocks. When Saul, played by Mayor von Brun, fell off his horse, blazing rocket powder set his pantaloons on fire. The Basel physician Felix Platter witnessed this stage accident as a boy and recalls it with delight in his autobiography.[41]

The best way to visualise early actors' costumes is through the religious art of the time. Until the seventeenth century, European artists did not historicise biblical figures but dressed them in fashions of their day. Pilate, Herod, and the Three Magi appeared as majestically accoutred kings and the High Priests Caiaphas and Annas as medieval bishops, their mitres sometimes twisted to resemble a pagan or Muslim half moon. Soldiers wore the armour and carried the weapons of their time. Young men playing women cross-dressed to hilarious effect in Carnival plays. Medieval specta-tors regarded nudity as outrageously funny, so when the script required nudity, as for example Adam and Eve in paradise, the patriarchs in limbo, or

Christ flogged and crucified, actors put on tight-fitting leather suits painted in body tones. This suit also hid the harness worn by the Christ actor, which, by hooking into a support bracket, allowed him to 'hang' for hours from the cross.

As in English Biblical pageants, divine and satanic characters routinely wore masks. When Wittenberg produced a Passion play in 1501, the director sent Lodewick Wilmar to the nearby town of Jüterbog to borrow several masks.[42] The young man playing the Virgin Mary usually had to don a mask because his face was not sufficiently sublime to represent the Mother of God. For the Dresden play of 1504, the painter Strassberger made a grotesque mask for Judas and masks for two Jews.[43] For reasons of 'public security', Nuremberg did not permit Carnival players to wear masks. In 1511, the controlling city council instructed actors to paint their faces instead and advised men playing women to cover their faces with a veil.[44] Wigs supplemented masks. The actor playing the one-time prostitute Mary Magdalene in the Vienna Passion wore a wig of such opulence that Wilhelm Rollinger, the director, pledged he would never permit any woman to wear it offstage 'for worldly joy and glory'.[45]

Stage properties tended toward the graphic. In 1514, Vigil Raber bought seventeen cattle tails for the devils to wear.[46] According to notes that Zacharias Bletz made for the 1560 Lucerne Passion, Judas represented his tortured soul by stuffing a live rooster, plucked of its feathers, under his yellow robe, releasing the poor fowl as he expired on the hanging tree.[47] Like much late-medieval art, Mathias Grünewald's Crucifixion panels for example, Passion and Corpus Christi plays featured graphic scenes of Christ's torture enacted with great ingenuity. In Lucerne, Longinus squirted pig's blood through a nozzle attached to the lance with which he pierced Christ's side. In the Freiburg Corpus Christ play of 1588, a gallon of blood flowed from tubes hidden inside the cross.[48] Such horrors were not presented for their shock value; rather they expressed a radical form of devotion, originating with Franciscan mendicants, known as 'affective piety'. This intensive worship required devout Christians to contemplate every cruel detail of Christ's redemptive suffering.[49] Commemorative monuments were raised to such devotional theatre. In 1492 and 1506, Frankfurt players erected the crosses on the Galgenhügel (Gallows Hill) flanking the road to Mainz where criminals were hanged, thereby turning the hill into Frankfurt's Golgotha. In 1498, players processed from the Römerberg over the Main river bridge to plant the crosses in a hillside cemetery and for years thereafter, townspeople and travellers saw the crosses looming over Frankfurt, reminding them of the city's theatre of devotion.[50]

Watching the play: The spectator as participant

When clerics and townsmen staged plays in marketplaces, thousands of people from all walks of life came to watch. Peasants flocked through the town gates, while the town council hosted the nobility from countryside castles and welcomed visitors from neighbouring towns. Only popular preachers like the Franciscan Berthold of Regensburg could rival religious theatre as a mass medium.

Since they authorised and subsidised the play, the town councillors claimed the best seats for themselves and friends. The Frankfurt city council watched the Passion play from the roof ramparts of the church of Saint Nicholas and from three town hall windows, both overlooking the Römerberg marketplace.[51] The audience, addressed as 'Christian people', did not just watch but were asked to participate by joining the actors in prayers and singing hymns and, at Corpus Christi, by processing with players and clerics. The church regarded this as a species of good works and offered indulgences to spectators.[52] The intense involvement of specta-tors in religious plays is best illustrated by an incident involving the Landgrave of Thuringia, Frederick the Arrogant. On 4 May 1321, he watched the *Five Wise and Five Foolish Virgins* staged by Dominican friars in the Eisenach marketplace. Following the parable in Matthew, the bride-groom Christ turned judge condemned the Five Foolish Virgins, who failed to do good works, to Hell, ignoring the pleas of the saints and his mother Mary. 'What use is it to pray to the saints', Landgrave Frederick shouted, 'when they are unable to help us on Judgement Day?' Not listening to councillors who pointed out that Judgement Day was not at hand, the count is said to have suffered a stroke and died.[53] However, in 1320 the Landgrave was already so ill that his wife had become regent for their minor son. Frederick actually died in 1323; nevertheless this story illustrates the power-ful effect this play – the only one to end as a Christian tragedy – must have had on pious believers.

During Carnival, young men invading houses and taverns to perform plays, interacted merrily with the revellers (fig. 2). They turned to them for advice, cast aspersions, begged for drinks and small change, and ended up dancing with the women. Players often improvised, like Bottom the Weaver, adding verses extempore and engaging the spectators in horseplay.

Carnival plays were set in the present, in the town, house or tavern where the ensemble performed. The scripts Vigil Raber wrote between 1510 and 1535 in Bozen and Sterzing provide good evidence of interactive theatre. Raber writes N (for *Nomen*, 'name') whenever he wants directors to insert names known to people watching the play –a local court clerk, for example, or the town's lutenist, a notorious lover, the local wine tavern or inn, or even the owner of the tavern where the ensemble is performing.

The licence of Carnival fools to improvise allowed ensembles to devise comic skits about townspeople they disliked or who were involved in scandals. After the Lübeck city council certified that business rivals had falsely branded the Mecklenburg merchant Johannes Westval 'a son of a skinner' (an untouchable profession), the Circle Confraternity, in 1432, staged a Carnival sketch demonstrating that 'Westval was [indeed] his father's son'.[54] At Carnival 1525, townsmen of Danzig/Gdansk performed a pastiche mocking Bartholt Hacke whose mother-in-law had taken back his wife, young daughter and the family jewels.[55]

Some characters in religious pageants were also prone to mingle with spectators, usually for comic purpose. Devils scared 'Christian people' by running into the crowd to grab playgoers, presumably hecklers, and drag them into Hellsmouth. Directors may have used devils to 'police' the crowd and keep unruly spectators in line.[56] The merchant or quack apothecary of the Easter plays often ran on stage from among the spectators and rejoined them afterwards so he must have seemed to the spectators to be one of them. Mentioning 'real' people by name occurred in the *Osterspiel von Muri* (c.1260) when the merchant hawked make-up and aphrodisiacs among ointments he offered the Marys for sale. He shouted out the names of Johannes Krumm and Rueli Statzen, probably known to the spectators in Zurich as local Don Juans.

When it came to Jews, this kind of 'reality show' turned sombre. At the end of the two-day Frankfurt Passion play, first staged around 1330, Saint Augustine baptised some Jews who had earlier vilified Christ. The script gives the names of prosperous local Jewish families – Lieberman, Kalman, Salman, Michilman, Secklin. Their synagogue stood near the square where the Passion play was being performed. The play's authors, clerics of the church opposite the synagogue, clearly longed for their conversion.[57] But this attitude, relatively benign as it was, did not last. The most painful fact concerning medieval religious theatre is its anti-Semitism, in French, Spanish, and Italian Passion plays as well as in German. The issue is less prominent in English plays only because the authorities had expelled all Jews from England by 1300. As they viewed Muslims during the crusades and the 'infidel' Turk in early modern times, European Christians regarded Jews as the Other, the enemy who had crucified Jesus. After the pogrom of 1349, Frankfurt consigned returning Jews to a walled ghetto and when, in April 1469, clerics and confraternity men staged an Antichrist play in the marketplace, Jews were ordered to remain in their houses and a guard was dispatched to lock the ghetto gate.[58] The processional Passion play performed by the Vienna Corpus Christi confraternity included no less than ninety men playing Jews with the cloaks and hoods that Jews were required to wear; printed paper sheets, attached to their costumes, invited ridicule.[59] Such anti-Semitism is not easy to overcome because the gospel writers depicted non-believing Jews as villains in the Passion story of Jesus, the Jewish prophet. Recent attempts to rid the Oberammergau Passion play of its anti-Semitism[60] and Mel Gibson's troubling 2004 film *The Passion of the Christ* show that the issue still confronts us today.

Controlling spectators was always a problem. The Strasbourg city council, in 1488, saw it necessary to impose fines on spectators who breached rules while watching the Passion play in the Rossmarkt. Spectators were not to bother the actors and should watch quietly without noise and commotion; if they brought stools, ladders, or wagons to help them see the play, they must not block the sight lines of the wealthier and worthier spectators sitting in the bleachers. No one could build an extra stand and charge people money for sitting there.[61] With large crowds jostling to see the play, accidents did happen. In February 1413 in Bautzen (Saxony), thirty-three spectators were crushed to death and many others injured when the roof of a house upon which they were standing to see a Saint Dorothy play collapsed.[62]

Since towns subsidised public plays, occasional attempts were made to collect money from spectators. In Dresden around 1500, the Kreuzschule placed collection boxes next to the platform in front of the Kreuzkirche, where teachers and students performed Saint Dorothy and other plays. The earliest instance of charging admission occurred in 1457 when Hans Jakob of Schweina took a Passion play he had written to Stolberg (Harz) where Heinrich Melse of Nordhausen joined him to produce a performance featuring five scaffolds. Stolberg collected fees at the town gates from visitors coming to see the play, but, as the council had to come up with funds to cover the deficit, not many can have come.[63] In Lent, around 1520,

Rostock made the first attempt to publicise a play by circulating a printed handbill, inviting people to come on a Sunday to the marketplace at 11.30 to see a unique play featuring the sacred number seven: the Seven Ages of Man, Christ's agonies linked to the seven canonical hours, the Seven Sorrows of the Virgin, concluding with an allegory of 'eternal happiness'. On the surviving copy of the broadside, a prospective spectator jotted the note, 'providing the weather turns fair'.[64]

Close to the Reformation, chroniclers and storytellers became fond of relating incidents of amateur actors going astray as they performed religious plays. In his *Facetiae* (*Facetious Tales*, 1508–14), Heinrich Bebel reports an embarrassing moment in Tübingen during a Passion play. When the actor who was playing Jesus saw Mary Magdalene, played by a young woman he dearly loved, standing under the cross, 'his male member began to rise'. Noting this with alarm, fellow actors led Mary away.[65] But we have no record of a Passion play being performed in Tübingen and the casting of a woman as Mary Magdalene would have been quite exceptional. Similar doubts arise from eye-witness reports about dignified performances being reduced to a sorrowful mess. The best known of these stories is found in the continuation of Thomas Kantzow's *Pommerische Chronik* (*Chronicle of Pomerania*). While the little town of Bahn was staging its Passion play, the townsman playing Longinus, nursing a grudge against the actor playing Jesus, thrust his lance straight into his heart, killing him instantly. The falling body crushed the actor playing the Virgin Mary to death. A friend of both victims, the actor playing St John, rushed over to strangle Longinus. Fleeing, the St John actor broke his leg leaping from a wall and guards arrested him. The Bahn council executed the murderer by breaking him on the wheel.[66]

In the thirteenth tale of Till Eulenspiegel's *Lustige Streiche* (*Merry Pranks*, 1511), a village priest asks Eulenspiegel to organize the annual Easter Matin play. The priest played the Resurrected, his one-eyed maid the angel at the tomb, and Eulenspiegel and two 'peasants' the three Marys. As the Marys approached the wooden sepulchre, the maid intoned *Quem queritis*. On Eulenspiegel's prompting, one of the peasant-Marys responded, 'We are looking for the old, one-eyed whore of a priest', which led to a punch-up between the priest, his maid and the peasants, while Eulenspiegel, as the woodcut testifies, slips away. Subjecting sacred rite to carnivalesque pastiche was only possible when people began to question the authority of the medieval church and the religious pageants that pious amateurs had been performing for centuries. These and similar reports of theatrical disasters signal the advent of the Reformation which would ultimately put an end to medieval religious theatre.

The end of medieval theatre: Survivals and revivals

As German towns and principalities introduced Martin Luther's reforms, the performance of plays at Christmas, Easter and Corpus Christi gradually ceased. Passion plays, Luther objected, might unintentionally turn a sacred moment into a joke. By stripping Christianity of its saints and legends, Lutherans also eliminated much of the subject matter of religious drama. Luther praised Terence, however, and believed that schools should continue to teach students by reading and staging plays. Although Protestant towns like Basel and Bern employed the stage to promote the new religion, most towns simply abandoned the old scripts, costumes, and props. Catholic towns in Bavaria and Austria continued to perform Christmas, Passion and Corpus Christi plays, while Lucerne sponsored magnificent Passion plays to affirm the old religion and defy neighbouring Protestant cantons. Ironically the Catholic church itself put an end to Christmas and Passion plays in the eighteenth century when it objected to raucous devils. The Oberammergau Passion play was the only one spared, surviving to this day as the sole example of early religious theatre.[67]

Tradition has it that after plague had killed scores of villagers in 1633, the Oberammergauers pledged to perform their old Passion play forever in the hope that plague would not return. The first extant script is based on three older Passion plays: the fifteenth-century Augsburg Passion, Hans Sachs's Passion *Tragedia* of 1558, and the Passion of a fellow master-singer, Sebastian Wild of Augsburg, published in 1566. Every ten years until the 1850s, Oberammergauers played only for local audiences, but then British and American travellers discovered in this 'remote, mountain-girt village' a religious Shangri-La, where simple and pious 'peasants', spurning modern materialism, enacted a medieval pageant to express their pure faith.[68] In fact, the 'peasants' turned out to be shrewd businessmen who knew how to market their play. In 2000, at the fortieth performance, all anti-Semitic references had been removed by the script director, Otto Huber, and between late May and early October 2000, half a million visitors, about 5,000 each day, witnessed over a hundred performances of the play.[69]

In 1730 the Leipzig professor Johann Christoph Gottsched, who would be a key figure in the establishment of professional theatre in Germany, was delighted to discover that the Germans of old had, like the ancients, written plays and, in 1757, published Schernberg's *Das Spiel von Frau Jutten* and Rosenplüt's Carnival plays. Later, in a poem written in 1776, the young Goethe rediscovered Hans Sachs, praising his 'Poetic Mission', and in the following year directed the Weimar Court Theatre in Sachs's Carnival play *Das Narren-Schneiden* (*Cutting Out Fools*). In *Faust*, Goethe imitated Sachs's rough-hewn four-beat lines (*Knittelvers*). Between 1903 and 1911, Hugo von Hofmannsthal rewrote the English Morality play *Everyman* subtitling it 'the play of the rich man dying'. He drew heavily on Hans Sachs's rendering of *Hecastus* (1539) by the Dutch Neo-Latin dramatist Georg Macropedius. Max Reinhardt first staged Hofmannsthal's play in Berlin in 1911 and, from 1920, produced it yearly at the Salzburg Festival, since when it has become the most frequently performed 'medieval play' of our time.[70]

In the twentieth century, directors like Erwin Piscator and Bertolt Brecht have revived or, more accurately, re-invented some staging and acting practices of early theatre. In his political plays, Piscator made use of the simultaneous place-and-scaffold stage, while Brecht employed 'estranging' figures in characters who introduce themselves and speak directly to the audience. Like medieval spectators, Brecht's audiences are to learn a message from what they see and should take action to change their lives. The irony is that Piscator and Brecht, who took his cue mainly from Chinese theatre, in fact knew little about early theatre.

Amateur ensembles, beginning with the *Wandervögel* movement preceding the First World War, have performed early plays with some regularity. The Redentin and Innsbruck Easter plays, the Hessian Christmas play, *Das Spiel von Frau Jutten* and Raber's Carnival comedies have been favourites. At British and North American universities, performance of early plays as a means of studying them has become a scholarly discipline. Because they have few theatre institutes, this has not yet happened at German universities, and studying theatre through performance is only now beginning to establish itself as a respectable discipline.

2 German baroque theatre and the strolling players, 1550–1750

GEORGE BRANDT

The term 'baroque' flows more readily from the pens of German-speaking than Anglo-Saxon scholars. Derived from the Portuguese word *barroco* (meaning a misshapen pearl), it originally had a derogatory meaning. But as baroque art came back into fashion towards the end of the nineteenth century, it shed its earlier connotation of the 'absurd' or 'grotesque'. Its critical usage is now so widespread that it covers a disparate range of activities and attitudes, from architecture, sculpture and painting to music and literature. Its meaning has become so broad that one may be tempted to feel that

> it is used as a general label for the period when this style flourished, broadly speaking, the seventeenth century. Hence such phrases as 'the age of Baroque', 'Baroque politics', 'Baroque science', and so on. This usage is probably more confusing than helpful . . . [1]

For some twentieth-century cultural historians, theatre in the widest sense, including opera and ballet, has been *the quintessential* expression of this 'baroque sense of life'. Some of these scholars' admiration, coming when the rationalist values of the Enlightenment have gone into decline, has perhaps been coloured by their seeing the ideology of baroque theatre as the affirmation of an absolutist, faith-bound, and stratified society, something they may have found congenial. The age of baroque was a period in which the Counter-Reformation sought to reverse the impact of Luther, Calvin, and Zwingli on popular beliefs and loyalties, and to restore an order which had been brittle for a long time. No less than the supremacy of the Church, the divine right of kings was asserted vigorously. The centralising tendencies of France under Louis XIV served as an example to many European monarchs, and the self-representation of ruling groups became increasingly extravagant. But it was an age of unceasing struggles only partially concealed by a glittering façade, an age of contradictions which make any over-arching generalisations hazardous.

Countries with different cultural traditions and class structures responded very differently to the *Zeitgeist*.

In surveying the German-speaking world in the baroque era, one is struck by its failure to develop its own theatrical idiom compared to the giant strides taken by Italy, France, Spain, and England. The emergence of a specifically German theatre was no doubt held back by the bloody though intermittent warfare between the Protestant Union and the Catholic League between 1618 and 1648. This devastating struggle known as the Thirty Years' War, which combined religious fanaticism with dynastic intrigue, left Germany in ruins for decades after it had ended. But that by itself is not sufficient to account for German theatre lagging behind the achievements of its Western and Southern neighbours. The Holy Roman Empire of the German Nation, that loosely structured territory in the heart of Europe, had emerged from the Reformation exhausted and racked by centrifugal forces, with no single urban centre, as in France and England, to provide the critical mass around which theatre could gather. The heritage of the master-singers, never professional in any case, had long been in decline; it led a mere phantom existence, which eventually ground to a halt in 1875 with the dissolution of its last 'school' in Memmingen: this consisted of a cobbler and two tailors.

Baroque court festivals

In the baroque era the gap between the entertainments available to different social strata was very wide. On the highest level there were the court festivals. Based in part on the Italian tradition of *trionfi* and in part on the French *ballets de cour*, they flourished throughout the baroque era with increasing ostentation and splendour; indeed they persisted well into the eighteenth century. These glittering celebrations of dynastic events – marriages, births, baptisms, and so on – aimed to exalt the ruling houses by impressing domestic and foreign elites with their wealth, power, and sophistication. They were framed in erudite mythological, astronomical, historical, geographical, and ethnographic references designed to flatter the spectators' understanding and confirm existing hierarchies as being God-given and hence 'natural'. Unlike English court masques, which employed a poet of the rank of a Ben Jonson, these German festivals conveyed their meaning less by the spoken word than by music, ballet, and visual spectacle. More often than not, leading roles in these self-aggrandising shows were performed by members of the court, including the prince himself.

A notable example of such a festival was held from 19 to 28 March 1616 in Stuttgart in order to celebrate the baptism of the son of Duke John Frederick and his wife Barbara Sophia of Württemberg. This event, which brought together Protestant rulers from different parts of the Empire, combined the spectacle of 'triumphal shows', song recitals, and elaborately choreographed dances with social entertainments such as banquets, jousting, a visit to the Duke's art collection, and two displays of fireworks.[2] Some of the songs and poems featured throughout the spectacle were composed by a well-known man of letters, the Duke's secretary and historiographer Georg Rudolf Weckherlin (1584–1653) who after the event wrote a description of the festivities in German and English, the latter as a tribute to a high-ranking guest, the Prince Palatine's wife Elizabeth, daughter of England's James I. But the festival's visual delights outshone its literary merits. The indoor spectacle, which included the entry of giant heads from which emerged twelve dancers of different nationalities, and a shop of mirrors, which was designed to reflect the beauty of womankind, was a 'guests-only' event, whereas the outdoor events, including emblematic processions of horsemen and triumphal cars, a movable bower and mountain, were witnessed by humbler onlookers as well. After a procession of the heroes of antiquity and assorted knights of different times and places, there sallied forth the ancient champions of Germany, including Arminius who had defeated the Romans, a role performed by the Duke Palatine himself. This appeal to national sentiment underlined the hidden agenda of the gathering, secret negotiations to disperse war clouds then looming on the horizon. Unfortunately these diplomatic efforts came to nothing: the Thirty Years' War broke out within two years anyway. However, the *Festspiel* had the effect of saddling Württemberg with a massive debt, which it took many years to pay off.

The war ruled out such extravagance for most rulers; but even while it lasted the Viennese court continued to celebrate family occasions theatrically. With the return of peace in 1648, festivities resumed in Vienna on an ever larger scale. The Emperor could afford to outdo lesser sovereigns in the splendour of shows designed to glorify the name of Habsburg and outshine the rival court of Louis XIV. On 24 January 1667 in the inner courtyard of the imperial residence, the Hofburg, an event entitled *La contesa dell' aria e dell' acqua* (*The Contest of Air and Water*) occurred to celebrate the recent marriage of the theatrically minded Leopold I (1640–1705) and the Spanish Infanta Margaretha Theresia, daughter of Philip IV.[3] The cost of this celebration was largely borne, at His Majesty's suggestion, by his loyal subjects. As its title suggests, the show was essentially an Italian affair, with a script by the Jesuit court poet Francesco Sbarra (1611–68) and music by court composers Antonio Bertoli (1605–69) and Heinrich Schmelzer (1620–80), it being natural for the largely Italian-speaking court to turn for inspiration to Italy. For the design and supervision of the horse ballet, which crowned the celebrations, two experts were imported from Florence and Ferrara. The theme of the elements competing for the honour of paying homage to the new empress was fairly trite, as was the idea of equestrian choreography. There had been a *festa a cavallo* in Florence in honour of the Grand Duke of Tuscany as long ago as 1615, and as recently as 1662 a three-day festival in Munich celebrating the birth of a son to the Bavarian Elector had featured a stylised tournament, *Drama Guerriero*, as the middle part of a trilogy linking Phaedra, Antiope and Medea. What made the Viennese event unique, not least in Leopold's own estimation, was its gigantic dimensions. The orchestra employed some 200 wind and string players alone, and more than 300 performers, all members of the highest nobility, acted the roles of the ancestors of the House of Habsburg. The equestrian ballet itself was climaxed by the appearance on horseback of Leopold impersonating himself. The costumes were of unparalleled splendour.[4] For once, some spectators just below the top echelons of society were admitted, but mere commoners who tried to sneak in were driven off with sticks.

Other princely courts also went in for lavish self-dramatisations. In the immediate post-war period, the Saxon Elector John George I (1585–1656) celebrated the double wedding of two of his sons with festivities in Dresden extending from 14 November to 11 December 1650. One of the high points was the *Ballet von dem Paris und der Helena* (*Ballet of Paris and Helena*) with 117 performers, in which both bridegrooms were involved. The story of the abduction of Helena resulting in the destruction of Troy, a calamity ultimately redeemed by the emergence of its successor state Rome, implied that Saxony would be restored to prosperity after the devastation of the recent war.

The next Saxon Elector, John George II (1613–80), a great patron of music and the arts, brought together the different branches of the ruling House of Wettin with an entertainment in Dresden lasting the whole of February 1678. This included processions, tournaments, hunts, fireworks, operas, and dances. The *Ballet von Zusammenkunft und Wirckung derer VII. Planeten* (*Ballet of the Reunion and Effect of the Seven Planets*) was designed by the outstanding German scenic artist of the period, Johann Oswald Harms (1643–1708), whose career also spanned Hamburg, Hanover, Brunswick and other places.[5] A notable contribution to the festivities was that of the *Prinzipal* (i.e. actor-manager) Johannes Velten.

The coming of the picture-stage theatre

German theatre had undergone a profound change around the middle of the century with the introduction of the scenic stage first developed in Ferrara, Parma, and Florence. The combination of backdrop, wings, and borders, all painted in perspective so as to create the illusion of three-dimensional space receding symmetrically to a central vanishing point, was to become the norm in a good many European playhouses. When this perspective scenery became changeable through flats being moved by machinery under the stage, exciting new visual possibilities opened up and the simpler staging methods of former times came to seem hopelessly antiquated. The evenly balanced stage picture gave the onlookers the image of an orderly universe; this was complemented in performance by grouping dancers and singers in similarly symmetrical patterns. A device characteristic of the German theatre until the end of the eighteenth century was the traverse curtain placed quite deep upstage, which could be closed to allow for scene changes out of the view of spectators while the stage action carried on downstage. But whereas in England and France the scenic theatre was soon occupied by professionals who threw it open to a paying public, in Germany it remained for a long time the exclusive domain of courts, schools, and religious institutions.

The first German to depart from the simplicity of humanist stage practice was Joseph Furttenbach (1591–1667). After a ten-year stay in Italy, where he studied theatrical inventions under Giulio Parigi (1590–1636) in Florence as well as many artistic innovations that the country had to offer, he published three books: *Architectura Civilis* (*Civil Architecture*, 1628), *Architectura Recreationis* (*Recreational Architecture*, 1640), and *Mannhaffter Kunstspiegel* (*The Noble Mirror of Art*, 1663). These treatises included a detailed exposition on the scenic theatre together with a good deal of other architectural and miscellaneous information. Furttenbach freely acknowledged his indebtedness to Italian examples, but developed quite a few ideas of his own. The last book in particular dealt with matters of stage management, including lighting effects of some sophistication.[6] In 1641 Furttenbach had a chance to put his theories into practice when he was commissioned to build a theatre for the Protestant *Gymnasium* (grammar school) in Ulm. Unfortunately this playhouse with a seating capacity of some 600 was rarely used.

The development of opera

The scenic theatre was introduced in the service of opera rather than spoken drama. Even open-air opera productions were adorned with scenery. Opera, which foregrounded the musical element even more than other court festival genres, originated in Italy together with the new staging methods. A short piece by Rinuccini on the Ovidian subject of Daphne, with music by Peri, had been produced in Florence in 1597 and the idea quickly caught on north of the Alps. In 1618, an Italian opera *Orfeo* – possibly Monteverdi's – was staged in an extraordinary venue, a theatre carved out of a mountainside in the park of Schloss Hellbrunn in Salzburg on the orders of Prince-Bishop Marcus Sitticus von Hohenems. This rock theatre, with ample space for performers and spectators as well as musicians and dressing rooms, exists to this day.[7] A German version of the Rinuccini libretto for *Dafne*, adapted by the poet laureate Martin Opitz (1597–1639) and with a new score by Heinrich Schütz (1585–1672), the leading German musician of the age, was premièred at Schloss Hartenfels in Torgau in 1627. This performance, the first of an opera in the German language, was occasioned by the wartime wedding of the Elector John George I's daughter, and it ended on a note of hope for the return of peace. The pastoral guise in which *Dafne* was cast would shape many of its successors.

The most dazzling developments in opera occurred at the imperial court in Vienna, though only for the benefit of the *crème de la crème*. As early as 1625, Eleonora of Mantua, wife of the Emperor Ferdinand II (1578–1637), arranged an Italian mini-opera to be performed for her husband's birthday. But it was the latter's successor, Ferdinand III (1608–1657), himself a composer, who initiated the glory days of baroque opera in Vienna when he summoned the brilliant theatre architect-cum-set designer Giovanni Burnacini (d.1655) from Venice. In 1652, Burnacini was instructed to build a theatre and supervise the production of an opera for the birthday of the Infanta of Spain. In 1653, Ferdinand had Burnacini erect a wooden opera house in Regensburg for a convention of German princes. Able to hold over one thousand spectators, this was later dismantled and transported to Vienna.

The magnificence of operatic productions reached its apogee in Vienna under Burnacini's son Ottavio Lodovico (1636–1707) whose versatility as a designer of scenery, costumes, as well as mechanical devices of every kind, found full scope during the reign of Leopold I. Initially, it had been planned

3 *Il pomo d'oro: Charon on the River Acheron.* Opera by Francesco Sbarra and Antonio Cesti, performed at the Habsburg Court in Vienna in 1668.

that the equestrian ballet, that high point of the Emperor's marriage celebrations in 1667, should be outshone by an even more ambitious operatic spectacle, *Il pomo d'oro* (*The Golden Apple*), with a libretto by Father Sbarra and music by Marc Antonio Cesti. But it took the younger Burnacini so long to prepare that the production could not be mounted until 1668. He tricked out the Greek myth of Paris awarding a golden apple to one of three goddesses with dazzling scene changes and startling lighting effects, flying machines and a wealth of costumes in rich and expensive fabrics (see fig. 3). The plot's dénouement was yet another act of homage to the young Empress: Jupiter gave the golden apple to *her* rather than to Pallas, Juno or Venus since she combined *all* the goddesses' virtues in her own person.[8]

Other courts for which opera houses were built included Munich (1651–4), Dresden (1664–7), Hanover (1687–9), and Wolfenbüttel (1688), where Duke Anthony Ulrich of Brunswick-Wolfenbüttel (1633–1714), a distinguished art collector, who took Louis XIV for his model as a ruler, lent a personal hand to opera productions as librettist, director, and performer, writing no fewer than ten German opera texts himself. These opera houses all reflected the existing social hierarchy in their tiered seating arrangements; the lower a spectator's rank the higher up in the house he or she would be accommodated. The prince was given the best view along the central axis of the sightlines, seated either on the auditorium floor at some distance from the stage or else placed in a raised, richly ornamented box at the back of the house, an arrangement which was soon adopted universally. Major courts kept out the lower orders altogether; lesser courts might admit citizens free of charge as long as they were decently dressed.

Operas that consistently used German rather than Italian texts flourished only in the Hanseatic city of Hamburg, from 1678 until 1738. Here opera was based not on princely patronage but on a share-owning scheme run by the wealthy business community. From time to time the opera's sponsors had to fight off vitriolic attacks by bigoted Lutheran clergymen. The driving force behind the Hamburg Opera was Reinhard Keiser (1674–1739), its conductor and musical director for over twenty years, who composed no fewer than 116 operas. The young George Frederick Handel worked under Keiser's guidance from 1703 to 1706.

Jesuit theatre

The worldly theatre of court spectacle, ballet, and opera addressed itself to a narrow elite, but religious drama, which was inevitably still prominent in an age of denominational strife, endeavoured to speak to wider circles. Various types of folk theatre and mystery plays lingered on after the Reformation, as did local saints' plays, at least in Catholic parts of the German-speaking world. But these efforts were soon overshadowed by more ambitious spectacles. Religious drama took on novel forms with the Counter-Reformation. From its foundation by Ignatius Loyola in 1539 until its dissolution in 1773, the Society of Jesus made play-acting in Latin an integral part of its educational programme. Not that teaching students to speak Latin fluently in public was altogether unprecedented. It was the legacy of humanism, the outstanding proponent of which was Konrad Celtes (or Celtis – his actual name was Bickel or Pickel, 1459–1508), a scholar anxious to revive the glories of Latin drama in performance. Crowned as poet laureate in 1487 by the Emperor Frederick III (1415–1508), Celtes was summoned to Vienna in 1497 to become the first director of the University's *Collegium poetarum* (Poets' College) by Frederick's successor Maximilian I (1459–1519). Celtes was determined to put into practice what he had learnt about the staging of Latin plays during his extensive travels in Italy, to such centres of learned theatrical activity as Ferrara, Bologna, and Florence. He not only wrote Latin plays as tributes to the imperial family – *Ludus Dianae* (*The Play of Diana*, 1501) and *Rhapsodia, laudes et victoria de Boemannis* (*Rhapsody, Praise and Victory over the Bohemians,* 1504) – he also had his students perform Terence's *Eunuch* and Plautus's *Aulularia* in the University's great hall to much acclaim in the winter semester 1502–3. The ambitions of fellow humanists were fired by these efforts, and authors like Jacob Wimpfeling and Johannes Reuchlin also wrote original comedies for their students to perform. The point of these exercises was not merely to raise proficiency in speaking Latin, the language of the Church and of scholarship, but to teach the students clear diction, decent deportment and the art of gesture, in other words oratory, with skills such as singing, dancing and the playing of instruments as added bonuses.

It was natural for the Jesuits to follow in the footsteps of the humanists as all these accomplishments would be invaluable in the station of life for which their pupils, the offspring of the aristocracy or high officialdom, were being educated. But the purposes of these dramatic performances was not merely one of self-improvement; their most vital function was the implanting at an emotional level, in performers and spectators alike, of those Catholic truths that the Society had been founded to propagate with the utmost militancy. By the time of Loyola's death in 1556, there were 33 Jesuit schools in Italy, Spain, Germany, and elsewhere. The first Jesuit school in the Holy Roman Empire was founded in Vienna in 1554; by 1588 it enrolled as many as 800 pupils. By 1640, out of total number of 16,000 Jesuit priests world-wide, including Latin America, 2,000 were in German-speaking lands.

Whilst the Society's educational rules of 1586 recommended the acting of comedies and tragedies in general, when they were revised in 1599 they insisted that no language other than Latin be used, that the subject matter be of a pious nature and that strict decorum be observed throughout. Women were to be excluded from the auditorium as well as the stage, and female costumes were banned. Over time some of these restrictions were relaxed. If they were well connected, women could attend plays, and some female characters, acted by boys, could appear in a play. The language barrier, too, was raised somewhat. German was used in the prologue to each act of a Jesuit play at Paderborn as early as 1604, and gradually German arias were introduced into the Latin play-text; by the end of the seventeenth century some plays were entirely in German.

Jesuit dramas were wordy at first. Jakob Gretser (1562–1625) called some of his plays 'dialogues' because of their rhetorical nature. But his *Dialogus de*

Udone Episcopo (*Dialogue Concerning Bishop Udo*), successfully performed in Ingolstadt in 1587 and Munich in 1598, gave dramatic shape to the story of an Archbishop of Magdeburg who, born a fool, was granted intelligence by the Virgin, but later cast into hell for abusing his position.[9] Characteristic elements of Jesuit drama were spectacular battle scenes and triumphs, magicians and ghosts, visions and dreams presented as *tableaux vivants*, the sufferings of martyrs rendered in gory detail, and the punishment of infidels. Locations that later Jesuit drama shared with the opera included the temple, the throne room, the inner courtyard, the street, the park, the forest, and the wilderness, a rock-flanked view of the open sea, its waves in illusory motion, and of course Heaven and Hell.

The first Jesuit performance in the German-speaking world was an import: *Euripus* by Lewin Brecht of Antwerp, first performed in Louvain (1549) and then revived in Munich (1560), Innsbruck (1563), Trier (1565) and Vienna (1566). Later such an exchange of play-texts would become uncommon. It was the duty of the Professor of Rhetoric to compose new plays in his capacity as *pater comicus* and then to direct them himself. Considered to be as ephemeral as sermons, these play-texts were not published after performance except on rare occasions.

Early Jesuit plays were large-scale open-air spectacles. Sensational processions through the streets were designed to astound and draw in the onlookers. One such parade featured 'giants, Jews, 160 German horses in armour and 130 Spanish horses, 230 foot soldiers in armour, drummers, pipers, triumphal carts, sleds, devils, men with lion's heads, Neptune, an elephant with Moors, and much else besides.'[10] Around 1600, performances withdrew indoors into the well-equipped assembly halls of Jesuit colleges, to be played mainly to elite audiences. They had large casts so as to involve as many students as possible, though the sons of the aristocracy would be given preference in the assignment of roles. The ability of most of the audience to follow Latin was taken for granted; but from 1597 onwards, programmes – at first only in Latin but later partly or even wholly in German – were designed to help the less erudite by giving the 'argument' of the play, a scene-by-scene synopsis, and a cast list. The letters O.A.M.D.G. – *Omnia Ad Majorem Gloriam Dei* ('To the greater glory of God') – invariably appeared at the end. These programmes were often delivered by way of invitation to leading citizens before the performance.

Jesuit drama inevitably reflected the *Weltanschauung* of its time. The Muslim world was represented as both a military and doctrinal threat, as in the *Drama de Godefrido Bullone duce Lotharingiae* (*The Drama of Godfrey of Bouillon, Duke of Lorraine*, Munich, 1596). This wholly mythologised story of the Christian commander in the First Crusade was reworked again and again in different texts and staged in Vienna, Innsbruck, Munich, Freiburg (Switzerland), and other places until as late as 1762. For Saracens contemporary audiences understood Turks, the bogeymen of the age. Another popular subject was that of Esther and Haman, over twenty versions of which can be traced between 1567 and 1768.[11] The *Book of Esther*, probably composed in the fourth century BC, is the legend of how the wife of the Persian King Ahasuerus saved her fellow Jews from extermination by their enemy Haman. One Esther play, performed in Munich in 1577, ran for three days and had a cast of 300. In some versions, like the one performed in Hall im Tirol in 1648, Esther was likened to the Virgin.[12] But there was no pro-Jewish bias in Jesuit dramas generally. A play by the Swiss-born Father Kaspar Rhey (1570–1625) about a youngster named Simon allegedly killed by the Jews was based on the age-old, frequently revived blood libel.

An early success in the indoor style of production was *Cenodoxus* by Jakob Bidermann (1578–1639). This tale of a learned Parisian lawyer, based on the legend of St Bruno of Cologne (1030–1101), was first staged in 1602 in Augsburg and revived in Munich and Lucerne in 1609, then in Ingolstadt (1625) and Vienna (1637); in 1636 it was even performed in Paris. A translation into colloquial German by Joachim Meichel came out in 1625.[13] Uniquely among Jesuit plays, *Cenodoxus* has had a twentieth-century revival, in Munich. When the first complete edition of Bidermann's dramas came out in 1666, the preface recalled the initial impact that *Cenodoxus* had had on its audience, as it provoked gales of laughter as well as thrills of deep horror. This story of a high-flying Doctor of Law mixes the genres; it begins almost farcically, but comic scenes alternate with increasingly ominous ones about the Doctor's salvation. The allegorical apparatus places Conscience and the Doctor's Guardian Angel in confrontation with Hypocrisy, Self-Love, and a clutch of devils led by one Panurgus. What Cenodoxus, no ordinary villain, suffers from is the deadly sin of pride. His pretended goodness is shown to be hollow; for example, he fails to help a shipwrecked mariner because there are no onlookers to admire his benevolence. Act V seals his fate at last: a heavenly tribunal composed of Christ, Peter, Paul, and the Archangels sits in judgment on his Soul while Cenodoxus in the flesh is laid out on his death-bed. The powers of Hell prepare to strike, and three times the dead man rises up from his bier to scream that he is about to be damned. But tragedy turns to triumph in that one of the bystanders, Bruno, has been so shaken by this miracle that he decides to lead fellow mourners into the wilderness where they will found the Carthusian Order.

This early Jesuit play probably employed what German scholars call 'cubic simultaneous staging', that is a platform serving as a neutral acting area with three cube-like curtained-off structures set upon it. These inner stages could be opened up to reveal specific locations, such as the Doctor's house, Heaven, or Hell. This arrangement, which was but a step removed from the humanists' traditional Terentian staging, would yield to full scenic presentation a generation later. The influence of Italian opera made itself felt in Jesuit drama, both in the greater visual sophistication of the settings and in the increasingly prominent part played by instrumental and choral music.

The Thirty Years' War did not put a stop to these college performances. By 1650 there were as many as 50 Jesuit theatres in German-speaking countries. The centre of gravity in play-making shifted south-east from Munich to Vienna. The Emperor Ferdinand III gave Vienna's Jesuit College a splendid theatre seating over 2000 persons, with a stage two storeys high that could work some dozen instantaneous scene changes. His successor, Leopold I, Jesuit-educated like his father, was even more supportive during the forty-seven years of his reign; he would regularly attend some six or seven performances during the school year. By then the Jesuit theatre had come to be a firm champion of imperial power. A prime example of the *Ludi Caesarei* (Imperial Plays) staged by the College in Vienna was *Pietas Victrix* (*The Victory of Piety*, 1659) by Nicolaus von Avancini (1612–86). In over forty years of dramatic activity, this Professor of Rhetoric and Philosophy who was also a court poet wrote numerous plays on allegorical, biblical, legendary and historical themes. *Pietas Victrix* celebrated a turning-point in Roman history, which established Christianity as the state religion, the Emperor Constantine's victory over Maxentius. This religious extravaganza deployed the full range of baroque stage technology: apparitions, visions, an aerial fight between a dragon and an eagle, flying serpents and furies, battles on land and sea, and assorted fire effects including flames spurting out of water – all marshalled in order to extol the House of Habsburg as the present-day champions of Christianity In German-speaking Switzerland, where there were no hereditary rulers, the Jesuit theatre celebrated not princely dynasties but saints and martyrs or the history of the Jesuits themselves. Thus, an open-air production in Lucerne in 1637 presented a fairly recent news item, namely the persecution of Christians in Japan.

The entire century was dominated by emblematic thinking in the visual arts as well as in literature. Father Jacob Masen (1606–81), a prolific playwright in the Cologne Jesuit school, compiled a volume of emblematic imagery available to playwrights in the 1120 pages of his *Speculum imaginum veritatis occultae* (*Mirror of Images of the Hidden Truth*), reprinted no fewer than eight times. His dramatic theory differed from Renaissance Aristotelianism in that it recognised only action as a valid criterion of unity, not time or place. He broadened traditional concepts by allowing as admissible dramatic genres 'comico-tragedy' (the fate of a person of middle rank that ends tragically) and 'tragicomedy' (the fate of a person of high rank with a happy ending).

The Jesuits were not the only Catholic teaching institutions to employ drama. The plays put on by the Benedictines, the oldest of all monastic orders, tended to portray divine justice as compassionate rather than vindictive. Unlike the Jesuits, the Benedictines allowed female roles on stage from the start, but portrayed by male students. The main sites for their performances were the University of Salzburg and the Kremsmünster *Gymnasium*, with Father Simon Rettenbacher (1634–1706) as the dramatist-director of both institutions. His language was far from the bombast that Avancini indulged in.[14] Other orders that used drama for educational purposes were the Cistercians and the Piarists, the latter being a secular order founded shortly before 1600.

We may gain some insight into the work of a Jesuit *choragus* from the posthumously published manual, *Dissertatio de Actione scenica, cum Figuris eandem explicandibus, et Observationibus quibusdam de arte comica* (*Treatise on Stage Action with Figures Explaining the Same and Some Observations on the Art of Acting*, Munich 1727) by Father Franz Lang.[15] This teacher had devoted some forty years of his life in the Society to writing and directing dramas. According to Lang, to have its desired effect, stage behaviour should be aesthetically pleasing and must appear natural but be tempered by art (§ II). The postures depicted by great sculptors and painters are recommended for imitation (§ III). Each part of the body is examined in turn so as to ensure its most effective management (§§ IV–IX). The actor's stance and gait are to be modelled on ballet positions. Standardised gestures are recommended to express specific emotions, with particular attention paid to the face, eyes, hips, arms and hands. Actors are enjoined never to turn their backs on the audience and never to act in profile. In dialogue scenes they are to speak facing the spectators while angling their bodies towards their interlocutors to convey the impression of conversation (§ IX).[16] These tenets, some of them still valid while others have obviously dated, are part of a tradition going back to Cicero and Quintilian In training his actors at the Weimar theatre, Goethe was to suggest a century after Lang that actors should use classical paintings and sculpture as models of gesture and deportment.

Protestant school drama

Some Protestant *Gymnasien* also had theatres, though as a rule they were less lavishly equipped than those of their Jesuit counterparts. Here plays were performed in German, but Latin was also deemed important. The Elizabethanum and Magdalenaeum in Breslau provided a regular platform for literary contributions by authors not on the staff of the school, notably the playwrights subsequently dubbed the 'Silesian School'. The outstanding talent among these was Andreas Gryphius (the Latinized form of Greif, 1616–64) who enjoyed high renown among his contemporaries both for his dramatic output and his Latin and German poetry. In his later years he was employed as a syndic (administrative officer) to his native town of Glogau (Silesia). Long foreign tours, including a six-year sojourn at Leiden University followed by travels in France and Italy, had acquainted him with the culture of other countries, in particular their theatre, which was further advanced than that available at home. His studies covered many fields; he was even alleged to know as many as eleven languages.[17]

With their dwelling on physical pain and spiritual suffering, Gryphius' tragedies reflected the Germans' wartime experience as well as his own. He located his tragic heroes among the ruling class in line with Renaissance genre theory as endorsed by Martin Opitz in his *Buch von der deutschen Poeterey* (*Book of German Poesy*, 1624). The protagonists' fate was clearly stated in the secondary title, a device also found in the titles of Jesuit plays and operas. *Leo Arminius oder Fürsten-Mord* (*Leo Arminius, or the Murder of a Prince*, publ. 1650) was a political intrigue based on Byzantine history; *Catharina von Georgien oder Bewährte Beständigkeit* (*Catherine of Georgia, or Constancy Proved*, publ. 1657) portrayed a Christian queen's martyrdom at the hands of the Shah of Persia, who desired her but demanded that she abjure her faith; *Ermordete Majestät oder Carolus Stuardus* (*Majesty Murdered, or Charles Stuart*, first version 1657) dealt with the execution of Charles I in which the king was glorified as a Christian martyr and, in the revised version of 1663, posthumously vindicated by one of the regicides going mad on stage.[18] In the preface to *Cardenio und Celinde oder Unglücklich Verliebte* (*Cardenio and Celinde, or Unfortunate Lovers*, published 1657) Gryphius apologised for the middle-class status, normally thought unfit for tragic treatment, of his two pairs of guilty lovers. *Grossmütiger Rechts-Gelehrter oder Sterbender Aemilius Paulus Papinianus* (*Magnanimous Lawyer, or the Death of A. P. Papinianus*, publ. 1659), told the story of an upright lawyer under the reign of the Emperor Caracalla, who paid with his life for refusing to bend the law. Gryphius sought to give tragic dignity not only to the remote past but also to such recent events as the death of the Georgian Queen in 1624 or the execution of Charles I in 1649.

Like other playwrights of the time, Gryphius was indebted to the ancients, especially Seneca. He used a five-act dramatic structure, choruses between the acts who comment on the action, prophetic dreams and ghosts, a typifying rather than individualising portrayal of character, and a highly rhetorical diction embracing both long monologues and stichomythic exchanges.[19] Like Opitz and the Dutch playwright Joost van den Vondel (1587–1679), whom he greatly admired, Gryphius employed alexandrines as the metre for tragedy, a practice retained by German playwrights until the second half of the eighteenth century. He was well aware of the effects made possible by changeable scenery: both *Catharina von Georgien* and *Papinianus* had thirteen scene changes; *Carolus Stuardus* called for as many as sixteen.

His comedies were located among the lower orders for whom prose was the appropriate medium. *Absurda Comica oder Herr Peter Squentz* (*Master Peter Quince*, publ. 1658) was indirectly based on the mechanicals' scenes in *A Midsummer Night's Dream* and proved a popular piece at court performances, on school stages, and with strolling players until as late as 1759. *Horribilicribrifax* (publ. 1663) poked fun at boastful soldiers and enabled the author to show off his language skills in polyglot dialogue. *Die geliebte Dornrose* (*Beloved Thorn-Rose*, publ. 1660) developed love complications in a rural setting and employed broad Silesian dialect.

Other playwrights close to Gryphius were his fellow Silesians, the diplomat Daniel Casper von Lohenstein (1635–83), whose alexandrine tragedies cast female protagonists such as Cleopatra, Agrippina, and Sophonisbe in a negative light and revelled in sensational scenes of horror, and the Breslau lawyer Johann Christian Hallmann (1640–1704) who delighted in even gorier scenes. Gryphius' reputation as a playwright was high during his lifetime: his plays were performed on popular as well as exclusive stages. *Papinianus* was adopted by some companies of strolling players, and it was also performed by the Benedictines in Salzburg. But in the following century his fame was to dwindle away, and there have been only sporadic attempts to revive a few of his works since.[20]

As the rector of the Protestant *Gymnasium* in Zittau, Saxony from 1678 until 1708, Christian Weise (1642–1708) wrote plays in his capacity as a schoolmaster. Adapting his output to the talent available among his charges, he provided his school with three pieces a year: a comedy, a biblical drama, and a history. He is now thought to have written some sixty plays altogether, not all of them published. His pedagogical aims were the standard ones – to endow his students with good diction and deportment as well as a firm moral backbone.[21] Writing a prose relatively free from bombast, he reflected life in a more down-to-earth manner than the Silesians, which may be why the two Breslau schools that staged the works of the latter do not seem to have performed any of Weise's plays.

Concurrent with these efforts was the development of so-called Purim plays among Jews in Germany and elsewhere, probably from the sixteenth century onwards. Purim, a celebration, on the fourteenth day of the month of Adar (roughly early March), of the legendary salvation of Persian Jewry, is essentially a family festival which included, and still includes, disguises and clowning. How these plays in Yiddish (*not* in Hebrew, the sacred language of religion) arose is uncertain because of the scarcity of original documents, the earliest complete text of the *Play of Ahasuerus* only going back to 1697. Some scholars have assumed a connection between this rough-and-ready play-making and non-Jewish folk drama such as German Shrovetide plays. A link with the more literary Italian-Jewish or Sephardic traditions seems doubtful. The obvious story material was of course that of Esther, but the repertoire also included other subjects such as the sale of Joseph by his brethren or David and Goliath. These partly improvised playlets, performed in family homes or public venues with minimal stage furniture, by itinerant clowns, failed yeshiva students and klezmer musicians, were often frowned upon for their scurrilous humour by the rabbinical establishment. In spite of the isolation of Jewish communities from the wider German public, a David and Goliath play performed by out-of-town actors in Frankfurt am Main around 1700 is alleged to have attracted crowds of Gentile spectators.

The influence of the *commedia dell'arte*

But what about the position of *professional* actors in the German-speaking world? Some attempts at professionalism had sprung up towards the end of the sixteenth century. For example, in 1615 a company led by Johannes Fridericus Virnius and Bartholomeus Freyerbott applied for permission to perform to the city council of Danzig. But without a native body of drama on which to build, such early attempts were still-born. So it was foreign companies who brought fresh theatrical concepts to the German-speaking world.

For well over two centuries the Italian players of *commedia dell'arte* enjoyed great popularity in Germany, just as they did elsewhere in Europe. Their usual comedic material depended for its success on the actors' improvisational skills. *Commedia* featured masked or half-masked character-types such as Arlecchino, Pantalone, the Dottore and the Capitano, as well as unmasked characters such as the pairs of lovers. Instantly identifiable by their costumes and attributes, these performers jigged their way through ever-renewed scenarios in different combinations of familiar plotlines. Oddly enough, the first visual documentation of *Commedia* is to be found in Germany – in the frescoes on the so-called '*Narrentreppe*' (the fools' staircase) and other mural surfaces of Castle Trausnitz, near Landshut. This lively sequence of illustrations was commissioned by Duke William IV of Bavaria in 1576 to commemorate the players who had entertained him there. In the very year these frescoes were completed, the illustrious company of the *Comici Gelosi* displayed their skills at the court of Emperor Rudolph II in Vienna. Other *commedia* companies performed at the courts of Stuttgart, Regensburg, Augsburg, and Linz. Throughout the following century, these companies would again and again visit the Empire, especially its southern, Catholic parts. Thus in 1628 the *Comici Fedeli*, led by the famous Giovan Battista Andreini (c.1578–1654) performed in Vienna and Prague. Francesco Calderoni, known as Silvio, went to Munich in 1687 where he stayed for four years; his company later performed in Vienna in 1706 and 1707. Sometimes relations between the Italians and their royal patrons went seriously awry. In 1697 Augustus, Elector of Saxony, nicknamed 'the Strong' (not least for his amorous prowess) commissioned Angelo Costantini (1655–1729), scion of a distinguished acting family and renowned as Mezzetino, to assemble and take to Dresden a company of some hundred actors. But once there, the star actor committed the *faux pas* of making love to the monarch's favourite mistress – and as a result found himself in prison for twenty years.[22]

The *Englische Komödianten* and others

Shortly after the advent of the Italians, visitors from England were to make an even deeper impact. With the opening of The Theatre (1576), The

Curtain (1577) and The Rose (1587), a new breed of fully professional players had sprung up in Elizabethan London. Due to growing competition at home, some groups crossed to the Continent. They achieved a lasting fame in Germany under the title of '*Englische Komödianten*' – meaning 'actors' rather than 'comedians' in the English sense. First among them were five actors from the Earl of Leicester's Men under the leadership of the comedian Will Kempe (d.1603). After playing in Denmark in 1586, this group travelled to Dresden to perform at the court of the Saxon Elector Christian I, not returning to England until 1587. Kempe was to join the Chamberlain's Men, Shakespeare's company, in 1594 where he created such immortal roles as Dogberry; but after quitting that company he visited Germany again. The next contingent of English actors was led by Robert Browne of the Earl of Worcester's players who made the first of many visits to the Frankfurt Fair in August 1592. His repertoire included such popular old chestnuts as *Gammer Gurton's Needle*. In 1595 his company were appointed players and musicians to Maurice, Landgrave of Hesse-Kassel (1572–1632). This ruler, a patron of the arts as well as a composer and playwright, was to erect the first German theatre building between 1603 and 1606, the Ottonium (named after his son Otto). Browne returned to London but continued intermittently to perform at the Frankfurt Fair and elsewhere on the Continent. Having spent the winter of 1619 in Prague at the court of King Frederick of Bohemia, he was last heard of in Germany at the Easter Fair in Frankfurt in 1620. The actor who was to succeed Browne as head of the company, John Greene, also had many noble patrons. His performance of a number of English plays at the imperial court in Graz in 1608 was enthusiastically described by the young Archduchess Maria Magdalena in a letter to her brother, the later Emperor Ferdinand II.[23] Greene was forced to leave the Continent in 1620 by the sequence of events that initiated the Thirty Years' War: the Bohemian noblemen throwing the Emperor's representatives out of a window in Prague Castle in 1618, the choice of Frederick of the Palatinate as the King of Bohemia in 1619, and the latter's defeat at the Battle of the White Mountain on 8 November 1620. But in spite of the relentless spread of warfare that followed these disasters, Greene came back to play in Cologne, Dresden, and Frankfurt as late as 1626–7.

Landgrave Maurice was not the only princely theatre enthusiast. Duke Henry Julius of Brunswick (1563–1613) wrote ten plays, some of which showed traces of English influence.[24] Thomas Sackville, a member of Browne's company who had settled at Wolfenbüttel, then the capital of

Brunswick, became a servant at the Duke's court. *Vincentius Ladislao* (1594) was a comedy written by the Duke about a boastful soldier which featured a clown called Johann Bouset (John Posset), a role created by Sackville using broken German for comic effect. Sackville went on a lengthy tour in Germany and then returned to Wolfenbüttel, with enough money to retire from the stage altogether in 1602. Like Sackville's, the stage names of other English Comedians were based on comestibles. John Spencer, who went over to the Continent in 1605 and performed at the courts of Saxony and Brandenburg, called himself Hans von Stockfisch (Sir John Dried Cod) in his clown roles, and in 1617 Robert Reynolds created the comic character of Pickelhering (Pickled Herring), a name that was to be adopted by German Comedians for over a century.

As for performance venues, the English Comedians would quickly put up stages anywhere they were permitted to perform – in the great halls of castles, in tennis courts, orangeries, town halls, fencing academies, monasteries, or wherever. As on the Elizabethan open stage, the downstage acting space would have a neutral connotation, while an inner stage might from time to time be used to discover specific locations. Some basic furniture would be all the scenery there was. What the English Comedians did offer by way of spectacle was the splendour of their costumes and, in the eyes of the German audiences, an amazing professionalism. They would play musical instruments such as lutes, cithers, viols, and fifes; they would dance, fence and perform all manner of acrobatics; above all they used their clowning to overcome the language barrier. Since they had to work with visual rather than verbal signals, fidelity to play-texts hardly mattered. Verse plays were mashed into prose; stage business tended to be coarsened, becoming violent in tragedy and obscene in comedy. As one might expect, among the ten plays in a volume of *Engelische Comedien und Tragedien* (*English Comedies and Tragedies* – Leipzig, 1620 and 1624) was the ever popular prose version of *Titus Andronicus*.[25] Biblical subjects struck a ready response: a comedy on the familiar subject of 'Queen Esther and haughty Haman' was included in this anthology. In *Romeo and Juliet* as performed by Greene in Dresden in 1626, we meet our friend Pickelhering as a servant in the Capulet household.[26] But the English Comedians did have the merit of being the first to introduce the plays, in however mangled a shape, of Shakespeare, Kyd, Peele, Chapman, Dekker, Beaumont and Fletcher, and their fellow playwrights to a Continental public. A significant item in their repertoire was Christopher Marlowe's *Doctor Faustus*, which was itself based on a

German chapbook published in Frankfurt as recently as 1587. The story thus repatriated to Germany in dramatic form was in turn to give rise to a puppet play, a perennial fairground favourite that would in time inspire the young Goethe to a lifelong effort, which he would abandon, take up again, revise, and complete only shortly before his death, to give this profoundly German myth its definitive literary form.

As long as the English actors were employed by a court they were the prince's servants. The patent thus granted did not give them a licence to appear before public audiences elsewhere: for this they needed the consent of the local council. They had to beseech the city fathers in humble terms to grant them the pleasure of serving so distinguished a community as theirs. Some towns welcomed the offer, others rejected it. The English Comedians were never allowed to perform in Zurich where the puritanical streak in Swiss Protestantism made all secular drama unacceptable. One fear was that strolling players would suck money out of a town to spend it elsewhere. If permission to play *was* granted, there were conditions attached. The players were obliged first to put on a so-called *Ratskomödie*, a closed performance for town councillors and their families, who could inspect the material for any offensive matter and be provided with a free entertainment. Other conditions imposed on players were that performances must not clash with any church services or official periods of mourning, and players had to donate a proportion of their takings to a charity such as the local poor-house.

To announce the afternoon's performance, it was customary to parade around town in the morning and make a merry din with trumpets and drums. Since that annoyed quite a few staid citizens, some companies got into the habit of putting up printed playbills. In fact, the oldest professional German playbill still extant announced an entertainment by English Comedians in Nuremberg consisting of a comedy followed by a ballet and a farce, a typical sort of programme in fact. (Unfortunately only the day of the month but not the year is listed, which leaves four possible dates between 1630 and 1652.)[27]

The English Comedians soon discovered they had to acquire a modicum of German or hire native assistants. Browne trained some young German actors while staying in Kassel. During the war, fewer and fewer English companies visited Germany. George Jolly, known as Jolliphus (*fl.*1630–1673), was among the last of the English actor-managers; he came over after peace had been restored in 1648, probably because theatres in England were closed under the Commonwealth. A pioneer, in that he had women in his company and used changeable scenery, he performed at the coronation of Leopold I in Frankfurt in 1658. But in the course of time the label of *'Englische Komödianten'* attached itself to companies that were partly or even wholly German. The last mention of such a company, by then probably English only in name, occurred as late as 1697.

As the English merged with the theatrical mainstream, another foreign influence briefly made itself felt – the Netherlands. The Dutch company leader Jan Baptista van Fornenbergh (1624–97) toured parts of Northern Germany – Hamburg, Flensburg, and Schleswig – where spectators who spoke or understood Low German would be able to follow the dialogue. The Fornenbergh repertoire included not only recent Dutch playwrights but also plays from the Spanish Golden Age, thus opening up another rich mine of new texts for the German public. What struck audiences about Fornenbergh and other Dutch actors was their device of freezing the action at key points in order to form static groupings called *vertoningen* (i.e. *tableaux vivants*); these would be imitated by some German companies.

An indication of future trends was the employment by the Bavarian court of a company of French actors in 1671, at a time when the drama of the *Grand Siècle* was gaining a Europe-wide reputation. Similarly, Hanover and nearby Celle jointly maintained a French court theatre from 1668 onwards. This development was to grow mightily in the eighteenth century when it was a matter of honour for German courts to maintain a French company for the spoken drama, a French dancing master for the ballet, and an Italian opera company.

The beginnings of German professional companies

With all these foreign influences, it is difficult to pinpoint the beginnings of the German acting profession, but it can be said to have emerged in the mid-seventeenth century. German actors were the heirs of the English both in terms of repertoire and performance conditions. Like them, they might be contracted for a spell as servants to a prince, in which case they would be obliged, as evidenced in an agreement with the Elector John George II of Saxony around 1670, not to depart from their master's residence without prior permission, to accept whatever role they were assigned, and to remain silent 'unto the grave' concerning any court business they happened to get wind of. In the absence of employment, they would travel from town to town in search of a venue and permission to play, still obliged to perform a *Ratskomödie* and contribute to a local charity. Acceptance of these foot-loose vagrants would differ from place to place. Clerical opposition, chiefly but not exclusively from Protestant ministers, often made life difficult. Parades to announce a forthcoming show would still take place, but playbills were becoming more and more common. The main difference between the early and mid-seventeenth century was that strolling actors were increasingly expected to provide something by way of scenic spectacle. The frontispiece of a volume of plays entitled, *Teütsche Schawbühne* (*German Theatre*) published in Strasbourg in 1655, gives an idea of what such a fit-up stage might have looked like (fig. 4) The illustration appears to represent a scene from Pierre Corneille's *Le Cid* in Isaak Clauss's version. Lit by two chandeliers, four fairly crude sets of perspectively painted wings represent a street scene with cloud borders suspended above, upstage of which an opened-up traverse curtain gives onto an inner stage that continues the street in illusory depth up to a central vanishing point. The spectators are standing, not seated, in front of this stage.

The status of German actors was morally dubious and professionally precarious. Many had second jobs not only as puppeteers and tightrope walkers, but as oculists, tooth-drawers and quacks of various kinds. One such dual practitioner still green in popular memory was Johann Andreas Eisenbart (1663–1721), a *Prinzipal* as well as a surgeon. The folk-song commemorating him as the medico who 'caused the blind to walk and the lame to see' and who trepanned a patient with an axe is less than fair: Eisenbart came from a family of surgeons and, though he never a qualified as a doctor, was successful in both his professions.

One of the earliest German *Prinzipale* to make his mark was Michael Daniel Treu (1634–1708) whose troupe began by touring around Northern Germany and Scandinavia, but which went south to Nuremberg and Munich in 1669 and became 'Comedians to the Bavarian Elector's Court'. Treu's repertoire comprised much standard English fare, such as Kyd's *Spanish Tragedy* and Marlowe's *Doctor Faustus*, not to mention *King Lear* and *Titus Andronicus*, but it also offered plays from the Spanish (Lope de Vega and Calderón) and the Dutch (Vondel) as well as Italian opera. It included a few German plays such as Gryphius' *Papinianus* and the political allegory, *Das Friede wünschende Deutschland* (*Germany Longing for Peace*, 1647) by the Protestant pastor Johann Rist (1607–67). But there was not much to draw upon in the way of German repertoire.

More important was the troupe of Carl Andreas Paulsen (1620– d. after 1679), which served as the training ground for many other professionals.

4 *Teutsche Schawbühne*, Strasburg 1655. Frontispiece of a book of plays.

A native of Hamburg, Paulsen embarked on his career in the early 1650s with a troupe mostly of students and a few actresses. One of the company's several names was the '*Hochdeutsche Comoediantenbande*' (The High German Company of Actors), which indicated that they performed neither in

English nor Dutch. This was to become a standard title for different troupes of strolling players for a century or so. The Paulsen company still featured many of the traditional English standbys but quite a few French titles had been added, especially plays by Molière, Corneille and Montfleury, whilst Lope de Vega and Calderón sounded a Spanish note. German drama was represented by Daniel von Lohenstein's Oriental melodrama, *Ibrahim Bassa* (*Pasha Ibrahim*, 1659). In addition to frequent visits to Copenhagen, Paulsen's tours covered a wide area of the German-speaking world. When he played at Danzig in 1669, the town councillor kept a diary noting eight of the plays he had seen, one item of particular interest being Paulsen's version of the Faust story.

Johannes Velten (1640–93?) raised the standing of German professional actors even higher than Paulsen. After obtaining the degrees of Bachelor and Master of Rhetoric and Poetry at the Universities of Wittenberg and Leipzig he joined Paulsen's company in 1665 and married Paulsen's daughter, Catharina Elisabeth, before forming his own group. Velten's troupe – twelve actors in addition to himself, his wife and his three children – took part in the previously described Dresden court celebrations in 1678, to which they contributed six German plays – four comedies, a tragicomedy, and a tragedy. They were officially appointed actors to the Saxon court in 1684 and performed as well in Nuremberg, Worms, Cologne and many other places, chiefly in Northern Germany. In their largely foreign-derived repertoire, German drama was represented by Gryphius' *Papinianus* and *Peter Squentz*. They outshone their rivals in the breadth of their repertoire: as many as eighty-seven items in it are known to us. Although it is difficult to define their acting style with any precision, the literary quality of their offerings may well suggest a higher performance quality compared to that of other troupes. But in spite of his high reputation, Velten met with fierce opposition from Protestant clergymen who even refused him holy communion as he lay dying in Hamburg. When his widow took over the troupe, she too was attacked for what some religious zealots saw as an 'immoral' way of life.

Another actor from the Paulsen Company was Andreas Elenson (d. after 1706) from whom sprang three further generations of actors. His daughter-in-law Sophie Julie Elenson first married his son Julius Franz, but after his death she married the *Prinzipal* Johann Caspar Haack (d.1722). When Haack died, she married the actor-manager Carl Ludwig Hoffmann (d.1731). This company was joined by Johann Neuber (1697–1756) and his wife Friederike Caroline (1697–1760), who in their turn went independent, and after the

dissolution of the Hoffmann troupe in 1726, took over some of the disbanded actors. The Neuber couple – particularly the better known wife who
has gone down in history as 'die Neuberin' – worked hard to bridge the gap
between theatre and literature, but this ambitious woman's occasional
attempts to eliminate the 'unliterary' figure of Harlequin were neither
consistent nor successful.

Varieties of improvised theatre

Curiously enough, the stock figures and plotlines of Italian comedy were
adopted quite late by German actors. When the *Comédie-Italienne* was
re-established in a permanent home in Paris in 1716, there was an upsurge
of interest in Germany in their more up-to-date form of the *commedia dell'arte*.
This led to the increased versatility of Harlequin, who in one play would
impersonate many characters in different disguises. Because of the virtuosity
required by his interpreters, Harlequin held sway on the German stage for
several decades in the early eighteenth century and even came to replace the
familiar Pickelhering. The Harlequin player Joseph Ferdinand Müller is
remembered for his bitter rivalry in the 1730s with Caroline Neuber for
the Saxon patent and a performance venue in Leipzig. Even the famous
Prinzipal Johann Friedrich Schönemann (1704–82), a champion of serious
German drama, played Harlequin roles at different times in his career. A
playbill for a comedy at Güstrow (Mecklenburg) in 1741 boasted that he
would undergo as many as eight transformations as Harlequin, including a
three-year-old child and a parrot.[28] The 'last German Harlequin' was Franz
Schuch (1716–64), yet another *Prinzipal* who played entirely literary as well
as improvisational roles.

Until well into the first half of the eighteenth century the mainstay of the
repertoire of most strolling players was not the high literary drama of
foreign, chiefly French, inspiration, but what was called *Haupt- und
Staatsaktionen*, i.e. 'principal and political plays'. The reason for this composite appellation was that the offering so described was the *chief* item in a
programme of several entertainments presented in one afternoon, and that it
involved matters of state. Plots illustrating the life-and-death struggles
among the great and powerful were of course largely the legacy of the
English Comedians. In contrast to French classical drama's restrained and
predominantly verbal treatment of such subjects, the *Haupt- und
Staatsaktionen* revelled in crass effects and extravagant histrionics. Gory and
rumbustious as they were, they left plenty of room for non-literary

improvisation, at times indulging in vulgar touches of comedy. Japes of this kind might well involve the popular Harlequin figure inserted as a counterfoil to the 'high' drama of the leading characters. Thus, in *Der Unglückselige Todes-Fall Caroli XII.* (*The Unfortunate Death of Charles XII*), a four-act play about the Swedish king's recent death in battle, written between 1720 and 1730 for the company of Johann Gottlieb Förster, there are slapstick episodes in an otherwise fully written-out script. When Harlequin enlists as a soldier together with his camp-follower friend Plapperlieschen (Little Miss Blabbermouth), their antics are in grotesque contrast with the bloody narrative of the Swedish king's downfall. No wonder Harlequin, resistant as he was to the discipline of the written text, became a key figure in the struggle to 'elevate' the German drama (see chapter 3). But the diamond-patterned zany was not the only *commedia* character on the German stage. Johann Peter Hilverding (b. *c.*1690), a member of a Viennese family of puppeteers, actors and choreographers prominent for well over a century, became known as the '*Berlinische Pantalon*' for his performance of the Venetian magnifico in the Prussian capital.

The improvisational tradition of strolling players took a characteristically Austrian form in Vienna. Joseph Anton Stranitzky, born in Graz in 1676, came to Vienna in 1705–6 with Johann Baptist Hilverding, father of the *Berlinische Pantalon*, as leader of a company that performed with marionettes and live actors. Stranitzky, who also practised dentistry on the side, gave up his puppets and created the stage character of Hanswurst (Jack Sausage). This was a traditional German name for a clown, but by making him into a Salzburg hog butcher, Stranitzky created a wholly new type in conspicuous contrast to Harlequin. Coarse and earthy but not so crafty as his Italian rival, this black-bearded figure sported a pointed green peasant hat, a pleated collar, a short vest with a heart-shaped red spot on it, and yellow trousers laced on the side with blue ribbons; the cross-band of his braces bore the initials 'HW'; his hair was tied in a top-knot; and he had a slapstick tucked in his belt.[29] Stranitzky was the first *Prinzipal* in the German-speaking world to have a theatre built for him, the Kärntnertortheater in Vienna, which he moved into in 1711 and where he performed until his death in 1728. He adapted familiar stories like Amphytrion, Faust, and Don Juan, and German versions of Italian operas, giving himself ample room for extempore gags. Hanswurst gained such wide popularity even outside Vienna that he was imitated by German strolling players like the dentist-actor-puppeteer Johann Ferdinand Beck (*fl.* 1703–36). Gottfried Prehauser

(1699–1769) who joined the Kärntnertortheater company in 1725, took over as the second Hanswurst after Stranitzky's death. He made Hanswurst less naïve and rustic and took a more cynical view of the life around him.

The survival of what some scholars regard as 'baroque' features into a different, more rationalist age provoked the so-called 'Hanswurst controversy' of the late 1740s which pitted the improvisers of the Kärntnertortheater against the French theatre next door, the forerunner of the famous Burgtheater. The sympathies of the Empress Maria Theresa (1717–80) were emphatically on the side of French literary drama and against vulgar buffoonery, so when she introduced theatre censorship in 1752 it was for reasons of taste as much as politics. This did not altogether clip Prehauser's wings, nor was the tradition of this essentially Austrian folk comedy destroyed entirely by the hostile polemics of the 'enlightened' journalist Joseph von Sonnenfels (1732–1817), though the Kärntnertortheater ensemble did decide after Prehauser's death to perform only 'regular' plays. Vestigial elements of this popular Viennese theatre can be discerned in the following century in the work of Ferdinand Raimund and Johann Nestroy.

But here we stray beyond any definition, however elastic, of the baroque.

Summary

Let us sum up the period and its long-term achievements. On the plus side we note a wealth of musical talent, both in composition and execution, and much ingenuity in design and staging, though largely of foreign inspiration; on the negative side we see an acting profession held back by its humble status, a peripatetic way of life, and the absence of any 'standing' theatres in which to perfect their art and secure a foothold in society. The lack of national unity, the country's hierarchical division of taste, and an educational system favouring foreign over German drama mean that theatre workers lacked both an indigenous repertoire and an educated public. Without a firm foundation, they could not build a robust tradition. It was the long and onerous task, then, of the following era to confront these shortcomings and overcome them.

3 Classical theatre and the formation of a civil society, 1720–1832
ANTHONY MEECH

In the mid-eighteenth century prospects for the development in Germany of a theatre to rival those of the other European states looked bleak. Parisians had been able to enjoy the canon of French drama at the Comédie-Française, in effect France's national theatre, since 1680, while in London, although theatre was run on more commercial lines, there was an established tradition of professional performance of English plays stretching back to Shakespeare's time a century and a half before.

Aristocratic and bourgeois theatre
Germany lacked a single capital city, which could attract writers and actors as well as provide a pool of informed audience members large enough to support significant theatre activity. Although there had been moves towards a confederation of German states, these had come to nothing, for, as W. H. Bruford suggests:

> The confederation would have had to include in the eighteenth century, kings of European importance like those of Austria and Prussia, the electoral princes, ninety-four spiritual and lay princes, one hundred and three counts, forty prelates, fifty-one free towns, in all some 300 separate 'territories'.[1]

Some of those rulers maintained court theatres, but there was little or no support for German language theatre among the nobility. They preferred French plays, often performed by French companies, or Italian operas sung by Italians. The more robust German-language theatre of the *Haupt- und Staatsaktionen* did not attract an educated, intellectual audience. As late as 1780, Frederick the Great, who famously regarded the German language as only fit for his dogs, could comment in his *De la Littérature Allemande* (*On German Literature*) that German literature would be of significance in the future, but he refused to acknowledge that any works of importance had been produced in the language so far. 'Frederick could not be persuaded, as

Schönemann wrote to Gottsched, that a German could write or German actors perform anything worth seeing on the stage, much less go to see a German play for himself.'[2]

What produced the conditions for the rise of a serious German language theatre in the mid-eighteenth century was the burgeoning self-confidence of the German bourgeois, mercantile class, whose influence and social importance increased with their wealth. Travelling German merchants who might have seen the neoclassical dramas of Racine and Corneille and the increasingly popular *comédies larmoyantes* of La Chaussée performed at the Odéon in Paris, or who might have enjoyed the performances of Garrick and Mrs Woffington in versions of Shakespeare at the Drury Lane Theatre on visits to London, would have been painfully aware of Germany's theatrical deficiencies.

Customarily excluded from court entertainment and mistrustful both of the form and content of Italian opera, neither the merchant class nor the numerous *Beamten* (civil servants attached to courts) sought to enter the cultural world of the aristocracy. Instead they were looking for a theatre that would dignify the German language while validating their world-view and embodying their values. The merchants used their business skills and the civil servants their administrative experience to make themselves indispensable to their rulers and, having established their economic and bureaucratic credentials, they were now looking for a vernacular theatre that could compete with those abroad. Above all they were looking for a theatre to which they felt they could take their families for an enlightening cultural experience. And for this they were prepared to pay.

Their self-confidence as a class was bolstered by the popularisation of ideas of the philosophers of the Enlightenment, amongst whom were the theologian Philip Jakob Spener (1635–1704) whose religious movement, Pietism, sought to replace the authority of the orthodox church by personal divine illumination. This confidence in humanity's ability to perfect itself, along with the widely held belief that God had not made the world perfect but had chosen to make the best of all possible worlds, engendered a new self-assurance in the middle classes and culminated in Kant's call for humanity to have the courage to use its own reason, rather than rely, as previously, on authority. No longer was humanity obliged to submit itself to an unalterable hierarchy in its view of the world. Humanity could stand, self-reliant, on its own two feet, and interpret the world for itself, using its God-given reason. And in this essentially anthropocentric universe, compassion would be promoted as the cohesive force in society.

Various attempts were made in Germany to acquire a national literature by imitation of foreign models. While poets emulated the sonnets of the Dutch poet Joost van den Vondel, in the theatre it seemed logical to turn to France, whose neoclassical drama was at the time accepted as the model in England and throughout Europe. The art critic Johann Joachim Winckelmann (1717–68) had awakened an interest in classical art in Germany. But this formulation of the qualities of Greek art, specifically sculpture, did not restrict itself merely to the aesthetic.

> The outstanding characteristic common to Greek masterpieces is, in the last analysis, a noble simplicity and a quiet grandeur, as much in the pose as in the expression. As the depths of the ocean remain calm, however troubled the surface, so too the expression of a Greek statue, however impassioned it may be, shows a great and serene soul.[3]

The 'grandeur' of art alludes to the stoical way in which the figures endure suffering, its 'simplicity' to the stripping away by the artist of all adornment, and the exposing of the essential humanity in his subject. These classical ideals of the primacy of form, control, and decorum were identified and admired not only in French writing but also in French thought, art, architecture, and even in the design of their gardens, which epitomised the Enlightenment's control over unruly nature. French gardens maintained a rigid distinction between paths and plants, much as French theatre subscribed to a rigid distinction between the genres of tragedy and comedy. Humanity's duty was to employ its God-given reason to impose order on nature. To this end, French dramatists regulated their plays in line with what they considered to be the classical unities of time, place and action, which they claimed to derive from Aristotle's *Poetics*.

Gottsched and a new classical theatre

The first effective call for a reform of the German stage came from Johann Christoph Gottsched (1700–66) who was appointed Professor of Poetry at Leipzig University in 1730, and Professor of Logic and Metaphysics from 1734. He was not alone in calling for a new drama for Germany. Christian Weise had earlier expressed ideas on drama similar to those of Gottsched and had worked them out in practice, but as his theatrical activity was limited to productions with schoolchildren, his influence was negligible. The Swiss critic Johann Jakob Bodmer (1698–1783) was vocal too in his rejection of opera in favour of realistic tragedy, but Gottsched's influence was greater due to his capacity to realise his ideas in practice by stepping out of the study and becoming involved with practical theatre production. He worked out his ideas on theatre during the 1730s with the old Elenson-Haack theatre troupe that was now based in Leipzig and had been given new life by the management of Caroline Neuber (1697–1760). He compiled a repertoire for this troupe, based on principles expounded in his seminal work *Versuch einer critischen Dichtkunst vor die Deutschen* (*The Critical Poetics*, 1730). In this Gottsched rejects the extravagant implausibility of much baroque theatre and grounds the plays he selects in a Theory of Probability, defined as 'the resemblance between what is written and what is accustomed to happen in real life'.[4] All poetry must be based on preordained rules, which are established by reason, and poetry can be judged as good or bad to the extent to which it accords with these rules. Gottsched chose as his inspiration dramas from France, which indicated at the time the quintessence of good taste. With his wife, Luise Adelgunde Gottsched (1713–62), he produced a number of translations from the French as well as six original tragedies. He recognised the value of comedies, but, unlike his wife, lacked the ability to write them. He did however establish something of a reputation as a writer of tragedy, which he describes as 'a picture of accidents which befall the great of this world and which they either heroically and steadfastly endure, or by which they are overcome, while retaining their greatness of spirit'. For Gottsched tragedy is important as it 'entertains insofar as it terrifies and distresses us. It teaches and warns us by way of unfamiliar examples; it uplifts us while giving pleasure, and sends its audience home more prudent and steadfast'.[5] The most famous of his plays, *Der Sterbende Cato* (*The Dying Cato*, 1732), is a verse tragedy, in part based on Joseph Addison's 1713 play *Cato*, written in the French manner in alexandrines – twelve syllable rhyming lines – with confidantes and strict observance of the unities.

The plays introduced onto the stage by the Neuber troupe were in alexandrines and this alone was responsible for a significant change in actors' attitudes to their roles, as they now had to learn their lines for each part instead of relying on their ability to improvise. Under Gottsched's guidance the Neuber company even staged a play in 1737 in which the most famous of the popular clowns Hanswurst was symbolically banned from the German stage. However, by 1741, Caroline Neuber, very much the practical theatre manager, had lost patience with Gottsched's prescriptive approach to the drama and the often lifeless scripts that resulted from observance of his advice, so they parted company.

In the light of future developments in German drama and theatre practice, Gottsched is all too frequently characterised as a prescriptive pedant, which he only became later in life. While it may be true that his ideas did not develop beyond his early championing of the precepts of the French neoclassical theatre in Germany, he did render the German theatre an immense service. In his work with Caroline Neuber, he raised the status of the theatre in Germany from that of an inn-yard entertainment to a serious art form. His success suggested that both actors and audiences in Germany were ready for a refined, poetic theatre, whose aims would extend beyond the merely entertaining to include the moral improvement of its audience. In his identification of its civilising potential, Gottsched claimed for the theatre an important new role, as well as new responsibilities for dramatists and practitioners alike. This new definition of the function of theatre would exercise theatre artists for the next fifty years and culminate in the aesthetic essays of Schiller at the end of the century.

Gottsched found an ally in his speculations on the theatre in the writer Johann Elias Schlegel (1719–49), who had come to Leipzig to take up a place at the university. While neglecting to attend any of the great man's lectures, Schlegel was an enthusiastic supporter of Gottsched's precepts, which he followed in writing his eight tragedies, amongst which *Hermann* (1743), is perhaps the best known. To a lesser extent he also followed the precepts in writing his six comedies, which enjoyed some stage success, and some, such as *Die stumme Schönheit* (*The Silent Beauty*, 1747), would later be praised by Lessing in his *Hamburgische Dramaturgie*. Schlegel is now better remembered for his critical writings on the theatre, for the first sympathetic view of Shakespeare in German, *Vergleichung Shakespeares und Andreas Gryphs* (*Comparison of Shakespeare and Andreas Gryphius*, 1741), in which he praises him for his creation of plays around characters rather than concentration on plot. He is best known, however, for his later essay, *Gedanken zur Aufnahme des dänischen Theaters* (*Thoughts on the Reception of the Danish Theatre*, 1747) written after his move to Copenhagen. Here he distances himself from Gottsched and prefigures some of the concerns of *Sturm und Drang* by calling for a drama on national themes and for characters drawn from a broader range of social class as the subjects of both comedy and tragedy.

Lessing and the Hamburg National Theatre

The desire amongst the bourgeoisie for a national culture led to a number of attempts to establish 'National' theatres in various states, even though there was no German nation. The first of these was the Hamburg National Theatre. When a group of Hamburg merchants decided to found this institution in 1765, they appointed a *Dramaturg* to fulfil the role of resident critic and literary advisor to the enterprise. Their inspired choice fell on Gotthold Ephraim Lessing (1729–81). During the brief life of the National Theatre, situated on the Gänsemarkt in Hamburg, Lessing's critical observations laid a firm foundation for the subsequent development of the German theatre.

The son of a protestant pastor, Lessing had been intended for the church but he abandoned his theological studies at the University of Leipzig in favour of medicine. The theatre was, however, his first love, and he spent much of his time backstage with the company of Caroline Neuber after her split with Gottsched. Here he learned the craft of stage writing and Neuber produced his first attempts at drama. Lessing had read widely in both the classics and contemporary literature and had translated treatises on acting and drama from the French and English. In 1755, inspired by Richardson's sentimental novel *Clarissa* and George Lillo's tragedy *The London Merchant* of 1731, he abandoned characters drawn from the aristocracy and introduced the bourgeois tragedy on to the German stage with his play *Miß Sara Sampson*, first performed in Frankfurt an der Oder in July 1755. This was the first tragedy in German to be drawn from contemporary life and written in unstilted prose dialogue, a harbinger of the realistic mode of theatre that would be so important in the nineteenth century (see chapter 4). *The London Merchant*, with its didactic, moralising tone and highly sentimental action, had enjoyed unprecedented success, not only in England, where it enjoyed regular revivals, but throughout Europe. *Miß Sara Sampson* exercised the same appeal as Lillo's play. To modern tastes, such plays may seem too long and over-imbued with sentiment, but eighteenth-century audiences were enraptured. This story of an errant daughter and her sorrowing father, set among the English middle classes, touched a nerve with its immediacy, its freshness, and its bourgeois characters.

The Hamburg National Theatre, which opened in 1767, was plagued by quarrels among the actors and found difficulty in attracting audiences. This, along with the paucity of German plays available for the repertoire, brought about the closure of the theatre after only two years. While working in Hamburg, however, Lessing produced the *Hamburgische Dramaturgie* (*Hamburg Dramaturgy*, 1769), which started as a collection of reviews of performances at the theatre, but quickly developed into a vehicle for his own ideas about the theatre. Lessing's views, cogently expressed in the *Dramaturgie*, were of vital importance for the subsequent development of the German theatre.

Lessing regarded theatre as the most complete of all art forms as it was a synthesis of bodies in space, as represented in painting, and action in time, as represented in poetry or music. For this reason, it had the greatest potential and was likely to have the greatest impact of any of the art forms. Lessing's *Dramaturgie*, his other critical writings and his plays laid a firm foundation for the extraordinarily rapid development of the German theatre in the 1770s and 1780s. He was unique in combining a critical sense of the highest order and an ability and willingness to read foreign texts in the original with the talent of a dramatist and an acute awareness of the practicalities of stage performance.

In July 1768, the Hamburg National Theatre staged *Richard III* by Christian Felix Weisse (1726–1804), a tragedy that, the author claimed, was not based on Shakespeare, and in which the character of Richard was so repulsive that it caused violent reactions among the audience and great relief when Richard received his just deserts at the end. This sent Lessing back to consult Aristotle in the original Greek. He was not convinced that the appearance of the central character in a tragedy should stimulate *Schrecken* (terror) in the audience, as was assumed at that time, a view endorsed by Gottsched. Instead he retranslated the Greek word *Phobos* more accurately as *Furcht* (fear).

> The word Aristotle uses means fear; fear and pity, he says, should be evoked by tragedy, not pity and terror. It is true that terror is a type of fear; it is a sudden, overwhelming fear. But this very suddenness, this surprise which is included in the idea of terror, plainly proves that those who here substituted the word terror for fear, did not understand what kind of fear Aristotle meant at all.[6]

This discovery led him to redefine the aim and purpose of catharsis in tragedy. The audience should empathise with the hero and pity him in his suffering and fall. Lessing reintroduced fear to the equation as the audience's pity turned on itself. Audience members might very well say, 'There but for fortune go you or I.' It was in this transference of pity felt for the hero into fear for oneself that Lessing saw the means by which tragedy can have a morally beneficial effect on its audience. The aim of tragedy was, therefore, to evoke compassion for the hero in the audience. Its moral intent can be adduced from the fact that, for Lessing, the most admirable person morally was the one with the greatest capacity for compassion. It was the importance of the audience's recognition of and identification with the hero, which led Lessing to ignore the requirement of the Greek classical hero that he should be admirable and therefore noble. He rejected Gottsched's magnanimous noble heroes, arguing that a bourgeois audience is more likely to identify with and be moved by the fate of a hero from their own class, someone like them. This idea is central to the concept of *bürgerliches Trauerspiel* (domestic or bourgeois tragedy) and was to be exemplified in Lessing's own *Emilia Galotti* (1772) as well as in Schiller's *Kabale und Liebe* (*Intrigue and Love*, 1784).

In his espousal of domestic tragedy, Lessing was happy to acknowledge the influence of the writings of the French dramatist and theorist Denis Diderot (1713–84), but for the neoclassical French theatre, admired and imitated by Gottsched, he had nothing but contempt. As ever, his argument was based on his research and soundly reasoned. It was certainly true that French writers attempted to observe the three classical unities of time, place, and action, and Gottsched had commended them for this, while vilifying Shakespeare for his lack of form and control in his dramas. Gottsched had maintained that German theatre should try to imitate the prescriptions of the French in order to engender a national repertoire, while Lessing argued that the unities should not be regarded as prescriptive and, as they were a product of the theatre of fifth-century Greece, no attempt should be made to apply them to contemporary western European drama. He proposed that each nation should find the drama that would be 'characteristic' of itself and its epoch. Thus it was that Lessing could claim that despite, or even because of his rejection of the unities, Shakespeare was closer to the spirit of Greek classical theatre than French dramatists were. His work as a translator and linguist convinced him that the English language was closer to German in form and structure than French was, and that English drama, such as the plays of Shakespeare, would therefore provide a better model for German playwrights than the stage works of Voltaire, which he found artificial and empty in their slavish adherence to rules he regarded as irrelevant.

While Lessing rejected French neoclassical tragedy, he was happy to draw on the *comédie larmoyante* (tearful comedy) imported from France and popularised by Christian Fürchtegott Gellert (1715–69) as it blunted the edge of the crude satire and ridicule of character types prevalent in German comedy at the time. The subtle effectiveness of his own play, *Minna von Barnhelm* (1767), owes much to the knife-edge on which the action balances between potential tragedy and the eventual happy ending. Lessing believed true comedy should both touch the emotions of the audience and make them laugh.

Lessing's readings in the art of classical Greece led him to disagree with Winckelmann's interpretation of the essence of Greek sculpture as residing in 'noble simplicity and tranquil grandeur'. In an essay on the newly rediscovered sculpture of Laocoön and his sons being attacked by snakes, Lessing points out that while the figures are still, they are by no means tranquil. He identifies the power of Greek sculpture as deriving from the struggle between enormous forces. We might now compare the work of art to a photograph, taken at the moment of stasis, of equilibrium in the struggle. In the case of Laocoön the balance is between the power of the snakes to crush and the failing strength of the father and sons to resist. This re-evaluation of the essence of classical art was an important development for the study of art history. It was also to prove significant for the later *Sturm und Drang* movement's appreciation of classical mythology.

Lessing considered himself to be neither a poet nor playwright. His plays were intended to be models to stimulate writers of genius into producing works of real quality. This they did, but Lessing was excessively modest in his appraisal of his work. Four of his plays have remained in the German theatre's active repertory and are still revived regularly, and in each of them his humanity and essential reasonableness shine through. In *Minna von Barnhelm*, the characters may belong to the minor nobility, but they embody the plain-speaking and straight-dealing central to the ideology of the middle classes. His tragedy *Emilia Galotti* (1772) may be set in Italy, but in a letter to Nicolai,[7] Lessing described Emilia as his 'middle class Virginia', intended to show that a German bourgeois girl can also espouse antique virtues traditionally associated with the aristocratic heroines of classical tragedy. His parable play *Nathan der Weise (Nathan the Wise*, 1779), one of the first works in which blank verse is used with effect in German theatre, is a powerful call for religious tolerance. As its central character is a wise and respected Jew, the play was widely staged in the aftermath of World War II as a means of bringing about national reconciliation.

While the Hamburg National Theatre, despite its short life, is of a particular importance because of Lessing's *Dramaturgie*, it was by no means the only theatre in Germany that attempted to spread Enlightenment values. The lack of an obvious centre for theatre led to the establishment of pioneering German-speaking theatres in various towns and cities. These reflected not only the demands of the bourgeois audience, but also a new seriousness among German actors towards their profession in the mid eighteenth century. Konrad Ackermann (1712–71), Konrad Ekhof (1720–78) and Friedrich Ludwig Schröder (1744–1816), while all involved in attempts to establish national theatres to satisfy the demands of a bourgeois audience, were nonetheless still compelled by financial necessity to accept the patronage of the aristocracy. Initially they were forced by economic circumstances to tour widely from city to city with the result that their new, more realistic and sensitive style of acting was seen by audiences in cities as far apart as Mannheim, Berlin, Vienna, and Weimar. In their concern both for the quality of their own performances and those of the company as a whole, they added a vital component to the development of the German theatre at the end of the eighteenth century.

Before this time there had generally been little semblance of unity of style in theatre companies. Actors were engaged to play and sing a limited range of predetermined roles in particular categories, such as romantic heroine and first soprano, comic old man and first bass. They would specialise early and expect to continue to play only a single character type for the rest of their careers. This type casting of stock characters, known as *Rollenfach*, allowed the company to present a large programme of plays, often with only very limited rehearsal. The frequent changes of programme, as well as the demands of touring led to much improvisation by actors, who often departed from the playtext. It was not until the establishment of standing theatres that the play-text came to be regarded as an aesthetic entity in itself, rather than the raw material from which the performance would be fashioned by the actors. A major factor militating against the impression of ensemble performance by companies was the practice of only issuing actors with their own parts, instead of full copies of plays. Indeed it was not unusual for actors not to know what happened at the end of a play in which they were performing only a minor role. Michael Patterson has suggested this was a security measure to prevent play-texts being pirated,[8] but this custom, coupled with the tendency at this time to rehearse only actors' entrances and exits, was the norm throughout Europe. It was regarded as unprofessional to waste a performance on an empty theatre. In fact, as late as the mid-nineteenth century, the English actor Macready provoked anger and derision from his actors in London when he asked them to read plays through in their entirety and to act during rehearsals.

Dalberg and the Mannheim National Theatre

The new generation of German actors did, however, spearhead change. Konrad Ekhof had toured northern Germany with the Schönemann company for 17 years from 1739 and in 1753 established with them an academy to discuss repertoire, the art of acting, and the social status of the actor. The academy may have lasted only thirteen months, but it served to initiate in the acting profession in Germany the serious consideration of theatre as an art form. Onstage too Ekhof was a notable innovator. Unsuited by his small and bony physique to the heroic characterisation of the dominant Leipzig school, he developed a new, more restrained style. 'While his colleagues in the Schönemann company were still sawing the air with their arms, he used less pronounced gestures, adopted a more relaxed pose, and articulated his words in a more subdued manner.'[9] He joined the Hamburg National Theatre, where his understated acting was an inspiration to Lessing. After the failure of that venture, he was invited by Duchess Anna Amalie to run the court theatre at Weimar, and after that theatre burnt down in 1774, he was invited to Gotha by Duke Ernst to run 'the first fully subsidized court theatre with a German-language repertoire'.[10]

In 1777 a National Theatre was opened by Duke Karl Theodor in Mannheim, with Baron Wolfgang Heribert von Dalberg (1750–1806) as its honorary director. After the death of Ekhof in 1778, Dalberg succeeded in attracting many of his actors from Gotha to strengthen the Mannheim company. He then set about trying to improve the quality of the theatre's performances through two principal means. The first was the issuing of a set of rules to govern the actors' behaviour, both in rehearsal and performance. Attitudes to rehearsal in the German theatre in general can be inferred from the rules stating that each actor is expected to arrive on time for read-throughs and rehearsals and at each dress rehearsal to 'rehearse without a script and know his part thoroughly' as well as 'play his or her role in character and at least in such a way that a sketch of the character is clearly recognizable.'[11] There was a complicated system of fines for offences such as refusing to take a minor role, damaging costumes, or improvising during performances. By these means Dalberg instilled professional discipline in his company, but his innovations extended far beyond regulations for his actors. He also made a major contribution to the advancement of theatre as an art form in Germany by interrogating theatre practice in a series of company discussion groups. The minutes of these meetings, the

Mannheimer Protokolle (*Mannheim Protocols*), show the company addressing a wide range of issues concerning the theatre, in particular the art of acting. Central to their concerns is the search for 'naturalness' in acting. Judging what a previous century might applaud as 'natural' in an actor's performance is, of course, impossible, but what can be gleaned from the *Protokolle* is a concern for authenticity in the presentation of character. Detailed discussion of the importance of study of emotion and the acquisition of technique, as well as the actor's knowledge of himself, is linked in a very eighteenth-century way to the concept of Nature being synonymous with perfection.

Schiller would later develop this argument to equate the beautiful with the good, while Goethe at Weimar would build on Dalberg's foundations to combine theory with the practice of acting and a canon of drama worthy of a truly national theatre. Despite Dalberg's pioneering recognition of Schiller's talent as a playwright by staging the première of his first play *Die Räuber* (*The Robbers*, 1782) and his subsequent employment of Schiller as theatre poet, the repertoire of the Mannheim National Theatre remained restricted by both the lack of high quality plays in German and the tastes of its audience. After Schiller's departure from Mannheim, it was dominated by the immensely popular sentimental plays of August von Kotzebue (1761–1819) and August Wilhelm Iffland (1759–1814), who was also the principal actor at Mannheim until his move to direct the National Theatre in Berlin in 1796. The content and style of these plays, along with the audience they attracted, shows the first flowering of a commercial theatre for the middle class in Germany.

Goethe, Schiller, and Weimar Classicism

The long association of Johann Wolfgang von Goethe (1749–1832) with the stage in Weimar exemplifies the development of the German theatre and drama in the late eighteenth and early nineteenth centuries. He first came to the fore as the leader of a historically important group of young writers known as *Sturm und Drang* (Storm and Stress), who idealised strength and genius, but also expressed deep sympathy for the trodden down and dispossessed. Their plays, which were rarely performed, showed the influence of Shakespeare and articulated a profound sense of social dysfunction. Having sung the praises of Shakespeare in his 1771 essay '*Zum Schäkespears Tag*' (*On Shakespeare's Day*), Goethe had gone on to write the two defining works of *Sturm und Drang*. The first was his immensely successful novel, *Die Leiden des jungen Werthers* (*The Sorrows of Young Werther*, 1774), in which he explores a character who is the embodiment of yearning – longing for what he cannot have. Imbued with the pathetic fallacy, the novel charts the hero's relentless downward path to suicide. The other was his play *Götz von Berlichingen* (1773). In this, Goethe chose a hero from the then unfashionable German history of the 'dark ages', a knight who tends to act first and think later – a true *Kraftmensch* (man of power) – the opposite of Werther and yet still a characteristic figure of *Sturm und Drang*. Believing himself to be emulating Shakespeare's disregard of rules in the construction of his plays, Goethe allowed himself a total of 54 scenes (20 in Act 3 alone) in 31 different locations, with a cast of 24 named characters, along with dozens of unnamed ones. This extravagantly conceived drama, centred on the character of Götz, would subsequently have an impact beyond *Sturm und Drang*, influencing, through Sir Walter Scott's translation, the English Romantics. This was not Goethe's only early attempt at writing drama to meet with success; both his drama *Stella* (1776) and the domestic tragedy *Clavigo* (1779) were widely performed.

Although he had become an internationally renowned author as a result of the success of these two works, in 1775 Goethe, who was only 26, accepted an invitation from the young Duke Karl August of Saxe-Weimar to come to live at his court in the little walled town of Weimar. There had been an opera house in the Wilhelmsburg castle in Weimar since 1696, and there was a tradition of support for theatre in the little state. In 1756, Karl August's father, Duke Ernst August Konstantin had invited Karl Theophilus Döbbelin (1727–93) and his resident troupe to perform German-language plays for the court, the first such arrangement in Germany. Ten years after Duke Ernst's death, his widow Anna Amalie reopened the castle theatre, under Gottfried Heinrich Koch (1703–75), whose 'natural' acting style had been praised by Lessing. In 1771, when Koch moved to Berlin, Abel Seyler (1730–1801) took over and invited Konrad Ekhof to join the company as his leading actor and financial manager. In the next three years the company performed *Miß Sara Sampson* and *Minna von Barnhelm*, as well as Gluck's *Alceste*. Unfortunately, as we have seen, the theatre was destroyed by fire a year before Goethe's arrival, and Ekhof and the professional company had had to move to Gotha.

When Goethe arrived in Weimar, theatrical performances were being staged by two amateur groups in the ballroom of the house of the master of the hunt. The two groups were strictly separate, one being composed of members of the court and one of the bourgeoisie, but Goethe, by virtue of his acting ability, was invited to perform with the court players, even though he was not from the nobility. He contributed occasional pieces for the company, in which the teenage Kotzebue performed, and directed the performances as well. Since spending many hours in his childhood playing with a puppet theatre, Goethe had developed a deep love for the theatre, but with no practical experience of production and few opportunities to attend performances, he had only a sketchy idea of the requirements of playable theatre texts. He did, however, have a painter's eye, and, in Johann Martin Mieding, the court carpenter, he found an important ally. Having no background in the theatre, Mieding was not bound by contemporary theatre practice and proved a willing interpreter of Goethe's sometimes unconventional staging ideas. Goethe immortalised his skill in realising his ideas for sets, both in the ballroom theatre and outdoors, in *Faust Part 1* and his poem *On Mieding's Death* (1782).

Fascinating insights into Goethe's views on the theatre can be gained from a reading of his novel *Wilhelm Meisters Lehrjahre* (*Wilhelm Meister's Apprenticeship*, 1795–96), which describes the adventures of a young man of business who falls in with a group of touring actors. Goethe started the novel *Wilhelm Meisters theatralische Sendung* (*Wilhelm Meister's Theatrical Mission*) in 1777, four years after finishing *Götz von Berlichingen*, but having worked at the manuscript intermittently for a number of years, he finally abandoned it, unpublished, in 1785. While extending Wilhelm's experiences considerably beyond the scope of the *Sendung*, the *Lehrjahre* retains the detailed characterisation of the members of Serlo's theatre troupe and their lively interactions. There is a description of the troupe's performance at the country house of a count, as well as an extended critical discussion of *Hamlet*, as part of the company's preparations for a production of the play.

The most significant of Goethe's writings for the stage from this period, is undoubtedly the prose version of *Iphigenie auf Tauris* (*Iphigenia in Tauris*, 1779), in which Goethe played Orestes and the Duke played Pylades. In *Iphigenie* Goethe turned his back on the licence and excesses of his *Sturm und Drang* period, and, inspired both by his reading of the classics and his rediscovery of French drama, wrote a play with five characters that observes the unities. He domesticated the story by dispensing with Euripides' chorus, but his other major change exemplified his view of the classical ideal and the civilising power of theatre. Where Euripides' Iphigenia is complicit in the theft of the statue of Artemis, only to be saved from King Thoas' wrath by the intervention of the goddess Athena, Goethe's Iphigenia tames the passions of the male characters and insists on revealing the planned escape to the King. Further, she is not satisfied when the King is reconciled to her leaving Tauris, but will only embark when she has received the King's blessing and promise of enduring friendship. In this play, as in his later *Torquato Tasso* of 1807, Goethe depicts the resolution of conflict and the achievement of harmony as the highest dramatic ideal.

> In *Iphigenie* new ethical conceptions applicable to all mankind, the respect for human life, truthfulness and trust in one's fellow-men are successfully asserted against the narrower loyalties of the family and the clan and older religious notions of jealous and vengeful deities.[12]

In the resolution of *Iphigenie*, in particular, we can hear echoes of Lessing's Enlightenment call for tolerance in *Nathan*.

The court theatre was rebuilt in 1780. In 1784 Joseph Bellomo installed a company of professional actors, which resulted in six years of theatre of indifferent quality, as Weimar was not sufficiently significant as a city or state to attract more distinguished performers. The repertoire was typical of a German language theatre of the day; it included plays by Lessing and Goethe, as well as versions of Shakespeare, but the majority of productions were of the sentimental plays of Iffland, Kotzebue, and Schröder.

Schiller, who had taken up a chair of history at the university in nearby Jena after his years as a theatre poet in Mannheim, came to Weimar in 1787. When Bellomo left Weimar in 1790 to take up a post in Graz, the Duke found it impossible to replace him and called upon Goethe to take over the direction of the theatre. Goethe was not in a position to refuse this request from the Duke and, if he wanted to see any improvement in the standard of performances at Weimar, the best way would be to take on the direction of performances himself.

The repertoire of the theatre had, at least at first, to reflect the taste of its relatively restricted audience. Goethe opened with *Die Jäger* (*The Hunters*, 1785) by Iffland and continued, both in Weimar and in the theatre at the Duke's summer residence at Lauchstädt, with a programme of popular plays. From the first, however, Goethe showed his intention to introduce more challenging work, with his production of Shakespeare's *King John* (in Eschenbach's translation) and Schiller's *Don Carlos*, although the latter had to be given in prose because the company was not capable of effectively delivering the blank verse version. Goethe managed to recruit Heinrich Vohs (d. 1804) from Düsseldorf, who, apart from being an accomplished actor, also acted as the theatre's artistic director for a number of years. It was Vohs who drew up the regulations for the theatre company, which imposed a professional discipline on the actors, both onstage and in their private lives, but he did nothing to improve the artistic level of the company. Goethe was disillusioned and, in December 1795, asked to be relieved of his post at the theatre, but this request was refused by the Duke.

The stimulus that reawakened Goethe's belief in the possibility of an improvement in the quality of the theatre at Weimar was the visit of Iffland, who gave twelve guest performances at Weimar in 1796. These were mostly of his own plays, but also included *Die Räuber* and Goethe's own *Egmont* (1787). As Weimar was such an insignificant state, Goethe had not yet had the opportunity, which he would have had, had he lived in a larger city, of observing such an experienced and exceptionally talented performer acting in different roles. He was very impressed by Iffland's versatility and his ability to appear to lose his own personality in whatever role he was playing and he admired his naturalness, variety, charm, power, and moderation. 'Iffland lives before the audience's eyes', Goethe wrote, 'a true picture of nature and art, while other actors, even if they do not perform badly, appear only as reporters, presenting alien situations from written records.'[13]

Goethe tried to persuade Iffland to remain at Weimar, but, although he returned to give guest performances in 1798, the attractions of the court at Berlin proved a more powerful draw than those of Weimar. Inspired by Iffland's performances, Goethe's first aim was to break his actors' habit of reverting to 'stock' characterisation. In this he was aided by the very lack of a tradition of professional practice such as existed in the established theatres of England or France. At that time, when a leading actor gave *his* Hamlet or Shylock on the London stage, he would expect to do it without rehearsal with the rest of the cast, wearing his own costume and using his own props. Goethe, however, could insist that senior actors take smaller roles as well, and, with his painter's eye, demanded historically accurate costumes, as far as his budget would allow. As a nascent stage director, he could also arrange his actors onstage in aesthetically pleasing groupings, rather than accede to the custom of the leading actor assuming a downstage centre position throughout.

It appears then that there were advantages for Goethe as an innovator in working in an environment devoid of employees who had developed set ways of doing things in their theatre. Goethe's actors were more receptive to his innovative ideas than they might have been elsewhere, and, as a result of his instruction, they were better able to undertake the more complex characters being written by Schiller in plays such as his *Wallenstein* trilogy, which was staged at Weimar in 1799. But a more natural, less stereotyped characterisation was not, in itself, sufficient to represent the poetic quality of Schiller's blank verse drama. Goethe was increasingly concerned that in the drive towards a more natural style of delivery, his actors were losing sight of the aesthetic demands of the texts. He wanted something more than realism from his actors, and to achieve this he instituted a new system of rehearsals. Until this time actors were accustomed to learn their parts on their own, only meeting the rest of the cast for perhaps three days of rehearsal before the first night. Goethe realised that he needed to direct his actors in speaking verse and called initial reading rehearsals for the whole cast at his house. At the first of these the play would be read through in turn by the actors, and then in subsequent rehearsals they would read their own parts. This meant that everyone in the cast had a chance to become acquainted with the complete play, while learning how to deliver verse under the direction of Goethe, who kept time by hitting a key on the table. Goethe also devoted considerable time to rehearsing individual actors, in particular assisting his younger actors with their speaking of verse.

Schiller's verse dramas may have provided the greatest challenge and achievement for Goethe as director of the Weimar theatre, but he also decided to educate his audience by extending the repertoire of the court theatre to include foreign plays, including Shakespeare, Calderón, and Schiller's versions of Gozzi's *Turandot* (1802) and Terence's *The Brothers*, for both of which the actors were masked. The Duke's predilection for French theatre manifested itself in his repeated suggestions of French texts, many of which were wholly inappropriate. Goethe had, however, been impressed by the artistry of the French actor François-Joseph Talma (1763–1826) and revised his earlier antipathy towards the French Classical canon. As a result the theatre staged Schiller's translation of Racine's *Phèdre* in 1804.

Now that his company was capable of sustaining a blank-verse tragedy such as Schiller's *Maria Stuart* (*Mary Stuart*, 1800), Goethe reworked *Iphigenie* in blank verse and staged it in 1802, along with Schiller's homage to Greek classical theatre *Die Braut von Messina* (*The Bride of Messina*, 1803), which used only four actors, but two choruses (see fig. 5), whose delivery Goethe conducted as if they were instrumentalists. In 1803, Goethe established an academy for a dozen actors who met for instruction and gave private

5 *Die Braut von Messina* by Friedrich Schiller, adapted and directed by Goethe, Weimar 1803. Aquatint by Johann Christian Ernst Müller after a painting by Johann Friedrich Matthaei.

performances at his house. It was at this time that Goethe dictated his *Regeln für Schauspieler* (*Rules for Actors*),[14] in which he laid down detailed requirements relating not only to the delivery of lines, but also to deportment and the creation of harmony in the stage picture. These rules offer a series of fascinating insights into Goethe's curriculum at his academy. The absence of an agreed German pronunciation at the time is highlighted by the first two of the rules, which deal with dialect. In the next 32 rules Goethe articulates his view of actors' delivery of lines. He stresses the need for an initial accurate memorising of the text and then a slow building up of intensity in declamation, always assuming that the actor's enunciation is clear enough for each word to be heard and understood by the audience. Throughout he lays great stress on poetic and rhythmical delivery, and the rules on speech abound with musical analogies. When he addresses the placing and movement of actors onstage, the emphasis is not on realism, but on the presentation of an idealised form of nature, in which the true is united with the beautiful. The rules go into considerable detail with regard to gesture and deportment, actors being encouraged to rehearse their parts in dumb show before a mirror to verify how well their gestures communicate the sense of the speech. It was this somewhat strict regulation of expressive movement, probably required for the less experienced members of his company, which would later develop into an ossified series of gestures and would be derided as the 'Weimar Style'. The behaviour that might routinely be expected of actors at the time can be inferred from some of the later rules, where Goethe bans male actors from rehearsing in outdoor boots and overcoats and female actors from carrying their handbags onstage. In particular he objects to actors blowing their noses and spitting during performances. His ideas on grouping and the movement of actors about the stage owe much to his artist's eye and in some ways prefigure the later ideas of Duke Georg of Saxe-Meiningen. Above all Goethe seeks a pleasing harmony, which will delight the audience's sense of the beautiful. He suggests that actors should view the stage as a chessboard and make diagonal moves to keep the stage picture always in balance. He also reminds his actors that they should behave offstage as if they were performing, as they are forever in the public eye and should not bring their profession into disrepute. The perception of the actor in German society had come a very long way in little more than half a century. Both by his *Rules* and the standards of offstage behaviour he demanded, Goethe made a significant contribution to the raising of the status of the actor, from mountebank to serious artist.

These changes in the way actors regarded their profession were as vital to the development of a serious theatre culture as were the changes in the German theatre repertoire. Goethe contributed to this repertoire, above all with his two classical masterpieces *Iphigenie auf Tauris* and *Torquato Tasso*, as well as *Faust*, but his major contribution to the development of the German theatre was his practical involvement in the direction of the theatre at Weimar and in the education of his company and his audience, through elevating their aesthetic sense of what the theatre could achieve as an art form. In this endeavour he was supported by Schiller, both through the dramas he wrote for the Court theatre and his philosophical essays. There remained, however, unreconstructed elements at court. Foremost amongst these was the beautiful and talented actress Karoline Jagemann (1777–1848), whom Goethe had brought to Weimar from Mannheim in 1797. She became the Duke's mistress and grew increasingly powerful in the running of the theatre. The Duke, who was quite autocratic, could and did interfere with the running of the theatre, making suggestions that had to be accepted. The end of Goethe's long association with the theatre came in 1817, and it was quite bitter as Jagemann insisted on a production featuring a performing dog, to which Goethe objected. Jagemann prevailed, which only highlights where, in a little state like Weimar, the true power resided. Goethe resigned and never returned, but his influence on the performance style and production values of the German theatre persisted. Some practitioners rejected, even caricatured the formal, elevated style, which Goethe had developed with his company to help them rise above the naturalistic acting style of the popular *Konversationsstück* (conversation play) and the plays of *Sturm und Drang*. Pius Alexander Wolff (1782–1828), however, who had created the part of Tasso at Weimar in 1807 and whom Goethe regarded as the only actor fully to have mastered the Weimar style, continued to practise this style to great acclaim in classical roles after his move to the Berlin Royal Theatre in 1816.

Iffland and the Berlin National Theatre

Berlin had been fortunate in its appointment of Iffland as director of the then Berlin National Theatre in 1796. During his directorship he raised the prestige of the theatre by staging, in addition to his own plays, lavish productions of plays by Schiller, Shakespeare and Goethe, with elaborate scenery and large casts. As an actor he continued his pursuit of nobility, decorum and truth in his performances, while in his *Almanach für Theater und Theaterfreunde* (*Almanach for Theatre and the Friends of Theatre*, 1807–12) he encouraged actors to seek harmony and humanity in their portrayal of characters, even villains. Iffland also made a major contribution to the rise in the status of actors in Berlin, being regularly welcomed into fashionable social gatherings. When Wolff arrived in Berlin he found a prestigious, wealthy theatre, proud of both its high artistic standards and its perceived role as a civilising force in society. With his command of the lofty Weimar style of acting, Wolff took the company's performances to new heights of nobility, above all in tragedy. In particular his interpretation of Hamlet, a role he played with gravity and lack of affectation, would prove a model for other actors for decades to come. Wolff was instrumental in maintaining the Weimar style of acting in Berlin, and was succeeded as its main exponent by Emil Devrient, who, encouraged by August von Lüttichau, the intendant of the Dresden Court Theatre, carried on the tradition until his retirement in 1868. As the fashion in acting moved progressively towards realism,

Devrient persisted with the Weimar style, not only in Dresden, but also on tour – notably with a company of German actors who brought productions of both Shakespeare and German classics to London in 1852 and 1853.

> By 1828, the year of Wolff's death, the 'idealist' approach to acting had been firmly established. While the harmonious and yet various image of humanity, conveyed through surface realism and an infinitude of nuances, was the ideal that many actors strove for, the idealism of the Weimar school became the predominant style for most actors until the end of the nineteenth century.[15]

Schiller

Goethe's efforts to elevate the level of the German theatre were assisted above all by his association with Schiller (his junior by ten years), whose plays raised the performances of the Weimar company to new heights and whose philosophical writings on aesthetics, and especially the stage, were crucial for the subsequent development of German theatre and culture.

The son of a military officer, Schiller had been sent by the Duke of Württemberg to his military academy in Stuttgart to train there as a doctor. It was while enduring the repressive discipline of the academy that he wrote *Die Räuber*, which he published in 1781, some six years after Goethe's move to Weimar. He escaped from Württemberg and found employment as theatre poet at Mannheim, where Dalberg premièred *Die Räuber* in 1782, albeit in a much modified form. Throughout his life, Schiller concerned himself with questions of freedom and nobility. In *Die Räuber*, the hero Karl Moor, having been tricked out of his inheritance by his brother, responds to this injury by taking the law into his own hands, setting up a robber band with the intention of righting society's evils by direct action, like Robin Hood intending to steal from the rich to give to the poor. As he attracts hard core criminal elements to his band, who commit rape and murder without remorse, he comes to realise that, however unjust his treatment at the hands of his brother, his rejection of the rule of law cannot be justified ethically. While Goethe's Götz maintains his defiance of the society with which he is at odds and dies with the word 'Freedom' on his lips, Schiller's Karl Moor recognises the imperative of justice and the rule of law and repents. At the end of the play, he seeks reconciliation with divine justice, and, by surrendering himself to a labourer with eleven children, allows the poor man to claim the thousand louis d'or for his capture. By this act of generosity, he attempts to atone for his career in crime. In this, the first of Schiller's plays, Karl's idealism in setting up the robber band is emotional and naïve and his eventual atonement appears somewhat contrived.

In his bourgeois tragedy *Kabale und Liebe* (*Intrigue and Love*, 1782–3), the happiness of the two lovers, Ferdinand von Walter and the commoner Luise Miller, is thwarted by Ferdinand's father and his henchman Wurm. In an ideal world the love of Ferdinand and Luise might transcend the disparity in their rank, but in the real world of petty, despotic German states of the late eighteenth century, Ferdinand's father plans to marry him off to his own discarded mistress. Ferdinand may belong, as Lesley Sharpe suggests: 'to a rootless generation, trying to throw off the shackles of the past and appropriate the victories of the Enlightenment over outmoded ways of thought',[16] but, despite their love, he and Luise do not possess the strength to transcend their social conditioning, nor to contend with the machinations of the evil Wurm.

Idealism, as well as the concept of atonement for past sins, figure as major themes throughout Schiller's writing. When his *Don Carlos*, on which he had been working for four years, was premièred at Hamburg in 1787, Schiller admitted that his extensively researched royal drama, initially intended as a family tragedy driven by the rival claims of King Philip and his son Carlos to the love of Elizabeth, was unbalanced by the introduction of a more fruitful confrontation. During the writing of the play, the theatrical interest shifted from the triangle of Philip, Carlos and Elizabeth to centre around the anachronistic encounter between the late eighteenth century idealism of the Marquis Posa and the absolutism of the Spanish king Philip II. 'What is enacted in the scene is one of the crucial political debates of the eighteenth century, in which Philip takes the conservative absolutist part and in which we hear echoes of Montesquieu and Rousseau in the speeches of Posa'.[17] As the play progresses, it is Posa who becomes the true antagonist of the king. He is an idealist, but not a simple one like Karl Moor. He is prepared to sacrifice his life in order for Carlos to win freedom for the inhabitants of the Netherlands, but Schiller weaves a more complex motivation for his character than merely love for his friend, or the political freedom of a nation. Posa's pride and conceit, the fanaticism of a man whose love is inspired by an ideal rather than a real object, lead him to engage in a web of intrigue, which eventually precipitates not only his own death but those of Carlos and the queen as well. 'In the completed work his death is still an act of self-sacrifice, in part inspired by a desire to protect his friend and in part to ensure the furtherance of his political ideals; it is also an act by which he hopes to rectify the mistakes he has committed in his dealings with the king and with Carlos.'[18]

So, in *Don Carlos*, the first of the plays of his maturity, Schiller presents us with a clash of ideologies represented not by a hero and a villain, but by two complex, flawed advocates of conflicting world orders. From *Don Carlos* onwards Schiller will choose his characters from history and make them wrestle with the conflicting demands of morality and politics.

> Schiller's language of moral heroism may seem suspect to us now, but beneath it there are issues of a kind that do not go away. Dilemmas still occur, moral decisions still demand to be made, the world of Realpolitik still needs to be confronted with a world of moral values. Drama which grasps these matters as supremely well as Schiller's stands out as a landmark and has permanent worth.[19]

It is the moral dimension to theatre and the beneficial effects which it may have on its audience which Schiller explores in the most famous of his theoretical writings on the theatre, his essay *Die Schaubühne als eine moralische Anstalt betrachtet* (*The Theatre Considered as a Moral Institution*, 1784), which has laid the foundation for the view many Germans have had of the theatre ever since. In this essay Schiller asserts that the stage supports both religion and the secular law by ridiculing vice and promoting virtue. 'What reinforcement religion and the law can gain when they join with the stage, where reality can be viewed as living presence, where vice and virtue, happiness and misery, folly and wisdom are reviewed in thousands of true and tangible images'.[20] Schiller agrees with Gottsched that the stage can assist us to bear the vicissitudes of life by offering us models of the ennobling effect of suffering stoically endured. He follows Lessing in asserting that it can educate us in tolerance and humanity, and that it can refine our sensibilities and make us more susceptible to pity and compassion by allowing us to suffer vicariously with the characters portrayed. The sight of a tragic hero attaining sublimity by way of acquiescing in his or her fate will not only give pleasure, but also have a morally uplifting and improving effect on the audience. This occurs most famously in *Maria Stuart* when Mary offers her execution (for complicity in the Mortimer plot) in an attempt to atone for her involvement in the earlier murder of her husband Darnley. In nobly enduring suffering, a character may achieve sublimity, but for Schiller this remains passive. To attain the higher state of active sublimity a character must consciously choose to accept a course of action which will involve them in suffering.

> By Active Sublimity he understands a condition in which the hero's suffering is brought about by his own volition. Either he chooses to follow a moral course which must entail suffering, or (an alternative form of Active Sublimity) he inwardly repents the evil of some past deed.[21]

Or, as E. L. Stahl formulates the distinction between the two forms of active sublimity:

> The suffering which an actively sublime person inflicts on himself can be one of two kinds. It can be an expression of moral freedom resulting from his choice to obey a moral principle, or it can be the expression of a moral necessity resulting from his decision to expiate a wrong he has himself committed.[22]

It is to allow Mary to achieve this second state of active sublimity that Schiller reverses history to make her complicit in her husband's death, but she is innocent of attempting to escape from her final incarceration. Through this vicarious experience of a character's acceptance of suffering, the moral effect of theatre on its audience is realised. By witnessing and sympathising with the dramatic suffering of a character on stage, an audience can be, as it were, inoculated, so that, when they too are faced with suffering in their lives, they are better prepared to endure it.

In *Maria Stuart* and his later tragedies, in particular the posthumous *Wilhelm Tell* (*William Tell*, 1804), Schiller sought to show historical characters exercising sublime freedom, in line with the philosophical precepts of Kant. In this he demonstrated that the theatre could have a moral purpose over and above support for the civil law. Such complex and ambitious aesthetic and ethical effects could now be realised through the elevated style of acting which Goethe had developed with the company at the court theatre and which informed the performance of tragedy in Berlin as elsewhere in Germany. The outstanding achievement of the period of Weimar Classicism in the theatre came from the alliance of the vision and the directorial skills of Goethe with the genius of Schiller as a playwright and a philosopher. Their legacy was the conviction that the theatre could and should function as a major factor in the creation of a civil society in Germany.

Theatre in Vienna

The leading proponent of the moral function of theatre in Austria was Joseph von Sonnenfels (1733–1817), a professor at the University of Vienna from 1763. Sonnenfels shared many of Gottsched's ideas for the reform of the theatre, and in his *Briefe über die wienerische Schaubühne* (*Letters on the Viennese Stage*, 1768), he called for the establishment of a national theatre and proposed the adoption of French models upon which to construct a serious, German-speaking theatre, devoid of the vulgarity associated with the popular theatre and the artificiality of the foreign repertoire of the court theatre, in short a theatre to which the bourgeois audience could relate. The repertoire was to be strictly controlled to ensure the morally improving nature of the entertainment. His intention was that the theatre should become a 'school of manners, courtesy and language'.[23]

The importance attached to the development of the theatre as an educative and moral institution in Austria was confirmed by the interest taken in it by the Emperor Joseph II. In an attempt to improve the moral tone of performances, in 1770 censorship was extended to the theatre. Of necessity this resulted in a de facto ban on improvisation on stage, an event that mirrored the exiling of Hanswurst from the stage in Germany by Gottsched and the Neubers in 1737. In 1776, the Emperor set his seal on Vienna's desire for a German theatre by installing a company of actors to perform German drama at the Burgtheater and granting it the title of National Theatre, in imitation of the Comédie-Française. In the same year another decree broke the monopoly of the court theatres and permitted the construction of new theatres outside the city walls. So it was that Hanswurst moved out of the court theatres and continued his career in the theatres in the suburbs, remaining a central character in the continuing tradition of Viennese popular comedy.

From the 1750s the repertoire of the Burgtheater had consisted largely of French drama and *opéra comique*, but the new Emperor Joseph's reorganisation of the court theatres in 1776 involved the consolidation of the German-speaking theatre at the Burgtheater. Joseph's enlightened educative intentions for the Burgtheater were apparent from the first. He dispatched J. H. F. Müller (1738–1815), one of the Burgtheater actors, to report on theatre activity in Hamburg and the other north German cities. Attempts were made to strengthen the Burgtheater by attracting actors from other established companies. Johanna Sacco (1754–1802) and Franz Hieronymus

Brockmann (1745–1812) came after spending time with the Hamburg company, but it was with the arrival of Friedrich Ludwig Schröder and his wife from Hamburg in 1780 that the Burgtheater began to develop its particular style. Smaller than the Kärntnertortheater, which would be given over to opera in the early nineteenth century, the Burgtheater proved an excellent home for Schröder's more intimate, conversational acting style, which would continue to inform the style of performance in the theatre long after he had returned to Hamburg. In the four years Schröder spent in Vienna, he succeeded in setting the Burgtheater on a path that would see it develop into one of the most stylish and influential German theatres for the next century. The Burgtheater also followed the lead of the National Theatre in Hamburg by establishing the post of dramaturge, the most famous occupier of this position being Kotzebue. Although he only held the post for some eighteen months before his resignation in December 1798, he was subsequently granted a pension of a thousand florins on the understanding that he would allow the theatre first refusal on each of his new plays. In all, forty-five of his plays would be staged at the Burgtheater; the actors' conversational style of acting was ideal for their successful presentation. The repertoire of the Burgtheater may have been limited by the strict censorship imposed by Joseph II, but its production values and stylish performances helped to set the tone of Viennese society and its attitude to the theatre as a civilising influence for many years to come.

The plays of Goethe and Schiller have maintained their position as the backbone of the canon of German drama; so too have their idealism and the belief that the theatre has above all a civilising function. 'The stage', as Schiller wrote, 'is an institution where pleasure is combined with instruction, rest with exertion, amusement with culture.'[24]

The philosophical essentials of the classical age have influenced the subsequent history of Germany and its theatre. There remains a conviction throughout German society that the theatre should be a forum for moral and ethical debate, and that, as part of a person's '*Bildung*' (cultural education), it can be a force for moral improvement. 'The highest merit of classical German literature lies in its expression in new symbols of this humanistic religion, which ... proved an inspiration to serious, cultivated men in Europe generally until late in the following century, and made Germany their spiritual home.'[25] This essentially idealistic view of the role of theatre can be traced directly back to Schiller's essays on theatre and aesthetic education, and led the governments of both Germanies after World War II to fund their theatres at a level far beyond that found elsewhere in Europe or the USA. Even in the less propitious economic conditions after unification in 1990, subsidy continues at a level which is the envy of artistic directors elsewhere. This allows theatre managements to stage plays they feel deserve to be produced for aesthetic, political or social reasons, despite the fact that they may not prove to be successes at the box-office.

In this way, the legacy of the writers, practitioners, and theorists of the classical period lives on in Germany. It was the achievement of the classical period to raise the German theatre from an inn-yard entertainment to a pre-eminent position in Europe, embodying the truly civilising message:

> When people from every stratum of society, casting off the chains of affectation and custom, freed from the pressures of fate, conjoined as brothers by an all-embracing sympathy and melded once more into a single race, forget themselves and the world and draw near their divine origins; each person takes joy in the rapture of all, which is reflected back, stronger and more beautiful, in a hundred eyes, and in his breast there is only room for one single sensation – that of being human.[26]

4 The realistic theatre and bourgeois values, 1750–1900

MARVIN CARLSON

At first glance it is difficult to distinguish between the 'classical' mode of German theatre that was influential until at least the end of the nineteenth century and the 'realistic' theatre that was also dominant throughout that century. In part this is because during the eighteenth century the seeds of theatrical classicism and realism were sown at the same time and by the same troupes and companies of players, in part because both classicism and realism shared the aesthetic goals of harmony and unity. But ultimately there are differences: Weimar Classicism viewed human existence through an idealistic perspective, while realism reflected human beings in their social context. Weimar Classicism fastened on the potential nobility in human beings, realism on their actual conduct.

The origins of realism

The origins of realistic theatre can be traced to the years following the split between Caroline Neuber and Johann Christoph Gottsched in the late 1730s; Neuber's fortunes gradually went into decline, but her leading actor, Johann Schönemann (1704–82), reconstituted her troupe in 1739, and the young actors who worked under him, Konrad Ekhof, Konrad Ernst Ackermann, and Sophie Charlotte Schröder (1714–92), went on to become the major figures of the next generation. In 1753 Ekhof founded the first German acting academy where he encouraged actors to develop a quieter and more realistic delivery. At the peak of his powers in the 1750s, his new approach was perfectly suited to the domestic tragedy that was appearing under English and French influence precisely at this time. As an actor he successfully combined an emotional, intuitive approach, later associated with the romantic style, with a well-controlled technique, a combination rarely found in a single performer. The inspiration of Ekhof's style and the influence of his academy earned him the title of 'the father of German acting'.[1]

In the mid-1750s, Ekhof and his follow actors in the Schönemann company presented three classics of the *bürgerliches Trauerspiel* – George

Lillo's *The London Merchant* in 1754, Edward Moore's *The Gamester* in 1756, and, in 1755, the first major German work in this new dramatic style, Lessing's *Miß Sara Sampson*. Ackermann and Sophie Schröder, who had split from Schönemann in 1741 to create their own company, continued to be identified with the new domestic tragedy. In fact they presented *The Gamester* in Breslau just three weeks before Schönemann first offered *The London Merchant* in Hamburg, and they followed his performances of *The London Merchant* with their own in Halle and Berlin. In Berlin they made the acquaintance of Lessing, who offered them *Miß Sara Sampson*, so it was Ackermann and Sophie Schröder rather than Schönemann's troupe who premièred it in Frankfurt an der Oder. Lessing's literary development followed a course that paralleled the growth of realism in contemporary German acting. As a student in Leipzig, he had studied under Gottsched and had written some light, French-style comedies, which were presented by the Neuber company. Later, as a journalist and theatre critic in Berlin in the 1750s, he began to turn away from the rather rigid French-oriented neoclassicism of Gottsched toward the less formal and more domestic drama of England, just as a number of leading actors were developing a style to complement this realism.

A crucial element of Gottsched's vision that remained even when his dramatic style and neoclassic theory were rejected was the idea of a theatre permanently based in some major urban, intellectual and political centre, where audiences could be developed, actors, subsidised and salaried, could be freed from the stress and burdens of continual touring, and more elaborate and detailed physical settings could be constructed. Gottsched's model was, of course, the Comédie-Française, which had flourished in Paris since 1680. The regular visits of Ackermann's troupe to Hamburg was one of the major reasons why a group of citizens, led by the local drama critic Johann Friedrich Löwen (1727–71), were inspired to raise the money in the 1750s for a permanent theatre. Löwen championed this cause by writing the first history of the German theatre, which he published in 1763.[2] The result of the citizens' effort was the establishment of the Hamburg National Theatre, which was directed by Ackermann, with Ekhof as the leading player. It opened in 1767, but foundered after only two years (see chapter 3), so the actors resumed their touring. It has often been said that the major contribution of this institution to the history of the theatre was Lessing's *Hamburgische*

Dramaturgie, as its championing of English drama and the new middle-class drama over the declining aristocratic neoclassicism of France was one of the major theoretical statements on the drama of the century. The *Dramaturgie* has since been considered by many as second in importance only to Aristotle's *Poetics*. But it was not the only legacy of the short-lived Hamburg National Theatre, because the ideas represented by this theatre provided an inspiration for a whole series of later ventures. The term 'National Theatre' came to be applied regularly to ventures on the Hamburg model, which may seem odd, as Germany would not become a nation for another century, but the label distinguished such theatres from court theatres and touring companies. In the eighteenth century the term 'National Theatre' implied a general public, with an audience primarily composed of members of the bourgeoisie, in a theatre that was sub-sidised, non-commercial, and permanently established. It also, naturally, reflected the moral concerns, the cultural aspirations, and the interest in an aesthetics of realism shared by the audiences. It was also national in the sense that it sought to promote German culture like other publicly supported educational and cultural institutions. Such stable theatre organisations were extremely important to the rise of realistic production techniques, since they not only allowed theatres to construct the detailed settings of realism but, by providing actors a long-term stable home, encouraged the development of a realistic ensemble.

The first of the German court theatres to be founded in the Hamburg mode as a permanent theatre no longer run for private profit was that of the Duke of Gotha in 1775. Once again, the formidable Ekhof was its leading player until his death in 1778. In 1776, the Habsburg Emperor Joseph II, inspired on the one hand by the Comédie-Française and on the other by the example of Hamburg, established the German National Theatre in Vienna. It was the first such theatre to be founded and subsidised by a major German state government and the first of all German companies to survive today, as the Burgtheater, one of Europe's oldest and most respected national houses and a rival to the Comédie-Française. The role of court sponsorship was recognised in a new desig-nation, the *Hof- und Nationaltheater* (Court and National theatre), a term applicable to Gotha, the Vienna Burgtheater, and to the Mannheim theatre founded in 1779, which inherited most of its actors from the short-lived Gotha venture and also became one of Germany's leading theatres during the later years of the eighteenth century.

Realism in *Sturm und Drang* and Weimar Classicism

While the first permanent subsidised companies in Germany were being founded in the 1770s, there was a significant shift in the types of dramas being created, which greatly aided the development of realistic theatre. Under the influence of English theatre and French writers such as Diderot and Germans such as Lessing, middle-class sentimental comedy and serious drama grew steadily in popularity. Alongside these appeared the drama of *Sturm und Drang*, which took its major inspiration from Shakespeare and was directly opposed in structure and approach to the French literary neoclassic tradition. The movement took its title from a play by Maximilian Klinger (1752–1805), *Sturm und Drang* (*Storm and Stress*, 1776), which was loosely based on *Romeo and Juliet*, though it was launched by the first important success of Goethe, the sprawling epic *Götz von Berlichingen*. When Goethe took up residence as a law student in Strasbourg in 1770, he fell under the influence of Johann Gottfried Herder (1744–1803), a nationalist and champion of Shakespeare, whose writings helped lay the foundations of romantic aesthetic theory. *Götz* clearly shows this influence. Its publication in 1773 and its frequent production on many German stages, a rare occurrence for a *Sturm und Drang* drama, spread Goethe's name across Germany. The stage première took place in Berlin in 1774, where Heinrich Koch, a veteran of the Neuber company, was struggling to establish a standing theatre. The larger project failed, but *Götz* itself was an enormous success. Six months later it was staged by Friedrich Ludwig Schröder, who, during this important decade re-established a standing theatre in Hamburg, which became a centre for *Sturm und Drang* drama. Before offering the unconventional *Götz*, however, Schröder took the precaution of first presenting a newer, but more traditional work by Goethe, *Clavigo* (1774) in the popular new style of middle-class tragedy. *Götz*, when presented, was adjusted to a less radical form, as was Schiller's *Die Raüber*, when it was offered in Mannheim in 1782. *Clavigo*, though one of Goethe's lesser works, made a number of important contributions to the developing realistic drama. Most significantly, as it was based on events in the memoirs of the French dramatist Beaumarchais, which had occurred only a decade before, it was an early attempt to set a tragedy in contemporary time amid contemporary society. Goethe also attempted, especially in the earlier scenes, to develop realistic debates on social issues that anticipated to some extent those of Ibsen and, later, Shaw. Similar hints of realism may be found in Goethe's *Stella*, written in 1775.

The major works of the *Sturm und Drang* fall within the ten-year period of 1773 to 1783, beginning with Goethe's *Götz*, ending with the three major contributions to the genre by Friedrich Schiller, *Die Räuber, Fiesko* and *Kabale und Liebe*. Although Goethe and Schiller's contributions to this movement are still regularly revived, the work of others has been largely forgotten. The most important of these was probably Heinrich Leopold Wagner (1747–79), whose middle-class tragedy *Die Kindermörderin* (*The Child-Murderess*, 1776) was among the most traditional contributions to the movement, and Jakob Michael Reinhold Lenz (1751–92), a friend of Goethe's during the period in Strasbourg when *Sturm und Drang* was developing. Lenz's *Anmerkungen übers Theater* (*Notes on the Theatre*, 1774) helped provide a theoretical base for the *Sturm und Drang* and his dramas *Die Soldaten* (*The Soldiers*, 1776) and *Der Hofmeister* (*The Tutor*, 1774) remain the best known *Sturm und Drang* plays after Goethe and Schiller's, due in part to the reworking of the latter in the twentieth century by Brecht. Thanks to the interest of *Sturm und Drang* authors in Shakespeare, the 1770s also saw the first flowering of Shakespeare productions on the German stage, most notably in Hamburg. Here between 1776 and 1779, Schröder offered no fewer than nine Shakespeare plays. All were heavily adapted to suit the taste of Schröder's largely middle-class audiences, strongly under the influence of eighteenth-century rationalism and sentimentality.[3] In tone and in their departure from the formal practice of the hitherto prevalent classical drama, they made their own contribution to the growing interest in realism on stage.

After their early contributions to *Sturm und Drang* Goethe and Schiller began to move toward the blending of older and newer forms that would compose Weimar Classicism, so they were heading away from realism toward the more idealised form of theatre even before they began their famous collaboration in Weimar. Schiller's watershed play had been his tragedy *Don Carlos*, which began as a realistic drama, 'a domestic tragedy in a royal household', but became in the second half the model for a new sort of German historical drama, elevated in tone, written in verse, and seeking to illustrate basic patterns of human relationships as, in this instance, a father-son conflict.

Realism was not entirely missing from Weimar. The great years of the Weimar stage began with the opening of a new building in 1798 with *Wallensteins Lager (Wallenstein's Camp)*, the first of a trilogy Schiller wrote on the great German military hero, and ended in 1805, with Schiller's death.

Although the poetic style of *Wallensteins Lager* was anything but realistic, the attention to the physical details of costuming and staging certainly was. In a letter to Goethe, Schiller called for a setting of 'fullness and richness as a picture of the character and customs' of the time and as a 'physical embodiment of a certain existence'.[4] During these years Goethe and Schiller, working closely together, developed, in playwriting, acting, and scenic design, a distinctive mixture of classic and romantic elements, which provided the basis for a scenic realism that proved to be highly influential for subsequent German theatre. In addition to directing and supervising scenery and costumes, Goethe wrote one major new work, *Die natürliche Tochter (The Natural Daughter*, 1803), set during the French Revolution. Schiller's more considerable dramatic contributions also provided substantial preparation for a realistic style, even though Goethe often resisted such realistic touches as the reddening of Lady Macbeth's hands in Schiller's adaptation of that work.[5] After Schiller's death, Goethe's interest in the Weimar stage waned, although he continued to direct it until 1817. Even so, the theatre's well-trained ensemble, headed by Pius Alexander Wolff, and the reputation it had built in the opening years of the century kept it among the most influential of the German stages of the period. Its repertoire set the model for other German theatres, as while it included German classics and translations of Shakespeare, it was composed primarily of sentimental comedies, middle-class dramas, early melodramas, ballets, operas, and operettas.

Iffland, Kotzebue and theatre in Berlin

In 1796, even before the arrival of Schiller, Goethe's interest in developing a more ambitious theatre in Weimar had been strongly stimulated by the visit there of one of the German stage's leading authors and actors, August Wilhelm Iffland. Iffland had been the leading figure of the recently closed *Hof- und Nationaltheater* in Mannheim and was on his way to Berlin, where Frederick William III had invited him to take over the direction of the Royal Theatre. Up until this point Berlin's theatre history had been quite undistinguished. During the eighteenth century, the city had been host to a number of companies, German, French, and Italian, which competed with each other in a series of unsuccessful attempts to establish a permanent theatre. Under Iffland's leadership, however, Berlin became for the first time a major theatre centre, gaining a prominence that befitted the capital of the powerful state of Prussia. Iffland's repertoire at the newly established Royal Theatre was essentially the same as at Mannheim and Weimar. The most popular and most frequently performed playwrights were Iffland himself and his somewhat younger contemporary, Kotzebue. Even in Weimar, where one might assume that the work of Goethe and Schiller would have predominated, Goethe in fact produced thirty-one of Iffland's plays and eighty-seven by Kotzebue as against a mere nineteen of his own, eighteen by Schiller, and eight by Shakespeare,[6] which argued that the realistic mode of theatre achieved greater popularity than the classical even in Weimar.

Iffland's works were perfectly suited to the bourgeois public that was the mainstay of the Berlin theatre – meticulous if rather sentimental depictions of middle-class home life called *Familienstücke* (family plays) and sentimental melodramas called *Rührstücke* (plays of emotion). In the political turbulence of the Napoleonic Wars, Iffland's works offered a kind of escapism as they carefully excluded any possibly disturbing references to politics, social problems, or history. Instead they demonstrated the inevitable triumph of persecuted virtue over vice and displayed the reward of deserving poverty with honour and prosperity, themes carried on into popular nineteenth-century melodramas. The most popular works of Iffland, such as *Die Jäger* (*The Hunters*, 1785), *Die Hagestolzen* (*The Old Bachelors*, 1791), and *Der Spieler* (*The Gambler*, 1796), were all frequently revived until late in the nineteenth century.

Kotzebue's work was different from Iffland's His range was broader, his humour lower, his catering to his audiences' prejudices and conceit more blatant, and his success proportionately greater than Iffland's. Born in Weimar, Kotzebue began writing plays at an early age, and enjoyed his first and greatest success in 1787 with *Menschenhass und Reue* (*Misanthropy and Repentance*), written while he was a civil servant in St Petersburg, but first performed at the Royal Theatre in Berlin. This tearful melodrama, known in English as *The Stranger*, gained him a European reputation rivalling that of Goethe. He rose to the position of director of the Court Theatre in St Petersburg, but on the death of his patron Paul I in 1801, he returned to Weimar, soon after Goethe and Schiller began their collaboration there. Goethe welcomed Kotzebue as a popular dramatist, indeed he was the author most often presented at Weimar, but as Goethe's taste was at this point for much more elevated fare in the classic mode, he considered Kotzebue a shallow and rather banal moraliser. After two years in Weimar, Kotzebue left for the more congenial atmosphere of Berlin.

By the time he arrived in the Prussian capital, he was already the author of more than fifty plays, but he would almost double that number before leaving Berlin in 1806 and then he would add another hundred before his death. In addition to finding a sympathetic director, Iffland, and a friendly public in Berlin, Kotzebue also enjoyed a far larger and better equipped theatre than in Weimar. The major state of Prussia could provide resources for Iffland that Goethe, in tiny Weimar, could only dream of. Iffland and the architect Carl Gottfried Langhans (1732–1808) built a totally new theatre in 1800–1, the *Königliches Schauspielhaus* with the most elaborate scenic equipment of any stage for spoken drama in Germany. Two new works by Kotzebue inaugurated this new theatre, which had clearly been created to show off its staging potential, one an elaborate historical drama, *Die Kreuzfahrer (The Crusaders)*, the other a spectacular fairy opera, *Des Teufels Lustschloss (The Devil's Pleasure Palace)*. Much of the drama Kotzebue created for Iffland provided further opportunities for this sort of display, but Iffland applied the same taste for spectacle to productions of Schiller and Shakespeare, who was just entering the German repertoire in the excellent translations of August Wilhelm Schlegel (1767–1845), Dorothea Tieck (1799–1841), and Wolf von Baudissin (1789–1878). Eight volumes of their translations appeared between 1797 and 1801 containing thirteen comedies, tragedies, and histories. Schiller's *Wilhelm Tell* was produced in 1804 with spectacular Alpine scenery and his *Jungfrau von Orleans* (*Maid of Orleans*, 1801) (see fig. 6) was staged with a cast of some eight hundred[7]. Stunning effects like this were far beyond the means of the humble Weimar theatre, where the size of the stage and its equipment were so limited that the company had had to present the premiere of *Jungfrau* in the better-equipped theatre in nearby Leipzig.

After the death of Schiller and the retirement of Goethe, the reputation of the Weimar stage rapidly diminished, but that of the Berlin theatre continued to grow under Karl Brühl (1772–1837), who became director after Iffland's death in 1814. During his administration, romanticism reached its full tide in the German theatre, especially in the acting of Ludwig Devrient (1772–1837), whose passionate, demonic style was often compared to that of his English contemporary, Edmund Kean, and which many considered to be almost an antithesis of the formal, patterned Weimar approach. Brühl's designer, Carl Friedrich Schinkel (1781–1841), similarly dominated the scenic design of the period, as well as leaving a lasting heritage as a painter and architect. His most famous designs were those

6 *Die Jungfrau von Orleans* by Friedrich Schiller, Berlin, Königliches Schauspielhaus 1818. Designed by Friedrich Schinkel. The set shows a hall with a view of the City of Rheims.

that allowed him to give free range to fantasy or historical spectacle, such as Mozart's *Die Zauberflöte* (*The Magic Flute*), Schiller's *Jungfrau*, or the triumph of German romantic opera, *Der Freischütz* (*The Marksman*) of Karl Maria von Weber, but as taste shifted from spectacular drama to light comedy and bourgeois drama, Schinkel found less opportunity to display his skills.

The deaths of Iffland in 1814 and Kotzebue in 1819 removed the two major suppliers of popular realistic drama, but imports from France, the rise of Kotzebue's major successor, Ernst Raupach (1784–1852), and the popularity of his leading interpreter, the actress Auguste Stich-Crelinger (1795–1865) responded to the continued public interest in such relatively undemanding fare. Like Kotzebue, Raupach wrote prolifically (117 plays in all) in a wide variety of genres without great literary merit but with great popular success. Among his most popular works were the Russian tragedy *Isidor und Olga* (1825), the domestic drama *Vater und Tochter* (*Father and Daughter*, 1828), and a sixteen-play cycle on the Hohenstaufen dynasty. One might have expected that the growing taste for contemporary material might have inspired a more realistic approach to scenic design, but that was not the case. Although the critic Louis Pujoulx as early as 1801 had called for box settings in realistic dramas in place of the traditional Italianate wings and drop, the first enclosed setting in Germany did not appear until 1819, when Schinkel provided a box set with realistic properties for Gretchen's room in a private performance of Goethe's *Faust*. In 1826 he designed a second box set for a comedy at the National Theatre, but the protests of both actors and audience that it interfered with lighting and sound caused him to give up such experimentation.

Theatre in Vienna

The other major German-speaking theatre centre of the early nineteenth century that fostered the ideal of an ensemble that became essential for successful realistic production was Vienna. Although Berlin had only one permanent theatre until the mid-1830s, Vienna began the century with four, headed by the Burgtheater. The other three in the Vienna suburbs – the Theater in der Leopoldstadt (founded 1781), the Freihaustheater auf der Wieden (founded 1787) and the Theater in der Josefstadt (founded 1788) – had opened after the popular comedy had been expelled from the centre of Vienna. These theatres specialised in a kind of theatre rarely, if ever, seen in the northern cities, stemming directly from the strolling players of the seventeenth and eighteenth centuries (see chapter 2). In these the traditions of folk farce and *commedia dell'arte* were combined with specifically Viennese characters. The most famous production from these theatres was Mozart's *Die Zauberflöte* (*The Magic Flute*, 1791), which had made a fortune for its director, Emanuel Schikaneder (1751–1812), the first Papageno, and enabled him to build one of the largest and best equipped theatres in Germany, the Theater an der Wien, in 1801. Kotzebue was invited to direct the flourishing Burgtheater in 1798 and during his brief administration (until 1802) he not surprisingly specialised in his own works and those of Iffland. His leading actress, Johanna von Weissenthurn (1773–1845) became, after his departure, a very successful author of dramas in the Iffland manner. Another actress discovered by Kotzebue at this time was Sophie Schröder (1781–1845) who in later years became Germany's greatest actress of romantic tragedy.

The opening years of the nineteenth century were difficult for all Viennese theatres, with severe censorship, and finally, in 1809, when Austria was conquered by the French under Napoleon, an outright ban on almost all German plays. Matters did not much improve until 1814, when the prominent

Viennese literary critic Josef Schreyvogel (1768–1832) was called upon to direct the Burgtheater. Schreyvogel remained effectively in charge of the Burgtheater until 1832 and by a combination of literary and theatrical taste, determination, managerial skills, and, perhaps most importantly, diplomatic tact, he managed to create the outstanding theatre in Germany of this period under one of the most conservative and rigorous censorships in Europe. The Burgtheater possessed the best ensemble and the most ambitious repertoire anywhere. His major actor was Sophie Schröder, now at the height of her powers. She was associated with many of the great roles in Schreyvogel's repertoire, which included Shakespeare, Calderon, a number of previously banned works by Schiller, the first major productions of Heinrich von Kleist, and, especially, the works of the greatest Austrian dramatist of the early nineteenth century, Franz Grillparzer. Grillparzer's ambitious poetic works often utilised classic themes, and his *Sappho* (1818) starring Sophie Schröder, caused him to be widely hailed as the greatest German-language dramatist since Goethe and Schiller.

Although Schreyvogel, once a student at Jena and a passionate devotee of the theatre in nearby Weimar, was clearly devoted to Goethe's ideal of a repertoire of significant foreign works and native ones of high literary and poetic merit, he did not neglect the wide public interest in middle-class comedy and drama. Iffland and Kotzebue were still often presented, along with the works of such followers as Johanna von Weissenthurn. A major actor in this genre was Heinrich Anschütz (1795–1866); it is testimony to the range and skill of Schreyvogel's company that Anschütz was just as successful and popular in domestic comedy and drama as he was at playing Theseus, Orestes, Wilhelm Tell or even King Lear opposite Sophie Schröder.

A strongly conservative reaction swept Europe after the Napoleonic Wars, stimulating a series of revolutions in 1830, followed in most cases by even more repression. The centre of European conservatism was Vienna, where Prince Clemens Metternich, the primary architect of this repressive era, was in power. When Schreyvogel departed in 1832, no director of comparable vision and diplomatic skill was available to replace him and the hitherto formidable Burgtheater went into decline. Between 1830 and 1850 the Viennese theatrical scene was dominated by the suburban theatres, whose light comedies and fairy and folk plays offered little to antagonise the powerful censor. This was the last golden age of the Vienna folk theatre, as Johann Nepomuk Nestroy (1801–62), building upon the foundations laid during the 1820s by the brilliant fairy tale fantasies of Ferdinand Raimund,

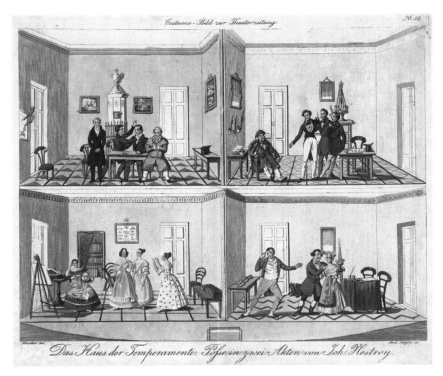

7 *Das Haus der Temperamente* by Johann Nestroy, Vienna, Theater in der Leopoldstadt,
1837. Four different appartments are shown at the same time.

elevated the Viennese folk play to a major literary form. Nestroy's first major
success, *Der böse Geist Lumpazivagabundus (The Evil Spirit Lumpazivagabundus,*
1833) was directly in the tradition of such romantic works as Raimund's *Der
Alpenkönig und der Menschenfeind* (*The King of the Alps and the Misanthrope,*
1828). His keen wit, rich language, exuberant comic imagination and
brilliant interpretations delighted his public even when the satire was at
their own expense. The fairy background of his early work not only related
him to a tradition, but helped disguise his social messages. By the mid-1830s
his popularity and developing skill allowed him to move into the contemporary world, beginning with the enormous success of *Zu ebener Erde and im
ersten Stock* (*On the Ground Floor and the First Floor,* 1835), a realistic comedy of
class relationships. The realistic staging showed the two apartments simultaneously, one above the other, a device extended to show four different
apartments at the same time in *Das Haus der Temperamente* (*The House of
Temperaments,* 1837) (see fig. 7). Despite their farcical tone, such plays, in

their preoccupation with contemporary social questions, reflected the concern for social justice which occupied so much of German thought in the years just before the revolutions of 1848. This tendency became even more marked in Nestroy's plays of the 1840s, which added more realistic and sentimental touches, resulting in what may be called comedic thesis plays, such as *Der Talisman* (*The Talisman*, 1840), a plea against the social intolerance of minorities. Other Viennese dramatists, most notably Friedrich Kaiser (1808–72), followed Nestroy's example, so that quite a flourishing school of realistic social comedy appeared in the suburban theatres of Vienna during this decade.

Young Germany

Although the uprisings of 1830 were largely unsuccessful, they inspired a generation of politically engaged writers, who, despite the oppressive policing of potential centres of resistance such as the universities and the theatres, risked prison and exile to produce writings that directly engaged contemporary themes and conditions. The most politically engaged writers in this group were christened *Das junge Deutschland* (Young Germany) by the artist Adolph Menzel (1815–1905). Although few of the plays of this group gained great distinction, they contributed significantly to the development of modern realistic and political drama. Instead of the grandiose characters of the romantic theatre, the authors of Young Germany presented persons from everyday life as accurately as social and psychological theory and observation would allow. Their favoured technique was that of the French well-made play, popularised during this same period by the Parisian Eugène Scribe and his followers and later utilised by masters of modern realism such as Ibsen. Thus in both subject matter and technique the dramatists of Young Germany anticipated the major directions of the modern realistic theatre.

The two leading dramatists of Young Germany were Heinrich Laube (1806–84) and Karl Gutzkow (1811–78). Both dramatists, like many of the leaders of this movement, were imprisoned for a time for their political writings. After Laube was released he travelled to Paris, where he was much impressed by Scribe's dramatic craft. His first play, *Monaldeschi* (1841), was a historical drama set in Sweden in the days of Queen Christina, a setting that assured he avoided censorship. It was a typical Young Germany drama, full of references that could be applied to the contemporary political situation, but its major impact came from its careful construction. It was primarily through this and Laube's later plays that the techniques of the French well-made play entered the contemporary German theatre, and, like Scribe, Laube often chose historical subjects, as in *Die Karlsschüler* (*The Students of Karl's School*, 1846) concerning young Schiller's struggle with the authorities over *Die Räuber*, *Prinz Friedrich* (1848), and *Graf Essex* (*Count Essex*, 1856). Although *Monaldeschi* was premiered with great success in Strasbourg, Laube had no real theatrical home during the 1840s and so had some difficulty in getting his early works presented.

Gutzkow was more fortunate, since he served as dramaturge to the theatre in Dresden during this decade and managed to present several of his plays there. His *Uriel Acosta* (1847), a plea for religious tolerance, has been the only play from the Young Germany movement to have a significant stage history. His dramatic range was far greater than Laube's, including Aristophanic tragicomedy (*Nero*, 1835), historical drama (*König Saul*, 1839), historical tragedy (*Jürgen Wullenweber*, 1847) and contemporary social dramas that anticipated the work of Ibsen such as *Ella Rose oder Die Rechte des Herzens* (*Ella Rose or the Rights of the Heart*, 1856). Gutzkow's major contribution to drama, however, was his arrangement for the publication of *Dantons Tod* (*Danton's Death*, 1835) by Georg Büchner. Doubtless the political tone of this epic of the French Revolution attracted Gutzkow, but Büchner rejected Gutzkow's invitation to join the politically oriented dramatists of Young Germany. Instead he pursued his own unique vision in his two subsequent plays, the coolly ironic *Leonce und Lena* and the grim fragmentary tragedy *Woyzeck*. In taking its protagonist from the dregs of society and presenting his suffering in almost inarticulate terms, *Woyzeck* looked beyond realism to the extremes of naturalism, but its striking juxtapositions, grotesque characters and situations and fragmented scenes and dialogue in fact anticipated even more closely the expressionist drama of the next century. None of Büchner's plays were produced in his lifetime and only *Leonce und Lena* during the nineteenth century. Only in the twentieth century was Büchner recognised as one of the most original and influential of German dramatists (see chapter 6).

The actor most associated with the Young Germany movement was Karl Seydelmann (1793–1843), now remembered as an early pioneer of realism and the first of the great German virtuoso actors who dominated the mid-century stage. On tour in Vienna in 1829 he dazzled and inspired the young Laube, who likened his powerful delivery to a Protestant sword thrust into mist-enshrouded romanticism.[8] Seydelmann was primarily associated with the Berlin stage, which he almost single-handedly restored in the 1840s to something of the prominence of the Iffland era. Indeed he was much closer to the calculating and deliberate Iffland than mercurial romantics, such as Ludwig Devrient. His most popular roles were the Shakespearean villains, Shylock and Iago, which he played with unequalled power. Both in his display of technical skill and in his compelling personality he set the style of the virtuoso actor, who often took precedence over script and production for mid-century German audiences.

The other major dramatist to appear during the 1840s had, like Büchner, an ambiguous relationship to the Young Germany movement. This was Friedrich Hebbel (1813–63) who had enormous difficulties at first in gaining any attention. Unlike Büchner, however, he came to be recognised as one of Germany's leading dramatists during his lifetime. He offered his first major play, a retelling of the Biblical story of Judith, to the Berlin Royal Theatre in 1840, where it gained the support of the theatre's leading actress, Auguste Stich-Crelinger (1795–1865). The modernist tone of this retelling gave it a certain similarity to the works of the Young German dramatists, but Hebbel had little interest in either the possible political implications of the story or in its religious dimension. He focused first on the story's social dynamics, but even more achieved a depth of psychological realism that was totally lacking in Gutzkow, Laube and their followers. It is doubtless on those grounds that the critic Georg Witkowski (1863–1933) in his study of the nineteenth century German theatre called Hebbel's *Judith* the first modern drama of the century.[9] It was, unfortunately, much too modern for Berlin in 1840. The censor found the psychological and sexual emphasis of the play unacceptable and insisted on extensive changes to bring the play closer to a religious or historical epic, thus totally distorting it and confusing its audiences. It was a failure that soon disappeared, not to be revived in the form Hebbel originally planned until more than half a century later, in 1896.

The failure of this first play clearly diminished interest in staging the works of this unconventional young dramatist. The next three plays he submitted to Stich-Crelinger were rejected. It took him two years to place the third of these, *Maria Magdalena* (1844), which ultimately became his most famous work, and this was at the distinctly minor theatre at Königsberg. This powerful prose tragedy of lower middle-class German life, with its strong social criticism, laid the foundations for much of the social drama of the rest of the century in Germany and elsewhere. In his preface to the play, Hebbel argued that contemporary Europe was experiencing for the third time in history – after the classical Greek and Elizabethan ages – a kind of social and philosophical transition that could produce great drama. During such periods of transition, the isolated champions of an emerging order confront, and in the case of tragedy, are defeated by the increasingly outdated but still powerful forces of the old order.[10] Hebbel's heroine is more passive and helpless and thus more pathetic than later suffering women in this play's successors, but there is a direct line from her to such later Hebbel heroines as Agnes Bernauer in the tragedy of that name (1852) or Queen Rhodope in *Gyges und sein Ring* (1854), and ultimately to the convention-challenging women of Ibsen. In a letter from Paris to Stich-Crelinger, Hebbel described *Maria Magdalena* in terms that could equally well be applied to the major works of Ibsen's middle period.[11] The aspects of the middle-class world view that he noted in it would become the central concerns of a play like Ibsen's *Ghosts*, an obstinate adherence to traditional patriarchal beliefs and an inability to accommodate to complex situations. The link between Hebbel and Ibsen was pointed out by the critic Herrmann Hettner (1821–82), who was largely inspired by the Berlin premières of *Judith* and *Maria Magdalena* to create the sections on middle-class drama in his book *Das moderne Drama* (*The Modern Drama*, 1852), which in its turn profoundly influenced the young Ibsen.

The political as well as the theatrical landscape changed abruptly in Germany in 1848, when another wave of revolts more vehement than those of the 1830 revolution swept across Europe. Metternich was toppled from power and the censor was abolished in Vienna. Franz Ignaz von Holbein (1779–1855), director of the Burgtheater since 1841, who had been systematically prevented from offering interesting new work, immediately opened his doors to Hebbel and the Young Germany dramatists. His first major offerings were revivals of *Maria Magdalena* and *Judith*, followed by premieres of new Hebbel dramas, the biblical drama *Herodes und Mariamne* (1849) and a contemporary tragedy *Julia* (1851), a kind of sequel to *Maria Magdalena*. This play has also been considered a forerunner to Ibsen's *Ghosts*, as it centres on a proposed marriage between the innocent heroine and the debauched Count Bertram, a precursor to Captain Alving. The heroine's father declares that such a marriage would be 'the mother of ghosts,' a striking line that anticipates Ibsen not only in theme but in image. The play's final act also contains a 'discussion scene,' a feature that Shaw later cited as the hallmark of the modern social drama and that he incorrectly thought had originated with Ibsen.

Laube and Dingelstedt

In 1849 von Holbein was replaced at the Burgtheater by a figure even more obviously committed to the new order, Heinrich Laube, already famous as one of the leading dramatists of Young Germany. Conservatives in Vienna feared that his appointment would mean a radicalisation of the national theatre, especially when Laube presented in 1850 the first production ever in Vienna of Schiller's iconoclastic *Räuber*, but his former Young Germany companions complained that he was too conservative. In fact between 1849 and 1867 he presented an impressive and varied repertoire, more ambitious than that of any other German theatre of the period, including classic German and Austrian authors such as Goethe, Lessing, Schiller, Kleist, and Grillparzer, but also the plays of Young Germany, Shakespeare, popular writers of comedy such as Friedrich Halm (1806–71) from Vienna, Roderich Benedix (1811–73) from Frankfurt, and Charlotte Birch-Pfeiffer (1800–68) from Berlin. He had a particular fondness for the contemporary French theatre of Scribe, Sardou, Augier, and Dumas *fils*; in fact, he produced almost every major new play from Paris, so that French drama eventually comprised almost a third of his repertoire. His audiences, dominated by culturally aspiring members of the bourgeoisie, strongly supported his French orientation, all the more in that the characters, the society, the moral concerns, even the settings of these plays bore a close resemblance to their own society and their own interests. The actor most associated with these plays was Adolf von Sonnenthal (1834–1909), who became known as the perfect salon hero, the very embodiment of Viennese high society and of the Laube style. He enjoyed a unique popularity during his remarkable career at the Burgtheater, which lasted from his first contract in 1856 until his death 53 years later. The presentation of these French works encouraged Laube, like his Parisian contemporaries, to develop a more realistic style, in which greater attention was paid to the physical details of everyday life by the acting ensemble. The ubiquitous salon settings of these plays also encouraged the development of the box set, which, under Laube, became common on the Viennese stage,[12] but he also experimented with more abstract scenic design, creating, for example, an imposing abstract flight of stairs for the climax of Grillparzer's *Des Meeres und der Liebe Wellen* (*Waves of the Sea and Love*) in 1849, which anticipated symbolist settings at the end of the century.

Laube's interest in the script and the acting ensemble meant that he had little tolerance for the kind of virtuoso style recently cultivated by

Seydelmann. He therefore quickly dismissed two actors who then went on to become leading virtuoso performers, Marie Seebach (1830–97) and Bogumil Dawison (1818–72). Dawison settled in Dresden, which was also home to the other most famous virtuoso actor of the period, Emil Devrient (1803–72), a nephew of the great romantic actor and the most celebrated practitioner of the Weimar style. The virtuoso actor, whose personality and individual approach tends to overshadow both the role and fellow actors, clearly cannot easily share the spotlight with a rival, and so Dawison and Devrient did not normally appear together, which presented no great problem for the Dresden stage as both were often on tour. In any case their styles were antithetical. Devrient had a smooth and elegant, if somewhat mannered delivery, excellent in contemporary drawing room plays, but also very effective in his most celebrated role, which was Hamlet. Dawison was closer to the romantic spirit, fiery, aggressive, and spontaneous. In a sense the tension between the cool Weimar classic style and the romantic intensity of actors like Ludwig Devrient continued to be apparent in these leading mid-century virtuoso performers.

Rapid industrialisation brought a huge influx of population into major cities in the mid-years of the nineteenth century, and nowhere was this more true than in Vienna, which attracted workers not only from the provinces but from throughout the Austro-Hungarian Empire. The city and suburbs went from a population of just under 320,000 in 1830 to over 600,000 by the end of the 1860s. Audiences altered significantly, particularly in the suburban theatres, which drew the majority of the new population. Although there was a certain continuity in both audiences and repertoire at the Burgtheater before and after 1848, the new audiences that came into the suburban houses had little interest in the traditional folk and popular entertainments that had long been the standard fare at these houses. Folk farces, Raimund-style comedies and magic plays continued to be produced, but to ever-diminishing audiences. Inflation followed by financial crises in the late 1840s and early 1850s made the situation in these theatres even more precarious so, like the Burgtheater, the suburban houses increasingly turned to French imports, in this case the lighter fare of vaudevilles, one-act farces, and, during the 1850s, a new form, the operetta. In 1856 Nestroy, now director of the suburban Karltheater, invited actors and singers from the Paris Gymnase and Variétés-Palais-Royale, who brought samples of the new operettas just then being introduced in Paris by Hervé and Jacques Offenbach. Their success was enormous and

Offenbach became the favoured composer of the Viennese suburbs. Nestroy enjoyed the greatest success of his final years, playing Jupiter in *Orpheus in the Underworld* by Offenbach and Offenbach himself directed his works at the Theater an der Wien from 1864 to 1867, professing himself more at home in Vienna than in Paris. This work prepared the way for the golden age of the Viennese operetta after 1870s, when Vienna replaced Paris as the home of this genre.

The only director in Germany in Laube's generation to rival him in importance was Franz von Dingelstedt (1814–81), whose career intersected with Laube's in a number of interesting ways. Like Laube, Dingelstedt in his early years was associated with Young Germany. While Laube was directing the Burgtheater in Vienna, Dingelstedt brought new prominence first to the Munich theatre, between 1851 and 1857, where he directed one of the first German productions of Wagner's *Tannhäuser* (in 1855), and then to Goethe's old theatre in Weimar, which he directed between 1857 and 1867. In neither theatre did he enjoy the flexibility in selecting a repertoire or the financial support available that allowed Laube such freedom of action in Vienna, yet Dingelstedt presented a repertoire that was almost as varied, including Goethe, Schiller, Hebbel, and Grillparzer, along with the more popular repertoire of Benedix, Eduard von Bauernfeld (1802–90), and Birch-Pfeiffer. Despite his comparatively limited means, Dingelstedt was more devoted than Laube to developing the visual side of his productions. He built a new theatre with gas lighting in Munich in 1864 and worked closely with local painters Friedrich Kaulbach (1822–1903), Karl Piloty (1826–86) and Hans Makart (1840–84) on costumes, settings and even stage compositions. There was thus a very close tie between Dingelstedt's stagings and the school of historical realism being developed on the vast canvases of these artists. This visual approach was carried on in the next generation by the Duke of Saxe-Meiningen, who spread the realistic historicist style to stages across Europe. Indeed the theatrical Duke was an enthusiastic spectator of the major achievement of Dingelstedt's Weimar years, a cycle of Shakespeare's history plays presented over a week in 1864. This event marked the foundation of the German Shakespeare Society and exercised a great influence over the next generation of German producers. The unified approach to production, especially the careful composition of crowd scenes, provided a model that would challenge and gradually supplant a theatre that was focused mainly upon the virtuoso star actor, who had dominated the German stage for most of the century.

The defeat of Austria by Prussia in 1866 caused a major upheaval in the Austrian government and a political drift to the right. Laube's liberal orientation now made him a subject of official suspicion and the Burgtheater was burdened with new regulations. The exhausted Laube resigned to be replaced by a popular dramatist with little administrative experience, Friedrich Halm (1806–71). Dingelstedt now set his sights on this prestigious position and, in order to be close at hand, assumed director-ship of the Vienna court opera to which he brought his usual emphasis on composed crowd scenes and unified visual spectacle. In 1870 he achieved his goal, being appointed director of the Burgtheater to which he brought new success and prominence. The audience of the Burgtheater changed greatly after 1870, as it was now dominated by a new moneyed class unfamiliar with the theatre's traditions and with interest in neither the French salon plays favoured by Laube nor his emphasis on language; Dingelstedt's penchant for spectacle was much more to their taste. In Vienna, as in Weimar, one of the high points of his directorship was a huge cycle of Shakespeare's history plays. The Burgtheater, however, commanded far greater resources than the small Weimar stage, and the 1875 cycle was generally considered one of the greatest series of productions ever seen at this theatre. It was revived six more times before the end of the century, even after Dingelstedt's death in 1881.

New plays did not fare so well in this administration. Unquestionably the leading Austrian dramatist of the 1870s was Ludwig Anzengruber (1839–89), who was introduced to the Burgtheater by Dingelstedt in 1873. Anzengruber had already won a major reputation in the suburban Theater an der Wien by invigorating the traditional folk drama of Nestroy and Raimund with the new interest in realism and social commentary, as in his popular peasant drama *Der Pfarrer von Kirchfeld* (*The Parson of Kirchfeld*, 1870). The success of this work gained Anzengruber a contract to create two plays for that theatre annually and also interest from Dinglestedt at the Burgtheater. Unfortunately, his attempts to adjust his work to the higher-class audiences of the Burgtheater by writing salon dramas set among the petit bourgeoisie, like *Elfriede* (1873) and *Die Tochter des Wucherers* (*The Userer's Daughter*, 1874) were only modestly successful. He returned to the suburban theatres and the mixture of folk elements and social concerns with which he had begun and after 1880 turned almost exclusively to the novel. Nevertheless his 1877 *Das vierte Gebot* (*The Fourth Commandment*) had suffi-cient social and naturalistic appeal to be revived with great success at the

Berlin Freie Bühne in 1890. In the meantime, the suburban theatres that had supported the folk tradition leading to Anzengruber were turning, even during the years of his greatest popularity, more and more to the operetta. Johann Strauss in the years between *Die Fledermaus* (*The Bat*, 1874) and *Der Zigeunerbaron* (*The Gypsy Baron*, 1885) achieved a European-wide reputation that eclipsed even Offenbach. Karl Millöcker (1842–89), who wrote incidental music for Anzengruber and a series of major operettas, was not far behind.

The Meininger and Wagner

Dingelstedt's interest in visual spectacle and crowd scenes and the attention to detail and impact of the ensemble, which he shared with Laube, were carried on most notably in the next generation in the work of Duke Georg II of Saxe-Meiningen (1826–1914). The Duke devoted his considerable private fortune to developing a company in his court theatre that would present classic dramas in meticulously researched productions in which the focus was on ensemble. To maintain the high level of production, the Meininger, as the company became known, had to tour, first in Germany and then throughout Europe, from 1874 to 1890. All the concerns that Laube and Dingelstedt had addressed in their productions were brought to their most complete expression in the most famous of the Duke's productions, *Julius Caesar*, which was added to the Meininger repertoire in 1867. When it toured to Berlin in 1874, the production's attention to physical detail dazzled the public and reviewers, who spoke of it in revolutionary terms. It was, however, not so much a revolutionary approach as the culmination of a greater concern with stage realism that had been developing throughout the century. Positivism was entering the theatre, as it had already entered science and historical study, and the romantic concern for beauty was being replaced by the realist concern with truth. Moreover, the bourgeois public of the 1860s and 1870s were much better informed on historical detail than their predecessors and had come, thanks to improvements in printing and especially graphics, to be increasingly aware of the look of past ages. This was the public that was dazzled by the accurate Roman togas, weaponry and armour of the Meiningen *Caesar* and was impressed by being informed exactly which views of imperial Rome were being accurately pictured in each of the seven scenes.

Every aspect of the production was conceived in the same spirit. The Duke encouraged his actors to interject groans, sighs, and cries into their lines for greater realism and even played the entire conspiratorial scene in Brutus' garden in whispers, much to the dismay of traditionalists. Among the most admired achievements of the Meininger were their realistic crowd scenes, to which the Duke gave special attention. Crowds were separated into small groups, each led by a more experienced actor, and they were provided with scripts showing exact positions and movements and containing specific realistic lines instead of the traditional vague cries and murmurs.[13]

During the decades when the company toured, they made a profound impression on the leading theatre artists of the period. In London in 1881 they were admired by Henry Irving, Ellen Terry, and Edwin Booth, and in Moscow, in 1885, they served as an inspiration to Konstantin Stanislavsky and Vladimir Nemirovich-Danchencko, the subsequent founders of the Moscow Art Theatre. Although they did not tour to Paris, their Brussels performances attracted the leading critics and experimental directors of France, André Antoine in particular being strongly influenced by their work. The Meininger productions, particularly of Shakespeare and the German classics, brought to culmination several lines of experimentation in the nineteenth-century German theatre and at the same time helped prepare the way for the new realist experiments of Antoine and Stanislavsky at the end of the century.

Shortly after the first Berlin tour of the Meininger came another major theatrical affirmation of the ideal of an artistically unified ensemble production. This was the production that opened Wagner's Bayreuth Festival in 1876, the monumental *Der Ring des Nibelungen* (*The Ring of the Nibelung*). The work of Richard Wagner (1813–83), like that of the Meininger, has often been spoken of as a culmination of experiments extending back through the entire nineteenth century, but, like the Duke of Saxe-Meiningen, his work can also be seen as the peak of the unified theatrical work sought by both Laube and Dingelstedt.

Thanks to the support of his most important patron, Ludwig, King of Bavaria, Wagner moved to Munich in 1864. Here were premiered *Tristan und Isolde* (1865) and *Die Meistersinger von Nürnberg* (*The Mastersingers of Nuremberg*, 1868), and Ludwig brought the leading architect Gottfried Semper (1803–79) from Berlin to build a major new opera house in Munich to house Wagner's work. All these plans were disrupted, however, by a growing aura of scandal surrounding the controversial composer. The close relationship between Wagner and the wife of Hans von Bülow

8 A view of the auditorium of the Bayreuth Festspielhaus in the nineteenth century.

(1830–94), was the excuse adopted by Wagner's enemies to exclude the composer from Munich. In actuality they were mainly alarmed by Wagner's influence over the impressionable young king. Over Wagner's objections, the new Munich theatre director, Baron von Perfall (1844–1909), was encouraged by Ludwig to premiere *Das Rheingold* (*The Rhinegold*) and *Die Walküre* (*The Valkyrie*), but the *Ring* cycle was not performed in its entirety until Wagner opened his long-planned festival theatre in Bayreuth in 1876. Wagner's staging of the cycle was fairly conventional, but the Bayreuth theatre itself was revolutionary and changed the European idea of theatre architecture (see fig. 8). The orchestra was placed out of sight in a pit extending back under the stage, an idea proposed but nor realised by Semper in Munich, and the traditional boxes and galleries were abandoned in favour of ranks of seats rising in semicircles facing the stage, with sufficient space between to eliminate the traditional aisles. This democratic fan-shaped seating arrangement provided a model for European theatre design and came to be known as 'continental seating'. Further, to focus attention on the stage, Wagner darkened the auditorium during the performance, for the first time in the German theatre. A second festival followed in 1882 for the première of *Parsifal*. During the 1880s the Bayreuth festival steadily grew into the national institution Wagner dreamed of, but did not live to see. He died the winter following the *Parsifal* première.

The coming of Ibsen

The same years that witnessed the establishment of the Bayreuth festival also saw the first major impact in Germany of those foreign dramatists, most importantly Henrik Ibsen, whose work would launch the modern drama. Ibsen was in fact closely connected to the German stage. The works of Hebbel and the theories of Hettner strongly influenced the family dramas for which he was best known, most of which were written in Munich, where he lived from 1875 to 1878 and again from 1885 to 1891. Here, during his first stay, he wrote the first of his revolutionary social dramas, *Pillars of Society* and began *A Doll's House* and during the second he wrote *Rosmersholm* (1886), *The Lady from the Sea* (1888) and *Hedda Gabler* (1890).

It was the pioneering Duke of Saxe-Meiningen who introduced Ibsen to the German stage, with his production of *The Pretenders*, which he brought to Berlin in 1876. That same year saw productions of Ibsen's *The Vikings at Helgeland* by Dingelstedt in Vienna and at the Munich Court Theatre. Although these dramas brought some German recognition to Ibsen, he was for a time quite overshadowed by his Norwegian contemporary Bjørnstjerne Bjørnson, whose realistic dramas of contemporary life were more to the taste of the times than Ibsen's romantic portrayals of Vikings and early Scandinavian monarchs. The Berlin productions of Bjørnson's *The Newly-Married Couple* and *A Bankruptcy* in 1875 were the first great successes of the new realistic drama of social comment, but they were quite over-shadowed three years later by *Pillars of Society*, Ibsen's first great work in this style and the play that established his German reputation. Five separate theatres presented it within a fortnight in Berlin alone, a record unrivalled in that city's history; the same year it was offered by twenty-two other theatres in Germany and Austria.

Productions of Ibsen's next play, *A Doll's House*, in Scandinavia during the winter of 1879–80 inspired both interest and apprehension among potential German producers, since the play's apparent attack on home and marriage aroused a storm of protest. The Berlin Residenztheater, which specialised in the realistic social drama of Augier and Dumas *fils* and which had offered *Pillars of Society* in 1878, was an ideal venue for the new drama, but its leading lady Hedwig Niemann-Raabe (1844–1905) agreed to present the role only after Ibsen wrote an alternative ending in which Nora remains with her husband and children. It was with this radically altered ending that the play was generally presented in Germany by those theatres bold enough to stage it, but it was still considered scandalous and was condemned by leading critics in Berlin and elsewhere as being more distasteful than even the coarsest of the French realists.

The protests aroused by *A Doll's House* were, however, nothing compared to those stirred up throughout Europe by Ibsen's next work, *Ghosts* (1881), dealing with even more shocking subject matter. Public presentation of the work was unthinkable. A group of young Munich authors sponsored its German première, a private showing in Augsburg in 1886. Later that year the intrepid Duke of Saxe-Meiningen staged it at his home theatre, but was prevented by the censor from bringing it to Berlin. The first Berlin showing was at a private matinee for charity at the Residenztheater, but the company's leading actors refused to perform in it, so the role of Oswald was played by the theatre's dramaturge, Franz Wallner (1854–98) and Mrs Alving by Charlotte Frohn (1844–88), the wife of Anton Anno (1838–93), the director.

Berlin, new companies and the naturalistic drama

In fact, this rather obscure Berlin première of *Ghosts* would be looked back upon as the beginning of the modern era in the German theatre. The next few years saw a steadily growing interest in Ibsen's work, which despite strong resistance from conservative critics and theatre directors, reinforced a spirit of change that was sweeping through the theatre world. In 1883 a major new artistic theatre was founded in Berlin by Adolph L'Arronge (1838–1908), the Deutsches Theater, on the model of the Vienna Burgtheater and the Comédie Française. Its distinguished company was headed by two of the leading artists of the new generation, Josef Kainz (1858–1910) and Agnes Sorma (1856–1927). Their simple truthful style was widely regarded as the perfect expression for the new drama, and they were widely heralded as the first 'modern' actors, the term having a great vogue in Berlin at this period, when artists and authors devoted to the new spirit of realism collectively styled themselves *Die Moderne*. Sorma's interpretation of Ibsen's Nora was much praised, but on the whole neither Kainz nor Sorma were comfortable with the underplaying and dark view of the human condition that was found in much of the new naturalist drama. They preferred instead to bring a new concern for realism and psychological depth to the classics, to Goethe, Schiller and Shakespeare.

The champions of the new drama soon realised that the Deutsches Theater, for all its high artistic goals, was not especially interested in dramatists like Ibsen, and even if it had been, there remained the continuing problem of censorship. An alternative example to that of the existing system was provided by Antoine's Théâtre-Libre in Paris, a theatre open only to members and therefore protected from police censorship and the commercial interests of the established theatre. The critics Otto Brahm (1855–1912) and Paul Schlenther (1854–1916) organised their own German 'free theatre', the Freie Bühne, in 1889. Its first production, fittingly, was the hitherto banned *Ghosts* and its second was *Vor Sonnenaufgang* (*Before Sunrise*), the first major drama of German naturalism by a young author who was to become the leading German dramatist of this era, Gerhart Hauptmann (1862–1946). Works by most of the leading new wave of European dramatists – Bjørnson, Tolstoy, Strindberg, Zola, and Becque – followed. Within a few years major commercial theatres were staging these authors so that the Freie Bühne disbanded in 1892, its mission largely accomplished. From time to time, however, Brahm continued to produce work under its title to avoid censorship, most notably Hauptmann's *Die Weber* (*The Weavers*) in 1893, the culmination of his social dramas and one of the greatest plays of the naturalist movement. When Brahm assumed directorship of the Deutsches Theater the following year, he opened his administration with this play, starring Kainz, displaying realistic settings and crowd scenes that made it one of the great realistic productions of the German theatre. The second leading actor in *Die Weber* was Rudolf Rittner (1869–1943). He and his frequent partner Else Lehmann (1866–1940) had played Oswald and Mrs Alving in the Freie Bühne *Ghosts* and came with Brahm to the Deutsches Theater to become leading interpreters of Ibsen and Hauptmann.

The working class message of Hauptmann's *Weber* reflected the growing influence of socialism in late nineteenth century Germany, particularly in Berlin. One of the aspects of social and cultural life that engaged the interest of this new movement was the theatre. The regular commercial theatre was well beyond the means of Berlin's proletariat, and during the late 1880s several socialist organisations began to develop plans for a workers' theatre.[14] The Freie Bühne provided both an inspiration and a model, and in 1891 the Freie Volksbühne, headed by Franz Mehring (1846–1919), opened at the suburban Ostend Theater, which had hosted the German première of Ibsen's *Enemy of the People*. The repertoire of the opening seasons clearly emphasised the new drama, with Ibsen as the dominant dramatist. In 1892 a disagreement among the directors resulted in the establishment of a rival organisation, the Neue Freie Volksbühne, headed by Bruno Wille (1860–1928). The mission and repertoire of the two organisations were not notably different, but Wille's operation, which offered a somewhat more traditional selection of plays, gradually began to attract a more middle-class public. In the years that followed, the Volksbühne movement spread throughout Germany and by the mid-1920s there were more than 200 Volksbühnen scattered across Germany, with a combined membership of more than 630,000, in some smaller communities ten to twenty-five per cent of the total population. Never before nor since has a popular theatre so fully achieved its goals.

Vienna and Berlin at the turn of the century

By the late nineteenth century Berlin had become the principal city of German-speaking Europe; Vienna, which had prevailed earlier, was much slower in responding to the new trends. Although a major new home for the Burgtheater was built in 1888 and the ensemble Dingelstedt had developed became famous throughout Europe, the years after Dingelstedt's retirement saw a series of directors and no clear artistic vision for the theatre. Finally in 1890 Max Burckhardt (1864–1937) assumed the leadership, and although his background was in government rather than theatre, he proved one of the Burg's great directors, opening its repertoire to the major new modern dramatists. His company was headed by Adele Sandrock (1864–1937) and Friedrich Mitterwurzer (1845–97) both of whom, significantly, had been previously considered too emotional or mercurial to undertake major traditional roles; in fact Dingelstedt had been unable to tolerate Mitterwurzer as a member of the Burg ensemble. But Burkhardt realised that they were ideal interpreters of the more complex and divided protagonists of the new drama. Among Mitterwurzer's most acclaimed roles were such self-divided Ibsen creations as Hjalmar Ekdal in *The Wild Duck* and Alfred Allmers in *Little Eyolf.*

Not surprisingly, Burckhardt introduced the plays of Hauptmann to Vienna and restored Ludwig Anzengruber to the Burgtheater. His realistic folk dramas, once scorned as too provincial by Dingelstedt, seemed much more at home among the new realistic dramas. Burkhardt's major discovery was Arthur Schnitzler (1862–1931), whose plays, like Anzengruber's, showed some influence of the Viennese folk tradition, but turned in the more fashionable current direction of ironic social drama. His best known and most typical dramas might all be given the name of his first success, *Liebelei* (*Light of Love*, 1895), since the psychology of love was his favourite theme, whether treated comically, tragically, or most notably, ironically, as in his major works *Anatol* (1893) and *Reigen* (*Round Dance*, 1903). No one ever better captured the brittle yet sentimental gaiety of old Vienna, though Schnitzler's range was far broader than his reputation suggests. *Professor Bernhardi* (1912), for example, is a taut drama dealing with anti-semitism, while *Der grüne Kakadu* (*The Green Cockatoo*, 1899) weaves a complex web of reality and illusion in French Revolutionary Paris.

Despite the success of Burkhardt's regime, the focus of German theatre towards the end of the nineteenth century was shifting from Vienna to Berlin, particularly to the Deutsches Theater, where Otto Brahm had gathered the most distinguished company in Germany with which he not only staged major revivals of the German classics, but the new repertoire of foreign dramatists like Ibsen and the two leading German dramatists Gerhart Hauptmann and Hermann Sudermann (1857–1928). Both these dramatists continued to contribute major works to the naturalist theatre but also to the symbolist or neo-romantic movement that followed it. The most innovative German dramatist of the 1890s, Franz Wedekind (1864–1918), was perhaps too experimental and involved with sexual themes to be acceptable to Brahm at the Deutsches Theater or even at the Berlin Freie Bühne, although one of his plays, *Erdgeist* (*Earth Spirit*), was produced before 1900 by the Freie Bühne of Leipzig in 1898. After 1900 Wedekind's reputation grew rapidly, primarily due to the promotion of his plays by Brahm's successor at the Deutsches, the outstanding figure in the German theatre at the beginning of the twentieth century, Max Reinhardt (1873–1940). Reinhardt joined the famous Deutsches Theater ensemble in 1894, playing mostly the parts of old men. In 1901 he founded a small experimental theatre, Schall und Rauch (Sound and Smoke). This was followed by two other important experimental stages, the Kleines Theater and the Neues Theater, the latter in the Theater am Schiffbauerdamm, which would later become famous as the home of the Berliner Ensemble. In 1905 Reinhardt became director of the Deutsches Theater and in doing so inaugurated a new era in the history of the German stage.

5 The romantic spirit in the German theatre, 1790–1910

SIMON WILLIAMS

Romanticism transformed German culture. For most of the eighteenth century there was a widespread sense in German-speaking Europe that in neither letters nor the arts had the Germans equalled the achievement of nations to their west, especially England and France. But romanticism changed that. It provided Germans with a greater sense of cultural individuality, so that they even began to provide paradigms that other cultures in turn would imitate and emulate. Romanticism was ultimately the most protean of movements, embracing almost all fields of imaginative and intellectual endeavour within Europe, but it had particular importance for the Germans.

Romanticism was foundational for the work of many playwrights and theatre artists of the nineteenth century. The realistic style of production, described in the previous chapter, stems in part from the interest of the romantics in reviving the life of the past, while the plays of social protest, discussed in the next chapter, originate, again in part, from revolt based on the romantic sense of subjective individuality. Also, as we shall see (in chapter 9), German nationalism, the theatre that fostered it, and the political movements that exploited it have been regarded as an outcome of the Romantic age. The Romantic Movement also introduced subjective perspectives that would be of crucial importance to the artistic development of the German theatre because they worked as an invigorating force within it, even though they could not easily be adapted to theatrical representation. But while theatre was renewed by romanticism, romanticism itself was often treated on stage as something to be interrogated. This chapter on the 'romantic spirit' will therefore explore romanticism as a phenomenon that surfaces fitfully throughout the nineteenth and even into the twentieth century and that informs plays and performance, but nevertheless is itself exposed to question.

The discovery of Shakespeare

Broadly speaking the German Romantic Movement arose in reaction to salient aspects of the Enlightenment and to a primarily classical, notionally aristocratic culture that had prevailed in Germany for much of the eighteenth century. The attempt to build a bridge between this culture and popular theatre had begun with Gottsched and culminated in Goethe's direction of the Weimar court theatre, but the point of departure from a predominantly classical understanding of theatre came in the middle of this process with the German discovery of Shakespeare. Lessing had read the relatively few Shakespeare plays that he knew – mainly the tragedies – as documents for the Enlightenment. He posited Shakespeare's plays as the model German playwrights should follow in contrast to the aesthetically correct drama of Racine or Voltaire and praised above all Shakespeare's capacity to express the sublime thoughts of tragedy in the language of the common people.[1] As a dramatist, Lessing did not follow Shakespeare, but the writers of *Sturm und Drang* did. They saw the English playwright as a formidable figure who opened up new visions of what theatre could achieve. But it would be several generations before these were realised on stage. The new paradigm of theatre suggested by Shakespeare was first explored in essays written during the 1760s and 70s. Heinrich von Gerstenberg's *Briefe über Merkwürdigkeiten der Literatur* (*Letters on Notabilities in Literature*, 1766–70) claimed that Shakespeare's plays were unlike those of the French neoclassicists in that they were not centred on actions in which each event led logically to the next; instead their appeal depended mainly on depth of characterisation, thematic contrasts, and a multiplicity of plots that brought together disparate social classes.[2] This was in contrast to the neoclassical drama that had a rigorously consequential action focusing solely on the ruling class and arguing for its inherent nobility. Goethe, in his *Sturm und Drang* days, was deeply engaged with Shakespeare, his most appealing and contentious statement about him being the first he ever delivered, a speech given at a family festivity, '*Zum Schäkespears Tag*' (*On Shakespeare's Day*, 1771), in which he described the effect of his first reading of Shakespeare as if he had been a blind man suddenly given the miraculous gift of sight. Through Shakespeare, Goethe felt his 'existence extended to infinity'. Shakespeare was the poet of nature, showing how humans are natural beings. Also, by demonstrating how good and evil are mutually exclusive and therefore dependent upon each other, he challenged the prevalently moralistic function of contemporary German theatre.[3] The most comprehensive *Sturm und Drang* statement on Shakespeare can be found in Johann Gottfried Herder's '*Shakespeare*' essay (1773), which not only contains an exhilarating description of Shakespeare as a mighty genius, but develops arguments, initiated by Gerstenberg, that each era and each society creates its own drama. Critics had assailed Shakespeare for breaching neoclassical decorum by ignoring the unities, combining tragedy and comedy, and mixing social classes on stage. These, Herder argued, were not irregularities but a natural development of the tradition of 'history and marionette plays' out of which he wrote.[4] Through the perspective offered by Herder, the neoclassical model appeared an arbitrary imposition on German theatre by the aristocracy and because Shakespeare challenged it, his plays both implied an artistic freedom and suggested radical values at a time when the power of the aristocracy was being called into question. But while Shakespeare's plays had resonant, even revolutionary implications for the Germans, it was their very political potency that kept them from the stage.

As most German theatres in the final decades of the eighteenth century were still under the patronage of the aristocracy and greatly influenced by neoclassical dramaturgy, this meant that when Shakespeare was staged, it was in fundamentally altered versions. *Hamlet*, for example, had, by 1781, found its way into the repertoire of most standing theatres, but the version that was played was a far cry from the original. Based upon a fairly accurate prose translation by Christoph Martin Wieland (1733–1813) that had been widely read, this was a *Hamlet* reduced to sentimental domestic drama with a small cast, fashioned in accord with the unities, with all political references excised, complexity of character reduced to a few clearly defined and unexceptional traits, and written in a style that avoided Shakespeare's unsettling tragicomic idiom.[5] The same can be said about other plays that found their way onto the boards in the late eighteenth century, mainly *Othello, King Lear, The Merchant of Venice*, and *Macbeth*. Most of the plays written by *Sturm und Drang* exhibited the influence of Shakespeare, but only two were performed in their time, Goethe's *Götz von Berlichingen* in Berlin in 1774 and Schiller's *Die Räuber* in Mannheim in 1782, and they had to be rigorously cut and adapted to succeed with audiences.

Romantic drama

It was not only in its veneration for Shakespeare that *Sturm und Drang* anticipated key themes of German romanticism. Romantic features of the work of these radically unconventional young men included a reverence for Rousseau's naturalism, elevation of the demands of emotion over the dictates of reason, a resistance to all attempts at social coercion of the individual, and a deep belief in subjective experience. But as the troupes of strolling players began to find permanent homes in the new standing theatres, the classical ethos of theatre as an agency of social cohesion came to the fore (see chapter 3), so these characteristics of *Sturm und Drang* did not exercise a wide appeal. Indeed, the respect for Weimar Classicism and the spread of realism in the course of the nineteenth century virtually prevented any performance of their plays until the beginning of the twentieth century. Searching social or political criticism or the expression of an outlook that rejected the very possibility of the individual coexisting with society was suspect in a theatre whose purpose was to further the ends of that society. In Germany after the Restoration in 1815, when rigorous censorship was imposed upon the theatre, the possibility of romantic subjectivity finding a stage was rendered even more improbable.

Clearly, therefore, there was an incompatibility between the practical theatre and the programme of the early romantic poets, centred in Jena and Berlin, who flourished over the turn of the eighteenth into the nineteenth century. Many had ambitions to make their mark upon the theatre, but none, despite their quite unusual prolificacy as writers of drama, managed to do so, and virtually none of their plays have been performed, in their own time or since. The early romantics were also given to dissolving rather than perpetuating the conventions of theatre. In hindsight, it can be argued that in doing so they were attempting, with virtually no practical experience of the theatre, to envisage what later came to be called the *Gesamtkunstwerk* or the total work of art, a stage production in which all senses are appealed to at once through the blending of words, music, and spectacle. Not only was the romantics' transgression of genre incompatible with the popular theatre; they also made no attempt to represent the world in the way that the conventional theatre did. For the romantics, self-expression and the capacity of the individual creative mind to interpret the world were among their most deeply held values and these could best be displayed through rich metaphors of lyrical poetry and the exercise of romantic irony, which involved a highly self-conscious display of the techniques and genres available to the poet or playwright and was intended to reveal the writer's imaginative fecundity and skill. This meant that the romantics paid attention first and foremost to elements of poetry, to complex word-play that could often be arcane, to the mixture of generic types, and to conscious breaches of theatrical illusion. Dramatic features of importance to the practical theatre, such as clarity of structure, consistent characterisation, and an economical and well-paced action were of secondary concern.

The fundamental incompatibility between German theatre and the early romantics meant that even the most theatre-struck of romantic writers could make little headway. Foremost among these was Ludwig Tieck (1773–1853), who throughout his career devoted considerable energies to the theatre, not only as a playwright but as a dramaturge, editor of Shakespeare translations and old plays, and stage director. His comedy *Der gestiefelte Kater* (*Puss-in-Boots*, 1797) is perhaps the most enduring of romantic plays not only because it deftly satirises the unromantic but extremely popular drama of Iffland and Kotzebue, but more memorably because it so ridicules audience expectations that by the end of the play our attentions are centred upon the playwright, whose ideal theatre we are encouraged to create in our imagination. *Die verkehrte Welt* (*The World Upside Down*, 1798) and *Prinz Zerbino* (1799), a 'six act concatenation of chaotic satire',[6] develop Tieck's paratheatricality to ever more dizzying extremes. He attempted to cram every known genre of drama into *Leben und Tod der heiligen Genoveva* (*The Life and Death of St Genevieve*, 1799) and, even more so, the gigantic *Kaiser Octavianus* (1804), which comprises both a romantic intrigue comedy and an epic on the conflict between Christianity and Islam. These plays are written in elaborate verse full of esoteric imagery. Only *Kater*, among all of Tieck's plays, has ever been performed, and even then infrequently.

Equally neglected by the theatre have been the plays of Clemens Brentano (1778–1842), though in the case of *Ponce de Leon* (1804) this may have been unjust, as this extraordinarily complex comedy of intrigue – at the end five couples are united – has achieved some critical acclaim and may have life on the stage. Brentano's dramatic *chef d'oeuvre* however, *Die Gründung Prags* (*The Foundation of Prague*, 1814), runs to almost 300 pages and, with a cast of 38 characters, is far too unwieldy for coherent presentation in the theatre. The most impressive mythological drama of the romantic period is perhaps the trilogy *Der Held des Nordens* (*The Hero of the North*, 1810) by Friedrich de la Motte Fouqué (1777–1843), the first play of which, *Sigurd der Schlangentöter* (*Sigurd the Dragonslayer*) covers much the same ground that Wagner would do in the latter two music dramas of his *Ring* cycle (1876). But Fouqué's trilogy remained unperformed, along with the seventy or so other dramas he either completed or sketched out, most of which have never been published. A. W. Schlegel argued that historical drama was the one genre in which the romantics might make their mark upon the theatre,[7] a form at which both Fouqué and Joseph von Eichendorff (1788–1857), with *Ezelin von Romano* (1828), tried their hands, but the only playwright who achieved a notable success in this regard was not associated with the romantics. He was Zacharias Werner (1768–1823), whose massive epic, *Martin Luther oder die Weihe der Kraft* (*Martin Luther or the Consecration of Power*) was a great success when it was produced by Iffland in Berlin in 1806. Werner, however, is perhaps better known for his grim one-act *Schicksalstragödie* (*Fate Tragedy*), *Der vierundzwanzigste Februar* (*The Twenty-Fourth of February*, 1810), which told a story, already familiar from George Lillo's *Fatal Curiosity* (1736) – and that would later be adapted by Albert Camus in *Le Malentendu* (*Cross Purpose*, 1944) – of a family curse that is fulfilled when a son returns to stay with his family in disguise, and they murder him for his money. This gruesome work carried unusual power on the stage and was widely performed and imitated.

The failure of the early romantics to find a theatre can, not unfairly, be attributed to their incapacity or refusal to impose limits on themselves by following conventional genres. But there was a further incompatibility between romanticism and the theatre that, while serving as an obstacle in the early years of the century, would, by the turn of the century, be a source of great enrichment to the theatre. Early in the nineteenth century, theatrical performance was universally based upon the assumption that action represented on stage was an imitation of reality, a representation, however stylised, of physical and social life, represented in a consequential chain of events from which a moral or practical lesson could generally be derived. In this performance, there should be nothing to remind spectators of their status as spectators. It was to this literalistic end, as well as in obeisance to French dramatic practice, that the unities continued to be adhered to in German theatre. The romantics, however, were not mainly interested in humans as social beings; indeed, one of the distinctive attributes of romanticism was its valorisation of the subjective experience of the feeling individual as a more authentic means of gaining access to basic truths than through an understanding achieved by social consensus. This subjective perspective, which is at the heart of much romantic art, could more effectively be expressed through lyric poetry, the *Lied*, orchestral tone poems, or atmospheric landscape painting than through theatre as it was currently practised.

Faust as romantic drama

The dilemma of performing romantic drama can be nowhere better illustrated than by the work that still stands in the minds of most Germans as the consummate drama in the language, Goethe's *Faust Part 1* (1808). Goethe would have challenged any attempt to label his tragedy 'romantic', as late in life he notably dismissed romanticism as a 'sickness'.[8] However, *Faust Part 1*, on which he worked periodically between 1771 and 1808, provides a virtual summary of the history of German theatre. The opening Prologue in the Theatre recalls the strolling players of the seventeenth century and the Prologue in Heaven the medieval religious drama before them; the rhymed *Knittelverse* in which much of the play is written is reminiscent of popular sixteenth-century poetry, as are the ballads sung by Gretchen; Shakespeare is recalled in the episodic nature of the action by which only high points of the story are represented; the small-town atmosphere of the Gretchen episodes has a pathos that recalls Iffland's *Rührstücke*; the polished rhyming verse of the study-scenes that lead to Faust signing his pact with Mephistopheles reflects Weimar Classicism; while the Witches' kitchen and wild scenes on the Brocken express an individual fantasy that is aligned to Gothic poetry. The extraordinary length of time taken in its composition and its stylistic variety mean that *Faust Part 1* has little apparent unity. If one is to be found it might be through imagining the drama as taking place within the mind of a single individual. Faust has many of the characteristics of the romantic idealist; he searches for new realms of experience, and as such his relation to the stage world is dynamic and changing. He may be viewed ironically as his constant wish for newness and change may appear little more than a desire to avoid the moral consequences of his action. His seduction of Gretchen is punctuated by episodes of escape into nature and the turmoil of Walpurgis Night; these may be read either as excursions into the supernatural or as dramatic metaphors for inner disturbance. The Walpurgis Night can also be read as a grotesque sexualized parody of the French revolution which put an end to the small-town idyll of Gretchen's world. *Faust Part 1* can also be interpreted as the conflict between the philosophies of life represented by Faust and Mephistopheles, or even as a struggle within a single consciousness.[9]

However it is interpreted, *Faust Part 1*, as it was published in 1808, was not suitable for performance, something Goethe himself recognised. The stylistic multiplicity of the text and the metaphorical strategy of representing the inner life of a character through stage action and setting were outside the practice and probably beyond the comprehension of most who worked in the theatre at that time. Even A. W. Schlegel, whose *Vorlesungen über dramatische Kunst und Literatur* (*Lectures on Dramatic Art and*

Literature, 1809–11) introduced the entire idea of romantic drama to a popular audience found it difficult to conceive of *Faust* in performance as it 'purposely runs out in all directions beyond the dimensions of the theatre'. He found scenes devoted to 'long soliloquies, or conversations, delineating Faust's internal conditions and dispositions' or 'rhapsodical fragments without beginning or end' to be inappropriate in a 'truly dramatic poem'. In such a poem 'the separate parts must be fashioned after the figure of the whole, so that … each scene may have its exposition, its intrigue, and winding up'.[10] *Faust*, for all its length, remained essentially a fragment and therefore unsuited for theatrical presentation. Eventually it was first performed not in Germany but in Paris and then London in 1828, where the text was adapted to allow maximum opportunity for elaborate spectacle. When it was staged in Germany in Braunschweig in 1829, all references to religion and the supernatural were excised and the play became what it remained for much of the nineteenth century, a realistic small-town melodrama about the seduction of an innocent girl by an older and more experienced man.[11] When this version was performed at the Weimar Court Theatre in honour of Goethe's eightieth birthday, the poet advised actors in preparation for the performance but did not see it himself. It was not until 1876 that a fairly complete version of *Part I*, along with the far more unwieldy *Part II*, was staged over two evenings by Otto Devrient in Weimar, but only in the twentieth century were stage techniques developed that allowed for satisfactory productions of the complete text. Max Reinhardt used a revolving stage to direct *Part I* in Berlin in 1909, followed by *Part II* in 1911, but it was only with the development of a 'simultaneous' stage in the vast space of the *Felsenreitschule* in Salzburg in 1933 that he managed to stage a completely integrated version of *Part I*.

The romantic as a subject for drama

But however difficult it was to accommodate romanticism in the German theatre, it was not ignored. Theatre was not suited to articulate the purely lyrical because the action of drama had been bred primarily on conflict. Hence, romanticism in its earliest years made its strongest mark upon the theatre not as a guiding or formative influence, nor as an artistic programme that provided a globalising perspective for the theatre artist, but as a subject for dramatic representation. Schiller began his tragedy *Don Carlos* (1787) as a plea for the rights of a young man suffering the oppression of his father, but in mid composition he turned his attention from the emotional rebellion of the eponymous hero to the sufferings of his father, Philip II, and the questionable idealism of the Marquis of Posa. In so doing, he created a tragedy that slipped its moorings in *Sturm und Drang* to elude the definitions of any artistic credo. The figure of the romantic hero was to recur in Schiller throughout his career. In his masterpiece of Weimar Classicism, the *Wallenstein* trilogy, the issue of romantic love, as embodied in Max Piccolomini and Thekla, is secondary to the tragedy of Wallenstein himself. After this, Schiller's interest was redirected toward the charismatic hold that the romantic hero can exercise over others. The confusing loyalties aroused by a romantic hero are apparent in the responses of characters to both Mary Stuart, in the otherwise classical *Maria Stuart*, and Joan of Arc in *Die Jungfrau von Orleans*. The ironic viewpoint that dramatic action compels us to take means that we question these characters as much as we admire them. We may wish to push them away even as we feel drawn to the power they exercise over others. The contradictions of the romantic hero are most in evidence in *Wilhelm Tell*. Schiller's final completed play has many romantic features such as the natural beauty of its setting among the Swiss Alps, the vivid representation of the Rousseauan closeness of the Swiss to nature, the pageant-like tableaux that epitomise the growing sense of national identity among the Swiss, and the myriad allusions to Shakespeare, the storm scenes in particular being riddled with allusions to *Lear*. There is no difficulty in deciding to whom one's sympathies are directed in the melodramatic confrontation between the freedom-loving Swiss and the cruel Austrians, who stand for the baleful forces of uniformity and modernity. But the melodrama is finally thrown into shadow by the strange figure of Tell, a romantic hero whose thoughts are all for family and solitude, whose calling in life is not, as it is in Rossini's better-known grand opera based on the play, to lead a triumphant national rebellion. Schiller's Tell finds that life will only have joy for him if he feels it constantly anew.

> *Rastlos muß ich ein flüchtig Ziel verfolgen,*
> *Dann erst genieß ich meines Lebens recht,*
> *Wenn ich mir's jeden Tag aufs neu erbeute.*
> (Restlessly I must follow a fleeing target/ As I only really enjoy life!/When I can capture it every day anew)[12]

He is not temperamentally given to action that is intended to have an outcome in the social or political realm. Against his will but according to what he perceives as necessity, he is driven to assassinate the Austrian governor Gessler. While the play ends with a chorus celebrating Swiss independence, it is clear that Tell's romantic freedom and the innocence that accompanied it have been irrevocably compromised by his action in the cause of family and nation. The romantic hero is essentially a lone figure; indeed his heroic status and integrity depend upon him sustaining that loneliness. He is not, therefore, at all suited to occupy the central role in any drama that is centred upon consequential action, because his very being denies consequentiality.

It is primarily as a subject for ironic scrutiny that the romantic spirit and the romantic hero are featured in the drama of the early nineteenth century. A central preoccupation of the romantics was that of the creative artist, who seemed capable of creating an entire world within his work, an imaginative whole that both had the potential to transform the social world and to allow the creator of it to withdraw from society, a paradox that has since become one of the major concerns of European drama. It was Goethe who initiated the theme with *Torquato Tasso* (1790), a play that, characteristically, he did not consider suitable for performance, though he was eventually persuaded to stage it at Weimar in 1807.[13] In this restrained neoclassical drama set in the Renaissance court of the Duke of Ferrara, the poet Tasso is a romantic artist who both creates from and relates to the world through instinct, feeling, and romantic love, all of which he expresses with effusive ardour. His subjective enthusiasm does not exist easily within the strict decorum of the court and Tasso is violently torn from the illusion that he is universally admired by the pronounced coldness of Antonio, a politician and man of affairs who has little time for art. Tasso's apparent submission to Antonio at the end of the play suggests that Goethe is casting doubt on the viability of the romantic artist, but this conclusion is questionable as the playwright shows an acute understanding of the imperatives that drive the creative artist, while the social world that seeks to contain him is not entirely disinterested either in the personality of the artist or in the use to which his work can be put.

Early romanticism is optimistic. The excursions of poets into the depths of human subjectivity and their explorations of the power of the individual imagination broadened and enriched understanding of the potential of the mind to create a better world. But as this optimism flagged, romanticism became tinged, ultimately possessed, by a darker vision, most completely characterised by the pessimistic vision of George Lord Byron, whose poetry most completely articulated Europe's growing disillusion at Napoleon's relentless conquest of Europe, at the failure of the promises of the revolutionary era, and the suppression of freedom of expression in the decades following his fall. Again, this is not a reaction that was comprehensively chronicled by the theatre, due to the prevalence of Weimar ideals and the imposition in the early years of the Restoration of rigorous censorship in German-speaking states. The decisively anti-romantic Young Germany movement of the 1830s protested against the complacency and narrowness of the time. Prior to this, however, the Prussian dramatist Heinrich von Kleist (1777–1811) and the Austrian tragedian Franz Grillparzer (1791–1872) wrote dramas centred on social dysfunction. Although neither can be classified as romantics – in fact both were great admirers of Weimar Classicism – their work engages romantic themes and techniques, above all by exploring the psychic strata opened up by romanticism. However, this exposure reveals the self-destructiveness of the psyche and a thorough dislocation between individual experience and the social world. In fact, both Kleist and Grillparzer, in their reflection of late romantic pessimism, serve as a link between the romantic period and the psychological drama that was to prevail in European playwriting later in the nineteenth century. Neither could escape the influence of Weimar, and Kleist in particular hoped for some recognition from Goethe, though his great full-length one-act comedy, *Der zerbrochene Krug* (*The Broken Jug*) was a decisive failure when it received its first performance at the Weimar Court Theatre in 1807.

The only other of Kleist's dramas to be performed in his short lifetime was *Das Käthchen von Heilbronn* (*Cathy of Heilbronn*) first staged at the Theater an der Wien in Vienna in 1810 and some months later in Bamberg. While Schiller explored the contradictions within the romantic hero, Kleist exposed the self-destructive conflicts. Hence, his Bacchic tragedy *Penthesilea* (1807, publ. 1808), another one-act play of over 3,000 lines that was first performed in an adapted version in 1876, centres upon the kinship between sexual desire and brutality in an action of extraordinary violence and fluidity that places great demands even upon the most technically sophisticated and versatile of stages. Even though his tragedy *Die Hermannsschlacht* (*The Battle of Arminius*, 1808–9, publ. 1821) was written to strengthen the resolve of the Germans to resist the Napoleonic occupation, it too was not performed until decades after it was written, in the 1860s. Even if it had been given in Kleist's lifetime, it would not have created the patriotic response Kleist intended, as the play exposes the fallacies of nationalism rather than its strengths. Kleist's last and most celebrated play, which is now at the centre of the German classic repertoire, *Prinz Friedrich von Homburg* (1810, publ. 1821) has also been read as a patriotic work, but it too questions the underpinnings of patriotism as the prince whose impetuous bravery wins the battle of Fehrbellin acts from romantic enthusiasm rather than discipline and love of country. The Elector in whose cause the battle was won condemns him to death for disobeying orders and it is only when the prince acknowledges the total nullity of his being that he is readmitted to life and the military. While Weimar Classicism authenticated those ideals that bind society, Kleist revealed their fallacies. His suicide in Berlin in 1811 robbed Germany of its most penetrating playwright.

Franz Grillparzer worked for most of his life as a civil servant in Vienna and to all appearances accommodated himself better to social life than Kleist, but many of his plays centre not on social or political issues but on characters who are possessed by a transformative romantic love they can do little to resist. When the object of their desire is denied them, darker forces take hold of them, and these drive the action to tragic denouements of unusual intensity. Grillparzer made his name with the *Schicksalstragödie*, *Die Ahnfrau* (*The Ancestress*), first performed in Vienna in 1817, but his reputation as a writer of high tragedy, who combined the elevation of Weimar Classicism with the sombre themes of late romanticism was based initially on a series of plays with classical Greek settings. *Sappho*, first staged with immense success at the Burgtheater in 1818, shares its theme with Goethe's *Torquato Tasso*, as both plays deal with poets in love and explore the interdependence of romantic love with artistic creativity. However, while *Tasso's* ending implies some accommodation between the poet and society, *Sappho* ends with the Greek poetess grandly throwing herself to her death so that the object of her desire, the warrior Phaon, is free to be united to her slave girl Melitta. If *Sappho* ends with an act of heroic altruism, Grillparzer's trilogy, *Das goldene Vließ* (*The Golden Fleece*), premièred at the Burgtheater in 1821, reflects more the harsh realities of failed sexual and familial relationships. The final play, *Medea*, covers the same ground that Euripides does, but there are no religious implications to the revenge Medea wreaks on Jason; rather she is driven by her fury at Jason's betrayal and her hatred of Greece, epitomised by the shallow Creusa and her heartless father Creon. But focus is as much upon Jason as it is on Medea; in fact, in this dramatisation of a dying marriage in which the middle-aged husband is unwilling to face up to the collapse of his youthful dreams, Grillparzer covers the same psychological terrain that Ibsen would visit later in the century. But while *Medea* seems ultimately to deny the viability of romantic love, Grillparzer's most popular play, the tragedy *Des Meeres und der Liebe Wellen* (*Waves of the Sea and Love*), first staged unsuccessfully at the Burgtheater in 1831, but revived to great acclaim in a production by Heinrich Laube in 1851, might appear to be the supreme hymn to the power of romantic love. This dramatisation of the story of Hero and Leander has been compared to *Romeo and Juliet*, but the parallel should not be taken too far. Hero, like Juliet, goes through considerable growth over the two days of the action; Leander, unlike Romeo, does not. The lovers are separated by the dictates of society, but while in Shakespeare these are arbitrary and exist without reference to the lovers, in Grillparzer Leander dies as a direct result of the intervention of the Priest, who extinguishes the light that guides him across the Hellespont. At the end, Hero does not commit suicide, but merely dies, it appears, at will, as a gesture, a *Liebestod*, that asserts that once one has experienced and then been denied the richness of the romantic experience, death rather than life is infinitely preferable. Grillparzer was also a noted writer of history plays such as *König Ottokars Glück und Ende* (*King Ottokar's Happiness and Death*, 1825), of political tragedy – *Ein treuer Diener seines Herrn* (*A True Servant of His Master*, 1828), and of the Viennese *Volksstück* – *Der Traum ein Leben* (*Life is a Dream*, 1834) and *Weh dem, der lügt* (*Woe to Him who Lies!* 1838). The failure of this last play at the Burgtheater persuaded him to abandon writing for the stage, and his last dramas remained unperformed until the realistic mode of presentation devised by Heinrich Laube at the Burgtheater suited them perfectly.

Certain traits of romanticism also found a genial host in the Viennese *Volksstück*, the popular comic tradition, originating in the English comedians and *commedia dell'arte*, that from the early eighteenth century on had dramatised the adventures of Viennese citizens in a magical world. The landscape of the *Volksstück* was drawn from the idyllic Alpine countryside and its actions provided characters with romantic adventures, the purpose of which was to reconcile them to their mundane lot in life and, not infrequently, to read them improving lessons. In the attractive plays of Ferdinand Raimund (1790–1836), especially *Das Mädchen aus der Feenwelt oder der Bauer als Millionär* (*The Girl from the Fairy World or the Millionaire Peasant*, 1826), *Der Alpenkönig und der Menschenfeind* (*The King of the Alps and the Misanthrope*, 1828), and *Der Verschwender* (*The Spendthrift* – 1834), the romantic scenery and the supernatural apparatus effectively relates to and even serves as a means of interpreting the actions of the characters, so that the metaphorical link between character and environment which lies at the heart of romantic theatre is effortlessly achieved.

Romantic acting

The reason why romanticism has been such a fluctuating presence in the German theatre is nowhere better demonstrated than in the phenomenon of romantic acting. In Germany, acting was practised as a discipline within a 'school', associated with a distinct style of presentation and manner of speech. Hence in the eighteenth century, the formal declamatory style of acting associated with reforms of Gottsched and Neuber was known as the Leipzig school, while the nimble virtuosic acting of Iffland was associated with Mannheim. Weimar Classicism developed a mode of acting akin to rhetoric that was influential throughout the nineteenth century. The advantage of such 'schools' was that they provided actors, who had had no formal training, none being available, with concrete techniques that, once they had mastered them, would enable them to represent their characters in a way that was accessible to audiences and stylistically consistent with other members of the company. But the 'school' approach to acting was inimical to the romantics for whom originality and the refusal to copy from models was an essential precondition for any creative art of value. 'Schools' of acting also encouraged a static theatrical dynamic as the actor's performance was fixed, controlled, and more devoted to projecting the 'worth' of the individual performing than to representing dramatic character.

One cannot speak of a 'romantic school' of acting as the romantic impulse by its very nature denies the concept of 'school'. But we can identify actors who were recognised by their contemporaries as 'romantic', even though their ties to each other are tenuous and haphazard. Elements of romanticism might be identified in the acting of Friedrich Ludwig Schröder, whose interpretation of leading roles in some *Sturm und Drang* and Shakespeare plays in Hamburg and other cities from 1776 until his retirement in 1798 established, ironically, a 'Hamburg School' of acting. But Schröder was noted mainly for the harsh realism of his powerful characterisations that did not attempt to resolve contradictions within the character. Tieck was a great admirer of Schröder, but felt more drawn to Ferdinand Fleck (1757–1801), who, after a few months acting in Hamburg with Schröder, spent the majority of his brief career at the Royal Theatre in Berlin, latterly under the direction of Iffland. Iffland was a visionary theatre director as he had the capacity to appreciate artists with a genius different from his own and, before he died in 1814, he had contracted to the Royal

9 Ludwig Devrient in *Die Galeerensclaven*, a melodrama by Theodor Hell with music by Johann Friedrich Schubert. Berlin, Königliches Schauspielhaus 1823. Act I, 'Hunger is tearing my intestines.'

Theatre the German actor whose career is more enshrouded in romantic myth than any other, Ludwig Devrient (1784–1832) (see fig. 9). Before going to Berlin, Devrient had achieved national fame for his portrayal of romantic heroes and for his exceptional comic performances at Breslau and on tour throughout Germany. Once in Berlin his opportunities for acting in tragedy were limited, because the theatre hired Goethe's favourite actor Pius Alexander Wolff soon after Devrient, and so the Weimar style prevailed. Nevertheless, despite his chronic alcoholism, Devrient continued to tour frequently, until his premature death. Vienna, like Berlin, was also a centre for romantic acting no doubt in part because the early plays of Grillparzer were in the repertoire and both Sophie Schröder and Heinrich Anschütz gave some moving performances before the realistic ensemble developed by Heinrich Laube began to prevail.

These romantic actors gave acting a new stature in the German theatre. While Lessing had written that the actor 'must think with the poet at all times, even think for him in places' (*Werke*, 2, 279), he never thought of the actor as working outside the limits of character indicated by the dramatist, nor did the Weimar actor. But Tieck, after he had seen Schröder, had different ideas. If actors, Tieck argued, were to be limited to 'the meagre and silly characters' offered them by the feeble imagination of the average writer of *Trivialdramatik*, they would never be able to display their powers fully. Actors were therefore justified in conceiving of these characters 'more freely and bravely' than the playwright.[14] This must have been eminently apparent in Schröder's interpretation of Shakespeare's leading roles, because he performed them in those severely adapted versions in which the tragedy was reduced to domestic melodrama and Shakespeare's complex characters were little more than ciphers. For example, the Hamlet in the text that he performed was a mild, comparatively uncomplicated character, but Schröder, who knew the English original, emphasised the anger of the man, highlighting the contradictions that destroy him in Shakespeare's tragedy, though not in the German adaptation, where he survives to rule Denmark. Schröder's Lear was also known for its titanic rage and was far from the rather doddery old man normally represented on stage. Above all, Schröder brought character to the fore often to the exclusion of all other concerns.

Emphasis on character alone does not identify acting as 'romantic'; rather the romantics were deeply involved in subjectivity. What was new about romantic acting was the representation of the psyche of the individual as the centre of dramatic conflict. Ludwig Devrient, whose interpretation of serious roles reached emotional extremes, had the reputation of being a 'demonic' actor, not because he represented villainous figures driven by demonic forces, but because his characters were possessed by powers that deprived them of the capacity to exercise their will. Hence his febrile Franz Moor from *Die Räuber* came to be torn between abject fear at what he had done and the sheer impulse to be cruel, between an awakening but sick conscience and a powerful urge ruthlessly to pursue his interests. His Shylock was both an immensely noble figure and an abject slave of his greed. Devrient did not represent dramatic character as a conglomerate of rational motives, so audiences were uncertain as to how to respond to his characters, which no longer articulated a moral, a point of view, or a general attitude. Character no longer stood for a clearly defined entity within the dramatic action, but it could confuse audiences by requiring them to exercise their imagination in order to understand it. In so doing, audiences often felt themselves being possessed and changed by the character's emotions, as if they had became part of his subjectivity.

One of the reasons successful romantic acting was so rare was that there was no known technique by which its effects could be achieved. E. T. A. Hoffmann, Ludwig Devrient's soulmate and drinking companion in later years, described how Devrient fastened his eyes on a member of the audience and then imagined a figure rising up between them, which then advanced to possess his soul;[15] Hoffmann also comments that Devrient often based his characters on dreams. This is a process that is, at best, haphazard and, by creating the myth that all depends upon the actor's inspiration, gave rise, no doubt, to many poor or uninteresting performances. Ferdinand Fleck was perhaps the most 'intuitive' of all romantic actors and when he was fully at one with the role he was playing, he filled it with a sense of immense life – his Wallenstein was considered to be fully equal to the world-historical figure of Schiller's tragedy. He often gave the impression of being possessed by forces external to him; his acting was described as 'demonic' and he performed 'as if a higher genius spoke out of him and gave itself being'.[16] But Fleck depended too frequently on his momentary mood to determine the intensity and scope of his interpretation and if he was in low spirits his performance could be entirely off. Meanwhile Devrient's addiction to the bottle not only led to passages of incoherence, but to him passing out, which put an end to the performance.[17] Romantic acting requires as intense a level of concentration from the actor as the more overtly technical modes of acting, but it might not seem to be that way. Consequently, as the great realistic actor Karl Seydelmann pointed out, there were several actors who, thinking that instant inspiration was all that matters, imitated Fleck and Devrient, but none did so successfully as none possessed the imaginative power of these artists.[18] Perhaps only Sophie Schröder had the capacity to incorporate within the same role the poise of Weimar Classicism with the raw emotional power required by drama that engages with romanticism. The apex of her career coincided with, perhaps might have been occasioned by, the appearance of the early plays of Grillparzer. Schröder was the first Sappho and, notably, Medea, a role to which she brought a tragic intensity that Weimar Classicism never tried to achieve. But by the time Des Meeres und der Liebe Wellen was first performed in 1831, Schröder had already left the company and the more uniform and less individualised acting required by the realistic ensemble was taking over.

Romantic stages

While the realistic style of staging that prevailed for most of the nine-teenth century was in part an outgrowth of the romantics' interest in detailed reconstruction of historical circumstances, it was anti-romantic in spirit. Theatre was ill-suited to represent the constant themes of romanticism, especially the subjective perspective of the individual creative mind. Theatre in the nineteenth century was fundamentally committed to realism and realism is based on the premise that the reality delineated on stage is social, not personal. The elaborate apparatus of realistic theatre can obstruct rather than express subjectivity. How, therefore, could theatrical practice be used to articulate the 'romantic' spirit of the drama?

It is in finding an answer to this question that Ludwig Tieck made his most lasting contribution to the development of theatrical practice. Although his own plays did not find their way to the stage, Tieck was closely involved with the theatre his entire life. As a translator he supervised the completion of the great verse translations of Shakespeare by A. W. Schlegel, Dorothea Tieck, and Wolf Graf von Baudissin; as an editor he published many historically significant plays, being responsible, among other projects, for the first complete publication of Kleist's drama; and as a dramaturge, first in Dresden (1825–42), then in Berlin (1841–53), he explored ways to stage Shakespeare based on his knowledge of the theatre for which Shakespeare wrote. Tieck's interest in Shakespeare was wider than that of most of his contemporaries. While the tragedies and, to some degree, the histories occupied most of the attention of directors in the middle decades of the nineteenth century, Tieck had always been more interested in the comedies. In his early critical works, he had argued that a Shakespeare play was an elaborately composed strategy on an audience, its intent being to create the illusion of an imaginary world, somewhat akin to a dream and, through carefully balancing all dramatic elements so that no single aspect of the play disturbs the others, it holds the audience within this dream-world.[19] However, in order to sustain the illusion successfully, the visual element should not be too insistent. Tieck conducted considerable research into the Elizabethan theatre and came to the conclusion that if Shakespeare's plays were to do their work upon the audience and appeal fully to their imagination, some degree of replication of Elizabethan stage conditions was necessary. In fact, Tieck's advocacy of the bare Elizabethan stage as an appropriate site for theatrical performance, largely contradicts the vision that is implied in many of his dramas, that theatre is a site where all the senses should be appealed to.

Tieck was not the first to experiment with a spare stage derived from Elizabethan models; this distinction fell to the novelist and playwright, Karl Leberecht Immermann (1796–1840), who briefly directed the Düsseldorf City Theatre (1835–7). After his tenure at the theatre, in 1840 he was commissioned to stage a production of *Twelfth Night* for Fasching (carnival). To do this he constructed a stage that resembled as much an ancient Roman as an Elizabethan theatre; it was wide, backed by two arches, two doors, and a small inner stage, where indoor scenes could be staged. This allowed Immermann to represent two scenes simultaneously, while the bare stage encouraged the blocking of characters in ways that highlighted and made clear their relations, thereby fulfilling one of the fundamental functions of the modern stage director, which had not until then been exploited. Immermann died only a few months after the *Twelfth Night* production; three years later, in 1843, Tieck, now a very old man, was commissioned by the Prussian monarch to direct a production of *A Midsummer Night's Dream* for his court theatre in Potsdam. This production did not involve a literal reconstruction of the Elizabethan stage either, but Tieck placed three tiers of galleries on stage and, through playing many scenes in these galleries and then by judiciously utilising scene drops in front of them, he created a production that was remarkable for its fluency (see fig. 10). In contrast to the realistic productions of Shakespeare that were universal at this time, the rhythms of the play were sustained and their momentum was never halted by cumbersome scene changes. For the first time, the dream-like illusion that Shakespeare's plays can conjure up in the audience became a possibility.

Despite the immense popularity of Tieck's production – it was staged regularly until 1885 – realistic rather than open staging remained the norm in the German theatre. Further experiments in the 'Shakespeare Stage' were made at the Munich Court Theatre towards the end of the century. In 1889, the director Jocsza Savits (1847–1915) and the designer Karl Lautenschläger (1843–1906) devised a configuration that was reminiscent of Immermann's *Twelfth Night*. It was used not only for the performance of Shakespeare but for other classics and incorporated a large forestage, the bareness of which intimidated many actors, and an inner stage in which scenery could be changed while action was occurring on the open forestage. Although this model was exploited with some resourcefulness, its mix of open and realistic staging was not popular and had to be abandoned after a few years. It did, however, lay the groundwork for the more radical work of the twentieth-century director.

10 *A Midsummer Night's Dream*, Potsdam 1843, directed by Ludwig Tieck. View of the stage.

Opera

In many ways, opera was the genre most suited to realising romantic experience in the theatre. Music provides more direct access to the subjective realm than words alone do, and it can sustain interest during static moments in the action, which is necessary if the action is to explore romantic subjectivity.

Opera had entered professional German theatre, like the spoken drama, as a foreign import, primarily of Italian origin, and until well into the eighteenth century it remained mainly the preserve of the courts. Only in Hamburg, between 1678 and 1738, did German-language opera flourish. But it was not until the latter part of the eighteenth century that a characteristic German form of opera emerged, the *Singspiel*, a term which had come to designate mainly comic opera with spoken dialogue; *Singspiele* generally provided a sentimentally Rousseauistic view of life in which the classes mingled without complications. The operas of Johann Adam Hiller (1728–1804), many set to libretti by Christian Felix Weisse, especially their major work, *Die Jagd* (*The Hunt*, 1770), did much to popularise the idea of opera in German. Goethe contributed the libretti to two *Singspiele*, *Erwin und Elmire* and *Claudine von Villa Bella* (both 1775), but it was Wolfgang Amadeus Mozart who raised the genre to a position of pre-eminence. He did this first with *Die Entführung aus dem Serail* (*The Abduction from the Seraglio*, 1782), a rescue comedy in which the clash between Christian and Islamic values leads to a moving articulation of the values of the Enlightenment. In *Entführung* the inventiveness of Mozart's score tends to overshadow the slight libretto, but in *Die Zauberflöte* (*The Magic Flute*, 1791), Emanuel Schikaneder's libretto sounds brilliantly vibrant when set to Mozart's music. In this crowing masterpiece both of the Viennese popular theatre and the *Singspiel* tradition, several colourful strands of eighteenth-century popular theatre are united in a sublime endorsement of Enlightenment values.

Mozart's relationship to the still nascent romantic movement is tenuous at best. His other operatic masterpieces, written to the Italian libretti of Lorenzo da Ponte, *Le nozze di Figaro* (*The Marriage of Figaro*, 1786), *Don Giovanni* (*Don Juan*, 1787), and *Così fan tutte* (*Women Are Like That*, 1790), display an unprecedented interest in the interior life of characters and generations have found emotional depths in them, but ultimately a strongly corrective sense of irony keeps the actions within the pale of Enlightenment drama. Beethoven's only opera, *Fidelio* (1805, 1806, and 1814), also in the *Singspiel* mode, was inspired by the ideals of the French Revolution, but while this great work touches depths of horror and magnificently celebrates human nobility and freedom, its characters remain two-dimensional.

The operas of E. T. A. Hoffmann (1776–1822), especially *Undine* (1816), introduced romantic themes to the German operatic stage. However, it was the works of Carl Maria von Weber (1786–1826) and Heinrich August Marschner (1795–1861) that most effectively explored the darker realms of folklore and the Gothic, and they quickly entered the repertoire. The supernatural elements in Weber's *Der Freischütz* (*The Marksman*, 1821) and Marschner's *Der Vampyr* (*The Vampire*, 1828) and *Hans Heiling* (1833), were undoubtedly introduced for grisly theatrical effect, but they can also be read as descriptive of states of mental confusion, anguish, and despair in the interior lives of the characters.

But the potential of romantic opera to penetrate and express the psychic world was not fully apparent until the music dramas of the late romantic composer, Richard Wagner. The range of his ten major music dramas was so broad and their appeal so wide that they changed the entire face of German, later of European theatre. Although his comparatively early works, *Tannhäuser* (1845) and *Lohengrin* (1850), are commonly regarded as the culminating works of German romantic opera, and his comedy *Die Meistersinger von Nürnberg* (1868) and his immense tetralogy, *Der Ring des Nibelungen* (1876), have been hailed as national dramas, a concern with romantic subjectivity runs throughout Wagner's work. This is apparent in his three most experimental music dramas – *Der fliegende Holländer* (*The Flying Dutchman*, 1843), *Tristan und Isolde* (1865), and *Parsifal* (1882) – in which the powerful subjectivity of the central characters have such a palpable influence upon the objective world around them that the stage can be understood as a metaphor for those characters' inner lives, a reading Wagner encouraged from *Holländer* onwards.[20] This process of making the action subjective probably reached its climax in Act 3 of *Tristan*, which comprises a painful and extended journey through Tristan's memories of his origins and parentage. The act climaxes with Isolde's celebrated *Liebestod* in which, like Grillparzer's Hero but with greater elaboration, she appears to expire out of sheer desire to be reunited with her lost lover. German theatre offers few passages through the subjective world as thorough as this.

But the stage upon which Wagner had to work ultimately defeated his purposes. His celebrated formulation of the romantic concept of the *Gesamtkunstwerk* in his major theoretical tract *Oper und Drama* (*Opera and Drama*, 1850–1) argued that all elements of the theatre – words, music, scenery, acting – are equal and should therefore draw the spectator's attention equally. However, in practice he realised that this equality was impossible to sustain and in his later essay 'Beethoven' (1870) began to suggest that the drama resided primarily in the music and that words were of secondary importance.[21] Wagner's priorities showed canny judgment as it is through rhythm and pure sound that audience attention is most effectively held, in the spoken as much as in the lyric theatre. However, the relentlessly realistic mode of nineteenth-century design and production both denied music its central function in the action and directed audience attention away from the rhythm of the action to the concrete actuality of realistic scenery. Although Wagner became increasingly aware of this problem, he could do little to solve it – his final production, of *Parsifal*, was entirely realistic. Nevertheless, it was his music dramas that inspired the French Swiss Adolphe Appia (1862–1928) to devise an approach to production and scenography that, while modernist in function, was to promote the realisation of the subjective tendencies of romantic drama. Appia was more effective as a visionary and theorist than as a practitioner and his ideas were first understood through books rather than production. In these he argued that the centre of performance in the theatre was the moving actor and that the entire scenic apparatus of the stage should be devoted to accentuating the actor's body and providing a space in which the audience could imagine for themselves the inner world of the character and the poetic core of the action. This led Appia to conceive of a scenic setting that was either abstract, being composed primarily of planes, verticals, stairs, and geometric shapes, or minimally realistic, as it included only the most characteristic details. Appia devised a stage that, by centring on the actor and allowing the dramatic action to appear with clarity, was similar in effect to the Shakespeare stage, but it was more versatile as his sets could work on the illusionist stage that was still uniformly in use at the end of the nineteenth century. Few theatres would, however, quickly take up the challenge offered by Appia. The Bayreuth establishment, headed by Cosima Wagner (1837–1930), the composer's widow, indignantly rejected his ideas as they did not accord with those of the great man himself. Among contemporary designers only Alfred Roller (1864–1935), in a series of revolutionary designs for the Vienna Court Opera in the 1900s, used the stage as a means of awakening the audience's imagination through an increasingly abstract design. It was not until well into the twentieth century that Appia's ideas would be fully realised.

Neo-romanticism

By the end of the nineteenth century, naturalism had become the dominant mode in the spoken theatre; even the verse plays of Goethe, Schiller, and Shakespeare, which were given in increasingly complete versions as the century progressed, tended to be delivered in a colloquial style that either brought the action closer to the experience of the audience or modernised it. Poetic drama in a neo-romantic vein was not entirely absent from the German stage, but, as with romanticism earlier in the century, one cannot speak of a coherent neo-romantic movement that establishes itself as a major genre of theatre.

Paris was the centre of theatrical experimentation, especially in the realm of poetic drama, at the end of the nineteenth century. The symbolist plays of the Belgian Maurice Maeterlinck (1862–1949), first staged at the Théâtre de l'Oeuvre during the 1890s, enjoyed quite a vogue in Germany. While naturalism revealed humans in the grip of social and biological drives, symbolism was devoted to exploring the metaphysical and the mystical, to showing how humans are subject to forces they cannot fully understand or control. Silence more than sound was Maeterlinck's main means to suggest the numinous world beyond immediate human ken. One-act plays such as *L'intruse* (*The Intruder*, 1890) and *Intérieur* (*Interior*, 1894) with their extended use of silence provided a parallel in playwriting to Appia's concept of abstract scenery, though they were still performed amidst realistic sets most of which suggested a natural or medieval environment. The German-language contribution to fin-de-siècle neo-romanticism was limited mainly to the writers of *Jung Wien* (Young Vienna) who, in the 1890s, produced a series of highly fanciful and poetically elaborate works that had some correspondence to the decadent literature of London and Paris. The most notable of these was Hugo von Hofmannsthal (1874–1929) whose early plays such as *Der Tod des Tizian* (*The Death of Tizian*, 1892), *Der Tor und der Tod* (*Death and the Fool*, 1894), *Der Kaiser und die Hexe* (*The Emperor and the Witch*, 1897), and *Das kleine Welttheater* (*The Little Theatre of the World*, 1897), are mainly remarkable for their intense, ornate verse. As with the romantics, however, Hofmannsthal's interests lay less in action, more in internal monologue, into which the action seems constantly to dissolve. These works have the form and quality of morality plays and anticipate Hofmannsthal's achievements in the theatre later in life, but they were only given coterie performances and had little impact upon the German theatre of his time.

Hofmannsthal is best known today, as librettist to the most frequently performed of all German twentieth-century opera composers, Richard Strauss (1864–1949). Strauss made his name with operatic adaptations of Oscar Wilde's *Salome* (1905) and Hofmannsthal's *Electra* (1909), which achieved notoriety for their graphic sexuality and colossal orchestration. In the violent juxtaposition between apocalyptic dissonance and lush romanticism, these operas seem to possess a profound kinship with expressionism. But once Strauss and Hofmannsthal teamed up, they withdrew from this modern idiom to produce a series of attractive works that either blended the milieu of the eighteenth-century comedy of manners with romantic subjectivity – *Der Rosenkavalier* (*The Cavalier of the Rose*, 1911) and *Ariadne auf Naxos* (*Ariadne on Naxos*, 1912 and 1916) – or employed symbolism to invest the traditional world of the fairy-tale with complex psychological meaning – *Die Frau ohne Schatten* (*The Woman Without a Shadow*, 1919). Strauss' last opera *Capriccio* was first performed in Munich in the dark days of 1942 and it concludes with a rapturous meditation of the relationship of words and music in art that is among the most complete articulations of romantic subjectivity.

The only neo-romantic German play that was widely performed well into the twentieth century was *Die versunkene Glocke* (*The Sunken Bell*, 1896) by Gerhart Hauptmann, better known for his naturalistic plays. This *Märchendrama* (fairy-tale play), which is full of echoes of *A Midsummer Night's Dream*, dramatises one of the most characteristic of romantic themes, the artist who is destroyed by the conflict between the demands of society, which expects him to conform, and his urge to live solely within nature, a realm that is highly eroticised. As he breaks free of social convention, Heinrich the artist acquires several of the features of the Nietzschean *Übermensch*, but at the end he is destroyed by a weakness that no *Übermensch* should ever admit to – guilt at the damage his career has done to others, especially his family.

The last romantic actors

Romantic modes of acting had been kept alive throughout the nineteenth century, most notably in the career of Bohumil Dawison, who was also celebrated for his strong, realistic characterisations. Some of the major actors of the turn of the century, notably Adalbert Matkowsky (1857–1909) and Josef Kainz (1858–1910) projected through their performance images of the self-contained individual as the dominant power within human society, and in so doing aroused associations with Nietzsche. Matkowsky, who spent the last twenty years of his career (1889–1909) as the leading actor of the by now very conservative Berlin Royal Theatre, was referred to as 'the last living example of the romantic actor'.[22] His bohemian way of life – he drank in the same pub that Ludwig Devrient and Hoffmann did – his habit of playing solely from instinct, and his leonine appearance and immense voice clearly marked him as an actor unsuitable for roles in realistic drama, so his repertoire consisted almost entirely of the classics. Unlike Devrient, however, he did not play characters torn apart by forces they can do little to control; rather he sought always to portray characters that were 'united in will and thought.' but with a spontaneity and lack of polish that was entirely opposite to the Weimar style, which, by the end of the century, was in its last throes. But according to Otto Brahm, it was Josef Kainz who really laid

the Weimar style to rest, when he gave his celebrated performance of Don
Carlos in Schiller's tragedy at the opening of the Deutsches Theater in
Berlin in November 1883.[23] Kainz would spend almost twenty years in this
company until his final decade when he returned to Vienna as a member of
the Burgtheater. For Brahm Kainz was significant as he was a modern and
a naturalist; he dispelled pomposity, tradition, declamation, and sentimentality from the stage; he was a 'nervous' actor who filled his roles with a
vitality that made them seem new to his audiences. But, unlike Devrient and
Matkowsky, Kainz had a superbly trained voice and flexibility of movement, a technique which he displayed on stage with the effect, somewhat
akin to that of the romantic ironist, of displaying an extraordinary control
over all means of expression. Hence tragic roles that were commonly
regarded as indicative of defeat, such as Romeo and Hamlet, became
epitomes of growth to maturity; Kainz's heroes died much fuller figures
than they were when they began, expressing defiance and a near savage joy
as they expired. Symbolic of Kainz's entire career was his performance of
Goethe's Tasso, the romantic artist who is brought to recognise and perhaps
accept the social limitations and conventions that hedge him in. Rather
than make Tasso into a figure of subservience, Kainz turned him into a rebel
from the start, one who had no difficulty in resisting both the blandishments
and the censure of his aristocratic patrons. In the final scene, normally
interpreted as the moment where Tasso submits to the social world, Kainz
pushed Antonio aside and defiantly strode down to the footlights, looked
out on the audience and declared that theirs was the world to which he
belonged.[24] The romantic hero, confident in his subjectivity, had, perhaps,
never been more effectively himself on the German stage.

6 The theatre of dissent from *Sturm und Drang* to Brecht, 1770–1920

HILDA MELDRUM BROWN

Dissent in the German theatre

The term 'dissent' covers a range of intensities, from mild to strong, on the scale of disagreement, often, but not invariably, in political or religious contexts. It implies a particular stance towards the status quo and a forceful articulation of opposition to that position. Traditionally, creative artists are especially sensitive to infringements by authoritarian forces upon what they perceive as individual or collective liberties. Cultural, political, social, or religious positions adopted by institutions will therefore be prime targets for dissent. For German expressionist dramatists, such as Georg Kaiser and Ernst Toller for instance, working in the years leading up to and following the First World War, dissent was focused on what was perceived as an inhumane, aggressive, spiritually bankrupt ethos prevailing in German society. However, in these cases the consequences and follow-up drawn from such a diagnosis are internalised and are presented in visionary terms, almost in the form of a spiritual crusade directed to the individual conscience. The utopian vision here side-steps the pressing practical issues, begging what are identified as difficult questions, such as, for example, the use of force to carry out radical new programmes. The more familiar form taken in the theatre of dissent tends, on the whole, to face these problems squarely. It grapples with the difficulties raised by attempts to reconcile the ideal and the real and to alter the status quo by means of reform or revolution. It is such examples of dissent in the German theatre on which I shall concentrate.

Of course the utopian element will always be lurking in any expression of dissent. What distinguishes the expressionist position from the other forms that I shall examine here is its tendency towards resolution, towards an ideal rather than a practical resolution. The other form of dissent may incline towards the opposite extreme, calling for practical solutions without regard for the consequences. Open expressions of dissent and the demand for practical implementation of ideals characterise the works of some writers who were directly involved in political agitation: the 'agit-prop' political theatre of the 1920s and the Piscator political theatre are notable examples. The case of Georg Büchner (1813–37) is an interesting one. Personally involved in political agitation in Hessen, writing and distributing among the populace a pamphlet, *Der hessische Landbote* (The Hessian Messenger, 1834) containing the inflammatory slogan '*Friede den Hütten, Krieg den Palästen*' (Peace to the cottages, war to the palaces), Büchner moved from a position of active dissent to the more muted but complex position embodied in *Dantons Tod* (*Danton's Death*, 1835) which could be regarded as an exemplary work in the mode. A reflective rather than an activist quality characterises the stance of many German dramatists from *Sturm und Drang* to Brecht. However, the dissenting impulse often acquires the sharp edge of satire and becomes focused on specific targets – laughter, albeit laced with the punitive quality of ridicule, being both a safety valve for the writer and a source of complicity with his audience. The phenomenon of dissent in the guise of 'inner emigration', which to some extent applies to the exiled Büchner, has often acquired such a form in the German tradition.

It has sometimes been argued that, paradoxically, the tension that is engendered in sensitive minds by a repressive, highly uncongenial environment can be creatively beneficial. This seems true in the German theatre though, as ever, examples of outstanding talent are always found in a few individuals only. The period of 'Restoration', which set in after the Congress of Vienna and Metternich's famous 'putting back of the clock in Europe', for example, could be described as one of unrelenting political and artistic repression, but the 1820s and 30s produced no more than one indisputably outstanding talent. When dissent appears in German theatre in contexts in which the possibility for change is negligible, it may be accompanied by a mood of disillusionment or the confident assertion of new norms and a programme for change.

Traditionally, drama, with its practical corollary theatre, has always been the major conduit for literary dissent. That is not to say that poetry and the novel have not also raised dissenting and eloquent voices, but drama – in its performing role – uniquely promotes direct access to an audience and has always had a special appeal to writers imbued with a sense of urgency and an overwhelming need to voice their concerns and disagreements. Given the Enlightenment notion of the theatre as a place for instruction, edification, and persuasion, it was not such a big step for writers like the youthful *Stürmer und Dränger* – seeking a platform for their revolutionary ideas – to reach for it naturally. Further prestige was added to the drama as a result of the extraordinarily long and fruitful reception process which Shakespeare's dramas underwent in Germany from the 1770s to the 1820s. Throughout the nineteenth century we find theorists and philosophers (e.g. Hegel) adopting a hierachical attitude towards the different art forms, according to which drama is invariably placed at the apex, as the 'highest' of all.

But of course where dissent and drama come together and where there is political oppression, there is bound to be conflict between writers and authority, which means censorship. Within the period covered in this chapter we can note three crucial phases. The first occurs in the period of Restoration (1820s and 30s) when Metternich's severe control of publicity in Vienna spread to Prussia, where, in 1819, repression was articulated in the 'Carlsbad Decrees'. The liberal ideas embodied in the youth movement led by the eccentric Turnvater Jahn, which culminated in the murder of Kotzebue by a student, produced a backlash on the part of the authorities towards any literature which contained the slightest hint of sedition. Later, after the July Revolution (1830), in response to an ever-mounting tide of political dissent repressive measures were taken by the police authorities in Hessen, involving the arrest of Georg Büchner's friends and collaborators, his own flight to Strasbourg, and his later move to Zurich as a political refugee. The next important phase of censorship strikes in the politically sensitive years of the 1880s and 90s, when the newly united Germany under Bismarck was showing all the symptoms of a politically jittery parvenu. Its chief targets were the Ibsen-inspired socio-critical dramas of the young Gerhart Hauptmann and its interventionist tactics led to Otto Brahm ingeniously putting on performances of such works before the members of the 'Freie Bühne' using various Berlin stages. In Munich things were no better: the main victim of censorship there was Frank Wedekind (1864–1918), whose expression of dissent took the form of an onslaught on the hypocrisy of German bourgeois society, especially in the area of sexual mores, leading to a total ban on the publication and performance of his dramas. Without the enlightened equivalent of a Brahm, Wedekind's most famous iconoclastic works *Frühlings Erwachen* (*Spring Awakening*, 1891), *Erdgeist* (*Earth Spirit*, 1895) and *Die Büchse der Pandora* (*Pandora's Box*, 1904) were withheld from the German stage for more than ten years, until they were rescued by the great pioneering director, Max Reinhardt. The last major example of the clash between the theatre of dissent and censorship is the most spectacular of all, the one that occurred during the 1920s and 1930s.

The incidence of the theatre of dissent within the period under consideration is by no means constant or predictable, and if we can talk of any tradition, it must be regarded as erratic. From the 1770s until the 1890s that literature is full of fits and starts and time-lags in the reception process as a result of censorship and delayed publication and performance. From a strongly defined starting point in *Sturm und Drang* the path veers sharply away during Weimar Classicism and romanticism, not to return seriously until Büchner, Christian Dietrich Grabbe (1801–1836), and *Junges Deutschland* focus attention on social and political issues. Here it is significant that Büchner seeks to link up with an earlier tradition by his appreciation of the gifted but uneven Jacob Lenz and his bold rejection of Schiller's classical works. Büchner's fellow-dissenter, Grabbe, on the other hand appears to reject all forerunners, to strike out on a completely novel path. But a surprising touch of continuity appears in the iconoclastic first drama of the young Brecht, *Baal* (1922), whose hero is a parodistic transposition of Grabbe as a character from Hanns Johst's drama *Der Einsame* (*The Lonely One*, 1917).

The large time-gaps between the transmission of Lenz's theatre of dissent to Büchner's, then to Hauptmann's, call for some comment. At various points along the way, the attention of German dramatists was focused on less concrete matters than social conditions or autocratic forms of governance. The Weimar Classicists, in their different ways, made their peace with the status quo, despite its inadequacies and set their sights on loftier matters; Schiller in particular was fascinated by the ethical and aesthetic issues which emerged from his combination of historical study and of the transcendental idealist philosophy of Immanuel Kant. Goethe, with his global view of Man's harmonious relationship with Nature, was less inclined to dwell obsessively on sources of conflict. Schiller's predilection led to a full-scale exploitation of the drama form throughout his career, but mainly within the context of tragedy, while Goethe's life-long Faust project, as we have seen, is hardly presented in terms of performable drama; instead it presents a 'celestial framework' which overarches the tale and exploits of the quasi-picaresque hero. The sense of final resolution created by this device is echoed in the numerous romantic dramas which offered 'reconciliation' through the intervention of divine, often Christian forces. Kleist and Grillparzer were too impressed by the combination of the Weimar and Shakespearian heritages to take their eyes off the task of producing German tragedy of high distinction along classical lines or to focus on the burning issues of the day. Classical forms and the mission of tragedy and more loosely structured anti-Aristotelian social and political dramas would box and cox for many decades, but the high ground was held indisputably by Weimar. The domestic tragedy managed to come close to achieving the impossible task of combining the necessary tragic pathos with the sheer ordinariness of the characters, who are deemed by their makers to be, in Lessing's words, 'of the same grist and grain' as ourselves. The domestic tragedy makes a last, somewhat melodramatic and self-conscious appearance with Hebbel's *Maria Magdalena*, but by 1840 it no longer has the breadth of focus or sharpness of dissent which had been *de rigeur* among the more gifted *Stürmer und Dränger*.[1]

The situation of German drama in the middle of the nineteenth century is both confused and complex. On the one hand much importance is laid at the popular level on the drama form and theatre-going had never been so popular.[2] According to *Junges Deutschland* writers, at times when continuing political disunity prevails, the theatre as an institution has the important task of demonstrating to contemporary audiences how progressive forces may emerge, as in Hegel's concept of the forward movement of the historical process. To this end – and not surprisingly since this was a period of raised historical consciousness – historical figures and situations are more favoured as material for drama than contemporary issues. But more often than not the outcome is merely '*Tendenzdrama*' (thesis-drama). This raises an important issue in one's consideration of the theatre of dissent: the pitfalls of over-commitment to ideas or ideologies that lie in the way of a dissenting writer are considerable, and it is instructive to examine how leading dramatists of dissent manage to avoid them.

It is a special feature of German drama – and German literature in general – that literary practice is firmly rooted in ideas and philosophical systems. This is evident in the long tradition of dramaturgical writing from Lessing, through *Sturm und Drang* and Schiller, all of whom had in turn drawn on the writings of Leibniz, Rousseau, and Kant. Beyond these eighteenth-century figures Büchner's laconic and scattered utterances in letters and the prose tale 'Lenz' present a surprisingly coherent aesthetic whose significance is out of proportion to its size. It is based on the replacement of Kantian idealism with a more pragmatic, materially based outlook which seems to be pointing forward to later materialist systems such as that of Büchner's brother Ludwig in *Kraft und Stoff* (*Power and Substance*, 1855), but is tempered by a more subjective, humanitarian ethos. By mid-century a plethora of aesthetic theories were spawned by Otto Ludwig (1813–65) and Gustav Freytag (1816–95), to name but a few, and dramatic 'rules' were codified to an extent unparalleled in the days of Lessing or Schiller, all based on the alleged models of Shakespeare and/ or Weimar Classicism. As Edward McInnes notes, there is a serious absence of interaction between '*Kritik*' (criticism) and '*kreative Tätigkeit*' (creative activity), and despite an instinctive tendency on the part of writers to engage critically with serious problems of the times, dramatic forms and styles of presentation remain rooted in a 'conservative-classical tendency'.[3] It is astonishing to think that Karl Gutzkow failed to encourage a performance of *Dantons Tod* (*Danton's Death*), which he recommended instead as a 'reading drama'. What might the course of late nineteenth-century German drama and in particular the theatre of dissent have taken had this work been accessible to the theatre-going public of the day? As things turned out, the public was deprived of performance of one of the greatest masterpieces of the nineteenth century until the year 1916. There had been readings of the work initiated by Hauptmann in the pioneering Berlin literary society, 'Durch', but by the time *Danton's Death* was performed, naturalism was long past. Much more significant was the play's liberating effect on expressionist drama and beyond because at long last the issues and critiques associated with dissent could find their complement in experimental dramatic structures. The abandonment of the Freytag model and substitution of a looser dramatic form[4] now opened the way for other aspects than character tragedy to come to the fore. This liberation of form would especially suit the paradoxical tendencies in Bertolt Brecht's thinking and pave the way for the development of his so-called 'epic' theatre.

True to the long-standing German theoretical tradition, Brecht would attempt to define and codify his ideas through numerous short essays and a longer treatise, the *Kleines Organon für das Theater* (The Short Organum for the Theatre, 1948). Surveying the continued prominence of such dramaturgical writings from *Sturm und Drang* onwards, one notes the increasing tendency to modify the application of philosophical systems to a distillation of key points, as in Brecht's adoption of Marxist principles. The effect is a narrower, more doctrinaire and ideological underpinning to aesthetic theorising. The classical Schiller and Brecht, however, share one important aesthetic principle, the demand for an anti-illusionist theatre, although their respective points of departure and desired outcomes differ greatly.

Sturm und Drang

This radical movement is the first example in German literature of a group of writers who share objectives in expressing their dissent towards the literary, political, and social status quo . That said, its cohesion is relative: the watchwords of its loosely defined 'programme', *'Freiheit'*, *'Gefühl'*, and *'Natur'* ('freedom,' 'feeling', and 'nature'), all greatly inspired by Rousseau, are variously and often contradictorily defined. The collection of essays *Von deutscher Art und Kunst* (On German Nature and Art, 1773), which includes Herder's essay on Shakespeare, provides, along with Lenz's *Anmerkungen*, such coherent literary programme as there is and sums up the collective endeavours of *Sturm und Drang* as a whole. This was the creation of a 'characteristic art' based on native German rather than imported sources, with the notable exception of Shakespeare and the English. The movement as such is of short duration (1770–80). Over it towers the figure of Goethe, whose charismatic personality attracted a number of lesser luminaries such as Gerstenberg, Klinger, Wagner, Leisewitz, and Lenz, with Schiller coming later as a special case. *Stürmer und Dränger* convey their 'dissent' with scant concern for good manners, or the *bienséances*, which had been a hallmark of the French classical theatre and had for so long held the Germans in its thrall. Even when the results were at their most extreme and uninhibited, the process of breaking out of the strait-jacket of the well-constructed drama, of writing a play in six acts (H. L. Wagner's *Die Kindermörderin* for instance) or abandoning verse form for a prose style, which sometimes comes close to the inflections of colloquial speech and makes some attempt to distinguish between different registers, was a liberating one and would leave its mark on the German theatre for years to come.

The targets for dissent among *Stürmer und Dränger* can mostly be subsumed under their overarching demand for 'freedom'. But, as has often been said, they are more interested in the negative rather than the positive aspects of freedom. The classical Schiller would claim 'freedom' too, but quite differently defined in moral and intellectual terms. *Stürmer und Dränger* claim freedom from the restrictions imposed by institutions and in so doing hit hard at examples of contemporary injustice: for instance, a legal system which deals so savagely with cases of infanticide, in the Gretchen tragedy in *Faust I* or *Die Kindermörderin*, or an arbitrary law such as primogeniture in Klinger's *Die Zwillinge* (*The Twins*), which flies in the face of natural justice, or a legal system riddled with pedantry and pettiness, such as the Bishop of Bamberg's court in *Götz von Berlichingen*. *Sturm und Drang* also attacked an educational system that shows scant regard for individuality by imposing rote learning on children at the expense of their developing perceptions of the world around them (*Götz*) and a religious system that imposes severe restrictions on sexual mores, thus infringing the natural rights of individuals to develop the emotional side of their personalities, the effects of which are graphically expressed by Bruder Martin in *Götz* and by the nun, Blanca, in *Julius von Tarent* by Johann Anton Leisewitz (1752–1806).

The sheer vehemence of the chorus of dissenting voices, together with the nature of the targets of dissent themselves, can, in many respects, be regarded as a function of *Sturm und Drang*'s major programme of self-definition. This focuses on the need to establish a distinctive profile to set against the weight of Enlightenment thought and literature, whose influence lingered well into the second half of the eighteenth century in German lands. The need to spread this mission is perceived as urgent, and all the verbal weapons of rhetoric and persuasion are deemed legitimate to this end. The polarisation of characters between the dynamic, male figures and the passive females, who are victims of their ambitions and lusts, almost invariably implies disastrous outcomes. Indeed the problematic consequence of unbridled self-expression is a point well taken by the greater writers of the movement and explains why often their dramas incline to the tragic mode. The insight of protagonists and audience into the limits set on the implementation of ideals will prove to be an abiding theme in the history of the theatre of dissent.

Among the various contributors to the movement, the most significant are Goethe, Schiller, and Lenz. Goethe's contribution is, not surprisingly, the most controlled and multi-faceted. His *Urfaust*, known only in manuscript form to a handful of close friends to whom he read sections shortly after his move to Weimar, is taken over virtually intact into the 'Fragment' of 1790 and *Faust Part I*, but its scope already goes far beyond the normal bounds of dissent. Through the complexity of the Faust figure, it becomes an examination of the human condition, its heights and its depths, rather than a critique of society, though to a certain extent that is its starting point. In its wonderfully free and supple form and in the succinctness and intensity of its emotional expression, it would inspire later dramatists with leanings towards dissent, such as Büchner. On the other hand, Goethe's *Götz*, despite retaining a more traditional five-act structure, turns out to be less cohesive, more diffuse and episodic. Paradoxically, its theme of untrammelled chivalric virtue contains nostalgic, even elegiac overtones, as the hero's death and failed attempt to maintain these values spells the end of a Golden Age and the beginning of a new bureaucratic and repressive order of society. The utopian prospect of their return at some future point dampens any sense of urgency, such as we might expect in the theatre of dissent.

For later dramatists who pursue the line of social critique, Lenz and Schiller offer much in the way of inspiration as models. Lenz's exposés of social evils are sharply focused though uneven and quirky. In the case of *Soldaten*, he even breaks the bounds of fiction supplementing the critique in the drama with a petition, '*Über die Soldatenehen*' (On the marriage of soldiers) urging Duke Karl August of Weimar to take drastic action in addressing the problems raised by incompatibility between soldiers and civilians and the damaging effects the military have on sexual mores and the lives of law-abiding citizens. The proposal to set up a 'nursery' of regimental harlots to satisfy soldiers' lusts seems both impractical and unlikely to produce the intended improvement in society. In his theoretical works such as *Anmerkungen* and within the context of his conscious rejection of traditional forms, Lenz proposes a form of drama, which he ambiguously calls '*Komödie*', which will present 'a painting of human society' and is above all a critical one. This is the first call for a specifically socio-critical form of drama in Germany. It would seem directly applicable to the well-established *Sturm und Drang* version of the domestic tragedy, but is broadly enough formulated to allow for other forms which will depart from the abiding influence of the Aristotelian unities. Thereby Lenz is setting up a powerful impetus for further developments in the theatre of dissent and pointing to the radical kind of dramatic form which this might take.

Schiller's *Die Räuber* went through a number of versions, including one specifically for performance (1782). The familiar *Sturm und Drang* theme of the two brothers competing for the exclusive favour of their father receives a new twist. The rejected son (Karl) uses this familial wrangle as a pretext to express a global dissatisfaction with his entire age – 'this ink-splattering century'. Taking the law into his own hands, he accepts command of a gang of robbers, malcontents, and drop-outs who roam around the countryside committing criminal acts and taking revenge on society. This somewhat adolescent approach to rebellion immediately highlights the problematic nature of dissent as expressed in the drama. Schiller himself seems aware of this since in the foreword he delivers something like an apologia, defending the amorality of his protagonist as a genius and the necessity of presenting realistic characterisations, warts and all, however much this may give offence to squeamish souls. Schiller pleads for an appreciation of his work as belonging 'among the moral books'. Referring to the criminal hero's final surrender to the legal authorities to receive due punishment for his many crimes he observes, 'the prodigal once more enters the ruts of the law'. This ending in 'poetic justice' would seem to nip dissent in the bud and has often been seen as a foretaste of Schiller's later development, in particular the foregrounding of the idea of repentance, which will form an important aspect of his classical theory of the sublime. Nevertheless, and despite the apparent watering down of the theme of dissent and highlighting character flaws, Schiller's contemporary audience was overwhelmingly enthusiastic, and his fame spread beyond the bounds of Württemberg. A climate of opinion was already in place, ready to respond to the impassioned language rather than bother about the details of the ending. The revolutionary impulse which would erupt at the end of the 1780s was already in the air. Possibly equally important was the means by which this mood was conveyed and the emphasis on realistic character portrayal, which would be a feature of later examples in the mode.

As can be seen, *Sturm und Drang* pioneers the form of social drama in various novel guises ranging from adaptation of the domestic tragedy, which it developed to become a sharpened satire and critique, to the creation of entirely novel dramatic forms – *Urfaust*. The single-mindedness with which these writers air their dissent in its multifarious forms and adopt theatre as the major means of doing so reflects a uniquely collective enterprise which would carry much weight with those of similar persuasions coming afterwards.

Biedermeier and Junges Deutschland: Grabbe and Büchner

A tide of optimism, in which Romantic writers participated, led up to the Wars of Liberation (1813–14), and a strong sense of national identity emerged for the first time in German lands, as the vast majority were united in the mission of driving Napoleon and the French off German soil. Fichte's *Reden an die deutsche Nation* (*Speeches to the German Nation*, 1808), reinforced at the popular level by E. M. Arndt's *Geist der Zeit* (*Spirit of the Time*, 1806–13), fuelled the revolutionary mood after the humiliation of Jena. Ironically, Napoleon, whose ambiguous profile and influence would haunt German writers for decades, had done more to unite a disunited people than anyone. But in the wake of the Congress of Vienna (1815) this bright hopefulness faded. An era of political reaction set in all over Europe, which would last until well into the century. The German 'Bund', consisting of thirty-eight states under the overall control of the Austrian Chancellor, Fürst Metternich, was a bureaucratic, backward-looking institution whose true mettle soon became clear when the repressive Carlsbad Decrees (1819) were introduced in Prussia and elsewhere. Abandoning the pre-1815 liberal reforming spirit which had prevailed under the leadership of its Chancellor, Hardenberg, Prussia was now forced into a strait-jacket of repression and started to take on some of the features of a police state in which all liberal stirrings were stifled. In such an environment the spirit of dissent seemed bound to flourish, but would, equally, meet with measures of uncompromising disapproval and severity in the German principalities. Georg Büchner's forced exile in Switzerland in 1834 in the politically sensitive period after the failed July Revolution encapsulates this dilemma vividly.

And yet, though the preconditions were there for a theatre of dissent, the post-1815 period did not in fact find more than a couple of writers of rank turning to drama as a conduit for expressing frustrations and rousing the general public to awareness of the need for radical change. The period 1815–48, which has been dubbed '*Biedermeier*' after the style of its furniture,[5] was characterised by a public possessed of few political aspirations and content with undemanding forms of literature which emphasised entertainment rather than intellectual challenge. Having been dominated in the early years by ultra-conservative writer-directors such as Iffland and Kotzebue, the Berlin Court Theatre continued to peddle politically correct dramas. From about 1830 the adherents of Young Germany, united in their desire to bring about political reform, adopted pamphlets and journals rather than drama to address their mainly middle-class audience. One of the few writers at this time to use drama was Karl Immermann, though his own work followed the prevailing trend for historical subjects, as it adopted a 'monotonous classicism' that has its roots in the overwhelming dominance of the Schillerian model.[6] The almost universal predilection for classical forms and historical subjects, many taken from German history, seems ill-suited to the problems of a rapidly changing society but even the 'domestic tragedy, which had been such a useful tool of social criticism for *Sturm und Drang*, made little headway. If theatre-going at this time was more popular with the German public than ever before, the dramas had never been more vacuous or less related to contemporary events.

The two exceptions to the decline of this form, which had been launched with such high hopes and carried along on the tide of the spectacular Shakespeare reception in Germany, are both talents of the highest order and among the most innovative and original dramatists ever to write in the German language. And they are, *par excellence*, representatives of the 'theatre of dissent' – Christian Dietrich Grabbe (1801–36) and Georg Büchner

(1813–37). These playwrights share a number of important features both in their choice of subject matter and in their use and development of a dramatic form appropriate to their new material. These bold spirits do not hesitate to explore revolutionary ideas, though neither preaches revolution as such or makes a break with the formal perfection associated with classical Weimar. There is a palpable urgency and desire to communicate in their works that is at times reminiscent of *Sturm und Drang*. Like their predecessors they seek to draw on near-contemporary events and bear witness to the socio-political trends that were shaping the course of history as groups of like-minded young fire-brands were building up a steady momentum for the revolution that erupted in Paris in July 1830, causing ripples over the length and breadth of the German speaking world as far as Vienna. Grabbe planned a series of dramas based on Hohenstauffen history, of which he completed two, *Kaiser Friedrich Barbarossa* (1829) and *Kaiser Heinrich der Sechste* (*Emperor Henry VI*, 1830). He also wrote *Napoleon oder die Hundert Tage* (*Napoleon, or The Hundred Days*, 1831), *Hannibal* (1835), and his own *Hermannsschlacht* (*The Battle of Arminius*, 1838). But while these plays adopt the currently popular mode of historical drama, they do so from a decidedly contemporary and critical perspective and their thematisation of the French Revolution and its aftermath in the Napoleonic Wars is presented from a perspective from which the outcomes of that recent event are still very relevant.

Both Grabbe and Büchner are fascinated by the phenomenon of power, the legitimacy, or otherwise, of the use of force, and the problematic nature of leadership. There is some debate as to whether Grabbe resolves these issues, particularly through the eponymous hero in *Napoleon*. Some commentators, such as Kaiser,[7] define the leader in terms of 'will and energy' and see Grabbe's stance as symptomatic of the driving forces of economic growth under capitalism so typical of nineteenth-century Germany, while others regard it as anticipating twentieth-century Fascism. The vexed question of Grabbe's popularity during the Third Reich has also been invoked in this connection.

In *Napoleon* the charismatic appeal of the heroic figure among the populace is evident as soon as it is rumoured that he has landed in France after his escape from Elba. It becomes clear, however, that the counter forces that have been unleashed through his years of imperialist expansion and warfare enabling the leading states in the coalition against France to join forces to crush his uprising, have now gathered such momentum that the time for any reinstatement of the leader, however popular nationally, is no longer ripe. Grabbe's Napoleon 'is smaller than the revolution',[8] a colossus thwarted by the times and brought down by forces beyond his control rather than by his own inadequacies, but he is nevertheless strong, heroic, and an example of all the dynamic qualities that the age has failed to appreciate. In a prophetic speech, Napoleon comments that the prevailing mood of mediocrity in Bourbon France – 'full of indecision, foolish false-hood and deceit' – will become the norm for the foreseeable future, until 'the waves of the Revolution and my empire' return. Here Grabbe permits his 1831 audience a glimpse of a future return to Napoleon's vision of greatness, projected far into the future. Even amidst Grabbe's dissent and his dissatisfaction with his own times, the protagonist's credo acquires a 'proscriptive quality'[9] taking on a quasi-mythical status as Napoleon addresses later generations even while expressing his disillusionment with the present situation.

Though the character of Napoleon may not 'shed light'[10] on the prob-lem of power in the way that Schiller had done in his brilliant exposés of its corrupting character and of the moral conflicts which this sets up, it is not appropriate to judge Grabbe's drama either in psychological or moral terms. The first three acts convey a kaleidoscopic impression of the complex and contradictory social and political circumstances in which Napoleon's bid to regain power is placed. It exposes not only the ineptness of the upper classes but also the fickleness of the mob, which is intellectually unemancipated and thereby unlikely to appreciate the alternative style of rule offered by Napoleon. Nor is it clear that Napoleon has any strategy or programme to liberate the masses. This externalisation of the situation and ability to convey an intricate configuration of interest groups by means of a brilliant and novel technique make *Napoleon* such an important work, though the battle scenes provide almost insuperable problems for staging. Grabbe's use of a new form of reportage, based on recently invented forms of media communication – newspapers and telegraph – to replace classical devices such as reports and stichomythia, has been hailed, not without justification, as evidence that he is a pioneer of modern theories of communication. Grabbe's other historical dramas, while showing signs of innovation in the handling of their material, by comparison seem, through their subject matter, rather more remote.

Georg Büchner (1813–37), one of the very greatest nineteenth-century dramatists, may seem on the surface to share many of Grabbe's attitudes and dramatic innovations. His technique for handling mass scenes in *Dantons*

Tod by means of short succinct and often witty episodes which move swiftly from one locality to another is often reminiscent of Grabbe's. His bitter-sweet comedy, *Leonce und Lena* (1836), with its underlying seriousness and satirical focus on social and political life in a small German principality reminds us at many points of Grabbe's pre-absurdist comedy, *Scherz, Satire, Ironie und tiefere Bedeutung* (*Joke, Satire, Irony and Deeper Significance*, 1827). But critics seem convinced that neither writer knew the other's work. However, their affinity was noted by Brecht who traced his own genealogy in the theatre of dissent back to *Sturm und Drang* via Grabbe and Büchner.[11] But a closer inspection of the treatment of the themes of leadership, power and revolution in *Napoleon* and *Dantons Tod* reveals very different approaches to the question of dissent. Danton's rejection of the status quo exudes ennui rather than thrusting energy and self-belief. He is racked by pangs of conscience for his part in the September Massacres, even while accepting that the revolutionary process has made puppets of those participating in it. He completely lacks Napoleon's ruthlessness and focus on action, indeed he is hyper-reflective to the point where, Hamlet-like, reflection actually stifles all desire to act. He is attuned to the problem of human suffering and moved by feelings of compassion, which are even more graphically displayed in *Woyzeck* (1835–7, publ. 1879). Finally, he agonises about the fundamental question of belief in the existence of God. So important is this matter to Büchner that he unhistorically introduces the character of Thomas Paine, placing in his mouth a case in favour of atheism that Paine never espoused, so that Danton and his friends can have a let-out clause for their religious doubts. The inconsistency in Danton's behaviour and his vain attempts to find a coherence in life as he oscillates between political indifference and a gut reaction to put his case and appeal to the people is a brilliant piece of characterisation. It contains more depth than Grabbe's portrayals of histor-ical figures, for while his charismatic leaders exhibit inconsistencies, they themselves are not prone to self-analysis.

Much has been said about Büchner's own inconsistency in throwing himself into an activist role prior to launching into an intensive programme of creative writing. Within the same year (1834) he could express in a letter to his fiancée his sense of 'the monstrous fatalism of history' and the futility of political endeavour as he reviewed the source material for Danton and at the same time set up the *Gesellschaft der Menschenrechte* (Society for Human Rights) in Darmstadt, following this with the publication of *Der hessische Landbote* which was intended to raise political awareness and encourage revolt.[12] This pattern of paradoxical behaviour also becomes the defining aspect of his characterisation of Danton, where it acquires depth and plausibility, reflecting an intractable conflict between the emotional and intellectual factors that make up the psychology of dissent, an aporia which Benn, quoting Ernst Toller, aptly sums up as a conflict between 'will' and 'knowledge'.

What makes *Dantons Tod* such a perfect example of the theatre of dissent is, firstly, the quality of Büchner's insights into political action and their intersection with human values and, secondly, the economy and brilliance with which he presents complex historical issues at a point of transition when revolutionary idealism is moving into its obverse, dictatorship. The interweaving of the personal dimension – exemplified by the female characters, Julie and Lucille, and the strong bonds of friendship between Camille and Danton – with the harsh driving force of ideology and historical inevitability – as represented by St Just and Robespierre – give the drama a unique breadth and completeness.

As for the much admired liberation from classical forms and substitution of an episodic or 'open' structure, such appearances may be deceptive because, while there is much scope for reflection, the action develops clearly to a climactic point – Danton's death on the guillotine – and the confrontation between Robespierre and Danton forms a peripatetic moment of no return similar to that of a classical tragedy. Even seemingly random episodes involving the crowd shed important light on the sense of fragility, which is an essential part of Danton's vision of an existential 'abyss' and extends the range of those characters who feel they have been engulfed by forces beyond their control. There is, finally, a striking use of symbolic 'cosmic' imagery throughout the drama which acts almost like a leitmotif.

Woyzeck is the first significant social drama featuring the proletariat. Not only does it provide some biting social satire directed at prevailing injustices and exploitation, it delivers this in a kaleidoscopic, uniquely terse and succinct form, based on short scenes. The hugely innovative potential for an intense form of drama developed here would be fully appreciated and exploited by the expressionists and in *Wozzeck* (1925), the operatic version by Alban Berg.

With Büchner the theatre of dissent finds one of its most eloquent and profound practitioners.

Naturalism

There is a considerable gap between Büchner's and Grabbe's contributions to the theatre of dissent and the next major examples which appear in the

1890s with Hauptmann and the naturalist movement. For a couple of decades (1850–70) at least it seemed as if Richard Wagner's music dramas would steal the thunder at the high cultural end of the theatre, following a series of tracts in which he set out his goals for revolutionising society through art. But despite Wagner's dissatisfaction with the mediocrity he perceived in the arts, politics and society of his day, his newly created hybrid form of music drama became a spur for metaphysical and mythological explorations of the human condition rivalling the grandeur and sublimity of Greek tragedy. All notions of dissent, traces of which can be detected in the earlier sketches of *Siegfried*, whose hero is celebrated as a free spirit, became subsumed in these grander purposes.

By the late 1880s and early 1890s, the euphoria created by unification in Germany had changed to disillusionment about its socio-economic effects, especially on the lower strata of society. Accelerated industrialisation, growing urbanisation of the work force, and poor and unsanitary living conditions, combined to rouse the attention and the sympathy of the more sensitive, mostly youthful members of the intelligentsia. Attempts were made to form new left-wing political parties, but these soon fell foul of the authorities and were outlawed by the introduction of measures such as the law against Socialists of 1878. It so happened that the young Gerhard Hauptmann's alertness to these problems coincided with the establishment of the short-lived but intense, European-wide movement of naturalism (1888–1900), which owed its origins to Zola in France and Ibsen in Norway, though at this point he lived in Germany. This meant that Hauptmann inherited a thoroughly debated aesthetic of realism from writers such as Arno Holz (1863–1929), Johannes Schlaf (1862–1941) and Wilhelm Bölsche (1861–1939), which drew its authority from the natural sciences and would prove a barrier to imaginative expression in the dramatic medium. In the case of Hauptmann, however, this did nothing to prevent his producing outstanding examples of the theatre of dissent in works like *Vor Sonnenaufgang* (*Before Sunrise*, 1889) and *Die Weber* (*The Weavers*, 1892). The first centres on the effects of an over-rapid access to wealth on a backward rural society, the second on a historical uprising in the 1840s, a kind of Luddite revolt by a community of Silesian weavers whose livelihood is threatened by encroaching mechanisation.

The heritage of scientific determinism inherent in the naturalist programme manifests itself in techniques that often seem more in place in the novel. Lengthy stage directions, often so detailed as to be impractical, set scenes that do not advance the action, and the assumption of a 'fourth wall' on stage to reinforce the illusion certainly create challenges for a director. The focus on a 'problem' and the application of an investigative analytical method of identifying it, together with the tendency of exposing it at a late stage when there is little prospect of any remedy, tend, unless expertly handled, to create a sense of overpowering gloom and claustrophobia. The predilection for the Ibsen-inspired figure of the 'messenger from afar', a *raisonneur* figure, whose role is that of the diagnostician, also creates difficulties as such mouthpiece-figures may come across as wooden and unconvincing. The tendency, especially noticeable in Hauptmann, of drawing attention to the discrepancy between the idealism of these figures and their ineffectuality, underlines a major motif in the theatre of dissent: the gap opened up between ideal and real, between the perceived need for change and the fragility of the means whereby change can be effected. The focus on such premises and their pessimistic implications continues the discourse so brilliantly articulated by Büchner. His treatment of scientific laws and determinism, his social concerns and humanitarian perspective, must have struck an especially strong chord in Hauptmann and may well have helped him utilise dramatic form in ways which, while remaining recognisably within the programme of naturalism, would also transcend its limitations.

Hauptmann's quality as a dramatist is brought into relief by comparing his works with the most extreme example of 'thorough-going naturalism', Holz and Schlaf's *Die Familie Selicke* (*The Selicke Family*, 1890). Despite its exhaustive examination of many social issues, which had become pressing since 1871 and which might have formed the basis for a dissenting perspective, Holz and Schlaf fail to convey this dramatically. It is easy for a modern reader to mock this work, but it is nonetheless interesting as an object lesson in how the lack of any clear focus for dissent, which might provide a wider perspective on events, leads to its failure as a drama. The desire of the theorist, Holz, to conform to the theories he had so painstakingly set out leads to protracted descriptive passages on a scale which detracts from the impact of what could be authentic glimpses of the predicament of lower middle class urban life in the Wilhelmian Era. The potentially suggestive contrast drawn between horror of the city and the idyll of a country parsonage is a promising theme which remains undeveloped.

Hauptmann's dramas, however, illustrate how palpable causes of dissent, imaginatively and sympathetically grasped, can coexist within a naturalist framework and yet at the same time make for theatre-worthy drama, creating differentiated, plausible characterisation and situations with which the audience can identify. Hauptmann summed up his position in the ongoing debate about 'art and nature' with a more cautious formulation than Holz, one which implies an aesthetic criterion: 'it is a step forward to represent more and more the undramatic dramatically'. This provides him with a powerful weapon as a contributor to the theatre of dissent and makes room for his strong humanitarian leanings towards the sufferings of the victims of society. He exploits the naturalist legacy of description while maintaining a sense of underlying dramatic momentum. At its first perform-ance, at the Freie Bühne, *Vor Sonnenaufgang* caused a sensation and fighting between the sharply divided factions in the audience. Building on the powerful social critique of Henrik Ibsen, Hauptmann's characters are more than mere vehicles for contemporary ideas about heredity and alcoholism. The idealistic Loth, the stranger from afar, comes to a country area in his professional capacity as a sociologist, to a region in which capitalist spec-ulation following the discovery of coal has brought sudden wealth to the local farming community. The incongruity of the impact of urban values on a backward rural economy is graphically summed up in small details, such as farm animals being equipped with marble mangers. In the wake of this, the emergence of social problems in the form of over-indulgence and alcohol dependency, whether environmental in origin or the result of heredity, is deliberately left ambiguous. The 'man from outside', who embodies the spirit of dissent towards the status quo and expresses his disgust with the degree of degeneration he encounters, becomes the focus of a real-life dilemma when he falls in love with the sister of an old university friend who himself is caught in the spiral of degeneration. Loth's principles of a general, but abstract and academic, humanitarian belief that his work will assist in the exposure of and provide a solution to social problems clash with the hypothesis that Helene herself may be tainted with alcoholism, which has become a modern version of the family curse.

Hauptmann injects dramatic significance into his presentation of the *nouveau riche* environment which carries an implied social critique, imposing on the would-be social reformer a moral obligation to act on his findings. But Loth's demonstration of human weakness in the face of crisis and his glib abandonment of his mission on the grounds that he might father alcoholic offspring appears to the spectator or reader as substituting self-interest for principle, and as such produces a potent and dramatically charged outcome. The problem receives further nuancing through the parallel characterisations of both Hoffmann and the doctor Schimmelpfennig alongside Loth. All three men have benefited from a university education, but have taken very different paths in life. The doctor provides the audience with a source of comparison to Loth, the dissenter who loses sight of the cause of humanity. Inured to a hardened cynicism through years of close contact with members of the depraved community who do not seem worthy of help, he nevertheless stays in their midst where he can at least alleviate some degree of suffering. Loth, therefore, in his abandonment of Helene and his mission, stands even more condemned by this contrast. Whether other means to meet the social problems might exist is not part of Hauptmann's remit. As a dramatist he is fascinated by a situation in which a potentially constructive manifestation of dissent is undermined by the frailties of human nature.

In any examination of the theatre of dissent *Die Weber*, based on a historical event dating from 1844, must stand as exemplary. Dissent, as so often, proves to be of no avail within the drama's terms of reference and its outcome; it could, however, be said to contain highly combustible material, thus serving as a conduit of dissent. At a time when there were no trade unions to represent workers, a band of destitute weavers conducts a poorly planned revolt against their employer, the factory owner Dreissiger, but cannot prevail against the muscle of capitalism. Dreissiger is keeping them below the poverty line, but is himself in the grip of industrial and mechanical change as well as market forces. The movement for change and justice peters out after a pitiful scene where the dissenting mass break into the opulent private home of the employer, gazing in disbelief at the luxury which they behold, only to be dispersed by the militia. Fate plays an ironic trick by making the only sacrificial victim a deeply religious elderly weaver who had dissociated himself from the uprising because of the violent methods. Once more Hauptmann leaves the audience pondering the problems posed by the theme of dissent. The leading spirits are two fiery young men, Jäger and Bäcker, and at a higher social level a lone voice of protest is raised by the young theology student Weinhold who, like Loth, utters platitudes about human and social needs but makes no headway with the bourgeois capitalists who are his employers and dismiss him from his post. Once more the voice of idealism and dissent is rendered impotent.

Die Weber stands in the tradition of mass drama pioneered by Grabbe and solves the dramatically difficult problem of how to convey an entire group – the drama famously has no single hero – by presenting a number of carefully selected tableaux in which representative figures are placed in their respective milieux — the factory, a weaver's home, an inn, the employer's home. The build up of dramatic tension within these scenes is carefully controlled and each act culminates in the singing of the emotionally charged, historically authentic Weavers' song with its apocalyptic vision of the Day of Judgement. The song encapsulates the frustrations and aspirations of the depressed and demoralised workers and acts as an emotional outlet for their pent up and otherwise barely articulated feelings. The deep irony in this situation is that in vandalising the mechanical looms in Dreissiger's and other factories in the belief that 'the entire misery comes from the factories', the weavers cannot hope to prevent technological advance or assist their own cause. A sense of hopelessness and futility about the poorly organised action is conveyed, though with deep sympathy and insight. Hauptmann presents this from the perspective of the weavers, emphasising and motivating the mass uprising in terms of a group of fundamentally peaceful people needing to find some outlet for their long festering discontent. Old Baumert, who had at first mooted the naïve possibililty that the weavers might travel to Berlin and demonstrate peacefully in front of the King and who is himself an unlikely candidate for revolution, nevertheless gets caught up in the tide of emotion released by the Weavers' song. Ansorge expresses this basic need in human beings to have a prospect of something better in life in the laconic phrase, 'each man has his own longing'.

Hauptmann shows how the hope of a better life and deliverance from an intolerable one underpins the decision of the weavers to take what to them is the huge step of drastic action. Because of their normally compliant attitude towards adverse circumstances they need a catalyst to stir them into action. Neither of the young firebrand leaders has any coherent plan: the stage directions indicate that there is not a little arrogance and self-esteem in the defiance of '*der rote Bäcker*', while Jäger, a former weaver who has now joined the army, seems keen to cut a figure among his former fellow workers.

At various points in the drama reference is made to revolution; the debate in fact extends on both sides of the divide. The weavers themselves point out ruefully, 'in France nothing has got any better', but in Act 4, when Dreissiger and his associates nervously await the outcome of the weavers' incursion, the timorous establishment figure of the pastor Kittelhaus voices fears that the violence perpetrated so far might indeed be a revolution in the making.

But the ineffectiveness of this challenge to the status quo and the attempt to right the social and economic wrongs caused by rampant capitalism would seem to make the first reference to revolution the more accurate. There is no hope for any positive outcome in political or social terms and the drama ends ambiguously with the death of the deeply religious and pacifist Old Hilse. The Kaiser, however, dismissed Hauptmann's play as 'dangerous socialist propaganda'.[13]

It is not the first time that the themes of religion, revolution, and dissent have been brought into close proximity. In *Dantons Tod* it is the religious questioning of Danton and his friends before they go to the guillotine, which is a sequel to the already palpable failure of a revolution and the overpowering sense of emptiness which this failure leaves. In Büchner, the issue is not presented in terms of a judgement of the living and the dead, but rather as a necessary consequence of a profound disillusionment and the questions it raises about the meaningfulness of human life. The debate might seem to be concluded in favour of atheism, but Danton is the eternal questioner. In *Die Weber* the sense of failure at the end produces a similar emptiness and the futility of Hilse's death can be read as a reflection of the futility of the whole uprising: either way, violence or quietism make no ripples on the relentless progress of historical or economic forces. For Hauptmann, as for Büchner, the human need to protest and express dissent is innate and cannot be muzzled, but it is pitted against such hopeless odds that it will often be defeated. These flickers of dissent, however, and their brutal extermination are in both cases presented with exceptional sympathy and understanding.

From Wedekind to Brecht

The dramas of Frank Wedekind (1864–1918), many of which were written in the 1890s and thus overlapped with naturalism, represent a new stage in the theatre of dissent. They take the debate away from the socio-economic or political arena and into the sphere of what is usually regarded as private mores, sexuality. In *Frühlings Erwachen* (*Spring Awakening*, 1891) and the 'Lulu' plays, *Erdgeist* (*Earth Spirit*, 1895), and *Die Büchse der Pandora* (*Pandora's Box*, 1905), Wedekind engages in a head-on confrontation with prudish and hypocritical attitudes in Wilhelmian Germany, which had become deeply ingrained and institutionalised. In this drama both family and the educational establishment conspire to ignore the needs of a group of adolescents to understand their sexual development, with tragic results. In the 'Lulu' dramas, the issue of sexuality is approached from another angle, namely the impact of an exploitative male-dominated society on a free-thinking child of nature. Lulu is compared in the Prologue to a wild animal, and the metaphor of a circus complete with a lion-tamer, provides a chilling frame of reference to what will follow, as Lulu's systematic exploitation by sugar daddies, pimps, freaks, and underworld figures culminates in her degradation and death in Soho at the hands of Jack the Ripper. Later dramas of Wedekind, for example, *Der Marquis von Keith* (1901), move away from the focus on sexuality to a character who paradoxically combines the aggressive entrepreneurial spirit of capitalism with a false idealism. Confusing messages are conveyed in these works, but Wedekind's subversive radicalism and his new profiling of gender conflicts reveals the general purpose of his dissent. His starting point is to unmask the pretensions and hypocritical attitudes associated with Wilhelmian society. But unlike most of his predecessors he offers no overarching ethos to place in their stead.

One clear perspective can be observed, however. This is Wedekind's break with and hostility towards the naturalist form of drama, which he explicitly thematises in both the programmatic episode of 'the man in the mask' in *Frühlings Erwachen* and the Prologue to *Erdgeist*. His dramas convince most in their exploration of the seedy underworld and the often grotesque characters inhabiting it, both of which he knew well. The dialogue, especially in *Erdgeist*, is terse, stylised, and staccato – it has been compared to the expressionist '*Telegrammstil*' – though sometimes marred with tendentiousness. Their subversive and satirical qualities are features we have found in earlier models of the theatre of dissent, for example Jacob Lenz's satirical diagnoses of specific shortcomings in eighteenth-century society, such as an equally repressive educational system in *Der Hofmeister* or the anti-social activities of the military, which plays havoc with the settled existence of burghers in *Die Soldaten*. In both instances, Lenz and Wedekind express strong dissent against the status quo and the destructive effects of repressive systems on individuals who dare to step out of line.

However, dissent here might better be described as subversion. The familiar motifs of disillusionment and travestied ideals and the laying bare of a gulf between what might and might not be possible find no exact equivalent in Wedekind. His approach of detached cynicism towards a bourgeois social order stands at a transitional point between that of his predecessors and the young Brecht. What links him particularly to Brecht is the ironic view he offers towards his own characters, even when, like Lulu, they are victims. The satirist's stance leaves no scope for compassion.

When examined under the rubric of 'theatre of dissent' the dramas of Bertolt Brecht (1898–1956) exhibit a much greater variety of modes than those of most other dramatists. We will conclude, however, with a consideration solely of the early works – *Baal* (1918, perf. 1923), *Trommeln in der Nacht* (*Drums in the Night*, 1918–20, perf. 1922), and *Im Dickicht der Städte* (*In the Jungle of Cities*, 1922). These early pre-Marxist dramas present a variant on the theme of dissent which is reminiscent of *Sturm und Drang*. In the first two the theme of individualism looms large. In *Baal*, without deigning to convey even a sketchy picture of any recognisable society, Brecht delivers a high-spirited denunciation of all bourgeois values – fidelity, decency, respect for religion etc. Even Karl Moor's indictment of his entire age and the colourful and obscene language Schiller employs, especially in the first version of *Die Räuber*, seem pale by comparison with Baal's torrents of abuse. The sheer range and scope of the invective, together with Baal's total indifference to all human suffering, is clearly a shock tactic perpetrated by a rebellious young writer. But the source of Baal's dissent is a general or existential malaise and it is counteracted by his ability to turn his experience into some highly expressive verse. This cathartic aspect of Baal's poetic mission to some extent distracts the reader or audience from the vaguely focused quarrel he is conducting with his particular age or society, redefining this in terms of '*le malheur d'être poète*' (the misfortune of being a poet), an idea which Brecht had imported from his studies of Rimbaud and Verlaine, themselves supreme representatives of the poet as dissenter.

Trommeln again focuses on a dissenting hero, once more an outsider from society, this time in the role of a returning soldier. It sets up a promising situation for protest as the beneficiaries of the war in the form of money-grabbing capitalists and a materialistic society can find no place for someone who, through years of sacrifice and hardship at the front, cannot easily adjust to the enormous changes that have taken place during his absence. The option of joining the Spartakus uprising – a Communist-inspired insurrection in 1918 in the Newspaper Quarter of Berlin led by the founders of the movement, Rosa Luxemburg and Karl Liebknecht – might have been an appropriate outlet for a dissenting misfit. But Brecht defies expectations by making Kragler swerve away from any such commitment to an idealistic programme. Cynically, the hero sells out to bourgeois materialism.

The theme of dissent is present too in *Dickicht*, a drama once more about the misfits and rejects of society. Garga, a bookish sort, and Shlink, a Malayan timber merchant, a seemingly ill-assorted pair, are mutually attracted to one another, but engage in what seems like a meaningless life and death struggle, involving endless verbal and physical rivalry and combat. The sexual and existential roots of this conflict are finally revealed to be a desperate attempt to find self-transcendence, a stepping beyond the bounds of isolation by which Brecht seems to be offering a critique of extreme individualism.

In these three dramas, dissent manifests itself chiefly through youthful, anarchic heroes in violent disagreement with the prevailing status quo in all its forms. But in *Baal* there is virtually no sense of a social dimension and critique gives way to the wider issue of creativity (and its murky origins). Only in *Trommeln* does Brecht's hero engage (negatively) with a defined social and political milieu, starting with the family, and then opening out on a contrasting dimension of collective action and nascent revolution along communist lines. There is in this work much caricature of the bourgeoisie and the grotesque portraits remind one of George Grosz's savage portrayal of capitalist figures in the early years of the Weimar Republic. But the hero's 'cop out' of the revolution puts paid to his embracing any social or political ideals. In *Dickicht* Brecht raises the modernist theme of the isolation of the individual, and, by implication, the problem of identity, but the working out of this issue, while providing satirical vignettes of a sleazy capitalist society in Chicago, points to an unexpected existential premise on which Brecht would not dwell further.

Conclusion

The examples which I have chosen to illustrate the theatre of dissent represent an identifiable and distinguished, albeit fitful, tradition in the German theatre. Individual examples though widely spaced chronologically, thus manifesting significant differences, can also be seen to share some important common ground. One question which has been raised is whether dissent can be expressed in the absence of any core values against which to set the perceived sources of concern and dissatisfaction. The case of Wedekind, as the most complete satirist among the dramatists considered, is the most marginal. *Sturm und Drang* displayed a remarkable unity of purpose, championing the cause of individual freedom, but in the most distinguished examples it also attempted to define its limits. The nineteenth-century dramatists approached the question of dissent from the other end. In line with contemporary thought they paid much more respect to a value-based social and political order and to the need for firm principles of leadership and direction of the masses than to individual liberties. However, they were still troubled by the apparent absence of any metaphysical under-pinning for such a programme and by a sense that history demonstrates that all action is futile. A purely materialistic conception of human aspiration could not fully satisfy their intellectual and emotional needs. The possibility that human suffering might be endemic or existential in origin opens up the spectre of nihilism, a state of mind with which Büchner occasionally flirts, creating a tension between the dissenting spirit and the disillusioned activist.

Twentieth-century representatives, driven by a post-Nietzschean, exclu-sively life-orientated and modernist outlook on the world, can lay aside the uneasy conscience that is characteristic of such religious questioning and focus instead on a purely secular frame of reference. This, it seems, provides evidence in plenty for the further expression of dissent and for the need for change in the political and social spheres. Marxist materialism has now supplanted transcendental or Christian-derived systems as the reservoir from which dissenting writers throughout the twentieth century will draw a new framework of values.

Thus while the targets of dissent altered continuously, as too did the intellectual, religious, and philosophical frameworks on which such dissent was based, the need to articulate dissent and the perceived existence of inadequacies in the world have remained fairly constant. This has enabled the greatest dramatists to produce theatrical works which are more than ephemeral commentaries on their times. The theatre of dissent during this period has, arguably, claimed for posterity some of the very greatest German dramas and demonstrated the resilience of the drama after the decline of traditional forms of tragedy.

7 The rise of the director, 1850–1939

CHRISTOPHER INNES

Over the twentieth century, the director has come to the fore as the major creative figure in German theatre; indeed, in the subsidised theatres, it can be argued that audiences are drawn to productions more by the name of the director than by the play itself. Indeed a major factor distinguishing German theatre history from the rest of Europe is the dominance of the director. There are historical reasons for this; to a greater extent than elsewhere, already in the early nineteenth century the German stage was a 'director's theatre'. The figure of the director emerged almost a half a century earlier in Germany than in France and Russia and a good century earlier than in either England or America. The effect was to make the German stage more open to aesthetic theory and to the development of new dramatic forms, even though, as we shall see, the official intention of this theatrical hierarchy may have been very different.

In a sense the function of the director is usually thought of as being called into existence only in the latter part of the nineteenth century, through the emergence of naturalism as the dramatic form of the age. This style of drama required objectivity in presentation and individualised characterization and placed significant emphasis on social context, both in environmental and biological terms. On the stage such qualities translated into scenic and psychological detail, creating a demand for something more than a stage-manager. It is no accident that Germany was the first country to stage almost every one of Ibsen's naturalistic plays outside Scandinavia, as in Germany a close equivalent of the artistic director had already been established at the top of the theatrical hierarchy long before Ibsen inaugurated the naturalistic movement with *A Doll's House* in 1879 (produced at Munich in 1880). This was in sharp distinction to the traditional actor-manager, who was still dominating stage production in other western countries, and in England would continue to do so until the early twentieth century. As the director was primarily an interpretative artist who controlled the theatrical event from offstage, the values this figure brought to performance were not only co-ordination of increasingly complex lighting and staging mechanisms around the actor, but conceptual and aesthetic unity as well, something that had already been called for by the greatest German theatre artist of the mid-nineteenth century, Richard Wagner. Further, it is quite notable that out of the three overarching stylistic movements of theatrical modernism initiated in the first half of the twentieth century – symbolism, expressionism, and epic theatre – two are specifically identified with Germany. While the first two of these forms may have had a primarily literary origin in the writings of Maeterlinck and Kaiser, the development of appropriate modes of staging was the prerequisite for their effectiveness. Again, the existence of a system of directors in Germany gave the theatre its capacity for innovation and greater experimental diversity in the repertoire. It is largely due to the official nature of this system that German theatre became publicly funded in the nineteenth century, quite unlike the situation elsewhere. This funding, which continued despite the intrinsically subversive nature of these theatrical movements, certainly made experimental staging more possible and allowed for the longer rehearsal times needed for the successful performance of any new type of drama.

All this can be seen, at least in part, as the result of Germany remaining a decentralised conglomeration of small independent states through much of the nineteenth century. The consequent predominance of competing court theatres led to the stage being financially subsidised and overseen by its patrons, the local prince or, in larger urban centres, the city council, who appointed their own representative to the theatre's administration to safeguard taste as well as morality. Such a set-up did not prevent several court theatres from being bankrupted by lavish spectacles, though the relative freedom from economic pressures had a distinctive result in terms of productions. Over the course of the twentieth century, the rest of Western theatre was to adopt the German concept of a director, but German theatre is still more subsidised than in other countries and is distinguished by the widespread dominance of directors.

Early instances of the director

Even in the eighteenth century, the organisation of German theatre was different from England or France. Until at least the 1770s German-speaking players were loosely gathered into wandering troupes, staging harlequinades, *Haupt- und Staatsaktionen*, improvised farces and musical entertainments. Signs of artistic development began to appear in the mid-eighteenth century. Johann Christoph Gottsched, disgusted with the crude level of stage performance by the strolling players, whom he saw as a source of moral pollution, developed strictly neoclassical rules for performing and writing drama. He patronised Caroline Neuber's acting company and wrote plays on Roman subjects for her to perform, but Neuber's record was one of failure when it came to changing the tone of drama. Even when she mounted the performance in 1737 in which the figure of Harlequin was driven physically from the stage, the public remained more attracted to the traditional farces and the current fashion for musical shows. Shortly after his association with Neuber ended, Gottsched set out his ideas in a weighty book: *Deutsche Schaubühne nach den Regeln und Exempeln der Alten* (*The German Stage Following the Rules and Examples of the Ancients*, 1740–5). As the title indicates, Gottsched assumed experience to be universal, nature static, and historical changes irrelevant, which ruled out any inclusion of current events in drama. Insofar as his rigid neoclassicism, which even heightened the French theories from which they were borrowed, was adopted, it made drama not only moralistic but politically safe. So while the so-called Leipzig style, associated with Neuber and Gottsched, helped to reform the stage by introducing aesthetic principles, it also helped to neuter German theatre as a political force.

This development initiated by Gottsched and taken further by such figures as Ekhof and Schröder, was continued by Goethe. When he was appointed to run the Weimar Court Theatre in 1791, it was the style of acting that most concerned him. Based on the premise that theatrical performances should not simply copy nature but unite it with the ideal and reflect hierarchical social concepts, Goethe's influential *Regeln für Schauspieler* (Rules for Actors) are designed to encourage beautiful poses and smooth movements, with 'the chest always in full view of the spectator'. But the Rules also clearly suggest that the kind of staging Goethe developed was highly stylised, since his positioning of actors followed principles of social hierarchy and privilege in the acting area. For example, 'the actor who stands on the left', he wrote, 'should be careful not to approach too closely to the one on the right [because] the person of higher social scale (women, elders, noblemen) always occupies the right side'. At the same time no attempt was made to create an illusionist stage picture, since actors were required always to show awareness of their audience and speak directly to them, while 'the stage is to be regarded as a figureless tableau for which the actor supplies the figure'. The other extreme of achieving pictorial effect was realised by Iffland at the Berlin Royal Theatre from 1796, where he staged a series of visually spectacular productions that were widely praised as extraordinary and set a standard to be emulated by subsequent German directors.

The *Intendant*

Both Goethe and Iffland were court officials with the title of *Intendant*. In the nineteenth century, it was these intendants, in effect superintendents or public bureaucrats, figures roughly equivalent to the modern artistic director, who determined what was put on the stage in contrast to the more humble and commercial managers who emerged in other European countries. After 1815, Intendants were instituted in almost all public theatres, but mainly as a means of censorship; as a result they have been blamed for the widespread decline of German theatre in the 1830s and 1840s.[1] Nevertheless, this unique feature of German theatre can be seen in the long run to have had an extremely positive effect on the development of the art of performance and upon the wider evolution of European theatre. Whatever may have been sacrificed in terms of limitations imposed on playwrights by the controlling function of these officials was made up for by their encouraging new developments in stagecraft.

Generally the Intendant also served as *Regisseur*, a loan word from French that includes the concepts of both stage director and stage manager, with all the connotations of conducting rehearsals and guiding actors. As they were part of the bureaucratic hierarchy, many intendants/regisseurs came from outside the theatre, and, once appointed, stayed backstage. They could be poets and novelists, like Heinrich Laube, or critics like Otto Brahm, or librarians like Franz von Dingelstedt. Sometimes they came from well-known theatrical families, as did Eduard Devrient (1801–77), the intendant of the Karlsruhe Court Theatre in the 1840s, though even he made his initial mark as a historian. Like Iffland, actors could also become Intendants, though when they did they often gave up performing altogether, something Max Reinhardt did shortly after taking control of the Deutsches Theater in 1905. The most influential Intendant of the nineteenth century was the Duke of Saxe-Meiningen, a ruling prince with his own court. All this meant that in Germany theatre was performed and rehearsed very differently than it was under the actor-managers of the English theatre, from John Philip Kemble at the beginning of the nineteenth century to the theatrical knights at the turn of the twentieth – Frank Benson, Herbert Beerbohm-Tree, and Henry Irving. Notoriously these figures organised every aspect of a performance around themselves, as for instance with Irving's *Faust*, where he made Mephistopheles (his own part) the leading role upon whom all eyes in the audience would be focused. Apart from the actor-director Gustaf Gründgens (1899–1963), who was an exception to the general rule that an actor gave up performing once appointed as an intendant, this kind of self-aggrandising production tended to be the exception in Germany. By contrast Heinrich Laube's aim was not only to reform the drama – one of his frequent comments to playwrights, who submitted their work to the Burgtheater, was that the play 'doesn't seem suited for presentation on this stage'[2] – but also to bring new standards to performance. He focused on ensemble, in which every role, however minor, was rehearsed with equal care – the exact opposite of the star system that produced the *monstres sacrés* of the English and French stages.

Laube, as intendant of the Vienna Burgtheater, was able to build on the ensemble approach established by Josef Schreyvogel, but where the performance style encouraged by Schreyvogel had been romantic, as epitomised in the acting of Sophie Schröder, Laube, as we have seen, developed a realistic style of non-rhetorical acting in which actors were trained to modulate their voices and moderate their gestures, creating a more naturalistic mode of expression as well as a more unified impression. This emotional restraint was both helped and to some extent enforced by the intimacy of the theatre itself, enclosed in the palace of the Hofburg. As the only German-speaking theatre at the time that could lay claim to being a national theatre of any kind, the Burgtheater had an influence far beyond the smallness of its stage. The company was noted for its understated elegance, even if to a modern eye their gestures and facial expressions would seem exaggerated and their vocal delivery declamatory. The Burgtheater style became widely imitated, spread by actors such as Adolf von Sonnenthal, who trained under Laube and was known for the gracefulness of his bearing into the early years of the twentieth century.

It is worth noting that when Laube left Vienna in 1867, eventually to take over the town theatre at Leipzig, it would still be eleven years before Zola published his influential essay *Naturalism in the Theatre*, thirteen before the new naturalistic drama burst onto the European stage with Ibsen's *A Doll's House*, and nineteen before Antoine founded the *Théâtre Libre* in Paris. Nevertheless, there is a good case for seeing Laube as a founding figure of naturalism in the theatre. Hermann Hettner's book of 'aesthetic explorations,' *Das moderne Drama* (1852), which called for psychological conflict to be made the basis of drama, was to have a great influence on Ibsen, and it was based primarily on the experience of observing performances at Laube's Burgtheater.

The Meininger

It was a short step, conceptually as well as chronologically, from the tonal unity achieved by Laube to the Meininger, who came to epitomise both ensemble acting and pictorial illusionism. Indeed their work overlapped, as Laube returned to Vienna in 1871 to found his own theatre, which was still running when the Meininger performed in Vienna in 1878. Duke Georg had been inspired by the work of Charles Kean, who, while in many ways a typical actor-manager, had established new standards for realistic stage production in the 1850s, so that when he inherited the small state of Saxe-Meiningen and took over its court theatre in 1866, he set out to emulate the meticulously researched and detailed accuracy that the English actor-manager had brought to his staging of historical drama. Just as Kean had consulted eminent architectural historians in designing his sets, documenting historical sources for each production with 30- and 40-page pamphlets, so the Duke created an archaeologically authentic classical Rome that was apparently accurate for Shakespeare's *Julius Caesar* in 1874, even moving Caesar's assassination from Shakespeare's symbolically significant setting of the Capitol to its actual historic location at the Curia of Pompey.[3] As a skilful painter, the Duke is reputed to have designed the scenes, props, and costumes for his early stagings at the Meiningen Court Theatre himself, but even after he hired the Scenic Atelier of Max and Gotthold Brückner in 1872, he continued to exercise influence on the highly dramatic settings they created for the series of major productions that made the reputation of the Meiningen Company. But the Duke also pursued the ideal of completely unified harmony between the various elements of stage performance, one of his so-called 'Meiningen principles' being that scenery must never overwhelm the rest of the work.

At the time, the visual effects in the Meiningen stagings were seen as being extremely realistic, even though folds on the backdrops might be visible. To modern eyes, however, the sharp perspectives and strong colours look strikingly romantic[4] (see fig. 11). But this impression of pictorial illusion seems due largely to the way in which crowd scenes were organised. The Duke also insisted that in any production a star, however famous, had to be ready to play a minor role if required. In fact this was a fairly rare

THE ILLUSTRATED LONDON NEWS.

REGISTERED AT THE GENERAL POST-OFFICE FOR TRANSMISSION ABROAD.

No. 2194.—VOL. LXXVIII.   SATURDAY, JUNE 4, 1881.   TWO WHOLE SHEETS | SIXPENCE. By Post, 6½d.

SCENE FROM "JULIUS CÆSAR," AS PERFORMED AT DRURY LANE THEATRE BY THE SAXE-MEININGEN COURT COMPANY.—SEE PAGE 56.

11 *Julius Caesar*, directed by Georg II of Saxe-Meiningen and Ludwig Chronegk, 1874. The Forum Scene. Marc Anthony declaiming over Caesar's dead body. Drawing from the Illustrated London News.

occurrence, but, being widely reported, it established the concept of a true ensemble. In addition, the financial resources of a whole dukedom were behind the theatre, allowing for an extensive period of rehearsal, which was practically unknown in European theatre. This allowed each of the figures in a crowd to be developed into individualised characters, while rehearsals – all conducted in full costume and with complete sets – enabled the performers to become so accustomed to their dramatic environment that they could 'live' it. The impression of actuality was accentuated by the identifying traits and personalised gestures for large groups of people, in which the Meiningen productions specialised. A further directorial innovation contributed to the illusion of realism. In the conventional staging of the time, groups tended to be posed in tight knots of people or spread across the acting area parallel to the proscenium; however, the Meiningen crowd scenes were orchestrated in a three-dimensional space extending diagonally from the audience or along multiple axes and off into the wings. The greater intricacy of this orchestration was not only closer to lived experience, but offered an aesthetic complexity that reinforced the harmony of other visual elements.

The Meiningen repertoire was composed of Shakespearean and romantic historical drama, with locations ranging from the classical Athens of *A Midsummer Night's Dream* or the pastoral Bohemia of *The Winter's Tale*, through medieval German Rhineland castles and the besieged city of Pilsen for *Die Räuber* and *Wallenstein*, the medieval churches of *Das Käthchen von Heilbronn*, and the archaic Jerusalem inhabited by Otto Ludwig's *Die Makkabäer*. Scenic details did not differ greatly from those used by Charles Kean. However, unlike Kean, Duke Georg combined pictorial accuracy with the realistic acting and blocking; in so doing, he completely superseded his English model. The human figure in movement became the primary visual unit. When Henry Irving saw the Meininger in London in 1881, his style of performance immediately changed. Irving's rehearsals for the Lyceum *Much Ado* of 1882 became meticulous in their attention to precise timing and positioning, clearly showing the Meiningen influence.[5] Indeed, the Duke, in cooperation with his third wife, Helene von Heldburg, a former actress known as Ellen Franz (d.1923), who served as his dramaturge and trained the actors, and the director Ludwig Chronegk (1837–1891), who served as tour manager, set the standards for stage realism across Europe. On their tours, the Meininger were seen by, among other notable figures of the theatre, Konstantin Stanislavsky, who was so impressed that he trained with the company for a year and adopted the same archaeological accuracy in staging historical drama. The Meininger also deeply influenced André Antoine, who spent time with the company while touring one of his early Théâtre Libre productions in Brussels. The Meininger also staged Ibsen's early heroic tragedy, *The Pretenders*, which was well suited to their historical realism, and after seeing their production in 1876, Ibsen's own stage practice changed so as to incorporate authentic detail in the settings of the sequence of plays initiated by *Pillars of Society* in 1877.

Arguably, without the Meiningen example there would have been little in the way of naturalistic stagecraft in Europe as a whole: the widespread change they introduced is neatly measured by the difference between the Stockholm premières of *A Doll's House* and *An Enemy of the People*. For *A Doll's House*, the Royal Theatre allowed just two blocking rehearsals, eight general rehearsals and one dress-rehearsal (with the inevitable recourse to acting clichés), but for *An Enemy of the People* at the same theatre just four years later, there were 32 rehearsals, twelve of which, echoing Meiningen practice, were devoted solely to the crowd scene of Act 4. Duke Georg learned from Ibsen too; he directed the original German production of *Ghosts* in 1886, and in correspondence with the playwright he dealt with the minutiae of wallpaper ('coloured, dark') and furnishings ('style of the First Empire; however … consistently darker') to recreate the exact ambience of a country house in Western Norway.[6]

Wagner

Details such as these clearly indicate that for Ibsen, as for Duke Georg, the focus was on emotional evocation rather than simply factual authenticity. So, despite the apparent contrast between realism and Wagnerian opera, it should not be surprising that there are close connections between Meiningen and Bayreuth; in fact Wagner and the Duke knew each other well and saw each other's productions. Even before Georg II came to the throne, there had been a series of *Tannhäuser* performances from 1855 to 1866 in the Meiningen Court Theatre, and the Meininger later staged *Das Rheingold*. When Wagner staged the premiere of the *Ring* in 1876, almost half of his Festival Orchestra came from Meiningen, and when the Wagner enthusiast Hans von Bülow was appointed conductor of the Meiningen court orchestra in 1880, he applied 'Meiningen principles' to musical performance, introducing individual rehearsals and meticulous work on scores in the search for a homogeneous musical style that produced a unique precision in presentation. Wagner also used the Coburg stage designers Gotthold and Max Brückner at Bayreuth so his stagings looked similar to those of the Meininger. Indeed Wagner's concept of a *Gesamtkunstwerk* was precisely what Duke Georg pursued so successfully in terms of action, scene, and lighting.

Arguably Wagner had just as much to do with the emerging prominence of the director in German theatre as did the intendant system. In the mid-nineteenth century when the mechanical hand of Eugène Scribe closed over the theatre in France and little that was original was being done on the English stage, Wagner's work presented a challenge and an opportunity unique to Germany. The first of his operas to be produced outside German-speaking countries during this period, the 1860 Paris *Tannhäuser*, was a spectacular failure, but from the first performance of *Rienzi* in 1842 in Dresden to the massive four-part cycle of the *Ring* with which he triumphantly opened the Bayreuth Festival Theatre in 1876, Wagner became the driving force for renewal in German theatre with regard to staging. The mythic material and heroic treatment of his librettos, the musical 'leitmotifs' that lent a dramatic complexity to his music dramas, and the sheer scale upon which the dramas were conceived required a unified presentation that could only be provided by an offstage director. In a very real sense Wagner's work could only be theatrically realised by a production method such as that created by the intendant system. Almost all the main intendants of the time had some connection with Wagner, from Laube to Dingelstedt who had been dismissed from the Munich Court Theatre for the expense of his elaborate *Tannhäuser* production. Indeed Dingelstedt introduced Wagner to the Vienna Opera before succeeding Laube at the Burgtheater, where he gained a greater reputation for creating a unified total art work on the stage than Wagner himself.

Almost as important in setting the context for a new style of production was Wagner's design for his Festival Theatre in Bayreuth. The undivided raked seating focused spectator attention solely on a strictly perspective stage instead of on other members of the audience, as in the standard boxes and tier configuration of the Italian opera house. It introduced a democratic symbolism into theatre that was to become the model for much twentieth-century theatre design and changed the relationship of each spectator to the scenic picture, since (as Wagner insisted), 'As soon as he has taken his seat [the spectator] truly finds himself in a "Theatron", a room designed for nothing else than for looking. Between him and the visible picture nothing definite or tangible exists: instead the architectonic device of the double proscenium gives to the stage the remoteness of a dream.'[7] These new architectural qualities helped to enforce the new standards of unity and verisimilitude in stage presentation but the visual impression was anything but appropriate to the mythic material of Wagner's operas. On the assumption that stage illusion should be so complete that an audience might lose itself in the performance, the settings for his gods and heroes were all too naturalistic with trees painted with every leaf on cut cloths or flat backdrops. The Ride of the Valkyries was staged with horses in mid-sky and a rolling 'swimming apparatus' together with clouds of steam provided the setting for the Rhinemaidens. With nothing left to the imagination, there was no room for the spiritual reality expressed in the music. Wagner's elaborate pictorial romanticism was to remain a standard part of German stagecraft, reappearing for instance in the forest (complete with live rabbits) of Reinhardt's famous *Midsummer Night's Dream* production, which remained in his repertoire from 1905 in Berlin right up to the Hollywood film of 1935. But the most significant offshoot from Wagner in terms of directing was Adolphe Appia, whose whole concept of theatre was based on his designs for Wagner's operas and on a repudiation of Wagner's principles of staging.

Appia and symbolist staging and design

Along with the English Edward Gordon Craig, the Swiss Adolphe Appia (1862–1928) marks the emergence of a completely new type of director: the theoretician with only a tenuous connection to practical stage perform-ance, but who serves as a visionary catalyst, promoting ideals of directorial approach and theatrical presentation in the abstract. Beginning in the 1890s, Appia produced theoretical writings, scenarios, and designs for the *Ring*, *Tristan und Isolde*, *Die Meistersinger*, and *Parsifal*, though he was only able to direct one of the operas over thirty years later, *Tristan*, which opened to a mixed reception at La Scala Milan in 1923. His designs for *Das Rheingold* and *Die Walküre* were used by the Swiss director Oscar Wälterlin in Basel in 1924 and 1925, but in productions that caused such vociferous opposition that plans to stage the rest of the *Ring* were abruptly cancelled; shortly after this Appia died. Indeed over his whole lifetime he had directed only three other productions and his designs were only used for the staging of two non-Wagnerian pieces. However his path-breaking publications, including *Musique et la mise en scène* (*Music and Production*, 1892; publ. German, 1899), *La Mise en scène du drame Wagnérien* (*Staging Wagnerian Drama*, 1895) and *L'Oeuvre d'art vivant* (*The Living Work of Art*, 1921), spread his ideas widely through the theatre world. These also described his unrealised scenarios and recorded his actual productions, while international theatre expositions in London, Amsterdam, Zurich, Magdeburg, and other German cities showcased his designs. Appia's stage was radically non-illusionistic; suggestive combinations of solid objects and empty space, light and shadow, replaced the painted scene-cloths of the Brückner brothers. If Appia's stage represented a real place at all, it did so only in the broadest of strokes, in conscious opposition to the detailed visual realism of Meiningen and Bayreuth. Appia's conceptual settings created an abstract but specifically theatrical environment from elements integral to the stage itself in a concrete realisation of symbolist principles.[8] However, his 'musical' dramaturgy of light had a wide international influence, being taken up particularly in the work of the French director Jacques Copeau or in Nikolai Okhlopkov's 'Realistic Theatre' in Russia during the 1930s. Appia's staging also had an immediate impact in Germany, through the flights of steps he introduced for his production of Gluck's opera *Orpheus and Eurydice* at Hellerau in 1913. This became the signature stage-form for expressionist directors like Leopold Jessner, who had attended the Hellerau performance, in the 1920s.

Even though Wagner's widow Cosima refused to allow any changes in the way Wagner's operas had been staged by the composer himself, Appia's concepts were gradually adopted piecemeal in Bayreuth in the 1930s although their importance was only acknowledged when Wieland Wagner (1917–66) took control in 1951, with the 'New Bayreuth Style' defined in the Souvenir Programme for 1955 as specifically deriving from Appia: 'a performance space fashioned out of the spirit of the music itself, and a sense of three-dimensionality ... the symbolic power of colour and of light, rhythmically coordinated with space'. [9]

Appia bridges the divide between the nineteenth-century German theatre and its modernist twentieth-century form in a way that points resolutely to the stagecraft of today. A line also runs from Duke Georg of Saxe-Meiningen to Otto Brahm, while Dingelstedt, with his 1864 production of the cycle of Shakespeare's history plays at the Weimar Court Theatre and spectacular stagings of German classics at the Burgtheater, foreshadows Max Reinhardt.

Naturalism

When the Théâtre Libre, an avant-garde naturalist company from Paris, directed by André Antoine, performed Tolstoi's *Power of Darkness* on tour in Berlin in February 1888, one of the people most impressed was Otto Brahm (1856–1912). Copying Antoine's model, in 1889 he opened the Freie Bühne, a producing organisation run on a subscription basis with neither its own stage nor acting company, which hired leading actors and rented available theatres. Dedicated to mounting the new naturalistic drama that he had championed as a reviewer for the *Vossische Zeitung* and *Die Nation*, Brahm opened with Ibsen's *Ghosts*. He produced the same international repertoire as Antoine – Tolstoy, Strindberg, Zola – but was also the champion of German naturalism. His second production was of Hauptmann's *Vor Sonnenaufgang* and, from then on, first at the Freie Bühne then at the Deutsches Theater, a large classically styled stage he took over in 1894, he staged the premières of all Hauptman's plays, gaining a reputation for psychologically naturalistic characterisation and realistically detailed domestic settings. Gordon Craig wryly commented:

> when lights have to imitate the hour of 5 p.m. and get down to 5.45 in an autumn evening, Brahm can absolutely wipe [Beerbohm-] Tree off the face of the clock – when the Stranger enters in *The Lady from the Sea*, you can bet it is not a spirit entering but . . . an ordinary man – you can even tell what class [rail] ticket he has in his pocket.[10]

Clearly Brahm's uncompromising naturalism had its limits, especially when applied to Ibsen's or Hauptmann's later symbolic plays.

Reinhardt

This was hardly the case with the theatrical entrepreneur Max Reinhardt (1873–1943), who had begun his career as a young actor under Brahm in 1894, and became his successor in 1905. Even though he made his reputation playing in the naturalistic works of Ibsen and Hauptmann, and the play he first chose to direct was Ibsen's *Love's Comedy* (in 1900), Reinhardt was by far the most eclectic of twentieth-century directors in his choice of styles. He controlled a theatrical empire unprecedented in its breadth, starting with the Deutsches Theater, which he took over from Brahm in 1905, to which he added a smaller stage, the Kammerspiele, specifically to house Strindberg's 'chamber plays' and other experimental works. It was Reinhardt who first championed Wedekind, using him as a poster-boy to promote Expressionism, much as Brahm had done with Hauptmann for Naturalism. In 1906, while defending his path-breaking staging of Wedekind's tragedy on the taboo subject of teenage sexuality, *Frühlings Erwachen (Spring Awakening)*, from police censorship, Reinhardt claimed 'the urgent artistic duty' that was to become characteristic of the whole European avant-garde movement, 'of performing a work of art which leaves the beaten track and suggests a new form of theatre'.[11] In Reinhardt's early repertoire, expressionism, characterised by the grotesque objectification of Wedekind's *Erdgeist* (*Earth Spirit*, 1901) and the quasi-religious subjectivity of Strindberg's dream plays, went side by side with the extreme naturalism of Maxim Gorki's *The Lower Depths* or Henri Becque's *The Crows* (both 1903), while the symbolism of Maeterlinck's *Pelleas and Melisande* (1903) paralleled the poetic excess of Wilde's *Salome* (1902 and 1903). But above all Reinhardt was a consummate showman, most clearly at home directing romantic mass spectacles – exotic orientalist (*Sumurûn*, 1911), classical Greek (*Oedipus Rex* and the *Oresteia*, 1910, 1911), medieval Gothic (*The Miracle*, 1913) – mounted in circus buildings or sports stadiums in Berlin and other European cities. For example, he transformed Olympia in London, a space designed for housing complete industrial exhibitions and Worlds Fairs, into a Gothic cathedral for *The Miracle*, in a space that was over 400 feet long and 250 feet wide, with a roof 100 feet above the floor and a circular stained-glass window almost twice the size of the rose window in Cologne, the city where the play was set.

The almost wordless script by Karl Vollmoeller (1878–1948) for *The Miracle* lent itself to grand processions, of capering peasants and marching knights in fantastically exaggerated medieval clothing, of dancing children, and sweeping files of nuns. It was literally theatre of the masses, prophetically anticipating in its medieval grotesque, the era of ideologically driven mass movements that was to be ushered in by the First World War, which broke over Europe just one year later. The whole production was on a vast scale, deploying over 2,000 actors and a choir of 500, plus a full orchestra with grand organ. There were also elaborately illusionistic stage-effects, rivalling the most extravagant of nineteenth-century *coups de théâtre*, such as the burning of the royal palace when the debauched Nun dances before the King, while streaming ribbons worn by masquers appeared to catch fire from the torches, and steam and air vented from below the acting area blew yellow and scarlet streamers high into the air; or there was the miracle itself when the statue of the Virgin Mary changed from stone to a real woman, who descended to comfort and redeem her devotees. But Reinhardt's production also offered a form of the *Gesamtkunstwerk* that Wagner and Appia had called for. There was harmony between the colours of the costumes and the lighting, which was dominated by rose and orange tints, and a progressive sequence of 'colour keys' was devised for each scene, so that greens and blues changed in the following scene to blues and violets, then to purples and vermilions, and so on.

The huge popular success of these spectacular productions led Reinhardt to conceive of the 'Theatre of Five Thousand', a figurative term for his idea of a mass theatre, which he then tried to realise in actuality in such spaces as the Circus Schumann, which he turned into the Grosses Schauspielhaus, in Berlin and the Ausstellungshalle in Munich; none of them actually seated five thousand. The sheer size of the auditorium imposed a specific style of directing. As his dramaturge described it, 'the vast space demands the simplest of forms, and strong, big, severe lines ... At the most, scenic decoration can only be frame, not function [and] lighting becomes the real source of decoration, its single aim to bring the important into the light and leave the unimportant in the shadow' so that the spectator became 'part of the whole, rapidly absorbed in the action, a member of the chorus.'[12] This fluid, plastic use of light, building on principles first suggested by Appia, became one of Reinhardt's most influential contributions to the German stage.

The Grosses Schauspielhaus lent itself to Classical Greek tragedy. Reinhardt opened this huge theatre with iconic productions of *Oedipus Rex* and *The Oresteia*. However, the highpoint of his mass spectacle came in the form of outdoor Festival theatre, a unique celebration of German culture initiated by the 1920 presentation of *Jedermann*, Hofmannsthal's modern version of the English morality play *Everyman*, in the Cathedral Square at Salzburg. This became an annual event, which to this day is a centrepiece of the Salzburg Festival. For Reinhardt, this 'drama for the people' was a revival of ritual drama for the modern age, with angels emerging onto the acting platform direct from the cathedral, while the audience was involved in its archetypal action through Everyman coming forward from among the spectators at the summoning. The actors' movements and gestures were patterned on the angularity of medieval woodcuts, and this apparent simplicity was combined with a sophisticated

12 *Jedermann* by Hugo von Hoffmansthal, Salzburg, 1920 or later, directed by Max Reinhardt. Death holds Everyman (Alexander Moissi) in his grip.

choreography that built emotional response through orchestrating comic human moments against the severe incantations of judgement, modulating from joyful celebration and song through a sudden perception of mortality to the stark entry of Death (see fig. 12). But the most effective part of this spectacle was the way the production extended beyond the stage. The entire city was turned into a stage, with criers calling from the Cathedral towers and distant church spires to the castle on its high cliff above the square. Reinhardt even enlisted nature, as the performance was timed to use natural light in a way that seemed almost miraculous; it started just before sunset and the rising moon made a ghostly effect. Flaming torches were lit as Faith strode out of the Cathedral and in the hands of the chorus they provided the main illumination for the action as darkness fell. As Hofmannsthal described it, 'One of these criers had been placed in the highest tower of a medieval castle, built far above the city, and his voice sounded, weird and ghostly, about five seconds after the others, just as the first rays of the rising moon fell cold and strange from the high heavens on the hearts of the audience.'[13] This communal drama, seeking to merge huge numbers of spectators into an emotional unity, was in many ways an artistic foreshadowing of the mass political movements that came to dominate then destabilise Germany in the

1920s and 30s. Although Reinhardt was protected to some extent by his international fame, on coming to power in 1933 the Nazis forced him to 'donate' all his German theatres to 'the German people', finally driving him into American exile in 1937. While Reinhardt's mass productions had democratic aims, his eclecticism makes him the least ideological of all the twentieth-century German directors.

Expressionism

By contrast, in the aftermath of the First World War, there were directors who quite consciously aligned their work with political movements, which they sought to express and even influence. This ideologically motivated theatre, which rejected bourgeois tradition in all its forms, went hand-in-hand with the attempt completely to renew the material and style of theatrical production, making the Weimar period one of the most experimental eras in the whole of European theatre. Away from the conventional stage, the Berlin Dadaists mounted interactive performance pieces in a public lavatory and disrupted parliamentary debates with 'guerrilla actions' in the Reichstag, while at the Bauhaus, Oskar Schlemmer (1888–1943) abstracted the human figure to geometric shapes, exploring movement in spatial relationships through architectonic ballets. But the most significant of these movements, Expressionism, emerged from the mainstream theatre as a style fostered by Reinhardt with his productions of Wedekind's *Frühlings Erwachen* (1906) and *Die Büchse der Pandora* (1918), and particularly Strindberg's later plays, from *The Dance of Death* (1912) or *The Father* (1915) to *The Ghost Sonata* (1916) and *A Dream Play* (1921). Indeed through Reinhardt's championing, Strindberg came to have a major effect on German theatre as more than 1000 performances of 24 Strindberg plays were given in 64 cities just between 1913 and 1915; and it was Reinhardt too who championed the later proto-expressionist poetic and religious dramas of Hauptmann such as *Rose Bernd* (1917) and *Und Pippa Tanzt* (*Pippa Dances*, 1919). In a clear demonstration of his political neutrality, Reinhardt also introduced the early grotesque expressionism of Reinhard Sorge's *Der Bettler* (*The Beggar*, 1917), as well as directing the first play in Georg Kaiser's anti-war and anti-capitalist *Gas Trilogy* (1918) and his expressionist classic *Von Morgens bis Mitternachts* (*From Dawn to Midnight*, 1919). He also directed Fritz von Unruh's *Ein Geschlecht* (*One Family*, 1918), *Die Maschinenstürmer* (*The Machine Wreckers*, 1922) by the imprisoned ex-president of the short-lived Bavarian Communist Republic, Ernst Toller, and plays of the leading expressionist painter, Oskar Kokoschka, such as *Job* (1919).

The term 'Expressionism' was first applied to theatre by the playwright Walter Hasenclever in a series of essays, published in *Die Schaubühne* in 1916, under the title of 'The Theatre of Tomorrow', which called for 'a spiritual stage'.[14] For these subjective and violent dramas of the subconscious, Reinhardt developed a technique of spotlight and gauze for dreamlike effects that facilitated scene changes without breaking the action, which it presented as 'stream of consciousness'. In addition, Reinhardt's influence can be seen in one of the most radical groups of the 1920s, *Das junge Deutschland*, since it was Reinhardt's dramaturge at the time, Heinz Herald, who promoted this movement.

But while directors such as Leopold Jessner (1878–1945), Jürgen Fehling (1885–1968), and the Reinhardt-trained Erich Engel (1891–1966) were heavily influenced by Reinhardt, they rejected his eclecticism. Jessner, who had begun as a naturalistic director and became intendant of the Berlin State Theatre in 1919, worked toward the creation of a plastic, three-dimensional acting space and introduced serried rows of steps onto the stage in a way that became so codified that they gained their own technical term: the Jessner-steps. Ruling out any scenery or stage-properties and imposing stylised movement, the Jessner-steps eventually filled the whole visual area, as in his staging of Shakespeare's *Richard III* (1920), a production which also marked the high point of expressionist acting with Fritz Kortner's performance in the title role. The expressionist style of staging also encouraged what came to be known as *Dramaturgie der Scheinwerfer* (spotlight-dramaturgy, corresponding to the free association of images in expressionist writing), which provided a context for the expressionist actor. Expressionist dialogue tended toward a condensed and staccato telegraph-ese, delivered as was the characteristically expressionist '*Schrei*', in a way designed to reflect the uncontrolled emotional depths of the subconscious, so as to appeal directly to the same pre-rational level in the spectators' psyches. The typical expressionist play becomes concentrated to the point where 'pure' emotion becomes so overwhelming that it breaks through dramatic structure.

Jürgen Fehling was brought to the Volksbühne in Berlin by Jessner, where between 1918 and 1922 he promoted anti-illusionistic theatre, while requiring highly physical performances from his actors in such strikingly expressionistic productions as Toller's *Masse Mensch* (*Masses and Man*, 1921). Later at the Berlin Staatstheater, he directed grotesque interpretations of Barlach's poetic religious plays, *Die Sündflut* (*The Flood*, 1925) and *Der blaue*

Boll (*The Blue Boll*, 1930). The continuing influence of the expressionist style can be seen in the career of Fritz Kortner (1892–1970), who even in the 1920s counted as a co-director for many of the productions in which he acted, particularly when working with Erich Engel. After his return from American exile at the end of the Second World War, Kortner became one of the directors at the Munich Kammerspiele, where he staged his own play *Donauwellen* (*Currents of the Danube*, 1949). However, expressionism also developed into very different theatrical forms that had far more influence on the whole of Western theatre.

Erich Engel, who made his name under Reinhardt as one of the leading expressionist directors, produced Brecht's early experiment in grotesque expressionism, *Im Dickicht der Städte* (*In the Jungle of Cities*, 1924), for the Kammerspiele at Reinhardt's Deutsches Theater. Here is a link between expressionism and epic theatre. Indeed Engel made his reputation as the director of the first production of Brecht's classic, *Die Dreigroschenoper* (*The Threepenny Opera*), in 1928 and became completely associated with his drama, putting into practice Brecht's developing ideas about 'objective' acting and non-illusionistic staging – and although from 1930 onwards he devoted himself mainly to films, he also subsequently served as Brecht's artistic director for the *Berliner Ensemble*. But far more important an influence on Brecht was Erwin Piscator (1893–1966), who originated the term 'political theatre' and was the first to define an 'epic' form of drama.[15]

Piscator can be grouped with other politically radical directors in the 1920s, such as Heinz Hilpert (1890–1967), who directed almost all the premières of Carl Zuckmayer's naturalistic satires and took over the Volksbühne in 1929, and Karlheinz Martin (1886–1948), founder of the very short-lived Proletarian Theatre, which lasted for a single performance. Martin made an immediate impact on arriving in Berlin with his production of Toller's archetypal expressionist drama *Die Wandlung* (*Transfiguration*, 1919) and then turned to film, becoming one of the most influential early German film directors with his 1920 classic adaptation of Kaiser's *Von Morgens bis Mitternachts* (*From Morn to Midnight*), starring Ernst Deutsch. He also collaborated with Piscator on experiments in integrating filmed scenes with live action on the stage, as with *Der letzte Kaiser* (*The Last Kaiser*) on the Piscator-Bühne in 1928. Martin continued to mount highly political productions in the Berlin theatre until he was banned from the stage by the Nazis in 1936, after which he turned exclusively to film work.

Epic Theatre

In strong and explicit contrast to the intense subjectivity of the expression-ists, the techniques of epic theatre were consciously developed to 'disillu-sion' audiences. Indeed Brecht later came to compare his *Mutter Courage und ihre Kinder* (*Mother Courage and her Children*, first produced in Zurich in 1941, then restaged in a revised version by Brecht himself in Berlin, 1949) to a withdrawal course for emotional drug-addicts. One of the most fully developed examples of epic theatre was his play *Mann ist Mann* (*Man is Man*), first conceived as a radio play, before being staged by Jacob Geis (1890–1972) in 1926, then by Engel in 1928, and in the most colourful and unrealistic production by Brecht himself in 1931. Using monstrous figures on stilts, discontinuous characterisation, fragmentary settings and harshly bright lighting, Brecht's production epitomised the qualities of the epic theatre that he had outlined in his pathbreaking essay, '*Das moderne Theater ist das epische Theater*' (The modern theatre is the epic theatre, 1930).[16] Engel's 1928 staging of *The Threepenny Opera* and Brecht's 1931 production of *Mann ist Mann* introduced most of the main elements of Brecht's epic dramaturgy: the half-curtain, which revealed the lights and stage machinery, use of projections instead of scenery, placards for commentary, the use of the grotesque and artifice, and the practice in rehearsal of having the actors speak their lines in the third-person, so that in performance they would present a critical attitude to the characters they were portraying. Brecht's concept of epic theatre has been ill-served by the English-language trans-lation of his central term *Verfremdung* as 'alienation' – with its implications of distancing and exclusion. For Brecht *Verfremdung* was more a political tool than an aesthetic one, a way of presenting content so as to challenge habitual preconceptions of the spectators, instead of a style of performance. So in his 'teaching play', *Die Ausnahme und die Regel* (*The Exception and the Rule*, first produced in Palestine, 1938) the opening chorus demands:

> *Betrachtet genau das Verhalten dieser Leute*
> *Findet es befremdend, wenn auch nicht fremd.*
> *Unerklärlich, wenn auch gewöhnlich.*
> *Unverständlich, wenn auch die Regel.*
> *Selbst die kleinste Handlung, scheinbar einfach*
> *Betrachtet mit Mißtrauen! Untersucht, ob es nötig ist*
> *Besonders das Übliche!*
> *Wir bitten euch ausdrücklich, findet*

Das immerfort Vorkommende nicht natürlich!
Denn nichts werde natürlich genannt
In solcher Zeit blutiger Erwirrung
Verordneter Unordnung, planmäßigere Willkür
Entmenschter Menscheit, damit nichts
Unveränderlich gelte.
(Observe the conduct of these people closely / Find it estranging
even if not very strange / Hard to explain even if it is the custom /
Hard to understand even if it is the rule / Observe the smallest
action, seeming simple / With mistrust ... / We particularly ask
you – / When a thing continually occurs – / Not on that account to
find it natural / Let nothing be called natural / In an age of bloody
confusion / Ordered disorder, planned caprice / And dehumanised
humanity, lest all things / Be held unalterable!) [17]

In a very real sense Brecht's concept of *Verfremdung* is the expression of his
belief that in a 'scientific age' like the twentieth century, where science has
the capacity 'to change nature to such an extent as to make the world almost
habitable, man can no longer [be presented] as victim'. So the first play he
directed, his *Mann ist Mann*, is a demonstration that character is not fixed but
malleable, and that it is possible to change anyone, such as the timid Galy
Gay, into a 'Human Fighting Machine' or the sadistic sergeant 'Bloody Five'
into a tearful sentimentalist, while in the last essay he wrote, Brecht was still
asserting 'the present-day world can only be described to present-day
people if it is described as capable of transformation'. As he states, epic
theatre is one possible method of achieving this. 'And you may perhaps
agree ... that the present-day world can do with transforming'.[18]

Misunderstandings about epic theatre are due to the way Brecht, as
Piscator once commented, was misled by logic, something that can be well
illustrated by the list that sets up epic theatre versus dramatic theatre in a
dualist opposition in his 'Notes to the Opera *Aufstieg und Fall der Stadt
Mahagonny*' (1930). Yet, as he repeated in several essays, for Brecht the
theatre's job was to entertain – *unterhalten* – and he emphasised that to
entertain was an active verb, and its second half meant 'to hold'. So his
aim was to grip the spectators more powerfully by engaging their whole
personality, their critical sense as well as their capacity to feel.[19] Indeed,
Brecht points out that spectators in his epic theatre should experience the
same range of emotions as those in the dramatic theatre, the only difference

being in the cause of response. They should say, 'That's great art: nothing obvious in it – I laugh when they [the characters] weep, I weep when they laugh', whereas one who feels traditional empathy will say: 'it all seems the most obvious thing in the world – I weep when they weep, I laugh when they laugh.'[20] Although politically the emotion he clearly wished to provoke was outrage at economic exploitation, social injustice, and oppression, he by no means avoided arousing empathy with his characters; and in Brecht's own productions, theatre was characterised by an electrifying vitality. So, in *Mutter Courage und ihre Kinder* the full title underlines the multiple focus of the production, even though in performance itself the balance was overwhelmed by sheer power of the actress Helene Weigel, who became identified with the title role. Brecht's production was notable for Eilif's soldier's dance, composed of breath-taking leaps, which took him high above the stage with his sword held in both hands over his head, and for Helene Weigel's 'silent scream' at the death of her other son Schweizerkas (Swiss Cheese), which communicated an unbearable intensity of grief beyond even cries or weeping. Particularly notable was the shooting of the dumb Kattrin as she stubbornly goes on beating her drum to save the children in the sleeping town of Halle by waking the defenders, in the face of increasingly violent threats from the invading soldiers, one of the most tear-jerkingly melodramatic sacrificial deaths in all modern theatre. What Brecht wanted to evoke was the same partisan enthusiasm, personal commitment and emotional involvement as displayed by crowds at a soccer match.[21] Yet, in contrast to the empty and inflated rhetorical emotions of the German stage during the Third Reich, we are never allowed to forget the reality of performance. Paradoxically, as on Shakespeare's stage, such an overt break in illusion can challenge the audience into a deeper imaginative involvement than naturalism does. As Brecht wrote:

> It's more important nowadays for the set to tell the spectator he's in a theatre than to tell him he's in, say, [the classical Greek setting of] Aulis. The theatre must acquire *qua* theatre the same fascinating reality as a sporting arena during a boxing match. The best thing is to show the machinery, the ropes and the flies.
>
> If the set represents a town it must look like a town that has been built to last precisely two hours. One must conjure up the reality of time.
>
> . . . The materials of the set must be visible . . . there mustn't be any faking. [22]

This emphasis on theatricality as a form of realism also aligns Brecht's epic theatre with the '*Neue Sachlichkeit*' ('new objectivity') movement, which was equally epic in its thrust, though emphasising fact-based functionalism. Promoted by a characteristically named theatre journal *Der Scheinwerfer* (*The Spotlight*), the theatrical application of *Neue Sachlichkeit* formed part of the wider artistic movement that included Le Corbusier's machine-architecture and Hindemith's utilitarian music. In stage direction, *Neue Sachlichkeit* was primarily initiated by Erwin Piscator.

Erwin Piscator (1893–1966), undoubtedly the most significant of these ideological and experimental directors, who wrote the highly influential book *Das politische Theater* (*The Political Theatre*, 1929), also brought together most of the main lines of development in early twentieth-century German theatre. Like Karlheinz Martin, in 1920 he founded a 'Proletarian Theatre', which presented agitprop pieces in workers' halls across Berlin, and in 1924 he moved to the Volksbühne where he dedicated himself to bringing out the social content of the new naturalistic drama. In 1926 Piscator mounted a historical revue at Reinhardt's Grosses Schauspielhaus, *Trotz Alledem!* (*Despite Everything*), about the murdered revolutionaries Karl Liebknecht and Rosa Luxemburg. Although Piscator would return to the extreme simplicity and directness of agitprop between 1929 and 1931 as the Great Depression destroyed the Weimar economy and the political situation became increasingly dire, for five years at the Volksbühne and, after 1927, at his own theatre, the Piscator-Bühne, he completely changed the nature of drama, experimenting with the integration of live actors and filmed sequences and with mechanising the stage to create a specifically modern theatrical image that reflected the two controlling forces in contemporary society: industrialisation and the media. It was a form of 'Total Theatre' (Piscator's term) very different from Wagner's *Gesamtkunstwerk* or Reinhardt's harmonies of colour and light. The subject of practically all Piscator's productions was political revolution, which gave thematic justification for his revolutionising of the theatre. This combination set the tone of German theatre for the most vital period of the whole twentieth century. Brecht worked with Piscator on several of his productions; for instance, they collaborated on the script for the Piscator-Bühne *Abenteuer des braven Soldaten Schwejk* (*Adventures of the Good Soldier Schweik*, 1928). As a leading figure in the *Neue Sachlichkeit* movement, Piscator had already risen to the challenge with his 1928 documentary/living newspaper staging of *Konjunktur* (*Business Cycle*, subtitled '*Petroleum*') just six months earlier.

SASHA STONE

13 *Rasputin, the Romanoffs, the War and the People who Arose against Them* after Alexei Tolstoy, Berlin 1927, Piscator-Stage in the Theatre on Nollendorf Square, devised and directed by Erwin Piscator, designed by Traugott Müller.

Trotz Alledem! was the first of the productions in which Piscator introduced documentary film into the *mise-en-scène*. But most characteristic of his new documentary theatre was the Piscator-Bühne staging of *Rasputin* in 1927. By turning Alexei Tolstoy's melodramatic script from a tragedy of individuals into a massive reconstruction of events in the crucial years from 1915, when the Tsar had taken personal control of the Russian military campaign, to the Russian Revolution in 1917, Piscator mounted a mechanised multi-media montage. The whole stage was occupied by an immense metallic half-globe, 49 feet in diameter, mounted on a revolve and divided into twelve internal acting areas, with a top section that could be lifted as a whole, or tilted, and with hinged sections of varying sizes in the curving shell that opened to reveal a scene being acted within (see fig. 13). Swivelling back and forth like a tank-turret, this dome served as a powerful symbol both for the mechanised horrors of the First World War and for the world the emperors of Germany, Austria, and Russia were fighting over. The image of this 'world' was technological, with its interior lattice of girders clearly visible in the openings, its extreme functional flexibility and its obvious seams echoing industrial manufacture. Painted in non-reflective silver, the hemisphere also served as a movie screen, across which documentary film was shown. In addition there was an eight-foot wide screen running the full height of the proscenium at one side of the stage, on which a 'calendar' of dates and events were projected as if on a continuously unrolling band; quotations from speeches or letters also appeared. This construction and the side-screen together offered multiple viewpoints, commenting on each other and providing shifting perspectives; while the filmed material extended the acted scenes into the widest social context, the size and dominance of its images effectively trivialised the individual characters played by the live actors. Basically the stage portrayed figures whose positions had made their names and faces familiar, in anecdotal and personal terms, while the film showed the faceless masses in action.

So in contrast to a staged scene that featured the Tsar in his headquarters alternately issuing inspiring exhortations to the troops and flirting with a nurse, the film showed battlefields covered with mangled Russian corpses and the side screen displayed an extract from a letter to the Tsarina: 'The life I lead at the head of my army is healthy and has an invigorating effect.' The multiple ironies made explicit commentary unnecessary, with the stark contrasts between scene, screen, and citation presenting the Tsar's egoism as blind and obscene. Film represented reality versus the cushioned life of the aristocratic characters displayed in the staged artificial scenes, as when the Tsarina histrionically ridicules reports of the communist revolution, while on the surface of the metallic globe directly above her head appeared a gigantic filmed reproduction of the shooting of the whole imperial family. By using a combination of movie-screen with black and white gauzes the live actors seemed to emerge out of the film to play their scenes and were dominated by the film image. This was also the case in the most iconographic moment in the production, where the figure of the Tsar appeared to be tiny against the towering shadow of the mad monk Rasputin that loomed above him with hands outstretched. The factual material and authentic nature of the presentation, with actors made up to resemble historical figures, induced the ex-Kaiser to claim defamation of character; he won a legal injunction, which forced Piscator to substitute a reading of extracts from the court judgment in place of an actor delivering the speeches of Kaiser Wilhelm. This was, if anything, still more to the point than the original, as it underlined the factual nature of the dramatic material.

Piscator and Brecht both liked to characterise their style as 'epic,' by which they meant scientific, rational, and objective, or documentary, or overtly theatrical, but the artist George Grosz (1893–1959), who had collaborated with both of them, commented on the 'Dionysian' effect of their work. The participatory nature of *Rasputin* was as intense as any of Reinhardt's mass spectacles, with a note in the programme emphasising that the audience were 'not merely spectators, but participants in the great drama of the collapse of imperialism . . . they form an undivided unity, one piece of world history: the theatregoer of 1927 and – *Rasputin, The Romanoffs, The War, and The People Who Rose Up Against Them*'. [23] Every performance ended with the audience, caught up in the sweep of events depicted, spontaneously rising to join in with the massed actors on stage when they sang 'The Internationale'.

The apparent contradictions, the enthusiasm, and the conscious modernity all represent the director's theatre of the first half of the twentieth century. But it was Brecht's misleadingly 'cool' theatre that had the most lasting impact, determining the style of American, and particularly British directors through the 1950s and 1960s; and even though Brecht is primarily known as a poet and playwright – possibly the only modern playwright to have his own company – he had a significant directing career with the *Berliner Ensemble* from 1949 right up to his death in 1956. As a director, his work was almost exclusively devoted to productions of his own plays, as well as to developing and demonstrating his epic principles. Indeed, although *Mann ist Mann* is the only play Brecht himself directed in the Weimar years, he was closely involved in the productions of his own plays from the beginning. But it was not until 1948 with his version of *Antigone* in Switzerland, or subsequently at his own theatre on the Schiffbauerdamm, that Brecht established his own presence as a director.

Outside Berlin

From the beginning of the twentieth century on, Berlin increasingly became a magnet for all the most exciting and innovative German theatre-artists and playwrights, and thus became the source and home for almost all of the most influential theatre movements. Yet German theatre remained far more regionally based than in France or England. An illustration of this is the career of Saladin Schmitt (1883–1951). From his first position, as an actor and dramaturge in the Stadttheater at Elberfeld, Schmitt became artistic director at the Freiburg Stadttheater, and, apart from a short stint at the

Deutsches Theater during the First World War, his career was entirely in regional theatres outside Berlin. He first directed in Brussels in 1916, then in Antwerp, and returned to Germany in 1918, where he was appointed the first intendant of the newly built Stadttheater in Bochum, a position he combined with the post of intendant at the Duisberg Opera from 1921 to 1934. He succeeded in making the mining district of Bochum a well-known theatre centre by initiating the whole idea of a 'Festwoche' and mounting a series of highly popular week-long summer theatre festivals devoted to the works of Shakespeare and the German classics, with the plays coherently linked together in a cycle. At the first of these annual festivals, in 1927, all ten history plays of Shakespeare were given in a single cycle, while, a decade later, the Shakespeare Week in 1937 presented all the Roman plays. In between came festivals devoted to Goethe (1928), Schiller (1934), and Kleist (1936). These continued into the beginning of the Second World War, with a Hebbel Week in 1939 and a Grabbe Week in 1941. During his tenure there, which lasted throughout the war, and ended in 1949, Schmitt forged what came to be known as the Bochum-style with his spectacular and decorative productions.

8 Naturalism, expressionism and Brecht: Drama in dialogue with modernity, 1890–1960

DAVID BARNETT

In an age in which the aesthetics of verisimilitude dominate television and cinema, it is perhaps difficult today to appreciate just how radical naturalist drama was in the late nineteenth century. Against a background of melodrama with its emphasis on sensationalism, and classicism, which stressed the ideal rather than reality, naturalism shocked its audiences with its unadorned depictions of human life and its confrontations with topical themes. Although a recently unified and industrially ambitious Germany lagged behind France and Scandinavia in terms of producing cutting-edge naturalist playwrights, the benefits of nationhood gave a boost to the repertoires of its growing numbers of theatres.

Naturalism

Naturalism sought to offer recognisable representations of everyday life yet this was something effectively unheard of in the recorded history of the stage. The rise of naturalism had much to do with seismic movements in society and the subjugation of nature to the principles of scientific inquiry. Developments in physics and mathematics drove the technology of the Industrial Revolution, which reorganised European society by creating new social formations. The increasing dominance of the bourgeoisie not only led to an accretion of vast wealth by a minority but also fostered an interest in a society that was becoming ever more complex, stimulating numerous fields of inquiry. The scientific method yielded palpable results in engineering, psychology, and economics, and a degree of certainty started to accompany human endeavour in these fields, while those affected by the Industrial Revolution and urbanisation were confronted with upheaval in their everyday lives. Technological progress suggested that great achievements could also be made in the field of artistic representation. The invention of photography in 1839 offered a remarkable degree of likeness to which fine art had been striving for centuries. Theatre, however, needed to find its own forms and subject matters. The then considerable influence of positivism was also an important factor affecting the problems of representing 'real life': the doctrine maintained that knowledge could only be derived from observation and experiment and not from metaphysical speculation. The scientific orthodoxies of the day treated human identity as a product of heredity and environment, and this determinism was an integral part of the worldview championed by the naturalists. Émile Zola (1840–1902) viewed literature as experimental in the sense that it became a laboratory in which various complex human compounds were mixed together to see how they would react with each other. A similar understanding was to be found in August Strindberg (1849–1912) and his 'Preface to *Miss Julie*' (1888). The presentation of character and action was given the stamp of scientific objectivity, as if it were real, witnessed by an impartial observer. German naturalists were also fascinated by the work of Georg Büchner (1813–37), especially his *Woyzeck* (1836–7), which offered a gritty realism hitherto unknown in the theatre. The play, which initiated the exploration of the lower classes and the use of slang, dialect, and expletives, was not performed until 1913, when naturalism had licensed the lower classes and the industrial proletariat as stageworthy.

Germany's great naturalist dramatist was Gerhard Hauptmann (1862–1946). An admirer of Büchner and Ibsen (1828–1906), he turned away from initial plans to write poetic dramas to explore subject matter closer to home, which could be realised through the new aesthetics of the naturalist stage. He excelled in presenting human beings with painstaking accuracy and without judging them, as befitted a scientist in the laboratory of determinism, and his stage directions were packed with detail and precision. *Vor Sonnenaufgang* (*Before Sunrise*, 1889) is a useful example of his early work in that it shows a *nouveau riche* peasant family going to ruin through greed and sensuality. The location of the play sets up one of Ibsen's favourite devices: the exposure of the moral morass behind the new prosperity of the industrial society. The action takes place in a village in rural Silesia, that is, on Hauptmann's native soil, which was then a province of the Second German Empire and is now a part of Poland. The village has struck it rich; coal deposits have been found under the fields, and thus the backwater is becoming something of a boom town. The sudden economic change allows the playwright to explore new moralities and social readjustments against a backdrop of economic expansion. The drama is initiated by the arrival of the outsider figure Alfred Loth, a social reformer, who is embarking on a fact-finding study, having recently graduated as an economist. His eye settles on Helene, an educated member of the Krause family whose farmland also contains coal seams. Over the course of the play, the Krauses' lifestyle is revealed as debauched and the root cause is a rampant alcoholism that runs through the whole family in true inherited fashion. Loth, a firm believer in eugenics, abandons the farming community, unable to consider marriage with a possibly afflicted woman, and Helene kills herself.

The play signals several of Hauptmann's stylistic motifs: firm divisions into acts which help to ratchet up the tension; dialect used to add veracity; an educated or enlightened person who struggles in vain to alter society; and a suicide or death concludes the events. *Vor Sonnenaufgang*, first given on 20 October 1889, caused something of a scandal, not only in its unembellished treatment of its provocative material but also in an off-stage birth that takes place in the final act. While Berlin's Lessing Theater, which very much promoted naturalism, had perhaps wisely decided not to have the actress scream out as the labour continued, a doctor in the audience had brought along his forceps and waved them around as a mark of his outrage. Such was the reception of the new aesthetics and subject matter among certain quarters that Hauptmann often met with disapproval and censorship.

Yet one should not forget the dramatist's sense of theatre and his belief that he was pioneering revolutionary new forms. His most famous play *De Waber* – the original dialect title of *Die Weber* (*The Weavers*, 1892) – dramatises the Silesian Weavers' uprising of 1844. The Kaiser was appalled by its treatment of social discontent and cancelled his box, but Lenin got his sister to translate and distribute it illegally in Tsarist Russia. Hauptmann's great dramaturgical innovation here was the use of a collective protagonist, the weavers, rather than an individual. The suggestion of a powerful set of forces beyond the characters shifted the audience's focus to broader socio-political issues: the hero of the piece is the nobility of labour put upon by the advances of technology and the pressures of the market. Despite the shift from the individual to the collective, the playwright retains a five-act scheme and engineers a human tragedy in the fifth act when a weaver who did not support the uprising is killed by a stray bullet. This event takes place shortly after another weaver comments on how action like this is never seen in the theatre. This self-congratulatory line gives a knowing nod to the audience and underlines the fact that they are watching something radical.

Hauptmann went on to write a great many plays, with only some of them repeating the success of the early years. He continued with socially realistic works, tried his hand at comedy, most successfully in *Der Biberpelz* (*The Beaver-skin Coat*, 1893), and experimented with allegory and neo-romanticism, for instance with *Die versunkene Glocke* (*The Sunken Bell*, 1896), which ironically became his most popular play of the period. Around the same time, a young Viennese doctor was starting to make a name for himself as a writer. While his work drew some inspiration from the naturalists and their willingness to explore taboo subject matter, he was not averse to writing ironically and taking up more stylised forms in his plays. Arthur Schnitzler (1862–1931) gained success with the *Anatol* cycle of playlets (1888–91). In these the well-to-do philanderer Anatol comes into contact with a range of women, all exhibiting different 'feminine' qualities while Anatol remains very much the same – behind his wordly façade a bored, distracted man. The plays are not naturalistic in the sense of Hauptmann's detail or detachment but they do offer a lively evocation of *fin-de-siècle* Vienna. Anatol himself is presented with an ambivalence equal to Hauptmann's in that his complexity is never reduced to simple categories of good or bad, and his contradictions are offered to the audience without moralising.

Schnitzler took the theme of sexual relationships further with his most famous play, *Reigen* (*The Round Dance*, 1896–7). The play is a series of ten scenes in which a male and a female character are seen pre- and post-coitus. A series of dashes across the page denotes the act itself. The ten scenes begin with the encounter between the Whore and the Soldier. The Soldier then moves on to the Chambermaid in the second scene, and she is together with the Young Man in the third. The pattern continues and the chain of sexual relations reaches the top of the social pile when the Actress meets the Count in the ninth scene. However, the tenth scene returns the action to the first one: the Count eyes the Whore. A simple dramaturgical idea based on a differentiated repetition of the action opens a broader set of issues that go far beyond the characters themselves. The circularity of the dramaturgy asks questions of a hierarchised society and the sexual mores that underlie it. The play is remarkable in the way that it contrasts well-observed naturalist dialogue with a series of generic character types, suggesting that the language itself is not individualised but rather a complex social code, predicated upon sex. The pairs of characters look to established linguistic formulations as a way of seducing each other and as a way of escaping their partners afterwards. The provocative themes meant that the play was first publicly performed in Germany at the Kleines Schauspielhaus, Berlin in

1920, a full seventeen years after publication, and when, bolstered by this, Vienna's Volkstheater produced it a year later, *Reigen* became something of a national scandal.

Schnitzler wrote other important works, such as *Das weite Land* (*The Vast Domain*, 1910) and *Professor Bernhardi* (1912). The former is a tragic-comedy that deepens the analysis of an Anatol-type character by exploring a marriage in which both the husband and the wife are having affairs. The focus, however, is very much on the husband, Friedrich, and his responses to his wife's infidelity rather than a more naturalist exploration of the circumstance of infidelity in itself. *Bernhardi* is a comedy based on an incident surrounding the eponymous Jewish doctor and a Catholic priest, whom he prevents from administering the last rites to allow a dying woman an unencumbered death. The play is a satirical and ironic exposé of anti-Semitic attitudes in Austrian society, although its subject matter (which also involves the ultimate dismissal of Bernhardi from his position) would seem to make the play a dark comedy at the very least.

While Schnitzler questioned the doctrines of naturalism indirectly, another playwright was altogether more recalcitrant. Frank Wedekind (1864–1918) saw the theatre as a place of artifice and considered this to be its great strength. His early masterpiece *Frühlings Erwachen* (*Spring Awakening*, 1890–1) similarly dealt with the theme of sex but this time focused on puberty and the interaction between teenage children and their parents. The play includes two masturbation scenes, an eroticised beating, a homosexual kiss and a rape. A teenage suicide and the death of the female lead, Wendla, from a botched abortion take place off stage. Wedekind certainly owed something to naturalism's interest in the seamier side of society and its willingness to depict all aspects of life but this is effectively where the connection ends. He uses a mixture of registers, including the poetic and the satirical; the action is episodic, including scenes which contribute nothing to the plot itself; the parents and teachers are grotesques; and the conclusion is fantastical: in a graveyard the suicide victim returns with his head under his arm and tries to convince the male lead, Melchior, to join him, until a mysterious Masked Man intervenes and takes Melchior off into the wide world. Despite the modulated language and the grand themes, the play takes a concrete social setting as its starting point. The children live in a provincial town, away from the vitality of the new cities. They (nearly) all come to grief because of the discrepancy between their parents' and teachers' outdated moral codes and their own sexual inquisitiveness. While the play was written well over a century ago, it continues to enjoy revivals due to the freshness of its generational conflicts, even if its ability to shock has waned somewhat in the decades since the sexual revolution.

Wedekind pursued his interest in sex in the *Lulu* plays, *Erdgeist* and *Die Büchse der Pandora* (*Earth Spirit* and *Pandora's Box*, 1895 and 1901 respectively). The central figure, Lulu, is a picture of rapacious sexuality, unbound by morality but also a slave to her drives rather than a calculating *femme fatale*. The plays plot her successive relationships and these were prefaced and provocatively contextualised by a prologue set in a circus ring. In it, the Animal Tamer considers the interchangeability of the humans and animals, and sets the scene for a dramatic examination of the control people have over themselves and others. Death haunts both plays, and the finale of *Büchse* sees Lulu murdered at the hands of Jack the Ripper. Wedekind also produced a remarkable comedy that is still performed today, *Der Marquis von Keith* (*The Marquis of Keith*, 1900). The play follows a bogus aristocrat and his scheme to build a vast entertainment emporium in Munich, which is nothing more than a confidence trick to line his pockets. When he is found out, he contemplates suicide before finding a way out. His and the play's curtain line 'life is full of ups and downs' reflects not only his own pragmatic *modus operandi* but also that of the society around him. He is neither worse nor better than his duped investors, as all are keen to turn a quick buck without considering broader ethical implications.

Expressionism

Wedekind is often fêted as a harbinger of expressionism in that his characters are too big and too vital for the more subdued cadences of naturalism. His poetic language is not interested in verisimilitude but the power of art, unfettered by superficial questions of slavish mimesis. Another proto-expressionist was Oskar Kokoschka (1886–1980), who is known more as a painter than a playwright. However, his *Mörder, Hoffnung der Frauen* (*Murderer, Hope of Women*, 1907) marks him as a more uncompromising dramatist than Wedekind. The play is barely five pages long and features short splutters of dialogue. Kokoschka, like Wedekind and Schnitzler, is investigating the relationship between male and female, but he chooses a radically pared down form to dramatise the confrontation between the sexes. The figures involved are all distillations: they are the Man, the Woman, and the choruses of Men and Women. Kokoschka also seeks to wrench the action away from a recognisable moment in history by setting it against a faux medieval-cum-primitivist backdrop, devoid of modern technology or mores. As with Wedekind, the central issue is that of human as animal, but *Mörder* strips away any vestige of realism. The primal conflict between the sexes takes on ritualistic features and gender stereotypes are upheld. The Woman manages to imprison the Man, having stabbed him, but ultimately she cannot hold him and he wreaks his revenge on all the cast. Eroticism and violence permeate a play which uses an abstract dramaturgy, devoid of psychology or character, to present its central conflict.

The earliest forerunner to what would become expressionism was the aforementioned unfinished play by Büchner, *Woyzeck*. While its language and setting had impressed the naturalists, it was the fragmentary form, struggling to keep up with the play's protagonist that appealed to the expressionists. German expressionism was not, however, a 'school' as such, and consequently its various manifestations present sometimes contradictory features. In short, like any 'ism', expressionism does not offer a checklist of boxes to tick in terms of either form or content. It can certainly be viewed as a reaction to and a rejection of naturalism: it refused to remain on the surface and was dissatisfied with the mere reproduction of outward appearances, and this led to a turn inwards. The expression of an experience and its distortion on the journey from within to without served as a stimulus to a range of dramatists of differing political and moral hues. Expressionism also marked a rupture with the naturalists' faith in the ability of art to represent reality in an unproblematic way. The expressionists found themselves in the thick of an intellectual revolution that systematically eliminated the certainties of the nineteenth century. This was an age of relativity, not only one sparked by Einstein in the scientific community, but across several fields of study. Karl Marx (1818–83) had posited a social relativity by asserting that consciousness did not precede being but that the opposite was true. In this sense, nobody was 'innately' noble, chivalrous, criminal or lazy; it was society that created the conditions for these qualities (often linked to social class by more conservative opinion) to emerge in individuals. Friedrich Nietzsche (1844–1900) undermined notions of absolute morality, maintaining that each age brought forth its own moral codex that matched the amount of truth its generation was able to tolerate. Sigmund Freud (1856–1939) undermined a belief in the rationality of human beings with the discovery of the unconscious mind. Men and women could no longer be depended on to act in accordance with anything but a mixture of conscious and unconscious faculties, thus making a singular definition of the human subject untenable. If one adds to this a suspicion of language which was famously manifested in Hugo von Hofmannsthal's *Ein Brief* (*A Letter*, 1902, also known as the *Chandos-Brief*) and flourished in the linguistics of Ferdinand de Saussure (1857–1913), one finds a Europe in which the apparent stability and certainty of the nineteenth century have been replaced by doubt and fluidity in the twentieth as these ideas began to permeate society.

These factors were aggravated by the rapid industrial and military expansion of Germany post-unification (1871). Swift urbanisation affected hundreds of thousands of people. Individuated rural identities became blurred as citizens found themselves among masses on streets and in factories. Prussian bureaucracy tried to tie people together by structuring society in delineated hierarchies in which social position was defined by rank within one's field of employment. Yet in a country in which rapacious capital was recreating communities in its own image, swathes of the populace sought collective identities through political affiliation. Parties developed for all hues of the social spectrum, and clashed, sometimes violently, in response to a range of crises before and after the Great War. Amid this social upheaval, expressionist dramatists were writing plays.

The undisputed masters of the genre were Georg Kaiser (1878–1945) and Ernst Toller (1893–1939). While their styles were quite divergent they shared a fondness for an angular language of violent outbursts and a thematic interest in what became known as the *Neuer Mensch* ('new human being'). The playwrights' interaction with their time was also crucial. Kaiser confronted the moral problems of an age in which traditional values were giving way to ones produced by an increasingly industrialised and anonymous society; Toller, a committed socialist, sought a reconciliation between the needs of the collective and those of the individual in a period of rapid social change.

Kaiser wrote prolifically, yet he is best known for his work of the second decade of the twentieth century and it is these plays which are still performed today. One of his first great successes was *Die Bürger von Calais* (*The Burghers of Calais*, 1913) which retells a famous incident from the Hundred Years' War in which Edward III of England offered to spare the city if six of its citizens agree to their own execution. The tension of the play arises from the clash between the military plans of Calais' commander, Duguesclins, and Eustache de Saint-Pierre, who volunteers himself as the first of the six. Over time another six citizens come forward pushing their number to seven. Come the day of the exchange, Eustache is missing and it is thought that his high-minded stance was little more than hypocritical bravado. However, Eustache's father enters with a coffin in which lies his dead son, who has killed himself to serve as a selfless example to the others. As it happens, a son is born to the English King that very morning and he spares the city, knowing nothing of the sacrifice that has taken place.

While the play broadly observes the unities, its language signals a rejection of everyday speech in favour of a clipped form, usually referred to as *Telegrammstil* (telegram style). Ornament and extraneous words cannot communicate the intensity of feelings or ideas, and while some of the speeches are indeed long, the formulation is always staccato, as if only the essentials are being ejected from the body. *Telegrammstil* is intimately linked to the utopian vision of the *Neuer Mensch* as incarnated in Eustache. Everyday language is simply not able to express the new morality and so it falls to a different form of syntax and diction to inspire change in the individual.

The individual is also at the centre of *Von Morgens bis Mitternachts* (*From Morn till Midnight*, 1912). This play helped to establish the very idea of an expressionist drama and stands as a testament to the imaginative resources Kaiser deployed to challenge the orthodoxies of naturalism. The play evokes contemporary society in a state of moral ruin, crying out for redemption. It uses both *Telegrammstil* and a generalised sense of place and character to wrench the action away from the particularity of naturalism. The play revolves around a nameless Cashier whose life is one of drudgery: at work in a bank, he is little more than an automaton, whilst his home life is a series of meaningless rituals. However, the sight of a wealthy lady's naked wrist causes him to rob the bank and use his ill-gotten fortune to buy as many new experiences as possible. He visits a bicycle marathon and a plush ballroom but both arenas fail to deliver. The fevered atmosphere of the sporting arena and the perpetual deferment of gratification in the *chambre séparée* offer an experiential theatre for the spectator in which garish images are conjured up by the ecstatic Cashier. The play concludes in a Salvation Army hall in which the Cashier hears confessional testimonies that remind him of his vain quest for fulfilment in a materialistic society, and finally he performs a speech of contrition and atonement. Yet when he strews his remaining money among the crowd, a riot ensues and, disgusted by what he finds around him, the Cashier takes his own life. As well as the distorted images of the modern city to which the Cashier flees, there is also a remarkable dialogue set in a snowy field in which the Cashier meets Death, whose grinning skull returns as an image in a chandelier just before the finale. The play is a metaphysical musing on the moral values of life in a society drained of spirituality, forever in the shadow of its own collapse. It also pioneers the form known as the *Stationendrama* (station drama, echoing the stations of the cross) in which the protagonist goes from scene to scene on a journey leading to a final, agonised passion. *Von Morgens* is one of the most ambitious and successful of all the expressionist dramas.

Kaiser expanded his focus in *Gas I* and *II* (1917 and 1918 respectively) with the introduction of massed crowd scenes and a foray into utopian socialist politics. Set in an enormous gas works, *Gas I* deals with a catastrophe when the gas, previously thought to be safe, explodes. The owner, the Billionaire's Son, plans to close down the plant and build an idyllic workers' housing-estate instead, but the Engineer can find nothing wrong with the formula of the gas and insists on a reconstruction of the plant. However, the gas has a life of its own and defies human control. Kaiser offers a bleak reflection on the nature of technology in industrial society. The typologised figures, present in Kaiser's earlier work as well, expand into crowds of workers who are part of the Son's profit-sharing company. Eventually they reject the Son's plans and opt for the Engineer with his promise of profit. Society has become faceless, although its pains and sufferings are brought into focus by representative speakers. At the end of the play, the Son takes his own life rather than suffer the rebuilding of the works, yet a ray of hope exists when his pregnant Sister says that she will give birth to the *Neuer Mensch*. This Grandson appears in *Gas II* as the Billionaire Worker, in a factory manufacturing poison gas for a great war taking place outside. Again, there is a clash between the humanism of the Worker and the technocratic zeal of the Chief Engineer. Unlike *Gas I*, the play ends in an apocalyptic disaster as the gas is released, killing everyone.

Kaiser was not, however, uniformly pessimistic and his *Hölle Weg Erde* (*Hell Path Earth*, 1919), as its title suggests, maps a more positive route from servitude to the establishment of the *Neuer Mensch*. The theme is varied in *Nebeneinander* (*Side by Side*, 1923) when the hero dies in an ecstatic triumph, elated in the knowledge that he has been able to help another suffering person. Kaiser continued to write prolifically until his death and perhaps the greatest work of his later years was *Das Floß der Medusa* (*The Raft of the Medusa*, 1942). The play charts the fortunes of thirteen child survivors in a lifeboat after their ship has been torpedoed. Again the focus is on human attempts to deal with extreme conditions and offers a range of possible routes that the children, representatives of a wider society, might take. While Kaiser dabbled with politics, in the form of the Son's co-operative gas works, though broadly preferring an examination of the dramatic conflicts engendered by human beings and a modern society, Ernst Toller had a more focused understanding of socialism and its principles. His drama was influenced by his patriotic willingness to join up in 1914, followed by a nervous breakdown in 1916 and his conversion to pacifism, and his active participation in the Munich Soviet in 1918, when the radical left briefly took power before being brutally suppressed.

Toller's first major play, *Die Wandlung* (*The Transformation*, 1919), is a *Stationendrama* in which the hero, Friedrich, makes his way through a grotesque and misery-laden series of scenes on his way to a recognition that hope is to be found in collective action. This belief in the brotherhood of man is also to be found in Kaiser, yet Toller proposes an organised political response to the human degradation of contemporary society. Toller also employs shadowy dream scenes in which figures such as talking skeletons and nameless mountaineers offer perspectives on the central action. Like Kaiser, the language is stylised and frequent use is made of free verse to articulate the rush of feelings coursing through the characters.

Toller's first real hit, *Masse-Mensch* (*Masses and Man*, 1921), follows the middle-class Sonja Irene L., a named character whose surname remains elusive, and The Nameless One, who shares her revolutionary aims but not her pacifist means. He advocates violence, and when the revolution fails and Sonja is to be shot, she delivers a final manifesto on the need to respect the individual while satisfying the needs of the collective. The play again features dream scenes that widen the play's ambit away from the central plot, and an ecstatic language that is always struggling to find expression for ideas that seek to transcend the play's conflicts.

Toller then turned his attentions to more concrete social issues and gradually tempered the more extreme elements of his expressionist style. His *Die Maschinenstürmer* (*The Machine Wreckers*, 1922) is something of an historical drama, set in the England of the early nineteenth century. *Der deutsche Hinkemann* (*Hinkemann*, or *Browbeaten the German*, 1923) lost its German specificity when published as *Hinkemann* in 1924. The play nonetheless caused a furore among nationalists in its portrayal of a war veteran who returns home having been castrated by enemy fire during the Great War.

While Kaiser and Toller were the most consistently successful expressionists, a wealth of others made often one-off contributions. *Der Bettler* (*The Beggar*, 1912) by Reinhard Sorge (1892–1916) follows an odyssey undertaken by the eponymous protagonist. It is not dissimilar to *Der Sohn* (*The Son*, 1913–14) by Walter Hasenclever (1890–1940) in that both deal with generational tension between fathers and sons, and both use a heightened language to convey the pain and anguish felt by their male leads. Yet whereas Hasenclever set his play against a background of bourgeois rebellion, the then left-wing Arnolt Bronnen (1895–1959) focused on the misery of a more working class milieu in *Vatermord* (*Patricide*, 1915). Hasenclever's son brings about his father's death – the latter dies of a stroke when the son draws a revolver; Bronnen has his son actually kill the father as an act of self-liberation.

There is also little coincidence that expressionism flourished during World War I: the scale, the means, and the consequences of the conflict changed perceptions of the terrible possibilities of human action, and this was reflected in the theatre too. However, the theme and setting of war was treated differently by Reinhard Goering (1887–1936) and Karl Kraus (1874–1936). Goering's *Seeschlacht* (*Battle at Sea*, 1916–17) takes place in the turret of a battleship during the Battle of Jutland and opens with a scream. It follows seven unnamed sailors as they experience the carnage unfolding before them and the stark awareness of their own mortality. Different perspectives are offered but the play ends in slaughter when an explosion tears through the structure and leaves the last sailors dying but conscious that the battle is far from over. Kraus's *Die letzten Tage der Menschheit* (*The Last Days of Mankind*, 1915–17) is an exercise in dramatic giganticism. The full printed version of the play totals 725 pages and encompasses five acts, a prologue and an epilogue. The vast panorama surveys a great war from a distinctly Austrian perspective. Whole strata of society are exposed to Kraus's satire, mainly through the recurring figure of *Der Nörgler* ('the man who carps' or 'the fault-finder'). This play, too, ends in catastrophe: the epilogue is tellingly called *Die letzte Nacht* ('the last night'). The sheer size of the play argues that the experience of war and its effects on language cannot be understood in a single evening's performance.

For the most part, German expressionist drama engaged with the social upheavals of a rapidly industrialising society and the experience of the Great War in work that was overwhelmingly bleak, even though the hint of redemption found its way into some of the plays. One writer, however, who used the clipped language of expressionism to a more comedic end, was Carl Sternheim (1878–1942). Although he started writing for the theatre at the very end of the nineteenth century, Sternheim rose to prominence with a cycle of plays which were collected under the heading *Aus dem bürgerlichen Heldenleben* ('From the Heroic Life of the Bourgeoisie'). *Die Hose* (*The Bloomers*, 1909–10) was the first of the Maske-tetralogy, which took as its protagonist Theobald Maske. The surname (English: 'mask') alludes to the bourgeois' ability to hide his rampant egotism and avarice behind a mask of respectability, a feature particularly evident in the Wilhelmine era before World War I. The bloomers in question belong to Maske's wife, come down and are lost at a public parade. The moment is witnessed by two bystanders who are sexually aroused and endeavour to approach her by lodging with the Maskes. Theobald fears for his job as a minor civil servant if this incident were to become known but manages to come out on top when he realises that the money from the lodgers' rent can support the couple's wish to start a family. *Bürger Schippel* (*Paul Schippel Esq.*, 1912) is similarly centred on the German middle class and deals with social mobility: a quartet of singers made up of middle-class men loses its fourth member on the eve of a major competition. In spite of their class prejudices they are forced to turn to Paul Schippel, a labourer of illegitimate birth, because of his wonderful voice. After much comic action, Schippel is finally accepted into the ranks of the middle class. While it would be difficult to identify Sternheim as a true expressionist, his use of language is never naturalistic and its clipped cadences suggest that language is being pushed away from puns and jokes into areas of linguistic experiment in the pursuit of comic tension.

Drama between the Wars

Expressionism was already established as the dominant genre of the day by the time the middle-class firebrand Bertolt Brecht (1898–1956) wrote his first full-length drama, *Baal*, in 1918, one year before the proclamation of the Weimar Republic. The play was a reaction to Hanns Johst's *Der Einsame* (*The Lonely One*, 1917), a maudlin expressionist depiction of the life of the play-wright Christian Dietrich Grabbe (1801–36). The eponymous protagonist of Brecht's play is a provocative writer who abandons the comfort of the bourgeois salon to give full rein to his enormous appetites, leading a debauched life, seducing women and men, betraying friends, and creating great poetry. The play is clearly not only in dialogue with Johst's work but also with the abstract idealism of the expressionists, being a wild celebration of the body and its desires. Baal is more amoral than immoral, unable to locate a fitting position within a society that is unwilling to accept his dubious standards. A counterpoint to Brecht's exploration of post-war morality may be found in Hugo von Hofmannsthal's comic masterpiece, *Der Schwierige* (*The Difficult Man*, 1920). Hofmannsthal (1874–1929) was closely associated with the Salzburg Festival where the first performance of his reworking of the medieval morality play *Jedermann* (*Everyman*, 1911) took place in 1920 and was to become an annual event there. *Der Schwierige*, however, a refined social comedy, was conceived as a swan song to pre-war Viennese values. The 'difficult man' of the title is an aristocrat who has seen action in the war and is hesitant about rejoining genteel society through a liaison with an eligible woman. The play is a comedy of manners and contrasts remarkably with Brecht's utterly uncompromising approach to the similar theme of navigating a course through post-war society.

The young Brecht continued to surprise with his often unorthodox approaches to playwriting. *Trommeln in der Nacht* (*Drums in the Night*, 1918–20) is set in the Berlin of the Spartacus Uprising and includes a third act whose omission Brecht condones if the director should decide it lacks pace in performance. *Im Dickicht der Städte* (*In the Jungle of Cities*, 1921–2) dispenses with psychology and motivation completely when a Malay timber merchant challenges a librarian's assistant to a duel in Chicago for no discernable reason. Brecht prefaces the play with a comment that would later illuminate his epic theatre: he asks the spectator to observe the process of the duel neutrally rather than getting involved with the characters themselves.

In the early 1920s Brecht spent time in both his native Bavaria and in Berlin. In 1924 he settled in Berlin and was appointed dramaturge at the Deutsches Theater. In another part of the city, the director Erwin Piscator (1893–1966) was helping to shape a new wave of political theatre that greatly influenced Brecht. Piscator pioneered a type of documentary theatre which used events from the news and recent history. Authentic detail brought plays and their staging to life, while newsreels were projected onto huge screens to heighten topicality and authenticity. Piscator directed Toller's *Hoppla, wir leben!* (*Hoppla, such is Life!*, 1927) with an emphasis on its actuality. The play drew heavily on Toller's experiences of the Munich Soviet and demonstrated the playwright's move away from expressionism to confront the political realities of the Weimar Republic. Toller advises directors to stage the play on a scaffold, divided into different spaces from which different scenes can be contrasted with each other. The use of such montage betrays a dissatisfaction with conventional linearity and reflects the compression of time and space engendered by modernity. The play tells of a small group of revolutionaries who are arrested after a failed uprising and follows Karl Thomas, who is imprisoned for eight years, as a way of comparing erstwhile political idealism with the rigours of a new society upon his release in 1927. Another popular dramatist of the time, Ferdinand Bruckner (pseudonym of Theodor Tagger, 1891–1958) also used the idea of simultaneous space in *Die Verbrecher* (*The Criminals*, 1927). This three-act play criticises the inequities of the legal system by contrasting different cases, their causes and their aftermaths. The first and third acts are set in seven rooms of a large house while the second takes place in six chambers of a court.

Around the same time, a different type of social drama was developing. Spurred on by Brecht, whom she had met in 1922, Marieluise Fleißer (1901–74) wrote *Fegefeuer in Ingolstadt* (*Purgatory in Ingolstadt*, 1924) and followed it up with *Pioniere in Ingolstadt* (*Military Engineers in Ingolstadt*, 1926–7). The two plays cast a critical eye over sexuality and bigotry in Fleißer's hometown and rely on a careful use of language to render relationships and social position. In such a way, Fleißer prefigures Brecht's political theatre in suggesting that language is specifically social rather than the ahistorical, always present expression of human identity. The works helped to revive the nineteenth century genre, the *Volksstück* ('play of the common people'), by equipping it with a new socially critical edge. Ödön von Horváth (1901–38), a Hungarian who came to Germany as a student and settled there, writing plays and prose fiction in German, developed the critical *Volksstück* further in plays like *Geschichten aus dem Wiener Wald* (*Tales from the Vienna Woods*, 1931) and *Kasimir und Karoline* (1932). *Geschichten* is probably Horváth's best known play and deals with the ill treatment of the working-class girl Marianne at the hands of various men. The action of the complex plot, as in the work of Fleißer, is constantly in tension with the language which is at once atmospheric and distancing. The jargon of the educated bourgeoisie pervades the lower-class speeches and catches its speakers in their socio-historical moment. Horváth's use of silence is also crucial because it allows the audience to take stock of what has been said as well as denoting a breakdown in communication. Both Horváth and Fleißer inflect their language with a social tone that calls the autonomy of their characters into question: the playwrights suggest that the characters' perceptions are hostage to their social position. They ask what can be done to alleviate such structures in society and liberate the characters from their involuntary narrowness of perspective. Horvàth's work in particular high-lighted the rise of Fascism and Fascist mindsets but managed to present it in a form that could be described as 'popular'. The marriage of sophisticated ideas, not reduced by simplification, and accessibility marks his drama as an attempt to bypass the perceived elitism of the theatre whilst avoiding the trap of patronising his audience.

Brecht's political theatre

While Piscator, Toller, Fleißer, and Horváth were experimenting with vari-eties of political theatre, Brecht was discovering Marxism and considering how it could be implemented in the theatre. The focus of his interest was the revolutionary potential of the dialectic. Following Hegel, Marx posited that all change was driven by the contradiction between a thesis and an antithesis. In each epoch of history, these antagonists were represented by a master class and a servant class. When the contradiction became too great, elements of both thesis and antithesis combined to form a synthesis. And because this was a dynamic process, the synthesis became a new thesis, ripe for challenge from a new antithesis and the forging of a new synthesis, and so on through history. The present struggle between labour and capital would hopefully be resolved in the synthesis of communism. The motor of such a theatre was therefore contradiction and its clear presentation on stage was the play-wright's goal. The Marxist dialectic offered Brecht a radical philosophy that affected almost all aspects of existence. Human beings were not constrained by an unchanging 'human nature' but were in constant dialogue with all their contexts. So, while free-marketeers argue that capitalism is a response to innate human greed, Marx counters that it is capitalism that encourages such a quality in the first place by valorising accumulation for its own sake. The corollary here is that socialism would bring forth more positive characteristics. Brecht, however, did not share Marx's confidence and was more concerned with formulating problems rather than offering solutions, even though his innovative forms accepted the dialectical nature of society as true.

Brecht's desire for a new kind of theatre was born of the view that naturalism did not present the world as a site of change. Indeed, the 'convincing' aesthetics of naturalism suggested a world of unquestioned surfaces in which characters and action were in some way inevitable because the stage never posited alternative ways of behaving. Contradictions were insurmountable and this led to the perpetuation of a vicious society. Brecht also realised that a theatre of social change would have to offer its spectators a new kind of experience, one in which they, too, were involved. The audience would never consider the possibility of acting themselves if they entered the theatre and merely accepted what they found there. Such passivity was typical of a society in which goods were consumed, and art was no different when considered merely another commodity. Brecht needed an active audience, not one that would just sit back and absorb the action. The theatre had to promote curiosity within the audience and give their minds a prod. It had to surprise spectators by presenting people and actions in all their contradictions, forcing a confrontation with material that would not yield simple, reductive answers.

Like Toller, Brecht had recognised that both time and space needed to be reconceived in a theatre of the modern industrial age, and with this in mind, he elliptically wrote that 'petroleum resists the five acts'.[1] In other words, capitalist work practices have collapsed linearity. The flow of petroleum affects a whole range of areas, from the production and price of the commodity to issues of supply and consumption which are not only economic, but social and political. Such stories are not to be told with a beginning, a middle, and an end, but are dispersed in different places while action may take place simultaneously. Brecht dramatised the machinations of such decentred capitalist production processes explicitly in *Die heilige Johanna der Schlachthöfe* (*Saint Joan of the Stockyards*, 1929).

One of Brecht's most concerted responses to Marx and modernity was the development of what he called 'epic theatre'. The 'epic' here, however, has nothing to do with a broad historical or thematic scope; it is a translation of the German 'episch', the adjective applied to the genre of prose fiction (following Aristotle's genre distinctions). Brecht wanted to combine the dramatic and the epic in a theatre which oscillated between the proximity of human characters and the distance of reflective narration. One of the early attempts to achieve this was *Die Dreigroschenoper* (*The Threepenny Opera*, 1928, with a score by Kurt Weill), an adaptation of John Gay's *The Beggar's Opera* (1728). While Brecht's version does not present a fully worked-through epic theatre, it points to some of its important features. Each scene, for example, is introduced by an 'epic banner', which sets the scene and/or describes what will happen so that the audience may regard the scene as a proposal being presented for their consideration rather than an all-enveloping emotional action. The deflation of tension is also engendered by the division of action within the scenes themselves. When, for example in the first scene, Peachum is about to reveal to his wife that their daughter has been stepping out with Mac the Knife, he is interrupted by a piece of parallel action. His announcement, after the short dialogue, no longer packs the same emotional punch as the build-up to it has been dissipated. The principle of interruption is central to Brecht's theatre as it promotes the readjustment of perception and an acknowledgement that nothing is necessarily as it seems. Brecht uses songs in the middle of scenes and at the end of acts as a way of interrupting the flow and inviting the audience to change their line of thought. The songs are occasionally sung out of character and they can offer commentary on the action. Yet while the play flits between different scenes, it retains a fairly linear plot, just like its forbear. Brecht's many and sometimes lengthy theoretical musings on epic theatre are perhaps best illustrated by the plays themselves, and I shall draw on some of the better known ones to consider some key facets.

Mutter Courage und ihre Kinder (*Mother Courage and her Children*, 1938–9) uses temporally distant episodes as a way of analysing how the character of Courage interacts with her circumstances over many years. However, in order to approach her, we must in some way relate to her, and empathise with her. Mother Courage has been dragging herself with her three children from one battle to the next as a sutler. At the end of the sixth scene Courage gives a grim appraisal of the Thirty Years' War and in her final line she curses the conflict. It would be difficult not to share her view, having experienced the brutality, hypocrisy, and cynicism of the earlier scenes. The seventh scene, announced by an epic banner telling us that Courage is at the height of her business powers, opens with Courage proclaiming that she won't have anyone spoil her war for her. The character with whom the spectator had just agreed is now openly contradicting herself, pushing the spectator away. There has been a turnaround in the character's reception by the audience, brought about by an unexpected juxtaposition; the spectator is implicitly expected to discover the reasons for the contradiction. The sudden change in the presentation of Courage illustrates Brecht's principle of *Verfremdung* – a term which has been mistranslated over the years as 'alienation' but which is better rendered as 'defamiliarisation' or 'estrangement'. Brecht wants the spectator to question that which was previously accepted and account for the difference. The audience's relationship with Courage changes continually throughout the play and the spectator should ultimately realise that the learning is taking place in the auditorium and not on the stage.

The *Verfremdung* of character is even more radical in *Der Gute Mensch von Sezuan* (*The Good Person of Szechwan*, 1939–41). Here an apparently good woman, Shen-Te, is financially rewarded by three gods for her kindness to them, yet her goodness is unable to survive the onslaught of demands on her purse strings by other characters. She is forced to invent a wicked (male) cousin, Shui-Ta, as a means of combating the supplicants Shen-Te would merely have given in to. While the audience is asked to consider what circumstances might produce such financial parasitism, Shen-Te's goodness is always thrown into relief whenever Shui-Ta arrives. They are the same human being and thus have the same capacity for being both nice and nasty. Her generosity can only survive in an unjust world if she nurtures a greedy side as well and becomes adept at exploiting her fellow citizens. Again, we find the oscillation between proximity and distance, between empathy and critical reflection. Through its dialectical treatment of its characters, epic theatre acts as a critique of 'the natural'. 'Nature' is always in dialogue with society and continually transforms itself to accommodate changes of circumstance.

The dialectic itself is perhaps most clearly dramatised in *Der kaukasische Kreidekreis* (*The Caucasian Chalk Circle*, 1943–4). The play starts with the successful resolution of a land dispute between two Soviet collective farms. As entertainment after the discursive and rational conclusion of the matter, one farm performs a play for the other. The play deals with other, less satisfactory treatments of conflict. The first involves the servant girl Grusche, who takes the Governess's son into her care when he is abandoned by his mother during a rebellion. By the end of the play, the birth mother and the surrogate mother attend a trial to see who should look after the child. The other major strand is the story of Azdak, a wily rogue, who will arbitrate in the final scene. He is appointed judge earlier in the play and we learn about his strange methods of discharging justice, generally favouring the underdog. He tries two cases at once and often mixes up the judgements. In effect, he is a dialectical magistrate, if one views the judgements as the syntheses of contradictions. Yet even once Azdak has given what the audience hopefully considers the 'right' verdict in Grusche's case by award-ing her the child, the Singer, the narrator of the play, calls Azdak's term of office an 'almost' just one. Motherhood and justice are the dialectical threads that run through the play and neither is satisfactorily synthesised at the play's conclusion. The audience is asked to consider why the birth mother is not fit to nurture her own child and why Azdak's justice is imperfect. A clue is given in that Grusche is advised to leave the city for the safety of her new family after the judgement: the nature of society itself is stifling the success-ful resolution of conflict.

Brecht went into exile when Hitler came to power in 1933 and it was in this period that he developed new conceptions of stagecraft to complement the epic dramaturgies of his plays. Much of the theory was set down on paper at a time when Brecht had little access to a real stage. While his contributions to stagecraft concern the ways in which the actor is to behave, the main focus of the work is always on the benefit to be drawn by the audience. Brecht developed a theory of *Gestus*, an untranslatable term which formed the basis of his 'new way of acting'. The gestic approach meant that actors had to give physical expression to their attitude at any given moment, taking social, historical and individual influences into account. The task involved capturing the particular of the character and the general of the character's class, occupation and/or biography to provide quotable indices that located the character in a concrete yet potentially changeable environment. Brecht also broke with the Stanislavskian idea of characters as psychological islands, cut off from the rest of the cast. Characteristics were defined by relationships, not by an individual, unchanging self. Thus rehearsal involved considering how a particular character might change when talking to, say, her boss as opposed to the people who worked under her, or her husband as opposed to her father. Brecht also wanted actors to comment on their characters, so that acting became a demonstration of the role at times. An actor was thus licensed to perform a role and then communicate his or her attitude towards it, breaking frame and offering the audience an open question as to whether they agreed. For building up a role the actors were recommended the 'not/but' technique, which asked them to consider what a character was not doing when undertaking something else. Grusche, for example, does *not* save her own skin *but* puts her life on the line when she decides to take the Governess's child. Such a tension can be shown on stage and can offer the audience further visual contradiction. If, then, Grusche keeps moving away from the child but finally takes it with her, the audience is presented with an option that the servant girl rejects, and is called upon to understand what moved Grusche to accept the burden. Brechtian stagecraft is grounded on presenting the world as contingent by undermining inevitability at every turn. The grand aim of all these approaches to acting is to destabilise the audience's accepting gaze and to suggest different ways of perceiving reality.

Epic theatre, however, presented more a compromise than an ideal as a form of political theatre for Brecht. The drawback was that it retained the barrier between the stage and the audience. Brecht believed that a more powerful dialectical theatre could be instituted by involving the audience in a far more active manner. The 'Lehrstücke' or 'learning plays' were designed and experimented with while Brecht was still in Berlin in the late 1920s and the early 1930s. These plays had the express aim of overcoming the actor/audience divide by letting the actors – mainly amateurs in a massed chorus – play for their own benefit, so they were their own audience and learnt about behaviour in extreme political situations by stepping into the parts themselves. The most radical Lehrstück was Die Maßnahme (translated as both The Measures Taken and The Decision, 1929–30, score by Hanns Eisler). The short play illustrates many features of the genre and constitutes its most provocative example. The play begins with a report from four Agitators that their revolution in China has been successful but that they had to kill a fellow agitator, the Young Comrade. The Control Chorus asks them to re-present the events that led to what amounts to a political execution, and so the Chorus is confronted with a series of plays-within-a-play. The inset plays are almost all very similar in that they show a variety of scenes in which the Young Comrade acts with his heart rather than with his head. He prefers the alleviation of misery for the few in the short-term to waiting for the right revolutionary moment to liberate the many from the shackles of capitalism. By eliminating the Young Comrade before the action starts, Brecht invites the actors playing the Agitators to take turns in playing him. They can thus experience his failings and then contrast them with their feelings when they are being let down by him in other roles. This is why the scenes are structurally repetitive. The Chorus is also involved in experiential theatre in that it has interrogative lines and songs to sing. Again, the performers are asked to reflect on what they say or sing and reach a decision on where they stand. The most highly charged point of the play is when the Agitators decide to kill the Young Comrade after he betrays their cause in a show of naïve revolutionary zeal. The Comrade agrees to his own execution, an act that led Adorno and others to believe that Brecht was sanctioning Stalin's show trials avant la lettre. Such critics failed to understand that this climactic moment was being presented to the Chorus for its consideration and not for its vindication. The Lehrstück is not designed to be performed before an audience (although the original production of Die Maßnahme was) but only to be rehearsed and discussed for the benefit of the participants who now 'include' the audience. Such an approach to the political stage was taken up and popularised by the Brazilian practitioner Augusto Boal (b. 1931) and he coined the term 'spectactor' for the switching roles of the participant involved in a theatre like this.

Brecht fled the Nazis in 1933 and while in exile in Scandinavia put most of his major plays to paper: in addition to *Mother Courage* and *Szechwan* he wrote *Leben des Galilei* (*The Life of Galileo, 1938*), a play about a scientist's responsibility for his work that underwent several transformations as the atom bomb was developed, *Herr Puntila und sein Knecht Matti* (*Mr Puntila and his Man Matti, 1940*) about a landowner who was a despot when sober but became more and more humane as he got drunk, and *Der aufhaltsame Aufstieg des Arturo Ui* (*The Resistable Rise of Arturo Ui*, 1941), a parody in a gangster setting of Hitler's rise to power.

Thingspiele

In the meantime in Germany, Joseph Goebbels, Nazi minister of Propaganda and failed expressionist playwright, promoted a type of drama that very much tapped into the aesthetics of expressionism. The '*Thingspiel*' or 'play of judgement' sought to ape the more collective practices of expressionism, although stylised language and new forms of expression ran counter to the didactic nature of the *Thingspiel*'s rigid subject matter. For the most part, the plays were about the new German nation and thus did away with the concept of the individual in favour of the mass and exemplary figures. The Propaganda Ministry was in charge of finding suitable locations for the new arenas which were to seat tens of thousands of spectators who would immerse themselves in the spectacles. The *Thingspiele* were supposed to foster a feeling of brotherhood and community, for Aryans only of course, and used pageant and very large casts to confront one mass with another. There was a ritualistic element that bordered on the cultic, suggesting a mystical bond of German blood. The plays both celebrated the new Reich and condemned the 'degeneracy' of the Weimar Republic. One of the better known *Thingspiele* is *Deutsche Passion 1933* (*German Passion 1933*, 1932–3) by Richard Euringer (1891–1953). It tells of a dead soldier who returns from the grave and is shocked that he cannot find the great Germany he had departed during the Great War. He meets representative characters who bemoan Weimar's emasculated and profligate values and criticise the provisions of the Treaty of Versailles. The 'agony' inflicted upon the soldier leads him to the revelation that only a strong leader can bring about a new Germany, and by the play's conclusion, even the Evil Spirit has to concede that the Third Reich is a real deliverance from the decadence in which he previously revelled. The *Thingspiel* phenomenon only lasted until 1936, by which time it had outlived its usefulness. This was the Nazis' only major contribution to drama, although such mystical propagandism is of historical rather than aesthetic interest.

Plays for a postwar theatre

In the dying years of the Second World War, German theatres were closed to mobilise all possible human resources. When the Reich was finally defeated, re-echoes of expressionism helped the theatre to confront a crisis of representation, similar to that which followed the Great War. One of the most popular post-war plays was *Draußen vor der Tür* (*The Man Outside*, 1947) by Wolfgang Borchert (1921–47). The drama deals with the return of a damaged soldier and steers clear of a critique of Nazism in favour of more existential concerns. The prologue is a discussion between an Undertaker and an Old Man, representing Death and God respectively. A dream scene follows in which the soldier, Beckmann, tries to commit suicide but is denied his drowning by a personified river Elbe. The Other Man takes Beckmann under his wing and tries to convince him that life is worth living. However, as the play progresses Beckmann is confronted by a series of defeats including the discovery of the suicide of his parents, and he is left asking why he should stay alive in such an empty, sick world.

The poet Else Lasker-Schüler (1869–1945), whose early work *Die Wupper* (*The Wupper*, 1909) mixed the naturalistic and the fantastical, also wrote the expressionist fragment *Ichundich* (*IandI*, 1940–1) that mixes biblical characters, a rewritten Faust, and the fall of the Nazis in an uneven six-act phantasmagoria, which nonetheless offers a breathless journey through Germany to Jerusalem, the playwright's own final resting place.

Another response to Nazism came in the three-act play *Des Teufels General* (*The Devil's General* – 1942, written in US exile) by Carl Zuckmayer (1896–1977). Zuckmayer was a popular dramatist before the war and had scored a huge hit with his comedy *Der Hauptmann von Köpenick* (*The Captain of Köpenick*, 1931) which was based on a true event. The play is a satire on Prussian servility to anyone wearing a uniform and follows the exploits of a down-and-out cobbler named Wilhelm Voigt who masquerades as a captain of the guards. *Des Teufels General* also deals with the military but in a very different context. Harras, the air force general of the title, is in charge of a fleet of aircraft which are failing because of mechanical problems. Sabotage is suspected but Harras is unable to trace the perpetrator and is himself under suspicion. His personal life offers him solace as he has just met and fallen in love with an actress, but he has to offset this happiness against his role in a corrupt state. Harras finally discovers the saboteur but decides not to betray him. Instead he takes to the air in one of the faulty aircraft and crashes to his death. The Nazis believe that the saboteur has killed himself, yet he is nonetheless to be given a state funeral. The play was, understandably, very popular but it is not without its problems. The role of 'the devil' is a convenient demonisation of the upper echelons of the Third Reich (a strategy also employed by Thomas Mann in his novel *Doktor Faustus*, 1943–7), and the final act's title 'Damnation' pursues the religious and moral theme rather than attempting a political or social analysis. Harras is also a sympathetic character and one that the audience can view positively: he finds himself in the service of the devil through his love of flying rather than mistaken political allegiance. He is thus an exceptional, untainted character, and one that audiences could easily use as a painless figure of projection. The play made no concerted attempt to come to terms with Germany's past.

After the division of Germany in 1949, Brecht had been given his own troupe, the Berliner Ensemble, by the Government of the German Democratic Republic. It started rehearsing and performing at the Deutsches Theater before receiving its own theatre, the Theater am Schiffbauerdamm in 1954 (at which the *Dreigroschenoper* was premièred in 1928). While Brecht continued to write plays and to theorise stage practice, his greatest achievement in his final years was his work as a director, implementing the theatre he had imagined during his years in exile. Landmark productions such as *Mutter Courage* in 1949 and *Der kaukasische Kreidekreis* in 1955 raised Brecht's profile as not only a writer but also as a practitioner of theatre. The gestic clarity, the attention to social detail, and the concentration on performing contradiction demonstrated the productivity of the theory in practice, and the Berliner Ensemble was warmly received as it toured Europe. At his death in 1956, Brecht had established himself as the principal figure of reference for theatre-makers the world over who were keen to move beyond the confines of naturalism.

9 Nationalism and its effects on the German theatre, 1790–2000[1]

STEPHEN WILMER

In his book *National Identity*, Anthony Smith differentiates between two types of nation that have developed since the eighteenth century, the rational 'western' and the emotional 'non-western' model. The western model, influenced by French rationalist philosophy, presumes that the individual is free to choose membership of a particular nation; the non-western model assumes national identity is prescribed by birth and is hereditary, with language and ethnicity as defining attributes. Members of a non-western nation form an extended family of which they will always remain a member. The western model is characterised by 'historic territory, legal-political community, legal-political equality of members, and common civic culture and ideology', whereas components of the non-western model are 'genealogy and presumed descent ties, popular mobilization, vernacular languages, customs and traditions'.[2]

The concept of the nation that developed in Germany from the end of the eighteenth century followed Smith's non-western model: the German nation was considered ethnic, linguistic, and organic; there was no single German state but a longing to create one, and belief had it that foreign cultures had dominated German values and traditions. After Napoleon's conquest of Europe, a united nation became an important goal for German nationalists, but after the Congress of Vienna in 1815 only a loose German Confederation was established. While pressing for political unification, nationalists employed cultural means to cultivate a sense of national identity and unity.

This chapter will discuss the influence of early forms of nationalism on German theatre in the eighteenth and nineteenth centuries that helped form a sense of national identity. It will then trace the impact on the theatre of the virulent nationalism beginning in the late nineteenth century, which asserted the superiority of the German people and the inferiority of other peoples during the Weimar Republic and the Third Reich. It will conclude by considering the residual aspects of nationalism in post-war German theatre.

The beginnings of German nationalism

In the middle of the eighteenth century a reaction against French cultural dominance gradually set in. Stimulated in part by the writings of Jean-Jacques Rousseau, who praised the natural in contrast to the civilised state of man and suggested that national differences were determined by climate, environment, and history, German intellectuals began to promote the cultural traditions of the common German people. They called in particular for a theatre that, in the words of Schlegel, should 'take into account the customs and the special characteristics of one's nation'.[3] The poet and visionary Friedrich Gottlieb Klopstock (1724–1803) urged Germans to create their own works of art and argued for a standardised language in all German-speaking theatres. Like J. E. Schlegel, he adopted the Cheruscian tribal leader, Hermann, as a national protagonist in a trilogy he wrote between 1769 and 1787. He described these plays as 'bardic', designed to 'encourage the love for the native country and patriotic moods of war and sacrifice'.[4] He also took interest in German mythology, depicting Teutonic gods in his odes. 'First of all I want to work for religion!' he wrote. 'After this the history of my country shall be my work so that I can contribute to remind our fellow citizens of the deeds of our ancestors and to revive the patriotism that inspired them.'[5] Behind the historic dress of Klopstock's plays lies a critique of contemporary German princes who, in forgetting German nationalism, are essentially unpatriotic.[6]

Theatre practitioners were also concerned about national identity. Lessing criticised French neo-classical influences, displayed an early interest in old German traditions, and advocated new German plays about humbler domestic characters: 'The misfortune of those whose circumstances come closest to our own must naturally invade our souls the deepest.'[7] Similarly, Konrad Ekhof persuaded German princes to support German forms of theatre rather than Italian opera and French drama. Many German writers, however, like Winkelmann, still looked to ancient classical civilisation for their models.[8]

But of all the early nationalists Johann Gottfried Herder (1744–1803) had the greatest impact. He not only warned of the danger of copying the French but discouraged Germans from imitating the classics,[9] arguing that genuine literature emanates from the natural community of the *Volk* and is based on a common language. He maintained that the Greeks were writing in a particular time and environment and imitating them would inhibit

Germans from creating their own national literature. Great literature was spawned by the individual speaking for the nation and expressing the national soul at a particular time. Herder encouraged Germans to take pride in their native language and peasant values, which had remained untainted by civilisation. He felt Latin literature had harmed the natural German character and Christian sectarianism had undermined German unity during the Reformation. He advised Germans to read Tacitus for a picture of the Germans, whom he described as 'a distinct unmixed race', free from the taint of inter-marriage, all with the same physical features, 'fierce blue eyes, red hair, huge frames, fit only for a sudden exertion'.[10] He urged his compatriots to acknowledge the German poets of the past and developed a theory of the organic growth of the nation, its language and *Volksgeist* (national spirit), as distinct and unique, placing his faith in cultural rather than political unity. He encouraged research into German folklore, myths, legends, and local history and argued that German culture would never come into its own unless it was based solely on traditional popular German culture. Like Klopstock and Goethe, he was impressed by the recovery in Britain of early folk tales and songs, and criticised German poets for not having used folk material as Chaucer, Spenser and Shakespeare had. To this end he encouraged them to make a 'complete critical study of the chronicles and legends of the Middle Ages'. As a result of his endeavours, Herder fostered a new respect for German folk traditions and so promoted a notion of national cultural unity.

Early national drama

Herder's nationalism had a deep appeal for *Sturm und Drang*. It spurred Goethe to dramatise German history in *Götz von Berlichingen* in which, according to A. W. Schlegel, he evoked 'the very language in which our ancestors themselves spoke. Most movingly has he expressed the old German cordiality.'[11] *Götz* spawned a whole genre of *Ritterdramen* (plays about knights), though Schlegel complained they lacked authenticity as 'nothing was historical but the names and other external circumstances. The sentiments were as modern as they were vulgar'. But by the end of the eighteenth century, Christoph Martin Wieland could write approvingly of the growing nationalist trend in the theatre:

> German history, German heroes, a German scene, German charac-
> ters, customs and habits were something completely new on

German stages. What could be more natural than German spectators feeling the liveliest pleasure at seeing themselves transferred, as if by a magic wand, into their own country, into well-known cities and areas, amongst their own people and ancestors – amongst people they felt at home with and who showed them, more or less, the features that characterise our nation.[12]

In the nineteenth century, German nationalism made its appeal by claiming that it stood for freedom for the individual who had been oppressed in feudal times. Schiller's *Wilhelm Tell* represented a passionate expression of nationalist feeling, as resonant for Germans as it was for the Swiss. The solidarity amongst the peoples of the three cantons, who unite against oppression in favour of greater autonomy and espouse democratic values, provided a striking model for the unification of Germany. A. W. Schlegel called the play a 'soul-kindling picture of old German manners, piety and true heroism'.[13]

Romantic nationalists responded to Napoleon's invasion of Germany in 1807 by reasserting pride in their history and customs. The nation, it has been argued, 'found solace from the humiliation it was suffering through the marvellous discovery of its culture. To forget their powerlessness they embraced everything Teutonic with a passion.'[14] In Jena, Friedrich Schlegel urged a cosmopolitan drama free from nationalism, while his brother August repeated calls for a national theatre and drama.[15] But, once again the romantics and the theatre proved to be incompatible, and the most successful work the romantics did in arousing national awareness was not through the theatre but through the transmission of German history and folklore, through poetry and the study of philology. Johann Gottlieb Fichte (1762–1814) took nationalism to a new extreme in *Reden an die deutsche Nation* (*Addresses to the German Nation*, 1807–8). He argued that political borders between Germans were unnatural. Heinrich von Kleist started the nationalist journal *Abendblätter* in Berlin as well as the *Christlich-deutsche Tischgesellschaft*. Kleist's dramas were highly ambivalent in their attitude toward nationalism, and he did not find theatres ready to produce them.

National theatres

The 'national theatres' that were founded towards the end of the eighteenth century were devoted primarily to cultivating the *Bildung* of the citizen and less to asserting the unique cultural characteristics of the Germans, though through the lack of a German repertoire, the absence of the German nation became apparent. In the final essay of the *Hamburgische Dramaturgie*, Lessing lamented the problem of

> getting the Germans a national theatre, while we Germans are not yet a nation. I don't speak about the political condition, but only about the moral character. One should almost say that this consists in not having one of our own yet. We are still the devoted admirers of the never enough admired French. Everything that comes to us from across the Rhine is beautiful, charming, lovely, divine.
>
> (Lessing, 2, 759)

In fact, Lessing's efforts for the Hamburg National Theatre did much to overthrow the Germans' taste for French drama. As A. W. Schlegel wrote, 'With such success were his labours attended, that, shortly after the publication of his *Dramaturgie*, translations of French tragedies, and German tragedies modelled after them, disappeared altogether from the stage'.[16] At the Mannheim National Theatre, a committee met regularly to discuss such issues as, 'What is a national stage in the true sense of the word? How can a theatre become a national stage? And is there really already a German theatre that deserves to be called a national stage?'[17] All of this led Iffland to define the difference between German and French styles of production: 'The French give performances. The Germans representations. Their paintings of passions are splendid, ours are true.' Schiller, who was briefly dramaturge at Mannheim, characterised the theatre as a forum of human knowledge and 'a school of practical wisdom' and argued that theatre could form as well as represent the nation, concluding that 'if we had a national stage, we would also become a nation'.[18] But, by the early nineteenth century, as the liberalisation of institutions caused by Napoleonic reforms was reversed, national theatres became court theatres,[19] the nationalist cause was defeated by the Congress of Vienna, and the assassination of Kotzebue in 1819 led to the Carlsbad decrees that strengthened the powers of the aristocracy.[20] Political unity remained a distant hope, so German intellectuals continued to seek unity through cultural and spiritual means. Ideas of nationalism and national character continued to spread, and, as George Mosse observed, a trend developed in the German lands towards a secular religion of democratic nationalism, aided by the growth of pietism. This tended to devalue sectarian differences between various religions and thereby promoted national unity. It also encouraged a link between religion and patriotism with emphasis on the sacredness of the fatherland.

Nationalist spectacles, festivals and festival plays

Throughout the nineteenth century, the desire for cultural and political unity was expressed though spectacles and festival plays. These integrated 'the spectators and the strengthening of their identity' and in patriotic plays especially 'the spectators [were] supposed to understand themselves as part of the "staged nation"'.[21] *Wilhelm Tell* was regarded as the forerunner for nationalist festival plays and was often staged by amateurs commemorating a historic event. Like Rousseau, who decried court theatres in comparison to the openness of ancient Greek society and advocated open-air festive performances, Schiller called for more public accessibility in art. To compensate for the secrecy and alienation in German society caused by social and political oppression, Schiller argued that art and culture should provide a sense of civic involvement.[22] His ideas were inspired by the celebrations and festivals of the French Revolution, such as *The Taking of the Bastille*, an oratorio staged at Notre Dame, and a series of open-air performances staged by Jacques-Louis David, culminating in the *Festival of the Supreme Being* in 1794, which denounced atheism and affirmed the new official religion of deism.[23]

In the early nineteenth century, Ernst Moritz Arndt (1769–1860) and others 'copied structures of the great French revolutionary celebrations, mixed them with Christian and Germanic pagan elements and reinterpreted them in a nationalist sense'.[24] Celebrations and open-air performances often accompanied the erecting of monuments to historic events or personages. The social historian Wolfgang Hardtwig explained the connection between the two types of events,

> During celebrations the gathered crowd experience themselves as a unity and articulate their dream of a new and better society, the monument presents historic-political thought patterns which – often fragmented and varied – can still be recalled more or less automatically. Both – monument and celebration – appeal to the senses. They mobilise hopes, desires, fears and aggressions. They provoke emotions of mutuality and differentiation. They confirm and strengthen the political belief in a way that today is almost unimaginable.[25]

Festivals and spectacles fostered the idea of national unity through mass theatrical events, often in the open air. In *Deutsches Volkstum* (*German*

Nationhood, 1810), the extreme nationalist Friedrich Ludwig Jahn (Turnvater Jahn) (1778–1852) advocated a return to Germanic dress. He developed mass gymnastic societies throughout Germany, which cultivated physical skills and promoted military preparedness. Nationalists emphasised Germanic clothes, folk songs and customs, utilised symbols such as the sacred oak, pillars of fire, and torchlight parades, and often organised these events of the newly emerging festival culture in historic landscapes to evoke a sense of the German past. The defeat of Napoleon at the Battle of Leipzig prompted numerous celebrations, including theatrical performances, such as Goethe's festival play, *Des Epimenides Erwachen* (*The Awakening of Epimenedes*), which was staged at the Royal Theatre in Berlin in front of the Prussian King in 1815. The Wartburg Festival of 1817, attended by about 500 people, was organized by Jena students to commemorate the tercentenary of the Reformation and the fourth anniversary of the Battle of Leipzig. A small group of Jahn's students organised a sensational book-burning of reactionary literature, including Kotzebue's works, and symbols of Prussian military power.

The Greek struggle for independence in the 1820s and the revolutions of 1830 in France, Belgium, and Poland encouraged further revolutionary activities in Northern and Central Germany in which political liberty was demanded. The mass gathering at the ruin of Hambach Castle in 1832 drew between twenty and thirty thousand participants from many parts of Germany, calling for German unity and constitutional reform. According to George Mosse, 'Dominating the processions were the black, red and gold emblems worn by everyone, the ancient German dress and costumes worn by the students, and many flags. These often displayed the emblems of the Roman fasci [sic] on one side as a sign of strength and determination, and a wreath of oak leaves on the other.'[26]

The centenary of Schiller's birth in 1859 provided an opportunity to celebrate a figure associated with nationalism and liberty in cities all over Germany. In Munich 500 students organised a torchlight procession which placed a bust of Schiller in the loggia at the Feldherrnhalle. Mosse writes:

> the Schiller festivals abounded in symbolic representations . . . The municipal theatres presented *tableaux vivantes* [sic] from Schiller's plays, always ending with his apotheosis: the poet ascends to Heaven and is crowned by his predecessors from Livy to Shakespeare. The national theme was crowded out in the theatre by the muses, but in the outdoor representations it was always present, Schiller and Germania proudly united.[27]

Open-air festivals and performances encouraged the notion of a 'Theatre of the Future' which would reduce barriers between audience and actors and promote a common unity in enacting German stories and legends. For example, the Swiss novelist Gottfried Keller (1819–90), who had been impressed with an open-air staging of *Wilhelm Tell*, proposed in *Am Mythenstein* (*By the Stone of Myth*, 1860) a theatre based on ancient Greek models, 'a community theatre, set in nature, which was to combine male choirs with Volk plays'.[28] The 'Theatre of the Future' could create cultic or ritualistic events with large casts and minimal scenery. The Passion Play at Oberammergau was seen as a model for this type of theatre because of its relationship to the *Volk*.

In the middle of the nineteenth century, Franz Dingelstedt formulated ideas for uniting the nation through using twelve of the best actors in the German-speaking world for a *Gesamtgastspiel* (an ensemble of guest artists) in a series of classic German plays in Munich in 1854.[29] As some of these actors happened to have regional accents (such as Emil Devrient from Dresden and Karl La Roche from Vienna), Dingelstedt tried to overcome the lack of harmony by using impressive scenography to frame the action and confine the actors to an authentic and specific location, conducting historical and ethnographic research for the costumes and set. This was not only an early development of the concept of a theatre festival in Germany, but a manifestation of the growing importance of ethnography, anthropology, and archaeology in the service of nineteenth-century nationalism. Simon Williams has suggested that in Dingelstedt's type of 'pictorial' direction 'the actor often served more as a component in a picture than as an independent artist in his own right'.[30] According to Heinz Kindermann, Dingelstedt's *Gesamtgastspiel* was 'the first attempt to present the most significant forces of the then available German dramatic art in the same performance, and so to give for the nation "the most perfect total image possible" of the contemporary condition of drama and theatre'.[31] The festival's repertoire suggested the formulation of a classic national repertory, including as it did Schiller's *Die Braut von Messina* and *Kabale und Liebe*, Goethe's *Faust I*, *Clavigo* and *Egmont*, Lessing's *Minna von Barnhelm* and *Nathan der Weise* and Kleist's *Der zerbrochene Krug*. In a parallel development H. Theodore Röttscher established the notion of the German character on the stage in his three-volume work *Die Kunst der dramatischen Darstellung* (*The Art of Dramatic Performance*, 1841–6).

Numerous festival plays celebrated the defeat of the French in the Franco-Prussian war of 1870–1 and the ensuing unification of Germany.

Among these were Friedrich Hoffmann's *Drei Kämpfer* (*Three Fighters*), which celebrated the first anniversary of the battle of Sedan on 2 September 1871 in the Neues Theater in Leipzig. It portrayed three generations of German soldiers from the same family: one who fought Napoleon, his son who fought in the 1848 uprising, and his grandson who defeated the French in 1870, all winning the Iron Cross for bravery. Another festival play, Max Jähns' *Preußisches Festspiel*, also adopted the convention of successive generations of German heroes in battle, from medieval times to the recent war, the performance ending with the singing of '*Die Wacht am Rhein*' ('The Guard on the Rhine').[32] Another way to express national unity was to represent soldiers in the front line speaking different dialects, conveying a sense of the different tribes of Germany coming together in the struggle for the nation.[33] Festival plays after 1870 often employed the myth of Kaiser Friedrich Barbarossa sitting inside his mountain, the Kyffhäuser, waiting for better times; in 1890, festival plays also celebrated the 700th anniversary of Barbarossa's death in battle. In 1896, on the twenty-fifth anniversary of the German empire, Franz Büttner Pfänner zu Thal used drawings by Kaiser Wilhelm as tableaux in a performance to celebrate the defeat of satanic forces by the German hero St Michael. According to the prologue,

> The Germanic Siegfried myth is transferred to the German St Michael. St Michael symbolises Germanness, German strength and German loyalty. He liberates Germania who is immobilised by foreign power and discord with the help of the German sword of unity which he has to weld together again himself. He leads her up to freedom and shows her the castle of Hohenzollern appearing at the horizon where she will be kept safe for ever under his protection.[34]

Opera and music

Opera successfully represented German characters and landscapes and expressed nationalist themes, especially Richard Wagner's music dramas in which Herder's ideas about folk poetry, legends, and local history were incorporated. Wagner celebrated traditional German poetry and song contests in *Tannhäuser* and *Die Meistersinger*, and employed the legend of the *Nibelungenlied* and Nordic mythology for the *Ring* in which a strong sense of German topography is evoked by the images of the Rhine and the Alps. Wagner wrote, 'To the operatic poet and composer falls the task of conjuring up the holy spirit of poetry as it comes to us in the sagas and legends of past ages.'[35] He also advised that artists focus on pre-Christian myths because, like Herder, he argued that Christianity had diluted the original popular spirituality. 'Through the adoption of Christianity the folk has lost all true understanding of the original, vital relations of this mythos.'[36] But his anti-Semitism led him to dangerous extremes in his thinking. With characteristic egotism, Wagner considered himself to be the most German of beings: 'I am the German spirit.'[37]

Unlike most composers, he wrote his own libretti, fusing his musical and dramatic ideas into the *Gesamtkunstwerk*. He felt art should express a national *Mythos*, approximate to Herder's *Volksgeist*.[38] By unifying the arts in a *Gesamtkunstwerk*, he felt he was helping unify the nation: 'The most imperious and strongest longing of the complete artist is to communicate to the highest level of his being with the most comprehensive community, and this he reaches with the necessary general breadth of understanding only in the drama.'[39] Wagner's communal notion of opera also affected his ideas about the audience which, rather than being split into traditional hierarchical divisions, should be part of an egalitarian community, which was reflected in the auditorium of the Bayreuth Festspielhaus. More controversially, he expressed a belief in the superiority of the German people and culture, something implied in the final act of *Die Meistersinger*, where he constructed borders of national identity by seemingly negative comments on foreign cultures.

While involved in the 1848 revolution and the 1849 Dresden uprising, Wagner proposed a national theatre for Saxony, which should operate as a democratic institution, with an elected rather than appointed director, but his proposal was rejected. The Bayreuth Festival, founded in 1876 with the aid of his patron Ludwig II of Bavaria in a specially built opera house in a rural setting, became a place for celebrating not only his work, but also the German cultural heritage. It grew into a sort of National Theatre to which Wagnerites made annual pilgrimages, a practice that continues to this day.

The Second Reich and the Weimar Republic

One might suppose that Bismarck's unification of Germany in 1871 would have satisfied nationalist aspirations. However, right-wing intellectuals and romantic conservatives became dissatisfied with the bourgeois, industrialised society of the new German empire under Kaiser Wilhelm and, drawing on the ideas of Herder, Jahn, and others, expressed longing for a *völkisch* society rooted in ancient myths, peasant stock, and idealised German virtues. Citing Tacitus as proof of the virtuous character and racial purity of the Germans, nationalists used theatre and other art forms to celebrate a pre-industrialised *völkisch* society. Some called for a 'sacred space' around national monuments to perform mass festivals and open-air performances. Ernst Wachler developed these ideas in his open-air Mountain Theatre, which opened in Thale in the Harz mountains in 1903.

> The plays he wanted to stage...were not traditional dramas. Actually they were embodiments of rites which would dramatize the *völkische Weltanschauung*. The titles themselves indicated the typical content – for instance, Wachler's own *Hohenstaufen* or *Walpurgis*. Other plays dealing with similar themes were also performed, especially the famous *Till Eulenspiegel*... It was one of the first serious attempts to objectify the ideological by means of the visual arts: to create a public cult for the dramatic presentation and reliving of German themes.[40]

In 1898, Adam Müller-Guttenbrunn, who had published an anti-Semitic pamphlet *Wien war eine Theaterstadt* (*Vienna was a Theatre City*, 1885) that blamed Jews and foreigners for the corruption of the theatre, became head of the Viennese Kaiserjubiläums-Stadttheater, which was dedicated to Aryan work. Social Darwinism, reinforced by ideas of eugenics, helped popularise the notion of an Aryan master race and the danger of its contamination by Jews and foreigners, setting the scene for the ultra-nationalist theatre of the twentieth century.

The Bayreuth Festival became a rallying point for extreme nationalists. The *Bayreuther Blätter*, founded by Hans von Wolzogen in 1878, was 'an ideological instrument to propagate a racist, anti-Semitic, chauvinistic, xenophobic and anti-democratic ideology'. According to Frederic Spotts, 'It would be difficult to find anywhere in the Western world in the late nineteenth century, even in the darkest corner of the French right, a publication so poisonous, so hate-filled, so spiritually demented.'[41] The Bayreuth festival and Wagnerian opera were used by an ultra-nationalist cult to express the uniqueness of the Teutonic race and the 'regeneration of the German soul'. Opposing the industrialisation, urbanisation, and Jewish assimilation of the Second Reich, conservatives engaged in an 'ideological rampage that translated Wagnerian opera into a national cultural religion with Bayreuth as its supreme place of worship'.[42] The production of *Parsifal* in the 1882 festival, for example, 'responded to the broad and deeply German longing for national salvation . . . to the *Bayreuther Blätter* what was important in *Parsifal* and the 1882 Festival was less the artistic aspect than what it regarded as the opera's message of German regeneration – that is, a Germany purified of Jews, liberals, democrats and indeed all modern influences'.[43]

While the Weimar period was noted for its experimentation, right-wing nationalists used theatre to project the more conservative image of home and roots, anti-Semitism and national identity, in *Völkische Weihespiele* (People's Consecration Plays), *tableaux vivants*, choral movement plays, and Nazi agit-prop. Nazi ideology found its way to the stage through the plays of Richard Billinger (1893–1965), Hanns Johst (1890–1978), and Erwin Kolbenheyer (1878–1962). Johst's *Der König* (*The King*, 1920) favoured brutal tactics by rulers and was seen many times by Hitler, while his later *Schlageter* (1933) was dedicated to Hitler and opened on his birthday. Even Goebbels tried writing nationalist plays; his *Der Wanderer* (*The Traveller*, 1927) was toured for two years by a Nazi experimental theatre company under the leadership of Robert Rhode.[44]

Following the Munich Beer Hall Putsch of 1923, the Bayreuth Festival became an ideological home for National Socialism. Winifred Wagner, the English wife of Siegfried Wagner – son of the composer and director of the festival – supplied paper to Hitler to write *Mein Kampf* while he was in prison, and she wrote to the press praising his political activities. Siegfried Wagner (1869–1930) became nervous of the close public association with the National Socialists, and from 1924 created a veneer of the festival being apolitical. But he and other members of the family joined proto-Nazi organisations, and Hitler continued to visit them regularly. The collaboration between Hitler and the Wagners was intensified following the death of Siegfried Wagner, when the Festival fell into Winifred's hands. She acted as Hitler's escort on numerous official occasions, and Hitler continued to stay with her in the summer in Bayreuth. Despite the dislike of other Nazis for Wagner and Bayreuth, Hitler continued to attend every festival until 1939. He maintained personal responsibility for Bayreuth, saving it from financial ruin and ensuring its musical reputation when it lost its Jewish and international audiences as well as many of its personnel, including Arturo Toscanini and Kirsten Flagstad, who refused to perform under the Nazis.[45] Bayreuth became effectively a Nazi shrine. According to Spotts:

> On arriving in the town, visitors were greeted by swastika banners hanging on every flagpole and from every house. Storm troopers

crowded the streets and cafés resounded to the Horst-Wessel-Lied, the Nazi anthem . . . If it was the first cycle of the season, the street was lined with armed SS guards and tens of thousands of onlookers heralding – and heiling – the arrival of government and party leaders, it now being socially obligatory for the prominent and the ambitious to put in an appearance.[46]

At the opening performance of *Die Meistersinger* in 1933, Joseph Goebbels broadcast on radio directly from the Bayreuth opera house claiming that *Die Meistersinger* was 'the incarnation of our national identity'. Everywhere in Germany, the National Socialists propagated the myth that the nation needed to be renewed and saved from decadence by the individual submitting to the national community and its leader. During the Weimar government, Nazis disrupted performances that they considered decadent, such as a film version of Lessing's *Nathan der Weise* (*Nathan the Wise*) and Křenek's opera *Jonny spielt auf* (*Johnny Strikes Up!*) with its jazz influence.

The Third Reich

Once in power, the Nazis used extensive government propaganda and strict censorship to impose their ideology and ensure order, discipline, and social uniformity. Culture was to become 'a weapon of the state'. In his opening speech as Minister of Propaganda, Goebbels announced that he would forge a *Gleichschaltung* (ideological coordination) between the government and the German people. His Ministry strictly controlled the theatre. Intendants who were members of the Communist or Social Democratic Parties or of Jewish origin were dismissed; by April 1933 thirty-six of them had been replaced.[47] Many theatre workers were sacked after the publication of the 'Nuremberg Laws' (1935), which revoked the citizenship of non-Aryans. Ultimately 4000 theatre people left the country, including Max Reinhardt, Bertolt Brecht, Erwin Piscator, and Ernst Toller. The Ministry for Propaganda ensured that theatres staged ideologically and aesthetically approved material by vetting all scripts and productions. The number of contemporary German plays in the repertoire was reduced from 35 per cent in the 1932–33 season to 5 per cent in 1933–4, while earlier 'patriotic or *völkisch*' plays such as 'dialect folk plays, farces and comedies' came to represent 58 per cent of the entire repertoire during the Nazi era.[48]

Some new drama was encouraged, especially plays on historical topics, which served as analogies for the nationalistic struggle, and those expressing support for 'the 'Führer Idea', such as heroic sacrifice for the 'people's community' and the inevitability of the 'racial struggle'.[49] Historical conflicts were represented so that 'they could be seen as mile stones on the way to the creation of the German National State'.[50] A major theme was the conflict between the German Reich and the Catholic Church, in which Germans heroically fought against the influence of the Vatican, such as in *Thors Gast (Thor's Guest,* 1937) by Otto Erler (1872–1943), *Uta von Naumburg (Uta of Naumburg,* 1934) by Felix Dhünen (1886–1939), and Kolbenheyer's (1878–1962) *Heroische Leidenschaften (Heroic Passions,* 1928) and *Gregor und Heinrich* (1934).[51] Audiences witnessed 'no new material or characters, but the old and accustomed through an everlasting regeneration of the human soul'.[52] The Nazis promoted plays that preached national unification and racial purity such as *Die Heimkehr des Matthias Bruck (The Homecoming of Matthias Bruck,* 1933) by Sigmund Graff (1898–1979) and Richard Billinger's *Der Gigant (The Giant,* 1937) as well as plays with cross-cultural historical heroes such as *Isabella von Spanien (Isabella of Spain,* 1939) by Hermann Heinz Ortner (1895–1956) and Johst's *Thomas Paine* (1927).[53] Performances were expected to display reverence for German history and from 1937 the comic portrayal of historical figures, such as Frederick the Great and Bismarck by circuses and variety theatres, were banned.

Nationalist plays under the Nazi government were not very successful aesthetically, while plays on current topics proved problematic because they ran the risk of showing Germans fighting amongst themselves or of depicting the devastating effects of war. By the mid-1930s the authorities tightened control over plays about the immediate political situation and numerous new plays by National Socialist or conservative dramatists about the Weimar period were banned as they portrayed a divided rather than a united Germany. With the introduction of universal conscription in 1936, the Ministry of Propaganda censored plays depicting the horrors of World War I, requiring instead plays glorifying self-sacrifice for the fatherland. In the mid-1930s, Goebbels concluded, 'Unfortunately we still don't have the playwrights who possess the visionary power to mould the mental substance of our age into dramatic form'.[54] Changing political circumstances, as friendly countries became enemies and vice versa, led to the withdrawal of previously favoured plays: *Der Marsch der Veteranen* (*Veterans' March,* 1935) by Friedrich Bethge (1891–1963) about a Prussian leader helping Russia during the Napoleonic invasion, suffered such a fate after the invasion of the Soviet Union.

Classic German plays by Lessing, Goethe, Schiller, Hebbel, and Kleist were acceptable to the Nazis, as many of these dramatists could be regarded as *völkisch* writers.[55] *Minna, Tell, Kabale und Liebe, Jungfrau, Hermannsschlacht, Homburg*, and Hebbel's *Die Nibelungen* were particularly popular, many being adapted to make a pro-Nazi statement. For example, *Homburg* was used to promote unquestioning loyalty to the military and the fatherland, being labelled 'a cornerstone of our repertoire of steely romanticism' and all theatres were required to stage it.[56] In a production directed by Jürgen Fehling (1938), the actors came to the front to emphasise the final patriotic lines about Brandenburg. Some classic texts proved too difficult to absorb, particularly *Nathan der Weise* and Hebbel's *Judith*, because of their sympathetic Jewish protagonists. Goethe was problematic because he had defended the concept of free will, but the Nazis eventually reinterpreted *Faust* as a *völkisch* hero and claimed that Goethe was anti-Semitic. After the war began, Hitler banned *Wilhelm Tell*, presumably because it justified murdering a tyrannical ruler. From 1939, all dramas by authors from enemy countries were banned and, during wartime, variety light entertainment was introduced to help swell audiences. Shakespeare was performed, however, because he was regarded as German in spirit.

Despite its strict control, the Ministry for Propaganda was inconsistent in its policies. While the government discouraged naturalism because of its association with socialism, Gerhart Hauptmann, who gave the Nazi salute and sang the Horst-Wessel-Lied in public, continued to write and enjoy success; *Die Weber*, however, was banned. The plays of Hugo von Hofmannsthal were not staged after 1934 because of his Jewish ancestry, but his opera libretti continued to be performed. Franz Lehár's operetta *Die lustige Witwe* (*The Merry Widow*) was very popular with Hitler, although its composer was married to a Jew. Alfred Rosenberg, the Nazi ideologue, publicly disagreed with some of Goebbels' cultural policies, while Hitler maintained a close interest in the artistic and financial affairs of the Bayreuth Festival, which hired Jewish and foreign performers. Moreover, Hermann Göring, responsible for the Berlin Staatstheater, allowed Gustaf Gründgens to remain as artistic director after Gründgens advised him of his homosexuality.

German theatre was affected by nationalism in other ways. Theatres were ordered to organise events to coincide with National Socialist festivals such as Hitler's birthday. From 1936, Goebbels banned theatre criticism. All French names used in the theatre were translated into German. Jews, who sometimes represented half the season-ticket holders, were, from 1938, forbidden from attending any 'concerts, cabarets, theatres, cinemas, circuses and lectures'. The *Jüdischer Kulturbund* (Jewish Culture Union) became the only legitimate organisation for Jewish theatre artists and audiences, and by 1938 its 'seventy-six branches had 50,000 members and had presented 1638 play performances'.[57]

The most original dramatic form developed under the Nazis was the *Thingspiel*, evolved from Gottfried Keller's *Am Mythenstein* and the idea of a 'sacred space' around national monuments for performances. The *Thingspiel* was based on the concept of a national community theatre. *Thing* plays incorporated German nationalist ideas and were mass open-air *Gesamtkunstwerk* performances with choral speaking and music. They dramatised German heroes sacrificing themselves for the fatherland, in front of huge audiences as if it were a cultic ritual. The *Thing* plays required a new dramaturgy and specially constructed venues on historical sites. Twenty *Thingplätze*, bearing a striking resemblance to ancient Greek theatres, holding as many as 50,000 spectators, were constructed throughout Germany. A further 400 were planned but were terminated because the art form did not achieve the success the Nazis had hoped for.[58] Mosse argues that Nazi drama failed because the National Socialists 'made them into large popular spectacles wherein the dramatic content of the performances was transformed into intense expressions of mass veneration for the actors on the stage . . . The drama that was permitted was subordinated in importance to the choral chants that periodically interrupted the action.'.[59]

Hitler considered opera one of the greatest forms of spectacle and Wagner's music dramas, like German classical historical dramas, were chosen to celebrate significant moments in the Nazi calendar. The inauguration of the Third Reich on 13 March 1933 ended with a gala performance of *Die Meistersinger* at the Berlin Staatsoper. Also the nineteenth-century tradition of the *Volksoper* was invoked to counter what was regarded as the influence of 'degenerate' Weimar composers such as Kurt Weill (1900–50), Paul Hindemith (1895–1963) and Ernst Křenek (1900–91). Because of his Jewish background, Offenbach's operas could not be performed, and his place in the repertoire of light romantic operas was filled by a revival of the operas of Albert Lortzing, whose 'simple melodious music and uncomplicated comic libretti' about such figures as Hans Sachs and Mozart appealed to the Nazis.[60] The direction and design of opera became noticeably more conservative. After the abstract productions of expressionism in the Weimar era, directors reverted to more naturalistic interpretations. New operas were also encouraged; according to Erik Levi, over 170 new operas were written between 1933 and 1944, those by Richard Strauss, Rudolf Wagner-Régeny (1903–69), and Werner Egk (1901–83) being the most successful. Composers were discouraged from experimenting and they addressed primarily romantic and nationalist subjects such as Nordic myth, German history, and peasant life, featuring such themes as 'the heroism and strength of the classical warrior, the self-sacrifice for a higher ideal, intimations of racial superiority, and a strong identification with the upright values of a peasant community'.[61] Some new operas caused problems. Richard Strauss lost his job as President of the *Reichsmusikkammer* because of his collaboration with the Jewish librettist Stefan Zweig on *Die schweigsame Frau* (*The Silent Woman*, 1935) and his next opera *Friedenstag* (*Day of Peace*, 1938) was regarded as disturbingly pacifist. Egk's version of *Peer Gynt* (1938) was considered subversive because of its depiction of the trolls as faintly reminiscent of Nazi Storm Troopers, until Hitler attended a performance and congratulated the composer.[62] Hitler was lamenting the insufficiency of theatres and operas as late as 1942, but in August 1944 Goebbels called for the closure of the theatres as part of the policy of 'total war'. Ironically, the German Propaganda Ministry, while encouraging classic German theatre and opera and the performance of ideologically correct plays, tried to curb some of the excesses of National Socialist expression. For example, the *Reichsdramaturg's* office censored anti-Semitism in a 1934 play because it was deemed 'completely superfluous with regard to domestic policy' (since Jewish influences had already been eliminated) and 'harmful to foreign politics'.[63] By the late 1930s, the Ministry banned all reference to politics, state religion, the police, and the army.

Goebbels not only used theatre but film, sports events, and mass rallies to provide an era of Nazi-style performance celebrating the racial, ideological and moral superiority of the German *Volk*. Spectacular events included the Festival of 1 May at the Tempelhof Airfield in 1933, the Nuremberg rallies, the enthronement of the Bishop of Berlin in the Berlin Sports Palace in 1935, and the Festival of Olympic Youth, staged by Hanns Niedecken-Gebhard with a cast of 10,000 at the Olympic Games in 1936 including a Dance for the Dead by Mary Wigman with 80 dancers. Niedecken-Gebard also staged the massive historical pageant, *Berlin in sieben Jahrhunderten deutscher Geschichte (Berlin in Seven Centuries of History,* 1937) with over 12,000 participants choreographed in symbolic formations, which culminated in '*Das neue Deutschland*' a gigantic display of Nazi army troops in uniform on the

14 *Berlin in sieben Jahrhunderten deutscher Geschichte,* a historical pageant staged by
Hanns Niedecken-Gebhard in 1937. The last scene displaying the Prussian Eagle
and the Nazi swastika.

stadium running track in the floodlit stadium, backed by performers creating the image of a giant eagle and swastika (see fig. 14). Such performances
conveyed the idea of an Aryan super-race and involved the idealisation of
the Nordic body in gymnastics and dance, which had been adapted from the
choreographic ideas of Mary Wigman (1886–1973), Émile Jaques-Dalcroze,
(1865–1950) and Rudolf Laban (1879–1958).

The staging of the 1936 Olympics challenged Nazi principles as the
Games' international spirit contradicted them. It was the Weimar government
that had committed to the Games, and some Nazis wanted to cancel them or
prevent black people from participating. The idea of individual competition
was at odds with the notion of personal self-sacrifice and with the
tradition of non-competitive sporting clubs such as the gymnastic societies
or *Turnvereine* of F. L. Jahn. Eventually, the government staged the Games on
an unprecedented scale, with mass pageantry and an impressive opening
ceremony. Furthermore, through holding the Games, the Nazis appeared
tolerant and inclusive while manifesting Aryan superiority. The inscription

on the bell tower, 'I call the youth of the world', could be read as both an invitation to the Olympics and a call for national self-sacrifice. Carl Diem, who organised the Games, combined neo-classical props, costumes, and staging devices, and introduced the custom of lighting the eternal flame as the climax of a torch relay from Olympia, which has since become an integral part of every Olympic Games.

Many mass events in the Third Reich were orchestrated like religious rituals, as the Nazis replaced the religious calendar and liturgy with party dogma. The traditional distinctions between theatre, ritual, and politics became blurred as stage techniques and ritualistic forms were used in political events. As Bettina Schültke has written: 'By means of theatrical devices the National Socialists succeeded in a cultic aestheticisation of politics.'[64] The Nuremberg rallies, which became week-long annual affairs, functioned as ideological performances and included spectacles of light, speeches by the Führer, Wagner operas, marching soldiers, choral singing, flag hoistings and commemorations of the dead. The enormous parade ground in Nuremberg was filled with hundreds of thousands of ranked men, moving like mass kinetic sculptures against a backdrop of monumental neo-classical structures. Benno von Arent's annual staging of the third act of *Die Meistersinger* as part of the Nuremberg rallies, displayed, with little attention to the drama, 'massed crowds and celebratory flags and banners, consciously mirror[ing] the events taking place outside the opera house'.[65] Hitler justified such events by claiming that their 'mass suggestiveness' dissolved the loneliness of the individual who 'is given here an idea of a greater community', in which 'the will, the longing, as well as the power of thousands of people are accumulated in every individual'.[66]

Annual pilgrimages to the Nuremberg rallies, the Bayreuth Festival, and mass community events and festivals took on the character of religious commitment. The Nazis devised their own liturgy and rituals, with Hitler as a Messiah and his fallen comrades in the Munich Beer Hall Putsch celebrated martyrs. As Günther Berghaus has written: 'Competition with the Church could only be won if a parallel cult could take over the functions that gave the Church such strong roots in society.'[67]

By manipulating the sanctioned national community, Nazis vilified the 'other' in society. They did this through spectacles such as the victimisation of Jews in *Kristallnacht*, film propaganda against the mentally and physically handicapped, book burnings, and the suppression of '*Entartete Kunst*' (degenerate art). The mass deportation of Jews, dissidents, itinerants, and homosexuals, the slaughter of 70,000 handicapped and old people, and the Nazis' decision in 1942 to kill all Jews in Germany and German-occupied lands represented the nadir of German nationalism.

Cold War and divided Germany

Following the war, German national identity was undermined by the division of Berlin by the occupying forces, the partition of Germany, and the trials of Nazi leaders for war crimes. The Western Allies sought to prevent a resurgence of cultural nationalism by establishing a federal government in West Germany with responsibility for education and culture devolving to the regions. National culture was decentred by moving the political capital from Berlin to Bonn and diminished by West Germany joining the Common Market.

In East Germany the communist government exonerated itself by laying the blame for the Nazi past on the German fascists. West Germans initially tried publicly to forget the Third Reich. While West Germany tried to mend fences with other parts of the world, nationalism continued to play an important role beneath the surface. The Bayreuth Festival proved to be one of the most extreme manifestations of the contradiction between a public avowal of internationalism and pluralism and a private complicity with extreme nationalism. After the war Wagner's works returned to the repertoire and Bayreuth reopened with Wagner's grandsons, Wieland (1917–1966) and Wolfgang (b.1919), taking over the Festival from their mother, without overt controversy. While Wieland initiated a style of performance that was deeply dependent on the ideas of Adolphe Appia with lighting and abstract scenery replacing the prevailing naturalistic style of production, the old guard still considered Bayreuth as the home for ultra-nationalist opinion, and the Bayreuth Festival book printed numerous articles by former Nazis. Moreover, the Wagnerites were dissatisfied with Wieland Wagner's new style, especially when in 1956 he relocated *Die Meistersinger* from historic Nuremberg to an imaginary poetic realm; audiences booed and devotees expressed their anger. 'Bayreuth', a 'Friend' of the Festival claimed, 'is a sacred German cultural shrine ... All your romantic internationalism cannot change any of that.'[68] Instead of taking their advice, the next time he directed *Die Meistersinger*, Wieland went even further and did it in Brechtian style, a production that was 'booed as nothing before in Festival history'.[69] While Wolfgang and Wieland endeavoured to ignore associations between the Festival and National Socialism and invited numerous Jewish artists to perform at the Festival, Winifred Wagner remained a Nazi sympathiser, inviting wives and daughters of famous Nazi leaders into her family box, and causing a scandal by praising Hitler in a long film interview in 1975.

> In its contradictions Bayreuth was a microcosm of the Federal Republic itself – a state where democracy and social welfare flourished but also a state where Nazis were not seriously purged from any profession, where concentration camp commanders and participants in mass murder went scot-free, where judges who had passed thousands of death sentences remained on the bench and where, in short, the desire to forget, and even to forgive, was overwhelming.[70]

Nevertheless, Walter Scheel, the President of West Germany, speaking at the centenary of the Festival (1976), urged the Festival to face up to and learn from the past and stop thinking that 'Bayreuth was only a place of culture without noticing that it had long since become an instrument for evil policies . . . Bayreuth's history is part of German history. Its mistakes are the mistakes of our nation . . . We simply cannot erase the dark chapter of German history and of Bayreuth's history.'[71]

During the Cold War, certain playwrights on both sides of the iron curtain called attention to the Nazi past, notably Bertolt Brecht, Rolf Hochhuth, and Heiner Müller. Brecht's *Furcht und Elend des Dritten Reichs (Fear and Misery in the Third Reich)*, which premièred in Paris (1938), was later shown in Germany (1948) and *Der aufhaltsame Aufstieg des Arturo Ui (The Resistible Rise of Arturo Ui)*, first performed in 1959, became part of the Berliner Ensemble repertoire. Rolf Hochhuth's *Der Stellvertreter: Ein christliches Trauerspiel (The Deputy: A Christian Tragedy* – 1963) caused considerable controversy by accusing Pope Pius XII of failing to condemn Hitler's victimisation of the Jews, while his *Juristen (The Lawyers*, 1979) exposed former Nazi judges who were continuing to hold influential positions in the 1970s, leading to the resignation of Hans Filbinger, the Prime Minister of Baden-Württemberg. Heiner Müller's *Germania Tod in Berlin (Germania: Death in Berlin*, 1971) chronicles the self-destructive history of Germany in the twentieth century, including a potent scene in Hitler's bunker in which a pregnant Goebbels is about to give birth with Germania as midwife and three magi in attendance, while a raving Hitler ties Germania to the mouth of a cannon and fires.

The director Adolf Dresen (1935–2001) provides an interesting example of an artist who felt strongly about the cultural unity of Germany and whose appeal for a national theatre based on the works of classical poets fell largely on deaf ears on both sides of the iron curtain. After causing scandals with productions of Goethe and Kleist in the East that were criticised for their lack of veneration, he was expelled from the SED party for his idiosyncratic views. He moved to West Germany where he became director of the Schauspiel Frankfurt am Main and produced *Minna* as 'a historical parable for intra-German reconciliation'.[72] However, failing to find support for his views on German cultural and political unity, he left the dramatic theatre to become a successful director of opera.

Reunification

With the fall of the Wall in 1989, intellectuals seemed unsure whether to celebrate the reunification of Germany. Botho Strauß captured this quandary in his play *Schlußchor* (*Final Chorus*, 1991), expressing the 'helplessness that was caused by the national unification 1989–90 not only on the western side of Germany'.[73] Despite the title, a reference to the final chorus of Beethoven's Ninth Symphony, there is no sense of utopia at the end of the play. 'Instead of the classic hope for reconciliation and wholeness, the play shows alienation and isolation.'[74] In a final image, the female character of Germania (Anita) is attacked by the shadow of an eagle representing the might of the Second and Third Reichs. According to the stage directions, 'When the lights go up again Anita stands up to her calves in feathers, with a bloody face, the bird's cut-off claws in her hand', with her repeating the word 'forest'.[75] This vanquishing of the imperial symbol and its replacement by a more peaceful and bucolic image suggests that Germany's self-destructive rapaciousness is now a matter of history, but that nationalism retains a potent voice. Sprengel asks about the ending of the play, 'What does this mean? Does one German myth here replace another one? ... The only thing that is clear and unquestionable is the aggressive, deadly-threatening nature of this turning towards the nationalistic. We can see in it the trace of astonishment, even of fear with which the intellectual élite in the West as well as the East reacted to the national unification of 1989–90.'[76]

While intellectuals remained relatively silent in the commotion that celebrated the reunification of the country, the people and the state did not. The state staged a celebration of reunification on 2 October 1990 in an atmosphere that already tempered the hoped for unity as it was clear the two halves of the country were seriously divided ideologically and economically. It involved speeches, the hoisting of a huge German flag by 14 young athletes, a performance of Beethoven's Ninth Symphony, and fireworks set off to Handel's Fireworks Music, with tens of thousands of participants lighting their own sparklers. This, rather than a festival play, served as a public performance for the audience to celebrate the reunification of the nation.

Since *Die Wende* (the change), many plays have been written dealing with the problems of reunification and identity,[77] especially as the East German state, along with the sense of a separate national identity and utopian communist ideology, has vanished and been absorbed into the capitalist western nation-state. The former East Germany is now regarded as an economic backwater. Plays by mainly western German writers, such as Herbert Achternbusch's *Auf verlorenem Posten* (*A Losing Battle*, 1990), Harald Mueller's *Doppeldeutsch* (*Double German*, 1992), John von Düffel's *Gelobtes Land – Eine schwarze Komödie* (*Promised Land – A Black Comedy*, 1992), and Lutz Rathenow's *Autorenschlachten oder War es ein Fehler die Römer zu vertreiben aus dem Teutoburger Wald* (*Battles of the Authors or was it a Mistake to Drive the Romans out of the Teutoburg Forest*, 1994) have all dealt with differences between East and West Germany and problems relating to its reunification. Similarly Christoph Marthaler's *Murx den Europäer! Murx ihn! Murx ihn! Murx ihn! Murx ihn ab!* (*Kill the European! Kill him! Kill him! Kill him! Kill him off!*, 1993) at the Berliner Volksbühne, which was regarded as a 'requiem for the GDR'[78] and his *Die Stunde Null oder die Kunst des Servierens* (*Zero Hour or the Art of Serving*) at the Deutsche Schauspielhaus Hamburg in 1995 on the fiftieth anniversary of the end of the war, which used verbatim documents to parody the new German leadership in an era of rapprochement, reflected the sense of anomie and powerlessness in German society resulting partly from the political changes. Likewise, Volker Braun's *Der Staub von Brandenburg* (*The Dust of Brandenburg*, 1997) and Heiko Buhr's *Ausstand* (*Stoppage*, 2000) have focused on the social and economic problems in the former East Germany.

Since the early 1990s, the topic of nationalism continues to cause unease and controversy in the theatre. Some directors thrive on controversy. The leftist director Christoph Schlingensief (b. 1960) has questioned nationalist attitudes by staging public events such as *Passion Impossible – 7 Tage Notruf für Deutschland. Eine Bahnhofsmission* (*Passion Impossible – Seven-Day Emergency Call for Germany. A Railway Station Mission*, 1997), which was about the homeless and drug addicts outside the Hamburg railway station. He also staged *Hamlet* in Zurich in 2001, with neo-Nazi actors performing the minor roles, singing neo-Nazi rock songs and frightening the audience with their slogans. Prior to the production Schlingensief had set up a volunteer association, which neo-Nazis could contact if they wanted to reintegrate into society. However, Schlingensief succeeded mainly in creating an uncomfortable event in which the audience was unclear about his motives. Many felt that members of the neo-Nazi cast, including Torsten Lemmer, a millionaire who had recently run for mayor of Dusseldorf, were simply using the play for publicity, so they reacted strongly against the use of the Zurich stage for these purposes.

In Vienna in 2000 Schlingensief created an event on the square outside the opera house during the Vienna Festival Week called *Bitte liebt Österreich* (*Please Love Austria*). He placed ten asylum seekers in a container and asked the public to vote for who should be deported and who should be allowed to marry an Austrian and gain the right to remain in the country. The events inside the container were transmitted via the Internet. Slogans associated with Nazis were affixed to the outside of the container such as '*Ausländer raus*' ('foreigners out') and '*Unsere Ehre heißt Treue*' ('Our honour is called loyalty'). The event caused a heated discussion in the press and the container was assailed by a crowd of people as it raised uncomfortable associations in connection with the Austrian support for Hitler during the Third Reich, as well as with the success of Jörg Haider's right-wing party, which had won a place in the ruling coalition the previous year. By creating events that have focused on the unemployed, the disabled, refugees, and neo-Nazis, Schlingensief has raised public awareness of the plight of the marginalised in society. On the other hand, his work enables publicity for right-wing factions and concerns, and this problem is compounded by the recurrent political activities of neo-Nazi groups and the intolerance towards foreigners.

Another controversial director, the East German Einar Schleef, who died in 2001, created many productions which were accused of instilling a violent and fascist aesthetic, such as Rolf Hochhuth's *Wessis in Weimar* (*West Germans in Weimar*) at the Berliner Ensemble in 1993, Brecht's and Wuolijoki's *Herr Puntila* at the Deutsches Theater Berlin in 1996, and his own work *Verratenes Volk* (*Betrayed People*) at the same theatre in 2000. According to Hans-Thies Lehmann, 'The extreme intensity of the physical – running, stomping, screaming, jumping, rhythmic patterns of movements, often frighteningly dangerous actions of the performers – conveys its physical and vocal painfulness in a vehemence hardly found elsewhere on German stages.'[79] For *Ein Sportstück* (*A Sport's Play*), Elfriede Jelinek's post-dramatic piece which premièred at the Vienna Burgtheater in 1998, Schleef used choral speaking with large casts dressed in black robes and white sports gear, executing disciplined movements. Moray McGowan observed that the play used 'sport as both allegory and concrete expression of the human propensity for fascism. Its structure highlights the tension between the body as reified object and the body as part of a choral collective.'[80]

Meanwhile, the drama and opera associated with the eighteenth- and nineteenth-century era of romantic nationalism continues to be performed. Even plays specifically associated with ultra-nationalism have occasionally been staged in experimental productions to raise questions about their rhetoric, such as Hanns Johst's *Schlageter*, and Hans Rehberg's submarine war play *Die Wölfe* (*The Wolves*, 1943), which caused demonstrations outside the theatre in Erlangen in 2003 when it was produced in connection with the Iraq war by a left-wing director. Furthermore, the Bayreuth Festival continues to produce Wagner for a devoted international following, but there have been highly unconventional productions like Heiner Müller's *Tristan* (1993) and Schlingensief's *Parsifal* (2005). As Germany enters the twenty-first century, reunited but with residual inequities between the former East and West Germany, both chauvinism and the need for reconciliation with the past are sometimes expressed in the theatre. For example, the co-production of *German Roots* (English title in the original) by the Hamburg Thalia Theatre and the Recklinghausen Ruhrfestspiele in 2004 attempted to investigate notions of national identity and the legacy of historical events in Germany. It reflected the research conducted collaboratively by the actors about their own families; and the resulting script by the director Nicolas Stemann and the dramaturge Bernd Stegemann, looked at Germany from both an outside and inside perspective. At the beginning of the play a Japanese television announcer in the future is introducing a show about Germany, which has become a fourth-world country. Various characters look back over their history and try to find their roots in 'a swamp of its guilt'.[81] The relationship between the characters is vague at the beginning, but gradually they unearth memories about the Nazi period, the liberalism of the 1960s, the terrorist Baader-Meinhof group, and the only aspect of Germany about which they are all proud – the German football team. The play criticises the current generation for its lack of idealistic commitment and for general inertia, which has resulted in Germany becoming impoverished. Members of each generation ask the previous generation 'why didn't you do anything?', while the play questions whether those who did act (e.g. the Nazis and the terrorists) were worse than those who were afraid to act. According to one reviewer, 'Never before has anyone of the generation of young contemporary German theatre-makers made the German culprits speak as victims. Here they are allowed to speak. The man tells about the death of German soldiers in the east. The woman tells how in 1945 in Berlin she was raped by Russian soldiers.'[82] Because of the postdramatic approach, which presents a number of different possible interpretations to the audience, one might argue that the form of the piece encouraged the company to investigate an awkward topic without having to take a clear position on it. The meaning of the play is left up to each member of the audience. Should the past be buried and forgotten or unearthed and addressed? Should the past perpetrators of Nazi atrocities be seen as the victims as well as the villains of their time? Is it better to be politically active regardless of ideology than to be passive and apolitical?

Conclusion

In its early days, nationalism tended to exert a relatively progressive influence in German theatre. From the middle of the eighteenth century the nationalist movement provoked Germans not to imitate foreign forms of theatre but to explore their own culture for dramatic material that expressed their history and customs and developed their language. Lessing, Schiller, Goethe, Kleist, and Wagner not only achieved national but international success, both because they were the first Germans to write world-quality drama and because they cultivated the attitude that the theatre should be primarily a place of education and culture rather than entertainment and commerce. Their development of a theatre infrastructure became exemplary for the Western world. However, after German unification in 1871, extreme nationalist factions began to gain a foothold in theatre and society. With the establishment of the Third Reich, many serious theatre artists left the country or were killed. Since the Second World War and the Holocaust, expressions of nationalism have been regarded with much more caution, and German theatre artists have tended to avoid extreme positions. Recent German theatre has avoided the positive images of the German character and German history that were common in nineteenth-century drama and, on the contrary, has tended to be critical about expressions of nationalism and nationalistic ideals. However, with the reunification of Germany, nationalism has become an important issue once again, as Germans seek ways to express a sense of patriotism without reverting to old formulas. It will be interesting to see how significant an ideological force nationalism will become in the theatre of the new millennium.

10 Experiments with architectural space in the German theatre

WILLIAM F. CONDEE AND THOMAS IRMER

Performance and space are inextricably intertwined. Experimentation in new modes of performance leads to the creation of new forms, and new theatres set the stage for new modes of performance. Until early in the twentieth century, performance space in Germany was, as in western theatre as a whole, almost exclusively centred upon the proscenium arch. While proscenium arches continued to be built in the twentieth century, German theatre architecture has been especially distinguished by its experimental use of space. Spaces have been devised in which the performance takes place throughout the theatre and engages the audience in a wide variety of spatial relationships. This chapter focuses primarily on those German twentieth-century theatres that exploit this concept of an open-space theatre.

Nineteenth-century experimental spaces

Nineteenth- and twentieth-century proscenium theatres are characterised by the two discrete, discontinuous spaces of auditorium and stage, separated by a wall that is pierced by an arch. The audience is gathered around a single, narrow viewing angle, oriented toward the stage. In an 'open space' theatre, on the other hand, audience and performers share the same space, with continuous walls and ceiling spanning both. While in the proscenium theatre the audience usually sits in a darkened space facing a brightly lit stage, in an open space the light commonly spills into the auditorium, uniting actor and audience. Examples of open space include the end-stage, similar to a proscenium stage; the thrust, with spectators seated on three sides of the stage; the arena, with the spectators fully surrounding the stage; the multiform stage, an adaptable space with a fixed number of audience-performance configurations; and the flexible or black-box stage, an open space with theoretically infinite audience-performance configurations.

The first efforts to create a unified audience-performance space in Germany occurred in the mid-nineteenth century when attempts were made to recreate the original performance conditions of Shakespeare's plays. Objectives of such experiments were the close proximity of actors and audience, minimal scenery, and a space that enabled continuous, fluid action. The architectural frame was unchanged throughout the course of the performance and included a forestage for acting, a gallery above, and a framed inner stage below for remnants of painted, perspective scenery.

Ludwig Tieck found nineteenth-century illusionistic production techniques to be inhibiting to the free-flowing action of Shakespeare's plays and considered the ubiquitous orchestra pit to be a barrier to actor-audience intimacy. In 1836, he collaborated with Gottfried Semper, the foremost nineteenth-century German theatre architect, to create a reconstruction of the Fortune, an Elizabethan playhouse. While the drawings do not reflect today's thinking about historical reconstruction, the project established the goal of recreating historical performance practice and searching for alternatives to the proscenium arch and changeable, painted scenery.

Karl Immermann, director of the Dusseldorf Theatre from 1834 to 1837, was influenced by Tieck and wanted to emphasise the actor and the text by employing simple sets and enhancing intimacy between actor and audience. In 1840, he produced *Twelfth Night* in an open hall using a single, unchanging set with a large, shallow forestage backed by doors and an inner stage. After Immermann's death, Tieck continued to approximate original performance conditions for Shakespeare's plays, in particular with the 1843 production of *A Midsummer Night's Dream* in Berlin, which was performed on a permanent set on the stage of a proscenium theatre and revived periodically up to 1885. Further experiments in staging Shakespeare were taken up in 1889 at the Munich Court Theatre by Jocza Savits (1847–1915) and Kurt Lautenschläger (1843–1906). To achieve the actor-audience intimacy sought by Shakespearean reformers, they placed a revolve – the first on a western stage – over the orchestra pit of the Munich Residenztheater and built a scenic wall with arches, windows, doorways, and a gallery. The forestage was an open area for acting, and the rear wall framed an inner stage for perspective scenery. Their effort, entitled the Munich Shakespeare-Stage, was used until 1906, only two years before the revolutionary Munich Artists' Theatre opened.

The other major nineteenth-century influence on later German theatre architecture was Richard Wagner's Festspielhaus in Bayreuth. While, as we have seen, this theatre was the epitome of the nineteenth-century illusionistic stage, its auditorium design influenced many later theatre reformers. Wagner's goal was to create as complete an illusion as possible for his music dramas, thus allowing the audience to throw itself imaginatively and emotionally into the action, while minimising their awareness of stage artifice and even of the theatre itself. So the steeply raked wedge shape of the Festspielhaus auditorium, reminiscent of a narrowed classical Greek amphitheatre or Roman *cavea*, drew the audience into the drama more effectively than conventionally designed auditoria. The seating-plan is 'democratic', with almost all the seats in a single bank facing the stage directly, so that everyone enjoys good sightlines and acoustics, and there is little class segregation, except for a few boxes at the rear. The goal is to focus the audience's attention on the stage, not on fellow spectators, as was the case in eighteenth- and nineteenth-century horseshoe-shaped auditoria. The orchestra pit is sunk beneath the stage and the orchestra's lights are masked from the audience's view, enhancing the audience's feeling of closeness to the stage. The side walls of the auditorium do not accommodate people in boxes; instead a series of wings or intervening arches lead the eye from the rear of the auditorium to the proscenium arch. The proscenium itself is a double arch that provides a transition from the world of the auditorium to the world of the stage. The result is a neutralised auditorium that throws the audience's focus onto the world of illusion on the stage. Although twentieth-century reformers avoided Wagner's illusionism, the Festspielhaus auditorium still provided the basis for most twentieth-century German theatres.

Munich Artists' Theatre

The first twentieth-century theatre in Germany to break the fourth wall of the picture frame was the Münchener Künstlertheater (Munich Artists' Theatre), built in 1908. The architect was Max Littmann (1862–1931), who worked from the ideas of Georg Fuchs (1868–1949), the theatre's first director. Fuchs is now primarily known for this formal innovation, but his change was based on a broader cultural and political agenda. Fuchs was a right-wing German nationalist, monarchist, supporter of the aristocracy, and an anti-Semite, his goal for the arts being the unification and invigoration of a homogeneous German people – the *Volk*. Inspired by Wagner and Friedrich Nietzsche, he wanted to create a theatre that united highbrow literary drama with modernised Dionysian cult rituals, medieval festivals, and popular, fairground entertainment. His agenda clearly anticipated fascism, in that it was anti-Semitic, sought to achieve racial homogeneity, and saw war as a viable means of achieving nationalist goals.[1]

Fuchs was opposed to the naturalism and illusionism of the time and believed that theatre was based on the rhythmic movement of the body in space, occurring in the midst of spectators and thus inducing a new communal experience. Fuchs's goal was to unify the audience by sweeping them into Dionysian intoxication with the performance. Because of his focus on these three aspects of theatre – the body, the space, and the audience relationship with the performance – his architecture endeavoured 'to contribute to the artistic effect of the whole production, so that the dramatic experience might enter the soul with such force and purity as to engender a complete and satisfactory artistic impression'.[2]

Fuchs's ideas on theatre architecture were influenced not only by the earlier Shakespearean reformers and Wagner's Festspielhaus, but also by Peter Behrens (1868–1940), a pioneer in modernist architecture and design and a leading member of the German Werkbund. In 1901, Behrens created a plan for a theatre that would emphasise performers' movements in relief, on a wide, shallow stage against a neutral background. He placed a circular orchestra – dancing place – at the centre and linked the stage and auditorium with wide steps at the sides. In 1904, Fuchs delivered a lecture on theatre reform in Munich, where he met Max Littmann, the designer of the Munich Schauspielhaus (Playhouse) as well as the Prinzregententheater (Prince Regent's Theatre), who would subsequently create designs to illustrate Fuchs' ideas in his book, *Die Schaubühne der Zukunft* (*The Stage of the Future*, 1904). Like Wagner, Fuchs advocated abolishing class divisions in the auditorium, focusing the audience's attention on the stage, and reducing social interaction in the auditorium. He used the fan-shaped, Bayreuth-style auditorium, with its egalitarian seating, acoustics, and sightlines, which had already been employed by Littmann at the Prinzregententheater. Littmann then designed the Künstlertheater, which incorporated Fuchs's idea of the 'relief stage', which was shallow with a neutral background, as a continuation of the audience's space, with the auditorium walls and ceiling tapering toward the stage to provide focus. Permanent doors on the sides provided entrances for the actors. An inner proscenium, with neutral walls and permanent doors and windows, framed the inner stage. The entire architectural unit was a simplified, more modernist version of the nineteenth-century Shakespearean stages (fig. 15).

On his relief stage, Fuchs sought to create forceful and immediate images that would be addressed directly to the audience with no 'spatial mediation'.[3] 'The purpose of the relief stage,' Fuchs claimed, 'is to intensify the

15 Künstlertheater in Munich, built in 1908 by Max Littmann for Georg Fuchs.

dramatic experience. This phenomenon does not occur upon the stage. It occurs in the mind and spirit of the spectator in response to the happenings upon the stage.' Without illusionism onstage, the audience would be less inclined to see the performance as a simulacrum of reality; instead, the stylized performance would inspire the spectator's imagination. The relief stage would communicate the performance 'directly and forcefully'.[4]

The Munich Artists' Theatre opened in 1908 as part of the 750th anniversary of the founding of the city, with a production of *Faust, Part 1*, which drew international attention but mixed reviews. Fuchs's first and only year as director proved to be a disaster. His subsequent book, *Die Revolution des Theaters* (*Revolution in the Theatre*), which described the Munich Artists' Theatre without reference to his failure, had widespread influence outside Germany. Fuchs was hailed as a pioneer in the effort to create a new theatre devoted to art and spirituality, not commerce. Kenneth Macgowan compared Fuchs to Adolphe Appia and Edward Gordon Craig, calling him 'the greatest theorist and builder of the modern German theatre'.[5] Mordecai Gorelik called Fuchs's forestage 'a battleground of dramatic theory'.[6] The

Munich Artists' Theatre was destroyed, except for the façade, by bombing in the Second World War.

Fuchs's and Littmann's theatre was a step toward breaking out of the proscenium model, but Adolphe Appia, the modernist set-designer, saw Littmann's theatres as a continuation of the nineteenth-century tradition. Appia had praised Wagner's Festspielhaus for its solemnity, harmony of lines and colours, and focus on the stage. He approved of the wide proscenium that formed an organic part of the auditorium, through which 'the mystical abyss' appears unlimited.[7] At Littmann's *Prinzregententheater*, on the other hand, Appia criticised the garish colors, bright statues and gilded proscenium frame, in which Littmann neglected 'the careful attenuation of colours and shapes, the cathartic luring of the eye into the stage perspective, and the organic incorporation of the auditorium to the acting sphere'. For Appia, the proscenium had a 'horrible feeling of narrowness', and caused 'a frightening impression of sitting in a big funnel that opens into the orchestra's dark hole'.[8]

Hellerau

Appia provided the inspiration for the first true open-space theatre in Germany, in a building of singular importance in architectural history (fig. 16). The Hellerau theatre outside Dresden was built for the work of Émile Jaques-Dalcroze (1865–1960), who developed Eurhythmics, a system of musical education based on rhythmic exercises. Jaques-Dalcroze wanted students to increase their awareness of the rhythm of music and to express that rhythm through free-form movement of the hands, feet, and body in space. Through Eurhythmics, students would gain musical sensitivity and physical coordination. Appia met Jaques-Dalcroze in 1906 and was attracted to his synthesis of music, movement, and space. The two collaborated over the next several years, with Appia creating renderings of 'Rhythmic Spaces' for performances of Eurhythmics.

In 1909, Jaques-Dalcroze conducted a Eurhythmics demonstration in Dresden, which was attended by Wolf Dohrn, an official in the Werkbund, a reform movement dedicated to advancing design and craft in everyday goods and architecture, as well as to improving the lives and working conditions of craftspeople. The Werkbund had founded Hellerau in 1907 as a 'model town' and factory. Dohrn invited Jaques-Dalcroze to use Hellerau as a centre for Eurhythmics and to open a theatre there 'to replace the missing church'.[9] Jaques-Dalcroze asked Appia to participate in the planning and design process and Heinrich Tessenow (1876–1950) was hired as architect.

16 Theatre in Hellerau near Dresden, the first genuine open theatre in Germany, built by Adolphe Appia and Heinrich Tessenow in 1912.

It is difficult now to tease out the relative contributions of Appia and Tessenow, but it is clear that at least the inspiration and overall design came from Appia. He was concerned that spectators had hitherto been passive absorbers of performance and that conventional theatre space encouraged the physical and mental posture of sitting quietly and inexpressively in a comfortable chair in a darkened room, separated from the performance. Appia saw Eurhythmics as an opportunity to create performances that encouraged active involvement: '*Eurhythmics will overturn this passivity!* Musical rhythm will enter all of us, to say: *you yourself* are the work of art.'[10] Appia also felt that conventional architecture enforced a barrier between audience and perform-ance, and he saw a unity in the theatre of ancient Greece that has since been lost: 'The spatial significance of our theatre is curtailed by the frame of the proscenium arch. The Greeks perceived a unity between the spectacle and its boundary; less fortunately, we have located the spectacle on the other side of the boundary because, not being artists, we separate ourselves off from the work of art.'[11] Appia is best known for his denunciation of illusionistic, two-dimensional painted scenery and his advocacy of a three-dimensional space sculpted by light, with platforms, ramps, steps, and towers that evoke the mood of the play: 'we shall no longer attempt to give the illusion of a *forest* but instead the illusion of a *man* in the atmosphere of a forest; man is the reality and the rest is of no importance.'[12] In order to create this involving, partic-ipatory, non-illusionistic performance, Appia needed a new space: 'Each of his [the poet musician's] dramas not only determines its own *production*, but the theatre as well.'[13]

The Hellerau theatre was a large rectangular box with nearly identical spaces at each end, platforms and steps for the performers, and tiered seating for the audience. Performers and audience shared the same space, separated only by an open void in the centre. The architectural distinction between the audience and the performance was abolished, except that the audience was at one end of the box and the performers were at the other. The performers and spectators were also united by light: the entire space was a glowing box, with fabric walls and ceiling lit from behind, creating a diffused daylight effect. Measuring 49 metres long, 16 metres wide, and 12 metres high, the theatre accommodated 560 spectators and up to 250 performers. There was nothing here of the conventional theatre: no proscenium arch, no orchestra pit, no fly space, no trap doors, and no wing space, and for the audience, no pit, no boxes, and no galleries. Appia described the theatre as 'an empty room, waiting'.[14] With only light, space, and levels, the focus was on the performer moving through space.

The house opened in 1912 with a programme that included Eurhythmic dancing and the second act of Gluck's *Orpheus and Eurydice*. Both performance and theatre were well received; artists from across Europe attended the first season and spread the reputation of this theatrical innovation. The project was short-lived, however. Dohrn died in a skiing accident in 1914, and Jaques-Dalcroze cut his ties to Hellerau following the outbreak of war later that year. During the post-World War II communist era the building became a sports hall for Russians stationed in Dresden. Today, the basic structure remains and has been partially restored. Hellerau is once again being used as a venue for experimental arts, performance, and exhibition, housing the European Centre for the Arts, under the direction of Udo Zimmermann.

The spaces of Max Reinhardt

Max Reinhardt was the first major German director to experiment with a large variety of theatre forms in the search to discover a specific space for each individual play. The word 'eclectic' has become welded to Reinhardt's name, and he surely did explore every known style. Throughout his career, he worked in both large and small-scale theatres and directed productions in a variety of non-theatrical spaces. According to Reinhardt, 'if the place corresponds with the play, something wonderful will be the outcome'.[15] Hugo von Hofmannsthal (1874–1929), playwright and frequent collaborator with Reinhardt, described the importance of theatre space for him:

> He considers place in the highest degree important. For months and sometimes for years he has dreamed of how a room will shut an audience in, whether with solemnity of height as in a church, or with solemnity of breadth as in the ancient theatre, or mysteriously, as in some grotto, or agreeably and socially, as in a pleasant, peopled salon . . . What he dreamed of was a house resembling as closely as possible the body of a violin and, like the violin, attuned to receive and respond to the slightest vibration.[16]

Arthur Kahane, Reinhardt's dramaturge and collaborator, later wrote that from the very beginning he expressed a desire for two theatres, a large one for classics and a small one for intimate drama, and, later, a huge third theatre for festival productions. In 1902 Reinhardt transformed his Berlin cabaret *Schall und Rauch* into the Kleines Theater (Small Theatre), and the following year he acquired the Neues Theater am Schiffbauerdamm, where he installed a revolve and sky dome. His career breakthrough came in 1905, when he was named director of the Deutsches Theater, which by this time had become the most prestigious theatre in Germany, which he ran, as he did his other theatres, with steadily decreasing involvement over the next twenty-five years. The following year, Reinhardt built the Kammerspiele within the Deutsches Theater as a site for chamber plays and as a counterpoint to the larger house next door.

His career then intersected with that of Georg Fuchs and the Munich Artists' Theatre. Reinhardt's company was booked into the Munich

Kammerspiele in the summer of 1908, and, following the dismissal of Fuchs, he was offered the leadership of the Munich Artists' Theatre for the 1909 summer season. He presented his Berlin productions at the Artists' Theatre, using the full depth of the stage rather than the shallow relief utilised by Fuchs. It was in Munich that he also presented the first of those large-scale mass spectacles, which he later dubbed 'Theatre of Five Thousand'. He directed Sophocles' *Oedipus Rex* in the Musikfesthalle in 1910, with over 3000 spectators on three sides of the thrust stage, with the central stage serving as a Greek orchestra. The production was a success and went on to be performed in the Circus Renz in Vienna and the Circus Schumann in Berlin. He continued to direct large-scale productions, including Aeschylus' *Oresteia* trilogy in Munich the following year and *The Miracle* at Olympia in London, with a cast of 1500 and an audience of 10,000. The production subsequently toured Europe and the United States, and, wherever it played, the entire space was transformed into a cathedral, with the audience as congregation. In 1919, Reinhardt converted the Circus Schumann into the Grosses Schauspielhaus (large playhouse), the first large multiform theatre in the twentieth century. Reinhardt, like other theatre reformers of the early twentieth century, wanted to unite audience and performance, a goal he described to the architect Hans Poelzig as follows:

> We must move out of the proscenium and eliminate the division between the actor and the public! But it is not enough to bring the stage into the auditorium; no, the whole tired tradition that the stage and the auditorium are two realms separate from one another must be destroyed. The viewer must feel that he is a participant in the development of the proceedings. But the curtain must disappear, the actor should, whenever it is possible, move through the auditorium, and it should be decorated in harmony with the scenery.[17]

Poelzig transformed the Circus Schumann by draping the entire structure with a new skin and covering the interior with plaster stalactites, which, when lit from behind, created a mysterious cave-like effect. The stalactites also served the practical acoustical effect of deadening the reverberation in the circus dome. The mysterious aura of the building was established in the lobby, by sculptural columns and indirect lighting, an effect carried through into the auditorium, which had small inset lights to create the effect of a night sky.

The permanent configuration of the theatre was a thrust, with the audience surrounding the stage on three sides in a U-shaped amphitheatre. To create a proscenium theatre, seats could be placed on the thrust stage, facing a wide portal that framed the scenic stage. The auditorium was divided into sections, but the effect was of a single, unified audience sharing one space with the performers. The stage consisted of a forestage and thrust – the former circus ring – backed by a wide portal, which could be closed off with screens for a solid background or opened up to the scenic stage behind. The backstage was equipped for scenery with a revolve, some capability for flying scenery, and a sky dome. Actors could enter through the portal at the rear of the stage or directly onto the thrust through tunnels from under the auditorium. The building was well received, as were the productions Reinhardt staged within it, which included the *Oresteia*, Rolland's *Danton*, and Schiller's *Räuber*.

While Reinhardt's mass performances did not contain an overt political message and Reinhardt was not a political or artistic radical, the spectacles were consistent with the revolutionary spirit of post-war Germany. The Grosses Schauspielhaus opened in 1919, shortly after the failure of the socialist Spartacist Revolt. Reinhardt sought to unite the audience and the performance, to bring all classes of people into the theatre, in order to reinvigorate it. Reinhardt considered the stage represented 'the most power-ful and direct form of art, the most powerful, because it appeals not to the individual only, but to the public in general, and because it has the power of mastering and influencing that public'.[18] Arnold Zweig described the powerful effect of this mass theatre:

> Does it not with its opening scenes, which create atmosphere, set the stage, dictate the conditions, the very laws, mould the thousands of individual preconceived ideas that each member of the audience has come with into one universal idea? One objective: the event; one attitude: ever more avid participation; one wish: the denouement; one frame of mind: abandon? With each action, each movement, does not the diversity of a thousand different interests give way to a unity, to one spirit, the spirit of the work? ... [T]he edifying, ennobling, consecrating power of such an evening performs the miracle of retransforming petrified, isolated individ-uals into a deeply moved, purified community.[19]

While there is certainly no cause and effect, Zweig's statement now eerily evokes the later large-scale Nazi spectacles. There are, however, critical differences; Reinhardt and Zweig were Jewish, the political context was socialist, and participation was not coerced. Nonethless, while the politics may have been radically different, Fuchs's relief stage, Reinhardt's 'Theatre of Five Thousand', and Nazi spectacles shared a common goal of transforming the individual spectators into a unified mass with a 'universal' idea.

Other Grosses Schauspielhaus productions, not directed by Reinhardt, were unsuccessful, and, after he left, the thrust stage was filled with seats and a compromised proscenium stage was the result. The change obliterated what had been unique about the theatre and exacerbated its existing problems. It worked well for Reinhardt's mass spectacular productions, but smaller shows were lost in the vast space. The permanent seats had encircled the thrust stage in a 'U' shape, which thus became the centre of the theatre. When the thrust stage was filled with seats that faced the wide proscenium stage, the sightlines from the side seats were poor and the space made no sense visually and structurally. In addition, even though the stalactites ameliorated the acoustical problems by cutting down on the echo, the space was still simply too huge for good audibility, and when actors moved upstage of the portal, there was yet more space to swallow up the sound. After the Second World War, the Grosses Schauspielhaus was used as a music hall, known as the Friedrichstadtpalast, until it was torn down in 1984 because of structural problems.

Simultaneous with the opening of the Grosses Schauspielhaus, Reinhardt established the Salzburg Festival, which was spread out across the city and was intended to incorporate a massive theatre designed by Poelzig; this, however, was never built. In 1920, the festival opened, albeit on a smaller scale than initially envisaged. Reinhardt's first production at Salzburg was Hofmannsthal's *Jedermann*, performed outdoors in front of the Cathedral, though the space of action implicitly included the greater city, with Everyman entering from the audience, other characters entering from adjoining squares, and bells and calls coming from church steeples across the city and from the castle above.

From 1922, Reinhardt also directed in another found space that he converted to theatrical purposes, the Redoutensaal in Vienna, a grand ballroom in the imperial palace, which offered a simple stage on a platform at one end with doors and curving staircases. Reinhardt's productions here included plays by Goethe and Calderon; the baroque space was well matched to the period styles of the plays, and the action was on a more human scale than it was in the Grosses Schauspielhaus.

During the 1930s, Reinhardt continued to match productions with found, non-theatrical spaces. In 1931, he directed *Twelfth Night* in his castle home, Leopoldskron, for a small invited audience. After emigrating from Germany following the Nazi rise to power, he directed *A Midsummer Night's Dream* in outdoor, garden locations, including the Boboli Gardens in Florence and a meadow outside Oxford in 1933. In the same year he created a 'Fauststadt' (Faust City) installation in the Felsenreitschule (riding school) in Salzburg. In 1934 he directed *The Merchant of Venice* on a canal in Venice and took *A Midsummer Night's Dream* to the US, where it was performed in the Hollywood Bowl and in the Faculty Glade at the University of California, Berkeley.

Bauhaus

A school of design, architecture, and applied arts, the Bauhaus was founded in Weimar in 1919 by Walter Gropius, but it moved to Dessau in 1925 when funding in Weimar was cut. While theatre was not in the original manifesto, it became central to the Bauhaus as a unifying art, and one of the Bauhaus books, *Die Bühne im Bauhaus*, was dedicated solely to theatre. Oskar Schlemmer, who led the workshop from 1923 to 1929, wrote that 'the aims of the Bauhaus are also the aims of our stage',[20] and Bauhaus artists sought to unite audience and performance in physical proximity and spiritual communion. As László Moholy-Nagy (1895–1946) wrote:

> in contemporary theatre, STAGE AND SPECTATOR are separated too much from each other. Their division into active and passive roles prevents a creative generation of relations and tensions between them. Finally, an activity has to be developed that keeps the masses from watching in silence, as well as from experiencing a solely inner excitement. Instead, this activity should encourage the spectators to enter and to participate actively in the action and eventually to merge with the stage action on the highest level of redemptive ecstasy.[21]

Schlemmer's best-known performance was the *Triadisches Ballett (Triadic Ballet)*, first performed in 1922 in Stuttgart and later at the Bauhaus. Schlemmer was interested in the human body as form, turning performers into doll-like automata devoid of individualising human features, and the movement of the body through space: 'SPACE as a part of the larger total complex, building (*Bau*). The art of the stage is a spatial art, a fact which is bound to become clearer and clearer in the future. The stage, including the auditorium, is above all an architectonic-spatial organism where all things happening to it and within it exist in a spatially conditioned relationship.'[22] Space, in Schlemmer's works, was a geometric volume defined by the human body moving through it. He stretched wires through the space and drew lines on the floor to delineate the performance space.

There was one actual theatre in the Dessau Bauhaus building, designed by Gropius, which had a stage with openings at the front and the back, onto the main hall and the dining room. The theatre was central to the Bauhaus, being literally at the heart of the building and figuratively central to the other art activities. The main hall (Aula) had 164 tubular steel chairs designed by Marcel Breuer in a single unified block facing the stage. The stage was 72 metres square, being made up of platforms that could be raised or lowered. Scenery or screens could be suspended from tracks on the ceiling, but there was no capability for the conventional scenery-changing devices of traps, flies, or wings. In addition, the entire Bauhaus building was turned into a performance space: a photograph by Lux Feininger, entitled 'The Building as Stage', shows the exterior of the building being used for performance, with performers in Schlemmer's costumes on the roof and hanging off the balconies The Bauhaus building, including the stage, has been restored and is currently open to the public.

Andreas Weininger, a Bauhaus architect, designed a *Kugeltheater* (spherical theatre) in 1924, with the audience on the inside of the sphere and the stage a rotating sculpture in the centre. According to Weininger, this was:

> an answer to the question of the space theatre, the problem of the theatre of the future. – The space stage and the space theatre as the home of the mechanical play. A sphere as architectonic structure in place of the customary theatre. The spectators, on the inner wall of the sphere, find themselves in a new relationship to space. Because of their all-encompassing view, because of centripetal force, they find themselves in a new psychic, optical, acoustical relationship; they find themselves confronted with new possibilities for concentric, eccentric, multidirectional, mechanical space-stage phenomena. – In order to realise its task completely, the mechanical theatre lays claim to the highest developments of functional technology. – Purpose: to educate men through the creative play of new rhythms of motion to new modes of observation; to give elementary answers to elementary necessities.[23]

This theatre was never built and would probably have been technically impractical, though it demonstrates the innovative scope of Bauhaus designers.

Farkas Molnár (1895–1945) designed another project for the Bauhaus, the U-Theatre, which was never built but was more in line with actual theatre practice, such as Reinhardt's Grosses Schauspielhaus and later thrust and multiform theatres. Molnár's 1,590 putative spectators would have been accommodated in a large U-shaped amphitheatre with balcony and boxes. The foremost section of the stage was a thrust surrounded on three sides by the audience, backed by a forestage with the capability of displaying three-dimensional scenery. A wide portal framed the scenic stage house at the rear. Above the stage was a gallery cantilevered over the main stage and connected to the auditorium balcony. As in Weininger's Kugeltheater, a cylindrical structure hung in the centre above the thrust; this raised and lowered equipment or performers, 'making aerial acrobatics possible'.[24] All areas of the stage and auditorium were connected by bridges, so the performance could flow easily from one area or level to another.

Walter Gropius, who designed the theatre in the Dessau Bauhaus and remodelled the city theatre in Jena in 1923, then went on to create one of the most influential theatre models of the twentieth century, the 'Totaltheater', for the productions of Erwin Piscator, which employed documentary techniques and socialist perspectives, and sought to change the audience's perception of theatre space through the use of projections and visual collage. According to Gropius, the aim of the Totaltheater was 'to overwhelm the audience'.[25] It should 'shake off its lethargy as soon as it experiences the surprising effect of the transformed room'. Gropius created in effect the first large-scale, mechanised multiform theatre, which would become the model for many subsequent post-war buildings. The idea was to create a single space that contained the potential for the major audience-performance configurations: proscenium, thrust, and arena. Instead of building three separate theatres, one space could be transformed into all three. According to Gropius, 'the contemporary theatre architect should aim at creating a grand keyboard for light and space, so clinical and adjustable that it would be susceptible to any vision ever imaginable by a stage director; a flexible construction whose space alone reshapes and recreates the mind'.[26]

The Totaltheater would have seated 2000 spectators in an ovoid space, connected to a rectangular stage house. One section of the auditorium was permanent, as was the stage house, but the central stage and audience blocks were placed eccentrically on rotating turntables, which could rearrange the space, even during a performance, to create the three configurations. Screens were mounted throughout the entire theatre, so that projected images could surround the audience in a total environment. However, the theatre was never built, in part because of the Depression, in part too because the mechanisms for shifting the audience and stage were too complex and impractical. Also, the sightlines, especially from the fixed bank of seating, may well have been poor.

The great modernist reform movement in theatre space had lost steam by the late 1920s. The experiments had run their course and neither the economy nor the energy of the artists could support new ones. National Socialist political and artistic policies stamped out any reforms in the 1930s and most major theatres were heavily damaged or destroyed in the Second World War.

Post-war theatre architecture

Many new theatres were built in the 1950s; most were reconstructions of destroyed theatres or multipurpose halls without a clear artistic mission. Almost every large town and city had a new theatre; up to 225 new or renovated theatres were constructed in former West Germany and 80 theatres in East Germany in the 40 years after the War.[27] In the immediate post-war era, some companies performed in minor houses or found spaces that were not in the destroyed city centre, and as these were redesigned for long-term use, provisional solutions often became permanent. In Leipzig, for example, the municipal theatre moved into a former music hall that was reconstructed in the 1950s for permanent use. This theatre is located on a side street outside the central ring and lacks any distinguishing façade. In other cases, the destruction of the inner cities and lack of heating in the immediate post-war years led to the phenomenon of *Kellertheater* and *Zimmertheater* (basement and apartment-room theatre), generally seating less than one hundred and with mini-stages suitable for plays with only a few characters. Many large theatres were rebuilt on their original sites, often on a main square or intersection in the city centre and are so prominent that they serve as major landmarks. In many cases, the wide open space around the theatre provides visual isolation and gives prominence to the building as a free-standing monument, symbolic of the city's cultural aspirations.

The exteriors of many of these reconstructions are for the most part modernist insofar as they avoid adornment in favour of clean, clear lines and are constructed of modern materials such as reinforced concrete, steel, and glass. The theatre space itself often follows the tradition of Wagner's Festspielhaus, Littmann's Prinzregententheater, and the Munich Artists' Theatre. The interiors are conventional mid-twentieth-century proscenium-arch constructions, and the backstage is usually equipped with up-to-date scenic technology. The architecture still enforces a separation of audience and performance, but this barrier is de-emphasised. The arch itself tends to be wide and nondescript, so that it blends into the auditorium; the effect is as if the auditorium side walls and ceiling simply end at the edge of the stage. The fourth wall is broken with a flexible apron and side stages, and the orchestra pit can be expanded or covered over as a forestage. In the auditorium, hierarchical order is largely abandoned in favour of undifferentiated banks of seats, with balconies stacked over the *Parkett* (stalls). Some theatres maintain an area of exclusive seats, whether a narrow loge or a few boxes, but the overall goal is egalitarianism in seating, sightlines, and acoustics. Lobbies tend to be spacious, if uninviting, with ample coat-check, bars, and toilets. The early twentieth-century reformist goal of greater intimacy between audience and performer is neither abandoned nor advanced. Many of these bland, uninspired theatres tend to perpetuate nineteenth-century conventions, while missing the point of the Festspielhaus's challenge to that tradition.

Several theatres do, however, continue to promote the innovative use of space, with varying degrees of success. These open-space theatres can no longer be labelled 'experimental', as they have by now become part of the institutional mainstream. Erika Fischer-Lichte attributes the development of the open-space theatre to changes in the nature of communication over the nineteenth and twentieth centuries: nineteenth-century drama was charac-terised by internal communication between characters, enclosed within the fourth wall of the proscenium-arch stage; twentieth-century theatre, on the contrary, forged a relationship between the stage and the auditorium, necessitating a shared space. The avant-garde in the first third of the twentieth century felt that this shift to external communication could 'win back the basic social and cultural functions of theatre'.[28]

The Mannheim National Theatre is one of the most frequently cited post-war German theatres in architectural journals and books on theatre architecture. The old building was destroyed by bombing in 1943, so in the early 1950s the city held a competition for a new house. Ten architects presented proposals, including Mies van der Rohe (1886–1969), who began his career working for Peter Behrens and was a director of the Bauhaus in the early 1930s. The commission went to Gerhard Weber (1909–1986), but his final design incorporated aspects of van der Rohe's proposal. The new complex opened in 1957 and comprises the Grosses Haus, seating 1200–1300 and used primarily for opera, and the Kleines Haus, seating 600–700 and used for drama.

For Hans Schüler, the first director of the new theatre, the goal was to enhance a 'feeling of community' among the audience and to create a sense of unity between spectator and performer, as postulated by the pre-war avant-garde.[29] According to Schüler, the 'highest law' for theatre design is 'Space, space, and again space!'[30] In the Kleines Haus, Schüler wanted 'the character of a lecture hall and meeting room in which the spectator is encouraged to participate in a creative discussion'.[31] The interior walls, made of uncovered perforated brick, enhanced this utilitarian feeling along with a rich, vivid colour. The Kleines Haus is designed as a unified space to be flexibly rearranged into a variety of audience-performance configurations. One end of the space is for the audience and the other is for the stage, but the walls and ceiling are continuous, creating a single unified space. Ramp-like stairs extend along the sides of the auditorium from the stage to the rear of the auditorium, which can also be used for staging, thus potentially surrounding the audience. A movable portal, consisting of two towers and a lighting bridge, with a variable width of 11 to 15 metres, can create a proscenium frame, or the portal can be moved away to create a single space theatre. The stage itself is 20 metres wide and 18 metres deep, or 23 metres if the forestage is added, and is made up of elevator platforms that can be configured for staging or for auditorium seating. In theory, and in early practice, the theatre could be configured into an end stage, with orchestra pit or steps, thrust, traverse, or arena. For the most part, however, the Kleines Haus has been used as an end-stage theatre, thus meeting the fate of most flexible theatres: they end up as de facto end-stage, with needless, expensive, and even counter-productive machinery and with none of the clarity of a well-designed single-purpose theatre. The theatre has proved to be important, however, as a site for Erwin Piscator's work after his return to Germany, including his production of Schiller's *Die Räuber*, which opened the theatre in 1957, and for the notable production of Arnolt Bronnen's *Vatermord*, directed by Jürgen Bosse, in 1979.

At its opening, the building was considered a showpiece of modernism and a milestone in the post-war reconstruction of Germany, but in its attempt to incorporate the ideals of pre-war modernism into the reconstruction of post-war Germany the design suggested cautious restoration, not radicalism. Fifty years later, however, it seems less like a fulfilment of early twentieth-century reforms and more like a series of functionalist compromises. Despite its frequent appearance in books and articles, the architecture has been sharply criticised as being cold. Even the first director of the theatre felt the complex was too bulky, and more recently Klaus Völker has called it a 'showy and unwieldy culture-bunker' that is 'constructed like a fortress on a giant air-raid shelter shielded against the city'.[32] Indeed, while in Mies's original proposal, a glass and open-truss structure lightened the mass of the building, the finished design is closed and heavy.

The Frankfurt Schauspielhaus is renowned as one of Germany's largest stages but has the infamous reputation as being one of the most difficult. The previous theatre was destroyed in 1944 and the new complex opened in 1963. It was designed by the architectural firm of Apel, Beckert and Becker, with the Grosses Haus seating a maximum of 700 and the Kleines Haus approximately 200. In addition, the theatre operates two other spaces, the Bockenheimer Depot, a former city garage now used as an open flexible space with variable stage and seating for up to 800, and schmidtstrasse 12, seating up to 300.

The theatre complex is situated in the centre of one of the world's major financial districts. 'Mainhattan', the nickname for Frankfurt am Main, is a challenging environment for theatre. The very façade displays this struggle, as it is dwarfed by the office towers that surround it. The financial district is virtually uninhabited after the banks, stock market, and offices close, leaving empty canyons of concrete and glass facades. Inside, the stage of the Grosses Haus is impressive for its vast size and extensive technology. Flexibility can be primarily found at the boundary between the auditorium and the stage. The basic arrangement of audience and stage, with the spectators in one seating block looking straight on at the performance area, is not disrupted, but the nature of the separation or unification can be varied. The proscenium frame itself can vary in size from 9 to 13 metres wide and 4 to 7.3 metres high. All three portions of the curtain-wall within the proscenium can be raised or moved to the back wall, thus creating an open space that is unified with the auditorium. This playing area is 25 metres wide and 21.5 metres deep. The edge of the stage is also variable and can be lowered to create an orchestra pit or raised to be used as a forestage. Stepped side stages extend out into the auditorium, which can be used for performance. The auditorium is a single bank of seats, with no balcony, and the side walls near the stage can be pivoted inward to focus on the proscenium arch or pivoted outward to create a single room with the stage.

The vastness of this stage, the widest in Germany, has swallowed up many productions, but it has also been used to impressive effect. Tom Kühnel and Robert Schuster's production of *Faust Parts I and II* in 1999, for example, emphasised the wide open space. Elisabeth Schweeger (b. 1954), the current artistic director, has successfully juggled a range of large-scale spectacles and chamber performances in the large and small theatres. In 2001, her first year, her productions on the main stage included Peter Greenaway's *Gold*, a multi-media show, with projections on curved screens, and Kleist's *Penthesilea*, in which the Austrian architects Coop Himmelb(l)au, rather than minimising or shrinking from the space, emphasised the great volume of the stage with massive cone-shaped tents.

The Staatstheater Darmstadt, designed by Rolf Prange and opened in 1972, provides a notable example of the problematic architecture of the 1960s and 1970s in West Germany. After Darmstadt's historic theatre had been destroyed by bombing in 1944, the company used a series of provisional non-theatrical spaces while planning for a new theatre that would suit all its needs and break with nineteenth-century traditions. The result is a complex that comprises the Grosses Haus, seating 956, the Kleines Haus, seating 482, a Werkstattsbühne (Workshop Theatre), seating 99, and a parking garage. The Kleines Haus has a *Parkett* and balcony, and can be transformed into a variety of configurations, including picture-frame proscenium, apron stage, thrust, arena, and open-space stage. The juncture of the auditorium and the stage can be reconfigured with a movable bridge overhead and with auditorium wall sections on pivoting wagons. The portal opening can be from 8 to 15 metres wide and from 5 to 7 metres high, the stage itself being 19 metres deep and 14 metres wide. The Werkstattsbühne is an open-space black box theatre with no fixed seats, measuring 15 metres wide and 20 metres long. The fortress-like building, designed in a concrete brutalist style, stands apart from its surroundings. While it was designed as a functionalist, democratic articulation of modern optimism during the affluent times of the 1960s and 1970s, the complex now seems like an indifferent imitation of government office buildings, ironically perpetuating the monumental style of dictatorship. A recent remodelling has aimed to brighten up the greying concrete and create a more distinctive entrance to the building.

The Ballhoftheater in Hanover exemplifies much of German theatre history. It was originally built in 1649 to house aristocratic pastimes and comprised a free-standing indoor tennis court with a central open space and a viewing gallery. It was converted for use as a theatre between 1752 and 1758, and then used for drama, opera, and balls, and even as a stable. It was used by the Hitler Youth in World War II and was a temporary theatre after the war. In 1975 architect Anton Meldau redesigned the space for the Niedersächsische Staatstheater Hannover (State Theatre of Lower Saxony) as the smaller venue for more innovative productions. Its immediate post-war use as an improvised, provisional theatre is typical of the period in which most major theatres had been destroyed and any existing space converted for theatrical purposes. But while most cities built new theatres in the concrete/steel/glass modernist style of the 1950s and 1960s, this temporary theatre survived long enough to be saved by the rise of interest in historic preservation during the 1970s. The restored space is now called *Ballhofeins* (Ballroom One), after a smaller adjacent theatre, *Ballhofzwei* (Ballroom Two), which seats 130 and was opened in 1990.

The goal of the conversion of Ballhofeins was to strip away the additions and renovations since 1679 and to create a functioning modern theatre. The conversion preserves the original building's exterior and creates adjacent modernised support spaces. The overall space is 12 metres by 28 metres. Part of the auditorium has fixed seating and part is moveable, allowing for end or thrust-stage configurations. The auditorium, which seats 300 to 400, has a Parkett (stalls) and galleries on three sides. The proscenium arch is movable and can be placed downstage as a conventional proscenium, framing the entire stage, or at mid-stage for an apron and frame combination, or be removed completely by being stored against the back wall to create an open-end stage. The stage itself consists of rectangular sections that can be raised or lowered, and the forestage can also be lowered to form an orchestra pit or provide extra seating. The Hanover Ballhoftheater is emblematic of theatre design trends in the last quarter of the twentieth century as it combines respect for historical tradition and flexibility but within strict limits. The galleries on the side create a 'courtyard theatre,' suggestive of theatre configurations from the Renaissance through the eighteenth century; these enhance audience intimacy without having spectators confront each other directly across the stage. The flexible stage and medium-size auditorium, housed within its historic walls, create a handsome venue for contemporary innovative performances.

The Basel Schauspielhaus provides a notable example of innovative use of theatre space. Theater Basel includes three theatres: the original Stadttheater, with its Grosse Bühne and Kleine Bühne, seating 1015 and

322 respectively, opened in 1975, in addition to the Schauspielhaus, which seats up to 530. The Schauspielhaus, designed by the architectural firm of Schwarz-Gutmann, with a glass façade that harmonises well with the Basel streetscape, was opened in 2002. The goal of the Schauspielhaus interior design is to avoid any formal separation of audience and performance, so the stage and auditorium are constructed as a single unit. Many configurations are possible, though most of the technical equipment is at one end of the space. A proscenium arch can be created out of two towers and a bridge, each of which can be raised individually or as an entire unit to create an open-space theatre. The stage is 14 metres wide with the portal or 16.5 metres without. The Parkett is stepped for seating, but a platform can be placed over it to make the entire space a flat expanse. Seats on the Parkett are on movable platforms that can be arranged into a variety of configurations, including picture frame, with orchestra pit or forestage; open thrust, with seats along three walls around a vast central flat space; 'Shakespeare stage', a thrust with a gallery above; traverse; or arena. Above this level are two permanent seating galleries and acoustical baffles can be adjusted for each of these configurations. In addition, an outside wall of the theatre can be opened so that the street space can be used for performance, which is viewed through an opening 3.5 metres high and 17 metres wide. The opening production of *Hamlet*, directed by Stefan Bachman, who was also the artistic director, emphasised the new venue as a total space, exploiting the full range of the theatre's capabilities. The complex design by Ricarda Beilharz employed metal containers with modern interiors that indicated the location of the respective scene, incorporated the auditorium gallery into the performance, enlarged the impression of space by projecting the water for Ophelia's drowning onto the huge concrete walls, and extended the performance into the street through the stage opening. On the following night the Swiss musical performer Ruedi Häusermann used the same space, but with the audience sitting where the stage had been before and the show taking place in what had been the auditorium.

The Schaubühne am Halleschen Ufer in Berlin was founded in 1962 and Peter Stein took over the artistic directorship in 1970. From the outset the company avoided conventional configurations. Their productions sought to bring the audience and the performer into close proximity, an example of what Fischer-Lichte has called the completion in the 1960s of the process begun by the historical avant-garde at the beginning of the century.[33] The Schaubühne performed in a variety of flexible, unified spaces that were not segregated and segmented into proscenium stage and auditorium. Many of their performances occurred in non-theatrical spaces, including the Olympic Stadium, exhibition halls, and film studios. Notable productions included *Shakespeare's Memory I and II* (1974 and 1976), directed by Stein in the empty Central Cinema Company building in Spandau, evenings that consisted of seven hours of lectures, readings, demonstrations, tableaux, and scenes from Shakespeare's plays, with the audience promenading around the open space. Ibsen's *Peer Gynt* (1971) was presented over two evenings, in an exhibition hall seating 700 spectators on two sides of the stage.

The artists of the Schaubühne found these appropriated spaces inadequate for their needs and the theatre on Hallesches Ufer too small, and by the mid-1970s, they were searching for a permanent open space that could be adapted for their own use. In 1981 the company opened the Schaubühne am Lehniner Platz, in a complex designed by Erich Mendelsohn (1887–1953) in 1927, which included a cinema, a cabaret, a hotel, and apartments. The building had been damaged in World War II and was converted into exhibition space and cinemas after the war. The architect for the Schaubühne conversion was Jürgen Sawade, with theatre consultant Klaus Wever. The exterior was largely restored to the original, but the interior was gutted to create one huge open concrete basilica-shaped space – a rectangular box with a semicircular apse – with plain reinforced concrete walls (see fig. 17). The overall space for theatre production is vast: 68.5 metres long and 33 metres wide, with a ceiling that is 6 to 12 metres high. This is the ultimate open-space, flexible theatre. There is no formal stage or auditorium: each production has its own space created for it by the use of movable walls, floor, and ceiling. The entire space can be used for one production, in which case it can house 2000 spectators or the whole space can be divided into three theatres with capacities of 300, 500 and 700 each. Heavy steel curtain-walls can separate the theatres from each other, with each space being used separately for performance, rehearsal, or scenery storage. A theoretically infinite variety of configurations is possible, including traverse (either axis), thrust, arena, end (either end), horseshoe, corner, etc. The floor, consisting of 7 by 3 metre platforms, can be raised, lowered, or raked in sections, or be built up with adjustable platforms for seating or stage. The walls have holes for attaching sets or wall panels, and the ceiling is equipped with a grid for lighting and/or scenery. Ancillary audience spaces are placed in a wide corridor that curves around the theatre and include the lobby, bar, cloakrooms and restaurant.

17 Schaubühne am Lehniner Platz, Berlin 1981. The auditorium of the converted cinema can seat 2000 but can also be divided up into smaller spaces.

The Schaubühne has been home to many notable productions, including a seven-hour, expanded version of *Hamlet* (1982–3), directed by Klaus Michael Grüber that used the full extent of the apse for the stage, with entrances at floor level and also higher up the apse wall. Johannes Birringer noted that the play was 'presented in its almost mythic grandeur', and that 'the physical space itself functions as a complex metaphor'.[34] Martin Graue described the range and complexity of productions at the Schaubühne in December, 1983, when four productions were running. *Cami*, a collection of short pieces by Pierre Henri Cami, was staged in a café with the audience in the centre at café tables and stages on all four sides; Jean Genet's *The Blacks* had the audience walking through the backstage, watching the actors putting on makeup, and then processing through a red velvet curtain to their seats, which were rows of benches around the apse; and Meredith Monk and Ping Chong's production of *The Games* had the audience sitting on low steps watching the performance in the apse. Finally, the company staged an adaptation of Aeschylus' *Oresteia* called *Antikenprojekt II*, directed by Peter Stein and designed by Karl-Ernst Herrmann, in a day-long per-formance that occurred in the large central space, with the audience sitting on low carpeted steps suggestive of a Greek amphitheatre, facing the palace façade that had an *ekkyklema* (small revolving stage) to display the dead bodies, a *machina* escalator for Apollo, and a cable and winch for Athena's entrance from the rear of the auditorium. More traditional productions have also been staged at the Schaubühne, such as *The Art of Comedy* by Eduardo De Filippo (1982) and *Kalldewey Farce* by Botho Strauss (1982), both of which were done on framed illusionistic stages within the larger space of the theatre. Graue praises this thoughtful use of space at the Schaubühne: 'Provocation, chaos and vitality had been replaced by elegance and beauty, calm and order. Productions at the Berlin *Schaubühne* have always shown, beside the attention given to scenography itself, an intense concern with the stage-spectator relationship. Spectators could be placed inside the scenic arrangements; open spaces could alternate with proscenium stages.'[35]

The current administration of Thomas Ostermeier (b. 1968) has continued the experimental use of the Schaubühne, especially in productions designed by Jan Pappelbaum (b. 1966), an architect who designed the stage as a plaza or Greek *agora*, a public site for debate and exchange. The Schaubühne remains a landmark of German theatre inside and out, with a unity of space that no other theatre in Germany has challenged. That there is no proscenium, even in its compromised post-reform post-war variants, is perhaps its greatest achievement.

The most recent architecturally notable theatre in Germany is in Potsdam, the new Hans-Otto-Theater, designed by the 86-year-old renowned architect Gottfried Böhm. Like many other cities – especially in the former East Germany – Potsdam had a series of interim theatres after its major theatre, established in 1795, was destroyed in 1945. The theatre company was founded in 1946 and later named after a German actor murdered by the Nazis because of his communist beliefs. The spectacular new structure, which opened in September 2006, is reminiscent of Jørg Utzon's Sydney Opera House, in that the soaring, shell-like roofline faces a waterfront (fig. 18).

The exterior has long horizontal stripes that rise to become three signature red wings overlooking a scenic lake. The exterior is also notable for its huge glass façade that provides a transition from the exterior realm of the lake and grassy terrace to the interior world of the lobby and the theatre. A second glass wall marks the transition from the lobby into the auditorium and provides the opportunity for daylight theatre or the incorporation of the outside landscape. The interior glass wall can also be made into a conventional wall to block off the auditorium.

18 The most recent theatre building in Germany: the Hans-Otto-Theater, Potsdam, built by Gottfried Böhm, opened in September 2006.

The theatre itself seats 470 to 485, and the stage is 240 square metres. The auditorium arrays the seats in a Bayreuth fan shape. In this regard, the theatre is consistent with normative patterns dating back more than a century, but it is also possible to lower the auditorium floor to the level of the stage, thus creating a genuine open space theatre. While flexible theatrical staging is possible, this flat-floor arrangement also allows the space to be used for ballroom festivities. Only future productions will tell if the theatre space is explored fully, with its opportunity for open space and its window to the world. The opening shows, under the artistic directorship of Uwe Eric Laufenberg (b. 1960), used Böhm's theatre in fairly conventional manner. In addition, the spectacular exterior brought the total cost to 26 million euros, so most of the interior walls have to be left in bare concrete. The resulting acoustics are problematic, though this is being addressed. What should not be overlooked, however, is that this building stands miles away from the uninspired *Kulturbunker* of the 1970s and represents a brave architectural solution to the multiple uses made of theatre space today.

These open-space theatres demonstrate the perils and opportunities for contemporary theatre design. Interiors and exteriors that attempt to fill every possible need, with no clear artistic vision, fail to achieve any definite form well. Many of these theatres are functionalist compromises, inside and out. Others present models of theatre design for the future. The Ballhoftheater incorporates historic architecture and audience involvement in a modern flexible theatre; the Schauspielhaus at Theater Basel offers limited choices of flexibility in a thoroughly modernist design; and the Schaubühne fulfils Gropius's vision of a 'grand keyboard of light and space'.

11 Revolutions in scenography on the German stage in the twentieth century

WILHELM HORTMANN

The story of scenography in modern German theatre begins, as does so much else, with Goethe. In 1803, Goethe decreed in his influential *Rules for Actors*: 'Theatre is a figureless tableau in which the actors are but figures in a landscape.' He regarded the proscenium arch as the frame and the painted backdrop and wing-flats as a picture to be completed and enlivened by human 'accessories'. These were warned never to step outside the frame, nor to move too far back as either would break the illusion created by perspective painting. Violent movement was frowned upon, as the painterly conception of the stage depended on slow transitions from one tableau to the next and required statuesque acting, noble poses, and declamatory delivery. Although this style was eminently suited to the performance of classical plays like Goethe's *Iphigenia*, it was also one from which the author of *Götz von Berlichingen*, written thirty years earlier, would have turned away in scorn.

Nineteenth-century scenography

The development of scenography on the German stage during the nineteenth century can best be understood as a conflict between two divergent impulses, the desire to provide opulent visual delights on the one hand and a lean theatre of reduction and concentration on the other. As early as 1824, Carl Friedrich Schinkel (1781–1841), the great architect of classicistic Berlin and builder of the Königliches Schauspielhaus (1818–1821), expostulated against too much decoration and praised the ancients for whom 'a symbolic indication of the place of action ... was quite sufficient to stimulate the productive imagination of the spectators'.[1] However, theatres were becoming part of a rapidly growing entertainment industry, and the laws of the market forced principals to give way to the public's demand for lighter fare and visual distraction. The theatres' limited means, however, no longer allowed them to cultivate the thrills that had been associated with the festive culture of the royal courts and the baroque opera. At best their production resources would include sets and costumes for the four styles

275

of antique, medieval, renaissance, and romantic, which would enable them to present a diversified programme of classical plays, romantic or sentimental comedies, farces, Gothic melodramas, plus, in many cases, operas and ballets. Any play would be given at the most two or three consecutive performances, so scenery had to be changed frequently and soon looked the worse for wear. In many cases theatre managers would buy whole outfits for certain types of play from specialised firms such as Baruch in Berlin or Brückner in Coburg where *maîtres-peintres* and their assistants produced scenery of standardised elegance or veristic realism. Towards the end of the century the advent of electric lighting for the stage showed up the make-believe character of these sets so that radically different solutions became imperative, but this was not before realism had reached its apogee in the historicism of the 'Meininger'.

When the Duke of Saxe-Meiningen took charge of his court theatre in 1866, he immediately dissolved the opera in order to concentrate all resources on drama. Under the customary repertory system at public theatres, with practically daily performances and a dozen or more different plays, a month's careful rehearsing was impossible. The Duke as his own producer and director changed all this and managed to make his theatre pay by bringing only a few productions at a time to perfection and then taking them on tour all over Europe, where they were praised, among other things, for the historical 'truth' of their costumes, scenery, and solid props. It took railway trains to move these, from Meiningen to Berlin, Copenhagen, Budapest, London, Moscow, and many other places. Henning Rischbieter in summing up their achievement calls the theatre of the Meininger,

> Janus-faced: it looks back into its century by fulfilling a pompous as well as painstaking historicism; it looks forward into a new epoch by discarding the unthinking and humdrum professionalism of the conventional acting style, striving instead to realise a unified artistic vision. This was achieved by filling again the position of director which, in the baroque era, had been occupied by the overall co-ordinator, the multi-functional theatrical architect.[2]

New beginnings

The period from 1880 to the First World War witnessed an upsurge of new ideas, initiatives, and experiments. They can be grouped around three central concerns: the creation of a higher form of theatre: a '*Kulturtheater*' as opposed to the '*Geschäftstheater*' (commercial theatres providing mostly light entertainment); advancement of the new, more spiritual kind of drama produced by neo-romantic or symbolist authors such as Hofmannsthal, Maeterlinck, Yeats, or Wilde (*Salome*), whose plays opened up worlds of dream, beauty and poetry; and finally, the devising of a simpler, uncluttered stage for swifter action, and thus ultimately the development of a new conception of scenic space.

These reform efforts were not separate issues, they often intermingled and their propagators might be active in several camps at once. The new generation of painters, architects, and theatre people were united in common rejection of the smooth academism and antiquarian historicism of the official schools of painting and their deadening effect on stage décor. Their endeavours were reinforced by the simultaneous paradigm-shift in the visual arts from representation and imitation to suggestion and evocation. Elements of impressionism, symbolism, Art Nouveau, even tentative abstraction, found their way into the scenery of the 'reformed' stages. In this sense the relatively short but vigorous phase of naturalism, with its ideological demand for stark social realism in the visuals, ran counter to the basic principles of art or artists' theatres in Moscow, Paris, Berlin, and Munich. These were private ventures and sometimes, to sidestep censorship, they operated as clubs with registered membership. Their performances were experimental in nature and dedicated to bringing modernity onto the stage, be it in content, acting style, or scenography. Instead of the jumble of styles that characterised productions in many public theatres the reformers aimed at artistic unity to be achieved by means of stringent simplification. In practice this meant having costumes and scenery correspond to one dominant 'style', turning the stage into an acting space which suggested what Georg Fuchs referred to as 'the power of reality ... with less realism'.[3]

The sets on the so-called '*Stilbühne*' no longer offered imitations of recognisable localities but various forms of 'neutral' stylisations, either in the painted scenery or by means of moveable devices at the sides of the stage, in the form of columns or pillars, the so-called '*Rollertürme*', which had been introduced by Alfred Roller (1864–1935), the versatile stage designer who worked for Reinhardt and was known for introducing greater abstraction into scenic design. The Roller towers, in combination with curtains, either monochrome or decorated with heraldic or abstract patterns, sectioned off different acting areas, and backdrops showing stylised landscapes for outdoor scenes or tapestries for indoor, formed the stock equipment of the *Stilbühne*. Together with the new advances in lighting, the basic elements for theatre as a non-representational spatial art were assembled. Directors who wanted an uncluttered stage to complement Shakespeare's dramaturgy took over many of these elements for their *Shakespearebühne*.

Audiences, however, were slow to alter their visual expectations: the first Munich *Shakespearebühne* of 1889 in the Court Theatre was regarded as too bare and had to be altered. Actors often felt exposed on these stages and at a loss without the customary props. Critics were not always convinced and were inclined to favour the actor against the scenographer. On the reformed stages the actor's star appeal was subordinated to the performance as a composite aesthetic event determined by the director and his scenographer. The public still preferred the star performer. There was, moreover, an unresolved contradiction at the heart of the *Stilbühne* movement. Dominated by adherents and practitioners of Art Nouveau, which denies depth for the sake of two-dimensional decorative form, the *Stilbühne* was often turned into a 'relief' stage. In practical terms this meant restricting the acting space to the narrow strip of the proscenium so as to create the impression of a tableau or of semi-sculptural relief. The relief stage proved an effective means to combat realism. It represented the belated consummation of the pictorial conception of the stage initiated by Goethe and Schinkel, with the victory of plane over space, of the painterly principle over the sculptural, of tableau over movement. Its success was short-lived for it was theatre's conquest of three-dimensional space that proved to be the decisive step.

Appia and Craig

At the beginning of the twentieth century most young theatre practitioners were intent on creating a new theatrical space, but it took Adolphe Appia and Edward Gordon Craig to work out a fundamental redefinition of theatre aesthetics. Although they worked independently of one another, they had much in common. They both discovered space as an independent aesthetic component of plastic and dynamic effects, both regarded lighting as a crucial element in suggesting spatial relations and significance, both were pioneers of abstraction on the stage, and both felt that the theatre had to liberate itself from the dominance of literature. For Appia light was a dynamic element and should be used onstage to suggest plasticity and spatial form. This meant that the actor would not only appear as an embodiment of 'character' or 'personality', but as a physical, sculptural presence in relation to abstract spatial volume and mobile light. The experiments in Eurhythmics in Hellerau explored the expressive value of the human body and also tested Appia's concept of 'rhythmic spaces',[4] which was stage space articulated by nothing more than platforms, ramps, staircases and landings, illumined to contrast shadowy areas with lighted ones and used to suggest 'the confrontation between man and the real volumes of the stage space'.[5] In Appia's designs the stage was resolutely divested of its decorative and pictorial character and turned into a plastic-architectonic acting space.

Edward Gordon Craig rejected both the hybrid form of the *Sprechtheater* in the service of literature as well as the *Musiktheater* in the service of music and song. For him drama originated in the dance, and to come into its own the theatre should return to its primal origins which in his mind were characterised not by a human actor playing roles but by a 'divine automaton', the '*Übermarionette*', performing a dance. Oskar Schlemmer of the Bauhaus realised some of these conceptions in the famous *Triadisches Ballett* in the twenties. Of far-reaching effect were Craig's designs for *Hamlet, King Lear*, and *Macbeth*, which were no longer meant to indicate the places of the action but to evoke the symbolic meaning of the drama. They show abstract, indefinable spaces indicated by tall pillars, outsize columns, massive, threatening walls, huge staircases, and articulated an abstract geometry of gigantic proportions symbolic of man's metaphysical dilemma to the neglect of his individual, historical and social position.

Appia and Craig had a profound influence through their radical rethinking of the basis of scenic presentation and their daring conception of a language of spatial relations. Many important stage-designers in Europe and especially in Germany owed, and still owe, something to their innovations. Robert Wilson (b. 1941), Erich Wonder (b. 1944), Wilfried Minks (b. 1931) and Gilles Aillaud (b. 1928) have all explored dimensions first opened up by Appia and Craig.

Max Reinhardt

Max Reinhardt's versatile genius was the most progressive force in the German theatre during the first two decades of the twentieth century. When he left Berlin for Vienna in 1920 not only had he produced practically all the important modern European dramatists, given a hearing to struggling young playwrights, assured a new lease of life for the Greek classics, and set new standards of rehearsing, acting and directing, he had also changed the visual aspect of performances. His stages could be bare or opulent, the décor illusionist or near-abstract. In every case it was the superlative inventiveness of his *mise-en-scène* which captivated audiences and (many) critics alike. Reinhardt's idea of theatre was all-inclusive: modern and experimental pieces, classical plays, festive spectacle; there was to be no restriction either in choice of play or production style, and he gave himself generous freedom to experiment, not for its own sake but in the service of a 'theatre of joy' capable of raising the public 'beyond the grey misery of everyday life into the serene and pure air of beauty'.[6]

The legendary forest that began to revolve on the stage of the Neues Theater in Berlin on 31 January 1905 to Felix Mendelssohn's music for *A Midsummer Night's Dream* wittily proclaimed the end of naturalism and all conventional forms of staging. When the run ended after more than two hundred performances Reinhardt's fame had spread throughout Europe, he was in charge of the prestigious Deutsches Theater, and had begun to lay the commercial foundations of his 'empire', which gave him the chance to operate in several theatres at once and offer an astonishingly high-quality repertoire. The characteristic most frequently attributed to Max Reinhardt's early work was suggestiveness, achieved either by means of full-powered illusionism as in his first *Midsummer Night's Dream* in Berlin or by mere scenic indications as when he took the same play onto the narrow relief stage of the newly opened Künstlertheater in Munich in 1909. Small stages or large, he filled them with movement, even if this meant merely suggesting invisible movement by sound when space was lacking. His *Bewegungsregie* (keeping actors moving instead of allowing them statuesque poses) conveyed the impression of burgeoning life through movement. Similarly, his *Massenregie*, put to the test in crowd scenes as in *Oedipus Rex* or *Julius Caesar*, was renowned for its choreography, for the turning of swarms of extras into articulated sculpted bodies and dissolving them in ordered movement and rhythm.

He did not follow one formula but tried out many, attracting many important designers and painters into his orbit. Edvard Munch (1863–1944), Lovis Corinth (1858–1928), George Grosz (1893–1959), Emil Orlik (1870–1932), Karl Walser (1877–1943), Alfred Roller, and others co-operated at various times. Munch's sketches and painting for Reinhardt's 1906 production of Ibsen's *Ghosts* are well-known. They thrilled Reinhardt who exclaimed to Ernst Stern (1876–1954), his congenial designer: 'The heavy armchair tells all . . . The dark colouring reflects the whole atmosphere of the drama. And then look at the walls. They're the colour of diseased gums. We must try to get that tone.'[7] Ideally for Reinhardt every play ought to be placed in its own visual cosmos. Set and scenery should be so designed as to reflect the atmosphere and particular inner pathos of the drama – a far cry from the stock sets in general use at the time. Reinhardt was fascinated above all by the challenge of different scenic realisations in new environments, performing in small, intimate spaces (*Kammerspiele*), on ordinary Stadttheater stages, in arenas and parks as well as in gigantic venues such as the Exhibition Hall in Munich or in circuses in Berlin, Budapest, St Petersburg and elsewhere. His zest for experiment was boundless. So were his plans for theatrical expansion. Before the First World War he branched out into international mammoth productions like *Sumurun* and *The Miracle*, a composite show of music, choric speeches, chanting, and processionals, for which, as we have seen, Ernst Stern had the Olympia Hall, seating 30,000, turned into a Gothic Cathedral, with an unbelievable 1,400 extras wheeled in on a specially constructed platform.[8] This show was a great success when revived after the war at the Century Theatre in New York and on tour throughout the United States.

Unlike Craig, Reinhardt was no theorist and he totally lacked Craig's desire to impose symbolic superstructures on his productions. He put his art unreservedly at the service of the dramatist. The road the German theatre was to take under the impact of expressionism was not for him. Its strident obsessions and blatant overstatements were antagonistic to the subtleties of his *Differenzierungskunst*, his art of exploring shadings and gradations. Nevertheless, he helped expressionism on its way. His theatre club '*Das junge Deutschland*' (Young Germany), founded in 1917, organised so-called private performances of young expressionist authors, beginning on 23 December with Johannes Sorge's *Der Bettler* (*The Beggar*), directed by Reinhardt himself, followed on 3 March 1918, after a smart battle with the censors, by Reinhard Goering's pacifist *Seeschlacht* (*Sea Battle*). Reinhardt left the directing of most of the other expressionist plays that were given their first public performance at one of his theatres to younger men: Heinz Herald (1890–1964), Ludwig Berger (1892–1969) or, in the case of Oskar Kokoschka (1886–1980), to the author himself. 'While, then,' in the words of Michael Patterson, 'it is clear that Reinhardt's relationship with Expressionism was a distant one, it is equally true that Expressionism could not have developed as it did without Reinhardt's contribution, especially in terms of a new understanding of stage space.'[9]

Expressionism – the 1920s
After the cataclysm of the Great War avant-garde artists realised that conventional realism was no longer capable of grasping reality. Dadaists and

surrealists were among the first to turn this to account. They demanded the total destruction of all established means of expression. Cubists, constructivists, futurists, and expressionists rejected the sensuous appeal of previous art by consciously deforming and defacing the natural subject, opting instead for pure structure or metaphysical passion. What is common to all these movements is their revolutionary fervour to create a new man, a new society, a new artistic language. Traditional society and art were regarded as beyond reform. They would have to be dismantled and reconstructed on a better plan. Conservative circles understandably feared the overthrow of traditional values and rose to defend their beloved heritage against 'cultural bolshevism'. A heated debate arose about the role of theatre in this new mental climate. The position of the new expressionist playwrights was unequivocal. The visionary young men in the plays of these 'ecstatic' expressionists are fired by the hope of a mankind made afresh in the glow of brotherhood. By contrast, the 'black' expressionists, disaffected materialist pessimists, regarded the world as a slaughterhouse. Images of decay abound in Gottfried Benn's poems; the early Brecht plays depict a jungle of subsocial amorality; in the paintings of Max Beckmann, Ernst Ludwig Kirchner and Otto Dix, the cartoons of George Grosz and John Heartfield's photomontages, mankind, exploited and forsaken, is reduced to the option between animality and criminality.[10]

Both ecstatic and black expressionists wanted to cut through bourgeois self-deception to achieve essential truth. The spirit of *Aufbruch*, or striking out for new horizons, not only produced a spate of extraordinary plays, it revolutionised scenography. Scenery with crazily slanting buildings proclaimed for everyone to see that the world was out of joint. Sets sprouting primitively shaped palm-trees and jungle plants in drawing rooms insisted on dissonance. Scenic expressionism had first gained ground in provincial centres like Dresden, Frankfurt, and Mannheim under the slogan '*Los von Reinhardt!*' (Let's move beyond Reinhardt) and as a reaction to the dominance of the Berlin theatre world generally. In scenographic terms this meant: no more fine shadings and smooth transitions but clear lines, strong, if need be garish colours, unmistakable visual statements. For a few years spectators wondered why actors' faces should be painted in all the colours of the rainbow, or why costumes showed blatantly symbolic colouring – white for innocence, black for death, red for evil, blue for victory etc. Such simplifications drove home the message that the new theatre was less interested in individual psychology than in general typology. Reinhardt had shaped individual characters, the expressionists projected typical role-bearers or addressed universal man.

In this process stages were emphatically uncluttered. They might even become completely bare. 'We don't want an audience ... but a congregation ... not a stage but a pulpit,'[11] Karl Heinz Martin stated as he announced the first expressionist season of his theatre, Die Tribüne, in 1919 to an as yet sceptical Berlin. Such rigour left little for stage designers to do. It was only when experienced directors like Leopold Jessner and Richard Weichert (1880–1961) approached the great plays of the traditional repertoire in the new spirit that expressionist stagecraft came into its own. It was not a style to be applied from without although lesser spirits found it easy to imitate some of its forms. The true expressionists, by contrast, worked from the inside out, burrowing deep for the 'central idea' or 'core' of the play, the *Regiegedanke* (a term coined by Jessner), and only after this had been found would they search for the corresponding forms. Time-honoured interpretations came under scrutiny and were discarded. Jessner had a clear idea of the themes he wanted to emphasise: in *Wilhelm Tell* the cry for freedom, in *Hamlet* the rottenness of the State rather than the melancholy of the prince. These were sensational re-interpretations, strictly for the present time. The new theatre should 'render the undisguised essence of things'.[12] In actual practice this ideological focusing demanded compressed texts, underlined by the staccato delivery of the actors, exaggerated gestures, abrupt movement, and sets of unremitting sternness.

The most resounding scandal occurred when Jessner opened his first season at the Staatstheater in Berlin (1919) with Schiller's *Wilhelm Tell*. Schiller's play was dear to the public for its homely patriotism and the picturesque Swiss scenery, but Jessner set it on an abstract set of ramps and stairs, bounded at the rear by a chilling geometric mountain range on the cyclorama between black curtains (see fig. 19). All topographical and historical realism had been expunged. To many older spectators the production was nothing but a wilful destruction of the cultural heritage. A year later, in *Richard III*, the famous Jessner-steps achieved a new dimension, a device ideally suited to symbolise the director's *Regiegedanke* of an exemplary rise to power through violence and murder. At the moment of triumph Gloucester stood at the top of the stairs and his scarlet robe seemed to connect the blood-coloured steps with the blood-red sky, as it were providing the final link in a now closed circuit of evil. Such congruence of the visual element and the interpretational concept required a brotherhood in spirit between director and designer: Jessner and Emil Pirchan (1884–1957), or Weichert and Ludwig Sievert (1887–1966).

19 *Wilhelm Tell* by Friedrich Schiller, Staatliches Schauspielhaus Berlin,1919, directed by Leopold Jessner, designed by Emil Pirchan. A sketch for Act IV, 'Eastern Shore', displays the famous 'Jessner-steps'.

Expressionist stagecraft was dominated by scenic symbols: steps indicated rise and fall, the bridge was an outreach towards fellow man, the spiral represented a tortuous way finally to overcome reality. But the repressed reality found its way back in demonic contortions. The deformations and the whirl of the falling lines in expressionist scenery revealed the stubborn opposition of the world. The industrial age entered the stage in visionary images of factories, sports arenas, engine rooms of ships, gasworks, petroleum fields ... traumatic images signifying the two basic experiences of this generation of theatre practitioners: the destructiveness of mechanised war and the fighting masses of workers during the November revolution.[13]

Constructivism, abstraction, Bauhaus

The competition between painter and set-designer in expressionist productions was never fully resolved. Sets were either dominated by strongly coloured expressive scenery or by functional stage architecture. This creative friction between plane and space reflected two important influences, that of the Ballets Russes under impresario Sergei Diaghilev (1872–1929) and his chief designers Léon Bakst (1866–1924), Mikhail Larionov (1881–1964), and Natalia Goncharova (1881–1962) and the Russian constructivists. From their first Paris season in 1909 to Diaghilev's death in 1929 the décor and costumes of the Ballets Russes had fascinated by the untrammelled primitivism of their colour and the daring vitality with which they combined motifs from Russian folklore and elements from Art Nouveau, symbolist, and more recent schools of painting. In France, Matisse, Picasso, Braque, Léger, and many other famous painters contributed, not only to the Ballets Russes but to numerous other avant-garde productions: a fascinating, if shortlived 'theatre of painters' which had no equivalent in Germany.[14] The Russian constructivists rejected all décor suggesting forms of organic life and concentrated exclusively on the abstract linear forms of the technical world. Their acting areas were occupied by complicated wooden or metal scaffolds and platforms, their cubist-influenced costume designs hid the human figure behind robot-like abstractions, and their cult of industrial production and of the machine-minding proletariat led them to propagate 'biomechanics' as the new acting style: actors were so to discipline their movements as to reflect the precision of the machine. Vladimir J. Tatlin (1885–1953), Vsevolod Meyerhold (1874–1940), Alexander Tairov (1885–1950) and many other avant-gardists at various stages from 1912 through the 1920s contributed to constructivist productions. Their influence on German scenography can be seen above all in the sets for Erwin Piscator's theatre of political agitation with pieces like Alfons Paquet's *Fahnen* (*Flags*, 1924) and *Sturmflut* (*Stormtide*, 1926) or Toller's *Hoppla, wir leben!* (*We're Alive!*, 1927). In these productions bare constructions of platforms and rostra provided the site for revolutionary action and inflammatory addresses, their impact being heightened by documentary film inserts or projection of stills. The unspoken message of such arrangements to German theatre-goers was that the theatre is no longer a place for private enjoyment in communion with the cultural heritage, but it is a place that deals directly with social reality, a political forum that reaches out to the masses. Theatre activists in Soviet Russia had shown the way by taking propaganda pieces on mobile constructivist sets to factory and farm workers. Berlin audiences, however, were composed primarily of the moneyed intelligentsia, and they appreciated the technical modernity of the visuals rather than the revolutionary messages.

Traugott Müller's (1895–1944) architectural sets for Piscator's political theatre negated illusion and made no attempt to imitate reality; they rejected the subtle suggestiveness of the Reinhardt scenes and proclaimed the new principles of abstraction and demonstration. The latter were to mark the staging of the early Brecht plays, from *Trommeln in der Nacht* (1922) and *Baal* (1923) to *Die Dreigroschenoper* (1928), the first designed by Otto Reigbert (1890–1957), the others by Caspar Neher (1897–1962), who also invented the typical *Kaschemmenbühne* (a set showing a low dive), which was the young Brecht's favourite scene of action. Neher's stages no longer hid but demonstrated the theatre's mechanics. Their collaboration culminated in staging *Dreigroschenoper* at the Theater am Schiffbauerdamm during the summer of 1928. This was the first production in which the idea of an entire staging achieved the status of a 'model', 'in the important sense that the setting could exist as a layer of meaning within the text.'[15] Their close co-operation was resumed after the playwright's return from exile in 1948 and played an important part in shaping Brecht's theories on stage design and the relation between dramaturgy and scenography.

Abstraction also governed the theatrical experiments conducted by teachers and students of the Bauhaus, which propagated *Neue Sachlichkeit*, the movement that promoted sobriety in the arts. Like the adherents of Art Nouveau at the beginning of the century, Bauhaus wanted to transform the everyday environment according to aesthetic principles, but their designs for furniture, lamps, household goods, and houses no longer showed the wavy lines and organic motifs of Jugendstil but spoke the unemotional language of geometric precision. The figurines for Oskar Schlemmer's *Triadisches Ballett* show stereometric puppets composed of cylinders, cones, and spheres, dehumanised figures executed on the drawing board. Putting live dancers into these stiff costumes for the *Bauhaustänze* (Bauhaus dances) realised between 1925 and 1929 explored theatre aesthetics at the extreme opposite of the vividly human and personal conception of theatre Reinhardt stood for. For a few years, Neue Sachlichkeit was even applied to romantic drama, especially in opera. László Moholy-Nagy constructed a tall, forbiddingly geometric set for Offenbach's *The Tales of Hoffmann* (Berlin, 1929) where several actors appeared in mid-air suspended from ropes. In the same year Ewald Dülberg devised a stark blocklike set in the manner of Adolphe Appia for Richard Wagner's *Der fliegende Holländer* (Kroll-Oper, Berlin, directed by Jürgen Fehling), a geometric abstraction in dark-red colours which radiated a laconic immediacy and a tenebrous presence (fig. 20).

20 *Der fliegende Holländer* by Richard Wagner at the Kroll-Oper, Berlin 1929, directed Jürgen Fehling, conducted by Otto Klemperer. A stage model by Teo Otto after a design by Ewald Dülberg.

Stage design under the Nazis

The Nazi regime and its policy of *Gleichschaltung* (subjection of all cultural activities to Nazi ideology) left no room for experimentation. Jewish and communist theatre people were dismissed, many had to flee for their lives but, strange to say, stage designers who did not belong to the incriminated groups were left fairly unmolested. Many had been trained in the modern styles of art, now forbidden and branded as 'degenerate', yet apart from general admonitions to artists to create from the depth of the German soul and produce works in line with the spirit of the newly risen *Volk*, they were left alone. There was no public any more for avant-garde experiments; even Goebbels had to give up his idea of installing a 'Nordic' expressionism. But since the regime wanted to preserve theatres as showcases of German culture there was a modicum of latitude which scenographers such as Caspar Neher and Traugott Müller could turn to account. Neher mostly worked for directors Erich Engel and Heinz Hilpert at the Deutsches Theater, Müller designed important productions at the Staatstheater in Berlin for Gustaf Gründgens and Jürgen Fehling. Müller's genius was at home in many styles.

For Gründgens' production of *Twelfth Night* (1937) he devised an illusionist set of great distinction and beauty, for Jürgen Fehling's production of *Richard III* (1937), *Richard II* (1939), and *Julius Caesar* (1941) he emptied the huge white-walled stage of the Staatstheater almost completely. In *Richard III* he employed only a row of stones, a few steel tube seats, an iron grid, and a central rostrum for the coronation, while Richard's body guards wore SS-type uniforms, a breathtaking piece of bravado. In *Richard II* abstraction, if anything, went even further, the crudely executed central platform contrasting expressively with the stilted refinement of Gründgens' poses. While Müller dared to disregard the official line, others sought a middle way between realism and indications of symbolic abstraction, and adherents of the regime such as Reichsbühnenbildner (Imperial Stage Designer) Benno von Arent (1898–1956) tried to project the official ideology of heroic idealism in their stage designs.

Post-war beginnings – *Das geistige theater*

When the war ended in 1945 roughly half of the theatre buildings had been totally destroyed, most others had been more or less seriously damaged, and few had escaped unscathed. Nevertheless, the immediate post-war years witnessed a tremendous upsurge of theatrical activity. New groups sprang up in the most unlikely places and made no pretence to imitate established theatre. They performed in whatever locations were available, calling themselves *Kellertheater, Zimmertheater, Junge Bühne,* or *Studiobühne* (cellar theatre, room theatre, young stage, studio stage) usually in combination with the town or the year in which they were founded. In many cases these semi-professional groups could only give dramatised readings, so the public came to 'hear' rather than see a play. Their repertoire contained a great deal of previously inaccessible foreign plays and works of formerly exiled German dramatists. Their contribution was above all to create an intellectual ferment among the audiences with which they were in close contact. This theatre excluded stars and promoted unpretentious acting. Their stage design, if it deserved the name, consisted of an unadorned acting area furnished with a bare minimum of props.

Scenography in the professional theatres did not attempt to recapture the opulence and gloss of the Nazi-sponsored theatres of the previous period. Events had not only shocked actors and directors, they had also chastened the designers. What people now wanted from theatres was reassurance, some form of hope, guidance, and clarity. Sets were frugal and spare, not only because so much equipment had gone up in flames, but also out of a kind of spiritual necessity. Audiences no longer hankered after illusionist realism, and designers such as Teo Otto (1904–1968), who returned from Switzerland, taught theatre-goers in Vienna and many other places how to enjoy the chaste beauty of functional stages with intelligently stylised décor. The most advanced stagings of the 1950s were to be found in the productions of the Greek classics, Shakespeare, and Kleist by director Gustav Rudolf Sellner (1905–1990) and his designer Franz Mertz (1897–1966) in Darmstadt. For Sellner, a follower of the philosopher Martin Heidegger, the great plays were 'ciphers of the totality of being', and the purpose of a performance was to bring out their essence, perceived in a kind of inner vision, through 'clarity, sincerity and transparency of means'[16] – a difficult task in which all theatrical arts, design above all, should be instrumental. His designer Franz Mertz, a determined anti-illusionist, radically cleared the stage, expunging all reference to local or historical details, with sets that were completely 'non-topographical'. For *Oedipus* and other Greek plays the *ortlose Bühne* (placeless stage) of Sellner/Mertz provided asymmetrically shaped white tiers for actors and chorus to stand on, the Austrian sculptor Fritz Wotruba (1907–75) occasionally contributing an outsize papier-mâché sculpture; the windy planes of Troy in *Troilus and Cressida* were indicated by a circular rake, a few spears sticking in the ground and a broken helmet; and, in *A Midsummer Night's Dream*, a three-tiered angular contraption as a set with kidney-shaped metal leaves sprouting on wires served for the magical wood. This non-committal visual austerity corresponded perfectly with the contemporary enthusiasm for abstract art and its applications in the non-representational patterns of curtains and furniture coverings typical of the period.

1968 and all that

When the Paris students' protests of May 1968 swept across the Rhine and turned German university towns into hotbeds of anti-authoritarian debate and action, the West German theatre revolution was already well under way. Plays like Rolf Hochhuth's *Der Stellvertreter* (*The Representative*, 1963), Peter Weiss's *Marat / Sade* (1964), Heinar Kipphardt's *In der Sache J. Robert Oppenheimer* (*In the Case of J. Robert Oppenheimer*, 1964) and many other accusatory pieces by a new generation of writers had already shaken the basis of consensus and compromise upon which West German post-war society rested. It was utterly destroyed when the nation's cultural heritage itself was put on trial under the slogan '*Buchenwald liegt bei Weimar*' (Buchenwald lies close to Weimar). Germany had boasted of its *Kultur*, but *Kultur* had not prevented Auschwitz. Buchenwald lay only five miles away from Weimar, the town sacred to the memory of Goethe and Schiller. Was this perhaps a symbolic coincidence, the propinquity of unspeakable horrors and the unthinking veneration of culture?

The new critical spirit found theatrical expression in a stern re-examination of the classics. Young Brechtians like Peter Palitzsch (1918–2004) and Egon Monk (1927–2007), or Piscator-trained directors like Hansgünther Heyme (b. 1935) subjected the plays to aggressive readings. The theatre was now an instrument of anti-bourgeois '*Aufklärung*', and under the impact of abrasive questioning by the young radicals even the most adored plays were made to yield up a hard core of shameful ideological complicities and unflattering human truths. In fact, the theatre, once a museum and a high altar, now became a battleground, a tribunal, a propaganda forum, a circus even. In other words something exciting, vital, anarchic, and instrumental, that could precipitate momentous changes in art and reality.

In this process the appearance of performances changed out of all recognition. In the climate of general emancipation, scenography could not remain in its previous subservient position. Designers of necessity became co-equals of directors, partly also because the break with tradition could best be demonstrated by means of disruptive visuals. Settings no longer supported the 'meaning' of the play because it was exactly the traditional meanings that were suspect. Settings, on the contrary, were employed as a means of subversion. A telling example was Peter Zadek's unorthodox rendering of *Henry V* at Bremen (1964), called *Held Henry* (*Harry, the Hero*). Zadek turned *Henry V* into a pacifist collage, an ahistorical multimedia show against heroism and militarism. The set pointed the message that patriotism is the product of manipulation and a hero the product of a cult. A screen at the back showed Hitler's troops marching into Paris and 'Harry' taking the salute; Lord Kitchener from a poster pointed a stern finger at skrimshankers from both sides; a backdrop showed fifty portraits of kings and queens, some of them changing into the heads of Hitler, Stalin, Billy Graham, Wernher von Braun, football stars etc. The heroic sentiments uttered by the protagonists were effectively undercut by what spectators saw.

From the mid-sixties to the end of the seventies, left-wing directors and their iconoclastic scenographers were busy destroying the hated icons of bourgeois *Bildung*: sacrosanct texts were mercilessly mutilated, the revered protagonists of classical drama disfigured, and the traditional iconicity of their portrayal on stage demolished. The theatre had become a laboratory in which plays were dissected and audiences subjected to various kinds of shock treatment to shake them out of their habitual passivity and 'culinary' expectations. Scenography played a central role in this process of re-education. No efforts were spared to achieve audience involvement. Orchestra pits were covered to lessen the distance between actors and spectators, thrusts covering the first rows of the stalls or even catwalks or gangways right through the auditorium gave the chance to act in immediate contact, a purpose also achieved by placing part of the audience on specially erected rises upstage. Radical iconoclasts considered such constructional alterations to be tame half-measures. In order to combat bourgeois cultural associations connected with traditional theatre-going, nothing less than transplanting productions from the municipal theatre buildings to altogether new environments would do. For a number of years classical plays or theatrical events were performed in disused factories and warehouses, in workshops, gasometers, even in sewage plants or, as in the case of Grüber's collage of texts from Hölderlin's *Hyperion-Fragment* entitled *Winterreise*, in the wide arena of Hitler's Olympic Stadium in Berlin (1977). Such exceptional translocations represented novel experiences for all concerned, awakened a new awareness of the possibilities of performance and incidentally tested the resilience of the classical repertoire against antipathetic surroundings.

Similar breaks with convention were achieved on traditional stages by filling an otherwise neutral acting space with dissonant objects. A thick neon-light rainbow, a heap of sand, and several Michelangelo statues comprised Wilfried Minks's set for Klaus Michael Grüber's *Tempest* (Bremen, 1970); a stage-floor simply full of tin cans was Matthias Langhoff's design for Heiner Müller's *Verkommenes Ufer, Medea-Material, Landschaft mit Argonauten* (*Derelict Shore, Medea Material, Landscape with Argonauts*) directed by Manfred Karge and Langhoff himself (Bochum, 1983). Random costuming left audiences guessing as to the period and place of the action, cross-dressing and gender-blind casting increased their uncertainty. These deliberate disjunctions ensured that the new practice did not develop into a style, style being suspect per se and limiting. Consequently, each production had to be an experiment, with scenography making inroads into the uncharted, mapping out the contours of a new de- or pluri-centred aesthetic in literally hundreds of individual approaches.

In spite of this tumultuous drive for originality and singularity in the scenography of the period, a few general trends can be made out. Political plays or productions intended to provide a critique of ideology demanded unequivocal sets that displayed the virtues of clarity and positive statement, a suitable site for lessons in the service of *Aufklärung* (enlightenment). Such purposes were best served by sets resembling tribunals, which had a direct affinity to the constructivist platforms of Piscator's political theatre of the 1920s. Another favourite setting for political drama was the plain white box, with walls sprayed with slogans and sparse furnishings; these sets might even include blackboards on which to write memorable phrases. Bert Kistner preferred his white boxes to be antiseptically tiled to suggest the clinical atmosphere of a laboratory, Wilfried Minks achieved the same effect with simpler means, namely rows of naked bulbs that accentuated the proscenium arch. His most impressive design during the 1960s provided Peter Palitzsch in Stuttgart with a highly practicable set for *Henry VI*, consisting of a white wall of sliding panels which shut off or opened up three acting spaces right, left, and centre, and was thus ideally suited for the many mirror scenes in that play. These could be exposed to view or cut off simply by sliding the panels across, thus enabling instant comment on a particular action by a corresponding or contrasting scene. The didactic intentions of the director were additionally supported by a memento-mori frieze that spanned the stage and displayed a gruesome assemblage of skeletons, hacked-off limbs, and broken implements of war, which reminded audiences of the inhuman price to be paid for the dynastic power games of the rulers.

By contrast, Zadek's productions at that time did not aim at analytical clarity but overwhelmed spectators with crude onslaughts on sense and sensibility, offering a wild mix of styles especially in the costumes, while presentational forms veered from Grand Guignol exaggeration to idiosyncratic theatricalisation. Zadek and his designer Peter Pabst (b. 1924) confronted audiences with a visual world of garish effects, full of the fury of the *nouveaux fauves*; the stage was no chessboard for calculated dramaturgic moves in the service of ideological instruction but as circus, whirlpool, or bear-garden for the lusty acting out of passions irrespective of taste or psychological coherence. Zadek's and Pabst's visuals often appeared unfinished and haphazard, deliberately retaining an element of rehearsal, which suggested process and work in progress rather than polished product.

There was nothing unfinished and slapdash about Karl Ernst Herrmann's (b. 1936) designs for Peter Stein's productions at the Schaubühne in Berlin.

The firm anti-bourgeois stance of the company was underpinned by a painstaking preliminary examination of the socio-critical content of each text, all members of the cast being alerted to the ideological aspects of their parts. The sets were intriguingly elaborated. For *Summerfolk* by Gorki, Herrmann devised a beautiful garden scene of panoramic extensions bounded at the rear by a thicket of live birch trees in real soil; at first this was a languorous retreat, but as the action progressed it could be increasingly perceived as a prison or a golden cage, ultimately unsafe, from which only the enlightened characters manage to escape. The set became the chief attraction during the long run, but the performance nonplussed English critics when it visited the National Theatre in 1977. Herrmann's designs also accounted in large measure for the success of Stein's twofold approach to Shakespeare during the 1970s. The first, called *Shakespeare's Memory*, was a seven-hour variety show presenting a medley of Renaissance texts, music, and acrobatics on two evenings in the vast halls of the CCC film studio in Berlin-Spandau; the second was the production of *As You Like It* (1977) in the same location. For *Shakespeare's Memory* the designer had provided the huge skeleton of a 'Ship of State', wagons as floats for the pageants, a Cabinet of Utopians (containing life-size models of utopian beings like the headless man, the hermaphrodite, the zodiac man), a Cabinet of Emblems, a planetarium etc., suggestive loci for the peripatetic audience to wander about in. The set for *As You Like It* also kept spectators on the move before they were allowed to reach the Forest of Arden. Once there, and seated on steep rises beside an L-shaped acting area, they could let their eyes wander from pond to cornfield, from a huge beech tree under whose branches the Duke's company rested to Audrey at the butter-churn and to the catwalks above where Robinson Crusoe shouting for Man Friday and the roaring Wild Man indicated that idyllic nature is an illusion. Herrmann's design of this semi-Arcadian environment was needed for Stein's careful examination of a combination of themes touching upon nature, nurture, civilisation, violence, primitivism, and culture, all of which left-wing critics found too remote. But then, in the words of Michael Patterson, 'Stein presented us with a vision not a political programme.'[17] In the following decades Herrmann worked above all for Claus Peymann, who served successively as intendant in Stuttgart, Bochum, and at the Burgtheater in Vienna. Here he created the sets for most of Peymann's many German-language premières of authors such as Thomas Bernhard, Peter Handke, Peter Turrini, and Elfriede Jelinek and affirmed his mastery in poetic realism as well as in the lean abstraction of the white box.

Culture as memory – postmodernist aestheticism, the 1980s

During the 1970s the suggestive realism of Peter Stein's Berlin productions was still the exception. It foreshadowed the return to aestheticism of the following decade when the rebellious Zeitgeist of the 1960s gave way to the so-called *neue Innerlichkeit* (new inwardness), as in the plays of Peter Handke and Botho Strauss. Perceptive directors realised that the ideological brain-washing of the classical repertoire had not only gained much-needed liberties, but also provided cover for artistic insensitivity. Further reduction-ism was impossible. There was, however, no simple going back. Theatre had become a self-conscious and self-reflexive art. An immense spectrum of presentational and scenographic choices was now at the disposal of its practitioners, but it took more than political convictions to use these mean-ingfully. For the scenographer especially the world's storehouse of images, from the visual arts to films and advertisements, all readily available through the electronic media, represented both a challenge and temptation. Television had trained audiences in the art of instantly decoding all manner of pictorial references and allusions; postmodern directors and scenogra-phers responded by turning these new opportunities to account. As often before, Shakespeare productions proved to be the testing ground.

Wolf Vostell (1932–98), a famous arranger of 'happenings', in co-operation with director Hansgünther Heyme, reacted to the change in cultural parameters by bringing out an 'electronic' *Hamlet* (Cologne, 1979). Vostell's set included the stuffed carcass of a horse hung up by its hind legs, a strip of eighteen TV monitors at the bottom of the iron curtain, and a video camera which actors occasionally turned on each other or themselves and whose pictures then appeared eighteen times in a row on the monitors. Electronic gadgets – transistors, pocket computers, walkie-talkies, microphones, cassette recorders – were handled by the actors during most of the scenes. They divided their attention between the action itself and the recording and transmitting of it by means of one of the media. The most extreme form of this schizoid division from self occurred in the figure of Hamlet. He was played by two actors. The Hamlet onstage was almost beyond speech, lost in the crude sexual fantasies of his subconscious, reduced largely to gestures and to a wondering preoccupation with his own body, while his alter ego in the auditorium – the director – nostal-gically declaimed the monologues over the theatre's amplifying system. Here the media were the message: the electronic robots were taking over, enmeshing all in their alienating spell. In a technically perfect media culture the unique event becomes reproducible and character de-individualised. A character like Hamlet is an anachronism. His unique individuality may make sense as a literary memory but its physical representation on stage can only be that of a madman, the victim of alienation.

The Heyme/Vostell *Hamlet* marked a caesura. Its radical deconstruction and stern rejection of individualism exemplified the iconoclasm of the period; at the same time it expressed the typically postmodern doubt of ever being able to give past art actual and vital presence again. Three years later Klaus Michael Grüber's *Hamlet* at the Schaubühne in Berlin proved the same point in a more sophisticated manner, by deconstruction through art. The aura of the hallowed classical text in the Schlegel translation was enhanced by an operatic kind of delivery: every soliloquy an aria, every speech a poem, the full text its own anthology of purple passages. Movement and gesture were carefully choreographed, designed to create beautiful tableaux. Other visual events were created by poses in deliberate imitation of *Hamlet* illustrations or of medieval, Renaissance, or Baroque paintings, which had also served as models for the sumptuous costumes. The stage thus became an exhibition room for living works of art. The characters were neither drawn on psychological lines nor meant to convince through the realism of their interaction. They were figures in a heraldic composition of studied artificiality. The calculated aestheticism of the presentation created distance through art. This effect was underscored by the unusual scenic space of the huge, half-circular stage of the Schaubühne and by the impressive lighting effects devised by Gilles Aillaud, the set designer. Both together created the illusion of unfathomable depth and unbounded distance, both necessary for what was meant to be a final *Hamlet* production, a *Hamlet* that recapitulated the history of its impact on German culture since Goethe, rendering the sum of its past significance without being concerned about its present meaning.[18] This was a profoundly postmodernist concept: a quotation of the cultural heritage rather than a vitalisation of it.

The 1980s were a period of searching. The old certainties were gone. Previously deconstructionist directors and designers began to prefer working in opera where the ideological pressures were less obvious. Achim Freyer (b. 1934) for instance, well-known painter and environmental artist, formerly one of Brecht's *Meisterschüler*, began staging and directing opera in 1980 with Gluck's *Iphigénie en Tauride* in Munich, soon followed by von Weber's *Der Freischütz* in Stuttgart, Mozart's *Die Zauberflöte* in Hamburg, and

Gluck's *Orpheus and Eurydice* in Berlin. 'He staged and designed all of them as scenic fairytales.'[19] Director Hans Neuenfels, however, with the help of Erich Wonder's designs, stripped Giuseppe Verdi's *Aida* (Frankfurt, 1981) of all monumentality, turning the performance 'into a severe critique of colonialism'.[20] Opera, however, generally proved more resistant to deconstruction than drama. Wonder works in both media, putting erratic sets into the box-like stage spaces, often with a thin gauze curtain between stage and auditorium, and creates enigmatic effects by means of coloured lighting. A radical realisation of this concept was his design for Wagner's *Tristan und Isolde* (Bayreuth, 1993), where the acting areas in the form of deliberately quoted Malevich squares were cut out of the dark stage space by coloured light. There was no indication of topography. Wonder's task, as he saw it, was 'transforming feelings into space ... *Tristan* is where there are very wide horizons and very lonely plains, where everything happens as in a glass case.'[21] For *Faust I* (Cologne, 1983) Wonder created ghostly atmospheres and deep mysterious spaces by means of painted gauzes as backdrops that were sometimes superimposed on each other 'allowing a variety of lighting effects and fast scene changes'.[22] Rolf Glittenberg (b. 1945) achieved similarly poetic effects with totally different means. His stages are near-abstract environments of studied artificiality; they show high walls painted in soft colours shading into each other and the entrances are sharply lit slits in the wall – colours, light and outside dimensions together suggesting both elegance and mysteriousness.

Lighting design began to play an increasingly important role. It reached its peak in the productions of Robert Wilson, especially *Death, Destruction and Detroit* (Berlin, 1979), *CIVIL WarS* (Cologne, 1984), and in his rendering of Heiner Müller's *Hamletmaschine* (Hamburg, 1986). Texts were reduced to a minimum and often fragmented for choric repetition. The overall impact of performances was almost exclusively visual: actors gliding through space against dark backgrounds, hovering in the air on swings, stepping like slow-motion dancers across the stage, positioned in groups for identical movements and gestures repeated automaton-fashion. These were visual events in their own right, not just a story in pantomime. In Wilson's productions the designer, draughtsman and choreographer took over from the dramatist, creating wonderful effects in an enigmatic, non-discursive theatre language.

In the course of the theatre revolution of the 1960s and 1970s scenography had become established as an autonomous artform and the highly subsidised German public theatre system provided the means even for expensive solutions such as Gisbert Jäkel's (b. 1954) subtle designs for Andrea Breth's evocative and profound productions. Spectators were showered with a succession of elaborated image worlds for a single play and invited to decode a wealth of pictorial allusions to famous paintings, avant-garde movies or recent theatre styles. At the opposite end of the scale designers at less affluent theatres and possibly influenced by Land Art brought sand, leaves, earth, water, and even plain rubbish onto their stages, opting for unadorned natural materiality rather than sophisticated cultural reference. Others again turned to painting styles of the period for their inspiration. Axel Manthey (b. 1945), for instance, cast the grim fate of Büchner's *Woyzeck* (Cologne, 1982) against a threatening backdrop of crudely executed vertical stripes in the manner of the *nouveaux fauves*, while for *Parsifal* (Frankfurt, 1982) he designed totally different sets ranging from strongly articulated quasi-expressionist signs for the gloomy world of the knights of the Grail, via colourful and pleasant patterns for the flower maidens' garden, to the cold geometry of a sharp-edged pointed rake in front of rows of tilted oblongs indicating 'a threatening aspect of Klingsor's domain'.[23] Whereas many designers freely move among different forms, others choose to follow their own unmistakable style. Rosalie (Gudrun Müller, b. 1953) creates astonishing sets from cheap plastic materials. Swaths of blue and green cellophane foil and hooped entanglements in brightly coloured tinsel suggest the dream-like unreality of the wood in *A Midsummer Night's Dream* (Wuppertal, 1983); in Strauss's *Die Frau ohne Schatten* (Dresden, 1994) a yellow half-circle wall at the back of the stage was pierced by red-rimmed bulls-eyes at different heights. When designing for less ambitious texts, Rosalie will fall back on plastic ready-mades – buckets, sieves, pipes, umbrellas – in the contrasting colours she likes, anything that is witty, bright, and fanciful: 'My style is simply being inquisitive and experimental.'[24]

Rosalie works as a loner, others prefer to collaborate. Eckart cites the longstanding and eminently productive collaboration between Dieter Dorn and Jürgen Rose (b. 1937) at the Munich *Kammerspiele* as an example of a *Belle Alliance* between director and designer. Prior to working at the *Kammerspiele*, Rose had collaborated with Rudolf Noelte whose poetic traditionalism demanded suggestively illusionist and basically realistic sets in an enclosed space or box. In cooperation with Dorn, Rose's stages 'not only became more open but also more abstract', as exemplified by 'an ingenious, highly variable yellow box for *Faust*, a realistic indication of a barn as the uniform set for *Die verkaufte Braut*, or the clinically white space with open passages for Mozart's *The Marriage of Figaro*.'[25] Abstraction also governed the plans for two widely acclaimed Shakespeare productions which may serve to show how the visuals contributed to the overall effect. Rose's design for *Troilus and Cressida* (Munich, 1986) was marked by deliberate indeterminacy. The sides of the stage were formed by white cloths daubed with many colours, at the rear a paper-covered sliding door of similar aspect served for the rapid exits and entrances, and on the floor were flat raised segments in an irregular pattern. The abstract quality of the set denied any representational orientation. Equally, Rose had kept the costumes from indicating place or period. The men wore what looked like battledress trousers, reinforced with greaves and pads, their bare chests were encased in tight leather belts and straps or covered by tunics of indistinct patterns somewhere between heraldic designs and camouflage spots, the more warlike sporting Indian braves' headbands. The Myrmidons, faceless under primitive Greek helmets, looked like dark-clad war machines. Pandarus and Cressida were dressed in flowing robes of rough weave and patterns derived from African and Mexican tribal textiles, their foreheads decorated oriental-fashion with strings of pearl – altogether a powerful blend of incompatibilities. The prevalent optical impression was of something archaic and passionate, of eruptive ferocity barely restrained, of a primitive culture in its harsh exoticism and thus blended in perfectly with the pace and dynamic character of the production as a whole. The set for *King Lear* (1992) showed evidence of a different approach. For this sinister end-of-the-world play Rose built a longish box in dark colours, parts of its sides looking like stable doors, other sections opening inwards like drawbridges. The whole structure suggested primitive, pre-civilised surroundings, but it functioned in a highly sophisticated manner. It allowed exits and entrances to be marked by the doors flapping open or snapping shut and by the drawbridge parts crashing down or being jerked up. This method of physically opening or closing a scene helped to structure and segment the action. The crashing and abrupt blocking off and opening up of the stage space evoked associations of an action whose progress was irrevocable. The suddenness with which the forbidding set thus came to life was in marked contrast to the slower pace of the unfolding of the human action. Together, they gave the impression of perfectly varied timing.

Scenography in East Germany

It is difficult to summarise the complex variety of German scenography since its emancipation in the 1960s and 1970s and quite impossible to do justice to the genius and achievements of literally hundreds of creative artists who give visible shape to thousands of texts. Although the two Germanys developed a markedly different theatre culture, the ideological rift had relatively little effect on stage design. In the early years of the GDR, theatres performed predominantly classics and a number of *Revolutionsstücke* such as *Sturm* by Wladimir Bill-Belotserkovsky and other propaganda pieces. Their staging was determined by the limitations of the prescribed style of socialist realism and rarely conveyed the aesthetic thrills older spectators remembered from the few revolutionary plays Piscator had produced in the 1920s. Brecht was of course a dominant figure on both sides of the iron curtain, with his theories as well as his practice constantly gaining in influence. Whoever staged his plays was recommended to follow the master's fairly rigid models, whether in the East or West, and directors were critically watched over by his heirs after his early death in 1956. The distanced acting style of epic theatre, which Brecht demonstrated in his production of *Der kaukasische Kreidekreis*, designed by Karl von Appen (1900–81), made European theatre history when it went on tour in 1956. In visual terms, however, it was the innovative choreography by Ruth Berghaus (1927–96) for the battle-scenes in Brecht's *Coriolanus* adaptation, staged by Joachim Tenschert and Manfred Wekwerth in Berlin in 1964, which represented a decisive departure. As a way of handling crowd scenes, this production had no match anywhere. 'The battle scenes demonstrated in exemplary fashion how particular arts contribute in their own way to telling the story so that a many-sided subject can be approached from different angles.'[26] The world-famous production was a break-through for Berghaus whose subsequent work as a director, especially in opera, was one of the landmarks of GDR theatre. Her productions at the Deutsche Staatsoper in East Berlin and soon at opera houses in the West, from Vienna to Frankfurt and Paris, expressed a radically contemporary consciousness in her interpretations for which top-rank designers such as Hans Dieter Schaal (b. 1943), Achim Freyer, Heinrich Kilger (1907–70), and Andreas Reinhardt (1937–2007) found congenial scenic metaphors.

Equally important GDR scenographers were Horst Sagert (b. 1934) and Volker Pfüller (b. 1939). Sagert, painter, dramatist, stage designer, was a unique loner in all these fields and is known above all for three sets: the fairy-tale political parable *The Dragon* by Yevgeny Schwartz, directed by Benno Besson at the Deutsches Theater, Berlin in 1965, which ran to 600 performances in the course of twenty years; *Dona Rosita the Spinster* by Garcia

Lorca, directed by Sagert himself in cooperation with Siegfried Höchst, at the same theatre in 1970; and *The Taming of the Shrew* at the Freie Volksbühne, Berlin, in 1986, directed by Peter Zadek. Sagert's art, reported Detlef Friedrich in *Berliner Zeitung* on the designer's 70th birthday, was 'celebrated, engraved, concentrated. He refined and alienated, and overwhelmed spectators by a pure imagination and fancy which was solely inspired by the content of the play. A creator of miracles.' Pfüller became famous with his set for *Dantons Tod* directed by Alexander Lang (Deutsches Theater Berlin, 1981), with whom Pfüller collaborated for many years before turning to book illustration as a professor of graphic design at the Hochschule für Grafik und Buchkunst in Leipzig. What Sagert and Pfüller, different as they are, have in common is that they broke away from the demonstratively symbolic or ironic use of individual elements favoured by Brecht and the stage designers under his influence. Sagert and Pfüller, by contrast, built their sets as a non-naturalistic, artificial totality.

The abrasive and ultimately cryptic texts of Heiner Müller have remained a standing challenge to designers to invent equally striking solutions. During the last months of the GDR (1989–90) Heiner Müller prepared a monumental production of *Hamlet* in combination with his own *Hamletmaschine* which was to portray 'the end of a civilisation for which *Hamlet* was the central myth',[27] the terrifying vision of a Hamlet traversing 'the history of the Earth from Ice Age to Heat Death', for which Erich Wonder conceived appropriate visuals. In the initial scene there was 'a stage-high cube of stretched gauze to represent an enormous block of ice, whose melting produced a constant trickle of water, to be waded through by the characters at various points'. The second part of the seven-hour mammoth presentation 'opened on the breath-taking vista of a tunnel through time. With astounding perspective effects, the arcades of a splendid Renaissance façade upstage merged into a gigantic subway tube downstage. Between Ice Age and Heat Death this represented the epoch of human civilisation.'[28] Poetic conception and scenic realisation worked together in impressive compatibility (see fig. 21).

End of the millenium, turn of the century

The present generation of stage designers is no longer primarily recruited from the painting or sculpture classes of art academies. Most of them receive their training directly in the stage design sections of the schools of dramatic art, either in three-year courses chiefly geared to practical requirements,

21 *Hamletmaschine* by Shakespeare and Heiner Müller, Deutsches Theater Berlin, 1990, directed by Heiner Müller. Erich Wonder's set for Act 1 shows an ice cube containing Hamlet (Ulrich Mühe), Gertrude (Dagmar Manzel), and Claudius (Jörg Gudzuhn) with parts of a gigantic crane in the foreground.

or in five-year courses in which stage design is a full academic study. Berlin, Hamburg, Leipzig, and Munich harbour the most reputed centres of instruction. With the growth of stage design as an autonomous artform, the extension of aesthetically acceptable possibilities and the introduction of high-tech electronic equipment, the curricula have increased both in volume and complexity. Aesthetic theory plays a more important part than formerly while the visual arts elements are reduced: stage designers no longer wield the brush but conceive scenic environments for an exclusively spatial art. Trained by the masters of their craft they can now use as everyday teaching material that which the previous generation had to battle for. But the new freedom has its drawbacks. There are no longer any models to follow and an almost absurd pressure for originality forces younger directors and stage designers to seek ever more particularist solutions. In 1938, Heinz Hilpert, head of the Deutsches Theater in Berlin, could still with some justification claim 'We present the text, not its interpretation.'[29] Under the pressure of having to be original at all costs, the situation has become reversed. Only exceptionally gifted and established teams such as those headed by Claus Peymann or Dieter Dorn have managed to balance the conflicting demands over longer periods.

Many younger directors and stage designers attempt to catch critical attention by outré presentations of wild hybridity. A not untypical example was the set of director Jürgen Kruse's production of *The Tempest* (Bochum, 1999), designed by Steffi Bruhn. It provided a jumble of allusions that placed Prospero's isle anywhere between Greece, Africa, and the Pacific Ocean. Shrunken heads sprouted on curling wires next to Easter Island stone sculptures, Greek statues flanked the stage portal, and Africa was brought in by a troupe of young girls in ballet dress with colourful umbrellas who circled the wrecked ship and sang out their names: 'Sunday, Monday, Tuesday, Wednesday, Thursday' etc. Obviously Goodman Friday had been there ten years before and peopled the isle. The director took the various references to the isle being filled with strange sounds and music as an invitation to drown the stage in his favourite pop tunes and bands, from the Beach Boys and Harry Belafonte to the Rolling Stones and Status Quo. This was hybridisation in sight and sound, and an overbearing director's concept determined all. What formerly constituted the subservient role of scenography in expressing the 'meaning' of the work at present frequently turns into the subservient role of the scenographer in fealty to the director's concept. It takes profoundly compatible minds and artistic temperaments to achieve lasting creative partnerships.

The most productive example in recent years is the co-operation of Anna Viebrock (b. 1951) with directors Christoph Marthaler (b. 1951) and Jossi Wieler (b. 1951). In their productions, in the beginning primarily in Basel and Zurich in their native Switzerland, from which they soon branched out into the centres of German and Austrian theatre activity, the auditory and visual elements so support and counterpoint one another that they achieve a strangely alienating, at once homely yet utterly inscrutable unity. The texts are mostly of the group's own devising or collages from various sources, but under Marthaler's direction they become strangely separated from their speakers. His actors employ words not as instruments of self-definition, but as elements in a ritual or items in a litany. Similarly, physical action onstage is not expressive of dramatic conflict, but consists of habitual gestures, unconscious actions repeated or echoed by most of the cast in turn. Movement is usually slow; a kind of cosmic lethargy prevails. Actors sit

22 *Murx den Europäer!* ... Volksbühne Berlin 1993, devised and directed by Christoph
Marthaler. A box set characteristic for the designer Anna Viebrock suggests time
standing still.

and brood, start pointless actions and return to their state of waiting, fall
asleep, or break into song, well-trained voices delivering madrigals and
chorales with the same expertise and equanimity as popular hits, national
anthems or marching songs. The productions are arranged around certain
themes or states of consciousness arising out of German history, yet are non-
aggressive, non-didactic, not intended to make a political impact. His
people are caught in a condition of lassitude, a paralysis of minds and
emotions. These states are perfectly embodied in Anna Viebrock's sets:
high-walled, often windowless interiors, the three sides covered in sheets
of brown artificial wood or equally ugly and non-committal wallpaper, a set
of iron stairs leading nowhere, a lift going up and down, doors that won't
open, a recess at the back leading to a toilet or bar, an outsize furnace, boiler,
or ventilator at inaccessible heights, writing on the wall whose letters drop
off at intervals, and on the stage floor an unprepossessing assortment of
furniture, preferably from the 1950s – the overall impression often is that of
a canteen or waiting room, or an over-furnished middle-class lounge, for
people in transit with nowhere to go and doomed meticulously to go
through the slow motions of their iterative yet incomprehensible scenarios.

Anna Viebrock's sets are strangely suggestive. At first their commonplace constituents evoke a feeling of familiarity. After a short while this vanishes completely. The number of evidently functionless items confirms that reality here is oddly out of joint, transmuted into an enigmatic game which director and stage designer play with the cultural memories of their audiences. They offer them well-known details, easily recognisable items, often from second-hand furniture markets – in an ultimately hermetic whole. What surprised audiences and critics alike is that the Viebrock formula described above not only worked for a production like *Murx den Europäer!* . . . (Volksbühne Berlin 1993) (see fig. 22) but was flexible enough to be applied and adapted to such divergent works as Debussy's *Pelléas and Mélisande* (Frankfurt, 1994), Verdi's *Luisa Miller* (Frankfurt, 1996), Chekhov's *Three Sisters* (Volksbühne Berlin, 1997), or Wagner's *Tristan und Isolde* (Bayreuth, 2005). In the course of the years Marthaler/Viebrock productions, examples of a successful interlocking of the highly personal styles of director and designer, have achieved cult status. Unfortunately, such felicitous pairings among Germany's younger theatre practitioners are the exception rather than the rule.

12 Playwriting in contemporary German theatre: Representation and its discontents, 1960–2006

DAVID BARNETT

In the wake of the Second World War, 'German theatre' became an ever more complex concept, as it not only included plays from Austria and Northern Switzerland but also from the two new Germanys, the Federal Republic (FRG), and the German Democratic Republic (GDR). By the 1960s, two very different paths were being beaten in theatres either side of the German-German border, both of which signalled conservatism, but in very different ideological forms. In the West, theatre was not in the mood for radical upheaval. Gustaf Gründgens, an *Intendant* during the Nazi period, set the tone for theatre production after the war. As Vice President of *Der Deutsche Bühnenverein* (the German Theatre Association, an organisation representing the *Intendanten*), he set out a cautious agenda in 1948 when he exhorted his fellow *Intendanten* to stage 'productions which were true to the text'.[1] While such a position may be something of an orthodoxy in English-speaking theatre, this was a remarkably tame manifesto for a theatre system famed for its inventiveness. This was, after all, a theatre that had provoked audiences by championing gritty naturalism in the 1890s, developed the breathtaking aesthetics of expressionism two decades later, and brought about the challenge of *Regietheater* (directors' theatre) in the heyday of the Weimar Republic. The 1950s had a 'business as usual' flavour, carrying on the Nazis' unimaginative work in the theatre, with little room for innovation. While high quality work was doubtless being offered, it did little to address social, political or historical issues. In the East on the other hand, hardliners fought against Bertolt Brecht and his so-called 'formalism' in favour of Soviet-prescribed 'socialist realism'. Official censorship was also to become tighter in the mid-1960s, although the system was not at all regularised and so betrayed many inconsistencies in its application. Yet despite the self and state controls imposed in the two Germanys, playwrights were to engage with the most fundamental issues of representation and its shortcomings and bring about some of the most challenging writing for performance in Europe.

Absurdism

The so-called 'theatre of the absurd', Martin Esslin's broad banner for a host of European writers, may well have been popular on the stages of West Germany, but few German dramatists took up this impulse. Wolfgang Hildesheimer's (1916–91) contribution to the genre, *Die Verspätung* (*The Delay*, 1961), was moderately popular and Günter Grass's (b. 1927) experiments such as *Onkel, Onkel* (*Uncle, Uncle*, 1956) or *Die bösen Köche* (*The Nasty Cooks*, 1957) mark an engagement with the absurd, but the plays found little resonance. The Swiss Friedrich Dürrenmatt (1921–90) did combine devices taken from Brecht's epic theatre with thematic and philosophical strands from the absurd in plays such as *Der Besuch der alten Dame* (*The Visit*, 1956) and *Die Physiker* (*The Physicists*, 1962). In both plays, and indeed others, the playwright takes an idea and pushes it to its often catastrophic limits. In *Die Physiker*, for example, a physicist, Möbius, who has unlocked the mysteries of the universe, passes himself off as mad to save the world from his potentially cataclysmic discoveries. The asylum, however, is not as safe as he thinks: the chief doctor, Mathilde von Zahnd, is revealed to be an insane megalomaniac who has stolen Möbius's formulae and plans to take over the world with them. The many ironies of the plot point to a sense of the absurd while the subject matter is eminently political. The mixture of the two yielded a variety of responses that both accused Dürrenmatt of neutralising the political and that praised him for developing a vibrant political form.

Fellow Swiss, Max Frisch (1911–91) also mixed variations of Epic Theatre with his own brand of comedy in plays that proved popular around the same time as Dürrenmatt. Frisch is perhaps best remembered for his plays *Biedermann und die Brandstifter* (*The Fire Raisers*, 1958) and *Andorra* (1961). *Biedermann* is subtitled 'a teaching play without a lesson' and presents a parable of a wilful refusal to confront catastrophic issues. Biedermann, the German for 'upright' or 'decent' man, is used ironically as such manners prevent or rather allow Biedermann to ignore the danger presented by two arsonists. His vicious and cowardly streaks nonetheless make him a figure of curiosity rather than empathy, and he is thus held at a critical distance from the audience. The play ends with an inevitable disaster, although Biedermann, as the subtitle suggests, has learned nothing. *Andorra* is similarly a parable yet it lacks the comic tone of *Biedermann*. The play focuses on identity and follows the persecution of Andri, who is rumoured to be a Jew. By the end, Andri dies at the hands of the invading Fascists and the various characters who helped perpetuate the lie of Andri's Jewishness are all found to have blood on their hands despite pleading either ignorance or misplaced good intentions.

It is difficult to say why Beckett, Ionesco, or Adamov had such a small impact on writing in West Germany (in the East absurdism was considered decadent and never had any major exposure until the 1970s), but it was likely to have been due to the significance, however repressed, of the events of the Nazi past. The politics of the 'absurdist' playwrights were at best ambivalent. Beckett deliberately avoided social or historical references and posited a timeless existential crisis. West German theatre was to be rudely awoken by a new wave of writing that announced a profound rejection of the political quietism that had dominated the period of the 'economic miracle'.

Documentary theatre

Documentary theatre, as it came to be known, took the theatrical establishment by storm. *Der Stellvertreter* (translated as both *The Deputy* and *The Representative*, 1963) by Rolf Hochhuth (b. 1931), *In der Sache J. Robert Oppenheimer* (*In the Matter of J. Robert Oppenheimer*, 1964) by Heinar Kipphardt (1922–82), and *Die Ermittlung* (*The Investigation*, 1965) by Peter Weiss (1916–82, from 1945 a Swedish citizen) were all directed by Erwin Piscator, who was then the intendant of the *Theater der freien Volksbühnen*, West Berlin. Hochhuth had studied the Vatican's own archives to indict Pope Pius XII for his lack of intervention in the deportation of Italy's Jews; Kipphardt and Weiss used official protocols and reports as the bases for their plays. In subsequent years, other writers would employ historical materials and studies, as Dieter Forte (b. 1935) did in his *Martin Luther und Thomas Münzer oder die Einführung der Buchhaltung* (*Martin Luther and Thomas Münzer or the Introduction of Book-keeping*, 1970), and newspaper articles, most notably Hochhuth. The nature of the 'document' was thus never uniform and the plays themselves were rarely similar in either their aesthetics or their politics. Hochhuth was far more a moralist than a political writer, and his preference for naturalistic dialogue, despite couching it in distinctly unpoetic verse, put the individual at the centre of the action. As Hochhuth pointed out: 'the theatre would be finished if it were ever to concede that a person in a mass were no longer an individual . . . It is *the* task of the theatre to insist that a person is a responsible being.'[2] Peter Weiss, on the other hand, sought to arraign a whole system in *Die Ermittlung*, which took its material from the 1964–5 Auschwitz trial. Nine anonymous and numbered witnesses deliver the testimony of several hundred, while eighteen named yet still numbered defendants offer their frequently callous responses. Despite their names, collective stage directions make it clear that they were part of a group that had been produced by a particular social and economic system.

The use of documents stems from the emergence of important questions concerning representation in the wake of historical events and advances in technology. In an interview in 1966 Kipphardt said: 'I don't deny that the [Brechtian] parable can describe a whole range of themes … I just don't believe that the parable as a form is suitable for all themes. I don't know if one can write a coherent parable … about Auschwitz or Hiroshima.'[3] The documentary appeared to present a way of processing material that touched raw nerves and national trauma through objective and unimpeachable sources. It was not, however, quite as unproblematic as its early advocates may have thought. Hochhuth's *Soldaten* (*Soldiers*, 1967) tried to demonstrate that Winston Churchill was complicit in a plot to murder the Polish general Władysław Sikorski in 1943 in a bid to keep Stalin on the Allies' side. However, after a successful libel action by the Czech pilot of Sikorski's plane in 1972, the disclosure of the sources in 1974 led to the conclusion that Hochhuth had actually misread them. Kipphardt, too, was unhappy about the status of documents when he revised *Oppenheimer* in 1977, and he developed a more sceptical dramaturgy that started to question the veracity and reliability of the evidence itself.

Peter Weiss had risen to prominence shortly before *Die Ermittlung* with *Die Verfolgung und Ermordung Jean Paul Marats dargestellt durch die Schauspielgruppe des Hospizes zu Charenton unter Anleitung des Herrn de Sade* (*The Persecution and Assassination of Jean Paul Marat as Performed by the Inmates of the Asylum of Charenton under the Direction of Monsieur de Sade*, better known as the *Marat/Sade*, 1963). Peter Brook famously directed the play in London in 1964 and helped to create an international hit. The play marks an attempt to synthesise the dialectical dramaturgies of Brecht with the visceral and sensual theatre theories of Antonin Artaud. The drama is set in 1808 in an asylum during the still victorious reign of Napoleon, where the Marquis de Sade stages a play depicting the murder of the revolutionary Jean-Paul Marat in 1793. The scenes present tensions between didactic control and the explosion of the irrational and meditate upon the efficacy of direct political action, the impotence of liberal reform, and the solace of radical individualism. Despite the series of plays-within-a-play, the thematic force of the piece very effectively addressed the issues of its time. Documentary theatre remained popular for much of the 1960s in the FRG, had offshoots in the GDR, for example, *Prozeß in Nürnberg* (*Trial in Nuremberg*, 1967) by Rolf Schneider (b. 1932), and continued into the early 1970s, although by then it had rather run out of steam.

The new *Volksstück*

A response to non-fictional sources was to be found in the revival of a much older genre, the *Volksstück*. The term is untranslatable: literally it means 'play for/of the people', and has been translated by Michael Patterson as 'the theatre of the common man' [sic].[4] The term has changed its meaning since the eighteenth century. Originally it denoted a play written for the common people and featured all manner of spectacle and slapstick. After further mutation in the nineteenth century, the form was reconsidered in the early twentieth as a critical examination of the lot of the common people. Two of the driving forces behind the *Volksstück* in the Weimar years, the Austro-Hungarian Ödön von Horváth (1901–38) and the South German Marieluise Fleißer (1901–74), were rediscovered in the 1960s and this inspired a wave of new plays. Just as with documentary drama, the new *Volksstück* cannot be understood by ticking a checklist of formal features. While there was a tendency to use dialect and to focus on characters at the lower end of the social spectrum, other strategies were open to negotiation. Martin Sperr (1944–2002) effectively reinvigorated the genre with his 'Bavarian Trilogy', consisting of *Jagdszenen aus Niederbayern* (*Hunting Scenes from Lower Bavaria*, 1966), *Landshuter Erzählungen* (*Tales from Landshut*, 1967) and *Münchner Freiheit* (which is a district in Munich and means 'The Liberty of Munich', 1970). The three plays treat very different themes: the first deals with the persecution of a homosexual man in a rural community in 1948; the second, set ten years later, focuses on two competing firms of builders, whose perspectives are certainly no less blinkered than the villagers of the first play; the third part, which plays in 1969, tackles issues of student rebellion in a capitalist society. The trilogy made use of an episodic structure, in acknowledgment that the act format used by the German naturalists of the late nineteenth century was no longer suitable to depict the lives of the characters in post-war Bavaria. Those who followed Sperr sometimes radicalised his premises. Rainer Werner Fassbinder (1945–82), for example, remained close to Sperr's themes in portraying a *Gastarbeiter* (immigrant worker) in his play *Katzelmacher* (1968), that is, an outsider, left to face the prejudices and often brutal whims of the young people of a provincial Bavarian town. Fassbinder, however, makes language the hub by practically eradicating plot from the play and shrinking the dialogue to little more than swiftly edited scenes from the cinema. In Austria, Wolfgang Bauer (1941–2005) and Peter Turrini (b. 1944) also developed the form and used the cadences of dialect to interrogate contemporary social themes.

The most famous and indeed most enduring of the *Volksstück* dramatists was Franz Xaver Kroetz (b. 1946). While his early work was mainly formalistic and at some distance from the aesthetics of Sperr, Kroetz encountered an adaptation of Fleißer's *Pioniere in Ingolstadt* when working with Fassbinder in 1968. Whether this episode or the general upsurge of interest in the form 'converted' Kroetz, he went on to become its champion and its main innovator in the 1970s. As with Fassbinder, language was a constant fascination, but he also considered that silence was just as important to characters who were unable to express themselves. His early play *Heimarbeit* (*Working at Home*, 1969) was subtitled 'an antidialogical play in twenty scenes'. Kroetz added in a note on the text:

> the main means of expression [in the play] isn't the dialogue but the action. ... Language doesn't work for my characters ... Their problems lie so far back and are so advanced that they're no longer able to express themselves in words. They are introverted. For the most part a society that pays them no attention and that lets them remain silent is to blame ... The primacy of dialogue in theatre is a prejudice.[5]

The dialectic of speech and silence runs through many of Kroetz's plays of the 1970s. It is important, however, to remember that, just like his fellow *Volksstück* writers, Kroetz was not advocating a return to naturalism. The scenes are clipped and the dramatist expressly asks that no elaborate decoration be afforded in production. In addition, one of the four characters in the play is Ursel, the two-year-old daughter of Willi and Martha. Kroetz gives no directions, as a toddler of that age cannot act: 'the important thing is the child's presence'.[6] He asks for a figure on stage that can contrast itself with the artifice of the theatricality demanded elsewhere. Kroetz plays an interesting game that pits a real child on the verge of speech against actors depicting characters who live in the abysses of language.

Kroetz was to develop as a dramatist over the years. His silent play, *Wunschkonzert* (*Request Concert*, 1971), is comprised of only stage directions and details how a lonely middle-aged office worker, Fräulein Rasch, returns home after a day at work and quietly and methodically prepares herself for suicide. Later on, the playwright modified his understanding of language, as he noted in 1981: 'dialects are the expression of work, landscape and society. Dialects are attitudes fixed in language ... unreflected appropriation of a dialect leads headlong into naturalism, aestheticising the dialect.'[7] The characters are no longer victims of language as such but its users, and have the possibility of changing (or indeed retaining) their means of expression through activity and engagement. Kroetz's plays also extend their reach beyond Bavaria and its isolated backwaters: his *Furcht und Hoffnung der BRD* (*Fear and Hope in the FRG*, 1983) is a twenty-scene kaleidoscope of experiences, which includes short dialogues, lengthy exchanges, and monologues. The title echoes Brecht's *Fear and Misery of the Third Reich* written forty-five years earlier. Kroetz delivered a 'state of the nation play', a form more common in British political theatre of the time, but far less so in the FRG. The playwright realised that representation had to survey language-encoded attitudes rather than characters themselves to gauge a broad set of political positions that transcended the individual.

Crises of subjectivity

In the middle of the 1960s, at a time when the *Volksstück* revival was yet to find a foothold, an alternative voice emerged from Austria in the form of the *enfant terrible*, Peter Handke (b. 1942). The writer had made a name for himself by haranguing the prestigious Gruppe 47 in Princeton in 1966 and reproaching them for 'descriptive impotence'. At a time when political commitment and a social conscience were very much the order of the day on the West German stage, Handke proposed an aesthetic revolution that was to start in the theatre itself. His cure for 'impotence' was to assault the theatre with forms that defied conventional signifying practices and helped to usher in a post-dramatic theatre, a theatre beyond representation. *Publikumsbeschimpfung* (*Offending* or *Insulting the Audience*, 1965) has no character attribution; there is only text to be divided up between four speakers. The paragraphs themselves are mainly meditations on theatre and the ways in which it does or does not work. The audience is directly addressed throughout and, as the title suggests, insulted. The textures of the speeches differ greatly from those of the documentarists and the writers of the new

Volksstück. Handke was not only a skilled writer but he also had elements that referenced the popular culture of the day, in the spirit of the happenings and pop art of the USA. His 'rules for actors' that preface the play mention football chants, the Beatles and the Rolling Stones, Westerns, and the top ten on Radio Luxemburg. Other 'characterless' plays followed, but the one that gained the greatest prominence in the wake of Handke's explosive debut was *Kaspar* (1966). *Kaspar* takes up the tale of Kaspar Hauser, the teenage boy found on the streets of Nuremberg in 1828, seemingly unable to speak. Handke does not, however, try to tell his story afresh; he uses the figure as a model for the acquisition of language. Over time, Kaspar is taught language by three anonymous prompters 'who bring Kaspar to speak through speaking'.[8] While Handke always distanced himself from Brecht (and wrote in 1990: 'Brecht? . . . Perennial futility'[9]), his treatment of language in the play is certainly dialectical. The play is driven by a move from the early to the later Wittgenstein: at first Kaspar is taught that there is an objective world and people merely attach words to it (the 'picture theory of language'). It becomes clear, however, that language is being coloured by all manner of ideological material as the 'teaching' progresses. The prompters are creating and not merely deriving meaning from speech. Handke may have been rebelling against the didacticism of Brechtian political theatre, yet *Kaspar* is actively involved in the *Verfremdung* of language. Kaspar is not a conventional character, but rather a vessel of language whose human materiality rather than psychology rebels against the strictures of the prompters. *Kaspar* was followed by *Ritt über den Bodensee* (*The Ride across Lake Constance*, 1970) which further problematised the business of human communication through a series of episodes performed and indeed mis-performed by a small ensemble of actors.

Handke, like Kroetz, went on to produce a sizeable corpus of work for the theatre, yet he rarely returned to the radicalism of his youth. Indeed, the play that marked his return to the stage, *Über die Dörfer* (*The Long Way Around*, 1981) after a hiatus of eight years, was something of a disappointment. Its use of more conventional character and its nature-mysticism leads back to unassailable divides between a poet and his family. Ever since then, Handke has oscillated between suggestions of a return to form and plays that get mired in the playwright's relationship to more fixed issues. *Die Stunde da wir nichts voneinander wußten* (*The Hour when We Knew Nothing of Each Other*, 1992) is, for example, a silent piece in which a broad host of figures traverse the stage in an impressionistic series of exchanges and missed opportunities. Handke became notorious for his sharp criticism of western engagement in the Balkans, and *Die Fahrt im Einbaum oder das Stück zum Film vom Krieg* (*The Journey in the Canoe or the Play about the Film of the War*, 1999) treats the attempt to make a film about the Balkan wars in a rather flat and one-sided fashion.

Handke's move away from the grand political themes of the late 1960s found echoes in the work of other writers at the time, despite the intensification of political plays around the key year 1968. Peter Weiss wrote his *Vietnam Diskurs* (*Vietnam Discourse*, 1968) assessing the larger geopolitical picture while, on a local level, Michael Hatry (b. 1940) penned his *Notstandsübung* (*Preparing for the State of Emergency*, 1968) as an agit-prop play that discussed the emergency laws brought in by the FRG government. In the same year one of post-war Germany's most prolific writers, Tankred Dorst (b. 1925), wrote *Toller*, a play combining documentary with absurdist effects, to reflect the helplessness of an intellectual in a revolutionary situation. Yet around the same time, Max Frisch scored a hit with *Biographie: Ein Spiel* (*Biography: A Game*, 1967) that effectively turned its back on his more political work of the 1950s and early 1960s in favour of an exploration of identity as a series of roles.

The turn inward away from affairs of state was to mark a movement that would reflect both the hangover of the student protests and a general concern with subjectivity in the 1970s. The shift to more personal perspectives can be traced in two major playwrights who started writing in the early 1970s, the Austrian Thomas Bernhard (1931–89) and the West German Botho Strauß (b. 1944).

While there was no sustained response to the absurdism of the 1950s in the German theatre, a more considered engagement took place in the prodigious work of Bernhard, which echoes yet develops the sense of an 'endgame', taken from Samuel Beckett. Bernhard's plays often feature lengthy monologues, a predilection for (blank) verse, and a series of situations that are bleak, desperate, and darkly comic. His first major play, *Ein Fest für Boris* (*A Party for Boris*, 1970), depicts a grim birthday celebration hosted by 'the good woman' for her legless husband, Boris. At the play's climax, he is presented with a pair of boots and a set of long-johns before a table of disabled guests. The figure of the artist is also a central motif, which continually questions the role and value of the works being performed. In *Die Macht der Gewohnheit* (*Force of Habit*, 1974), a peculiar set of musicians try to produce a decent rendition of Schubert's 'Trout' Quintet but never achieve their goal. The play, like many of his others, uses repetition extensively to vary and compound the hopelessness of the exercise. *Die Macht der Gewohnheit* also points to the central role of musicality in Bernhard's plays, not merely as a theme but as structuring principle. The dramas are like pieces of music that introduce phrases, develop them, return to them, and combine them with others. The obsessive and the compulsive colonise the individual and construct a set of relations on stage that undermine the representation of the sovereign self.

The repetitions and the circularity of the plays' form dwell on existential issues for sure, but as Bernhard matured, the political also intruded upon the claustrophobic scenes. *Vor dem Ruhestand* (*Eve of Retirement*, 1979) features Rudolf Höller, a former SS-officer involved in the death camps, who has become an eminent judge. He is adored by one sister, the ironically named Vera (Slavonic for 'faith'), and criticised by the other, the wheelchair-bound Clara. It is Himmler's birthday, a celebration repeated annually. The tensions of the play, however, culminate in Rudolf's death. Clara's position is ambivalent as her silence towards the end provokes the heart attack, yet her silence that failed to inform the authorities of Rudolf's rampant political sympathies similarly leaves her a guilty figure. History as trauma also occurs in Bernhard's final play, *Heldenplatz* (*Heroes Square*, 1988). The play was a commission for the Burgtheater and its intendant Claus Peymann, with whom Bernhard had worked productively since the mid-1970s. The play is about a Jewish family who fled the Nazis. On the fiftieth anniversary of the *Anschluß*, the *pater familias* commits suicide by jumping from the family apartment onto Heldenplatz, a location in Vienna where Hitler was received as a conquering hero in 1938. His widow suffers from an auditory complaint that haunts her for the duration of the play – she cannot stop hearing the cheers that greeted Hitler all those years ago – until she falls dead into her soup at its conclusion. While the play reuses many formal features mentioned above, its focus on history and memory makes it a more nuanced meditation on helplessness and politics. Nuance was not, however, to be found in the parts of the public response to the première in Vienna. Bernhard was accused of befouling his own nest by a vocal and broad group of conservative, nationalistic protesters.

Botho Strauß emerged from his job as a critic for the most important West German theatre magazine, *Theater heute* (1967–70), and as the director Peter Stein's most trusted dramaturge (1970–5), to become one of the country's leading dramatists in the 1970s. Unlike the writers of the *Volksstück*,

Strauß tended to concentrate on more middle-class characters, as in *Trilogie des Wiedersehens* (*Reunion Trilogy*, 1977), which is set at a vernissage to which friends of the gallery have been invited. The exhibition is called 'Imaginings of Reality', which functions as a *mise en abîme*. The seventeen-strong cast flit in and out, displaying their neuroses and involving themselves in dalliances, as the minimal action of the play unfolds. *Groß und Klein* (*Great and Small*, 1978) expanded the lens by reducing the *dramatis personae*. The play focuses on Lotte, a single woman who traverses the FRG against a backdrop of crumbling values. The spiritual desert she inhabits extends to all aspects of her life, which itself unravels as the play progresses, and marks a pessimism and a longing for a past now lost, themes which run through Strauß's work as a whole. With the onset of the 1980s, Strauß moved from social observation into different realms, drawing upon more mythical and literary reference points. The most famous and well-received example of this shift was *Der Park* (*The Park*, 1984) which presents a contemporary version of *A Midsummer Night's Dream*. The play is an exploration of love, and while Oberon and Titania do indeed appear on stage, it is more the spirit of Shakespeare that resonates through the rest of the action rather than direct quotation from the play. Motifs from the myth of Pasiphae as well as the narrator of a cycle of stories by the Romantic writer E. T. A. Hoffmann intermingle in a city park. The play is, again, concerned with disappointment and the hollowness of contemporary life. The myths wilt and fade against a backdrop of new gods, replacing the older archetypal structures.

The breakdown of dramatic form

Towards the end of the 1960s, intendant Kurt Hübner gathered a group of talented young directors around the Theater Bremen, foremost among them Peter Zadek and Peter Stein, who, together with a host of others beyond that city, were to revolutionise the practice of theatre in the FRG. The role of the director was hypostatised, and the play itself became a flexible material for radical reinterpretation. The frequent target for such productions was the classic text, and while this tendency did not do away with new writing per se, it nonetheless had an inhibiting effect upon it. Come the 1980s in the West, the playwrights already discussed were still producing work, but there was also an underbelly of interesting plays that have not always found their way onto many of the FRG's highly subsidised stages.

Rainald Goetz (b. 1954) can hardly be described as a prolific writer for the theatre. His *Krieg* (*War*) appeared in 1986; it was followed by *Festung*

(*Fortress*) in 1993 and *Jeff Koons* in 1999. His remarkable achievement is that on each occasion that he offered a text for performance, he won the most prestigious award for new writing for the theatre in the FRG, the Mülheim Dramatikerpreis. Both *Krieg* and *Festung* are three-part works in which different elements combine to produce a complex whole. *Festung*, for example, starts with *Kritik in Festung* (*Critique in the Fortress*) in which a family is investigated under a cold and distant lens. The second play, itself entitled *Festung*, is a meditation on the Wannsee conference of 1941 in which the fate of millions of European Jews was sealed by the upper echelons of the SS. The text features too many characters to enumerate and takes the format of a talkshow of sorts. Figures from pop-culture rub shoulders with those from history and a variety of other sources in a display of dense and staccato textures. The third play is a monologue, *Katarakt* (*Cataract*), which features an old man who may be dying or already be dead. All Goetz's work for the stage is predicated upon the following thoughts articulated in an interview in 1995:

> – Clarity: the new terror of comprehension – that which is too quickly assimilated is also boring – on the other hand the correctness of the demand: oppose the mythicisation of art, oppose deliberate obscurity . . .
> – the most fleeting forms of cognition: *real* reality as lack of precision, lack of depth – pre-formed by the reality of the media's flow.[10]

Plot and character become highly unstable and can hardly be said to exist in Goetz's plays. Rather, one is confronted by a welter of material that almost defies an interpretive production concept from a director. Goetz is far more interested in the experience of text than its subordination to a limiting frame and thus confronts representation with its own shortcomings. Language and its mediatisation course through the plays in a self-consciously harsh and uncompromising way, eschewing conventional categories of plot and character in a bid to present a world in which the individual is subordinated to forces beyond his or her control.

Ginka Steinwachs (b. 1942) is another playwright whose output is sporadic, although she appears regularly as a performance artist of her own shorter texts. Her two major plays, *Georges Sand* (1980) and *Erzherzog Herzherzog* (*Archduke Duke of Hearts*, 1985), which has never been staged, are demanding and interrogate the lives of Georges Sand and Archduke Ludwig

Salvator of Habsburg-Lothringen, an aristocratic explorer, scholar, and author. Both plays contrast dialogue with prose and focus on the associative power of language. Steinwachs is fascinated by puns, playfulness, and allusion and suffuses her texts with a richness of material that repeats motifs and varies them in a style reminiscent of Bernhard's musical compositional form, but with considerably more verve and optimism. Again, one finds little in the way of plotting; rather her plays are composed of episodes from her central characters' lives, which are replete with anachronism and multiple perspectives. Conflict is lacking, just as with Goetz, and is replaced by a rush of language. Both playwrights display an open challenge to the dramatic 'rules' in a bid to call representation into question and to posit new forms that value language and its embodied articulation as the primary mode of theatrical performance. Their positions, however, owe much to a figure writing from the other side of the iron curtain, Heiner Müller, and so it is to the GDR that we turn to survey some of the developments within a very different ideological context.

Theatre and authority in East Germany (Kippphardt and Hacks)

Theatre in the GDR in the 1960s was one in which playwrights worked under the tension of loyalty to socialist ideals on the one hand and a growing vexation at restrictions on the other. The doctrine of socialist realism demanded certain features in a work of art that stifled its ability to function critically on its own terms. *Parteilichkeit* (partiality) called for the active demonstration of support for the Party's interpretation of socialism; *Volksverbundenheit* (solidarity with the People) prescribed that the arts should speak directly to working people, and this marked an implicit exclusion of formalist dramaturgies in the case of theatre. It is not surprising, then, that several prominent playwrights found themselves in direct conflict with the authorities. Heinar Kipphardt, one of the early documentarists, had voluntarily resettled in East Germany in 1949 and initially worked as a doctor before moving to the Deutsches Theater in 1950 as chief dramaturge. Despite winning a prize for his play *Shakespeare dringend gesucht* (*Desperately Seeking Shakespeare*, 1953), a humorous satire on GDR cultural policy, he was attacked for his more critical work *Esel schreien im Dunkeln* (*Donkeys are Screaming in the Dark*, 1958), which calls petit-bourgeois attitudes in the GDR into question. Kipphardt departed his country of choice in 1959. Peter Hacks (1928–2003), who left the FRG to settle in the GDR in 1955, produced a large body of work popular both in the East and the West. His plays are mainly modelled on German classicism albeit with a good flavour of Brechtian irony. Together with Heiner Müller he revived blank verse for contemporary drama, a feature peculiar to GDR theatre that was taken up by Volker Braun (b. 1939), Hartmut Lange (b. 1937), Jochen Berg (b. 1948), Lothar Trolle (b. 1944), and others. Hacks also suffered interference and censure at the hands of the SED (Socialist Unity Party). *Die Sorgen und die Macht* (*Worries and Power*, 1959, revised 1962) seemed to be a play very much of the type favoured by the Party: it deals with the lot of working people in two factories and concludes with a resolution of the contradictions between them. It was, however, the contradictions that preceded the happy end that provoked the SED's functionaries. His next play, *Moritz Tassow* (1961), which transplants Goethe's *Torquato Tasso* into an East German village during the land reform, fared little better: it was staged in 1965 and cancelled after a few performances. Hacks was forced to resign his position of dramaturge at the Deutsches Theater in 1963 in the wake of the *Sorgen und die Macht* affair. He then kept away from contemporary themes, preferring to clothe his criticism in classical and biblical guise, *Prexaspes* (1968), or *Adam und Eva* (1972) for example. His rewriting of the Amphitryon myth in 1967 and the even more popular one-person play *Ein Gespräch im Hause Stein über den abwesenden Herrn von Goethe* (*A Conversation in the Stein Household about the Absent Herr von Goethe*, 1974) made Hacks a well-known figure on both sides of the Berlin Wall. His basic political commitment was to the GDR, and his open support for the expatriation of the songwriter and poet Wolf Biermann in 1976, contrary to the stance of a sizeable number of prominent East German artists, led to a boycott of his work in the West for the most part, which had a drastic effect on further productions of his plays.

Heiner Müller and other GDR playwrights

Heiner Müller (1929–95), the greatest and most innovative GDR play-wright, also started his career in the theatre by causing friction with the authorities. His first major work, *Der Lohndrücker* (*The Wage-Squeezer*,[11] 1956), was a dialectical piece set in a factory, which was both awarded a state prize and banned from further production. His play on collectivisation, *Die Umsiedlerin oder Das Leben auf dem Lande* (*The Female Re-Settler or Life in the Country*, 1961), was pulled from an amateur stage after its first performance, and *Der Bau* (*The Building Site*, 1964) was cancelled before it ever reached production in 1965; it was not staged in East Germany until 1980.[12] All the early plays engaged with the social and economic problems of the GDR, just like those of Hacks, with a view to sharpening an awareness of socialist society. Müller, like Hacks, was a committed socialist, yet Müller's forms and his use of language presented a stylised theatre in which words and actions extended their reach far beyond the work-a-day locations into metaphorical realms that addressed issues of politics and subjecthood.

Müller's problems with the SED led him to ask larger questions of his society, and he began to engage with German history in the 1970s. While *Die Schlacht* (*Slaughter*, 1951–74) stages fragmentary episodes from the Second World War, *Germania Tod in Berlin* (*Germania Death in Berlin*, 1956–71) goes all the way back to Germanic mythology and the Prussian legacy while offering parallel scenes from the GDR's own history. The play attempts to excavate a complex of historical forces that might account for the stultification of the present. In both plays, episodes replace linear plot and characters are far more like representatives or ciphers of attitudes and positions than autonomous psychological entities. The spectre of history, which was always evident in the early plays, becomes a central presence in Müller's works from the 1970s onwards. One of his most radical texts, *Die Hamletmaschine* (*The Hamlet-machine*, 1977), is a meditation on socialism among other things. The five-act, ten-page play opens with a characterless monologue suffused with intertext, continues to a third act which contains unrealisable stage directions, and concludes with the figure of Ophelia declaring that she is Electra, with a speech about liberation couched in the language of others. There is precious little in the way of plot as Müller traces a set of historical impasses through representative and associative figures taken from *Hamlet*. Brecht had questioned the status of unchallenged representation in the theatre on ideological grounds. Müller sought to suspend the very act of representation for similar reasons: to posit a world was to give it a legitimacy that may preclude more fundamental political change. Such a position meant that Müller's plays, which were much performed in the FRG, Europe, and beyond, hardly made it onto the GDR's stages. Only a handful of productions emerged in the final years of the state, shortly before its collapse in 1989 and its liquidation a year later.

Müller had been fascinated by Brecht's idea of the *Lehrstück* or 'teaching play'. He admired 'a new type of institution without spectators, whose actors are simultaneously listeners and speakers', as a dynamic site of conflict in which there was no division between the stage and the auditorium, and actors could learn through the act of performance.[13] Müller's experiments started in the 1960s with his version of Sophocles' *Philoctetes* (1958–64), through a revision of Brecht's *Die Maßnahme* (*The Measures Taken* or *The Decision*) as *Mauser* (after the gun of the same name, 1970) but he called a halt to the possibility of education in the theatre in 1977 in an open letter to the initiator of serious scholarly research into the *Lehrstück*, Rainer Steinweg. Several plays later, with the advent of Gorbachev in the Soviet Union, Müller returned to the *Lehrstück* form. The time for learning had returned, and Müller composed the *Wolokolamsker Chaussee* cycle (*The Road of Tanks*, 1983–9). The five plays all concern central crises in the recent history of socialism, starting in the dark days of World War Two, via the GDR workers strike of 1953, to the Prague Spring of 1968. The conflicts and contradictions are never resolved, and the plays never attribute character to text. This dramaturgical strategy, used earlier in his career as well, encourages production teams to locate voices in the texts, to empower directors and actors to play with the text and its meanings in a bid to develop productive attitudes towards the thematic impasses of the plays themselves.

Müller's later dramaturgies did much to provoke the theatre and were to prove extremely influential in both Germanys and further afield. Characterless speeches, plotless scenes, and extreme brevity defined a fundamental collapse of conventional representation in his political theatre. He was convinced that 'literature must resist the theatre' and that it should not be easily consumed but duly processed by both its realisers and the audience.[14] His theatre sought to suspend representation and to present the spectators with uninflected material that could not be simply digested but forced them to make choices, to interpret on their own terms, not on those of the theatre's. This, of course, was something of a utopian aspiration, but on occasion, Müller's productions, which were sometimes directed by the author himself, attained that level of distance that sought to open up the textual material in a bid to present and not to represent.

Other writers from the GDR were to emerge in the wake of an apparent 'thaw' in cultural policy, when Erich Honecker succeeded the dogmatic Walter Ulbricht as first secretary of the SED in 1971. While this proved something of a false dawn, despite Honecker's promise of a 'literature without taboos',[15] some interesting work was nonetheless done. Volker Braun started writing for the stage in the early 1970s and was strongly influenced by Brecht. His *Großer Frieden* (*The Great Peace*, 1979) is set in China and closely follows the tenets of the epic theatre. To an extent, Braun was influenced by Müller. *Simplex Deutsch* (1981) bears more than a passing resemblance to *Germania Tod in Berlin*, and his play on German emigrants in occupied France, *Transit Europa* (1985), leans on features found in Müller's *Der Auftrag* (*The Mission*, 1979). Braun's own voice is more distinctive in some of his other plays such as *Die Kipper* (*The Dump-Truck Drivers*, 1962, revised 1972), which is set in the GDR. One may see just how erratic East German censorship was when the play was performed at the prestigious Deutsches Theater, Berlin in 1972. One of the characters says of the GDR: 'This is the most boring country on earth'.[16] This was performed dozens of times until it was reported in a West German paper; whereupon the authorities had the line cut. Perhaps Braun's greatest play is *Die Übergangsgesellschaft* (*Transitory Society*, 1982). Taking Chekhov's *Three Sisters* as a model, Braun uses his characters and their longings for a better future as a means of questioning the GDR government's basic pronouncements about its people's place in history. Braun suggests that socialism has not been attained and that the GDR is still in a period of transition. The comedy points to the absurdity of party dogmatism while exposing the desires of the characters for a different life. The stasis of the nation is reflected in the three sisters' intention to move on and their failure to do so. Yet the characters themselves are consciously theatrical: they first appear under sheets of gauze, which emphasises their unreality, as if dust covers are being taken off figures from the drama's past.

Christoph Hein (b. 1944), a dramatist who emerged in the GDR in the mid 1970s but developed a more confident style in the 1980s, also meditated on the possible demise of the state in his *Die Ritter der Tafelrunde* (*The Knights of the Round Table*, 1989). Hein employs characters from Arthurian legend to comment on the movement of history. The search for the Holy Grail has been long abandoned and the knights are now looking for meaning in a stagnating environment. The characters represent a range of views from the conservative to the progressive. While the play has been interpreted as a parable about the end of the GDR, as well as a more encompassing exploration of historical forces, the allegorical nature of the piece places it far beyond any sense of a character study. Ulrich Plenzdorf (1934–2007), actually a script writer whose film *Die Legende von Paul und Paula* achieved cult status, was equally successful with his play *Die neuen Leiden des jungen W.* This reworking of Goethe's *Sorrows of Young Werther* in a contemporary setting opened in Halle in 1972 and was played by almost every theatre up and down the country.

Germany reunited

The collapse of the GDR and the reunification of Germany on 3 October 1990 led to something of a crisis in German-language drama as a whole. Müller would not write another full-length play until 1995, and the other major writers produced little of merit. Hochhuth's *Wessis in Weimar* (*West Germans in Weimar*, 1993), Kroetz's *Ich bin das Volk* (*I am the People*, 1994) and *Wartesaal Deutschland Stimmenreich* (*Waiting Room Germany Realm of Voices* or *Rich in Voices*, 1995) by Klaus Pohl (b. 1952) all present collages composed of mainly unrelated scenes, snapshots of a new Germany. Hochhuth's crude realism provides little more than a ham-fisted critique of Western acquisitiveness; Kroetz is a touch more subtle, focusing on the rise of xenophobia and probing formal strategies that occasionally undermine the realism that characterises the play. West German Pohl takes a documentary approach and assembles a variety of verbatim responses and testimonies to the *Wende* from erstwhile citizens of the GDR. Despite its 'authenticity', the play nonetheless has something of a Western bias in the voices that were selected and the themes they address. Positive aspects of the defunct state are hard to find in the text. Botho Strauß also engaged with the *Wende* in his *Schlußchor* (*Final Chorus*, 1990) and produced a comic triptych of unconnected acts which considered the recent political events, various modes of observation, and a set of missed opportunities. In each act, someone shouts 'Deutschland!', and this is the only concrete link between the triptych's parts. The word, however, is something of an empty signifier in the play, opening its meaning to a wealth of interpretations from the audience. Its ambivalence and its more negative and threatening connotations were developed in Strauß's essay 'Anschwellender Bocksgesang' ('Swelling Goat-Song', 1993) which gave an ambiguous political prophecy of a Europe overcome by foreign influence and rent of its traditional values; it was received for the most part as a manifesto for the new right. Its 'difficult' and slippery style also proposes it as a text for a readership that was sufficiently sophisticated to penetrate its formulations. Strauß's play *Ithaka* (*Ithaca*, 1996) seemed to offer the same kind of political fare, using Odysseus as a front for more of the same political thought.

A more knee-jerk response to the *Wende* came from the maverick and highly productive dramatist Herbert Achternbusch (b. 1938), who allegedly penned the farce *Auf verlorenem Posten* (*A Lost Cause*, 1989) in three days over Christmas. The play focuses on 'a man', who may or may not be a former general of a GDR artillery battalion, and his crumbling marriage. Associative material pervades the self-consciously theatrical monologue that opens the play, which is followed by apparently random episodes that combine news of the Romanian revolution, the Christmas nativity story, including the stage direction for the presence of a real camel, which was adhered to at the premiere in Munich 1990, and the effects of manic consumerist freedom on East German citizens. The latter may be seen when the man encounters a GDR Trabant car packed with sixteen people on its way to enjoy the perceived riches of the FRG. By its conclusion, the man's contentment is brought about through a liaison with a woman, 'Das Glück' (Happiness). The anarchic play clearly eschews psychological realism in favour of amassing comic, grotesque, and phantasmagoric moments in a quick-fire assault on the sensibilities of the audience. Coherence and causality are dispensed with as Achternbusch uses the theatre as a site in which material is stockpiled and launched at an audience which is itself unable to make sense of its own place in the welter of historical events.

A concern with xenophobia has also run through the early 1990s and has accompanied the rise of neo-Nazi groups and violent attacks on foreigners. While Fassbinder's *Katzelmacher* had been produced widely at this time, younger writers were exploring the phenomenon as well. *Heilige Kühe* (*Holy Cows*, 1992) by Oliver Czeslik (b. 1964) focuses on two skinheads who kidnap a left-leaning documentary film-maker. Czeslik is more concerned with the media's reporting of the far right's activities in this play, in which identity becomes unstable and nothing really is what it seems. John von Düffel (b. 1966) treats the problem differently in two plays of the mid 1990s. In *Oi* (1995), language is the focus, as well-heeled racists speak a pseudo-German as a secret language for identifying each other and excluding foreigners and those who do not share their views. *Solingen* (1995) is a response to an arson attack on a Turkish family in the city of the same name in 1993. The play is less grotesque than *Oi* and deals with an experienced German teacher and a trainee and their inability to deal with xenophobia in their school. Political correctness and an intellectual distance mean that the problem is never really dealt with, and when the arson attack is reported in the final pages of the play, the two characters withdraw to the safety of the world of literature, quoting lines from Shakespeare to each other. Speech and silence play an important role here. Only the unnamed teacher and the trainee are given lines, but the additional character, 'the silent majority', makes various appearances at certain junctures, and although the two main figures speak all the time, they never discuss the most important matters. Multiculturalism was, however, the theme of one of the most successful plays of the early twenty-first century, *Die arabische Nacht* (*The Arabian Night*, 2001) by Roland Schimmelpfennig (b. 1967). The playwright creates a dreamlike atmosphere on the seventh floor of a block of flats, as acts of narration transfigure everyday drudgery. A small group of German and Turkish characters imagine a series of events that blur the boundaries between the here-and-now and an altogether more sultry and magical place.

Austrian experiments with language

While the Germans were overwhelmed by the momentous events unfolding before their eyes, the Austrians were presenting a vibrant challenge to the theatre through a broad range of formal innovations. Elfriede Jelinek (b. 1946), who started writing for the stage in the late 1970s, had been making a name for herself in the 1980s. Her *Burgtheater* (1984) is a savage satire on an acting dynasty, the Hörbiger-Wessely family, and its connections with the Nazis, written in a parodistic Viennese dialect. *Krankheit oder moderne Frauen* (*Illness or Modern Women*, 1987) draws on Emily Brontë's *Wuthering Heights* to offer a grotesque disquisition on gender relations featuring vampires and a frightful gynaecologist. The women inhabit the ranks of the undead, embodying Jelinek's view that women's existence is neither fully living nor completely expunged in a patriarchal society. The slightly earlier *Wolken. Heim* (*Cloud. Land*, 1986) presented what would later be described as *Sprachflächen* (planes of language). The text, written in the first person plural, approaches issues of nationalism and encounters with the Other from a partisan and insular perspective, taking its material from philosophers (Hegel, Fichte, and Heidegger), writers (Hölderlin and Kleist) and from the letters of the Rote Armee Fraktion, also known as the Baader-Meinhof Group. The text has no stage directions and is presented as an object in itself. The 'we' extends beyond the stage and makes connections with the audience and its collective identity in the German-speaking theatre. The architecture of the play declares its own artifice whilst not necessarily divorcing itself from its speaker; the language cannot simply be dismissed as parody as its construction is so complex and far reaching. The texture is wont to change, allowing the 'planes' within one section to offer resistance to others, despite the common theme. Other plays by Jelinek develop this technique, such as *er nicht als er* (*he not as him*, 1998), an elliptical consideration of the Swiss author Robert Walser, or *Bambiland* (2003) and *Babel* (2005), both on the war in Iraq. The *Sprachfläche* is not only restricted to the monologue form. In the more dialogic *Stecken, Stab und Stangl* (*Stab, Staff and Stangl*, 1995), characters defer to an ideological script that transcends their individual existences. The play is about the public response to the racist murder of four Romany men in Oberwart, Austria, in 1995. The text posits two archetypes, the aggressive Herr Stab and the demure Frau Margit, who become functions of a language that both produces neat gender role models and frames them within nationalist discourse. The media, another of Jelinek's preoccupations, are also present as the play is being filmed for live television broadcast. The 'characters', who are only referred to in generic terms, such as 'the butcher', 'the first customer' or 'someone else' are undone by the language that 'speaks' them and present attitudes that are no longer their own.

The 1990s also heralded the arrival of the Austrian Werner Schwab (1958–94). Very much an *enfant terrible*, he burst onto the theatre scene in 1990 with his much produced play *Die Präsidentinnen* (*First Ladies* or *The Chairwomen*, 1989), only to die of alcohol poisoning on New Year's Day, 1994. In this short period of time he wrote fourteen full-length plays, most of which were performed either in his lifetime or shortly after his death. The popularity of Schwab's work stems from its visceral and violent treatment of language: his German is as tortured as the characters. Modal verbs accumulate, the most peculiar compound nouns proliferate, and spatial prefixes transform the geography of many a familiar verb. The distinctiveness of the language led critics to dub it 'Schwabish'. The characters themselves are mainly neurotic or damaged, carrying traumas and depression into insalubrious locations. Plotting is basic with the characters preferring to exchange opinions, insults, and abuse rather than engage in action as such. Indeed, dead characters are sometimes brought back to life in the final scene as if nothing had happened: the action is very much secondary to the language. The artificiality of Schwab's theatre is sometimes marked by metatheatrical devices. While *Endlich tot, endlich keine Luft mehr* (*Dead at Last, No Air Left at Last*, 1993) is set in a theatre, *Die Präsidentinnen* takes place in a dingy flat, owned by one of the three female pensioners in the play. By its conclusion, two of them have turned on the wise fool Mariedl and sawn her head off. The stage directions then call for a second performance of the whole piece with three young and attractive actresses while the original cast watches and then demonstratively leaves the auditorium. Character, as in Jelinek, is subjected to a thorough examination which rejects its apparent autonomy. For Schwab, the basest instincts (his first collection of plays was called *Fäkaliendramen – Faecal Plays*) determine action away from accepted morality or social convention.

New writers for performance

While the Austrians were making much of the running in the theatre of the early nineties, a stimulus from the other side of Europe would enliven German writing from the mid-1990s onwards. The work of Sarah Kane (*Blasted*, 1995) and Mark Ravenhill (*Shopping and Fucking*, 1996) was received as a shot in the arm for the cause of new writing, and ever since the 'British invasion', there has been a rapid expansion in the number of new plays produced. While the stage had mainly been supported by well-known writers from earlier decades, all of a sudden, there was an interest in the promotion and the nurture of young talent. The never terribly successful invention of the mid-1970s, the *Stückemarkt* (marketplace for plays), has been reinvigorated in various German cities in the past few years, especially as part of the annual Theatertreffen in Berlin. At these events new material is presented in rehearsed readings, and opportunities are opened up for the aspiring and the more established to produce new work in front of real audiences and members of the theatrical establishment. Stipends and commissions for playwrights are also a staple of the contemporary theatre landscape and have played their part in breathing new life into the business of writing for performance.

Foreign imports have certainly proved popular, with, for example, the plays of the Norwegian Jan Fosse accompanying the British; yet home-grown playwrights have become ever more popular as well. The first national and indeed international success as a response to the new impetus was *Feuergesicht* (*Fire Face*, 1998) by Marius von Mayenburg (b. 1972), a play that tapped into the perceived brutalism of Kane and Ravenhill. Set in the thin atmosphere of a nuclear family, the play focuses on teenager Kurt and his alienation from the norms of society, as represented by his parents. His pyromania leads to the complete burning of his face, hence the work's title. The rift between young and old becomes intolerable for Kurt, and he kills his parents in their sleep before dowsing himself in petrol and striking a match. Mayenburg's form is filmic in that it flits between fairly short scenes and monologues. Its language is clipped but mainly relies on its action and an interest in the family and its dysfunctional relationships. Mayenburg took up the shock effects from his British counterparts, but other playwrights have sought a more formally experimental relationship with contemporary reality.

While many of the writers about to be discussed were active before new writing became vogue, they found resonance and popularity for the most part in the period after Mayenburg's success. Perhaps the most performed of these playwrights is René Pollesch (b. 1962), who started writing while still a student on the Practical Theatre course at the University of Giessen in the mid-1980s. He only really rose to national prominence in the late 1990s with his *Heidi Hoh* trilogy and went on to win the Mülheim Dramatikerpreis in 2001 with his seven-part 'theatre soap' *www-slums* (2000). While a soap opera might make one think of action and characters, neither is all that evident in Pollesch's work. Pollesch is one of the most theoretically and politically attuned writers in the German theatre today. His plays are lightning-paced explorations of globalisation and its discontents. As a director, he has developed a particular style for delivering his texts, which are written in two modes: conventional orthography or capitalised letters. While one may wish to interpret these in a variety of ways, Pollesch is clear about how they are to be given in performance. The standard printing is spoken very quickly and neutrally; the capitalised words and phrases are shouted out hysterically. The two modes relate to information overflow and the stress it puts upon the individual. Yet individuals can hardly be said to exist in Pollesch's theatre: the dialogue dominates its speakers, pouring out of their mouths. In many ways, Pollesch's subject matter is secondary to his form. Whether he is discussing the influence of town planning on citizens *Stadt als Beute* (*City as Spoils*, 2001) or the situation of the third world in global capitalism *Pablo in der Plusfiliale* (*Pablo in a Branch of Tesco/Wal-Mart*, 2004) the overwhelming factor is the experience of a completely canalised language. As we have already noted with Müller and others, the tendency to present language as a focus often displaces the traditional role of conflict in theatre. The contradictions of modern life are never overtly acknowledged in Pollesch's many plays and this blithe acceptance in the speakers creates a jarring effect in the audience.

While Pollesch has distinguished himself as a playwright and a director, it may be useful to consider further elements of the contemporary writing scene by concentrating on some of the themes that have arisen in recent years and the forms that have been used to approach them. The German past, for example, has proved fertile ground for much recent theatre. In a period of political impotence, in the face of an all-devouring consumerism and the collapse of ideological alternatives to the market, some playwrights have looked to the radical upheavals of the 1970s. *Leviathan* (1993) by Dea Loher (b. 1964) deals with the immediate aftermath of the formation of the Baader-Meinhof Group. The play is set in Christine's flat and features discussions concerning the nature of political action in society. The play does not present itself as historical, as the 'real' musings of the group's members; it prefers to use its space for a discussion of ideas in which the need for change and the means to achieve it are the centrepiece. The characters are clearly ciphers for debates taking place in the present of the performance, and the articulation of contradictions, between revolution and reform, the public and the private, has a particularly pointed resonance today. Düffel's *Rinderwahnsinn* (*Mad Cow Disease*, 1999) is a witty meditation on the radicalism of the past and its roles in the present. The characters with names like Karlmarx and Mothermeinhof present a consciously theatrical and concertedly comical version of the dilemmas of *Leviathan*. The Grips Theater, Berlin's premier theatre for children and young people, also resurrected and extended its *Eine linke Geschichte* (*A Story of the Left*, 1980) by Volker Ludwig (b. 1937) and Detlef Michel (b. 1944), a play about the 1968 generation of student radicals and what became of them. The director Armin Petras (b. 1964), under the pseudonym of Fritz Kater, has also probed the past in a trilogy of plays that examined the legacies of the GDR, the country where he spent most of his life until he returned to the FRG in 1988. The third of these, for example, *WE ARE CAMERA/jasonmaterial* (2003), takes up the themes of observation and surveillance and follows an East German spy who is about to be exposed and the plight of his family. The main action takes place between New Year's Eve 1969 and New Year's Day 1970 as the family are hurried out of their home to flee Finland for the safety of the GDR. Yet Kater intersperses the linear plot with flashes forward that frustrate a simple understanding of the events. In addition, the jumps in time do not demand different actors for the same temporally scattered roles, and so grown actors play younger children and are able to show the differences between the ages in a consciously theatrical fashion. The intermingling of the personal and the political, the scars the relation leaves, and the complex operations of memory run through the play, whose remit clearly extends beyond its GDR setting.

Elsewhere, frustrations with contemporary life in a globalised, media-tised Europe manifest themselves in two particular areas: the question of what can be accepted as reality and the experience of the economy, work, and unemployment. While the work of Pollesch clearly acknowledges that the spheres of reality production and the economy are intimately connected, other playwrights have chosen to focus on particular areas.

Albert Ostermaier (b. 1967) deals with the compact between the media and what Adorno called 'the culture industry' in *The Making of. B-Movie* (1999) in which a mediocre poet makes a name for himself by indulging in apparently scandalous public displays of rebelliousness. This fairly satirical and definitely intertextual plot is itself framed by the constant presence of a television crew on stage: everything is consciously observed and one is left to wonder how much of the action is being played to the camera. A set of filmic stage directions precedes every scene, but the author notes:

> the stage directions are not to be understood as literal guides for the construction of character and the construction of space in a classical sense. They are rather an attempt at creating an atmospheric road movie, a surreal filming of the reality of the stage.[17]

Ostermaier went one step further with *Death Valley Junction* (2000), in which a supposed revenge drama is suffused with cinematic intertexts and events that cannot logically cohere (such as the deaths and reappearances of certain characters), so that the very basis of the reality experienced is always unstable. Falk Richter (b. 1969), on the other hand, locates his *Electronic City* (2003) in a television studio and follows the construction of two apparently fictional characters who inhabit what Baudrillard called hyper-real space. The irony of the casting is that the two 'characters' have names while the speeches of the TV crew are only marked by dashes indicating a change of speaker. The Swiss playwright Thomas Hürlimann (b. 1950) places the action of *Synchron* (*In Sync* or *Dubbing*, 2002) in a recording studio in which the flow of time and its effects on memory become the dominant themes. The need to synchronise dubbing (for sex movies) bleeds into synchronisations of romantic relationships between three couples. The compression and indeed the collapse of linear time presents a series of déjà-vus in which it is never quite possible to understand how time is being structured. The internet, of course, is also the subject of investigation and is perhaps most prominent in *norway.today* (2000) by Prague-born, German-writing Igor Bauersima (b. 1964). Julie searches the internet for people to join her in a suicide pact and finds August. They meet on an icy cliff in Norway with a view to taking their own lives and to film the event.

Yet the filming and their consciousness of performing presents them with a different take on their reality, and they end up throwing only their recorded suicide notes into the abyss. The plays exploit the stage's implicit artificiality and never fully guarantee the 'reality' of the events themselves. The inability to offer anything but signs and performance allows theatre to revel in the uncertainty of the texts and to throw questions of authenticity and veracity back at the audience.

The economy also presents fundamental problems for representation in that its so-called 'invisible hand', especially in an age of virtual markets and assets, resists by its very definition realisation on stage in a concrete form. Playwrights have thus sought to understand the effects of modern economic logic on their characters and figures as a way of approaching the abstract functioning of the market. The play that raised the curtain on this subject was the international hit *Top Dogs* (1996) by the Swiss Urs Widmer (b. 1938). The text is a loose montage of scenes that deals with a small group of unemployed senior executives. The question that underlies the whole piece is why the group is so keen to return to a system that has so mercilessly rejected them. Widmer avoids psychology and makes the figures on stage appear both individual and as nothing but faceless ciphers in a bid to broaden the ambit of the play. The Austrian writer Kathrin Röggla (b. 1971) also sets her play *wir schlafen nicht* (*we don't sleep*, 2004) amongst the champions of globalisation by choosing to deal with management consultants. While primarily taking her speeches from a series of interviews she conducted, Röggla nonetheless transposes almost the whole of the play into indirect speech. This means that the actors can never refer to their characters as 'I' and are always presenting linguistic material at a remove. There is little in the way of plot either: the scenes are more an exploration of a language that has colonised its speakers. While resistant strains can be detected, the promise of an alternative is never delivered, and even the figure who leaves the firm, the trainee, is unable to cast off its idiom. Ostermaier's *Erreger* (*Pathogen*, 2000) is a similar examination of language. In his play, a stockbroker finds himself in an isolation tent, infected with a mysterious virus. The play is a monologue in which the trader seeks to understand the nature of the disease. His speech is pervaded by a failure to understand his own implication in the world of stocks and shares and also includes thought and opinions written in italics that suggest other voices whilst still being articulated by the trader. The protagonist becomes a language-machine, presenting a pathetic, embattled individual struggling to preserve a semblance of self-control in the face of ever-strengthening discourses whose origins are the markets in which he works. A broader sweep of the interface between the economy and the subject is found in *Täglich Brot* (*Daily Bread*, 2001) by Gesine Dankwart (b. 1969) in which five speakers present stream-of-consciousness accounts of their working day. The disconnectedness of the different experiences and the internalisation of market-oriented behaviours help to generalise representative attitudes towards work and unemployment, while not excluding the remnants of individual perspectives. The journey from waking to sleep encompasses a day's experiences, of course, but telescopes away from the specificity of the speakers and creates a disconcerting circularity, that this day is not that different from any other. In this group of plays, there is a clear dramaturgical attack on the sovereign subject; autonomy is diminished by language and by mindsets that help construct the struggling neo-liberal, self-regulating subjects. Alternatives are removed and the individuals share a helplessness that is inscribed by ideological interpellation. Again, the playwrights play on the stage's obvious artifice as a way of presenting speakers who are not restricted by verisimilitude and are allowed to create contradictory signs on stage without ever having to explain themselves.

German-language writing for the stage since 1960 has produced some remarkable plays and texts and has developed strategies that have called conventional representation into question and posited realities that break with surface realism again and again. The collapse of character, plot, and dialogue has been noted in the plays of many languages in this period. It is, however, the German-language tradition that has displayed the most consistent will to experiment and the most sustained engagement with non- and anti-realistic dramaturgies in the face of the representational crises of recent decades. This continuity seems to owe more than a passing acknowledgement to the material riches of a highly subsidised and decentralised theatre system. The freedom to play and the virtual detachment of the theatres from the economy in the years preceding the fall of the Berlin Wall promoted an approach to making theatre that included the director, the audience, *and* the playwright in equally radical measure. While German theatre now faces a stricter financial regime with reductions in staffing levels and closures of theatres, a sophisticated audience and a daring (and, at times, self-indulgent) collection of directors will still expect texts that broaden and extend concepts of dramaturgy. At present, it does not look like either group will be disappointed.

13 Directors and actors in modern and contemporary German theatre, 1945–2006

MICHAEL RAAB

German theatre is dominated by the director. Many leading representatives of this profession tend to value plays in terms of how much of their own vision and personality they can project into them. If they do this successfully, they will earn high marks from the critics, thus enhancing their chances for further employment or even the artistic directorship of a theatre. The highest ambition of a director is to be invited to the Berlin Theatertreffen where, every year since 1964, the previous season's most remarkable productions from Germany, Switzerland, and Austria are shown. To be chosen means an enormous career-boost as all the major critics attend. Well-made plays are not particularly appealing to directors who are keen to demonstrate their own uniqueness. In their attempts to be original they will be supported by reviewers who welcome any kind of transgression and are likely to refer to a very good production of a tightly constructed text as being 'merely solid'. No wonder that directors who see their main function to be the bringing out of the inherent structural principles of a play and to disappear behind their work lead a tough life in the German theatre. Careers have been made by directors taking on the world première of a half-baked new German text in the hope of getting the credit for having turned it into a bearable evening in the theatre or by deconstructing a classic out of all recognition. The market has become so overheated that after a mere handful of successful productions a young shooting star might receive the offer of running a theatre himself.

After World War II, Germany was divided into two separate states and, in each, theatre developed along different lines, although there was some interplay between the two and a great deal of defection from East to West. In 1961 the GDR erected the Berlin Wall, which only fell in 1989, prior to reunification a year later. Throughout this time there was strong cultural rivalry between the two halves of the city.

The director in post-war GDR

Initially, East Germany received an enormous boost through an influx of progressive theatre people who had been exiled or had been in 'inner emigration' during the Nazi period. These 'nineteenhundreds', as they were called, because they were all born around 1900, included Ernst Busch (1900–80), Walter Felsenstein (1901–75), Wolfgang Heinz (1900–84), Wolfgang Langhoff (1901–66), Helene Weigel (1900–71), and the composers Hanns Eisler (1898–1962) and Paul Dessau (1894–1979). They helped to shape an astonishingly liberal cultural climate in East Berlin until the mid-sixties. The most important impulse came, of course, from Bertolt Brecht, who decided to settle down in East Berlin after his return from America. Brecht and his wife Helene Weigel formed their own state-subsidised company in 1949. After a period of uncomfortable co-existence with the Deutsches Theater, they were given their own house at the Schiffbauerdamm and achieved international acclaim as the Berliner Ensemble. Brecht's 'epic theatre' became a by-word and was more or less successfully emulated the world over. Brecht's *Theaterarbeit*, which documented the first six productions of the Berliner Ensemble, served as a Bible for East German theatre people for years to come.[1]

In spite of his successes, Brecht was viewed with suspicion by GDR hardliners who favoured the traditional Stanislavskian methods of work. He was subjected to attacks in the press and party philosophers quarrelled with his concept of 'realism'. However, the company's successful trips abroad helped to check such carping. In 1956 Kenneth Tynan was overwhelmed by performances of *The Caucasian Chalk Circle*, *Mother Courage*, and *Trumpets and Drums* at the Palace Theatre in London:

> I defy anyone to forget Brecht's stage pictures. No steps or rostra encumber the platform; the dominant colours are browns and greys; and against a high, encircling, off-white backcloth we see nothing but solid, selected objects – the twin gates in *The Caucasian Chalk Circle* or Mother Courage's covered wagon. The beauty of Brechtian settings is not the dazzling kind that begs for applause. It is the more durable beauty of *use*. The same applies to the actors. They look capable and practical, accustomed to living in the open air.[2]

One of Brecht's best and most celebrated productions, in cooperation with designer Caspar Neher (1897–1962), was not of a play of his own but an adaptation of Lenz's *Der Hofmeister* (*The Tutor*, 1950). In marked contrast to official demands for realistic illusionism the director thought it timely to emphasise 'the poetic element in the plays and the artistic side when producing them'.[3] Accordingly in one of the scenes he turned Lenz's unfortunate pedagogue literally into a figure skater, with Hans Gaugler (1913–97) playing him as a character desperately trying to control his sexual urges, often contorting his body into positions that threatened to tear his ligaments. For Brecht, the teacher, who ends up castrating himself rather than losing his job, was a typical example of what he called the tradition of 'German misery'.[4]

After Brecht's death in 1956 Helene Weigel was able to maintain standards for a while. In 1959 Manfred Wekwerth (b. 1929) and Joachim Tenschert (1928–92) directed Brecht's Hitler-parody *Der aufhaltsame Aufstieg des Arturo Ui (The Resistable Rise of Arturo Ui)* with a virtuoso performance by Ekkehard Schall (1930–2005) in the main part. Five years later they did a lucid, dynamic version of Shakespeare's *Coriolanus* in an adaptation by Brecht and themselves with Schall and Hilmar Thate (b. 1931) as the antagonistic generals. The production, with its monumental black and white gate in the centre of the revolve and battles choreographed by Ruth Berghaus, was one of the Ensemble's last great achievements. Afterwards it began to stagnate, as directors like Wekwerth stuck to formal Brechtian principles and the Brecht estate vetoed any attempt to depart from the hallowed model. Berghaus was able to give a blood transfusion to the company, which she headed from 1971 to 1977. Her production of Heiner Müller's *Zement* (*Cement*, 1972) was deemed the start of a post-Brechtian era at the Schiffbauerdamm. Einar Schleef (1944–2001) and B. K. Tragelehn (b. 1936) directed Frank Wedekind's *Frühlings Erwachen (Spring Awakening)* and Strindberg's *Miss Julie* in an avant-garde, deconstructive manner, which led to both directors being barred in 1975 from further work in the GDR. Not for nothing was East German cultural policy often referred to as a dictatorship of petit-bourgeois tastes. After leaving the Ensemble, Berghaus switched to directing operas, staging many works by her husband Paul Dessau. Her 1968 production of Rossini's *The Barber of Seville* with a set by Achim Freyer (b. 1934), a target of official criticism at the time, was still in the repertory of the German State Opera in 2008. Berghaus's former colleague Schleef in the 1980s began a new career in the West and was particularly influential there by using strong choric elements in his work.

The Deutsches Theater, five minutes' walk from the Schiffbauerdamm, housed the other main company in the East German capital. Regarded as the national theatre, it was the most architecturally splendid and heavily subsidised house with a star-studded company of some 70 actors led by Ernst Busch, Fred Düren (b. 1928), Elsa Grube-Deister (1926–2001), Wolfgang Heinz, Inge Keller (b. 1923) and, later, Kurt Böwe (1929–2000), Eberhard Esche (1933–2006), Dieter Franke (1934–82), Christian Grashof (b. 1943), Dietrich Körner (1926–2001), Dieter Mann (b. 1941), Klaus Piontek (1935–98), and Jutta Wachowiak (b. 1940). From 1946 to 1963 it was run by Wolfgang Langhoff, who had returned after years of internment in a concentration camp and exile in Switzerland. In contrast to Brecht, he adhered to the more orthodox Stanislavskian methods. Although in no way provocative as a director himself, in 1962 Langhoff found himself in trouble with the authorities over his production of Peter Hacks's *Die Sorgen und die Macht* and was forced to stand down. This mildly critical play gave a portrayal of life in a socialist factory that was allegedly counterproductive to the aims of the SED. Langhoff's dismissal was an ignominious ending for an Intendant who had built up the most distinguished company in the GDR.

Under his successor, Wolfgang Heinz, the Swiss director, and former Brecht assistant Benno Besson (1922–2006) triumphed with light and elegant productions which were all the more effective as lightness and elegance are not qualities normally associated with German theatre. Besson did not forget the lessons learnt from Brecht but he added his own brand of Romanesque wit and imagination. His staging of *Der Frieden (Peace)* by Peter Hacks after Aristophanes was a revelation. The applause at the première in 1962 lasted for a full 45 minutes. Fred Düren depicted the hero Trygaios as a lecherous old man whose only objective was to go to bed with a certain young lady in time of war and he had to bring about peace to achieve his aim. The production on a spare set by Heinrich Kilger (1907–70) sparkled with artistry. It hardly seemed possible for Besson to improve on this but he did three years later with Yevgeny Schwartz's *Der Drache (The Dragon)*. In this Russian fairy-tale the eponymous Dragon, played by the highly versatile comic Rolf Ludwig (1925–99), terrorises a city and demands the sacrifice of a virgin once a year. Lancelot, played by Eberhard Esche, kills the dragon, only to find that the former Burgomaster has become the new dictator. He realises one heroic deed is not enough, people must continuously fight for their freedom. The association with Stalinism was

23 *The Dragon* by Yevgeny Schwartz, Deutsches Theater Berlin 1965, directed by Benno Besson, designed by Horst Sagert. A scene with the maiden Elsa (Katharina Lind), the hero Lancelot (Eberhard Esche) and the Dragon in the shape of an old man (Rolf Ludwig).

obvious. Horst Sagert's (b. 1934) imaginative set was full of lace and feathers and produced a strange but menacing fairy-tale atmosphere (see. fig. 23). The ingeniously constructed dragon reared its three heads in the air during the fight with Lancelot, and they went on talking even after they had been cut off. The play remained in the repertory for almost 20 years.

The 1960s were the heyday of the Deutsches Theater. Heinz himself was an excellent director for plays by Chekhov and Gorki and as an actor he was acclaimed for his Nathan in Friedo Solter's (b. 1933) production of Lessing's play. Adolf Dresen (1935–2001), who had got into trouble with the authorities after his staging of *Hamlet* in Greifswald (1964), in 1968 did a courageous production of *Faust I* in cooperation with Heinz, a text officials were particularly ambivalent about, because they saw it as pivotal for their theory of cultural heritage. This staging caused one of the biggest theatre scandals in the GDR. The official view of Faust was that of a Renaissance character with lots of willpower and energy, but Dresen firmly refused to show a positive hero. Fred Düren instead portrayed a disingenuous intellectual racked by self-doubt. Dieter Franke's Mephistopheles was no demonic seducer but a pragmatic down-to-earth devil, a fat perspiring plebeian. The production used many elements of fairground theatre. A West German critic called it 'the most cheerful *Faust* ever'.[5] When Dresen and Heinz tried to stage *Faust II* a year later, pressures from outside were so strong that the production team broke up and Heinz resigned as Intendant in consequence. Adolf Dresen remained the only GDR-director who still considered theatre as a means of reviving national awareness; his policy could be described as 'opposition via the classics'. After directing Isaak Babel's *Marija*, he developed his ideas about the fate of an artist in a repressive society with Goethe's *Clavigo* on a set by Achim Freyer. The production was banned because of alleged hippie-influences, so he redid the play in an austere fashion on a new set, again by Freyer, but this was not officially liked either. He produced Kleist's *Prinz Friedrich von Homburg* and *Der zerbrochene Krug* in one evening with Dieter Franke, Alexander Lang (b. 1941) and Bärbel Bolle (b. 1941) taking the main parts in both plays. Finally he adapted Kleist's novella *Michael Kohlhaas* with Kurt Böwe before going to the West. There in 1981 Dresen became the first East German to be made Intendant of a theatre, the Frankfurt Schauspielhaus, which had seen its most interesting post-war period under the former Brecht assistant Peter Palitzsch (1918–2004) in the 1970s. Dresen's aspirations for a national theatre were frustrated in the West, just as they had been in the East, but for different reasons. He stood down prematurely in 1985 and afterwards only directed opera.

At the Volksbühne Benno Besson became a leading director between 1969 and 1974 and was Intendant from 1974 to 1980. His point of departure from Brecht was marked by a grotesque staging of *Der gute Mensch von Sezuan*. Before that he had directed Hacks's *Moritz Tassow* (1965) with Jürgen Holtz (b. 1932) which was banned after a few performances. Manfred Karge (b. 1938) and Matthias Langhoff (b. 1941) did a provocative *Räuber* with a critical slant on the student rebels in the West. Jürgen Gosch (b. 1943) produced Büchner's *Leonce und Lena* as an artistic and poetic parody of socialism, where the Privy Council consisted of a dozen blind nonagenarians stumbling around with sticks. Many Heiner Müller plays premièred at the Volksbühne, including *Die Bauern* and *Der Bau*, both directed by the former agricultural labourer turned actor Fritz Marquardt (b. 1928). Müller himself (with Ginka Tscholakowa) in 1982 staged his aesthetically controversial reworking of *Macbeth* showing the whole world as a slaughterhouse; Hermann Beyer (b. 1943), Michael Gwisdek (b. 1942), and Dieter Montag (b. 1949) shared the title role, and Corinna Harfouch (b. 1954) was Lady Macbeth.

The Maxim Gorki Theater, the smallest of the four main East Berlin theatres, successfully occupied a niche with new Russian plays and also specialised in comedies and naturalist drama. Matthias Langhoff's older brother Thomas (b. 1938) achieved his breakthrough there in the late 1970s.

The director in post-war West Germany: Peter Zadek and Peter Stein

Berlin did not enjoy as prominent a position in the West as in the GDR. In contrast to East Berlin the Western part of the city was not the capital, the government of the FRG being sited in Bonn. West Berlin was an enclave surrounded by the GDR and subject to a number of special legal regulations due to the four power status of the city. West German theatre in the 1950s and 60s was dominated by artistic directors who ran their buildings like fiefdoms over long periods of time. Gustaf Gründgens (1899–1963) had briefly appeared as an actor at the Deutsches Theater in 1946, but then went to Dusseldorf and finally to the Deutsches Schauspielhaus in Hamburg where he successfully reworked his earlier versions of *Faust*. *Faust I* was filmed and became required viewing for generations of German school-children. Many critics rated Gründgens's own Mephistopheles the definitive interpretation of the part. His mercurial energy and smooth rapid-fire delivery made life on stage rather difficult for Will Quadflieg's (1914–2003) Faust, a stiff and ponderous academic. Among Gründgens's most notable colleagues Gustav Rudolf Sellner (1905–90) worked at Darmstadt, Hans Schalla (1904–83) at Bochum and Karl Heinz Stroux (1908–85) took over at Dusseldorf after Gründgens. These directors liked to talk about the stage as 'a metaphysical space' and wanted to let plays speak for themselves. However, as Peter Brook put it so succinctly in *The Empty Space*: 'If you just let a play speak, it may not make a sound.'[6] Emigrants returning to the West like Berthold Viertel (1885–1953) referred to the acting in these productions as *Reichskanzleistil* (Reich Chancery Style).[7] This opinion was shared by Fritz

Kortner (1892–1970); he was the towering exception among stage directors in the West German theatre of the 1950s and 60s, because he rigorously examined every word of a text for hidden meaning over unusually long rehearsal periods. Nevertheless, a Kortner production rarely seemed finished at the first night, and his last minute changes were many an actor's nightmare. In contrast to Sellner, Schalla, or Stroux he never showed 'man himself', but specific characters 'denuded down to minute stirrings of the soul and their most basic, unreflecting everyday behaviour'.[8] The Jewish Kortner, who had been one of the major actors of the Weimar Republic, felt understandably bitter when he witnessed how Nazis and fellow travellers continued to work in the theatre seemingly without any second thoughts or regrets. In a profession where many tend to prize themselves on their moral standards, memoirs by directors and actors often make sad reading when it comes to the period of the Third Reich. In contrast Kortner's *Aller Tage Abend* (*At the End of the Day*, 1959) is one of the most searching and beautifully written autobiographies by a German director. No wonder he was a role model for the new generation who in the late 1960s and early 70s took over from the old guard. Piscator was less influential. He enjoyed no more than a brief renaissance with the vogue for documentary theatre at the Freie Volksbühne Berlin, his only well-known pupil being Hansgünter Heyme who followed in his mentor's footsteps with heavily politicised versions of Schiller, such as *Wilhelm Tell* at Wiesbaden in 1965. Particularly innovative was his 'media-*Hamlet*' developed together with the installation artist Wolf Vostell in 1979 in Cologne. But the two most important productions signalling the breakthrough of the post-war directors' theatre premièred both at Bremen, and the men responsible for them could not have been more different: Peter Zadek (b. 1926) who directed *Measure for Measure* in 1967 and Peter Stein (b. 1937) who staged *Torquato Tasso* two years later.

Zadek, the son of Jewish refugees, grew up in England, where he studied at the Old Vic School and was influenced there by Tyrone Guthrie. He had his early training in British weekly rep and left London in 1957 when his world première of Genet's *The Balcony* at the Arts Theatre turned into a scandal. After seeing a run-through the author protested vehemently, threatened to shoot the director, and was barred from attending the first night. Zadek brought an English sense of showmanship and revue to the German theatre, which was unusual for an artistic institution that was strongly marked as educational, in the sense expounded by Schiller ('The Stage as a Moral Institution'). Zadek stated: 'Shakespeare is characterised by an elementary curiosity, whilst Brecht and Schiller always know everything better from the outset. Probably that is the big difference between the Anglo-Saxon attitude towards theatre and life and the German one.'⁹ The director's eclectic and iconoclastic approach was first demonstrated with Brendan Behan's *The Hostage* at Ulm in 1961, a theatre at which Kurt Hübner (1916–2007), the Intendant responsible for the 'Bremen theatre miracle', had previously worked. To make Ulm and Bremen into leading theatrical German cities was tantamount to establishing the Bolton Octagon as the most important British theatre. With *Measure for Measure*, Zadek attempted to translate Shakespeare's play into body language, savagely cutting and rewriting the text to include a final massacre that left most of the characters dead. To show their mutual dependence, Angelo and Escalus had a shouting match standing unsteadily on the same chair whilst desperately clinging to each other. Isabella jumped at Angelo from behind, screamed hysterically into his ear, and crawled all over him while trying to persuade him to pardon her brother Claudio. When she wanted to prepare Claudio for his death, she sat behind him on the floor and slung her legs around his hips. As if to break his inner resistance, she then tried to force his thighs open. The set was basically empty with just a few chairs and a proscenium frame of coloured light bulbs. The young cast wore everyday jeans and T-shirts, the only costume in the traditional sense being the cowl for the disguised Duke. Designer Wilfried Minks (b. 1930) introduced developments in modern art that had not previously been seen in the theatre.

Minks also worked with Stein on *Torquato Tasso*. For Goethe's play he created a highly artificial environment, down to the lawn covering the stage-floor, which was framed by 'perspex screens through which shimmered dull gold walls and pillars'.¹⁰ There was hardly any furniture, and the lighting had a Brechtian clarity. In marked contrast to Zadek, despite cuts and transpositions, Stein left the text basically intact. He had already made a name for himself with his very first production, a Bavarian dialect version of Edward Bond's *Saved* at the Munich *Kammerspiele* in 1967. He sees philology as a main ally and does not mind if his theatre is compared to a museum. Often he rails against Artaud-inspired voodooism and objects when directors foist their own ideas and sentiments on a play, as if they are superior to anything in the play itself: 'I am of the almost militant persuasion that in the European theatre the text is essential and nothing else.'¹¹ Still he himself was capable of radical reinterpretations worthy of Kortner. In his production of *Torquato Tasso*, Stein showed the eponymous hero, played by Bruno

24 *Torquato Tasso* by Goethe, Bremen 1969, directed by Peter Stein, designed by Wilfried Minks. Tasso (Bruno Ganz) in rapturous conversation with Leonore von Este (Jutta Lampe).

Ganz (b. 1941), as a Weimar court jester and 'emotional clown'[12] kept for the delectation of the two Leonores (see fig. 24). He and the company saw their concept as a reflection of their own role as subsidised theatre practitioners in the FRG, governed from 1966 to 1969 by a 'grand coalition' of Conservatives and Social Democrats led by a Chancellor who had been a member of the Nazi Party.

Stein and Zadek remained high-profile rivals throughout the 1970s. Bruno Ganz, Edith Clever (b. 1940), and Jutta Lampe (b. 1943) had worked with Zadek in *Measure for Measure* as well as with Stein in *Torquato Tasso*. They formed the nucleus for Stein's future company which moved to Berlin in 1970, when he took over the Schaubühne am Halleschen Ufer after a short and troublesome period in Zurich. Zadek stalwarts over the years were Ulrich Wildgruber (1937–99), Angela Winkler (b. 1944), and Ilse Ritter (b. 1944), who had also worked with Stein, as well as Eva Mattes (b. 1954), Rosel Zech (b. 1942), and Hermann Lause (1939–2005). The director established a kind of travelling circus with a permanent group of actors he brought with him, a system the critics labelled 'Lufthansa Theatre'. This proved to be not only costly, but caused a lot of internal problems for the theatres he worked at. Even in Zadek's acclaimed productions, whole scenes might be carelessly arranged while the most detailed attention was paid to others. His work was improvisational and he wanted it to be different every night, as if it were free jazz or a football match. With modern classics like Ibsen or Chekhov he kept the text as he found it, but Shakespeare inspired him to spectacular directorial ideas. In his *Merchant of Venice* (Bochum, 1972), Hans Mahnke's (1905–78) Shylock appeared to be taken straight out of the vicious Nazi propaganda paper *Der Stürmer*. Zadek's point was: only if you accept this Jew as he is, can tolerance be worth its name. An interpretation like that would have been impossible from a non-Jewish director. Until Zadek, and even afterwards, as in Thomas Langhoff's version with Fred Düren at the Deutsches Theater in 1985, Shylock was generally presented as a kindly old gentleman who only very reluctantly resorted to the cutting of Antonio's flesh. The biggest scandal of Zadek's career was *Othello* at the Deutsches Schauspielhaus in Hamburg in 1976. His protagonist, Ulrich Wildgruber, was costumed as a grotesque caricature, a mixture of King Kong and black minstrel, wearing a shaggy and matted wig and a garish uniform jacket. Whenever he touched Desdemona, his generously applied body make-up rubbed off on the young woman, who after she arrived in Cyprus sported no more than a tiny bikini. Zadek confronted the audience with their own stereotype of a black man. With Wildgruber's Othello, he cast a heavily perspiring leading actor known for his elocution problems. During the first night there were a number of angry calls demanding a greater clarity of verse speaking from Wildgruber. In one instance he calmly stepped from the stage, walked up to the heckler and repeated the passage in question exclusively for his benefit before returning to the play. What infuriated the Hamburg audience even more was the treatment of the murder scene. After the line 'Put out the light', the stage remained dark for a couple of minutes while Othello hunted down Desdemona who desperately shouted for help. She was sexually violated as she was murdered, rather than suffocated tastefully with a pillow as was usually the case. After his prolonged ranting and raving, Othello 'suddenly turned silent, sat down on the edge of the bed, next to the dead Desdemona, and seeming to be greatly amazed asked in his most harmless childlike tone: "Who killed her?" And one realised (if one wanted to) that in a tragedy people get utterly destroyed, not only the theatre, the scenery and good taste.'[13] For part of the audience, the moment of worst taste was Othello throwing Desdemona's dead and naked body unceremoniously over a washing line. Zadek aimed for the biggest possible contrast between moments of terrifying rage and intense calm on stage. Somebody like Wildgruber had to maintain his dignity against all the odds that the director staked against him, from costume to staging. He also played the title roles in Zadek's *King Lear* (at only 36) and *Hamlet* in Bochum, neither of which had quite the sheer raw power of *Othello*, but these interpretations, together with *The Merchant of Venice*, added up to the most impressive quartet of Shakespearean productions in the German theatre of the 1970s. Wildgruber, who committed suicide in 1999, was the unlikeliest protagonist the German theatre had known in decades. It took enormous courage on the director's and the actor's part to brave the occasionally nasty reactions of the audience. Finally, in the 1980s and 90s, Wildgruber became one of the great favourites at the Deutsches Schauspielhaus Hamburg and elsewhere.

There was no love lost between Peter Zadek and Peter Stein. Stein called Zadek's productions 'Shakespeare in underpants',[14] and Zadek considered that any spark of life in Stein's work was stifled by a cold perfection achieved by grindingly hard work. In retrospect he claimed sneeringly: 'It's unbelievable how somebody can achieve so much with such limited talent.'[15] While Zadek's periods as Intendant were usually marked by absentee landlordism, Stein made the Schaubühne am Halleschen Ufer the indisputedly leading West German theatre of the 1970s. He excelled with big ensemble pieces like Gorki's *Summerfolk* and a *Peer Gynt* in which no less than six actors were cast as Peer. Productions were diligently prepared through reading lists worthy of a university course or exploratory journeys to Greece and Russia by the whole company. His most successful production was Heinrich von Kleist's *Prinz Friedrich von Homburg* in 1972. Stein and his dramaturge Botho Strauß called their version *Kleists Traum vom Prinzen Homburg* (*Kleist's Dream of Prince Homburg*). The crux of the play is the final scene when Homburg learns to abandon his individual quest for glory and to submit to the rules of war as set out by the Elector. Instead of being executed as he expects, he is pardoned and given the hand of the ruler's niece. It was this final reconciliation of an individual's deepest wishes to the demands of the state that post-war German directors often took objection to, especially as the last line of the play shouted by the Prince and all the officers, which renews war with Sweden, is 'Into the dust with all the enemies of Brandenburg!' In Stein and Strauß's version, the blindfolded Homburg awaited his execution and could hear the firing squad's preparations. On being pardoned he sank to the ground as if he really had been shot. He was roused and crowned with laurel by Natalie, the Elector's niece, in a dream-like state that resembled the somnambulism of the first scene. Then with an ingenious directorial touch Stein split the stage persona of Homburg. A puppet was lifted up by the officers and borne away in triumph as the Prince, but Bruno Ganz, the actor playing Homburg, had fallen to the ground, and lay in the dust, passed over just as the unfortunate Kleist had been in his own life. A meditative female voice on a PA system (Jutta Lampe, who played Natalie) stated that the playwright committed suicide six months after completing *Homburg*. Ganz stood pensively in front of the grave that had been dug for the Prince and left the stage in a visibly shaken manner. The epilogue pointed back to the mimed opening sequence during which Homburg had moved as a sleep-walker across a stage bathed in violet dusk and in slow motion had picked up the laurel wreath from the ground while the meditative female PA-voice read out the author's name, the title of the play, and the dedicatory poem to a Prussian Princess Kleist had written in 1811. From the beginning, therefore, Stein directed the play with the intimacy of a studio piece, as if he were staging the author's mind. The black curtains of the walls of the auditorium emphasised the fact that the spectators were witnessing a dream piece. This was the dramatic utopia of a sensitive bourgeois individual at the beginning of the nineteenth century. Designer Karl-Ernst Herrmann (b. 1936) drew upon the works of the romantic painter Caspar David Friedrich for his views of the plains on which the battle is fought, thereby enhancing the period feel. The Schaubühne's version marked one of the high points of the collaboration between a top-rank director and a dramaturge who rigorously questioned inherited assumptions about a text while adhering faithfully to it.

Stein's thoroughly intellectual approach served him well for works as different as *Homburg, The Oresteia,* or his Botho Strauß premières. His bitterest defeat in Berlin concerned the author he probably revered most and with whom his rival Zadek had triumphed a number of times: William Shakespeare. So huge was the Schaubühne's respect for the Bard that they did not dare just do one of his plays. They researched pre-Shakespearean dramatic writing and the philosophical and ideological background of the Elizabethan age for months on end and then presented their findings in 1976 in the Spandau CCC-film studio. *Shakespeare's Memory* was a rather drearily didactic affair which must rank as the most expensive and exhausting evening class in the whole of German theatre history. When Stein directed *As You Like It* a year later, again in the Spandau film studio, the result was a big disappointment. Dwarfed by an inappropriately gigantic forest environment, the company appeared overawed in every possible sense. The central love scenes between Rosalind and Orlando in particular lacked the charged sexual energy that characterised a Zadek Shakespeare; indeed, one secretly longed for the occasional glimpse of some underpants!

But Stein had a rare quality in artistic directors, which more than made up for set-backs like *As You Like It.* He encouraged colleagues who were at least as highly regarded as himself to work at his theatre, so that his company could get to know the methods of directors aesthetically different from himself. From Bremen he brought Klaus Michael Grüber (b. 1941), whose work, in marked contrast to Stein's analytic clarity, achieved a mystically brooding quality, employing strong visual statements by designers like Eduardo Arroyo (b. 1937), Gilles Aillaud (1928–2005), or Antonio Recalcati (b. 1938). His most spectacular production for the Schaubühne was *Winterreise* (*Winter's Journey*) based on Hölderlin's *Hyperion* as a reaction to the political situation in Germany at the height of the Baader-Meinhof terrorism. This was staged for 800 spectators on six freezing winter nights in 1977 in the Berlin Olympic stadium. Despite the topicality of *Winterreise,* Grüber did not seem particularly keen on the Schaubühne's leftist policies, which included compulsory classes in Marxism/Leninism for the company.

The only truly conservative West German director of high reputation during that time was Rudolf Noelte (1921–2002). He saw Büchner's *Dantons Tod* as a statement against any kind of revolutionary change and in productions of Chekhov tried to tone down the visions of a more just society so fervently voiced by this author's student characters. Noelte's work was noted for the amazing precision of its detail. He excelled in productions set in closed rooms as with Hauptmann's *Michael Kramer* (Thalia Theater Hamburg, 1983), but his detractors claimed they always appeared to be the same room, down to the very lighting. His almost fanatical perfectionism made it increasingly difficult for Noelte to find theatres willing to agree to his demands, and he virtually retired to a provincial Bavarian summer festival run by his former wife.

The prosperous 1970s and 80s

In the late 1960s and early 70s the West German theatre profited from the impact of the student rebellion and chancellor Willy Brandt's wish 'to risk more democracy'. The 1970s were the most fruitful post-war period for the theatre as directors and dramaturges explored plays for hidden subtexts, often turning them inside out in the process. But as West German society became more business-like under Helmut Schmidt and later Helmut Kohl, the theatre continued to flourish with the help of generous subsidies from cities that were themselves thriving thanks to taxes from a booming economy. Dieter Dorn (b. 1935) at the Munich Kammerspiele, Jürgen Flimm (b. 1941) in Cologne and at the Thalia Theater in Hamburg as well as Claus Peymann (b. 1937) in Bochum and at the Vienna Burgtheater established companies with which they worked for years, a continuity of enormous benefit to directors and companies alike. They managed to hire some of the most important German-speaking actors and actresses on a long-term basis. Dorn had the best 'old guard' company anywhere in the country, with Rolf Boysen (b. 1920) and Thomas Holtzmann (b. 1927) playing everything from Lear and Gloucester to the juggler and the actor in Thomas Bernhard's *Der Schein trügt (Appearances Are Deceiving,* 1983). Until his death in 1988 Peter Lühr (b. 1906) completed an outstanding male triumvirate with Gisela Stein (b. 1934), Doris Schade (b. 1924) and Christa Berndl (b. 1932) as their female counterparts. Flimm's doyen was Will Quadflieg who had played Faust to Gründgens's Mephistopheles and enjoyed a remarkable comeback in the 1980s. The favourite old actor of the important directors of the 1970s and 1980s was Bernhard Minetti (1905–98) who proved more open to innovation than Quadflieg; he could be seen as Grüber's Faust and Lear, while he played the protagonist in a string of world premières of Bernhard's plays, usually directed by Claus Peymann. George Tabori (1914–2007), a playwright as well as a director, worked for Dorn, Peymann, and Flimm, sometimes with a 'laboratory' of his own. Luc Bondy (b. 1948) briefly ran the Schaubühne, as did Andrea Breth (b. 1952) later. Bondy, who like Besson is

Swiss, has some of the older man's Romanesque lightness, while Breth in a way is Noelte's brooding successor. Both moved to Vienna, Bondy working as Intendant of the Festwochen and Breth as resident director at the Burgtheater.

It is unusual for a major director to stay for a long period of time in the same city, particularly if it is only a regional one. The big exception in this respect is Pina Bausch (b. 1940) who established the Tanztheater Wuppertal in 1973 and has stayed there ever since. Bausch is far more than a mere choreographer and her work often includes spoken language and a remarkable use of her dancers' personal experiences. Her invitation to the Berlin Theatertreffen for the first time with *Arien* in 1980 marked a huge boost for the whole West German dance scene. She brought *Bandoneon* to Berlin in 1981 and four years later her variations on *Macbeth* under the title *Auf dem Gebirge hat man ein Geschrei gehört* (*A Cry has been Heard on the Mountains*). Often Bausch's work is researched and first performed abroad before transferring to Wuppertal where she and her company have built up an unusually loyal audience. This was far from the case during her early years there when she was even spat at and physically attacked by members of the audience while watching her own shows in the auditorium. A number of her dancers became stars and developed careers of their own. Other choreographers apart from Bausch whose work has been honoured by an invitation to the Berlin Theatertreffen are Reinhild Hoffmann (b. 1943), Johann Kresnik (b. 1939), Jo Fabian (b. 1960), Sasha Waltz (b. 1963) and Joachim Schlömer (b. 1962).

Some of these choreographers as well as a number of theatre directors turned to opera, perhaps because in this more conservative medium experimental devices still make an impact. That was particularly evident at the Frankfurt Opera in the 1980s, where Hans Neuenfels (b. 1941), Ruth Berghaus, and a number of colleagues from the straight theatre staged productions under the artistic directorship of the conductor Michael Gielen (b. 1927). This created an era of experimentation not known in German opera since Walter Felsenstein's legendary days at the Komische Oper in East Berlin during the 1950s and 1960s when he insisted on the theatrical potential of opera and rejected an approach solely pleasing to the ear. The breakthrough for the new aesthetics at Frankfurt was Hans Neuenfels's version of *Aida* in 1981, one of the biggest theatrical scandals of the decade. The director turned Radames into a museum clerk and Aida into a charwoman complete with bucket and cleaning rag. Under the parquet floor Radames discovered a sword and the sculpted head of Aida, and the production was presented as if it were an attempt at archaeological reconstruction. On the first night, the appearance of the enslaved Ethiopian princess as a cleaning lady set off howls of protest even before she had sung her first syllable. The level of hostility increased markedly when Neuenfels depicted the cynical Egyptian spectators at Verdi's triumphal march as the mirror image of the opera audience. The prisoners were clad in rags, some of the women were pregnant after violation by the victorious army, and everybody was severely starved. The culturally superior Egyptians tried to teach the Ethiopians proper table manners, but they just grabbed the food with their bare hands. Neuenfels saw the Egyptian clergy as a kind of fascist camarilla; they killed Radames and Aida by pumping gas into the tomb where they were imprisoned. The director received death threats even before the production had opened, and protesters tried to stop the first night. They showered leaflets from the dress circle, threw stink bombs, and used whistles so that it was impossible to hear a word from the singers for whole minutes. But the cast battled through the evening, and the production became one of the biggest critical and box-office successes the Frankfurt Opera has ever known.

Emotions like that in the eighties could only be coaxed from an opera audience, in the theatre hardly a single taboo was left to break. Increasingly all the possible subtexts of the classics had been discovered and attempts at finding new approaches became strained, even ludicrous. Directors made cross-references to the work of their colleagues in other cities, and many spectators reacted with bewilderment to this kind of artistic inbreeding. Sometimes texts were so distorted that one had to know the original very well to understand the directorial concept, though this knowledge could no longer be taken for granted with the younger generation. No wonder one of the last successful reinterpretations along the lines of Stein's *Homburg* in 1982 was a play by Kleist that had fallen completely from the repertory, *Die Hermannsschlacht*. Kleist's play celebrates the victory of the Germans over the Roman occupational forces in AD 9, and the author had hoped for a similar triumph over the French in his own time. Not surprisingly it had been a great favourite with the Nazis. Claus Peymann in Bochum rescued it from oblivion by showing the price that Arminius as the leader of the German guerrilla-army had to pay. Gert Voss (b. 1941) played him as a Che Guevara-like figure, who wins the war but ruins his life, health and marriage on the way. A particular success with the audience was the subplot concerning Arminius's wife Thusnelda who almost falls for the charms of the Roman diplomat Ventidius. As Thusnelda, Kirsten Dene (b. 1943) established herself as a major comic actress, a rare breed in Germany.

Western critics saw the eighties merely as a decade of 'continuation and variation ... No innovations, no inventions, no fresh starts.'[16] In 1931 Julius Bab had stated: 'There are people who run a theatre for 30 or 40 years, but the good and important time even for the most gifted does not last much more than ten years.'[17] The situation was the same in the 80s, but was exacerbated by the fact that the former revolutionaries of 1968 who had ousted the old regime in the 1970s themselves mutated into patriarchal if not outright authoritarian characters. They effectively kept out possible successors in the next generation, none of whom were very keen to take on administrative responsibilities. Ivan Nagel (b. 1931), who as Intendant of the Deutsches Schauspielhaus Hamburg had invited Zadek to direct *Othello*, put it bluntly: 'The generation born between 1945 and 1955 did not exert much influence ... Peymann or Stein around 1970 would have attacked every worthy older Intendant in a dark alley with a knife if they had been assured of his succession. But around 1985 one might have incited a young director to commit suicide by threatening to hand him the artistic directorship of a municipal theatre. In the meantime the 68ers turned into sexagenarians: Wotans waiting in vain for their Siegfrieds.'[18]

From the GDR and the Federal Republic to a united Germany

Heiner Müller, the most important dramatist of the GDR, had often been in conflict with the authorities. Later in his career he turned to directing himself and after reunification became head of the Berliner Ensemble. Müller's creed as a writer was: 'Only if a text is impossible to stage in the current state of our theatre can it be productive or interesting.'[19] He did not believe that coherent stories and plots were still able to reflect an increasingly fractured reality. His stage directions were deliberately impossible to execute and he thereby forced directors to desist from illustrating his work. He was happiest when, for example, Robert Wilson produced his *Hamletmaschine* by having the words read over a PA system with the company executing a series of movements that seemed not to have the slightest connection with them (Thalia Theater Hamburg, 1986). *Hamletmaschine* also featured in the last big GDR production in 1990 at the *Deutsches Theater*, when Müller inserted it into his eight-hour version of

Hamlet with Ulrich Mühe (1953–2007) playing the Prince. The rehearsal period took place during the huge early November 1989 demonstrations and a mass rally in East Berlin, which some of the company helped to organise.

Although Müller's work was frequently banned by the authorities, he stayed in the East, but as his reputation grew he was able to travel more or less freely. A substantial number of directors, actors, and authors, however, defected to the West due to the repressive cultural policy of the regime. The East's loss was the West's gain, as directors like Adolf Dresen, Jürgen Gosch, Manfred Karge, Matthias Langhoff, Einar Schleef, and B. K. Tragelehn lost any hope that things would change for the better. There was a time when Bochum in the Ruhr valley under Claus Peymann's artistic directorship (1979–86) was jokingly called 'the second-best GDR theatre', as so many former East Germans were employed there. In the GDR a few hardliners like Hanns Anselm Perten (1917–85) at Rostock and Karl Kayser (1914–95) at Leipzig remained ensconced as Intendants, but in the younger generation innovative critical theatre held sway.

The most influential directors of the 1980s were Alexander Lang, Thomas Langhoff, Wolfgang Engel (b. 1943), and Frank Castorf (b. 1951). Lang, formerly a well-known actor, cultivated an extremely artificial, almost choreographed style. He is a very conceptual director who likes to think big by, for instance, combining Grabbe's *Herzog Theodor von Gothland* and Goethe's *Iphigenia in Tauris* as a double bill (1984), in which he neatly juxtaposed the former's *furor teutonicus* and the latter's appeal for rational humanism. In his production of Büchner's *Dantons Tod* in 1981 at the Deutsches Theater, Christian Grashof stunningly played Danton as well as his rival Robespierre on an almost monochrome red set designed by Volker Pfüller (b. 1939). Lang's programme notes have a high intellectual quality. This was particularly the case with his essay for *A Midsummer Night's Dream* (1980). His production focused on the quartet of lovers so often neglected by other directors. At the Deutsches Theater they were no longer young and hopeful but already well into their thirties with a life characterised by boredom, moroseness, and latent aggression. This disillusionment is even further emphasised during the course of the play. As a result 'all four for the rest of their lives will regard their spontaneous and direct feelings with fear and suspicion'. Exhausted and indifferent they watch the performance of the mechanicals 'who are demonstrating the consequences of a love which is not domesticated. This is the reason for the youngsters' verbal sarcasm. You try to ridicule what you fear.'[20] Productions like *A Midsummer Night's Dream* also led to a growth of interest in Lang's work in the West where his biggest success was a *Don Carlos* at the Munich Kammerspiele in 1985; in this production the generation of the grandfathers easily quashed a childish rebellion by a crassly inefficient younger generation. Obviously this referred to the ossified gerontocracy determinedly clinging to their posts in the East.

Thomas Langhoff followed in his father's footsteps as Intendant of the Deutsches Theater, which he took over in 1991. He is more of a psychological realist and mistrusts any kind of flashy invention. At the Maxim Gorki Theater he directed a version of Chekhov's *Three Sisters* (1979), which ran for fourteen years. Volker Braun was so impressed by the quality of the acting company that he wrote his modernisation of the story, *Die Übergangsgesellschaft (The Transitory Society)*, for the same cast, depicting the GDR as every bit as stagnant as Chekhov's Russia had been. Langhoff is primarily interested in the contradictions of characters whose weaknesses he never denounces. At the same time he does not allow actors a kind of identification that can all too easily become sentimental. *Three Sisters* and *Übergangsgesellschaft* earned him his reputation as an expert in female psychology since actresses like Monika Lennartz (b. 1938), Ursula Werner (b. 1943), Swetlana Schönfeld (b. 1951), and Ruth Reinecke (b. 1957) trusted him to an unusual degree. The danger for Langhoff is a tendency to blandness, which was less marked in East Berlin than in his guest productions at the Munich Kammerspiele in cooperation with the latter's star designer Jürgen Rose during the 1980s. In 2006 his version of Botho Strauß's *Schändung (Violation)* after Shakespeare's *Titus Andronicus* at the Berliner Ensemble was rated inferior to Luc Bondy's world première production in Paris the year before, because, in contrast to Bondy, Langhoff stuck to a literal illustration of the action's gruesome proceedings instead of translating them into convincing stage pictures.

Occasionally there were interesting developments in the regions of the GDR. Provided local apparatchiks were not too narrow-minded, a courageous Intendant could schedule subversive productions that might have been banned in the East Berlin showcase. Christoph Schroth (b. 1937), in Schwerin from 1974 to 1988, produced work such as Hacks's *Moritz Tassow*, both parts of *Faust*, with four actors playing Faust and Lore Tappe (b. 1934) as Mephistopheles, and *Antike-Entdeckungen* (*Classical Greek-Discoveries*) incorporating plays by Aeschylus, Euripides, and Aristophanes. This represented an ambitious attempt to establish a quality Volkstheater, but sometimes his ideas seemed altogether too facile, as for example when he identified Erich Honecker with the dreaded tyrant Gessler in Schiller's *Wilhelm Tell* in 1989. In Halle, Horst Schönemann (1927–2002) had a huge success with Ulrich Plenzdorf's play about a young dropout, *Die neuen Leiden des jungen W.* (*The New Sorrows of Young W.*, 1972), which drew on Goethe's *Werther*. Criticised by hardliners for its irreverent reworking of Goethe's novella, the play nevertheless made it to almost every one of the GDR's sixty theatres. Schönemann moved on to Dresden, which was the most interesting of the Perestroika theatres.

In Dresden in 1986 Wolfgang Engel interpreted Kleist's *Penthesilea* as 'the meeting of two people from extremely different social systems who try to act in accordance with their respective ideology. They fall in love, and their ideology is forgotten only on the battlefield, in a kind of political no man's land for a few utopian moments, but then it hits back all the more strongly and destroys them both. Seen in this way Kleist's play appeared very modern without the slightest need to update it.'[21] The clash of two cultures, represented in the confrontation between Penthesilea and Achilles, meant that the GDR audience experienced Kleist's text as if it had been written in 1986. Penthesilea was played by Cornelia Schmaus (b. 1946), her friend Prothoe by Hannelore Koch (b. 1951). As the queen of Amazons, Schmaus achieved an almost unbearable intensity. At the end she sat alone, legs parted, hands pressed to her knees, transported to a different kind of reality before she gradually realised that it was she who in a delirious frenzy had killed and partially eaten Achilles. When she recognised her former beloved in the mess of gore and blood in front of her, her only resort was to kill herself by autosuggestion: 'Now I step deep down into my bosom / As into a shaft and dig up, cold as ore / An annihilating feeling.' Engel also directed the first East German production of *Waiting for Godot* in 1987. When the central committee discussed the request by the Intendant Gerhard Wolfram (1922–91) to allow the production to go ahead, one of the functionaries brandished an A–Z of plays printed in 1956 and asked: 'Are we really giving up all we stand for and allow this decadent piece to be staged?' At the first night interest was so overwhelming that the perform-ance began late. Those already seated got restless and started clapping, but someone from the circle shouted: 'You've waited for 35 years, so what's the harm in waiting another ten minutes?'[22] Christoph Hein's *Ritter der Tafelrunde* was as explosive as Braun's *Übergangsgesellschaft* had been. It depicted the circle around King Arthur as a tired senile clique whose achievements are derided by their own children and who are hugely disappointed when they have to admit that even the returning Lancelot did not find the Holy Grail. In Klaus-Dieter Kirst's (b. 1940) production the parallels to the aged party leadership were obvious. Engel, Kirst and Schönemann were lucky in having Gerhard Wolfram as a very supportive Intendant, particularly when in 1989 the whole company demonstrated for free speech, an end to travel restrictions, and a democratic GDR. There were similar demonstrations at many houses, notably in Berlin. This was one of the few moments in the twentieth century when German theatre really had a position at the forefront of things, and artists risked their personal liberty for what they regarded as the greater common good.

Frank Castorf only briefly enjoyed help from a sympathetic Intendant with Gerhard Meyer (1915–2002) in Karl-Marx-Stadt, now Chemnitz. His production of Ibsen's *An Enemy of the People* (1988) fiercely attacked the GDR's disastrous ecological record and his interpretation of Heiner Müller's *Der Bau* in 1986 was probably the most radical indictment of the political situation in the GDR allowed to see the light of day. It contained a particularly breathtaking moment when two characters, to the accompaniment of the Internationale, were unceremoniously whisked off the scene by the simple expedient of accelerating the revolving stage – as it turned out, a pertinent preview of events to come three years later. One of the most eloquent of German directors, Castorf claims:

> Germans like to construct mental barriers in the Hegelian sense against the discontinuity of their history. They attempt to create an alternative world in their minds, a system secure and independent of reality. In the theatre they want to be told stories which develop straightforwardly in a certain way – with a reassuring end product telling them: this is the way things got to be! But my theatre has to have a dose of anarchy, of negation, of questioning. It is important for me to state a thesis, then vigorously negate it and instead of pressing for some kind of synthesis leave matters open to doubt.[23]

As a result, Castorf cuts texts radically, moves lines around and uses rock and pop music to address his audience's feelings as directly as possible. He rejects accusations of arbitrariness: 'This method of disruption is vital to me: On the one hand I need extreme triviality, clowning, slapstick, on the other hand moments of peace, the drawing of a deep breath, like a wind passing through trees. I look for this kind of effect, for the clash of opposites. That is my form of eclecticism.'[24] His productions tend to be very long, sometimes lasting between five and six hours. Not every minute of them can claim maximum attention, but even after a prolonged, boring patch, the evening regains intensity. In addition, Castorf employs the most unusual actors in the German theatre. In their performances, it is extremely difficult to draw a line between where the private side of the performer ends and the character he plays begins, 'character' being a term that is anathema to Castorf, one he apparently disallows in rehearsal. Henry Hübchen (b. 1947), who serves as a form of director's alter ego, excels at slapstick and improvisation. He is particularly suited for weak men like Goethe's Fernando who is torn between two women in *Stella* or the male lead in a stage version of Fellini's *City of Women*. Almost as important are Herbert Fritsch (b. 1951), Bernhard Schütz (b. 1959), and Martin Wuttke (b. 1962), who joined Castorf's troupe after a period at the Berliner Ensemble, where his career had been crowned with his internationally acclaimed Arturo Ui in Heiner Müller's production (1995). The female protagonists are Kathrin Angerer (b. 1970), Astrid Meyerfeldt (b. 1960), and the eccentric Sophie Rois (b. 1961). Castorf is influenced less by the Russian theatre revolutionaries of the 1920s or by movements like Futurism, Dadaism, and Surrealism – though he likes to invoke them all – than he is by Pina Bausch. The drawback of his method is a tendency to repetitiveness, using the same elements in a patchwork approach for different productions.

When, after 1989, the Berlin theatre scene was restructured, a report suggested the Volksbühne should be handed over to a young company. Castorf was appointed and led not only a theatre, but an institutionalised social experiment with young people of alternative tastes. The Volksbühne organises concerts, discos, discussions or symposia and, in contrast to the other Berlin theatres, sustains a clearly defined artistic, intellectual, and political identity. But, apart from Dimiter Gotscheff (b. 1943) and Christoph Schlingensief (b. 1960), too few directors working there are strong enough to compete with Castorf who over the turn of the century triumphed with a quartet of adaptations of Russian novels: Dostoevsky's *The Demons*, *The Oppressed and the Insulted*, and *The Idiot* and Bulgakov's dissident masterpiece, *The Master and Margarita*. To avoid the danger of stagnation and repetition, Castorf increasingly uses video in his productions. His distinctive style inspired a number of rather unfortunate imitators, lacking his intelligence and sense of rhythm. Still, in the 1990s the *Volksbühne*'s only serious rival was the Deutsches Schauspielhaus in Hamburg run by Frank Baumbauer

(b. 1945), not a director himself. Castorf himself worked there along with Christoph Marthaler, a former stage composer who occasionally came to the Volksbühne, where his musical-metaphorical reflection on German reunification *Murx den Europäer! Murx ihn! Murx ihn! Murx ihn ab!* designed by Anna Viebrock achieved cult status. In keeping with his Swiss origins, he developed a style of slowness punctuated by mournful communal singing and gentle slapstick, which differed markedly from Castorf's more abrasive humour. His production of Horváth's *Kasimir und Karoline* in 1996 at the Deutsches Schauspielhaus had an outstanding performance by Josef Bierbichler (b. 1948) as Kasimir, a redundant chauffeur. Bierbichler movingly managed to project the immense effort it takes his character to come to terms with the new situation, the sheer fight to find halfway adequate words for something that fundamentally eludes him.

Among the older generation of directors Zadek and Stein continued their rivalry. Zadek's best production of the 1990s was *Ivanov* at the Vienna Akademietheater, the Burgtheater's smaller second auditorium. He has, however, become more and more allergic to theatricality for its own sake, and when he directs Chekhov he elicits from his actors a kind of underplaying that in its best moments appears to emulate real life on stage. Gert Voss played Ivanov as a highly mercurial character, forcing the audience to ask which of his personal assertions he actually believes himself:

> What is overwhelming imagination, what is only exaggeration, comedy, playacting? . . . Gert Voss and Peter Zadek don't pretend to know it themselves. Quite possibly it is always only the other side of the coin. But how do you show that? Gert Voss neither criticises Ivanov nor does he turn him into a melodramatic character. He does not judge and he does not defend. He doesn't try to uncover more of the text than it yields of its own, he only contradicts it from time to time – considered and emphatic – with his own words. When Chekhov repeatedly stipulates: 'He shouts', Voss remains rather quiet, the voice velvety and nevertheless sharp, the foil kept in the sheath . . . Agitation for him does not mean loudness, but a kind of inner glowing of the nerves, like embers beneath ash, the same ash in which this Ivanov likes to stir around, but so gently that not too many sparks are generated . . . The synthesis of Stanislavsky and Brecht here wears the names of Peter Voss and Gert Zadek.[25]

Voss's partner, the self-righteous doctor Lvov, was Ignaz Kirchner. This tandem had already acted together in Tabori's *The Goldberg Variations* (1991), had played Othello and Iago, and went on to do Hamm and Clov, Claire and Solange in Genet's *The Maids*, as well as Al Lewis and Willie Clark in Simon's *The Sunshine Boys* – one of the benefits of a permanent company. Meanwhile, Zadek's old rival Peter Stein resigned from the directorate of the Schaubühne in 1985 after overseeing its move out of its previous building at the Hallesches Ufer to the Lehniner Platz. Stein continued to direct at the Schaubühne until 1990 and divided critical opinion with productions of *Three Sisters* and *The Cherry Orchard* that were effectively homage to Stanislavsky's work at the Moscow Art Theatre. But in the 1990s he increasingly fell out of favour and was accused of bombastic neo-classicism. He dedicated years of preparation and fundraising to a 21-hour production of the full text of Goethe's *Faust I* and *II*, even though the author never conceived of Part II for the stage, let alone uncut. Zadek saw four hours of a run-through and unsurprisingly labelled it 'the most boring production I saw in my whole life'.[26] The reviewers too called the show merely illustrative, comparing it unfavourably to Stein's work at the Schaubühne in the 1970s, a body of achievement about which in hindsight the director himself is unnecessarily scathing. Despite the hostile press, the unusual event in 2000 was a success with the audience, particularly with spectators who were fed up with more and more desperate attempts at taboo breaking elsewhere. Feeling misunderstood at home, Stein now predominantly works abroad, particularly for Welsh National Opera and the Edinburgh Festival. In Edinburgh in 2005, unusually for him, he directed a contemporary play, David Harrower's *Blackbird*, which deservedly transferred to the West End a year later.

New developments after the turn of the century

At the beginning of the new millennium, German theatres still receive generous allocations from the state, the provinces, and the cities, but a growing amount of that money goes into salaries and less remains available for production costs. The situation became particularly difficult in the regional theatres in the five new provinces where, after reunification in 1989, subscriptions collapsed and even today are far below former levels. The theatres lost their strong bond with those spectators who felt tacitly encouraged in their opposition to the State. As regards smaller cities, in western Germany there is still a large enough bourgeois audience that regularly patronises its local theatre, but in eastern Germany continuously low attendance figures are indicative of a major economic crisis more than a purely artistic one. Nowhere in Germany at present is there an undisputed leading company. Munich at least can claim impressive audience figures.

In Munich in 2001, Dieter Dorn moved across the road from the Kammerspiele to the Bavarian State Theatre taking almost the entire company with him. Frank Baumbauer (b. 1945) took over as Intendant. During his uneven first year at the Kammerspiele, one production stood out, that of Euripides' *Alkestis* directed by the Swiss Jossi Wieler. Wieler, one of the foremost directors of his generation, equally at home in opera as in spoken drama, has been particularly successful at the Stuttgart Opera, where Klaus Zehelein (b. 1940) guaranteed, until his retirement in 2006, a continuously high level of artistic quality that is generally missing in spoken theatre. Apart from Wieler and Hans Neuenfels, the most important director working in Stuttgart was Peter Konwitschny (b. 1945). His politically and aesthetically radical concepts are more controversial with audiences than Wieler's more discreet approach. Both directors are very much in demand at other prestigious opera houses, too. In the straight theatre only Jürgen Gosch works regularly on a similarly high level without any ambition to lead a company himself.

Politicians, looking for somebody to run their theatres, increasingly turn to talented managers who do not spend a huge part of their budget on their own productions. Managers who are particularly sought after, apart from Baumbauer, include Friedrich Schirmer (b. 1951), who took over at Hamburg's Deutsches Schauspielhaus in 2005, after thirteen years as Intendant of the Schauspiel Stuttgart and Ulrich Khuon (b. 1951), who will move from the Thalia Theater Hamburg to the Deutsches Theater Berlin in 2009. People like Baumbauer, Schirmer, and Khuon compete for the same pool of creative talent, for directors such as Stefan Bachmann (b. 1966), Andreas Kriegenburg (b. 1963), Christina Paulhofer (b. 1969), Christiane Pohle (b. 1968), Stefan Pucher (b. 1965), Nicolas Stemann (b. 1968), and Michael Thalheimer (b. 1965). These young artists might be praised to the skies today only to be torn to pieces tomorrow, because they have not had the time or opportunity to develop properly in a smaller or medium-sized theatre like their predecessors. When Peter Stein in 1969 saw Torquato Tasso's position at the Court of Ferrara as a reflection of his own situation in German society, he knew very well the story he wanted to tell with Goethe's play. Today's young directors are often attacked because they have technical brilliance, but they do not know what to do with it. Günther Rühle (b. 1924), the doyen of German theatre critics, characterises the new generation as follows:

> They are good, often astonishingly expert craftsmen, creators of multiple effects, great talents – but without any intellectual ambitions. They try to compensate for the loss of meaning, in self-evidence, atmosphere, psychology and the power to move and disturb, as well as the loss in aura and language, with bizarre set designs, artifice, irony, implants from foreign texts and the rhythms of rock music. One asks oneself: what will the next generation of theatre practitioners, who have learned their craft from these directors, end up doing?[27]

It is grist to Rühle's mill when somebody like Tina Lanik (b. 1974) nonchalantly claims in an interview that as a rule she reads every play only once before starting to direct it[28] – a strange basis for working at such renowned houses as the Deutsches Theater in Berlin or the Bavarian State Theatre in Munich. But elsewhere not all is indiscriminate deconstruction. In 2005 and 2006 the municipal authorities at Stuttgart, Bochum, and Dusseldorf installed three representatives of 'careful modernisation' as their Intendants: Hasko Weber (b. 1963), Elmar Goerden (b. 1963), and Amélie Niermeyer (b. 1965), who is the most sought-after female head of a theatre. The three of them are in their early 40s, they stand for text-based work and in contrast to their colleagues born ten years earlier are not shying away from administrative responsibility. Weber and Goerden have not held positions of this kind before, but, during her intendancy at Freiburg, Niermeyer was a great success with the audience and the press, a combination increasingly rare in the German theatre. Goerden inherited Bochum from Matthias Hartmann (b. 1963), who moved up the career ladder in 2005 to Zurich where he tries to lure back spectators, something his predecessor Marthaler failed to do. A rather bland director, Hartmann had managed previously in Bochum to create the right mixture of German premières, star-studded revivals, and pure entertainment. But after only one year in Switzerland he was appointed to become Intendant of the Vienna Burgtheater in 2009, another example of the increasingly hectic pace of the so-called 'merry-go-round for artistic directors'. His successor in Zurich will be Barbara Frey (b. 1963). Martin Kušej (b. 1961) will take over from Dieter Dorn at the Bavarian State Theatre in 2010. Finally now that Thomas Ostermeier (b. 1968) runs the Schaubühne am Lehniner Platz, Armin Petras (b. 1964) the Maxim Gorki, and Karin Beier (b. 1965) Cologne, nine directors of the younger generation already are or will be in charge of major theatres. All of them strenuously contradict Rühle's cultural pessimism with their individual work as well as their overall policy.

The annual critic's survey in the influential magazine *Theater heute* includes among its categories 'most frustrating experience in the theatre'. Increasingly respondents do not give as their answer the artistic disaster of an individual director or the lamentable decision by politicians to cut subsidies. Instead, from the combined responses there can be heard one deeply felt collective sigh: 'old men'.

14 Patterns of continuity in German theatre: Interculturalism, performance and cultural mission

ERIKA FISCHER-LICHTE

As can be concluded from the previous chapters, German theatre has changed considerably over the centuries and so has our understanding of it. In spite of all changes, we can discern three tendencies that, though not always present, do recur markedly. First, there is the tendency towards interculturalism, i.e. the incorporation of plays and theatrical devices from other cultures; second, a tendency towards a particular emphasis on the performance as an autonomous work of art; and third, a high esteem of theatre, founded on the conviction that it has an important cultural mission.

Interestingly, it was Goethe who not only reflected on these three tendencies but also greatly contributed to intensifying them. Thus, I will discuss each in turn by proceeding from Goethe's reflections and practices.

German theatre as intercultural theatre

In conversation with Eckermann on 31 January 1827, Goethe remarked: 'National literature means little nowadays, the era of world literature is at hand, and each of us now must help to hasten its arrival.'[1] This insight, delivered five years before his death, already informed the programme that he had elaborated and followed as director of the Weimar National and Court Theatre (1791–1817) more than thirty years earlier. Then one of his most important objectives was the preparation and realisation of a repertoire that would consist of what he considered to be the most significant plays in world literature. He began, therefore, to develop a repertoire for his small, somewhat provincial theatre in Weimar that would encompass dramas from European theatre history alongside contemporary literary plays, principally his own and those of Friedrich Schiller but also Heinrich von Kleist's *Der zerbrochene Krug*, as well as the unavoidable trivial 'daily bread' productions he so despised. Thus, Sophocles' *Oedipus* and *Antigone*, plays by Terence and Plautus, Shakespeare's *Hamlet, Henry IV, Romeo and Juliet, Macbeth, Julius Caesar,* and *Othello* were performed alongside Calderón's *The Constant Prince* and *Life is a Dream*, Pierre Corneille's *Cid*, Jean Racine's *Phèdre*, Molière's *Miser*, comedies by Carlo Goldoni and Carlo Gozzi, and tragedies by Voltaire and Lessing. All of Mozart's operas were also included. Here theatre became a means of mediating between Goethe's own and other European cultures.

Goethe did not consider it important to have the plays of other cultures performed in literal translations. In fact, he regarded translation in general as a kind of a cultural brokerage: 'If you read the same portrayal in the original, then it looks quite different and prevents us from enjoying and using it fully in our foreign situation: in translations, our reading is aided, as at a trade fair where the dealer brings the foreign wares to us.'[2] However, this kind of brokerage did not seem sufficient. Goethe was eager for the contemporary audience to feel the full effect of the foreign play directly. To this end he was prepared to make far-reaching alterations so that, ultimately, he did not produce translations but adaptations. In this enterprise, he was energetically supported by Schiller. Out of consideration for the moral standards of the Weimar audience, for example, Schiller cut the porter scene from *Macbeth* entirely, as he considered it obscene, replacing it with a pious *aubade*. Goethe revised *Romeo and Juliet* for similar reasons and to such an extent that his version was described by a later Shakespeare scholar as an 'amazing travesty'.[3] But a particular success was Schiller's adaptation of Gozzi's *Turandot* (1802). Schiller was able to write new riddles for each performance by drawing on a wealth of suggestions sent to him by enthusiastic spectators. Goethe explained his approach in a letter to Charlotte von Wolzogen: 'The maxim that I followed was to concentrate on the interesting parts and to harmonise them, for Shakespeare was forced by his genius, his age, and his audience to add much disharmonious confusion in order to reconcile the ruling theatre genius.'[4]

Through this approach, Goethe succeeded in bringing plays from other cultures to his audience and making them a vibrant component of the theatre of his time. In this way he contributed to the emergent interweaving of theatres and cultures. On his production of *The Constant Prince* he wrote to G. Sartorius: 'This time we have a play that was written nearly 200 years ago in a quite different climate, for people of a quite different culture, and it is performed in such a fresh way that it might have come hot from the oven.'[5]

The repertoire at the Weimar theatre was made up exclusively of European dramas even though Goethe had expressly wanted to bring about a theatre that drew from world literature. This contradiction was not the result of a purely Eurocentric perspective, however, as one might suspect, nor did it stem from a lack of knowledge about theatre traditions outside Europe. Not only had Goethe read the drama *Sakuntala* by the Indian poet Kalidasa in a German translation of 1791 by Georg Forster, but his acquaintance with it also had 'a very great influence on [his] whole life'.[6] He showed his enthusiasm in the now famous distich:

> *Willst du die Blüthen des frühen, die Früchte des späteren Jahres*
> *Willst du was reizt und entzückt, willst du was sättigt und nährt,*
> *Willst du den Himmel, die Erde mit Einem Namen begreifen –*
> *Nenn ich Sakuntala dich, und so ist alles gesagt.*
> [If you wish for the blossoms of spring, as well as the fruits of autumn,
> If you wish for charms and delights, wish for what satisfies and
>   nourishes,
> If you wish to grasp both heaven and earth in one name,
> I name, *Sakuntala*, thee, and thus is everything said.]
>
> (Goethe, *Werke*, 4, 122)

Goethe's enthusiasm for *Sakuntala* also found expression in his own work as he took the idea of the 'Prelude in the theatre' in *Faust* from the Indian drama. Despite this, he shied away from adapting and incorporating the whole play into his Weimar repertoire. With regret he decided 'that our sensibilities, customs, and ways of thinking have developed so differently from those in this Eastern nation that even an important work such as this ... can have little success here'.[7]

Goethe not only incorporated plays of other cultures into his repertoire, he also experimented with theatrical devices originating in other traditions, as for instance, the use of masks in his production of Terence's *The Brothers*. Considering the rather small population of Weimar and neighbouring Jena, the fact that the house sold out each time the play was performed suggests the enormous interest which the audience took in Goethe's experiments. He also repeated the experiment with equal success with Schiller's *Turandot*.

The interculturalism in Goethe's theatre was by no means a new phenomenon on the German stage; it had been characteristic of German theatre from the beginning of professional theatre. From its very inception, German professional theatre was intercultural, because, as we have seen, it was founded by strolling players from Italy, England, France, and the Netherlands. In the course of the seventeenth century, as the members of the troupes from different cultures met, they were forced to negotiate common concerns about performance. Even after German companies were established, they originally maintained the repertoire of the English players. In the eighteenth century, they widened their repertoire by incorporating *comedias* by Lope de Vega, Calderón, and Tirso de Molina available to them in French and Dutch adaptations, plays by Joost van den Vondel and Jan Vos, by Corneille and Molière, by Cicognini, and many translations of Italian opera libretti, which formed the basis of *Haupt- und Staatsaktionen.* From Reinhart Meyer's documentation on the plays printed and performed in German-speaking countries throughout the eighteenth century,[8] it is notable that French, Italian, Latin, Spanish, English, and even Czech plays were printed and performed in translations as well as in the original language. French and Italian comedians and Italian opera troupes performed at the provincial courts. German companies, however, were only rarely invited, which is small wonder when rulers such as Frederick the Great of Prussia denounced the German language as barbarous and did not permit German companies at court.

This was the situation in the 1760s when the idea of a 'national theatre' first took root. Significantly, as we have seen in earlier chapters, 'national' in this context had little to do with German nationalism, rather it meant a theatre where plays written in German would be performed, a theatre for the citizens of the towns and cities rather than the aristocracy – that is to say, a 'national theatre' as had already existed for two centuries in England, Spain, and France. However, the follow-up to the first national theatre, to the so-called *entreprise* in Hamburg in 1767/8, the establishment of 'national and court' theatres in Vienna (1776), Mannheim (1777), Berlin (1786), Munich (1789), and Weimar was in effect a hollow compromise arising from the lack of financial resources in the courts. The courts had had to dismiss the expensive Italian opera troupes and French comedians and faced the choice of either remaining without theatre or being content with the much cheaper German companies. They opted for the German-speaking companies, but their court theatres were named 'national and court theatre' only for strategic reasons; citizens were admitted to them as paying 'guests'. 'National' only meant the particular state in question, as Lessing noted, when, on the occasion of the foundation of the Mannheim national and court theatre he wrote to his brother: 'With the national theatre, it is nothing but wind, and in Mannheim, there never was another idea linked to it than that there would be a German national theatre in which only actors born in the Pfalz may appear.'⁹ Goethe's programmatic development of a world repertoire was directed against such provincialism.

In the nineteenth century, translations and adaptations of plays from other European cultures continued to be used. These were not always only the 'most significant' works, as proclaimed by Goethe, but popular plays, such as those from the French boulevard theatres. In addition, experiments by figures such as Tieck and Immermann kept alive the intercultural aspects of German theatre. Germany's contact with other cultures intensified over the turn of the century, as the repertoire of the Freie Bühne in Berlin included plays by Ibsen, Björnson, Gorki, Maeterlinck, Wilde, Yeats, Galsworthy, and Shaw, which were played alongside the work of Hauptmann, Hofmannsthal, and Wedekind. Plays from Japan, China, and India also began to find their way to the German stage. *Terakoya or the village school* by Takeda Izumo, Namiki Senryu, and Miyoshi Shoraku was performed in Cologne (1907), Dresden and in Max Reinhardt's Berlin Kammerspiele (1908), while *Sakuntala* was seen in Cologne (1925) and Vienna (1926) as was the Sanskrit play *Vasantasena* in Lübeck and Graz (1920) and Frankfurt (1924). The Chinese play *The Chalk Circle* by Li Xingdao, a Yuan dynasty poet, was performed in 1925 in an adaptation by Klabund (1890–1928) at a number of theatres. In one production of this play, in Frankfurt, the director Richard Weichert experimented with Chinese stage devices, such as having stage hands appear on stage.

Max Reinhardt was a master at using stage devices taken from other theatrical traditions. He tried to revive the *commedia dell'arte* in his famous production of *A Servant of Two Masters* at the opening of the Theater in der Josefstadt in Vienna in 1924, a production, which, as Georgio Strehler acknowledged, inspired his legendary production of the play in 1947 in the Piccolo Teatro, Milan. Moreover, Reinhardt also used stage spaces that drew heavily on ancient Greek and Japanese traditions as well as from the Chinese theatre. In his productions of *Oedipus the King* (1910) and the *Oresteia* (1911) at the Circus Schumann in Berlin he used an arena stage that was reminiscent of the ancient *orchestra*; in the pantomime *Sumurun* (1910) he employed a *hanamichi* for the first time, which he used to create a theatre that challenged the traditional modes, habits, and perspectives of perception. The critics either admired or harshly condemned the new effects. In 1912 the production toured through the United States. A New York critic wrote:

> In *Sumurun* there is a narrow runway reaching from the back of the orchestra over the tops of the seats and onto the stage. Most of the characters in *Sumurun* [enter] ... along this runway. This is a daring device for one who is working on your imagination and creates the effect of delusion. And it is all the more tribute to the acting of the German company who present *Sumurun* and to the staging that, although some of the audience could put out their hands and touch the garments of the actors as they passed them, none of the spell that enveloped the actors on the stage left them as they crossed the runway at the end of the play and made their way back.[10]

This positive judgement of the *hanamichi* is decidedly contradicted by another critic, who writes that the *hanamichi* 'distracts the audience's attention', because 'the actors make their entrance at some vital point in each scene of the play.' This is fatal, since no spectator is able 'to resist the temptation of turning round or looking skyward as a flock of very fat eunuchs or a bevy of gaily fledged ladies of the harem come clattering down the center of the theatre just two feet above your head'. The critic comes to the conclusion that the *hanamichi* was not only totally superfluous but, moreover, counterproductive: 'It destroys a great deal of the illusion and it makes the audience miss many points of the play.'[11] Both critics were missing the point that Reinhardt made. He was not interested in an illusionist theatre but, quite the contrary, used the Japanese device in order to create a theatre that challenged the traditional modes, habits, and perspectives of perception.

Reinhardt used Chinese stage devices in his production of Hazelton/Benrimo's *Yellow Jacket* (1914) to similar ends. Here, the device was understood by the critics. One wrote: 'It became obvious that we may expect anything from our imagination.'[12] And another concludes that the devices as elaborated and demanded by the Chinese stage may be seen as 'the complete emancipation from the illusionist mechanics of our occidental box set stage'.[13]

Reinhardt's 'intercultural' productions used the devices taken from other theatrical traditions so as to re-theatricalise theatre, through reflecting on its theatricality by means of theatre itself. Theatre is not the representation of reality, but a reality of its own. The recourse to theatre traditions of other cultures served his purpose of creating a new theatre. In general, it would seem that during the first three decades of the twentieth century, non-Western as well as past Western theatre traditions were used to do away with the 'old' theatre of representation, in the interests of creating quite a new kind of theatre, which in Reinhardt's case, was a theatre of the senses and sensations.

For Brecht, theatricalisation was a constitutive element in the process of elaborating his new epic theatre, a theatre for the scientific age. In October 1930, a Japanese troupe, led by Tsutsui Tokujiro, gave guest performances in Berlin. According to Elisabeth Hauptmann, Brecht saw the troupe perform. Among his papers one finds the following fragmentary note, probably written down as a direct reaction to the Japanese performance:

> we should attempt to examine certain elements of foreign perform-
> ance art for their usefulness. This attempt will be carried out within
> the very specific situation of our theatre, where our own theatre is
> not sufficient to accomplish its tasks (tasks of a new kind). These are
> the tasks demanded of the performance art by the epic dramatic
> structure. Now the above mentioned foreign technique has long
> since been in the position to accomplish similar tasks – similar, but
> not the same ones. The technique must be separated from those
> highly essential prerequisites, transported and subjugated to quite
> other conditions. In order to undertake such an analysis, one must
> take the viewpoint that there is a kind of technical standard in art,
> something that is not individual, not already developed, but some-
> thing one can build in, something transportable. This statement
> should suffice to show that we are convinced of this. Anyway, this
> technique cannot be considered to be that 'form ... which is only
> valid insofar as it is the form of its own content.' Japanese perform-
> ance technique ... can naturally only mean something to us insofar
> as it is able to know our problems. The 'Japanese' in it, moreover, its
> whole 'character' or 'individual worth', etc. is irrelevant to this
> analysis.[14]

This analysis was not carried out. However, in his Berlin production of *Mann ist Mann* (1931) Brecht used two such devices, which he had come to know through the Japanese guest performance. First, he characterised the different states of development or emotion in a figure by letting the actor don different masks; and second, he indicated the change from one state to another by having the actor hide behind a table top (in the Japanese performance behind a cloth), where the change is performed.

It is interesting to note how the critic Herbert Ihering related the Japanese performance to the state of the German theatre and in particular to Brecht's experiments.

> The poles of world theatre are Max Reinhardt and the Japanese ... But we ourselves stand to win a different approach toward the German stage, if we view it from the viewpoint of the enormous tradition and the huge achievements of Japanese theatre. We realise the aims of many experiments, as for example those of Brecht. Not toward the individual disintegration of the stage art, but toward the creation of a basic style, a basic behaviour, a form, a tradition. The fundamental situation and the mimic stations in Japanese theatre show what we are lacking and what we must yet achieve.[15]

When Brecht saw the Chinese actor Mei Lanfang perform in 1935 in Moscow, he once again grew interested in theatrical devices 'as *transportable techniques* (as an artistic device detachable from the Chinese theatre)'.[16] In his reflections *Verfremdungseffekte in der chinesischen Schauspielkunst* (Alienation effects in the Chinese art of acting), which later formed part of his *Messingkauf*, Brecht focuses on devices which have the effect of making 'the things' which the actor presents appear to the spectator as 'something astounding': 'Things of everyday life, by this very art, are lifted out of the sphere of the natural, the self-evident.'[17] According to Brecht, they allow the spectator to take a distanced stance towards what is presented, to perceive it in a new way and so accord it new meanings. Elaborating a new theatre by having recourse to theatre traditions of other cultures now gained a new quality. What Brecht explored theoretically in the 1930s, became a practical experiment in the 1950s after World War II on the stage of the Berliner Ensemble. In *Der kaukasische Kreidekreis*, for instance, Brecht experimented with the relationship between musical (music by Paul Dessau) and scenic devices. While the actor playing the governor (Erwin Geschonnek, 1907–2008) presented the fall of the governor in a slow motion, almost dance-like pantomime, the singer (Ernst Busch) who was also present on stage, described this fall in a solemn melody. While Grusche and Simon became silent when standing at the brook and slowly turned away from each other, the singers placed at the background of the stage expressed the thoughts and emotions of the unhappy couple. The action was performed simultaneously as a gestural and a musical proceeding. This artistic device, which Sergej Eisenstein had also admired so much in Japanese Kabuki theatre[18] here fulfilled the function of emphasising the independence of the two theatrical systems – acting and music – a function which Brecht had elaborated and stressed in the *Kleines Organon*. He also tried out some other theoretically developed devices and presented the results in Paris and London as well as Berlin.

Nowadays, interculturalism of diverse kinds is widespread in German theatre life. Not only do stage directors from various cultures work with German ensembles, many international co-productions are mounted and festivals throughout the year present performances of all kinds from all over the world. Theatres such as the Hebbel Theater in Berlin and, until 2004, the Theater am Turm in Frankfurt am Main offer groups from various cultures a space to perform and all kinds of cooperative aid. In addition, the Haus der Kulturen der Welt in Berlin presents performances, exhibitions, poetry readings, and other performances from the most diverse cultures all year long. The aim now is not to use the devices of other traditions to elaborate a new theatre of one's own but rather to explore processes of interweaving and of cross-fertilisation between German theatre and theatres of different cultures of the world. So, what is at stake now, is the collaboration of German theatre artists with those from other cultures.

Performance as an autonomous work of art

In Goethe's dialogue *Über Wahrheit und Wahrscheinlichkeit der Kunstwerke* (On the truth and verisimilitude of works of art, 1798), an advocate of opera and a spectator have a discussion on the question why an opera performance provides its spectators with such a lively and complete pleasure. The advocate succeeds in convincing the spectator that this pleasure is not due to any kind of imitation of nature but to the effect of the work of art alone. The spectator concludes: 'When the opera is good, it creates a little world of its own, in which all proceeds according to certain rules, a world, which must be judged by its own laws, felt according to its own spirit.'[19] Here, the performance is not regarded as an imitation of nature nor of social reality nor as a means of 'mediating' or even 'reproducing' something else, namely the literary text of a drama, but as an artwork in its own right. It is conceived as a 'whole', which is 'complete' only on the condition that all its elements are perfectly attuned each with the other. According to Goethe, these are the general criteria that must be met if the status of a work of art is given to a poem, a painting, a sculpture, or a symphony. If a performance meets these criteria, it is to be regarded as a work of art.

In his essay on *Proserpina*, Goethe suggested that the different elements that have to be attuned to each other include the following: '1. stage design; 2. recitation and declamation; 3. bodily movement; 4. the contribution of clothing; 5. music ... All these are 6. concluded and completed by a *tableau*.'[20] Thus, when the performance is conceived as a 'whole', whose elements are harmonised, the function of directing, of *mise-en-scène*, is foregrounded. The concept of harmony had not played a prominent role till this time in German theatre, although actors such as Conrad Ekhof and Friedrich Ludwig Schröder had at least partly tried to fulfil it. In fact, for the reasons outlined in earlier chapters, Goethe can be regarded as the first director in the modern sense of the word. Above all he accorded the status of an autonomous work of art to the performance. It seems that when his criteria were met, he regarded theatre performance as the greatest art work possible, because it is the only one that encompasses all the arts. In *Annalen* (1815) he wrote:

> In an ideal way, theatre is so great that almost nothing that man can create with his genius, spirit, talent, technical skills or practice can compare. Just as poetry is admirable, with all its ground rules through which imagination gains its laws and orientation; as rhetoric with all its historical and dialectical demands remains in high regard and is indispensable; and just as a direct oral lecture cannot do without appropriate facial expression: then we shall see how theatre empowers these giant prerequisites of mankind with ease. If we were to add the fine arts as well, i.e. what architecture, sculpture, painting all contribute to the completion of the stage image, and add to that the special ingredient, music, then one can see what wealth of human glory lies to rest on this tiny spot.[21]

Thus for Goethe, the play, the space, the design, the actors, the costumes, and the music, everything serves as material from which the performance as an autonomous work of art is created.

In the nineteenth century, this concept of Goethe's proved highly influential. Richard Wagner developed it even further when elaborating his idea of the *Gesamtkunstwerk* in which the individual arts, in particular, dance, music, and poetry, are united. However, such a 'union of the arts' presupposes that all elements of the performance are subordinated under the banner of artistic unity. The *Gesamtkunstwerk* was conceived as 'a chain of organic links'.[22] But the idea of an 'organic unity' takes another turn here.

For although the individual arts contribute to the constitution of 'organic links', they are no longer identifiable as individual arts. Thus, it is the orchestra and the singers, i.e. music, movement, and language, which together form the complex link of 'action' or 'dramatic character'. A union of the arts, on the other hand, transforms the individual arts. While music, movement, and gesture become semantic, language loses its semantic quality. In this sense, it is not a question of accumulating the different arts into one, but rather transforming all arts in a way that together they bring forth a new 'whole'.

However, to complete the *Gesamtkunstwerk*, the spectator needs to learn a new art of spectating. Wagner thought that neither empathetic identification with the dramatic characters as in the bourgeois illusionist stage, nor a desire purely to be entertained, nor even the assumption of aesthetic distance that allows for reflection, were adequate attitudes towards the *Gesamtkunstwerk*. This new art of spectating is based on the condition of 'concentration' and 'participation'. The *Gesamtkunstwerk* requires an active spectator who is not only supposed to act as an 'organically participating witness',[23] but, also, to advance to the 'necessary co-creator of the work of art'.[24] It is within the spectator, in his state of 'dawning imagination, a dream come true of something never experienced'[25] that the *Gesamtkunstwerk* is completed.

Thus Goethe and Wagner celebrated performance as the most complete artistic experience. Such an understanding became very influential. Although, at the turn of the twentieth century, Reinhardt was admonished by some critics for allegedly proceeding 'from the principle that the director is everything, the poet nothing',[26] nothing, as we have already seen, could stop the director from becoming the leading figure in theatre. The importance of stage directors in the first decades of the twentieth century, thus, seems to be a consequence of the concept of performance as an autonomous work of art as rooted in Goethe's thought and developed by Wagner. It was precisely this understanding of theatre that also made radical experiments such as those by the Dadaists or the Bauhaus possible.

In the 1960s the so-called *Regietheater* sprang up as a continuation of the concept of performance as a work of art in itself. However, this was ignored by most critics. The term is not synonymous with the expression 'director's theatre'. Rather, it means a theatre that not only freely uses the text but also the actors' bodies and space as a material that has to be worked upon and transformed in the process of *mise-en-scène*; this allows the performance to come into being as an art work *sui generis*. In this sense, *Regietheater* is firmly rooted in a tradition that goes back to Goethe. It aims at imagining, discovering, and realising new ways of creating performances that are able to affect deeply or even to scandalise today's audiences. However, there are still some critics who continue to lament that the productions by Frank Castorf, Christoph Marthaler, Jürgen Gosch, Michael Thalheimer, Stefan Pucher, Stefan Bachmann, and many others are 'not true to the text'. They overlook the simple fact that theatre in the German tradition is not regarded as derivative but as an art form by itself. What productions by directors such as those listed above do achieve is to invent new forms and practices so that, even in the world of mass media, theatre can continue to be not only a live art but a lively art that is able to arouse fierce and heated debates among audiences as well as in the *feuilletons* of newspapers.

Theatre's cultural mission

Even when Goethe adapted plays for his stage he did not intend the spectator to consume the performance mindlessly. Quite the contrary, he thought it necessary

> for the spectator to learn to accept that not every play is to be seen as a coat which must be fitted to each man according to his present needs. One should not always only think about satisfying the immediate spiritual, romantic or sensual needs of oneself or one's neighbour; one could more appropriately conceive of oneself as a traveller who, in visiting strange places and countries for one's education and pleasure, does not find every personal comfort as at home.[27]

This amounted to saying that the new repertoire taken from 'world literature' as well as the performance as a 'whole' had to fulfil a particular cultural mission: theatre was meant to contribute to the *Bildung* of the spectators.

In fact, it was Goethe's concept of *Bildung* that changed the very grounds upon which theatre was discussed and justified. For almost the entire eighteenth century, the moral usefulness of theatre was emphasised. Gottsched stated that tragic theatre in particular 'teaches and warns through other examples. It strengthens through pleasure and sends the spectator home more intelligent, more prudent and more steadfast than ever before.'[28] The argument that theatre is a moral institution, a school of ethics, was repeated throughout the eighteenth century in ever new variations. At the opening of the Hamburg National Theatre on 22 April 1767, Madame Löwen began with a prologue, written by her husband, which characterised and listed theatre's moral benefits, culminating with the words: 'Beneficial to the state, it will turn/angry and wild men into human beings, citizens, friends and patriots.'[29] In a lecture delivered in 1784 to the German Electoral Society in Mannheim and later published as *Die Schaubühne als eine moralische Anstalt betrachtet*, Schiller summarised the argument: 'The theatre is, more than any other public state institution, a school of practical wisdom, a guide through our middle-class lives, an infallible key to the most secret passages in the human soul.'[30] Both Löwen's Prologue and Schiller's lecture promote the 'republican argument' that theatre even has the power to correct a ruling prince when he has not acted in an enlightened way.

Theatre was accorded a cultural mission to raise the moral standards of citizens and to teach them, and those in power, ethics. The opponents to theatre, who had been particularly dominant in Protestant towns and cities, lost their influence, as a result of which it became common understanding that theatre is morally useful. The concept of theatre as a school of morals and ethics had even already become commonplace as can be seen from Zedler's *Großes vollständiges Universallexikon aller Wissenschaften und Künste* (*Universal Encyclopedia of All Sciences and Arts*, 1752) where the term 'Schau-Spiele' is explained in this way: The spectator is 'drawn into a school from which he can derive the best lessons and make the prettiest rules ... Even if he only comes to the theatre willing to pay attention, with the intention of using everything he sees for his own benefit, then the theatre can help.'[31] No matter whether people went to the theatre to be entertained, taught morals, or moved to tears, theatre, in general, became a respectable institution, whose moral usefulness was beyond doubt.

It was precisely against this usefulness, against the plain applicability of theatre's morals as taught in and by performance that Goethe set his idea of *Bildung*. In his view theatre is not supposed to convey teachings that can easily be applied to the solution of everyday problems. Rather it has to contribute to the process of unfolding the potential of each individual, of his development into a personality. By creating the performance as an autonomous work of art, using plays taken from cultures and traditions somewhat unfamiliar to the spectators, theatre is able to induce a particular aesthetic distance in the spectator, which is the best conceivable prerequisite for the process of *Bildung*.

Und bietet aller Bildung nicht die Schauspielkunst,
Mit hundert Armen, ein phantast'scher Riesengott,
Unendlich mannichfalt'ge, reiche Mittel dar?
[And does not the art of performance offer a way/With a hundred
arms, a fantastical giant god, /Infinite, manifold, and rich?] [32]

Schiller systematically elaborates and explains this idea in his writings
on aesthetics at the end of the century, in particular, in *Über die ästhetische
Erziehung des Menschen* (*The Aesthetic Education of Humanity*, 1795). Here, he
unfolds his concept of the three stages of world history. In the beginning
there was no opposition between an individual's right to develop his
potential freely and the real conditions in society. This was the age when
Greek culture flourished. Here, 'the individual was able to grow into the
genus',[33] and 'timebound man could coincide with the idea of man'.[34] The
process of civilisation tore this unity into fragments. This not only had
impact on the relationship between individual and society but also on the
state of man:

> Forever bound to a single fraction of the whole, man can become
> nothing but a fraction himself. With only the same eternal monot-
> onous sound of the wheel on which he turns in his ear, he shall
> never be able to develop the harmony of his being and instead of
> cultivating humane qualities, he merely becomes the imprint of his
> business, his knowledge.[35]

Schiller regarded his age as the beginning of an era that will give back to
each citizen the possibility of developing his personality freely and in all
respects. In his view, it is not revolution that will accomplish this but the
arts, and in particular, theatre. He accords theatre the function of restoring
to man the totality which was broken and lost in historic-social reality. For
'man can only play when he is a human being in the full sense of the word
and *he can only be a human being when he plays*.'[36] This is precisely why a theatre
performance has to act and to be regarded as an autonomous work of art.
For only the autonomous work of art is able to represent the ethically
reasonable in a sensuous manner and, thus, to provide the spectator with
an opportunity to 'develop the whole of our sensuous and spiritual powers'[37]
with aesthetic distance. Art alone is able to bring about the passage into the
third stage of human history, when free individuals will unite into a free
state, for 'it is through beauty that one must pass on the way to freedom'.[38]

This idea, that theatre performance as an autonomous work of art is the only means by which humans can regain the totality they have lost in the process of civilisation, was taken up by Wagner. In this process not only was the unity of humanity fragmented, but also the unity of the arts. In the *Gesamtkunstwerk*, when poetry, music, and dance are reunited, then, simultaneously, the person of reason, of emotion, and of the senses will be reunited. Humans are restored to their original totality, although on another level. But while Schiller accorded priority to the arts as the prerequisite of a free state, Wagner believed in revolution as precondition to the existence of the *Gesamtkunstwerk*. On 12 November 1851 he wrote to his friend Theodor Uhlig:

> I can only conceive of a *performance after the revolution*. Only a revolution can provide me with artists and spectators, the next revolution must bring our whole *theatre business* to an end: They must and shall all fall apart, I cannot help that. From the ruins, I shall call for what I need: and I will find what I am looking for *only then*. I shall build a theatre on the Rhein and I shall invite everyone to a great dramatic festival: after a year of preparation, I shall have my entire oeuvre performed in only *four* days. With that, I will help the people of the revolution realise the *meaning* of their revolution in its most noble sense. *This audience* will understand me; the present one simply cannot.[39]

Wagner still believed that the potential of the *Gesamtkunstwerk* was political, that it was something to be unfolded and realised by the revolution. Thus, in the 1850s, after the failure of the revolution in 1848, he conceived of a theatre festival which was meant to celebrate and display the liberating force and potential of the *Gesamtkunstwerk* as a democratic meeting. The festival building was to be the meeting place of a 'free, beautiful public celebration'.[40] However, when the foundation stone on the Green Hill was laid at Bayreuth, and not, as originally planned, on the meadows on the banks of the river Rhine, on 22 May 1872, Wagner's opening speech compared the building to a temple, indicating that he intended to accord his art the status of something close to religion. With the performance of *Parsifal* (1882), this re-evaluation was accomplished. The great democratic festival had changed into a kind of divine service. Bayreuth became a place of pilgrimage to which the disciples of Wagner's art from all over the world would travel.

In the twentieth century, the idea of theatre as a festival was taken up again, with reduced religious and stronger political undertones. Peter Behrens[41] and Georg Fuchs[42] hailed theatre as a festive celebration of life, to be realised at special festivals like the one in Darmstadt in 1900 and the Munich Volksfestspiele. It was here that Reinhardt conceived of the 'Theatre of Five Thousand', which was designed to fulfil the 'original purpose' of theatre realising itself as 'festive play'.[43] Such thinking was also behind the foundation of the Salzburg Festival at the end of World War I. Theatre as festival, as conceived by Behrens, Fuchs, and Reinhardt was, in a way, a transformed continuation of Goethe's, Schiller's, and Wagner's ideas of the cultural mission of theatre. It is in participating in festive play that totality is restored in the participants when actors and spectators were united in a festive community.

A contrasting idea of theatre as festival was taken up in the 1920s by the Social Democrats, Communists, and members of the Unions for whom theatre became *the* constitutive element of Union festivals, workers and sports festivals and May Day celebrations. The performances were organised as mass spectacles in which up to 5,000 performers and 65,000 spectators participated. They were held on cycle racetracks, open spaces on fair grounds, in stadiums, amusement parks and so on. The mass spectacles of the Leipzig Union festivals, for instance, featured *Spartakus* (1920), followed by *Der arme Konrad* (1921), a play on the farmers' war in the sixteenth century, *Bilder aus der französischen Revolution* (*Scenes from the French Revolution*, 1922, text by Ernst Toller), *Krieg und Frieden* (*War and Peace*, 1923, text by Toller), and *Erwachen* (*Awake*, 1924, text by Toller and Adolf Winds). It was the aim of the mass spectacle 'to unite author, player and spectators into a great community of shared experience', as the critic of the *Leipziger Volkszeitung* (14 August 1923) wrote on the performance of *Krieg und Frieden*.

The Nazis continued this tradition by channelling the amateur and open air theatre movement which was already active from the beginning of the century and, like the English Pageant Movement between 1905 and 1917, propagated a theatre of the people, by the people and for the people into the *Thingspiel* movement. It was meant to transform all participants, performers and spectators alike, into members of a *Volksgemeinschaft* (Volk community). Since the *Thingspiele* failed to accomplish this, the state subsidies were withdrawn only two years later. The mass spectacles, which the Nazis continued to celebrate, became the *Reichsparteitag*, the *Reichstrauertag der Partei*, and similar festivals.[44]

Even beyond festivals, theatre in the 1920s strikingly often turned into political theatre. Stage directors such as Erwin Piscator, Leopold Jessner, Karlheinz Martin, and Bertolt Brecht used the high esteem and great reputation which theatre enjoyed within German culture to have political impact. Apart from Piscator's two political revues *Revue Roter Rummel* (*Revue Red Fun Fair*, 1924) and *Trotz alledem!* (*Despite Everything!*, 1925), which were commissioned by the Communist Party and in which the majority of the audience consisted of labourers, the performances staged by these directors were also visited by members of the middle and the upper classes. However, these audiences tended to enjoy and to judge these performances as autonomous works of art, celebrating the new stage devices, the novel art of acting, and the striking use of technology as original and remarkable artistic innovations. Whether anyone joined the Communist Party after participating in a Piscator performance is not known.

The Nazis abused the traditional high esteem of theatre. By appointing renowned artists such as Gustaf Gründgens and Heinz Hilpert as directors of the Staatstheater and the Deutsches Theater in Berlin, they secured excellent quality and high artistic standards in performance. It was nothing but a strategy which allowed them to claim that the government respected and supported the arts – and, in particular, theatre.

But even after twelve years of the Nazi regime, the atrocities of World War II and the *Shoa*, the general belief of the German public in the civilising and humanising force of theatre was not diminished. As we have seen, although most cities and towns lay in total ruins, the theatres, which had been closed on 1 September 1944, reopened almost immediately after the end of the war. Theatre quite clearly was as necessary as daily bread. And not only in Berlin, but across Germany – in big cities such as Hamburg, Dusseldorf, Cologne, Munich, and Leipzig and smaller towns such as Trier, Koblenz, Kamenz, or Weißenfels.

Today, theatre continues to play an important role in German culture. Each year, the Berlin Theatertreffen documents this. Theatre is still regarded as a major factor in German cultural life. These performances, and many others, are recorded and shown on the television, and not only on the 'Theatre Channel', a television channel which exclusively transmits recordings of performances and related discussions, but also on the 'major' channels. In this way theatre reaches out to millions of people in a mediatised version. Theatre continues to matter. It is still seen to accomplish an important cultural mission.

But this mission no longer aims at moral improvement nor does it restore a long since lost wholeness nor does it establish a community, be it quasi-religious, ideological, social, or political. Rather, theatre's mission today is to expose spectators to new, mostly disturbing experiences, to destabilise them, even to plunge them into a crisis without showing them a way out or any kind of guidance or reorientation. Be it productions like Frank Castorf's *Puntila* (Deutsches Schauspielhaus Hamburg, 1996), Einar Schleef's *Sportstück* (Burgtheater Vienna, 1998), Michael Thalheimer's *Emilia Galotti* (Deutsches Theater Berlin, 2001), or Jürgen Gosch's *Macbeth* (Düsseldorfer Schauspielhaus, 2005), they all deeply disturb their spectators by various transgressions which until recently were unheard of.

The same holds true for the so-called audiotours of the company Hygiene heute (director Stefan Kaegi) that send the spectators to a tour through a town under very special circumstances or for the productions by the company Rimini Protokoll led by Daniel Wetzel and Helgard Haug who work with amateurs, as for instance in the production *Sabenation* cast from the employees of Sabena; or in the site-specific productions *X Apartments Berlin 2004 – Theater in Private Spaces*, initiated by Matthias Lilienthal. Here, in the Berlin neighbourhoods of Kreuzberg, Schöneberg, and Lichtenberg, 22 productions arranged by different directors in private homes were visited by groups of two to three people.

All the productions named above are exemplary for contemporary German theatre as they succeeded in transgressing all kind of boundaries, allow for the most disturbing experiences, and transfer the spectators into a state of liminality. In fact, the cultural mission German theatre has to accomplish today is to bring about transgression, liminality, crisis, and transformation.[45]

15 Theatertreffen 2007

MAIK HAMBURGER AND SIMON WILLIAMS

As mentioned in chapter 13, every year in May, the ten productions of the German-language theatre judged by a panel of experts to have been the most outstanding of the season are invited to Berlin to participate in a festival, the Theatertreffen. Hence, in any given year it is possible to gain a bird's-eye view of the current trends and tendencies and strengths and weaknesses of the German theatre. We would like, therefore, to conclude this history by surveying the Theatertreffen for 2007. In doing so we hope to identify characteristic features of the contemporary German theatre and to determine, if possible, how far the German theatre today is in continuity with its past, and how far it has rejected it.

In the early twenty-first century, the scripted drama is often considered to be an endangered species, and the very idea of a canon of plays forming the backbone of a theatrical culture has been consistently questioned. On first glance, the selection of plays for Theatertreffen 2007 seemed to contradict this, as it was dominated by scripted plays, six of which were classics and two of which were key works of the modern theatre; only two plays were new. In actuality, however, the productions offered homage neither to canons of the past nor to the centrality of the dramatic text in performance.

In German-speaking theatre, to a greater degree than elsewhere, the idea of 'post-dramatic theatre' has taken a firm though not undisputed hold upon performance. 'Post-dramatic theatre', as theorised by Hans-Thies Lehmann, is a theatre in which 'sense and synthesis has largely disappeared',[1] which challenges the assumption of a sacrosanct text or a meaningful storyline, is intensely self-reflexive, and depends as much upon employing the spatial and visual aspects of performance as it does upon the spoken word. If there is a primary artist in this theatre, it is the stage director. This development is somewhat loosely called *Regietheater* (directing theatre), though this term was originally coined in the 1920s to describe the work of Reinhardt, Jessner, and Piscator; the more correct term for today's avantgarde would be *Regisseurstheater* (director's theatre). In contrast to *Regietheater*, a theatre historian notes, 'Regisseurstheater is not interested in interpretation, explication or discovery. It does not develop its results from the play but shows the play as the director's ego sees itself within it. It becomes the material of his or her ego, is broken up, cut, condensed, distanced, enlivened by wild emotions or ideas of the directing subject. [The question is] not, who is Shakespeare's Hamlet, but how do I see this Harlequin, this fellow who doesn't manage to do anything? Isn't he a clown? A funny little crosspatch? That's the way I see him and therefore the way I show him. As a result the play is dispersed, loses its significance, its immanent philosophy.'[2]

However, it would be a mistake to assume that in post-dramatic theatre the dramatic text is nullified; rather, as Lehmann suggestively comments, this theatre might even revivify the written text which is, he plausibly claims, 'under more threat from museum-like conventions than from radical forms of dealing with it'.[3] But post-dramatic theatre does redirect our attention, from the dramatic text to 'theatrical performance as an ephemeral, a performative experience. As a result, the performance is no longer to be understood as a work, but as a process, as an experience, which is marked by the signs of transience, fleetingness, unrepeatability, and singularity.'[4]

At Theatertreffen 2007, the post-dramatic perspective was perhaps most apparent in two productions directed by Andreas Kriegenburg. One was of Dirty Hands (Thalia Theater, Hamburg), Jean-Paul Sartre's rigorously didactic examination of the circumstances in which action endows life with a sense of reality. Kriegenburg cut the play loose from its moorings in realism and the well-made play and transformed it into a piece in which whimsy, impulse, and the arbitrary initially seemed to prevail. The set, an anodyne space of modern wooden panels, lacked specificity. At the start we were reminded that all performance is artificial; stage directions were read out and actors in street clothes delivered their lines at great speed with little attention to character, speaking them more as running narrative than dialogue. This denial of the dramatic (and of sense) was sustained only in the opening act, which frames the main action in which a young man struggles with himself as to whether he should or should not assassinate a political leader to whom he serves as secretary. However, even when the action was entered into, the continuity of Sartre's play was constantly disrupted, by the adoption of contrasting acting styles that ranged from farce through absurdism to bourgeois tragedy, by the refusal to find any psychological consistency in the characters, by frequent rewritings and interpolations, and by the raucous eruption of contemporary popular music, all of which was designed to dispel any illusion of consistency and continuity. Any action committed by an individual was presented as arising from a potentially infinite number of choices. Accordingly the political ramifications of the play were denied. It was only towards the end that the feasibility of consequential action was offered as a possibility, and for the first time one felt a corresponding sympathy towards the characters.

If *Dirty Hands* highlighted the randomness of human action, Kriegenburg's production of Chekhov's *Three Sisters*, from the Munich Kammerspiele, was centred upon *one* of the play's many themes, which he explored via numerous stylistic variations. He fastened on the propensity of the three sisters and their brother Andrei to regress to childhood, by reducing Chekhov's many-faceted symbol 'Moscow' to a code that represents the siblings' yearning for the happy days of infancy. Any movement forward, any urge to keep up with the relentlessly moving times, and any fear of being left sitting in the house for ever was excised. Thus the sisters seemed to lack maturity and the depth of emotion to be found in Chekhov's play was missing. Such a strategy is quite acceptable to proponents of post-dramatic theatre, who, denying the primary authority of the text, require each performance to be judged on its own merits.[5] (see fig. 25)

The performance started with the sisters dancing in front of the iron curtain, like birds of passage, unable to take off. They were difficult to tell apart as all wore black wigs and were clad in creamy summer lace dresses with black boots. When the curtain rose they continued their nostalgic play in a salon that was disturbingly surreal. A chandelier sprouting from the ceiling like a huge menacing flower poured an unending stream of nutshells on Olga, who behaved as if this was the most natural thing in the world. For the rest of the evening the shells crunched under the actors' feet.

Kriegenburg followed Chekhov's text but broke up the narrative structure and obviated characterisation through changing perspectives and presentational modes. At a moment's notice the action, built as series of vaudeville acts, jumped from slapstick to tender musicality, from caricature to Stein-like realism. For example, Andrei, who, as the text hints, has been putting on weight, was padded to enormous proportions, while Natasha, a mere slip of a girl, was well-nigh crushed under his huge belly during a sex scene. A dialogue became a soliloquy recited by Olga in a sing-song tone, as if it were an interminable daily ritual. Irina constantly banged her head as if in a routine of self-aggression. Occasionally the characters put on oversized childrens' heads with large sad eyes and spoke their lines like children; later,

25 *Three Sisters* by Anton Chekhov, Munich Kammerspiele 2006, directed and designed by
Andreas Kriegenburg.

they played tunes on toy instruments culminating in 'Yellow Submarine', a
tune so often repeated during the evening that it became a metaphor for
their entombed existence. This stylistic fragmentation dispensed with the
meaningful silences commonly regarded as 'Chekhovian'. In fact,
Kriegenburg swung the pendulum to the opposite extreme, filling the static

action with stage business and pushing it towards the farcical. The set went through symbolic changes from act to act. In the first act Irina pinned pieces of paper to the wall like a list of birthday wishes; in the second act these pieces of paper covered all the walls to the ceiling; in Act 3, the back wall disappeared behind a pile of rags and clothing; and in Act 4 the stage was filled with white balloons hovering in mid-air, unable to fly to Moscow because they were tied to Irina's sheets of paper.

The first act was a brilliant *tour de force* but Kriegenburg's concept could not sustain the whole evening, which ultimately became repetitive, even wearying. The greatest impact was made by the haunting children's masks which, coupled with stiff gestures, conveyed the impression of a sophisticated marionette theatre. The contrast between the monstrous children's heads and the delicate period dresses provided a sense of poignancy that had a distinctly Chekhovian quality.

Not only do directors feel free to emphasise one theme to the exclusion of others, they regularly and often ruthlessly cut dramatic texts to only a fraction of their original length. In 1980, when Peter Stein put on an almost uncut version of Aeschylus' *Oresteia* at the Schaubühne, his meticulous ten-hour production charted the evolution of an autocratic society ruled by terror into a democratic one ruled by law. In 2006, Michael Thalheimer's staging at the Deutsches Theater reduced the same trilogy to 100 minutes and provided no notion of historical progress. The luxurious nineteenth-century auditorium of the Deutsches Theater was made to look bare and hostile; doors stood wide open, the golden light of the sconces was replaced by the glare of incandescent tubes, and the proscenium was boarded up from top to bottom with raw planks splashed with blood. Two ledges running along this wooden wall provided the only space for the actors.

Clytemnestra, squatting almost naked on the upper shelf, poured blood, presumably Iphigenia's, over her head and body, Iphigenia having been sacrificed by her father Agamemnon ten years before. It quickly became apparent that the large blot of blood on the wall behind the actress came from previous performances, so the ugly stain got larger and deeper each evening; because of this the red plush of the auditorium seats and walls assumed a bloodstained look as well. Clytemnestra, freezing and wet, smoked a cigarette and drank a can of beer (see fig. 26). Agamemnon, on returning from the wars, first had sex with his wife against the wall, then addressed his subjects with his pants still at his ankles. Eventually Clytemnestra slaughtered her husband, having previously killed his mistress

Cassandra who, before dying, bit off her own tongue. At intervals a chorus in the second gallery commented on the action and rhythmically chanted Zeus' slogan: 'Act, suffer, learn'.

When Orestes arrived, he was so terrified he wet his trousers, but after much subterfuge the unfortunate youngster succeeded in fulfilling the behest of the gods to kill his mother and her lover Aegisthus. All this time the blood-covered body of a not yet dead Agamemnon crawled at a snail's pace from one side of the stage to the other. Having committed the two murders, Orestes in terror yelled for Athene to help him. In Aeschylus' play she does, by setting up a court of law to exculpate Orestes from blood guilt, but Thalheimer practically eliminated the final play of the trilogy; instead, Orestes' appeal to Athene went unheard, and the Chorus's final crescendo, 'Peace for ever', sounded rather like 'enduring freedom', which suggested that the chain of blood feuds represented by Aeschylus has never been broken. Orestes was seen to squat miserably in his gore with no hope, the curse of the Atreides weighing on him and mankind from mythical times to this day (see fig. 26).

The spectator could only conclude that the Apocalypse we are facing today has been with us from earliest times; we have to acknowledge that all hopes of progress, humanity and enlightenment are illusions. Thalheimer's *Oresteia*, like much of the foremost theatre in Germany today, had no time for differentiated arguments, multi-layered discourses, or shades of emotional engagement. It was a production that almost luxuriated in pessimism. Thalheimer and his designer, Olaf Altmann, made no appeal to the impartial, democratic viewpoint of the Greek spectator, who surveyed the action, as it were, from above; instead they intimidated the audience with monumental images. Rather than argument, reasoning, and the clash of opinions, it is the archaic vision of blood and slaughter that remains imprinted on the memory of the spectator.

The Bulgarian-born Dimiter Gotscheff (b. 1943) is an earnest and politically engaged artist, clearly alarmed by the current state of the world, but while his younger colleagues express their disgust by ridiculing all political attitudes, Gotscheff is not afraid of making a political statement. His *Tartuffe*, from the Thalia Theater, was acted on a totally empty stage, and Molière's text was used to demonstrate how easily a hedonistic society can fall under the spell of fundamentalist ideology. The two-hour production began with a solo by Dorine as a Bulgarian charwoman making fun of her employer. To festive music, the Orgon family entered in neo-baroque

26 *The Oresteia* by Aeschylus, Deutsches Theater Berlin 2006, directed by Michael Thalheimer. Clytemnestra (Constanze Becker) sits with a can of beer by her bloodstained imprint on the wall.

finery – pink hotpants, skimpy tennis outfits, sequined gowns, and leisure suits. Cannons shot confetti and streamers into the air and the floor was inundated with coloured paper, which littered the stage for the rest of the evening and stood for the self-absorbed decadence of the family. Orgon's family was a collection of spoilt, indecisive individuals, impervious to Cleante's attempts at rational argument. Only Dorine, a bundle of wit and energy, had her head screwed on right; she even half seduced Tartuffe to get her own way. Orgon was at once hard-headed business man and dupe, so totally infatuated by a religious guru that he walked around quoting the Bible, dressed in nothing but a sheet and sandals. Tartuffe was a deceivingly pleasant young man, glibly able to talk himself out of each and every difficulty. His brown suit and Orgon's tendency to sing snatches of the *Horst-Wessel-Lied* suggested ties between religious fanaticism and fascism.

Religious paraphernalia, hymns, chants, and modern songs like 'O happy day when Jesus was', replaced the relics of Enlightenment, a point driven home by interpolations of apocalyptic passages from Heiner Müller. Orgon's ominous coffer, which was stolen by Tartuffe, no longer contained evidence about helping a friend to escape, but was full of incriminating material, such as child pornography, Gazprom shares, and arms deals with Libya. Valère's offer to help the family flee was cut and the happy ending with the King's pardon deleted. Instead, the victorious Tartuffe cut the throat of Madame Pernelle and commented, 'Where I come from, we call this the laughter of the lambs', whereupon he drove the whole family downstage, crawling on all fours and bleating like sheep, a possible reference to Brecht's parody of the *Horst-Wessel-Lied*, in which the followers of the Nazis are shown as calves marching to the slaughterhouse. Gottschef's bitterness drove the comedy out of the play, but this technique destroyed any subtlety of language, character, or structure, and even though his intention is a political one, the aesthetic impact does not differ significantly from that of the more deconstructive *mise-en-scènes* of the younger directors.

Post-dramatic theatre thrives on the mixture of genres, which was most apparent in Theater Basel's unique hybrid of drama and opera in its production of *Dido and Aeneas. A Musical Play Project after Purcell's Opera and Christopher Marlowe's Tragedy 'Dido Queen of Carthage'*, an adaptation co-authored by the director Sebastian Nübling (b. 1960) and a team of musicians, designers, and dramaturges. In contrast to other offerings at the Theatertreffen, which ignored the historical contexts of older drama, this production played up the interaction between past styles and contemporary modes and exploited the cross-over of theatrical and operatic genres.

The flexible stage of the Schaubühne provided an ideal venue for this performance. The two-and-a quarter-hour action without intermission took place in a traverse staging that spanned the entire auditorium. Orchestra and chorus were placed at one end of the strip, opposite them a goodly-sized kitchen range. From the start the performance had a strong culinary component. As the audience took their seats, actors were busy chopping vegetables and meat for a four-course meal to be cooked on stage and served up in the course of the action. The chef Jupiter had a crush on his kitchen-boy Ganymede and had to be called to order with a fly-swat by his wife Juno. The basis for the *mise-en-scène* was an opulent banquet at a long table at which Dido caroused with her courtiers, among them her possessive fiancée, Iarbas, her alcoholic sister Belinda, and a transvestite Venus. Whenever the situation threatened to get out of hand, Jupiter diverted attention by having the next course served. The unexpected appearance of Aeneas with his son Ascanius, impoverished fugitives from the Trojan war, and his account of the atrocities perpetrated there thoroughly upset the festivities, but as Aeneas was of royal blood he was invited to the top of the table. His passionate affair with the queen was elaborated through dialogue and operatic arias. Whereas most actors and actresses both played and sang their roles in virtuoso style, the part of Dido was shared by an actress and a similarly dressed operatic soprano. Dido had, as it were, two bodies, the mortal one of flesh and blood and the immortal one represented by the music. Thus in a moving moment the actress Dido launched upon a passionate aria, which was then taken up and heightened by her operatic alter ego. The love affair between the queen and Aeneas was broken up by Iarbas who hatched a plot to despatch his rival to Italy. Dido did not commit suicide, as in traditional versions, but sat petrified at the table with her new husband, Iarbas, a modern couple bored to death with each other.

Purcell's score remained grounded in opera, and although it was given a contemporary sound, it still contrasted effectively with the popular hits and the songs of Bob Dylan sung by the cast in the roles of present-day cooks. When Aeneas, who had a southern appearance and spoke in Arabic to his son, performed a courtship dance with Dido, Purcell's music assumed an oriental tone. The problems and opportunities of multi-culturalism were integrated into the fabric of the story. Although it made no explicit political statement, this enthralling performance both aroused gritty associations with the contemporary world of the wealthy North and the poor, war-infested South and told an absorbing tale of love in times of war.

Increasingly today, the term 'performance' implies something different from and perhaps more than the presentation of plays. Drama as a self-contained entity no longer holds sole monopoly over the German repertoire.

A telling example of this was *Die Leiden des jungen Werthers* (*The Sorrows of Young Werther*), presented by the Gorki Theater of Berlin. Goethe's *Sturm-und-Drang* novel, among the most frequently adapted non-dramatic works in the history of German theatre, was here presented half as narrative, half as enactment, on the bare forestage in front of a closed curtain, which was identical in design with the walls of the theatre. Thus the virtual 'fourth wall' of naturalistic theatre became a real wall with the action taking place in front instead of behind. This had the effect of turning the bright white walls of the auditorium, distinctly reminiscent of the German Enlightenment, into a prison.

In the hands of the lanky Hans Löw, Goethe's sentimental hero was constantly on the verge of a nervous breakdown, but Löw never represented Werther as a dramatic character in a self-contained world. Rather, using Goethe's words, he spoke directly to the audience as if he were in dialogue with it. This strategy had a most unnerving effect, as Werther's intense anxiety gradually but palpably infected the audience, a condition aggravated by the claustrophobic environment of the auditorium. It was made both to experience and be complicit in Werther's mental crisis.

Nothing weakened the perturbing grip of this performance. Lotte and Albert came out of the audience, as if they were somehow its emissaries. Lotte, a torn and irresolute figure, became the object of intense competition between the men, and Albert, using Goethe's words, assailed Werther in tones suggestive of the brash pop culture of the twenty-first century. Although this performance approximated public address more than it did representational theatre, the director Jan Bosse (b. 1969) did not hesitate to employ strong, even outrageous theatrical effects, above all at the point where Werther tries to escape from Lotte into the world of petty diplomacy, when stagehands noisily tramped through the auditorium carrying on to the forestage gigantic mirrors, which were then set up so the audience could contemplate reflections of itself, as if it was the society whose snobbery and indifference would drive Werther back to his obsession with Lotte. In concert with the non-representational nature of the performance, his suicide was not shown realistically, but by him kicking a hole in the proscenium curtain – now seen to be made of paper – and disappearing into the darkness behind it.

This was a disquieting evening because the anguish generated by Werther's relentlessly egotistic assault upon the world and then himself became the experience of the audience. But it had disconcerting aesthetic implications as well. Is the act of representation, this performance seemed to ask, no longer adequate to communicate the inner or outer crises of our lives? Must 'performance' necessarily step beyond the aesthetic bounds within which the theatre has so far largely contained itself?

This question also lay behind the third production from the Thalia Theater, *Ulrike Maria Stuart* by the Austrian Nobel Prize laureate Elfriede Jelinek. This was not a drama in the usual sense of the word, but a running text of about 150 pages, which Jelinek intended to be used as a basis for theatrical production, directors being invited to hew their own independent work of art out of this mass of semi-formed material. To emphasise that the work has no existence over and above concrete stagings of it, Jelinek does not permit the text to be published. Its first production, by the Thalia Theater, included the director, Nicolas Stemann (b. 1968), as co-author of the work and each subsequent staging will in turn be a new play, of which the new director will be a new co-author.

The title conflates the names of the modern terrorist Ulrike Marie Meinhof and Maria Stuart of Schiller's tragedy. The piece is conceived as a 'drama of four queens' – Meinhof, queen of the left-radical RAF (Red Army Fraction), her fellow revolutionary, Gudrun Ensslin, Queen Elisabeth I, and Mary Queen of Scots. Jelinek is not interested in explicit parallels between these two pairs of queens, but in reproducing the hyperbolic style of Schiller's blank verse explores the phenomenon of language bringing forth idealistic attitudes. As she comments, 'the characters are not themselves but products of ideology'; hence members of the cast were only sporadically associated with individual characters.

The production mixed true and fictional elements from terrorist activities of the 1970s with reminiscences of English history some 400 years earlier. In particular the ideological and sexual rivalries between Meinhof and Ensslin were contrasted to those between Mary and Elisabeth. Themes included the struggle against capitalism, the rationale of violence in politics, whether the end justifies the means, structures of female power play, the loss of ideals, and the alleged incompatibility of motherhood and politics. The production on a bare stage, on which stood a small proscenium arch theatre, was a hodge-podge of quotations, dialogues, revolutionary songs, pop, folk, English renaissance madrigals, and contemporary political satire. Meinhof was shown committing suicide, but she and Ensslin also appeared as crippled old women with walking aids, as they might have been today had they survived. There was a film sequence, *Der Untergang* part 2, an ironic allusion to the movie about Hitler's end; there was some nudity and splashing of variously coloured liquids (a seemingly indispensable feature in modern productions); there was some interaction with the audience, who were handed water-bombs, which they were encouraged to throw at cardboard replicas of today's politicians and an Intendant known for his aversion to the post-dramatic – an allusion to the real assassinations of 'reactionaries' perpetrated by Meinhof and her followers. Occasionally the author herself was the object of parody. In one scene two performers supposed to represent Jelinek and another Austrian woman writer, attired in vagina-like capes, spouted out clichés about feminism and femininity; and at the end of the play the (male) director came on with a Jelinek hair-do and quoted passages from her work. This post-dramatic production bristled with ironic references. Some points may have been lost on an audience without knowledge of the historical facts but the pure entertainment value kept interest going.

This was a 'performance' with no plot, no story, no chronology. It carried no 'authority' as there was no authorial position; indeed, Jelinek's intention for the piece may have been quite different. The main aim of Stemann's production seemed to be the avoidance of the clichés and ideological propaganda that has been disseminated ever since the terrorists began to operate. Perhaps it was touched by nostalgia for the times when political engagement seemed to matter, even to the point of risking one's life. But as in Kriegenburg's production of *Dirty Hands*, actions and arguments that once carried political weight are ridiculed as the basis for any political or social change.

As is clear from several of these productions, there is a resolutely pessimistic, if not apocalyptic strain in much of German theatre today and this was nowhere more effectively displayed than in the production of Ferdinand Bruckner's *Krankheit der Jugend* (*Malady of Youth*, c. 1926), a production, directed by Tilmann Köhler (b. 1979), from the National Theatre in Weimar, which was staged at the Sophiensaele. This venue is the sort of site that currently enjoys great popularity in German theatre; despite its opulent sounding name, it is a barebones hall in an abandoned building in the centre of the city, an icon of post-industrial grunge. In fact, it provided a most appropriate setting for Bruckner's expressionistic diatribe on the anguish experienced by young people as they confront but disastrously fail to come to terms with their realisation that sexual desire and violence spring from a common source. In all ways, this performance by a troupe of youngsters was an uncomfortable event. The set, surrounded on four sides by stark bleachers, resembled an empty, derelict swimming pool; within this desolate spot was one prop, a steel table on wheels, which served a multiplicity of functions, from a slab at the morgue, to dining-room table, to park bench, to a bed where couples occasionally met in desolate embrace or sour discord. The audience were made to feel like medical students watching a dissection in the anatomy theatre. The production eliminated any sense of material reality that might underlie Bruckner's text as it forced an exclusive focus on the trauma of the characters. All social differences between them had been eliminated, and any vestige of linear development in the action had disappeared, to be replaced by the ceaseless repetition of the paradigm of sex and violence.

This was a calculatedly disheartening evening of theatre. Dialogue was delivered as if it were a species of armed conflict rather than a medium of conversation. Harsh rock music stemming from the well-known 'Tocotronic' band and performed by the actors themselves interrupted the action. No one smiled, everyone was afraid, at violence from others or from within themselves. The only alternatives for the women appeared to be the street or suicide. It would be difficult to imagine a theatrical event more removed from the mission of *Bildung* that was once, but is perhaps no longer, the energising force in the German theatre. In these terrified, deeply unattractive people, put forward as characteristic of modern youth, there was no trace of generosity and goodness. It was a world in which happiness was not possible.

The great crowd-pleaser of the Theatertreffen was Jan Bosse's production of *Much Ado About Nothing* from the Vienna Burgtheater. Here was a production that so consistently celebrated its own theatricality that its main purpose seemed to be reflection on the nature of spectacle. The set was under construction as the audience entered the auditorium; then, half way through the performance, in a coup of flamboyant theatricality, an army of stage hands transformed the stage into a *faux* Hawaiian wedding, complete with waterfall, an event greeted by a huge round of applause from the audience; and at the end the same stage hands dismantled the set. There can have been no doubt in anyone's mind that this production was a construction.

Self-conscious theatricality was apparent too in the presentation of the text. As is now common throughout German-speaking theatre, the text was substantially cut or compressed; indeed, the performance was trimmed to what seems to be a standard length for the German theatre at present, two hours without intermission. Songs were interpolated, and characters eliminated, in this instance Dogberry and Verges. Some of their knockabout comedy, but not their words, were transferred to Shakespeare's more serious characters. This had the effect, again very common in Germany today, of reducing the heroic and romantic to the trivial and everyday. The Burgtheater could not, however, be accused of trivialising the text. In fact, refreshingly, they made no bones about Shakespeare's sudden plunging of the plot into the darker realms of near-tragedy. The action began with a spectacle of macabre poor taste, as coffins were brought on stage; characters began mourning, only to be shocked by the returning soldiers jumping like maniacs from their coffins. The ambivalent atmosphere was sustained throughout the perform-ance. Beatrice and Benedick attacked and wooed each other with an energy that at one and the same time recalled Strindbergian tragedy and the comic tropes of the music-hall. Comedy was always belied by an atmosphere of threatening sleaziness and bursts of distasteful egotism from the socially superior characters. Hence, it was quite within the bounds set up by the production for the dispute over Hero's chastity to reach levels of unsettling violence. The production's highlighting of Shakespeare's juxtaposition of the lightly comic with the ferociously melodramatic heightened our awareness of how the play is put together from fundamentally different and probably irreconcilable elements. Accordingly, the production made no attempt to project an illusion of aesthetic wholeness. Throughout it was clear that the performance was being held together by seams that were threatening to come apart, the danger offered by this threat giving the production much of its edge and energy.

The Parisian Yasmina Reza, one of today's most successful playwrights, clearly has great confidence in German directors, as, for the fourth time, she entrusted the world premiere of one of her plays to a German, this time Jürgen Gosch, who first produced *The God of Carnage* in Zurich, whence it made its way to the Theatertreffen. Gosch's production of *Macbeth* from Dusseldorf, acted by seven nude males squirting blood at each other from bottles and defecating on the floor, had been a sensation at the previous year's Theatertreffen. However, the versatile director's approach to Reza's comedy was far more conventional and employed a high degree of psycho-logical finesse. The comedy, running 90 minutes without an interval, was enacted in a non-realistic set by Johannes Schütz, an almost empty white box on which all the props were stored at the rear, from where they were brought forward when required.

The predictable plot turns on the fact that two kids had a fight in which one lost two teeth. Their educated parents meet to discuss the situation in a civilised manner, but before long they start quarrelling and the archaic God of Carnage is re-enthroned. Each character argues with the others and as the conflicts gain in acerbity, all middle-class decorum is dropped and the drawing room becomes a battleground with constantly changing alliances and confrontations. The action includes one of the characters engaging in what must be the longest and most profuse vomit in the history of theatre. Where the usual boulevard comedy would nicely hint at nasty realities, Gosch gave them to us in all their excruciating detail, while drawing unrestrained laughter from the audience.

Gosch stuck to Reza's text but did not accentuate the political dimension nor the subliminal tragedy that seems to run parallel with the comedy. Thus the production, in spite of its biting wit, did not transcend its origins in high-class boulevard theatre. One critic, seeing shades of Ibsen and Albee and referring to a symbolic hamster in the action, renamed it *Who's Afraid of Hedda Hamster?*[6] This production adopts features of post-dramatic performance without actually belonging to this category, as it follows a clear narrative line and the four top-notch actors are able to present exquisite character studies.

Although the Theatertreffen occupies the limelight in Berlin throughout the month of May, the city's theatres continue to flourish. To judge from many of the productions playing in tandem with the Theatertreffen, the post-dramatic theatre does not rule unchallenged in contemporary Germany. For example, Thomas Ostermeier's production of *Hedda Gabler* at the Schaubühne, which had been selected for Theatertreffen 2006, followed Ibsen's text closely. It was given in an absolutely contemporary setting, and scrupulous efforts were made to find modern parallels to Ibsen's nineteenth-century artefacts, which ranged from Aunt Juliane's visor for her hat to a laptop for Ejlert Løvborg's manuscript. The result was a telling of Ibsen's tale that was tense and compelling, extraordinarily so, because one constantly savoured the skill and ease of the updating. Hedda, played by a diminutive, ruthless, but sexually confused Katharina Schüttler, destroyed Løvborg's laptop with a hammer, which elicited gasps from the audience; destroying digital technology is today, it seems, the ultimate taboo. But while Ibsen's narrative was maintained intact, powerful images, which are the speciality of contemporary German directors and the mainstay of post-dramatic theatre, were what stayed in one's mind after the performance – the rain that poured down the windows throughout the action and the last three minutes, where the stage revolved, displaying a dead Hedda, while Tesman, Thea, and Brack, unaware of her death, covered the living room and veranda in yellow post-its. Metaphorically the audience knew Hedda's death would never be discovered, a powerful image for alienation in today's society.

Certainly post-dramatic theatre has powerful critics and detractors, most notably Peter Stein, in the 1970s the leader of the German avant-garde. For Stein, the most important feature of European theatre has been and still is the classic text. Great literature of former times, he contends, is still highly significant. While in his younger years he extracted contemporary social implications from the text, his aim now is primarily aesthetic, to allow the words of a play to come over as effectually as possible, a procedure he calls *Verräumlichung* ('spatialisation') of a written drama. He has in the past decades produced a number of marathon-like events including his 22-hour *Faust Parts I and II* (Hanover and Berlin, 2000).

Theatertreffen 2007 had scarcely ended when Stein presented both as a coda and as a dissenting voice the entire *Wallenstein* trilogy by Friedrich Schiller in a converted brewery in Berlin-Neukölln. The production was run under the patronage of the Berliner Ensemble, the Intendant of which, Claus Peymann, another dissenter to the current post-dramatic orthodoxy, regards his own theatre as a Noah's Ark where real values are being saved from the deluge. The three plays that compose *Wallenstein* (*Wallensteins Lager, Die Piccolomini* and *Wallensteins Tod*), a historical epic about the mightiest and most ambivalent general of the Thirty Years' War, were written as independent plays, but Stein ran them together, which resulted in a performance lasting well over ten hours. The cast of over a hundred was headed by Klaus Maria Brandauer, an actor who achieved international notice in the film *Mephisto*. With straggly shoulder-length hair – a holdover from the 1960s? – Brandauer played the intransigent general like a formidable alien from some distant world. The extreme width of the stage and the rigorous historicism of the costumes meant that the production bore a certain resemblance to a film epic. The full breadth of the proscenium was used for the mass scenes, while the more intimate *intérieurs* were played in smaller spaces defined by sliding screens, which achieved a cinematic zoom effect. Not only did Stein let the rhetoric of Schiller's verse sparkle but his direction also coupled imaginative group scenes with psychologically subtle portraits. He unfolded a panorama of military exploits, victories and defeats, of intrigues, treacheries and murders, of paranoia and of love in war-time. The production was dismissed by some critics as a museum piece but acclaimed by others as a stirring contemporary interpretation of a great classic, and one, perhaps, that Goethe and Schiller might have approved of as well.

Conclusion

The current divide in German-speaking theatre between proponents of a 'dramatic' theatre, in which the prime purpose of theatre is the production and performance of scripted plays in a representational manner, and practitioners of a 'post-dramatic' theatre, in which the text of the play is neither sacrosanct nor necessarily central to the performance, is the most pressing artistic issue of the time. Advocates for a 'dramatic' theatre accuse those whose work is primarily 'post-dramatic' of self-indulgence and foresee incipient chaos when the underpinnings of a dramatic repertoire have been removed. Furthermore, given the intense suspicion among 'post-dramatic' directors of the rhetorical nature of theatrical representation and their frequent avoidance of even a trace of illusion on stage, it is difficult to imagine that theatre even has a future if the 'post-dramatic' were to become the sole mode of theatre in Germany. But as in any mature theatre culture, various genres of theatre are constantly laying claim to precedence, and the vitality of the culture depends primarily on competition between modes rather than the prevalence of one over all others.

The German theatre has been particularly fortunate in that the generous subsidy that it has received since the latter part of the eighteenth century has allowed theatre practitioners from Goethe through Wagner and the Duke of Saxe-Meiningen to Brecht and contemporary directors to engage in wide-ranging experiments that enabled them to discover newer and more radical theatrical languages, without paying too much attention to the box-office. As the Theatertreffen for 2007 and in previous years has displayed, the German tradition of theatrical experimentation is still alive – and still very much a bone of contention for critics, audiences, and practitioners alike. Again, controversy is far from new to the German theatre: from Gottsched's assault upon the figure of Harlequin in the eighteenth century through the impassioned responses aroused by Wagner's music dramas in the nineteenth to the continual arguments over the pre-eminence of the director in the twentieth and twenty-first centuries, German theatre has been invigorated by constant polemics.

The slinging of mud (and other unpleasant substances) on stages today has led to a good deal of mud-slinging in the media. Whereas, for instance, Peter Stein's classical production of *Wallenstein* was regarded by one critic as 'the last groan of the *Titanic* before sinking',[7] he himself countered by stating that young directors were so uneducated today they could only stage 'the itch on their foreskins', stating that nowadays actors had to endure 'being smeared with shit or having to wank on the forestage for half an hour'.

Things came to a head last year when an arch-conservative critic attended an opening of a Ionesco play staged by a notoriously avant-garde director at Frankfurt. The critic's muttered imprecations in the first row so incensed one of the actors that he dropped a stuffed chicken into the critic's lap and snatched his spiral note-pad; the critic fled the theatre, pursued by a volley of abuse from the actor. Of course this had repercussions in the press and conservative reviewers are now called the 'spiral note-pad faction'.[8]

Perhaps the most dispiriting aspect of the Theatertreffen 2007 was the emergence of an attitude negating every outlook for a change. Several productions expressed mistrust in all involvement in political issues and, by implication, in any chance of progress in the world. Examples of political endeavour as addressed in several plays were exposed to devastating irony or pure ridicule suggesting that political commitment, even today, was merely an act of naïve stupidity. Owing to the self-referential strategy of directors and their aesthetics of the present moment, the historical dimension was being eliminated from stagings of old plays. History was being expelled from the theatre in favour of the unique magic encounter between the performance and the audience.

Another disquieting feature was the frequent recourse to violence, both in overtly gory productions such as Thalheimer's *Oresteia* or nominally comic productions such as Bosse's *Much Ado About Nothing*, disquieting not because it was gratuitous, but because the implication seemed to be there was no alternative way of tackling the world's problems – a total reversal of the ideas of German theatre since Lessing.

Does this indicate that the mission of *Bildung*, which, as many of the earlier chapters of this book have shown, has been one of the central purposes of the German theatre, is no longer relevant because society no longer values or believes in it? On the evidence offered by the Theatertreffen, the answer seems to be 'yes'. Certainly these productions opened up our minds to unusual images and metaphors, but this on its own does not constitute *Bildung*. *Bildung* is an essentially positive concept; it considers the individual to be one who can be educated and culturally enriched so that ultimately the community can contain those forces that subvert society and lead us into an unending spiral of violence. At present it is not easy to find that confidence in the German theatre, primarily, one suspects, because that confidence cannot be found in the world outside it.

Notes

Introduction

1. As, for example, Hans Knudsen partly did in *Deutsche Theater-Geschichte* (Stuttgart, 1959).

Chapter 1

1. Bernd Neumann, *Geistliches Schauspiel im Zeugnis der Zeit. Zur Aufführung mittelalterlicher religiöser Dramen im deutschen Sprachgebiet*, 2 vols. (Munich and Zurich, 1987) and Eckehard Simon, *Die Anfänge des weltlichen deutschen Schauspiels, 1370–1530. Untersuchung und Dokumentation* (Tübingen, 2003).
2. Neumann, *Geistliches Schauspiel*, 3624.
3. Stephen K. Wright, tr., *Medieval German Drama. Four Plays in Translation. The Innsbruck (Thuringian) Easter Play, The Innsbruck (Thuringian) Corpus Christi Play, The Mühlhausen Play of St Catherine, The Play of Lady Jutta*. (Fairview, NC, 2002).
4. Eckhard Bernstein, *Hans Sachs, mit Selbstzeugnissen und Bilddokumenten* (Reinbek bei Hamburg, 1993).
5. Simon, *Anfänge des weltlichen deutschen Schauspiels*, 252.
6. Neumann, *Geistliches Schauspiel*, 563, 576, 585, 600.
7. Kurt Ruh, Burghart Wachinger *et al.* (eds.), *Die deutsche Literatur des Mittelalters: Verfasserlexikon*, 2nd edn, 11 vols. (Berlin, 1978–2004), 2, 808f.
8. Simon, *Anfänge des weltlichen deutschen Schauspiels*, 505.
9. Ruh, *Deutsche Literatur des Mittelalters*, 7: 97.
10. Ibid., 6: 684f.
11. Ibid., 1: 959.
12. Neumann, *Geistliches Schauspiel*, 2370.
13. Ibid., 2285.
14. Ibid., 2653, 2656.
15. Ruh, *Deutsche Literatur des Mittelalters*, 3:608.
16. Simon, *Anfänge des weltlichen deutschen Schauspiels*, 2.
17. Ruh, *Deutsche Literatur des Mittelalters*, 1:978.
18. Neumann, *Geistliches Schauspiel*, 2834, 2844.
19. Ibid., 1234.
20. Ruh, *Deutsche Literatur des Mittelalters*, 8: 911–13.
21. Wolfgang F. Michael, *Frühformen der deutschen Bühne*. Schriften der Gesellschaft für Theatergeschichte 62 (Berlin, 1963), 84f.

22. Neumann, *Geistliches Schauspiel*, 2524.

23. Ibid., 2099.

24. Simon, *Anfänge des weltlichen deutschen Schauspiels*, 243.

25. Stephen K. Wright, *The Vengeance of Our Lord: Medieval Dramatizations of the Destruction of Jerusalem* (Toronto, 1989), 68–96.

26. Ruh, *Deutsche Literatur des Mittelalters*, 7: 120, 123.

27. Neumann, *Geistliches Schauspiel*, 1532.

28. Ruh, *Deutsche Literatur des Mittelalters*, 5: 1098.

29. Neumann, *Geistliches Schauspiel*, 3369.

30. Ibid., 2332.

31. Glenn Ehrstine, *Theater, Culture, and Community in Reformation Bern, 1523–1555* (Leiden, Boston, Cologne, 2002), 38.

32. Neumann, *Geistliches Schauspiel*, 2527.

33. Ibid., 211–12, 541, 543.

34. Ibid., 1050.

35. Ibid., 2494.

36. Simon, *Anfänge des weltlichen deutschen Schauspiels*, 477–85.

37. Ruh, *Deutsche Literatur des Mittelalters*, 7: 98.

38. Neumann, *Geistliches Schauspiel*, 2527.

39. Ibid., 541.

40. Ruh, *Deutsche Literatur des Mittelalters*, 5: 364–8.

41. Neumann, *Geistliches Schauspiel*, 3372.

42. Ibid., 1252, 1254.

43. Simon, *Anfänge des weltlichen deutschen Schauspiels*, 442.

44. Neumann, *Geistliches Schauspiel*, 3013.

45. Ibid., 546, 597.

46. Ibid., 2116.

47. Ibid., 1907.

48. Ehrstine, *Theater, Culture and Community*, 17.

49. Wright, *Vengeance of Our Lord*, 29.

50. Neumann, *Geistliches Schauspiel*, 1511, 1517, 1537.

51. Ibid., 1510, 1522.

52. Ruh, *Deutsche Literatur des Mittelalters*, 5: 447.

53. Neumann, *Geistliches Schauspiel*, 1483.

54. Simon, *Anfänge des weltlichen deutschen Schauspiels*, 168.

55. Ibid., 78.

56. Ruh, *Deutsche Literatur des Mittelalters*, 1:265.

57. Klaus Wolf, *Kommentar zur 'Frankfurter Dirigierrolle' und zum 'Frankfurter Passionsspiel'* (Tübingen, 2002), 82–6, 215, 273–9.

58. Wolf, *Kommentar*, 291–3.

59. Neumann, *Geistliches Schauspiel*, 3142–3.

60. James S. Shapiro, *Oberammergau: The Troubling Story of the World's Most Famous Passion Play* (New York, 2000).

61. Neumann, *Geistliches Schauspiel*, 2650

62. Ibid., 50

63. Ibid., 2647/1.

64. Ibid., 2371.

65. Ibid., 3714.

66. Ibid., 3737.

67. Shapiro, *Oberammergau*, 65–70.

68. Ibid., 114f., 120.

69. Ibid., 11.

70. Andreas Thomasberger (ed.), *Hugo von Hofmannsthal, Jedermann. Das Spiel vom Sterben des reichen Mannes* (Stuttgart: 2000), 81–93; Martin Stevens, 'The Restaging of Everyman: Hofmannsthal at Salzburg', *Germanic Review* 48 (1973), 117–31.

Chapter 2

1. *The Oxford Dictionary of Art*, new edn (London, New York, Sydney, Toronto, 1999), 44.

2. See Ludwig Krapf and Christian Wagenknecht (eds.), *Stuttgarter Hoffeste. Text und Materialien zur höfischen Repräsentation im frühen 17. Jahrhundert*, 2 vols. (Tübingen, 1979).

3. See Hilde Haider-Pregler, 'Das Rossballett im Inneren Burghof zu Wien', *Maske und Kothurn* 15 (1969), 291–324.

4. George W. Brandt (ed.), *German and Dutch Theatre, 1600–1848* (Cambridge, 1993), 44–5.

5. See Horst Richter, *Johann Oswald Harms. Ein deutscher Theaterdekorateur des Barock* (Emsdetten, 1963).

6. See Barnard Hewitt (ed.), *The Renaissance Stage: Documents of Serlio, Sabbattini and Furttenbach* (Coral Gables, 1958).

7. Brandt, *German and Dutch Theatre*, 25–6.

8. See Heinz Kindermann, *Theatergeschichte Europas*, vol. 3 (Salzburg, 1959), 500–3.

9. Johannes Müller, *Das Jesuitendrama in den Ländern deutscher Zunge*, Schriften zur deutschen Literatur, 2 vols. (Augsburg, 1930), vol. 1, 34–5.

10. Ibid., vol. 1, 19.

11. Ibid., vol. 2, 106.

12. Evi Butzer, *Die Anfänge der jiddischen* purim shpiln *in ihrem literarischen und kulturgeschichtlichen Kontext* (Hamburg, 2003), 21–2.

13. Reprinted in Willi Flemming (ed.), *Das Ordensdrama*, Barockdrama, vol. 2 (Leipzig, 1930).

14. See Artur Kutscher, *Das Salzburger Barocktheater* (Vienna, Leipzig, Munich, 1924) for a history of the Salzburg Benedictine theatre.

15. Available in German translation in Alexander Rudin, *Abhandlung über die Schauspielkunst* (Bern, Munich, 1975).

16. Brandt, *German and Dutch Theatre*, 57–61.

17. Willi Flemming, *Andreas Gryphius: Eine Monographie* (Stuttgart, Berlin, Cologne, Mainz, 1965), 43.

18. The edition of *Carolus Stuardus*, ed. Hugh Powell (Leicester, 1955) is useful.
19. Flemming, *Andreas Gryphius*, 189–91.
20. See Erika A. Metzger and Michael M. Metzger, *Reading Andreas Gryphius: Critical Trends 1664–1993* (Columbia SC, 1994).
21. Peter Behnke and Hans Gert-Roloff (eds.), *Christian Weise. Dichter – Gelehrter – Pädagoge* (Bern, Berlin, Frankfurt, New York, Paris, Vienna, 1994).
22. Allardyce Nicoll, *The World of Harlequin* (Cambridge, 1963), 30, 35, 79, 192.
23. Brandt, *German and Dutch Theatre*, 47.
24. Albert Cohn, *Shakespeare in Germany in the Sixteenth and Seventeenth Centuries* (London, 1865), XL–LVIII.
25. Ibid., 155–235.
26. Ibid., 305–406.
27. Eike Pies, *Einem hocherfreuten Publikum wird heute präsentiret eine Kleine Chronik des Theaterzettels* (Hamburg and Dusseldorf, 1973), 11–14.
28. Ibid., 30–1.
29. Otto Rommel, *Die Alt-Wiener Volkskomödie: Ihre Geschichte vom barocken Welt-Theater bis zum Tode Nestroys* (Vienna, 1952), 345–51.

Chapter 3

1. W. H. Bruford, *Germany in the Eighteenth Century: The Social Background of the Literary Revival* (Cambridge, 1965), 7.
2. W. H. Bruford: *Theatre, Drama and Audience in Goethe's Germany* (London, 1950), 93.
3. Johann Joachim Winkelmann, *Kleine Schriften und Briefe* (Weimar, 1960), 44.
4. Johann Christoph Gottsched, 'Die Ähnlichkeit des Erdichteten, mit dem, was wirklich zu geschehen pflegt', *Versuch einer kritischen Dichtkunst vor die Deutschen* (Leipzig, 1751; facsimile repr. Darmstadt, 1962) 198.
5. Johann Christoph Gottsched, *Schriften zur Literatur*, ed. H. Steinmetz (Stuttgart, 1972), 5.
6. Gotthold Ephraim Lessing, *Gesammelte Werke*, ed. Paul Rilla, 10 vols. (Berlin, 1968), vol. 6, 377.
7. Lessing, *Werke*, vol. 9, 157.
8. Michael Patterson, *The First German Theatre: Schiller, Goethe, Kleist and Büchner in Performance* (New York and London, 1990), 18.
9. Simon Williams, *German Actors of the Eighteenth and Nineteenth Centuries: Idealism, Romanticism and Realism* (Westport, 1985), 18.
10. Ibid., 16.
11. Patterson, *First German Theatre*, 161.
12. Bruford, *Theatre, Drama and Audience*, 278.
13. Johann Wolfgang von Goethe, *Werke* ser. IV vol.13, 130, letter 3786.
14. For a complete translation, see Marvin Carlson, *Goethe and the Weimar Theater* (Ithaca, 1978), 309–18.
15. Williams, *German Actors*, 47.
16. Lesley Sharpe, *Friedrich Schiller, Drama, Thought and Politics* (Cambridge, 1991), 48.

17. Ibid., 89.
18. E. L. Stahl, *Friedrich Schiller's Drama* (Oxford, 1954), 32.
19. T. J. Reed: *The Classical Centre: Goethe and Weimar, 1775–1832* (London, 1980) 149.
20. Johann Friedrich Schiller, *Sämtliche Werke*, 16 vols. (Stuttgart and Berlin, 1904/5), vol. 11, 90.
21. John Prudhoe, *The Theatre of Goethe and Schiller* (Totowa, NJ, 1973), 21.
22. Stahl, *Friedrich Schiller*, 64.
23. David G. John, 'From extemporization to text', *Momentum Dramaticum*, ed. Linda Dietrick and David G. John (Waterloo, Ont., 1990), 124.
24. Friedrich Schiller, *Werke*, 4 vols. (Leipzig, 1962), vol. 1, 750.
25. Bruford, *Theatre, Drama and Audience*, 115.
26. Schiller, *Werke* (Leipzig, 1962), vol. 7, 750–1.

Chapter 4

1. Adolf Winds, *Der Schauspieler in seiner Entwicklung von Mysterien zum Kammerspiel* (Berlin, 1919), 71.
2. Johann Friedrich Löwen, *Geschichte des deutschen Theaters* (Hamburg, 1766; repr. ed. Heinrich Stumcke, Berlin, 1905).
3. See Simon Williams, *Shakespeare on the German Stage* (Cambridge, 1990), 81–7, for an account of Schröder's adaptations of Shakespeare.
4. Fritz Jonas (ed.), *Schillers Briefe*, 7 vols. (Stuttgart, 1892), letter 1382, vol. 5, 431.
5. Eduard Genast, *Aus dem Tagebuche eines alten Schauspielers* (Leipzig, 1865), I, 113.
6. Carl August Hugo Burckhardt, *Das Repertoire des Weimarischen Theater unter Goethes Leitung* (Leipzig, 1891).
7. Carl Zelter, *Briefwechsel zwischen Goethe und Zelter* (Berlin, 1833), I, 84.
8. Quoted in S. Troizkij, *Karl Seydelmann: Die Anfänge der realistischen Schauspielkunst* (Berlin, 1949), 98.
9. Georg Witkowski, *The German Drama of the Nineteenth Century*, tr. L. E. Horning (New York, 1909: repr. 1968), 71.
10. Fredrich Hebbel, *Werke*, 5 vols., ed. Gerhard Fricke, Werner Keller & Karl Pörnbacher (Munich, 1963), vol. 1, 308.
11. Friedrich Hebbel, *Gesammelte Ausgabe*, 20 vols. (Bern: 1970), 21, 347–9.
12. Rudolph Lothar, *Das Wiener Burgtheater* (Vienna, 1934), 163.
13. See Ann Marie Koller, *The Theater Duke* (Stanford, 1984), 85–114 for a detailed description of the Meininger production technique.
14. See John Osborne, *The Naturalist Drama in Germany* (Manchester, 1971), 56–74 for an account of the *Volksbühne* movement.

Chapter 5

1. Gotthold Ephraim Lessing, *Werke*, 3 vols. (Munich, n.d.), vol. 2, 861.
2. Heinrich Wilhelm von Gerstenberg, *Briefe über die Merkwürdigkeiten der Litteratur* (Schleswig & Leipzig, 1766–7 and Hamburg & Bremen, 1770; repr. Hildesheim & New York: Olms, 1971), 215–69.

3. Johann Wolfgang Goethe, *Sämtliche Werke*, 21 vols., ed. Karl Richter *et al.* (Munich, 2006), vol. 1.2, 414.

4. Johann Gottfried Herder, *Werke in Zwei Bänden*, ed. Karl-Gustav Gerold (Munich: n.d [1953]), vol. 7, 884.

5. See Simon Williams, *Shakespeare on the German Stage, 1586–1914* (Cambridge, 1990), 69–81 for an account of the different versions of *Hamlet* played at the end of the eighteenth century.

6. Roger Paulin, *Ludwig Tieck: A Literary Biography* (Oxford, 1985), p. 114.

7. August Wilhelm von Schlegel, *A Course of Lectures on Dramatic Art and Literature* (London, 1846), 528–9.

8. Johann Peter Eckermann, *Gespräche mit Goethe in den letzten Jahren seines Lebens, 1823–1832*, 2 vols. (Leipzig, 1835), 348.

9. A good introduction to the generic problems of *Faust* is provided in Chapter 1 of Jane K. Brown's *Goethe's Faust: The German Tragedy* (Ithaca and London, 1986).

10. Schlegel, *A Course of Lectures*, 518–79.

11. Julius Petersen, *Goethes Faust auf der deutschen Bühne* (Leipzig, 1929), 15–21.

12. Friedrich Schiller, *Sämtliche Werke*, 5 vols. (Munich, n.d.), vol. 2, 383.

13. Marvin Carlson, *Goethe and the Weimar Theatre* (Ithaca and London: 1978), 233.

14. Ludwig Tieck, *Kritische Schriften* (Leipzig, 1852), 3: 64–5.

15. E. T. A. Hoffmann, *Gesammelte Werke*, 5 vols. (Berlin and Weimar, 1977), vol. 3, 387.

16. Ludwig Tieck, *Schriften*, 28 vols. (Berlin, 1828–54), vol. 5, 469.

17. Karl von Holtei, *Vierzig Jahre*, ed. Max Grube, 4th edn (Schweidnotz, 1898), 1, 74.

18. Williams, *German Actors of the Eighteenth and Nineteenth Centuries: Idealism, Romanticism and Realism* (Westport, 1985), 95.

19. Ludwig Tieck, *Ausgewählte kritische Schriften*, ed. Ernst Ribbat (Tübingen, 1975), 1–38.

20. Richard Wagner, 'Remarks on Performing the Opera *The Flying Dutchman*', in *Judaism in Music and Other Essays*, tr. William Ashton Ellis (London, 1907; repr. 1995), 209.

21. Richard Wagner, 'Beethoven,' *Actor and Singers*, tr. Ellis, 104–5.

22. Max Grube, *Adalbert Matkowsky* (Berlin, 1909), 13.

23. Otto Brahm, *Theater, Dramatiker, Schauspieler*, ed. Hugo Fetting (Berlin, 1961), 139.

24. Erich Kober, *Josef Kainz: Mensch unter Masken* (Vienna, 1948), 295.

Chapter 6

1. *Pace* Ladislaus Löb in Ronald Hayman, ed., *The German Theatre* (London, 1975) 80, who makes a case for what he describes as 'a masterpiece of Realism'.

2. See Edward McInnes, *Das deutsche Drama im 19. Jahrhundert* (Berlin, 1983), 32.

3. Ibid., 29.

4. A critique of Volker Klotz's categorisation of 'open' and 'closed' forms in drama can be found in John Guthrie, *Lenz and Büchner: Studies in Dramatic Form* (Frankfurt-am-Main and New York, 1984).

5. See Peter Stein, *Epochenproblem Vormärz (1815–1848)* (Stuttgart, 1974) for a discussion of periodisation and definitions between 1815 and 1848.

402 | NOTES TO PAGES 156–84

6. Hartmut Steinecke, *Literatur des Jungen Deutschland: Entwicklungen, Tendenze, Texte* (Berlin, 1982).

7. Herbert Kaiser, 'Zur Bedeutung des Willens im Drama Grabbes', in *Grabbe und die Dramatiker seiner Zeit*, ed. Detlev Kopp and Michael Vogt (Tübingen, 1990), 224.

8. Lothar Ehrlich, 'Grabbe und Büchner. Dramataturgische Tradition und Innovation,' ibid., 178.

9. Wolfgang Rothe, *Deutsche Revolutionsdramatik seit Goethe* (Darmstadt, 1989), 5.

10. McInnes, *Das deutsche Drama*, 65.

11. Ehrlich, 'Grabbe und Büchner', 171.

12. Maurice B. Benn, *Georg Büchner. The Drama of Revolt* (Cambridge, 1975), 18.

13. J. S. Styan, *Max Reinhardt* (Cambridge, 1982), 6.

Chapter 7

1. See Eduard Devrient, *Geschichte der deutschen Schauspielkunst* (Leipzig, 1848–1874), and Simon Williams, *Richard Wagner and Festival Theatre* (Westport, 1994, 36–7.

2. See Andrea Hofmann-Wellenhof, ' – *das Stück scheint für die Darstellung auf dieser Bühne nicht geeignet': Schriftsteller und ihre am Burgtheater eingerichten Theaterstücke 1850–1870* (Vienna, 1996). (Unless otherwise indicated, all translations are mine.)

3. See Inge Krengel-Strudthoff, 'Das antike Rom auf der Bühne und der Übergang vom gemalten zum plastischen Bühnenbild', in *Bühnenformen – Bühnenräume – Bühnendekorationen* (Berlin, 1974).

4. For an excellent impression of the backdrops painted by the Brückner brothers for the Meiningen productions, see www.meiningermuseen-thueringen.de/mmuseeneng/kerntext.html#ziel2.

5. See Christopher Innes, *Edward Gordon Craig – A Vision of Theatre* (Amsterdam, 1998), 13.

6. Quoted Christopher Innes (ed.), *A Sourcebook on Naturalist Theatre* (London, 2000), 77.

7. Richard Wagner, *Das Bühnenfestspielhaus zu Bayreuth* (Leipzig, 1873), quoted Herbert Barth (ed.), *Der Festspielhügel* (Munich, 1973), 11. For a fuller discussion of the Bayreuth Festspielhaus and its stage, see Williams, *Richard Wagner and Festival Theatre*, 117ff.

8. For a more detailed discussion of Appia's connection to Symbolism, see Richard Beacham, *Adolphe Appia: Theatre Artist* (Cambridge, 1987), 3–5.

9. Souvenir Programme, Bayreuth: cit. Karl Reyle, 'Adolphe Appia and the New Stage', *American-German Review*, Aug–Sept. 1962, 19.

10. Letter, 25 November 1904, cit. Innes, *Edward Gordon Craig*, 110.

11. Quoted by J. L. Styan, *Max Reinhardt* (Cambridge, 1982), 35.

12. Arthur Kahane, 'Glossen zum Theater der Fünftausend', trans. Huntly Carter, *The Theatre of Max Reinhardt* (London: 1914), 112–73 and 124.

13. Hugo von Hofmannsthal, cited in Oliver M. Sayler, *Max Reinhardt and his Theatre* (New York, 1924), 25–6. For a detailed analysis of the *Jedermann* production, see Styan, *Max Reinhardt*, 86ff.

14. 'Das Theatre von Morgen', *Die Schaubühne* (11, 18, 25 May 1916), 453ff., 474ff. and 499ff.

15. Christopher Innes, *Erwin Piscator's Political Theatre: The Development of Modern German Drama* (Cambridge, 1972), 189–96.

16. Published as 'Notes to the Opera *The Rise and Fall of the City of Mahagonny*' in 1930.

17. Bertolt Brecht, *Werke 3, Stücke 3*, 30 vols., ed. Werner Hecht, Jan Kopf, Wertner Mittenzwei and Klaus-Detlef Müller (Berlin, Weimar and Frankfurt-am-Main, 1988). Translation from *The Exception and the Rule* in *The Jewish Wife and Other Plays*, tr. Eric Bentley (New York, 1965), 111.

18. 'Kann die heutige Welt durch Theater wiedergegeben werden?' ('Can the Present-day World be Reproduced by Means of Theatre?', 1955), in *Brecht on Theatre*, tr. John Willet (New York, 1964), 274–5.

19. See for example 'Vergnügungs-oder Lehrtheater?' ('Theatre for Pleasure or Theatre for Instruction?', 1936 – unpublished until *Schriften zum Theater*, 1957), in *Brecht on Theatre*, 73.

20. Ibid.

21. 'Notes to the *Threepenny Opera*', in *Brecht on Theatre*, 44.

22. Undated note (Brecht-Archiv 331/173), in *Brecht on Theatre*, 233.

23. Leo Lania, programme-essay, Piscator-Bühne 1927. See too Christopher Innes, 'Piscator's *Rasputin*' and Marianne Mildenberger, '*Rasputin*: A Technical Recreation', in *The Drama Review*, 22 No. 4 (T80), 83ff.

Chapter 8

1. Bertolt Brecht, 'Über Stoffe und Form', in Brecht, *Werke*, vol. 21.1, *Große kommentierte Berliner und Frankfurter Ausgabe*, ed. Werner Hecht, Jan Knopf, Werner Mittenzwei and Klaus-Detlef Müller (Berlin and Frankfurt/Main, 1992), 302–4, at 303.

Chapter 9

1. I am indebted to Katrin Wächter, Anna Lohse, and Hana Pecharová for their assistance in researching this essay. Translations from primary German texts are by Anna Lohse unless indicated otherwise.

2. Anthony D. Smith, *National Identity* (Reno, 1991), 11 and 13.

3. J. E. Schlegel, *Canut: Ein Trauerspiel*, ed. Horst Steinmetz (Stuttgart, 1967), 76.

4. G. E. Grimm and Frank R. Max (eds.), *Deutsche Dichter: Aufklärung und Empfindsamkeit* (Stuttgart, 1990), 3: 162.

5. *Geschichte der deutschen Literatur: Von den Anfängen bis zur Gegenwart*, H. de Boor und R. Newald. Sechster Band: *Aufklärung Sturm und Drang, Frühe Klassik*.

1740–1789, ed. S. A. Jørgensen, K. Bohnen, P. Ährgaard (Munich, 1990), 6: 248.

6. Ibid., 250.

7. Gotthold Ephraim Lessing, *Hamburgische Dramaturgie*, No. 14, in *Lessings Werke*, 20 vols. (Berlin, 1925) 5, 76.

8. Henry Hatfield, *Aesthetic Paganism in German Literature: From Winckelmann to the Death of Goethe* (Cambridge, MA, 1964) 7.

9. See Herder, *Sämmtliche Werke*, ed B. Suphan, 33 vols. (Berlin, 1877–1913), 2: *passim*.

10. Tacitus, *Complete Works of Tacitus*, ed. Alfred John Church, William Jackson Brodribb and Lisa Cerrato (New York, repr. 1942).

11. A. W. Schlegel, *A Course of Lectures on Dramatic Art and Literature*, tr. John Black (London, 1846), 514–15.

12. C. M. Wieland, *Werke*, 3 vols. (Munich, 1967), 3: 478.

13. Schlegel, *A Course of Lectures*, 522.

14. Alain Finkielkraut, *The Defeat of the Mind*, tr. Judith Friedlander (New York, 1995), 9.

15. A. W. Schlegel, *Kritische Schriften und Briefe*, 7 vols. ed. Edgar Lohner (Stuttgart, 1966), 5: 34.

16. Schlegel, *A Course of Lectures*, 510.

17. M. Martersteig, *Die Protokolle des Mannheimer Nationaltheaters unter Dalberg aus den Jahren 1781–1789* (Mannheim: 1890), 259.

18. Schiller, *Werke*, 3 vols. (Munich, 1976), 1: 728.

19. Erika Fischer-Lichte, *History of European Drama and Theatre*, tr. Jo Riley (New York and London, 2002), 201.

20. Lothar Gal (ed.), *Milestones, Setbacks, Sidetracks: The Path to Parliamentary Democracy in Germany* (Berlin, 2003), 35.

21. Peter Sprengel, *Die inszenierte Nation: Deutsche Festspiele 1813–1913* (Tübingen, 1991), 19.

22. Ibid., 33.

23. See Donald Roy (ed.), *Theatre in Europe: A Documentary History, Romantic and Revolutionary Theatre, 1798–1860* (Cambridge, 2003), 284.

24. Sprengel, *Die inszenierte Nation*, 50.

25. Wolfgang Hardtwig, *Geschichtskultur und Wissenschaft* (München, 1990), 265–6.

26. George L. Mosse, *Nationalization of the Masses* (New York, 1975), 84.

27. Ibid., 88.

28. Ibid.

29. Heinz Kindermann, *Theatergeschichte Europas*, 10 vols. (Salzburg, 1965), vol. 7, 162.

30. Simon Williams, *German Actors of the Eighteenth and Nineteenth Centuries: Idealism, Romanticism and Realism* (Westport, CT, 1985), 146.

31. Kindermann, *Theatergeschichte*, vol. 7, 161.

32. Sprengel, *Die inszenierte Nation*, 55.

33. Ibid., 61.

34. Franz Büttner Pfänner zu Thal, 'Der deutsche St. Michael' (Leipzig, 1897).

35. Quoted in Harold C. Schonberg, *The Lives of the Great Composers* (New York, 1970), 256–7.
36. Albert Goldman and Evert Sprinchorn (eds.), *Wagner on Music and Drama* (London, 1970), 139.
37. Schonberg, *Lives of the Great Composers*, 264.
38. Mosse, *Nationalization of the Masses*, 10.
39. Richard Wagner, 'The Work of Art of the Future', in George W. Brandt, *Modern Theories of Drama: A Selection of Writings on Drama and Theatre, 1840–1990* (Oxford, 1998), 10.
40. George L. Mosse, *The Crisis of German Ideology: Intellectual Origins of the Third Reich* (New York, 1964), 81.
41. Frederic Spotts, *Bayreuth: A History of the Wagner Festival* (New Haven, 1994), 84.
42. Ibid., 131.
43. Ibid., 84.
44. John London (ed.), *Theatre under the Nazis* (Manchester, 2000), 7.
45. Ibid., 10.
46. Spotts, *Bayreuth*, 173.
47. London, *Theatre under the Nazis*, 12.
48. Thomas Eicher's *Spielanalyse der Deutschen Schauspieltheater 1929–1944* (Freie Universität, Berlin) summarised by Barbara Panse in 'Censorship in Nazi Germany', in *Fascism and Theatre: Comparative Studies on the Aesthetics and Politics of Performance in Europe, 1925–1945*, ed. Günter Berghaus (Providence and Oxford, 1996), 144.
49. Ibid., 147.
50. Ibid., 146.
51. London, *Theatre under the Nazis*, 23.
52. Mosse, *Nationalization of the Masses*, 103.
53. London, *Theatre under the Nazis*, 23; Panse/Berghaus, *Fascism and Theatre*, 153–4.
54. London, *Theatre under the Nazis*, 25.
55. According to John London, 'Proposals for a new national theatre under the Nazis, such as Richard Elsner's *Die deutsche Nationalbühne*, were full of references to previous German writers' aspirations to the supposedly identical notion (of a national theatre)' (*Theatre under the Nazis*, 48, note 72). See also Richard Elsner, *Die deutsche Nationalbühne* (Berlin: Heyer, 1934), Series 2, Deutsche Zukunft.
56. Berghaus, *Fascism and Theatre*, 300.
57. London, *Theatre under the Nazis*, 28.
58. See William Niven, 'The Birth of Nazi Drama?' in London *Theatre under the Nazis*, 73–90.
59. Mosse, *Crisis of German Ideology*, 81.
60. Erik Levi, 'Opera in the Nazi Period', in London, *Theatre under the Nazis*, 145.
61. Erik Levi, 'Towards an Aesthetic of Fascist Opera', in Berghaus, *Fascism and Theatre*, 262.
62. Ibid., 266–7.

63. London, *Theatre under the Nazis*, 12.

64. In Berghaus, *Fascism and Theatre*, 159.

65. Ibid., 143.

66. Ibid., 60.

67. Ibid., 59.

68. Spotts, *Bayreuth*, 221.

69. Ibid., 226.

70. Ibid., 265.

71. Ibid., 269.

72. Ernst Schumacher, in *Freitag. Die Ost-West-Wochenzeitung*, 20.07.01, available at www.freitag.de/2001/30/01301501.php

73. Sprengel, *Die inszenierte Nation*, 9.

74. Ibid.

75. Ibid., 10.

76. Ibid.

77. See Jutta Wolfert, *Theatertexte zwischen Medien und Revolution, 1989–1996* (Berlin, 2004).

78. Stefanie Carp, *Slow Life is Long: On the Theatre of Christoph Marthaler*, www.kunstenfestivaldesarts.be/en/2003/art/art02.html, accessed 21 January 2006.

79. Hans-Thies Lehmann, 'Theater des Konflikts: EinarSchleef@post-110901.de', www.theaterderzeit.de/content/arbuech11b.php, accessed 17 July 2006, translated by Katrin Wächter.

80. Moray McGowan, 'German Theatre in the Late 1990s', www.new-books-in-german.com/featur18.htm, accessed 17 July 2006.

81. Maike Schiller, 'Deutsche Wurzelbehandlung', *Hamburger Abendblatt*, 3 September 2004.

82. Ronald Meyer-Arlt, 'Wurzelgemüse, süss-sauer', *Hannoversche Allgemeine Zeitung*, 4 September 2004.

Chapter 10

1. Peter Jelavich, *Munich and Theatrical Modernism: Politics, Playwriting, and Performance, 1890–1914* (Cambridge, MA, 1985), 198.

2. Georg Fuchs, *Revolution in the Theatre: Conclusions Concerning the Munich Artists' Theatre*, tr. Constance Connor Kuhn (Ithaca, 1959), 44.

3. Jelavich, *Munich and Theatrical Modernism*, 196.

4. Fuchs, *Revolution in the Theatre*, 67.

5. Kenneth Macgowan, *The Theatre of Tomorrow* (New York, 1921), 189.

6. Mordecai Gorelik, *New Theatres for Old* (New York, 1940), 286.

7. Adolphe Appia, 'Der Saal des Prinzregenten-Theaters', *Die Gesellschaft* 18 (1902), 200.

8. Ibid., 203.

9. Mary Elizabeth Tallon, 'Appia's Theatre at Hellerau', *Theatre Journal* 36 (1984), 496.

10. 'Eurhythmics and the Theatre', in Richard C. Beacham, *Adolphe Appia: Artist and Visionary of the Modern Theatre* (Chur, 1994), 129.

11. 'Music and the Art of Theatre', in Beacham, *Appia*, 54.

12. 'Ideas on a Reform of Our *Mise en Scène*', in Beacham, *Appia*, 18.

13. 'Music and the Art of Theatre', in Beacham, *Appia*, 55.

14. Cited in Tallon, 'Appia's Theatre', 498.

15. Max Reinhardt, 'The Theatre Through Reinhardt's Eyes', in *Max Reinhardt and His Theatre*, ed. Oliver M. Sayler (New York, 1926), 64.

16. Ibid., 24–5.

17. Cited by Yvonne Shafer in 'Preface' to Anthony Hostetter, *Max Reinhardt's Grosses Schauspielhaus – Its Artistic Goals, Planning and Operation, 1910–1933* (Lewiston: 2003), ii-iii.

18. Sayler, *Max Reinhardt*, 57.

19. Cited by Julius Posener, *Hans Poelzig: Reflections on his Life and Work*. ed. Kristin Feireiss, tr. Christine Charlesworth (New York, 1992), 129.

20. Oskar Schlemmer, László Moholy-Nagy, and Farkas Molnar, *Die Bühne im Bauhaus* (Munich, 1925, repr. Mainz, 1965), 85.

21. Ibid., 54–5.

22. Ibid., 85.

23. Ibid., 89.

24. Ibid., 74.

25. Walter Gropius, 'Theaterbau,' *Reale Accademia d'Italia* 13 (1935), 12.

26. Walter Gropius, 'Nachwort: Die Aufgaben der Bühne im Bauhaus', *Die Bühne im Bauhaus*, 91–2.

27. Colby H. Kullman and William C. Young (eds.), *Theatre Companies of the World: United States of America, Western Europe (excluding Scandinavia)* (Westport, CT, 1986), 578.

28. Erika Fischer-Lichte, *The Show and the Gaze of Theatre: A European Perspective*, ed. and tr. Jo Riley (Iowa City, 1997), 43.

29. Hans Schüler, 'Beitrag für das Programmheft der bühnentechnischen Tagung vom 27. bis 30. Juli 1959 in Mannheim von Dr. Schüler', 1–7. Archive of the Mannheim Nationaltheater, 4.

30. Hans Schüler, 'Gedanken des Intendanten zum Neubau des Nationaltheaters', 1–13. Archive of the Mannheim Nationaltheater, 7.

31. Schüler, 'Beitrag', 4.

32. Klaus Völker, 'New Theatre Buildings', in *The German Theatre: A Symposium*. ed. Ronald Hayman, tr. Nicholas Hern (London and New York, 1975), 241.

33. Fischer-Lichte, *The Show and the Gaze*, 57.

34. Johannes Birringer, *Theatre, Theory, Postmodernism* (Bloomington, 1991), 104.

35. Martin Graue, 'West German Scenography', *TDR* 28 (1984), 95–7.

Chapter 11

1. Quoted in Ernst Schumacher, 'Szenographie der Veränderung, Szenographie in Veränderung', in *Maske und Kothurn*, 27 (1981), 361.

2. *Bühne und bildende Kunst im XX. Jahrhundert. Maler und Bildhauer arbeiten für das Theater*, ed. Henning Rischbieter (Velber bei Hannover, 1968), 9.

3. Georg Fuchs, theatre reformer and propagandist for the Munich Künstlertheater in 1914. Citation from Paul Marx, 'Shakespeare und die modernen Bühnen probleme (seit 1907)', in *Shakespeare Jahrbuch*, 51 (1915), 61.

4. See *Adolphe Appia 1862–1928, acteur – espace – lumière*, ed. Denis Bablet and Marie-Louise Bablet (Zurich, 1981), 11–13.

5. Denis Bablet, *The Revolutions of Stage Design in the 20th Century* (Paris and New York, 1976), 45.

6. Quoted by Günther Rühle, '*Der Sommernachtstraum* Max Reinhardts', in *Shakespeare Jahrbuch* (West), 1976, 102.

7. Hugh Morrison, 'Max Reinhardt and Ernst Stern', in *Max Reinhardt: The Oxford Symposium*, ed. Margaret Jacobs and John Warren (Oxford, 1986), 63.

8. Gisela Prossnitz, 'Bühnenformen und Spielstätten bei Reinhardt', ibid., 75.

9. Michael Patterson, 'Reinhardt and Theatrical Expressionism – or the Second Wall Removed', ibid., 53.

10. See Richard Hamann and Jost Hermand, *Stilkunst um 1900* (Berlin, 1967), 67–81.

11. Quoted by Julius Bab in *Das Theater der Gegenwart. Geschichte der dramatischen Bühne seit 1870* (Leipzig, 1928), 178.

12. 'Das Theater. Ein Vortrag' (1928), in Hugo Fetting (ed.), *Leopold Jessner. Schriften: Theater der zwanziger Jahre* (Berlin, 1979), 98.

13. Hans Peter Doll and Günther Erken, *Theater: Eine illustrierte Geschichte des Schauspiels* (Stuttgart, 1985), 107.

14. See *Die Maler und das Theater im 20. Jahrhundert*, exhibition catalogue published by Schirn Kunsthalle (Frankfurt, 1986), ed. Denis Bablet and Erika Billeter, *passim*.

15. Christopher Baugh, 'Brecht and stage design,' in *The Cambridge Companion to Brecht*, ed. Peter Thomson and Glendyr Sacks (Cambridge, 1994), 236f.

16. Gustav Rudolf Sellner, *Theatralische Landschaft* (Bremen, 1962), 198.

17. Michael Patterson, *Peter Stein: Germany's Leading Theatre Director* (Cambridge, 1981), 149.

18. See Robert Weimann, 'Shakespeare on the Modern Stage: Past Significance and Present Meaning', *Shakespeare Survey* 20 (1967).

19. Martin Graue, 'West German Scenography', in *TDR*, vol. 28 (summer 1984), 81.

20. Ibid., 82.

21. Quoted by Nora Eckert, *Das Bühnenbild im 20. Jahrhundert* (Berlin 1998), 170.

22. Graue, 'West German Scenography', 85.

23. Ibid., 92.

24. Eckert, *Bühnenbild*, 180.

25. Ibid., 143.

26. Sigrid Neef, *Das Theater der Ruth Berghaus* (Berlin, 1989), 19.

27. Maik Hamburger, 'Shakespeare on the Stages of the German Democratic Republic', in Wilhelm Hortmann, *Shakespeare on the German Stage: The Twentieth Century* (Cambridge, 1998), 429.

28. Ibid., 430–7.

29. Eckert, *Bühnenbild*, 115

Chapter 12

1. Gründgens, *cit*. Knut Lennartz in *Theater, Künstler und die Politik. 150 Jahre Deutscher Bühnenverein* (Berlin, 1996),122. All translations from the German are mine.

2. Rolf Hochhuth, 'Soll das Theater die heutige Welt darstellen?', in Helmut Kreuzer (ed.), *Deutsche Dramaturgien der Sechziger Jahre* (Tübingen, 1974), 38.

3. Heinar Kipphardt, *In der Sache J. Robert Oppenheimer: Ein Stück und seine Geschichte*, ed. Uwe Naumann (Reinbek bei Hamburg, 1987), 232.

4. Michael Patterson, *German Theatre Today: Post-War Theatre in West and East Germany, Austria and Northern Switzerland* (London, 1976), 88.

5. Franz Xaver Kroetz, *Heimarbeit*, in Kroetz, *Heimarbeit: Stücke*, vol. 2 (Hamburg, 1996), 9.

6. Ibid., 12.

7. Franz Xaver Kroetz, *Nicht Fisch nicht Fleisch*, in Kroetz, *Drei Stücke*, ed. Jochen Ziller (Berlin, 1986), 6.

8. Peter Handke, *Kaspar*, in Handke, *Stücke*, vol. 1 (Frankfurt/Main, 1972), 99–198, at 111.

9. Peter Handke, 'Brecht?', *Volkszeitung*, 13 July 1990, 13.

10. Rainald Goetz, 'Lieber Diederich', *Spectaculum*, 59 (1995), 284.

11. Often incorrectly translated as *The Scab*.

12. The professional première of *Die Umsiedlerin*, renamed *Die Bauern* (*The Peasants*) for tactical reasons, was in Berlin in 1976.

13. Bertolt Brecht, '[Institut ohne Zuschauer]', in Rainer Steinweg (ed.), *Brechts Modell der Lehrstücke* (Frankfurt/Main, 1976), 54–5.

14. Heiner Müller, 'Literatur muß dem Theater Widerstand leisten', in Müller, *Gesammelte Irrtümer*, vol. 1 (Frankfurt/Main, 1986), 18.

15. Erich Honecker, '[Schlußwort Erich Honeckers auf der 4. Tagung des ZK der SED Dezember 1971, Auszug]', in Gisela Rüß (ed.), *Dokumente zur Kunst-, Literatur- und Kulturpolitik der SED 1971–1974*, (Stuttgart, 1976), 287–8.

16. 'Die Kipper', scene 4, in Volker Braun *Texte in zeitlicher Folge*, vol.1 (Halle/Leipzig, 1990).

17. Albert Ostermaier, 'Bild-Regie. Eine Vorbemerkung', in Ostermaier, *The Making of Radio Noir. Stücke* (Frankfurt/Main, 1999), 15.

Chapter 13

1. Berliner Ensemble/Helene Weigel (ed.), *Theaterarbeit. 6 Aufführungen des Berliner Ensembles*, text by Ruth Berlau, Bertolt Brecht, Claus Hubalek, Peter Palitzsch and Käthe Rülicke (Berlin, revised third edition 1967).

2. Kenneth Tynan, *A View of the English Stage 1944–63* (London, 1975), 196.

3. Berliner Ensemble/Weigel, *Theaterarbeit*, 93.

4. Bernd Mahl, *Brechts und Monks Urfaust – Inszenierung mit dem Berliner Ensemble 1952/53* (Stuttgart and Zurich, 1986), 29f.

5. Manfred Leier, quoted in Adolf Dresen, *Wieviel Freiheit braucht die Kunst? Reden. Briefe. Verse. Spiele 1964 bis 1999*, ed. Maik Hamburger (Berlin, 2000), 83.

6. Peter Brook, *The Empty Space* (Harmondsworth, 1972), 43.

7. Berthold Viertel, *Schriften zum Theater* (Munich, 1970), 266f.

8. Ernst Wendt, quoted in Henning Rischbieter, *Durch den eisernen Vorhang. Theater im geteilten Deutschland 1945–1990* (Berlin, 1999), 81.

9. Mechthild Lange, *Peter Zadek* (Frankfurt/Main, 1989), 59.

10. Michael Patterson, *Peter Stein. Germany's Leading Theatre Director* (Cambridge, 1981), 21.

11. *Theater 1993*, Jahrbuch der Zeitschrift *Theater heute* (Seelze, 1993), 20.

12. Goethe *et al.*, *Torquato Tassso. Regiebuch der Bremer Inszenierung*, ed. Volker Canaris (Frankfurt/Main, 1970), 135.

13. Benjamin Henrichs, *Beruf: Kritiker. Rezensionen, Polemiken, Liebeserklärungen* (Munich and Vienna, 1978), 69.

14. *Der Spiegel*, 20 December 1976, 132.

15. Klaus Dermutz, *Die Außenseiterwelten des Peter Zadek* (Salzburg, 2001), 41.

16. Georg Hensel, *Spiel's noch einmal. Das Theater der achtziger Jahre* (Frankfurt/Main, 1990), 20.

17. Julius Bab, *Das Theater im Lichte der Soziologie* (Leipzig, 1931; repr. Stuttgart 1974), 151.

18. Ivan Nagel: 'Die Kinder an die Macht', *Frankfurter Allgemeine Zeitung*, Bilder und Zeiten No. 155, 6 July 1996, 1.

19. Heiner Müller, *Gesammelte Irrtümer. Interviews und Gespräche* (Frankfurt/Main, 1986), 18.

20. Alexander Lang: *Abenteuer Theater*, ed. Martin Linzer (Berlin, 1987), 96.

21. Michael Raab, *Wolfgang Engel* (Frankfurt/Main, 1991), 40.

22. Ibid., 46. Adolf Dresen had planned a production of *Godot* at the Deutsches Theater in the 70s but a West German journalist overheard him discussing this in the Green Room and his premature disclosure thwarted the attempt.

23. Siegfried Wilzopolski, *Theater des Augenblicks. Die Theaterarbeit Frank Castorfs. Eine Dokumentation* (Berlin, 1992), 220.

24. Ibid., 193.

25. Peter von Becker, in *Theater 1990*, Jahrbuch der Zeitschrift *Theater heute* (Seelze, 1990), 60.

26. Dermutz, *Peter Zadek*, 41f.

27. Günther Rühle, 'German Theatre at the Beginning of the New Century', in *The Actor Today. Light and Shadow, the 5th European Theatre Forum 2000, du théâtre*, Special Issue, No. 12 (February 2001), 235.

28. *KulturSPIEGEL*, 27 October 2003.

Chapter 14

1. Johann Peter Eckermann, *Gespräche mit Goethe in den letzten Jahren seines Lebens*, ed. Otto Schönberger (Stuttgart, 1994), 238 (tr. Jo Riley).

2. Letter to Josef Stanislas Zauper, 7 September 1821, *Goethes Werke*, ed. Großherzogin Sophie von Sachsen, 143 vols. (Weimar, 1887–1919, repr. Munich 1987), 4, 35, 74f.

3. W. H. Bruford, *Theatre, Drama and Audience in Goethe's Germany* (London, 1950), 319.

4. 4 February 1811, quoted in Walter Hinck, *Goethe – Mann des Theaters* (Goettingen, 1982), 19.

5. Ibid., 14.

6. J. W. Goethe, *Sämtliche Werke*, 18 vols. (Zurich, Artemis 1961–66) , vol. 11, 205.

7. Tag- und Jahreshefte, in Goethe, *Werke*, 4, 937.

8. Reinhart Meyer, *Bibliographia dramatica et dramaticorum* (Tübingen, 1986), 28 vols have been published, the last one, for 1772, in 2005.

9. Letter of 25 May 1778, in G. E. Lessing, *Sämtliche Werke*, ed. Karl Lachmann, 3rd amended edn., 23 vols. (Leipzig/Berlin, 1886–1924, repr. 1968), 18, 24.

10. Unidentified review with the date 4 February 1912 from the archive of the Vienna Theatre Museum.

11. 'Why Lot's Wife Could not Have Sat out "Sumurun". The pedestrians on that bridge would have aroused her curiosity so that she would have turned into twenty pillars of salt'. Unidentified review from the archive of the Vienna Theatre Museum.

12. E. K., *Frankfurter Zeitung* (1914).

13. Richard Elchinger, *Münchner Neueste Nachrichten*, 11 July 1914.

14. Bertolt Brecht-Archiv, *Bestandsverzeichnis des literarischen Nachlasses*. 4 vols. ed. Herta Ramthum (Berlin/Weimar, 1969–1973), 158/44 (tr. Jo Riley).

15. Herbert Ihering, *Von Reinhardt bis Brecht: Vier Jahrzehnte Theater und Film*, 3 vols. (Berlin, 1961), 3, 95 f.

16. Bertolt Brecht, *Gesammelte Werke*, 20 vols (Frankfurt Main, 1967), 16, 626.

17. Ibid., 621.

18. Sergej Eisenstein, "Hinter der Leinwand", in: *Nô – Vom Genius Japans*, ed. and introd. by Eva Hesse (Zurich, 1963), 264–82.

19. *Goethes Werke* (1887–1919), 47, 260. Tr. as "Aesthetic Education of a Playgoer" in *A Source Book in Theatrical History*, ed. A. M. Nagler (New York, 1959), 438.

20. *Goethes Werke* (1887–1919), 40, 108.

21. Ibid., 36, 278f.

22. Richard Wagner, *Gesammelte Schriften und Dichtungen*, 2nd edn., 10 vols. (Leipzig, 1887–1888), 4, 196.

23. Ibid., 192.

24. Ibid., 186.

25. Richard Wagner, *Gesammelte Schriften*, ed. Julius Kapp, 14 vols. (Leipzig, 1914), 9, 340.

26. Paul Goldman on Reinhardt's production of *Oedipus Rex*, *Neue Freie Presse*, November 1910.

27. *Goethes Werke* (1887–1919), 40, 73–85.

28. Johann Christoph Gottsched, *Schriften zur Literatur*, ed. Horst Steinmetz (Stuttgart, 1972), 5.

29. Gotthold Ephraim Lessing, *Hamburgische Dramaturgie*, ed. Klaus L. Berghahn (Stuttgart, 1981), 40.

30. *Schillers Werke*, Nationalausgabe (Weimar, 1962), 20, 95.

31. Quoted in Hilde Haider-Pregler, *Des sittlichen Bürgers Abendschule* (Vienna and Munich, 1980), 7.

32. 'Was wir bringen', 16. Auftritt, Weimarer Ausgabe, vol. 13, 73.

33. *Schillers Werke*, 20, 312.

34. Ibid., 316.

35. Ibid., 323.

36. Ibid., 359.

37. Ibid., 376.

38. Ibid., 312.

39. Richard Wagner: *Briefe*, ed. Hanjo Kesting (Munich/Zurich, 1983), 224–6.

40. Wagner, *Gesammelte Schriften*, 6, 273.

41. Peter Behrens, *Feste des Lebens und der Kunst* (Leipzig, 1900).

42. Georg Fuchs, '*Die Schaubühne – ein Fest des Lebens*', *Wiener Rundschau*, III, 1899.

43. Quoted in Arthur Kahane, *Tagebuch des Dramaturgen* (Berlin: Cassirer, 1928), 119.

44. See Erika Fischer-Lichte, *Theatre, Sacrifice, Ritual: Exploring Forms of Political Theatre* (London and New York, 2005).

45. Erika Fischer-Lichte, *The Transformative Power of Performance: A New Aesthetic* (London and New York, 2008).

Chapter 15

1. Hans-Thies Lehmann, *Postdramatic Theatre*, tr. and intro. Karen Jürs-Munby (London and New York, 2006), 25.

2. Günther Rühle, 'Verwandlungen des Theaters – Die Zerstörung der Zeitmaschine', *Berliner Zeitung*, 25 May 2007.

3. Lehmann, *Postdramatic Theatre*, 52.

4. Gabriele Klein, 'Der entzogene Text: Performativität im zeitgenössichen Theater', in *Ulrike Maria Stuart*, ed. Ortrud Gutjahr (Würzburg, 2007), 65.

5. See chapter 14.

6. Matthias Heine in *Die Welt*, 3 December 2006.

7. 'Esther Slevogt", 'Offene Bürgerwunde', www.nachtkritik.de, 20 May 2007.

8. See for instance: Gerhard Stadelmaier, 'Ein Angriff', *Frankfurter Allgemeine Zeitung*, 18 February 2006 and Christine Dössel, 'Deckname Beckett', *Süddeutsche Zeitung* 25–26 March 2006.

Select bibliography

General histories

Brandt, George W. (ed.), *German and Dutch Theatre, 1600–1848*, Cambridge, 1993

Devrient, Eduard, *Geschichte der deutschen Schauspielkunst*, ed. Rolf Kabel and Christoph Trilse, Berlin, 1967

Fischer-Lichte, Erika, *History of European Drama and Theatre*, tr. Jo Riley, New York and London, 2002

The Show and the Gaze of Theatre: A European Perspective. ed. and tr. Jo Riley, Iowa City, 1997

Kurze Geschichte des deutschen Theaters, Tübingen, 1993

Hayman, Ronald (ed.), *The German Theatre: A Symposium*, London, 1975

Kindermann, Heinz, *Theatergeschichte Europas*, 10 vols. Salzburg, 1957–74

Knudsen, Hans, *Deutsche Theatergeschichte*, Stuttgart, 1959

Michael, Friedrich and Hans Daiber, *Geschichte des deutschen Theaters*, Frankfurt, 1990

Patterson, Michael, *German Theatre: A Bibliography from the Beginning to 1995*, New York, 1996

Roy, Donald (ed). *Romantic and Revolutionary Theatre 1789–1860*, Cambridge, 2003

Rühle, Gunther, *Theater in Deutschland 1887–1945*, Frankfurt Main, 2007

Stahl, Ernst Leopold, *Shakespeare und das deutsche Theater*, Stuttgart, 1947

Warrack, John, *German Opera: From the Beginnings to Wagner*, Cambridge, 2001

Williams, Simon, *Shakespeare on the German Stage, Vol. 1. 1586–1914*, Cambridge, 1990

Medieval theatre

Borcherdt, Hans Heinrich, *Das europäische Theater im Mittelalter und in der Renaissance*, 2nd edn., Reinbek bei Hamburg, 1969

Ehrstine, Glenn, *Theater, Culture, and Community in Reformation Bern, 1523–1555*, Leiden, Boston and Cologne, 2002

Neumann, Bernd, *Geistliches Schauspiel im Zeugnis der Zeit. Zur Aufführung mittelalterlicher religiöser Dramen im deutschen Sprachgebiet*, 2 vols. Munich and Zurich, 1987

Scheel, Katja (ed.), *Et respondeat: Studien zum deutschen Theater des Mittelalters*, Leuven 2002

Shapiro, James S., *Oberammergau: The Troubling Story of the World's Most Famous Passion Play*, New York, 2000

Simon, Eckehard, *Die Anfänge des weltlichen deutschen Schauspiels, 1370–1530: Untersuchung und Dokumentation*, Tübingen, 2003

Tydeman, William (ed.), *The Medieval European Stage, 500–1500*, Cambridge, 2001

Sixteenth- and seventeenth-century theatre

Baur-Heinhold, Margarete, *The Baroque Theatre*, New York, 1967

Cohn, Albert, *Shakespeare in Germany in the Sixteenth and Seventeenth Centuries*, London, 1865

Haekel, Ralf, *Die englische Komödianten in Deutschland*, Heidelberg, 2004

Heine, Carl, *Johannes Velten*, Halle, 1887

Limon, Jerzy, *Gentlemen of a Company: English Players in Central and Eastern Europe, 1590–1660*, Cambridge, 1985

Rommel, Otto, *Die Alt-Wiener Volkskomödie: Ihre Geschichte vom barocken Welt-Theater bis zum Tode Nestroys*, Vienna, 1952

Eighteenth-century theatre

Barnett, Dene, *The Art of Gesture: The Practices and Principles of 18th Century Acting*, Heidelberg, 1987

Brandes, Johann Christian, *Meine Lebensgeschichte*, 3 vols., Berlin, 1799–1800

Bruford, W. H., *Theatre, Drama and Audience in Goethe's Germany*, London, 1950

Carlson, Marvin, *Goethe and the Weimar Theater*, Ithaca, 1978

Christ, Josef Anton, *Schauspielerleben im achtzehnten Jahrhundert: Erinnerungen*, Munich and Leipzig, 1912

Daniel, Ute, *Hoftheater: Zur Geschichte des Theaters und der Höfe im 18. und 19. Jahrhundert*, Stuttgart, 1995

Devrient, Hans, *Johann Friedrich Schönemann und seine Schauspielergesellschaft*, Leipzig and Hamburg, 1895

Eichhorn, Herbert, *Konrad Ernst Ackermann: Ein deutscher Theaterprinzipal*, Emsdetten, 1965

Fetting, Hugo, *Conrad Ekhof: Ein Schauspieler des achtzehnten Jahrhunderts*, Berlin, 1954

Flemming, Willi, *Goethe und das Theater seiner Zeit*, Stuttgart, 1968

Hermann, Wilhelm, *Thaliens liebster Sohn: Iffland und Mannheim*, Mannheim, 1960

Iffland, August Wilhelm, *Meine theatralische Laufbahn*, Leipzig, 1798

Lamport, F. J., *Lessing and the Drama*, Oxford, 1981

    The German Classical Drama: Theatre, Humanity and Nation, 1750–1870, Cambridge, 1990

Maurer-Schmock, Sybille, *Deutsches Theater im 18. Jahrhundert*, Tübingen, 1982

Münz, Rudolf, *Das 'andere' Theater: Studien über ein deutschsprachiges teatro dell'arte der Lessingzeit*, Berlin, 1979

Oelker, Petra, *'Nichts als eine Komödiantin', Die Lebensgeschichte der Friederike Caroline Neuber*, Weinheim, 1993

Pascal, Roy, *The German Sturm und Drang*, Manchester, 1967

Piens, Gerhard, *Conrad Ekhof und die erste deutsche Schauspielerakademie*, Berlin, 1956

Prudhoe, John, *The Theatre of Goethe and Schiller*, Totowa, NJ, 1973

Reden-Esbeck, Friedrich Johann von, *Caroline Neuber und ihre Zeitgenossen*, Leipzig, 1881

Reed, T. J., *The Classical Centre: Goethe and Weimar, 1775–1832*, London, 1980

Robertson, J. G., *Lessing's Dramatic Theory*, Cambridge, 1939
Sharpe, Lesley, *Friedrich Schiller, Drama, Thought and Politics*, Cambridge, 1991
Williams, Simon, *German Actors of the Eighteenth and Nineteenth Centuries: Idealism, Romanticism and Realism*, Westport, 1985

Nineteenth-century theatre

Altman, Georg, *Ludwig Devrient: Leben und Werke eines Schauspielers*, Berlin, 1926
    Heinrich Laubes Prinzip der Theaterleitung, Dortmund, 1908
Bab, Julius, *Adalbert Matkowsky*, Berlin, 1932
Barnay, Ludwig, *Erinnerungen*, Berlin, 1954
Bauer, Oswald Georg, *Richard Wagner: The Stage Designs and Productions from the Premieres to the Present*, New York, 1983
Burckhard, Max, *Anton Friedrich Mitterwurzer*, Vienna, 1906
Carlson, Marvin, *The German Stage in the Nineteenth Century*, Metuchen, 1972
Claus, Horst, *The Theatre Director Otto Brahm*, Ann Arbor, 1981
Costenoble, Carl. L., *Aus dem Burgtheater, 1818–1837*, Vienna, 1889
Devrient, Eduard, *Aus seinen Tagebüchern*, ed. Rolf Kabel, 2 vols. Weimar, 1964
Dietrich, Margarete, *Das Burgtheater und sein Publikum*, Vienna, 1976
Gross, Edgar, *Johann Friedrich Ferdinand Fleck*, Berlin, 1914
Houben, Heinrich Hubert, *Emil Devrient: Sein Leben, sein Wirken, sein Nachlass*, Frankfurt-am-Main, 1903
Innes, Christopher (ed.), *A Sourcebook on Naturalist Theatre*, London, 2000
Jacobs, Monty, *Deutsche Schauspielkunst*, new edn., rev. Eva Stahl, Berlin, 1954
Klingemann, August, *Kunst und Natur*, 3 vols. Brunswick, 1819–28
Kollek, Peter, *Bogumil Dawison: Porträt und Deutung eines genialen Schauspielers*, Kastellaun, 1978
Koller, Anne Marie, *The Theater Duke: Georg II of Saxe-Meiningen and the German Stage*, Stanford, 1984
Laube, Heinrich, *Schriften über Theater*, ed. Eva Stahl Wisten, Berlin, 1959
Litzmann, Berthold, *Friedrich Ludwig Schröder*, 2 vols., Leipzig and Hamburg, 1890–4
Lothar, Rudolf, *Sonnenthal*, Berlin, 1904
Martersteig, Max, *Das deutsche Theater im neunzehnten Jahrhundert*, Leipzig 1904
    Pius Alexander Wolff, Leipzig, 1879
McInnes, Edward, *Das deutsche Drama des 19. Jahrhunderts*, Berlin, 1983
Osborne, John, *The Meiningen Court Theatre, 1866–1890*, Cambridge, 1988
    The Naturalist Drama in Germany, Totowa, NJ, 1971
Patterson, Michael, *The First German Theatre: Schiller, Goethe, Kleist and Büchner in Performance*, New York and London, 1990
Richter, Helene, *Kainz*, Vienna and Leipzig, 1931
Schlegel, A. W., *A Course of Lectures on Dramatic Art and Literature*, tr. John Black, London, 1846
Schreyvogel, Josef, *Tagebücher, 1810–1823*, ed. Karl Glossy, Berlin, 1903

Schreyvogl, Friedrich, *Das Burgtheater: Wirklichkeit und Illusion*, Vienna, 1965

Schumacher, Claude (ed.), *Naturalism and Symbolism in European Theatre, 1850–1918*, Cambridge, 1996

Spotts, Frederic, *Bayreuth: A History of the Wagner Festival*, New Haven, 1994

Sprengel, Peter, *Die inszenierte Nation: Deutsche Festspiele 1813–1913*, Tübingen, 1991

Troizkij, S., *Karl Seydelmann: Die Anfänge der realistischen Schauspielkunst*, Berlin 1949

Williams, Simon, *Richard Wagner and Festival Theatre*, Westport, 1994

Yates, William Edgar, *Theatre in Vienna: A Critical History, 1776–1995*, Cambridge, 1996

Twentieth-century theatre

Bab, Julius, *Kränze der Mimen*, Emsdetten, 1954

    Schauspieler und Schauspielkunst, Berlin, 1926

    Das Theater der Gegenwart: Geschichte der dramatischen Bühne seit 1870, Leipzig, 1928

Bablet, Denis, *The Revolutions of Stage Design in the 20th Century*, Paris and New York, 1976

Barnett, David, *Rainer Werner Fassbinder and the German Theatre*, Cambridge, 2005

Beacham, Richard, *Adolphe Appia: Theatre Artist*, Cambridge, 1987

Behrens, Peter, *Feste des Lebens und der Kunst*, Leipzig, 1900

Berghaus, Günther (ed.) *Fascism and Theatre: Comparative Studies on the Aesthetics and Politics of Performance in Europe, 1925–1945*, Providence, 1996

Bonnell, Andrew, *The People's Stage in Imperial Germany: Social Democracy and Culture, 1890–1914*, New York, 2005

Braulich, Heinrich, *Die Volksbühne: Theater und Politik in der deutschen Volksbühnenbewegung*, Berlin, 1976

    Max Reinhardt: Theater zwischen Traum und Wirklichkeit, Berlin, 1969

Canaris, Volker, *Peter Zadek: Der Theatermann und Filmemacher*, Munich, 1979

Davies, Cecil W., *The Volksbühne Movement: A History*, Amsterdam, 2000

Dermutz, Klaus, *Die Außenseiterwelten des Peter Zadek*, Salzburg, 2001

Drews, Wolfgang, *Die grossen Zauberer*, Vienna and Munich, 1953

Fiebach, Joachim, Christa Hasche and Traute Schölling, *Theater in der DDR*, Berlin, 1994

Fuchs, Georg, *Revolution in the Theatre: Conclusions concerning the Munich Artists' Theatre*, tr. Constance Connor Kuhn, Ithaca, 1959

Gropius, Walter (ed.), *The Theater of the Bauhaus*, tr. Arthur S. Weninger, Middleton, CT, 1961

Hensel, Georg, *Das Theater der siebziger Jahre*, Stuttgart, 1980

    Spiel's noch einmal: Das Theater der achtziger Jahre, Frankfurt/Main, 1990

Hortmann, Wilhelm, *Shakespeare on the German Stage: The Twentieth Century*, Cambridge, 1998

Ihering, Herbert, *Von Reinhardt bis Brecht: Vier Jahrzehnte Theater und Film*, 3 vols., Berlin, 1961

    Reinhardt, Jessner, Piscator oder Klassikertod?, Berlin, 1929

Innes, Christopher, *Edward Gordon Craig: A Vision of Theatre*, Amsterdam, 1998

Erwin Piscator's Political Theatre: The Development of Modern German Drama, Cambridge, 1972

Jacobs, Margaret and John Warren (eds.), *Max Reinhardt: The Oxford Symposium*, Oxford, 1986

Jelavich, Peter, *Munich and Theatrical Modernism: Politics, Playwriting, and Performance, 1890–1914*. Cambridge, MA, 1985

Kalb, Jonathan, *The Theater of Heiner Müller*, Cambridge, 1998

Kennedy, Dennis, *Looking at Shakespeare: A Visual History of Twentieth-Century Performance*, Cambridge, 1993

Kitzwegerer, Liselotte, *Alfred Roller als Bühnenbildner*, Vienna, 1959

Kortner, Fritz, *Aller Tage Abend*, Munich, 1979

Kuhns, David F., *German Expressionist Theatre: The Actor and the Stage*, Cambridge, 1997

Kuschnia, Michael (ed.), *100 Jahre Deutsches Theater Berlin 1883–1983*, Berlin, 1983

Lange, Mechthild, *Peter Zadek*, Frankfurt/Main, 1989

Lehmann, Hans-Thies, *Postdramatic Theatre*, tr. Karen Kürs-Munby, London, 2006

Lennartz, Knut, *Theater, Künstler und die Politik. 150 Jahre Deutscher Bühnenverein*, Berlin, 1996

Ley-Piscator, Maria, *The Piscator Experiment: The Political Theatre*, New York, 1967

London, John (ed.), *Theatre under the Nazis*, Manchester, 2000

Luft, Friedrich, *Berliner Theater 1945–1961*, Velber bei Hannover, 1962

Melchinger, Siegfried, *Theater der Gegenwart*, Frankfurt Main, 1956

Minetti, Bernhard, *Erinnerungen eines Schauspielers*, ed. Günther Rühle, Stuttgart, 1985

Müller, Heiner, *Gesammelte Irrtümer: Interviews und Gespräche*, Frankfurt Main, 1986

Nagel, Ivan, *Kortner – Zadek – Stein*, Munich, 1989

Neef, Sigrid, *Das Theater der Ruth Berghaus*, Berlin, 1989

Niessen, Carl, *Der Szeniker Ludwig Sievert: Ein Leben für die Bühne*, Cologne, 1959

Patterson, Michael, *Peter Stein: Germany's Leading Theatre Director*, Cambridge, 1981
    The Revolution in German Theatre, 1900–1933, Boston, 1981
    German Theatre Today: Post-War Theatre in West and East Germany, Austria and Northern Switzerland, London, 1976

Riess, Curt, *Gustaf Gründgens: Eine Biographie*, Hamburg, 1965

Rischbieter, Henning (ed.), *Bühne und Bildende Kunst im XX. Jahrhundert*, Velber bei Hannover, 1968
    (ed.), *Durch den eisernen Vorhang, Theater im geteilten Deutschland 1945–1990*, Berlin, 1999.

Rühle, Günther, *Theater für die Republik im Spiegel der Kritik*, Berlin, 1988

Sayler, Oliver M., *Max Reinhardt and his Theatre*, New York, 1924

Sievert, Ludwig, *Lebendiges Theater*, Munich 1944

Styan, J. L., *Max Reinhardt*, Cambridge, 1982
    Modern Drama in Theory and Practice, 3 vols., *Expressionism and Epic Theatre*, Cambridge, 1981

Thomson, Peter and Glendyr Sacks (eds.), *The Cambridge Companion to Brecht*, Cambridge, 1994

Viertel, Berthold, *Schriften zum Theater*, Munich, 1970

Völker, Klaus, *Fritz Kortner. Schauspieler und Regisseur*, Berlin, 1987

    Brecht: A Biography, tr. John Nowell, New York, 1978

Wekwerth, Manfred, *Notate*, Berlin and Weimar, 1967

Willett, John, *The Theatre of the Weimar Republic*, New York and London, 1988

    The Theatre of Bertolt Brecht, rev. edn., London, 1977

Wilzopolski, Siegfried, *Das Theater des Augenblicks*, Berlin, 1992

Wolfert, Jutta, *Theatertexte zwischen Medien und Revolution, 1989–1996*, Berlin, 2004

Zadek, Peter, *Das wilde Ufer. Ein Theaterbuch*, Cologne, 1990

Index